"Amazingly easy to use. Very portable, very complete."

—*Booklist*

♦

"The only mainstream guide to list specific prices. The Walter Cronkite of guidebooks—with all that implies."

—*Travel & Leisure*

♦

"Complete, concise, and filled with useful information."

—*New York Daily News*

♦

"Hotel information is close to encyclopedic."

—*Des Moines Sunday Register*

Frommer's®

3rd Edition

Maryland
&
Delaware

by Denise Hawkins Coursey
and Matthew Coursey

Macmillan • USA

ABOUT THE AUTHORS

Denise and Matt are Maryland natives, Orioles fans (of course), and frequent travelers. They are both always happy to apply their writing skills to their home state and its lovely neighbor, Delaware. Denise is a former New York City publishing career woman who enjoys debunking misconceptions about her second hometown, Baltimore. Matt writes for local newspapers, is an avid canoeist, and (when he dries out) loves to explore little-known historic sites.

MACMILLAN TRAVEL

A Simon & Schuster Macmillan Company
1633 Broadway
New York, NY 10019

Find us online at **www.frommers.com**.

ISBN 0-02-862080-1
ISSN 1072-8015

Editor: Jeff Soloway
Production Editor: Carol Sheehan
Design by Michele Laseau
Digital Cartography by Jim Moore and Ortelius Design
Photo Editor: Richard Fox

SPECIAL SALES

Contents

List of Maps

AN INVITATION TO THE READER

In researching this book, we discovered many wonderful places—hotels, restaurants, shops, and more. We're sure you'll find others. Please tell us about them so that we can share the information with your fellow travelers in upcoming editions. If you were disappointed with a recommendation, we'd love to know that, too. Please write to:

Frommer's Maryland & Delaware, 3rd Edition
Macmillan Travel
1633 Broadway
New York, NY 10019

AN ADDITIONAL NOTE

Please be advised that travel information is subject to change at any time—and this is especially true of prices. We therefore suggest that you write or call ahead for confirmation when making your travel plans. The authors, editors, and publisher cannot be held responsible for the experiences of readers while traveling. Your safety is important to us, however, so we encourage you to stay alert and be aware of your surroundings. Keep a close eye on cameras, purses, and wallets, all favorite targets of thieves and pickpockets.

WHAT THE SYMBOLS MEAN

✪ Frommer's Favorites

Our favorite places and experiences—outstanding for quality, value, or both.

The following abbreviations are used for credit cards:

AE	American Express	DISC	Discover
CB	Carte Blanche	MC	MasterCard
DC	Diners Club	V	Visa

FIND FROMMER'S ONLINE

Arthur Frommer's Outspoken Encyclopedia of Travel (www.frommers.com) offers more than 6,000 pages of up-to-the-minute travel information—including the latest bargains and candid personal articles updated daily by Arthur Frommer himself. No other website offers such comprehensive and timely coverage of the world of travel.

The Best of Maryland & Delaware

Maryland and Delaware are small states, so how difficult could it be
to decide where to go? Well, that depends. Are you coming to explore the mountains and raging rivers of Western Maryland? Are you
a Civil War buff looking to visit the sites of some of the war's greatest
battles? Perhaps you're planning a trip to the nation's capital and
want to see the outlying areas or take a jaunt out to Baltimore or
Annapolis. Maybe you want to catch a glimpse of the lives of
Delaware's rich and famous, the du Ponts, in the Brandywine Valley. Or maybe you've come for the waters and the seafood of the
Chesapeake Bay, which comprises much of Maryland's over 3,000
miles of shoreline.

We think you get the picture. Don't let the size of these two states
fool you. They're packed with exciting and interesting adventures,
and they've got lots of special nooks and crannies—museums, historic sites, small towns, natural wonders, spectacular vistas, and opportunities for outdoor adventure—that you may or may not know
about. So in planning a trip to Maryland and Delaware, you're faced
with two issues: finding out exactly what the region has to offer and
then deciding what to do first. While the rest of the book will help
you to discover what awaits you in Maryland and Delaware, this
chapter will entice you with what we believe is the best of the nooks
and crannies.

1 The Best Views & Vistas

- **Baltimore Harbor from the elevators in the Hyatt Regency:**
  Many of the Hyatt's rooms offer an unsurpassed view of
  Baltimore's beautiful Inner Harbor—gleaming water, yachts, sailing ships, shopping centers, and the National Aquarium. However, if you are not staying at the Hyatt, try to sneak up their glass
  elevator; it serves almost as well. See chapter 5.
- **Annapolis Harbor from the water:** There are few scenes that we
  find more memorable in Maryland than entering Annapolis Harbor by boat. A mecca for sailboats and yachts, the city's harbor is
  often cluttered with bobbing masts and brightly colored sails. Add
  to this Annapolis's historic skyline featuring the great domes of the
  Maryland State House and the Naval Academy Chapel and you
  feel like you're seeing the harbor as it looked 200 years ago, when

it was bustling with trade and sailing vessels of the nonrecreational kind. Luckily, you don't have to own your own boat to enjoy this; many companies offer cruises of the harbor and nearby academy. See chapter 6.

- **Bay Bridge:** Riding east from Annapolis on Route 50 you hit the over-4-mile-long William J. Preston Memorial Bridge, better known locally as the Memorial or Bay Bridge. It is the fastest way to cross the Chesapeake and offers a magnificent look at the bay from above. For a good view of the bridge itself, try the public beach at Rock Hall near Chestertown on Maryland's Eastern Shore.

- **Sidling Hill:** In the late '80s, the engineers of the new Interstate 68 blasted straight through the mountain known as Sidling Hill and in the process unwittingly created an impressive vista. Now from the visitor center you can see easily 50 miles to the east over numerous mountain ridges. The gash the workers cut through the hill reveals layer upon layer of mutlicolored rock strata, some of which date back to the age of dinosaurs. See chapter 9.

- **Jefferson Rock:** This is a vista with a presidential name and seal of approval. High above Harpers Ferry, West Virginia, Thomas Jefferson visited this precariously leaning rock and looked down from it on the confluence of the mighty Shenandoah and Potomac rivers. He is reported to have said that the view was worth crossing the Atlantic to see. See chapter 9.

- **Great Falls:** Just outside the Washington, D.C., beltway, the Potomac River crashes into the Mather Gorge through the turbulent cataracts called Great Falls. These falls have long been the hidden natural wonder of the capital area, but for over 20 years the bridges to the best overlook lay in ruins after a disastrous flood. Recently, however, the National Park Service restored the bridge over Olmsted Falls and once more the main falls can be viewed in all their glory from a rocky overlook on Olmsted Island. See chapter 9.

2 The Best Hiking

- **Calvert Cliffs State Park:** This park offers several trails for moderate-length day hiking and, more importantly, a wide variety of unique wilderness scenery. The trails wind through rolling forests and then descend into a primordial tidal marsh filled with grasses, waterfowl, and cypress trees. Most hikes also include at least one view of the Chesapeake Bay either from atop the cliffs or from a small beach at the base of the marsh. See chapter 6.

- **Maryland Heights:** Just across the Potomac River from Harpers Ferry, West Virginia, is a towering gray-black cliff with a 19th-century ad for tooth powder etched, perhaps forever, on its face. The trails that wrap around and help you conquer this peak are at times steep, but the view of Harpers Ferry from the top is well worth the effort. See chapter 9.

- **Paw Paw Tunnel:** Hiking along the Chesapeake and Ohio (C&O) Canal towpath is always fun, but the section of the towpath that leads through Paw Paw Tunnel takes the experience to a new level: the weird. The tunnel is a three-quarter-mile-long, arching, brick-lined underground passage where both the canal and towpath (and you the hiker) disappear into almost total darkness even in the middle of a summer day. An interesting circuit hike can be made by taking the steep ridge trail over the mountain and then making the return trip through the tunnel. See chapter 9.

- **Swallow Falls State Park:** A great place for families to hike in Garrett County, this park's short trails wind through dark, peaty forest and offer relatively easy access to some stunning scenery. There are overlooks to three waterfalls—Swallow Falls, Tolliver Falls, and the 63-foot-high, cascading Muddy Creek Falls. See chapter 9.

- **Big Savage Trail:** This rugged hiking trail extends 17 miles along the ridge of Big Savage Mountain, passing several impressive vistas along the way. A tough hike through almost total wilderness, it's our choice for serious backpack camping in Maryland. See chapter 9.

3 The Best Public Gardens

- **Sherwood Garden** (MD): Visit this neighborhood garden in mid-May, when the brightly colored yellow and red tulips are in full bloom. This little gem in north Baltimore is one of the city's best-kept secrets, hidden among the grandiose old homes just south of Loyola College. And it's the only truly public garden on our list of bests: It's free. See chapter 5.
- **Longwood Gardens** (DE): The largest and most elaborate of the Brandywine Valley/du Pont gardens, Longwood covers 1,050 acres with a 4-acre indoor conservatory, fountain displays, topiary gardens, a waterfall and chiming tower, and even a children's garden. Seasonal displays, like Acres of Spring, the Festival of Fountains, the Chrysanthemum Festival, and the Christmas Display, make this attraction a year-round delight. See chapter 11.
- **Nemours Mansion and Gardens** (DE): Although Nemours is one of the least visited of the du Pont attractions, the gardens of this Louis XVI–style château are among the finest examples of French-style gardens in the United States. The gardens, including the beautiful Sunken Garden, extend for almost a third of a mile along the main vista of the house. See chapter 11.
- **Winterthur Museum and Gardens** (DE): Winterthur is best known for its immense collection of decorative arts, filling 175 rooms of the Winterthur mansion. But the mansion sits on   a 983-acre estate surrounded by a vast collection of native and exotic plants, including rare rhododendrons, azaleas, and conifers. The garden is accessible on foot via miles of paved and woodland trails or by a garden tram that also offers narration about the gardens. See chapter 11.

4 The Best Outdoor Adventures

- **Off-road vehicle trips on Assateague Island:** Most people who visit Assateague see only the 4- or 5-mile stretch of guarded beach and the federal and state camping facilities. Unfortunately, they've missed the best part: the 20 miles of wild, undisturbed, unpopulated beaches. This part of the island is only accessible on foot, by canoe or kayak, or over the miles of beach off-road vehicle trails, the fastest way to get to those secluded areas. See chapter 8.
- **Rafting the Yough:** The Youghiogheny River (generally just called the *Yock*) is Maryland's contribution to the great white-water rivers of the Southeast. Its churning waters race through numerous class III–IV rapids, with daunting names like Gap Falls, Bastard, Triple Drop, Meatcleaver, Lost and Found, and Backbender. The water levels are controlled by dam release so that the river is runnable almost year-round. See chapter 9.
- **Cross-country skiing in Western Maryland:** For years, Marylanders have been spending winter weekends at New Germany and Herrington Manor State Parks in Garrett County, taking advantage of the excellent cross-country skiing facilities. There are 20 miles of trails between the two parks, both of which have cozy stone "warming rooms," ski-rental facilities, and best of all, cabins for rent at affordable prices. See chapter 9.
- **Sea kayaking anywhere with Delmarva Dennis:** Dennis Little, naturalist and sea kayaker extraordinaire, leads numerous guided trips throughout the coastal waters

of the Delmarva Peninsula. A circumnavigation of Burtons Island in the Rehoboth Bay is an excellent starter trip and a great way to sneak up on some waterfowl or to do a little kayak fishing. Dennis also offers daylong kayak surfing lessons off the coast of Assateague Island, cypress-tree tours of Trapp Pond on the Nanticoke River, and kayaking with the dolphins along the Delaware coast. See chapter 13.

5 The Best Fishing & Crabbing

- **Point Lookout State Park** (MD): Location is everything at this peninsular state park with the Chesapeake Bay on one side and the Potomac River on the other. You can fish either from the pier on the bay, just about anywhere on the shore, or from a boat rented at the little camp marina. So if the fish aren't biting in the bay, just stroll over to the Potomac side of the park and try again. See chapter 6.
- **Wye River** (crabbing/near St. Michaels, MD): Whether you are wading out with crab pots or chicken necking from the side of a boat, the Wye River is the place to go crabbing. Not because there are lots of crabs but because for some reason the crabs caught in this river just tend to taste great. What better reason do you need?
- **Casselman River** (fly-fishing/near Grantsville, MD): Ecology and environmental cleanup efforts in this area have really paid off. The beautiful and wild Casselman River, once empty of fish because of local acid mining, is now teeming with trout. We've heard rumors of people catching as many as 40 fish a day (yeah, we believe that). One thing is for certain though, the Casselman is once again a great place to fish. See chapter 9.
- **Delaware Bay off Cape Henlopen:** During our recent visit to this area, the locals told us they were throwing tuna back, having caught their limit in half the time they expected. Of course, there's no guarantee that the catch will be as plentiful every year, but the waters are pretty consistent and the facilities (the pier at Cape Henlopen and the charter fishing companies) are always good. See chapter 13.

6 The Best Birding & Wildlife Watching

- **Calvert County** (MD): Driving down Route 2 through Calvert County, you'll see signs every few miles for a park or wildlife area. All of them are great places to glimpse native birds, small mammals, reptiles, and amphibians. Our favorite stops along this strip: Battle Creek Cypress Swamp Sanctuary, Flag Ponds Nature Park, and Calvert Cliffs State Park. See chapter 6.
- **Blackwater National Wildlife Refuge** (MD): The entire Delmarva Peninsula is dotted with wildlife refuges and protected lands, creating havens for migrating waterfowl and other wildlife. Blackwater is the largest and most popular of these refuges. During peak migration season, you'll see many species of ducks, tundra and mute swan, and snow geese, as well as the ever-present herons, Canada geese, and osprey, and the occasional bald eagle. If you explore the wooded areas of the park, you may even catch sight of the endangered Delmarva fox squirrel. See chapter 7.
- **Eastern Neck National Wildlife Refuge** (MD): You'll see a lot of the same species of birds and mammals at all the refuges along the peninsula, but each park has its own character. Eastern Neck is smaller than Blackwater to the south, but it also gets fewer human visitors and has a greater portion of its 2,285 acres accessible by road or hiking trails. See chapter 7.
- **Bombay Hook National Wildlife Refuge** (DE): The largest of Delaware's wildlife refuges, Bombay Hook, just northeast of Dover, comprises nearly 16,000 acres of

tidal marsh, freshwater pools, and timbered swamps. Again, you'll see a lot of migratory waterfowl, but after waterfowl season, in April, May, and June, migrant shorebirds and songbirds appear. See chapter 12.

- **Whale and dolphin watching along the Atlantic coast:** Although it may seem odd, the Atlantic coast of Maryland and Delaware, especially near Cape Henlopen State Park, is a good place to spot whales and dolphins. The Great Dune at Cape Henlopen offers a great vantage point (though you should bring a pair of binoculars), and several companies along the Delaware shore offer whale- and dolphin-watching cruises, or even sea kayaking with the dolphins. See chapter 13.

7 The Best Festivals & Events

- **Fells Point Fun Festival** (Baltimore, MD): For over 30 years this outdoor street festival, usually held the first weekend in October, has entertained residents and visitors of Baltimore's coolest neighborhood. There are 2 full days of arts, crafts, music, and food, and if that isn't enough, when it all closes down at 7 there are still the restaurants and bars of Fells Point to enjoy. See chapter 3.
- **Maryland Renaissance Festival** (Crownsville, MD): This 3-month-long re-creation of a 16th-century English festival features more colorful reenactors than any tyrant could hope to oppress. Also present are a ton of food and craft shops, dozens of quirky performances, and of course, jousting. Jousting is Maryland's state sport (no, we're not joking), and it usually involves spearing small (dime-size) rings with a lance while riding a horse. Here, however, they also practice the ever-popular knock-'em-off-the-horse variety. See chapter 3.
- **National Hard Crab Derby and Fair** (Crisfield, MD): The hottest place to be in Maryland and Delaware over Labor Day weekend is the seafood town of Crisfield for this festival in honor of Maryland's favorite entree, the crab. Join this crowd of people in the late summer sun, and you'll be in for great seafood, music, rides, fireworks, and contests, including the famous hard crab race and the crab-picking contest. See chapter 7.
- **Rocky Gap Music Festival** (near Cumberland, MD): Country music fans flock to this major summer outdoor concert held at or near Rocky Gap State Park. To give you a feel for the extravaganza, here's a list of a few past Rocky Gap performers: Dolly Parton, Willie Nelson, Roy Clark, Travis Tritt, Alabama, Kathy Mattea, Mary Chapin Carpenter, Bocephus (Hank Williams Jr.), etc. See chapter 9.

8 The Most Unusual Sporting Events

- **Jousting at Maryland's Renaissance Festival:** Jousting is the official sport of the state of Maryland (in fact, Maryland is the only state that has a state sport), and you'll find that jousting tournaments and demonstrations occur frequently throughout the state. But for a sure bet, you'll always be able to witness this unusual sport at the Maryland Renaissance Festival. See chapter 3.
- **St. John's College vs. Navy Croquet Match** (Annapolis, MD): This genteel contest pits midshipmen from the U.S. Naval Academy against the St. John's croquet team. St. John's team members and spectators don Gay '90s attire for the event, and apparently they've bested Navy 7 years running.
- **Annual Canoe Joust** (Snow Hill, MD): For 10 years, the town of Snow Hill has been practicing its own mutated form of Maryland's state sport. It's a simple concept: six men or women, two canoes, and two giant padded "lances" (that is, oversized Q-tips). Three minutes on the river, and, in the end, the dry team wins. See chapter 8.

- **World Championship Punkin' Chunkin' Contest** (Lewes, DE): It's a bit of a stretch to call this a sporting event; this annual competition is more a test of physics, ingenuity, and creativity to see whose mechanical contraption (no explosives allowed) can launch an 8- to 10-pound pumpkin the farthest and with the greatest accuracy. The current distance record is 2,710 feet. See chapter 13.

9 The Best Family Activities

- **Orioles baseball:** Some major league ballparks have to designate family sections; this isn't necessary at Oriole Park at Camden Yards. The Baltimore fans are notoriously loyal but also friendly and well behaved, making a trip to the ballpark a fun and generally wholesome experience for the entire family. See chapter 5.
- **Collecting fossils at Calvert Cliffs State Park:** The 30-foot bay-side cliffs for which this state park was named are the primary attraction here, but the park is also a great place for the whole family to hike, picnic, and of course, search for fossils along the beach below the cliffs. See chapter 6.
- **Biking on the C&O Canal:** The Chesapeake and Ohio (C&O) Canal and its towpath runs parallel to the Potomac River for 184½ miles, from Georgetown to Cumberland. Any stretch of it makes a great place for a family biking excursion. The dirt and grass towpath is flat and untrafficked by motorized vehicles, making for a safe and easy ride through the scenic floodplain forests. See chapter 9.
- **White-water rafting on the Shenandoah/Potomac:** Maryland offers some great white-water adventures, but a lot of it is a bit too rough for your average 8-year-old. However, the class II and III rapids of the Shenandoah and Potomac rivers near Harpers Ferry are exciting enough to keep adults interested and tame enough for the whole family. (There is a minimum weight requirement, so inquire before you make reservations.) See chapter 9.

10 The Best Small Museums

- **Calvert Marine Museum** (MD): It seems every town on the eastern or western shore of the Chesapeake Bay has at least one small marine or maritime museum, but this one is by far the most impressive. With fossil exhibits, several aquariums, a pair of playful river otters, the Drum Point Lighthouse, and even regular harbor tours aboard a bugeye (a traditional Chesapeake sailboat), this is a great place to bring the whole family. See chapter 6.
- **Ward Museum of Wildfowl Art** (MD): This unique museum, in a brand-new building beside Schumaker Pond, is much more than a simple collection of decoys. It houses some truly amazing sculptures, including the winners of the World Championship Wildfowl Carving Competition, past and present. See chapter 8.
- **Brandywine River Museum** (PA): This popular Brandywine Valley attraction contains the largest collection of Wyeth (N. C., Andrew, Jamie, and family) paintings in the country, as well as the works of many other Brandywine artists. The museum is set in a sleekly restructured old mill right next to the Brandywine River. The third-floor gallery is devoted to the works of Andrew Wyeth, who still lives and paints in the Brandywine Valley, and occasionally stops by the gallery to touch up and rearrange some of his paintings. See chapter 11.

11 The Best Places to Get Away from It All

- **Waterloo Country Inn** (Princess Anne, MD): When innkeepers Theresa and Irwin Kraemer moved from Austria to this 1775 Georgian manor on Maryland's Eastern

Shore, their intention was to turn it into the quintessential country inn. Slowly but surely, they have succeeded. This charming inn on the banks of Monie Creek offers seclusion, peace, and tranquility whether you're wandering the inn grounds, canoeing the lovely tidal creek, or biking the back roads of Somerset County. See chapter 7.

- **Merry Sherwood Plantation** (Berlin, MD): Even though this intriguing inn is only minutes from the modern resort town of Ocean City, you'll feel like you've been transported to another century. This 1859 plantation home is decorated from top to bottom with Victorian antiques; in fact, it's probably more elaborately and beautifully furnished today than during its heyday in the late 19th century. See chapter 8.
- **Stone Manor** (Jefferson, MD): This 1760s manor home set on a 114-acre working farm is ideal for quiet, romantic weekends not too far away from the big city. It has all the ambience of a historic country inn and the conveniences of a modern luxury hotel, including a Jacuzzi in each room and a fine restaurant. See chapter 9.
- **Inn at Montchanin Village** (Wilmington, DE): This former du Pont workers' village has been transformed into an elegant yet comfortable and relaxing inn, a great place from which to tour the sites of the Brandywine Valley or Wilmington. But the guest suites are so warm and cozy, you may find it difficult to leave your room. See chapter 10.
- **Eli's Country Inn** (near Greenwood, DE): Within Maryland and Delaware, this is about as far away from it all as you can get (with the Waterloo running a close second). A family of seven sisters runs this truly country inn in the farmhouse their father built and they grew up in. It's a simple inn, but you will forget the cares of the world while you're in these women's capable hands. And the home cooking is wonderful. See chapter 13.

12 The Best Camping

- **Janes Island State Park** (MD): For sunset views over the Chesapeake Bay, the campsites at this state park just north of Crisfield can't be beat. Many of the sites sit on the water's edge, offering unobstructed views and easy access to the park's canoe trail. If you prefer less primitive accommodations, there are even a few waterside cabins. See chapter 7.
- **Rocky Gap State Park** (MD): Maryland's second largest state camping facility, Rocky Gap boasts 278 wooded and lakeside campsites, all generously spaced and well maintained (30 sites have full hookup). Campers enjoy a private beach, camp store, clean bathhouses with showers, and laundry facilities. This is a popular campground that fills up completely on summer weekends, so reserve well in advance. See chapter 9.
- **New Germany State Park** (MD): This wooded campground has the distinction of being the cleanest, most well-kept campground we've ever stayed in. It's small, with only 39 sites, but they're well spaced and offer easy access to hiking trails, fishing spots in the park lake, and the facilities of several other state parks and forests. There are also 11 cabins, which are great options for winter cross-country skiing trips. See chapter 9.
- **Potomac–Garrett State Forest** (MD): For primitive camping in a beautiful mountain setting, head to these little-known state forests in southern and western Garrett County. Nearly all the campsites are within walking distance of one of the forests' mountain streams, and they're so spread out, you'll probably never know if you have camping neighbors. See chapter 9.

- **Cape Henlopen State Park** (DE): Summer beach camping is always a tenuous venture, with the heat, the bugs, and the sand. But the facilities at Cape Henlopen make for the best beach camping experience on the Maryland and Delaware shore. There are 159 wooded sites, several with full hookup, and all with access to bath-houses and running water. Within the park, you'll find several miles of hiking and biking trails, guarded beaches, and great fishing. See chapter 13.

13 The Best Shopping

- **Inner Harbor, Baltimore:** Although often criticized as little more than a big shopping mall, Baltimore's Inner Harbor is, in our books, a combination of *at least* two big shopping malls in a great setting. The Gallery and the Pratt Street Pavilion offer retail shopping with everything from The Sharper Image to Ann Taylor, while the Light Street Pavilion has a plethora of eateries as well as fresh seafood, pastries, and fudge. See chapter 5.
- **Downtown Annapolis:** Annapolis's Main Street is one of those increasingly rare locations in Maryland's increasingly suburbanized landscape: a truly vibrant outdoor shopping district. People from the area come here rather than go to the mall. It has jewelers, art galleries, antique shops, retail shops (like Banana Republic and Gap), gift shops, hippie shops, and even tackle shops if you're planning to hit the water. See chapter 6.
- **Frederick/New Market, MD:** Whether you're into browsing for antiques in tiny dusty shops or in sprawling antique malls, few places have as many opportunities as close together as Frederick and New Market. Frederick has dozens of antique shops featuring mostly 19th- and early 20th-century furnishings and doodads of all sorts. There are also quite a few fun consignment-type shops featuring things that may be considered antiques someday. The nearby village of New Market is more refined and considerably smaller; it offers shops specializing in furniture, estate jewelry, old books, tools, and glassware. See chapter 9.
- **Rehoboth Outlets:** Delaware is the state for tax-free shopping, and the Rehoboth Outlets center is the place to beat retail prices. Over 150 shops fill three sprawling strip-mall complexes, making this the third largest outlet center in the U.S. It boasts names such as Tommy Hilfiger, L.L. Bean, Mikasa, Lenox, Pfaltzgraf, Guess, Levi's, Ann Taylor, Liz Claiborne, J. Crew, and more. See chapter 13.

14 The Best Crab Cakes

If you ask 10 people in Maryland and Delaware who makes the best crab cakes, you'll easily get 10 different answers. That's because there are a lot of good crab cakes out there (and a lot of bad ones). And also because there are a million ways to make a crab cake, ranging from the basic crab, bread crumbs, and Old Bay spice variety, to gourmet crab cakes held together with salmon mousse, to Southwest crab cakes filled with peppers and topped with homemade salsa. So the answer will depend on the taste of the person you ask.

Our preference is for the basic, down-home, fried or broiled variety—heavy on the crab, light on the filler, and just the right amount of spices. Without a doubt, my great aunt Marie makes the best of this type of crab cake, but since she won't cook for just anyone, here are some excellent substitutes.

- **Stoney's Seafood House** (Broome Island, MD): This place has all the makings of your basic crab shanty—it's a small, casual restaurant right on the water in the middle of nowhere (on a place called Broome Island, no less). But it's a little more upscale than that, and the crab cakes are good—huge balls of crab (I couldn't find any filler), with not so much Old Bay as to overpower the crab's flavor. The crab cakes alone are worth the drive, but the view isn't bad either. See chapter 6.

- **Robert Morris Inn** (Oxford, MD): James Michener believed this restaurant had the best crab cakes on the Eastern Shore, so of course, we had to check it out for ourselves. And we weren't disappointed. They're the perfect blend of gourmet taste without all the fancy ingredients. Even if you don't like crab cakes (perhaps because you've been burned by one too many of the bad, overdone, overfilled, crab-shanty variety), these are worth a try. They might just change your mind. See chapter 7.

- **Suicide Bridge Seafood House** (Secretary/Hurloch, MD): This family restaurant overlooking Cabin Creek served us our first really good, restaurant-prepared crab cake, and therefore holds a special place in our hearts. These hefty crab cakes are moist, lightly spiced, and have lots of slightly shredded lump crabmeat. It's not an easy place to find, but you can get directions from just about anyone in the area. They all know the place, and they all know the crab cakes. See chapter 7.

- **Bayard House** (Chesapeake City, MD): Ask for the New Age crab cakes off the appetizer menu. They're the only nontraditional crab cakes to make our list of bests. This Santa Fe–style treat is lightly breaded with a spicy blue cornmeal and served with a tangy cream sauce. Our one complaint: The New Age crab cakes are only an appetizer, and we wanted more. And unfortunately, they're not a regular item on the menu, but maybe that'll change. See chapter 7.

- **Old Mill Crab House** (Ocean View, just outside of Bethany Beach, DE and Delmar, DE): If you're not up to the famous all-you-can-eat steamed crab dinner, try their first-rate crab cakes. They've got all the makings of a great crab cake we've already mentioned plus a bit more seasoning for a little extra zing. Delawareans claim the crab cakes at the Bethany Beach location are toned down for the tourists, so if you've got the time and think you can handle it, visit the Delmar location. See chapter 13.

2 Getting to Know Maryland & Delaware

Maryland and Delaware call to mind different things for different people. For many, it's water—the Chesapeake and Delaware bays, filled with sailboats, yachts, skipjacks, tankers, charter fishing boats, fish, oysters, mussels, clams, and crabs. Alongside the glistening waves stand cottage-style screwpile lighthouses, looking out over marsh grass for vessels wandering too close to shore. This image of maritime life mixes seamlessly with that of the area's bustling ports: Annapolis, a city little changed since Jefferson called its brick-lined streets the best in the colonies; and Baltimore, "Charm City," where the Inner Harbor shimmers under the glass peaks of the National Aquarium. The maritime ways live on in the Eastern Shore's historic towns, from Chestertown to St. Michaels and Smith Island, where James Michener toured while writing *Chesapeake* and watermen still reap the harvest of the bay in skiffs and crab shanties, just as they have for over 200 years.

But all the water isn't in the bays. For some the Atlantic beaches are where the action really is. Ocean City has its miles of wide, white strand, rippling heat, and almost constant summer parties. Assateague Island boasts almost 30 miles of pristine beaches, rolling dunes, grassy marshes, sika deer, and wild horses. The quieter resorts of the Delaware shore have their star in sophisticated Rehoboth, where you can gaze at the night sky from a quiet boardwalk, dine elegantly at first-class restaurants, and shop the day away tax-free. Others prefer Cape Henlopen, where you can peer down from the Great Dune at the three lighthouses off in the distance and the whales and dolphins swimming in the surf.

Still others remember the more turbulent side of Maryland, when it was the crossroads of the Civil War and saw the war's bloodiest single day of battle at Antietam, where 23,000 men fell. Outside Maryland but near its borders, the battles of Gettysburg and Harpers Ferry also shook the state.

Farther west the Allegheny Mountains form the state's frontier. These rolling and rumbling hills turn bright red and orange in autumn, drawing visitors to their trails, waterfalls, and steam-powered train, *Mountain Thunder*. In winter, cross-country and downhill skiers explore the quiet, snow-padded forests and hillsides.

Hidden in these hillsides is, once again, the water. As the winter snow melts, it feeds the Chesapeake, and, through the Ohio River, the Mississippi—this is wild water. Through deep, forested valleys, the Savage and the Youghiogheny rivers flow through rapids and over boulders, cataracts, and falls, inviting rafters, kayakers, and canoeists to come from all over and test their mettle.

The best thing is that all these images are true to life. They are real. They are as real as the opulent oil paintings on palatial walls in the du Pont mansions of Northern Delaware, as real as the sweet chocolate desserts in Baltimore's Little Italy, as real as the dappled wild horses that walk right up to your car window on Assateague Island, and as real as the roar of Great Falls on the Potomac. So pick an image or maybe two or three, come visit, and see how real they are.

1 The Regions in Brief

Western Maryland   This thin panhandle of land wedged between West Virginia and Pennsylvania in some ways has much more in common with these neighboring states than with the rest of Maryland. Unlike the bulk of Maryland, where the distinguishing geographical element is water, Western Maryland is a mountainous region, marked by long, cold winters and short, mild summers. It's a year-round paradise for outdoor and adventure-sports enthusiasts. The raging waters of the Youghiogheny and Savage rivers in Maryland, and the Cheat and Gauley in West Virginia, offer some of the best rafting and kayaking on the East Coast; and the Allegheny Mountains provide the only downhill skiing in the state, as well as extensive cross-country trails. Frederick has historically been considered the gateway to Maryland's western counties: Washington, Allegany, and Garrett. But though geographically it still belongs to Western Maryland, Frederick is really a suburb of Washington, D.C., offering easy access both to the attractions of the nation's capital and to points west.

Central Maryland   This region encompasses the Baltimore/Washington metropolitan area and is the most densely populated region in the state. Baltimore and Washington (not covered in this book), though they make up one metro area, are quite different and economically separate. Nonetheless, residents of each city travel frequently to the other for its cultural amenities and nightlife. Annapolis is an interesting mix of a government seat, tourist destination, and sailing town. Perhaps because it is Maryland's capital, Annapolis is much more closely tied in terms of culture and economy to Washington. Most of the rest of central Maryland is simply suburbia, with little of interest to the tourist.

Southern Maryland   The term *Southern Maryland* perplexes outsiders. It refers to that section of the state on the western shore of the Chesapeake that is south of Washington. Didn't know there was anything south of D.C.? Don't worry—we grew up in Western Maryland and didn't know it existed until our late teens. Much of Southern Maryland is either D.C. suburbs or, farther south, vast tracts of farmland. However, Calvert County, a peninsula wedged between the Chesapeake Bay and the Patuxent River, is home to the largest charter fishing fleet on the bay; and Solomons, at the tip of the peninsula, is a locally popular boating and tourist destination.

Eastern Shore   The term *Eastern Shore* is also somewhat confusing, referring to the Chesapeake's Eastern Shore, not the Atlantic coast. More than any other part of Maryland or Delaware, every aspect of life here is influenced by the Chesapeake Bay and surrounding wetlands. The Eastern Shore's vast area, comprising nine counties and 36% of the state's landmass, can be subdivided into smaller segments that vary significantly in geography, culture, and character. The southern counties, Somerset, Wicomico, and parts of Dorchester, are home to the traditional crabbing and

Maryland & Delaware

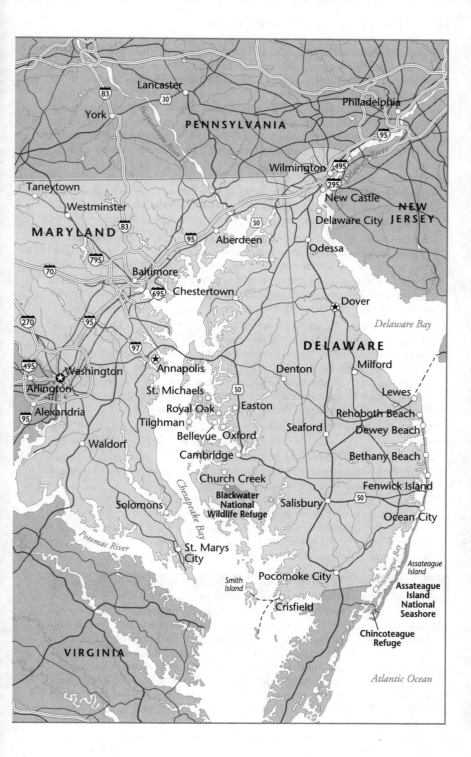

13

fishing communities. The land is flat and the elevation so low that vast wetlands, havens for migrating waterfowl, cover much of the shore. Most of the communities are welcoming and tourist-friendly, but you'll not find many first-class hotels or 4-star restaurants (though there are a few).

The higher Central Shore—Talbot County, Kent Island, and Dorchester County along the Choptank—is the most developed part and the most tourist-friendly. Though fishing and crabbing are important, the main industry here has historically been shipbuilding. Talbot County is where you'll find the highest density of hotels, inns, and restaurants.

Queen Anne's, Kent, and Cecil counties comprise the North Shore, an area of highlands and rolling hills. This area, along with the Central Shore, is home to many of the region's more affluent residents, retirees from across the bay. The countryside is beautiful, but accommodations for travelers are few and far between.

Atlantic Coast   Consisting of two barrier islands, Ocean City and Assateague, in Maryland, and five resort towns and three state parks in Delaware, the Atlantic coast is the most developed tourist area in the two states. Each of the towns and beaches is distinct, offering everything from the wild beaches and ponies of Assateague to the high-rise hotels and condos and crowded beaches of Ocean City. The Delaware beach towns fall in between in terms of development, size, and summertime population.

Central Delaware   Kent County, which is primarily farmland, is Delaware's central county and home of Dover, the state capital. Bombay Hook National Wildlife Refuge on the Delaware Bay is another stop along the east coast for migrating waterfowl and is less developed than Blackwater on the Eastern Shore. Dover, a striking contrast to Annapolis, is usually a quiet town, with a few interesting museums and historic sites, but twice a year on race weekends Dover and most of the state fill up with tourists visiting for the big NASCAR auto races.

Brandywine Valley   This is du Pont country. The American branch of the du Pont family has been living and working in this region since E. I. du Pont opened his black powder mill on the banks of the Brandywine River in 1802. The legacy of the du Ponts is everywhere, from Longwood Gardens to the Nemours Mansion. You could easily spend 2 weeks here and not see all the sights.

It's not hard to see why the du Ponts or anyone would settle here: The countryside is spectacular, with gently rolling hills, fertile land, and of course, the river itself, all of which have served as inspiration for the region's other famous family, the Wyeths. Wilmington lies at the mouth of the Brandywine River and is a good place from which to explore the attractions of the valley.

2 Maryland & Delaware Today

The curious thing about Maryland and Delaware is the tremendous diversity of culture in such a small region. The states sit at the Mason-Dixon line, which traditionally demarcates the end of the North and the beginning of the South. The catch is that though Maryland and Delaware are at identical latitudes, Delaware is considered to be in the North and Maryland squarely in Dixie. Both states are populated by a strange mixture of Northerners, Southerners, and that new category, Suburbanites. There are currently, at the very least, four distinct accents in the region, ranging from the Philadelphia clip spoken in Wilmington to the West Virginia grind of Western Maryland.

Central Maryland (the Baltimore/Washington metropolitan area) and Northern Delaware around the Brandywine Valley (including Wilmington and Newark) are lands of suburban sprawl, affluence, and big-city culture. They represent what seems most Northern about the area. We would never presume to imply that Baltimore or Wilmington is like Philadelphia or New York; that woeful inaccuracy would irritate all parties involved. But both of these are cities of industry: Baltimore of blue-collar workers and trading, Wilmington of banking and chemicals. If you make the trip from Baltimore to D.C., you definitely get the feeling of crossing over from a Northern working-class city of industry and business to a more Southern one of politics and gentility.

Baltimore today is facing the same difficulties as many cities across the country, aggravated by the financial problems of Washington, D.C. One concern is urban flight. As people leave Baltimore and Washington for the suburbs, Suburbanites themselves flee in turn, creating new suburbs farther and farther north and west. Officially, according to the census bureau, the Baltimore/Washington metropolitan area now extends all the way to Hagerstown, Maryland, almost a 1 1/2-hour drive from either city. Outside the cities the ever-growing suburbia is encroaching on the traditional farming communities and small historic towns of Western Maryland and even beginning to move across the bay to Maryland's Eastern Shore. Needless to say, tension between the old and the new is building.

Nevertheless, Baltimore itself is doing fine. Oddly, even while its population has been shrinking, its amenities, cultural and otherwise, have been improving. A new marine research center and a Hard Rock Cafe have opened on the Inner Harbor near the National Aquarium. A new stadium is being built for the Ravens football club next to the already immensely popular Oriole Park at Camden Yards. And Baltimore's restaurants, theaters (including its renowned regional theater, Center Stage), shopping, and bar scene are all first rate.

Wilmington, by contrast, is doing great economically but doesn't have nearly the robust culture of Baltimore. Not to be too hard on Wilmington, but it could be said that the city has a heart of gold—the hard, cold kind. Long in the shadow of its larger neighbor Philadelphia, it exists in many ways simply as a tax-free, politically pliable haven for large banks and mammoth chemical and pharmaceutical companies.

Not surprisingly, by catering to the truly rotund of the corporate fat cats for centuries now, Wilmington has amassed some world-class amenities suitable for the noble and near noble in wealth (luckily most of these attractions are open to the public for only a small price), including the nearby palatial mansions and gardens of the Brandywine Valley and Wilmington's elegant Hotel du Pont and 19th-century Grand Opera House. Today one of Wilmington's challenges is to make the town a suitable home for those not bankers or billionaires, and to its credit it has made great strides. A revitalization effort is under way on the city's waterfront, spearheaded by the 1997 launch of the *Kalmar Nyckel,* a re-creation of the first sailing vessel to land in Delaware. Also, the area's nightlife got a big boost with the recent opening of the Big Kahuna nightclub, which has managed to attract several up-and-coming nationally known rock bands.

The two regions of the Delmarva Peninsula, Maryland's historic Eastern Shore (the shore of the Chesapeake Bay) and the Atlantic coast of Maryland and Southern Delaware, are unlikely neighbors. The Eastern Shore has often been called a world apart—it's conservative, traditional, and struggling, with strong family ties and an enduring work ethic. It contrasts sharply with the resort areas on the Atlantic coast, where fun-seekers go to golf, fish, and relax, and youth go to celebrate, party, and just be young. In recent years, however, Eastern Shore working families of watermen and farmers have struck a very successful balance with the area's own emerging tourism trade. Some old farmers have opened bed-and-breakfasts (or not complained when their neighbors did), and many small fishing communities now use charter fishing to supplement their economies.

The beaches are as always the beaches. Assateague Island and its ponies are wild and beautiful, and Ocean City is just wild. Recently O.C. (as it is called by most locals) appears to have reached its critical mass for party tourism and mellowed just a little bit. Instead of new bars, O.C. has lately seen the creation of new golf courses, earning it the title "The Myrtle Beach of the mid-Atlantic." Attention has also shifted away from Ocean City to the quieter resorts to its north in Delaware. Rehoboth, in particular, with its mix of laid-back beach resorts, eclectic fine dining, and tax-free shopping, has become quite the summer hot spot.

Western Maryland was only made easily accessible to the rest of the state in 1991, with the creation of Interstate 68. Before this, only Frederick and Hagerstown could be reached from Baltimore without spending hours on winding mountain roads. Today we know a kayaker in Annapolis who brags she can make it to the Youghiogheny River in Friendsville in 2½ hours. (We don't recommended you try this yourself, because Maryland State Troopers are quite diligent.) The result of this newfound accessibility is that far Western Maryland—Cumberland, Deep Creek Lake, and the surrounding wilderness—is experiencing a boom in tourism as people discover all the fun to be had on the area's ski slopes, wild rivers, lakes, and mountainsides. The area's newest attraction and its first 4-star resort, the Rocky Gap Golf Resort and Lodge, opens in April 1998. It will feature an 18-hole Jack Nicklaus signature golf course, open completely by October 1998.

3 A Look at Maryland's Past

Dateline

- 1634 English colonists sail into the Potomac and found St. Mary's City, Maryland's first capital.
- 1649 Puritans find a home in Annapolis.
- 1729 Baltimore founded.
- 1767 Mason-Dixon line completed.
- 1783–84 Annapolis becomes capital of colonies for 9 months; Treaty of Paris signed at Annapolis in 1784.
- 1788 Maryland ratifies constitution and becomes seventh state.
- 1814 "Star-Spangled Banner" written at Baltimore.
- 1829 Chesapeake and Delaware Canal completed.
- 1845 U.S. Naval Academy founded at Annapolis.
- 1850 Chesapeake and Ohio Canal (C&O) reaches terminus at Cumberland.

continues

EARLY EXPLORATIONS & SETTLEMENT

The area that is present-day Maryland was initially settled by various Native American tribes including the Algonquin, Lenni Lenape, and Nanticoke. The first European to catch sight of the coast of Maryland was probably the Dutchman Henry Hudson as he sailed in from the Atlantic and along the body of water now known as Delaware Bay.

After Hudson, the Dutch made their mark several more times in the New World and as early as 1629 were attempting to establish a whaling colony in Delaware. While the Dutch were busy in Delaware, the English set their sights on neighboring territory, on the southern rim of what is now Maryland. In 1634 more than 140 English colonists arrived at the mouth of the Potomac River on two ships, *The Ark* and *The Dove.* These stalwart settlers set up a community that served as the state's first capital until 1694. It was Lord Baltimore's brother, Leonard Calvert, who christened the land in honor of Henrietta Maria, wife of King Charles I, calling it "St. Marie's Citty" (or St. Mary's City). Among the achievements of this early city was the enactment of the first laws recognizing religious tolerance.

PURITANS ESTABLISH A BASE In 1649 another group from England, the Puritans, came on the scene. They landed first in Virginia, but, encountering religious intolerance there, moved northward to what is now Annapolis and settled at the mouth of the Severn River. These early inhabitants called their new settlement Anne Arundel Town, after the wife of the second Lord Baltimore, proprietor of the colony of Maryland. In 1695 the town was renamed Annapolis in honor of Princess Anne of England, and the colonial government of Maryland was moved here from St. Mary's City; it has been Maryland's capital ever since. Shortly afterward, another city began to take shape on the Patapsco River—Baltimore, named after Lord Baltimore of England and founded in 1729.

STRUGGLE FOR INDEPENDENCE Although Philadelphia was the capital of the colonies for most of the period from 1774 to 1800, during the First and Second Continental Congresses and the major part of the Revolutionary War, Maryland's colonial hub also took a turn as capital. As the hostilities of the war drew to a close, Philadelphia relinquished its preeminence and Annapolis reigned as the first peacetime capital of the United States (from November 26, 1783, until August 13, 1784) and served as the site for the ratification of the Treaty of Paris, the document in which Great Britain formally recognized the independence of the United States.

After almost 9 months in Annapolis, the capital was once again firmly established in Philadelphia, and in 1787 a Federal Convention of 55 delegates gathered at Independence Hall to debate and revise the Articles of Confederation and ultimately to write the Constitution of the United States.

- 1852 Baltimore and Ohio Railroad (B&O) reaches the Ohio River.
- 1861 Abraham Lincoln passes through Baltimore's President Street Station on the way to his inauguration. "First Blood of the Civil War" shed at Baltimore.
- 1862 Battle of Antietam.
- 1875 Ocean City, Maryland, opened as beach resort.
- 1876 Johns Hopkins University founded in Baltimore.
- 1925 Deep Creek Lake created.
- 1952 William Preston Lane Jr. Bridge opens up the Eastern Shore.
- 1980 Harborplace debuts in Baltimore.
- 1992 Oriole Park at Camden Yards opens in Baltimore.
- 1996 Cleveland Browns football franchise moves to Baltimore, renamed the Ravens.
- 1997 Baltimore celebrates its 200th anniversary with the opening of new $150 million Convention Center at the Inner Harbor.

STATEHOOD, EARLY GROWTH & A NATIONAL ANTHEM Maryland ratified the Constitution on April 28, 1788, becoming the seventh of the original 13 colonies to do so. The post–Revolutionary War era was one of growth and expansion for the new states, and farming was pivotal to the development of all the states, including Maryland.

Transportation avenues blossomed—the 19th century soon became the age of the railroad, the steamboat, and the canal, and rivers were harnessed for milling and industrial use. National roads were built and Western Maryland via Cumberland became a gateway to the West. In 1829, the completion of the Chesapeake and Delaware Canal provided a shortcut from Chesapeake Bay to the Atlantic. The Chesapeake and Ohio Canal, stretching westward across Maryland from Georgetown, reached Cumberland in 1850, and the Baltimore and Ohio Railroad (B & O) reached the Ohio River in 1852.

This was a relatively peaceful era for the region, with the exception of the War of 1812, which began with a British blockade of the Chesapeake and Delaware bays. By 1813 much of the action had shifted westward toward the Great Lakes, but one of the war's most notable events occurred in Baltimore in 1814 as the Americans were holding off a siege of Fort McHenry by the British. Francis Scott Key, a native Marylander, was inspired to write the words of the "Star-Spangled Banner," the song that would become the country's national anthem.

CIVIL WAR YEARS   The Civil War (1861–65) was to have a great effect on the entire mid-Atlantic area including Maryland. On February 23, 1861, Abraham Lincoln passed through Baltimore's President Street Railroad Station on the way to his first inauguration. A few months later, the Sixth Massachusetts Union Army Troops and the Pennsylvania Volunteer Washington Brigade passed through the same station on April 19, 1861, on their way to the nation's capital. While the troops attempted to march to nearby Camden Station, a mob quickly gathered and blocked their passage. The skirmish resulted in the deaths of four soldiers and 12 civilians, and the incident became known as the "First Blood of the Civil War." More than a year later one of the war's most significant battles took place in the state. On September 17, 1862, the Battle of Antietam at Sharpsburg, Maryland, became the bloodiest single-day battle of the war, with the dead and wounded on both sides exceeding 23,000.

MODERN MILESTONES   In the 35 years from the Civil War's end to the dawn of the 20th century, the United States moved quickly from a war-torn nation to a leading industrial power. The first major tourist destinations in Maryland developed at about the same times on opposite sides of the state. On July 4, 1875, Ocean City officially opened as a beach resort, and a few years later, the first summer-resort hotel opened in Oakland (Garrett County), along the B&O railroad lines in 1876. Later, in 1925, the construction of the 12-mile-long Deep Creek Lake would establish Garrett County as a year-round water- and winter-sports playground.

In 1952 the William Preston Lane Jr. Bridge (commonly called the "Bay Bridge") was built, stretching from Annapolis to Kent Island, making the Eastern Shore and Ocean City truly accessible to the rest of the state. And in 1980 the cornerstone of waterfront urban development in Baltimore, Harborplace, was opened. This spurred further expansions of the waterfront area, encouraging investment in many new restaurants, hotels, and attractions including the National Aquarium in 1981, the Pier Six Concert Pavilion in 1991, Oriole Park at Camden Yards in 1992, and a $150 million Convention Center in 1997.

4 A Look at Delaware's Past

Dateline

- 1609 Henry Hudson explores Delaware Bay area.
- 1610 Delaware is named for the governor of Virginia, Lord de La Warr.
- 1629 Delaware's first town is settled by the Dutch.
- 1638 The *Kalmar Nyckel* lands near Wilmington and "New Sweden" is established.
- 1655 Peter Stuyvesant establishes Fort Casimir.
- 1664 The English rename Fort Casimir as New Castle

continues

EARLY EXPLORATIONS   This tiny area was initially settled by the Lenni Lenape and Nanticoke Indian tribes. The first European to arrive was probably Henry Hudson, in 1609, when he sailed in from the Atlantic and along the Delaware Bay. He might have stepped off the *Half Moon* to explore, but the sight of dangerous shoals persuaded him to turn his ship northward, where eventually he discovered the Hudson River in New York.

The following year, an English sea captain, Samuel Argall, sailed into the same waters by accident while en route to Virginia. It is said that he named the body of water in honor of the governor of Virginia, Thomas West, Lord de La Warr (1577–1618). The name *Delaware* was later also assigned to the land around the bay.

FIRST SETTLEMENTS   In 1631 a small group of Dutch fishermen settled on the curve of land between the bay and the ocean. They called their settlement Zwaanendael, or Valley of the Swans. But soon thereafter a misunderstanding arose between the Dutch and the Lenni Lenape Indians, and in the ensuing dispute the colonists were massacred. Now the town of Lewes (pronounced LOO-is) lies at the site of their settlement.

In 1637 two Swedish ships, the *Kalmar Nyckel* and the *Vogel Grip,* sailed into Delaware Bay and continued northward almost 60 miles, entering a smaller river. The people on board named this new body of water the Christina River, after their queen, and in time they built a fortress and called their settlement New Sweden. The Swedes adapted well, using local trees to build log cabins, said to be the first in the New World. They also raised livestock and grew corn, a staple introduced to them by the Indians. Although the settlement prospered, it was not to remain under the Swedish flag for long. By 1655, the Dutch, led by Peter Stuyvesant, had succeeded in establishing a stronghold at Fort Casimir, 7 miles to the south. Anxious to extend their power, the Dutch sent warships and soldiers and forced the surrender of the Swedes, but they allowed them to keep their settlement near Fort Christina.

THE COMING OF THE ENGLISH   The tides of history changed in 1664, when the English overpowered the Dutch and took over most of the eastern seaboard, with settlements stretching from New England to Virginia. The English, like the Dutch, allowed all previous settlers to stay. They also made a few name changes, and Fort Casimir became New Castle. Because of its location, New Castle soon evolved into the first capital of Delaware and a major colonial seaport.

Shortly afterward, William Penn crossed the Atlantic to claim extensive lands that were granted to him and his Quaker followers. He dropped anchor first at New Castle, in 1682, and then sailed farther up the Delaware River to found Philadelphia. At the time, Delaware's territory was considered part of Penn's lands, and so he divided the area south of Philadelphia into three counties: New Castle, Kent, and Sussex. As the three lower counties took shape, they also developed a sense of separateness from the rest of Pennsylvania. Recognizing this, Penn agreed to give them their own assembly in 1704.

As more English colonists poured into the counties, new cities and towns began to develop, including Wilmington (where Fort Christina once stood), named in honor of the earl of Wilmington, and Dover, plotted in 1717 according to a street plan devised by Penn. Dover would become the state capital 60 years later.

THE STRUGGLE FOR INDEPENDENCE   In 1776, as the colonies began their struggle for independence from England, Delaware assumed its part. At one point it was feared that a deadlock would develop in the vote for independence at the Continental Congress, but a Delaware man, Caesar Rodney of Kent County, rode 80

- and it becomes the first capital of Delaware.
- 1704 William Penn grants Delaware its own assembly.
- 1717 Wilmington is plotted as a city.
- 1777 Revolutionary War battles are fought near Newark and, later, in the Brandywine Valley.
- 1787 The U.S. Constitution is drafted; Delaware is the first state to ratify the document, on December 7.
- 1792 Dover becomes the capital of Delaware.
- 1802 Du Pont chemical enterprises are established in America.
- 1829 Chesapeake and Delaware Canal (C&D) completed.
- 1897 A new state constitution is adopted.
- 1940s Route 13/Du Pont Highway is completed.
- 1981 Delaware enacts Financial Center Development Act.
- 1995 C&D Canal Bridge (from Route 1) opened.
- 1997 *Kalmar Nyckel,* an authentic re-creation of the original ship, is launched.

miles through a storm-filled night on horseback from his Dover home to Philadelphia to cast his crucial vote.

As the Revolutionary War got under way, Delaware quickly raised an army of some 4,000 men, who became known for their blue uniforms. In their gear, some of the soldiers carried blue hen chickens (so called because of their blue-tinged feathers), which they used for cockfights. Today, the blue hen chicken is the official Delaware state bird.

The fighting of the war largely bypassed Delaware, except for a skirmish in 1777. A large army from England had landed near Elkton, Maryland, close to the Delaware border, and General Washington moved his forces into Northern Delaware to meet it; a short encounter took place at Cooch's Bridge near Newark, southwest of Wilmington, after which the British headed north. They met Washington's army again at the Battle of Brandywine, one of the largest battles of the Revolutionary War, just north of the Delaware line in Pennsylvania.

STATEHOOD & EARLY GROWTH   The war ended in 1783 with independence from British rule, but a new country waited to take shape. In Delaware, as in the other former colonies, the citizens felt the need for a new form of government to replace the Articles of Confederation under which they had banded together to fight the war. In September 1787 a Constitutional Convention, meeting in Philadelphia, adopted a new Constitution and then submitted it to the states for approval. Delaware was the first to ratify the document, on December 7.

As the 19th century dawned, Delaware began to prosper, as did other states on the eastern seaboard that had fostered trade with Europe. Early citizens of New Castle County were quick to harness the fast-flowing waters of the Brandywine River for milling, while the people of Kent and Sussex counties farmed their fertile lands. New immigrants from Europe arrived daily, among them a Frenchman, Eleuthère Irénée du Pont, who started a black-powder (gunpowder) mill on the banks of the Brandywine in 1802. This establishment was the foundation of a family empire that was to become the largest chemical company in America and a powerful influence, to this day, on the state of Delaware.

Wilmington, fast growing into Delaware's largest city, soon became a hub of industrial development and a shipping center. With the coming of the railroads and the steamboat, farm products, from soybeans and corn to peaches, were moved ever more swiftly up from Sussex and Kent counties to northern markets. In 1829 the completion of the Chesapeake and Delaware Canal (C&D), a waterway that flows west to east across the entire state, provided a shortcut from Chesapeake Bay to the Atlantic. In the early 1900s the du Pont family, branching out into chemical and aerospace enterprises, also sponsored a new highway, Route 13, which runs the length of the state, from north to south.

MODERN MILESTONES   In recent times, the industrial northern part of the state has taken on an added dimension. The Financial Center Development Act of the 1980s freed banks from restrictions on credit-card interest rates and provided tax advantages for banks moving assets to the state. This legislation drew many of the nation's largest banks to Delaware, as well as other businesses, earning Delaware the title of "corporate capital of the world." Currently, thousands of businesses are incorporated in the state, including more than half of the companies on *Fortune* magazine's Top 500 list and more than a third of the companies listed on the New York Stock Exchange.

Planning a Trip to Maryland & Delaware

aryland and Delaware are relatively tourist-friendly states—they're compact and have good roads, fair public transportation, and three international and one national airport within a single 3-hour drive. But even in such an accessible region, a little advance planning can make your visit run much more smoothly. This chapter will answer many of the questions you may have while planning your trip: When is the best time to visit? Which festivals and events will coincide with my trip? How much will it cost? What's the best way to get there?

1 Visitor Information & Money

VISITOR INFORMATION

For information about Maryland, contact the **Maryland Department of Business and Economic Development,** Office of Tourism Development, 9th Floor, 217 E. Redwood St., Baltimore, MD 21202 (☎ **800/MD-IS-FUN** or 410/333-6611). They also have a good website with links to all the county websites at **www.mdisfun. org**. For information on Baltimore and the vicinity, contact the **Baltimore Area Convention and Visitors Bureau,** 100 Light St., 12th Floor, Baltimore, MD 21202 (☎ **800/343-3468** or 410/659-7300). If you're looking for information on Maryland's state parks, forests, and wildlife refuges, write or call the **Maryland Department of Natural Resources,** Tawes State Office Building E-3, 580 Taylor Ave., Annapolis, MD 21401 (☎ **410/974-3771**), or you can check out their website at **quantum.gacc/dnr/**.

The **Delaware Tourism Office,** 9 Kings Hwy., P.O. Box 1404, Dover, DE 19903 (☎ **800/441-8846** or 302/739-4271), can provide general information, a state calendar of events, and a state map. But for detailed information, the local tourism offices and chambers of commerce are much more helpful. In Southern Delaware contact the **Sussex County Convention and Tourism Commission,** P.O. Box 240, Georgetown, DE 19947 (☎ **800/357-1818** or 302/856-1818). For information on Wilmington and the Brandywine Valley, write or call the **Greater Wilmington Convention and Visitors Bureau,** 100 W. 10th St., Suite 20, Wilmington, DE 19801 (☎ **800/422-1181** or 302/652-4088). On the Internet, you can find information at **www.state.de.us/tourism/intro.htm**, the Delaware State Tourism site, or at **www.visitdelaware.com**, the Sussex County site.

What Things Cost in Baltimore	U.S. $
Shuttle from BWI to Inner Harbor	11.00
Economy class rental car from Budget for a week (unlimited mileage)	185.00
Double room at the Harbor Court Hotel (very expensive)	210–250
Double room at the Admiral Fell Inn, Fells Point (expensive)	155–215
Double room at the Holiday Inn Inner Harbor (moderate)	139–159
Double room at Gibson's Lodgings, a B&B in nearby Annapolis	78–98
Lunch for one at Paolo's at the Inner Harbor (moderate)	11.00
Lunch for one at Women's Industrial Exchange Tea Room (inexpensive)	5.00
Dinner for one, without wine, at Hamptons (very expensive)	40.00
Dinner for one, without wine, at Tío Pepe (expensive)	27.00
Dinner for one, without wine, at Bertha's (moderate)	17.00
Dinner for one, without wine, at Troia, The Bistro at the Walters Cafe (inexpensive)	12.00
Typical full day's parking at the Inner Harbor	12.00
Typical Orioles' game parking	5.00
Local phone call	.25–.35
Roll of ASA 200 Kodacolor film, 24 exposures	5.89
Adult admission to the National Aquarium	11.95
Inner Harbor water taxi fare for one adult, all day	3.50
Glass of Coca-Cola	1.25
Cup of espresso (latte) at Louie's Bookstore Cafe	1.84
Dessert at Vaccaro's	3.75–7.50
Movie ticket at the Senator theater	7.00
Upper deck ticket to an Orioles' game at Camden Yards	11.00–14.00
Pint of beer in Fells Point	2.50–5.00

MONEY

In addition to the details below, foreign visitors should see "Preparing for Your Trip" in chapter 4.

Automated teller machines (ATMs) are all over the place, including most supermarkets, so getting cash is almost never a problem. For locations of machines on the Cirrus system, call ☎ **800/424-7787;** for the Plus network, call ☎ **800/843-7587.** American Express cardholders can write a personal check, guaranteed against the card, for up to $1,000 in cash at any American Express office (see "Fast Facts" in the city chapters that follow for locations of offices).

Major credit cards are accepted at most establishments throughout both states, as are U.S. dollar traveler's checks.

2 When to Go

The best time to visit Maryland and Delaware varies with each region. Obviously, the resort towns on the Atlantic are most popular in the summer, though usually quite crowded. The fringe season, May and especially September, is the optimal time for cheaper rates, comfortable temperatures, and quieter beaches. Peak season for the Eastern Shore, Annapolis, and Southern Maryland is April through October, when the weather clears up for boating and the fish start biting. Most everything is open in Baltimore year-round, though because of its boating culture and baseball season, summer is the most popular and most crowded time to visit.

Western Maryland has something for visitors year-round. Summer temperatures are generally 5° to 10° lower in the Allegheny Mountains, offering a much-needed break from the summer heat of Baltimore and the shore areas. Peak time for fall foliage is approximately the third week in October, and you'll find a lot of local festivals this time of year. From the first snow in November to about mid-March, Garrett County has the state's only downhill skiing and cross-country skiing. The only downtime for this region is April through June, when there's not enough snow for skiing and it's too cold to do anything else; it seldom reaches 70° before July in Garrett County.

Wilmington and the Brandywine Valley also are good year-round destinations. Most of the attractions in the area hold interesting festivals and events yearlong. In the chart below, Baltimore information also applies generally to Wilmington and the Brandywine Valley; expect summer temperatures to be slightly higher on the southern Eastern Shore and on the coast. Also, remember that monthly averages can be deceiving. Even though the average temperature in Baltimore during July is 77°, days in the 90s are not uncommon.

Baltimore's Average Monthly Temperatures and Precipitation

	Jan	Feb	Mar	Apr	May	June	July	Aug	Sept	Oct	Nov	Dec
Temp (°F)	31.8	34.8	44.1	53.4	63.4	72.5	77	75.6	68.5	56.6	46.8	36.7
Temp (°C)	0	1	6	11	17	22	25	24	20	13	8	2
Precip (in.)	3.05	3.12	3.38	3.09	3.72	3.67	3.69	3.92	3.41	2.98	3.32	3.41

Cumberland's Average Monthly Temperatures and Precipitation

	Jan	Feb	Mar	Apr	May	June	July	Aug	Sept	Oct	Nov	Dec
Temp (°F)	30.3	33.4	43.2	53.6	63.1	71.0	75.1	73.9	66.7	54.8	44.6	34.6
Temp (°C)	0	0	6	12	17	21	23	23	19	12	7	1
Precip (in.)	2.38	2.29	3.08	3.19	3.66	3.34	3.37	3.30	3.08	2.77	2.76	2.61

MARYLAND & DELAWARE CALENDAR OF EVENTS

January

- **Annapolis Heritage Antiques Show.** Quality antiques, spanning centuries, shown at the Medford National Guard Armory. Call ☎ 410/222-1919. Last weekend in January.
- **Welcome Spring, Longwood Gardens,** Brandywine Valley. Conservatory displays featuring thousands of colorful, fragrant spring bulbs indoors. Call ☎ 610/388-1000. Late January through April.

February

- **Winterfest at Wisp,** Deep Creek Lake. A weekend celebration of winter, with ski races, snowboarding, torchlight parades, fireworks, entertainment, and more. Call ☎ 301/387-4911. Late February or early March.

March

- **Maryland Days,** St. Mary's City. An annual celebration commemorating the founding of Maryland, with addresses by state and city officials and entertainment. Call ☎ 800/SMC-1234. Third weekend in March.

April

- **Great Delaware Kite Festival,** Lewes, Delaware. Kite-flying demonstrations and competitions on the beach at Cape Henlopen State Park. Call ☎ 302/645-8073. Good Friday.
- **Annapolis Spring Boat Show.** Staged along the waterfront, this is the region's largest boat show, featuring new and used powerboats and sailboats plus boating, fishing, and water-sports equipment. Tickets are $6 for adults, $3 for children age 12 and under. Call ☎ 410/268-8828. Third weekend in April.
- **Ward World Championship Wildfowl Carving Competition,** Ocean City. Display and judging of over 1,000 wildfowl sculptures, with $93,000 in prizes. Call ☎ 410/742-4988. Third weekend in April.

May

- ✪ **Annapolis Waterfront Festival.** More than 100 artisans and craftspeople display their work along the waterfront, in an atmosphere of celebration, featuring a flotilla of historic boats and tall ships; boat races; sailboat mini-lessons; and performances by barbershop quartets, chorale societies, and folk, gospel, and rock groups. Call ☎ 410/268-8828. First weekend in May.
- ✪ **Old Dover Days.** Dover's leading colonial, Federal, and Victorian homes, mostly private residences and gardens, are all opened to the public. There's also a full program of parades, music, maypole dancing, refreshments, and craft demonstrations. Guides in period costumes greet visitors and answer questions. Call ☎ 302/734-1736. First weekend in May.
- ✪ **Preakness Celebration.** The best known of Maryland's annual festivals, this citywide event revolves around the Preakness Stakes race at the Pimlico Race Course. The Preakness, the middle jewel in horse racing's Triple Crown, is regarded as one of the prime sporting events in the world. The weeklong hoopla includes a 5-K run, music festival, hot-air balloon races, polo match, golf tournament, frog hop, boating, food-eating contests, and waterside activities at the Inner Harbor. On the eve of the big race, there is also a parade with floats, drill teams, and marching bands. You must reserve seats to the race in advance. Call ☎ 410/542-9400. Mid-May.
- **Delmarva Hot Air Balloon Festival,** Milton, Delaware. This annual event attracts over 20 balloons and features craft, antique, and food vendors, live entertainment, and balloon rides. Call ☎ 302/684-8404. Second Saturday in May.
- ✪ **Mid-Atlantic Maritime Festival,** St. Michaels. A 3-day nautical celebration featuring exhibits and demonstrations of ship models, paintings, photographs, nautical crafts, and collectibles, plus music, seafood, a parade of tall ships, and more. Call ☎ 410/820-8606. Third weekend in May.
- **A Day in Old New Castle.** For more than 70 years, the residents of this historic district have opened their doors for an open-house tour of the town. On this day, the town's private homes, public buildings, gardens, churches, and museums are all open to the public. Other events include maypole dancing, carriage rides, musical programs, and bell-ringing. Tickets are $10 for adults, $5 for age 12 and under. Call ☎ 302/322-5744 or 302/328-2413. Third Saturday in May.
- **Chestertown Tea Party Festival,** Chestertown. This is an annual reenactment of a 1774 event, with crafts, parade, art show, and entertainment. Call ☎ 410/778-0416. Fourth Sunday in May.
- ✪ **Dover Downs NASCAR Weekend.** This 2-day, action-packed stock-car racing competition draws dozens of top drivers from around the world to Dover Downs, nicknamed the "Monster Mile." Tickets range from $20 to $72 and should be

purchased in advance. Call ☎ **800/441-RACE** or 302/674-4600. Late May or early June.

June

- **McHenry Highland Festival,** McHenry, Maryland (Deep Creek Lake). A celebration of the area's Scottish heritage with musical performances, dance competitions and workshops, and athletic contests. Call ☎ **301/334-1948.** Early June.
- **Zwaanendael Heritage Garden Tour,** Lewes, Delaware. A 1-day tour of the historic houses and gardens of Zwaanendael Park and historic downtown Lewes. Call ☎ **302/645-8073.** Third Saturday in June.

July

- **Old-Fashioned Ice Cream Festival,** Rockwood Museum, Brandywine Valley. A refreshing event with major entertainment, band music, games, hot-air balloons, fashions from the past, a baby parade, an antiques show, Victorian crafts, and a chance to sample more than two dozen flavors of locally made ice cream. Admission is $5. Call ☎ **302/761-4340.** Second weekend in July.
- **Delaware State Fair,** State Fairgrounds, Harrington. The annual showcase for state and local produce, agricultural wares, and crafts, as well as stock-car races, a demolition derby, Paramutuel harness racing, rides, games, and concerts by top-name entertainers. Admission is $3. Call ☎ **302/398-3269.** Third week of July.

August

- ✪ **Rehoboth Beach Sand Castle Contest.** Held on the north end of the beach, this annual competition includes categories for both adult and child competitors in sand castle, whale sculpture, and free form. Call ☎ **302/645-2265.** First Saturday in August.
- **Annual Canoe Joust,** Snow Hill, Maryland. This unusual sporting event takes Maryland's state sport to the water. Contestants actually stand in canoes and try to knock each other into the water with giant Q-tips. Call ☎ **410/632-3110.** First weekend in August.
- ✪ **Rocky Gap Country/Bluegrass Music Festival,** Rocky Gap State Park, near Cumberland. This annual jamboree features nationally known music stars—such as Willie Nelson, Hank Williams Jr., and Dolly Parton—local music acts, musical workshops, arts and crafts, and sports activities. Tickets are $66 and up for a 3-day pass or from $20 to $30 per day for adults. Call ☎ **800/424-2511** or 301/724-2511. First weekend in August.
- **Kunta Kinte Heritage Festival,** Annapolis. African-American connections and achievements in Maryland are the focus of this 2-day festival of arts and crafts, cuisine, and music. Call ☎ **410/349-0338.** Second weekend in August.
- **White Marlin Open and White Marlin Tournament,** Ocean City. These two competitions draw fishermen from far and wide to the "white marlin capital of the world." Call ☎ **410/289-9229** or 410/289-2800. Early to mid-August and the last weekend in August or first weekend in September.
- **Bethany Beach Boardwalk Arts Festival.** The major annual happening for the "Quiet Resorts" of Delaware's lower shore, this juried show attracts craftspeople, artisans, and spectators from near and far and takes up the entire length of the boardwalk. There are competitions for wood carving, photography, handmade jewelry, batik, metal sculpture, calligraphy, oil and watercolor painting, toys, dolls, and painted porcelain. Call ☎ **302/539-2100.** Last Saturday in August.
- ✪ **Maryland Renaissance Festival,** Crownsville, Maryland. Maryland's state sport of jousting is featured at this annual 8-weekend event, along with all types of entertainment, from musicians and singers to mimes, jugglers, magicians, fire-eaters,

stilt-walkers, and actors dressed in medieval costume. Call ☎ **800/296-7304** or 410/266-7304. Late August through early October.

September

○ **National Hard Crab Derby and Fair,** Crisfield, Maryland. Since 1947 this has been a major fixture on the late summer calendar. The focal point is a crab race in which crustaceans from states as far away as Hawaii try to match the speed of the Eastern Shore crabs. Other highlights include crab-picking and crab-cooking competitions, tennis and fishing tournaments, a beauty contest, fireworks, and a parade. Call ☎ **410/968-2682.** Labor Day weekend.

• **Brandywine Arts Festival,** Wilmington. Held on the grounds of the Josephine Gardens, this event is a showcase for local craftspeople, artisans, and musicians. Call ☎ **302/656-8364.** First weekend in September.

○ **Dover Downs NASCAR Weekend.** This action-packed 2-day stock-car racing competition, like June's NASCAR event, draws dozens of top drivers from around the world to Dover Downs. Tickets range from $20 to $72. Call ☎ **800/441-RACE** or 302/674-4600. Third weekend in September.

• **New Market Days,** New Market. The "antiques capital of Maryland" hosts a 3-day celebration of crafts, music, and food. Call ☎ **301/831-6755.** Fourth weekend in September.

October

○ **Fells Point Fun Festival,** Baltimore. This annual street festival features four stages with musical performances, as well as arts, crafts, and food vendors. Call ☎ **410/675-6756.** First weekend in October.

• **Boast the Coast,** Lewes, Delaware. A celebration of the town's maritime heritage with arts-and-crafts vendors, seafood sampling, and a lighted boat parade on the canal. Call ☎ **302/645-8073.** First weekend in October.

• **Coast Day,** Lewes, Delaware. An "open house" day focusing on the marine environment of the Delaware coast, sponsored by the College of Marine Studies of the University of Delaware. Call ☎ **302/645-4435.** First Sunday in October.

• **U.S. Sailboat and Powerboat Show,** Annapolis. Staged at the City Dock, this event is a showcase for new sailboats and products from the world's leading manufacturers. Call ☎ **410/268-8828.** Second weekend in October.

• **Olde Princess Anne Days,** Princess Anne, Maryland. More than 20 historic 18th- and 19th-century houses, mansions, and cottages—from Federal and Victorian to Italianate and Georgian—open their doors once a year for this open-air walking tour celebration, with narration by costumed guides. Tickets are $10 per person. Call ☎ **800/521-9189** or 410/651-2968. Second weekend in October.

• **Catoctin Colorfest,** Thurmont. More than 350 arts, crafts, and food vendors fill the streets and parks of Thurmont. Call ☎ **301/271-4432.** Second weekend in October.

• **Autumn Glory Festival,** Oakland, Maryland. The peak of fall foliage is celebrated at this 3-day event, with banjo and fiddle championships, a tournament of bands, parades, Oktoberfest, arts, crafts, antique sales, and concerts. Call ☎ **301/334-1948.** Second weekend in October.

• **Autumn Jazz Festival,** Rehoboth Beach, Delaware. Some of the top names of international jazz gather for a weekend of oceanfront concerts at the boardwalk bandstand as well as continuous sessions at hotels, restaurants, clubs, and bars throughout the town. Call ☎ **800/29-MUSIC** or 302/226-2166. Third weekend in October.

○ **Sea Witch Halloween Festival and Fiddlers' Convention,** Rehoboth Beach, Delaware. A celebration of Halloween by the beach. Halloween.

November

○ **World Championship Punkin' Chunkin',** Lewes, Delaware. This contest offers a chance to break a world's record for pumpkin throwing, using handmade or professional catapults and centrifugal devices. Call ☎ **302/645-8273.** First weekend in November.

○ **Waterfowl Festival,** Easton, Maryland. A major Eastern Shore fixture since 1971, this 3-day event is attended by waterfowl artists, carvers, sculptors, photographers, collectors, and anyone interested in waterfowl. Activities include duck- and goose-calling contests; workshops; auctions of antique decoys; dog trials; and exhibits of waterfowl paintings, artifacts, books, carvings, duck stamps, and memorabilia. Call ☎ **410/822-4567.** Second weekend in November.

○ **Yuletide at Winterthur.** Celebrate the holidays in 19th-century style, with a festive program at the Brandywine Valley's premier museum, featuring extensive decorations, entertainment, and guided tours. Call ☎ **800/448-3883** or 302/888-4600. Mid-November through early January.

December

• **Yuletide in Odessa,** Odessa, Delaware. Holiday decorations and observances in 18th-century style in a small town in central Delaware. Call ☎ **302/378-4069.** Throughout December.

• **Christmas in Historic Chestertown and Kent County,** Chestertown, Maryland. Walking tours of historic homes decorated for the holiday season. Admission $15. Call ☎ **410/778-6890.** Third weekend in December.

3 The Active Vacation Planner

Maryland and Delaware are not often thought of as great outdoor destinations, and this is unfortunate. Between the Atlantic Ocean, the Chesapeake Bay, and the mountains of Western Maryland, there's an awful lot of outdoor activities to fill your vacation. It's just that they've been overlooked by casual tourists until recently.

The Maryland Department of Natural Resources is a helpful source of information for all activities that you can do on state lands in Maryland, and they maintain a great website at **quantum.gacc/dnr/.** In Delaware, contact the state or tourism agency and ask for a copy of "Delaware Discoveries" and "Delaware Outdoors." The Delaware Department of Parks and Recreation also publishes "Summer Sensations," a guide to all the state parks and a listing of their summer programs.

ACTIVITIES A TO Z

BICYCLING/MOUNTAIN BIKING   Maryland and Delaware offer cycling options for all ages and abilities, and both states provide good maps for cyclists indicating safe, bicycle-friendly roadways. March through October is the best time to be cycling in both states, though summer everywhere east of Hagerstown, Maryland, is generally hot and humid, sometimes in the 90s, so bring plenty of water. Maryland law requires all cyclists under age 16 to wear helmets; otherwise, laws in both states are fairly standard. For a complete list of bicycle regulations contact the Bicycle and Pedestrian Coordinator, State Highway Administration, 707 N. Calvert St., Baltimore, MD 21203 (☎ **800/252-8776**), in Maryland; or the Bicycle and Pedestrian Coordinator, Delaware Department of Transportation, P.O. Box 778, Dover, DE 19903 (☎ **302/739-BIKE**), in Delaware.

The Delmarva Peninsula—that is, the Eastern Shore, Southern Delaware, and the Atlantic coast—is generally flat and light in traffic on the back roads. Southern Delaware is especially good to cyclists, with an excellent bicycle map of Kent and Sussex counties available and even a small biking inn-to-inn program (see chapter 13). It's also home to Cape Henlopen State Park, a great place for family biking, with designated paved trails for cyclists and pedestrians only. On Maryland's Eastern Shore, the best places to cycle are in the state parks and wildlife refuges, though the scenery is beautiful throughout the region. If you plan to cycle outside the parks, contact the county tourism agency where you wish to bike and get a good map before you start out. In many of the more rural communities, roads are seldom marked and it's easy to get lost.

Perhaps the most popular place to bike in the two states is the C&O Canal towpath, which runs along the Potomac River and the C&O Canal for 184 miles from Georgetown to Cumberland. It's slightly more challenging than bike routes on Delmarva but still a good family biking destination. The towpath is a wide dirt trail through floodplain forests, but it is generally flat and closed to vehicular traffic.

Mountain biking is a quickly emerging sport in the mountains of Western Maryland. The state forests and parks of Garrett County offer miles of multiuse trails and designated mountain biking trails, and there are even a few guide services. For experienced mountain bikers, try the trails at Potomac–Garrett State Forest or Savage River State Forest.

Cycling clubs throughout both states can provide information and maps. In Delaware, contact the **White Clay Bicycle Club,** 49 Marsh Woods Lane, Wilmington, DE 19810 (☎ **302/529-7929**), for New Castle County; **Diamond State Bicycle Club,** P.O. Box 1729, Dover, DE 19903 (☎ **302/697-0430**), for Kent County; or **Seaside Cyclists,** 205 Stockley St., Rehoboth, DE 19971 (☎ **302/227-3427**), for Sussex County. Maryland has too many clubs to list here, but contact the Bicycle and Pedestrian Coordinator at the State Highway Administration address given above and ask for a copy of "Bicycling in Maryland," a very helpful booklet that lists all the clubs in the state by region as well as the appropriate government contact in each county.

BIRDING & WILDLIFE WATCHING   The Delmarva Peninsula is a prime location along the Atlantic Flyway, and as such both Maryland and Delaware have many wildlife refuges that offer ample opportunities for birding and wildlife watching. Of course, the best time to see migrating waterfowl is early spring (February and March) and fall. The largest and most visited of the refuges is Blackwater National Wildlife Refuge, just south of Cambridge on Maryland's Eastern Shore. In addition to flocks of Canada geese, tundra and mute swan, and several species of ducks and widgeons, you may also catch a glimpse of the endangered Delmarva fox squirrel, peregrine falcon, or bald eagle. At the smaller refuges you're likely to see the same types of wildlife (except the Delmarva fox squirrel) with fewer human visitors around. In Maryland, these include Deal Island, south of Blackwater, and Eastern Neck, near Chestertown. Delaware's largest refuges are Bombay Hook and Prime Hook, but Fort Delaware State Park on Pea Patch Island outside of Wilmington is a good place to spot waterfowl as well as muskrats and other mammals.

For information on birding in Delaware contact the **Delaware Audubon Society** (☎ **302/428-3959**), P.O. Box 1713, Wilmington, DE 19899, or call the Delaware Birding hotline at ☎ **302/658-2747.** In Maryland contact the **Maryland Ornithological Society** (☎ **800/823-0050**), Cylburn Mansion, 4915 Greenspring Ave., Baltimore, MD 21209.

CAMPING   The people of Maryland and Delaware love to get outside and sleep under stars, as evidenced by the fact that it can be quite difficult to find an empty campsite on a summer weekend. Campers can find accommodations throughout both states from $5 to $18 per night depending on amenities and location. RV camping is available at most parks, though not in state forests, and sites with full hookup are especially plentiful at the parks along the Atlantic coast in both states. You can always find a campground that's open year-round, but many of the parks along the coast close down for the winter or offer limited sites. Several campgrounds are open during the winter in Western Maryland, though this certainly isn't the best time for camping unless you want to camp in the snow. Also, many of the beach campgrounds have significant mosquito and biting fly populations in summer. (There are those who believe there are more mosquitoes per square foot on Assateague Island than on any other place on earth, and we're among them.)

The largest campgrounds are at Assateague Island and Rocky Gap State Park in Maryland and at Cape Henlopen State Park in Delaware. Reservations are highly recommended at Rocky Gap and an absolute necessity if you want to camp at the federal campground at Assateague. Cape Henlopen and Assateague State Park do not accept reservations. For information about camping in Maryland contact the **Maryland Department of Natural Resources,** State Forest and Park Service, Tawes State Office Building E-3, 580 Taylor Ave., Annapolis, MD 21401 (☎ 410/974-3771), or the individual parks. In Delaware contact the **Delaware Division of Parks and Recreation,** 89 Kings Hwy., P.O. Box 1401, Dover, DE 19903 (☎ 302/736-4702).

FISHING   The region's fertile waters are one of its biggest attractions, not to mention industries. Charter fishing, freshwater fishing, fly-fishing, deep-sea fishing, surf fishing, and even ice fishing—Maryland and Delaware have so much to offer anglers it's difficult to cover it all here, but here's a quick rundown of the best places.

On the Atlantic, Ocean City is the place to go for charter fishing in Maryland. Nearly all the charter operations run out of the Shantytown Marina or the Bahia Marina in Ocean City. In Delaware, nearly all the charter fishing operations are run out of Lewes and fish the Delaware Bay as well as the Atlantic. State lands along the coast, such as Assateague Island and Delaware Seashore State Park, offer the best surf fishing because the beachgoing crowd is smaller.

Chesapeake Beach on the western shore of Chesapeake Bay, in Calvert County, has the bay's largest charter fishing fleet, and Solomons to the south is not far behind. If you prefer to fish from the shore, Point Lookout State Park in St. Mary's County has a large fishing pier on the bay as well as designated areas for shore fishing in the bay and on the Potomac.

For freshwater and fly-fishing, head west to Deep Creek Lake and the rivers of Garrett County. The Casselman River is reportedly the best place for fly-fishing in the area, but the Youghiogheny and the North Branch of the Potomac are also good bets. Ice fishing is also growing in popularity in and around Deep Creek Lake.

For information and fishing regulations in Maryland contact the **Department of Natural Resources** at ☎ 410/974-3558 for tidewater fishing and ☎ 410/974-3061 for freshwater fishing. In Delaware contact the **Delaware Division of Fish and Wildlife** at ☎ 302/736-4702, or for fishing, weather, and visitor information call ☎ 800/345-4444 (out of state) or **800/345-4200** (in state).

GOLFING   New golf courses are popping up all over the region, but the Atlantic coast still has the highest concentration in the two states. Most are in and around Ocean City, Maryland, or just across the border in Delaware. **Ocean City Golf Getaway** (☎ 800/4-OC-GOLF) publishes a handy guide to all the area courses and can arrange golf vacation packages with many area hotels and courses. They also maintain a helpful website at **www.oceancitygolf.com**.

However, there is one important new addition to the golfing scene and it isn't along the Atlantic coast: Rocky Gap Lodge and Golf Resort at Rocky Gap State Park near Cumberland, Maryland. This 18-hole Jack Nicklaus signature course is scheduled to open in October 1998 and promises to be among the state's best. And it's certainly in a beautiful location, next to Lake Habeeb in the Allegheny Mountains.

HIKING & BACKPACKING Opportunities for hiking abound in both states, but for serious hikers and backpackers, Western Maryland offers the most challenging and scenic trails. The Appalachian Trail runs through Maryland along the border of Frederick and Washington counties and is a popular place for backpackers hiking through or for a short day hike. Farther west, Savage River State Forest offers miles of hiking and multiuse trails and welcomes backcountry campers. The Big Savage Trail, a 17-mile hike along the ridge of Big Savage Mountain, is a good option for backpackers.

The C&O Canal towpath, a popular route for cyclists, is also a good place for a less strenuous hike. It runs along the canal and the Potomac River from Georgetown to Cumberland and is generally flat. You can also pick up the trail from several places near Frederick. The **Mountain Club of Maryland (MCM),** 4106 Erdman Ave., Baltimore, MD 21206, provides information about specific trails and schedules hikes that nonmembers can participate in for a small fee. For information and a copy of the hike schedule call ☎ **410-377-6266.**

HOT-AIR BALLOONING Southern Delaware's open countryside and the predictable wind patterns off the Atlantic make it a good spot for hot-air ballooning. An annual festival held in Milton, Delaware (☎ **302/684-8404**), features tethered and untethered balloon rides, or you can contact the **First State Hot-Air Balloon Team** (☎ **302/684-2002**) to schedule a trip, as the weather permits, of course. Maryland also hosts a balloon festival in La Plata in Southern Maryland the first weekend in October. For information on this festival contact **Charles County Tourism** at ☎ **301/934-9305.**

HUNTING Though it's not exactly a politically correct pastime anymore, hunting is still a popular sport in both states. Because of its location on the Atlantic Flyway, the Eastern Shore, especially Talbot County and Cambridge, is a popular destination for duck and goose hunting. Many hotels and inns there cater to hunters, and outfitters will plan hunting vacations.

Several state parks and federal wildlife refuges in Delaware are open at selected times for small game, deer, and wildlife hunting. For information on hunting in Delaware contact the Department of Natural Resources and Environmental Control, 89 Kings Hwy., Dover, DE 19901 (☎ **302/739-4506**). This organization produces a quarterly magazine called *Outdoor Delaware* that contains feature stories and information on hunting on state lands. It costs $2.50 per issue or $5 for a 1-year subscription.

RAFTING/CANOEING/KAYAKING Again, the region offers river trips for all ages and skill levels, ranging from flat-water trips in Southern Delaware and the Eastern Shore to the raging class IV and V rapids of the Youghiogheny and Savage rivers in Western Maryland. The best time for all river adventures is March through June, after the snow melts and the river levels rise. Summer trips are also quite popular, but the falling water levels make white-water trips considerably tamer.

There are many beautiful rivers on the Delmarva Peninsula that are good places for flat-water canoeing. The Nanticoke River canoe trail in Southern Delaware at Trapp Pond State Park is perhaps the most beautiful, meandering through the northernmost stand of bald cypress in the country. On Maryland's Eastern Shore the waters around Blackwater National Wildlife Refuge and the Pocomoke River north of Snow Hill (the *Pfiesteria* outbreak on this river was farther south) are also good scenic canoe runs. On all flat-water trips in summer, you should come prepared to deal with the mosquito and biting fly populations.

But Maryland is best known for its abundance of good and exciting white water in its western counties. In general, the farther west you go, the rougher the water, so for novices and first-timers, the creeks and rivers in Frederick and Washington counties are best. Several outfitters offer rafting trips down the Shenandoah/Potomac, a class II/III river, as well as canoeing, kayaking, and tubing trips on nearby creeks. More experienced paddlers will want to head to Garrett County, to the Youghiogheny and Savage rivers, both class IV/V. There are many outfitters in Maryland and nearby Ohiopyle, Pennsylvania, that offer rafting trips on the Youghiogheny and nearby rivers in West Virginia. The Savage is a dam-release river, only runnable during snow-melt, after heavy rains, or following adequate dam releases. For a release schedule call ☎ **410/962-7687.**

You don't need any experience to take a raft trip down these rivers with an out-fitter. However, the Savage and much of the Youghiogheny are very dangerous rivers and should not be run by inexperienced paddlers without a trained guide. If you are an experienced paddler and would like to run these or any of Maryland's and Delaware's rivers or creeks on your own, pick up a copy of *Maryland and Delaware Canoe Trails* (Seneca Press, 1996) by Edward Gertler. It is the definitive paddler's guide for this region.

SAILING Annapolis is often called the "sailing capital of the world," and not with-out good reason. In 1997 Annapolis hosted sailors from around the globe before send-ing them off on the eighth leg of the Whitbread Round the World Race. But even on a regular day, sailing vessels fill the Annapolis harbor. There are five full-scale sail-ing schools in Annapolis, countless places to charter bareboat or crewed sailboats, and several companies that offer daily sailing/sightseeing trips on the harbor and in nearby waterways. Some companies even offer overnight "boat and breakfast" trips and 2- or 3-day excursions on the bay.

SEA KAYAKING With easy access to the ocean and the many bays and inlets along the coast, the beach resorts on the Atlantic coast offer a good base from which to do some sea kayaking. **Delmarva Dennis' Sea Kayaking Adventures** (☎ **302/ 537-5311**) is the only full-service outfitter in the area and offers trips on Rehoboth Bay, the Atlantic, the waters around Assateague, and several other seasonal trips. You can also rent a boat and go it on your own; Chincoteague Bay at the Maryland end of Assateague Island is a favorite and fairly calm place for kayakers with some pad-dling experience.

SKIING Maryland is not a great skiing destination, but it does have one downhill ski resort and several miles of cross-country trails. Wisp operates the state's only downhill skiing resort, near Deep Creek Lake, with 23 trails and a vertical rise of 610 feet. You'll find the best trails and facilities for cross-country skiing at New Germany State Park and Herrington Manor State Park, also in Garrett County. The season for both runs from about the end of November through mid-March. For ski conditions call ☎ **301/387-4000.**

OUTFITTERS & ADVENTURE TOUR OPERATORS

Because the region is relatively compact and easily accessible, most outdoor adven-tures can be planned through local outfitters as day trips. Generally you'll have to make reservations a few days to a week in advance for sea kayaking and white-water rafting or kayaking trips. To charter a fishing boat or a sailboat, you should reserve even farther in advance (a month or more) for peak season, especially summer weekends. A complete list of outfitters for specific sports can be found in the appropriate regional chapters.

If you're trying to plan a more extensive adventure vacation, there are a few places you can contact. The **Adventuresports Institute,** P.O. Box 151, 687 Mosser Rd., McHenry, MD 21541 (☎ **301/387-3032**), is actually a division of Garrett Community College, but its classes are open to the general public. The institute offers weekend classes in white-water paddling, rock climbing and mountaineering, mountain biking, orienteering, camping, ropes, cross-country and Alpine skiing, sea kayaking, sailing, and even fly-fishing. Classes generally cost about $300 for out-of-state students. The only downside is you have to plan your vacation to coincide with the class you wish to take.

Allegany Adventures, 14419 National Hwy., LaVale, MD 21502, will help you plan weekend (or longer) hiking or cycling trips May through October, tailored to your skill level. For information and reservations call ☎ **301/729-9708. Allegany Expeditions,** Route 2, Box 88, Cumberland, MD 21502, can organize a variety of outdoor adventure trips, including hiking, biking, cave explorations, canoeing, backpacking, and rock climbing. Call ☎ **800/819-5170** or 301/722-5170 for information and reservations. Hunting and fishing trips on the Eastern Shore can be arranged through **Albright's Sportsman's Travel Service** (☎ **800/474-5502**), based in Easton, Maryland.

4 Health & Insurance

STAYING HEALTHY Maryland and Delaware don't pose any unusual health risks to the average visitor. If you're hiking or camping east of Washington, D.C., be aware that this is deer tick country, and deer ticks can carry Lyme disease. Not much can be done to protect yourself from the ticks; they're small and difficult to see. The best you can do is wear long sleeves and cover your head, and inspect yourself for bites after the trip.

Travelers to the Eastern Shore, especially anglers and boaters, should be aware of the fish kills caused by *Pfiesteria* during the summer of 1997. *Pfiesteria* is a microscopic marine organism that under certain circumstances releases a chemical toxin that causes lesions on fish and even large-scale fish kills. Some human health effects, including skin lesions, light-headedness, short-term memory loss, and headaches, have been documented among researchers working closely with high concentrations of the organism and among watermen working in affected areas.

Pfiesteria has been detected in several parts of the Chesapeake Bay and nearby rivers and, in fact, is known to occur all along the coast from the Gulf of Mexico to the Delaware Bay. However, the mere presence of the organism is not cause for alarm; certain conditions that are not yet understood must be met in order for the organism to become toxic to fish and harmful to humans. Visitors should simply avoid those waters recently affected by fish kills (in 1997, this was the lower Pocomoke River and Pocomoke Sound, Kings Creek off the Manokin River, and the Chicamacomico River in Dorchester County) and use common sense. Do not swim, water-ski, etc., in an area closed due to a fish kill. Do not handle fish with lesions. Any fish or shellfish you buy in the grocery store or at restaurants is safe to eat, but if you're catching your own, never eat fish with sores or fish that seem diseased.

For more information on health issues related to *Pfiesteria,* call Maryland's Department of Health and Mental Hygiene at ☎ 410/767-6677 or Maryland Department of the Environment at ☎ 800/633-6101, ext. 3906. To report fish lesions in

Maryland waters call the Department of Natural Resources' 24-hour hotline at ☎ **888/584-3110.** The University System of Maryland sponsors a website that can provide detailed and up-to-date information on *Pfiesteria* and any newly affected rivers at **www.mdsg.umd:80/fish-health/pfiesteria/**.

INSURANCE   Before embarking on a trip or spending money on expensive travel insurance, check all your existing policies to see what they'll cover. Make sure your health insurance or HMO will cover any emergency medical care you might need while you're away. If you have a homeowner's or renter's policy, check to see if it covers off-premises theft or loss. Some credit cards offer automatic flight insurance, covering death or dismemberment in the event of a crash, when you purchase the ticket with that card.

Also, check your credit cards to see if any of them pick up the collision/damage waiver (CDW) when you rent a car. The CDW can run as much as $12 a day and can add 50% or more to the cost of renting a car. Check your automobile insurance policy, too; it might cover the CDW as well.

If you've prepaid a lot of your travel expenses, you may want to consider a trip-cancellation policy. Most travel agents offer this type of coverage, combined with insurance against lost or stolen baggage, and even short-term health insurance.

If after checking all your existing insurance policies you decide that you need additional insurance, ask your travel agent about your options and check with local banks and your personal insurance carrier to compare costs. You can also try **Teletrip (Mutual of Omaha),** at Mutual of Omaha Plaza, 7th Floor, Teletrip, Omaha, NE 68175 (☎ **800/228-9792**). This company offers several different travel insurance policies, including medical, baggage, trip cancellation or interruption, and flight insurance against death and dismemberment. All policies last from 1 day to 6 months.

5 Tips for Special Travelers

FOR TRAVELERS WITH DISABILITIES   Most hotels in Maryland and Delaware, including many bed-and-breakfasts and inns, offer accessible accommodations, but be sure to ask when you call to make reservations. Nearly all of the states' museums are also accessible, with the exception of some historic buildings and sites. The state and county tourism offices listed in "Visitor Information" above can help you locate accessible facilities.

Rick Crowder from the **Travelin' Talk Network,** P.O. Box 3534, Clarksville, TN 37043-3534 (☎ **615/552-6670** Monday through Friday from noon to 5pm), organizes a network for disabled travelers. An eight-page newsletter is available for any contribution. A directory listing people and organizations around the world who are networked to provide the disabled traveler with firsthand information about a chosen destination is available for $35.

The **Maryland Relay Service** (☎ **800/735-2258**) links standard voice telephones with text-telephone users, and the **Maryland Department of Natural Resources** (☎ **410/974-3771;** TDD 410/974-3683) has a TDD (Telephone Device for the Deaf) line where hearing-impaired travelers can get information about recreation and camping at state parks. Several state parks in Maryland and Delaware offer wheelchair-accessible facilities.

FOR GAY & LESBIAN TRAVELERS   Baltimore has two gay newspapers, the *Baltimore Gay Paper* (☎ **410/837-7748**), P.O. Box 225, Baltimore, MD 21203, and the *Baltimore Alternative* (☎ **410/235-3401**), P.O. Box 23, Baltimore, MD 21203.

CyberDeals for Net Surfers

It's possible to get some great deals on airfare, hotels, and car rentals via the Internet. So go grab your mouse and start surfing before you hit the real waves in Hawaii— you could save a bundle on your trip. The websites we've highlighted below are worth checking out, especially since all services are free (but don't forget that time is money when you're on-line).

Microsoft Expedia (www.expedia.com) The best part of this multipurpose travel site is the "Fare Tracker": You fill out a form on the screen indicating that you're interested in cheap flights to Hawaii from your hometown, and once a week they'll e-mail you the best airfare deals. The site's "Travel Agent" will all steer you to bargains on hotels and car rentals, and you can book everything, including flights, right on-line. This site is even useful once you're booked: Before you go, log on to Expedia for oodles of up-to-date travel information, including weather reports and foreign exchange rates.

Preview Travel (www.reservations.com and www.vacations.com) Another useful travel site, "Reservations.com" has a "Best Fare Finder," which will search the Apollo computer reservations system for the three lowest fares for any route on any days of the year. Say you want to go from Chicago to Honolulu and back between December 6 and 13: Just fill out the form on the screen with times, dates, and destinations; and within minutes, Preview will show you the best deals. If you find an airfare you like, you can book your ticket right on-line—you can even reserve hotels and car rentals on this site. If you're in the preplanning stage, head to Preview's "Vacations.com" site, where you can check out the latest package deals for Hawaii and other destinations around the world by clicking on "Hot Deals."

Travelocity (www.travelocity.com) This is one of the best travel sites out there. In addition to its "Personal Fare Watcher," which notifies you via e-mail of the lowest airfares for up to five different destinations, Travelocity will track the three

---

Also in Baltimore is the **Gay and Lesbian Community Center** (☎ **410/837-5445**), 241 W. Chase St., Baltimore, MD 21201.

Rehoboth Beach, Delaware, is a gay-friendly community. The *Rehoboth Beach Gayzette* (☎ **302/644-1032**) is a good source of information. They also maintain a very informative website at **www.gayrehoboth.com/rbg.html**.

FOR SENIORS Nearly all hotels and motels, and several airlines, now offer senior discounts, so be sure to ask for the reduction when you make your reservation. Always carry photo ID as proof of age to avail yourself of discounts at attractions, hotels, restaurants, and public transportation.

6 Getting There

BY PLANE The gateway to Maryland is **Baltimore–Washington International Airport (BWI),** situated 10 miles south of Baltimore and 20 miles north of the state capital at Annapolis. Hundreds of domestic and international flights a day land and depart from this gateway. Most Maryland cities and towns are also convenient to Dulles International Airport and Ronald Reagan Washington National Airport.

Most of the major **airlines** fly into BWI, including **Air Canada** (☎ 800/776-3000), **American** (☎ 800/433-7300), **British Airways** (☎ 800/247-9297),

lowest fares for any routes on any dates in minutes. You can book a flight right then and there, and if you need a rental car or hotel, Travelocity will find you the best deal via the SABRE computer reservations system (a huge database used by travel agents worldwide). Click on "Last Minute Deals" for the latest travel bargains, including a link to "H.O.T. Coupons" (**www.hotcoupons.com**), where you can print out electronic coupons for travel in the U.S. and Canada, including Hawaii.

Trip.Com (www.thetrip.com) This site is really geared toward the business traveler, but vacationers-to-be can also use Trip.Com's valuable fare-finding engine, which will e-mail you every week with the best city-to-city airfare deals on your selected route or routes.

Discount Tickets (www.discount-tickets.com) Operated by the ETN (European Travel Network), this site offers discounts on airfares, accommodations, car rentals, and tours. It deals in flights between the U.S. and other countries, not domestic U.S. flights, so it's most useful for travelers coming to Hawaii from abroad.

Airline Websites Here's a list of airlines and their websites, where you can not only get on the e-mailing lists but also book flights directly:

- **American Airlines:** www.americanair.com
- **Continental Airlines:** www.flycontinental.com
- **TWA:** www.twa.com
- **Northwest Airlines:** www.nwa.com
- **US Airways:** www.usairways.com

Epicurious Travel (travel.epicurious.com), another good travel site, allows you to sign up for all of these airline e-mail lists at once.

—Jeanette Foster

Continental (☎ 800/525-0280), **Delta** (☎ 800/638-7333), **Northwest** (☎ 800/225-2525), **Southwest** (☎ 800/435-9792), **TWA** (☎ 800/221-2000), **United** (☎ 800/241-6522), and **US Airways** (☎ 800/428-4322).

In addition, commuter flights operate into **Salisbury/Ocean City Regional Airport** on Maryland's Eastern Shore and into **Cumberland Regional Airport** (from Pittsburgh International Airport) in the western part of the state.

Delaware does not have its own major airport for regularly scheduled passenger flights. The following airports, however, are located within easy reach: **Philadelphia International Airport,** 30 minutes from downtown Wilmington and 1 1/2 hours from Dover; **Baltimore–Washington International Airport,** approximately 1 1/2 to 2 1/2 hours to most points in Delaware; **Dulles International Airport** and **Ronald Reagan Washington National Airport,** approximately 2 1/2 to 3 hours to most points in Delaware. In addition, **New Castle County Airport,** about 10 miles south of Wilmington, serves private and corporate craft and some limited commercial flights.

BY TRAIN **Amtrak** (☎ 800/USA-RAIL) offers convenient daily service into Baltimore at Pennsylvania Station (downtown) and BWI Airport Rail Station and into downtown Wilmington at the Amtrak station at Martin Luther King Boulevard and French Street. There is also limited service into Cumberland in Western Maryland.

In addition, **Maryland Area Rail Commuter (MARC)** (☎ 800/325-RAIL) service runs between Washington, D.C., and Baltimore during the week. MARC also serves Western Maryland in Brunswick. There are plans to extend the line to Frederick.

BY BUS　Greyhound (☎ 800/231-2222) and **Trailways** (☎ 800/343-9999) both serve major points in Maryland and Delaware, including Wilmington, Dover, Rehoboth Beach, Baltimore, Ocean City, Easton, Frederick, and Cumberland.

BY CAR　The eastern seaboard's major north–south link from Maine to Florida, **I-95,** passes through both states via Wilmington and Newark in Delaware and Baltimore and central Maryland. Other interstate highways that traverse Maryland are **I-83,** which connects Baltimore with Harrisburg and points north; **I-70** and **I-68,** which connect Western Maryland to the rest of the state and to Pennsylvania, West Virginia, and Ohio. There are no other interstates in Delaware, but to access the state from Maryland and points south, use U.S. Routes 13 or 113.

BY FERRY　The Cape May–Lewes Ferry travels daily between southern New Jersey and the lower Delaware coast. This 70-minute crossing is operated on a drive-on, drive-off basis and can accommodate up to 800 passengers and 100 cars. Full details are given in the Lewes section of chapter 13.

7　Getting Around

BY CAR　The most practical way to see both Maryland and Delaware is by car. Because the states are small, it usually doesn't take long to get from one place to another. Depending on traffic, it takes approximately 2 hours to get from Wilmington to Lewes; 1 hour and 15 minutes from Wilmington to Baltimore; 1 hour from Baltimore to Frederick; 2¹/₂ hours from Frederick to Cumberland; and 2¹/₂ hours from Annapolis to Ocean City.

Rentals　Major car-rental agencies with offices in Baltimore and Wilmington include **Avis** (☎ 800/331-1212 in Baltimore, 302/654-0379 in Wilmington); **Budget** (☎ 800/527-0700 in Baltimore, 302/764-3300 in Wilmington); **Enterprise** (☎ 410/787-9210 in Baltimore); and **Hertz** (☎ 410/850-7400 in Baltimore).

Maps　The tourism agencies in Maryland and Delaware both produce good, free maps that you can get at most highway tourist information centers and from the tourism agencies listed earlier in this chapter. However, if you plan to do any extensive driving on Maryland's Eastern Shore, you'll need more detail than the state maps provide. Contact the county tourism agencies (especially Somerset, Dorchester, and Talbot) for free county maps.

BY PLANE　Commuter flights within Maryland are operated from Baltimore–Washington International Airport to Salisbury/Ocean City Regional Airport.

BY BUS/RAIL　You can travel within Baltimore on the metro, light rail, or by bus, all operated by the city's MTA (☎ **410/539-5000**). In Wilmington and the Brandywine Valley, DART First State (☎ **302/577-3278**) operates daily buses between the downtown business section and outlying suburbs and tourist attractions.

FAST FACTS: Maryland & Delaware

American Express　In Baltimore the office is located at 32 South St., Baltimore, MD 21202 (☎ **410/837-3100**); in Annapolis contact the office in the Annapolis Mall on Bestgate Road (☎ **800/788-3559** or 410/224-4200). In Wilmington contact the Delaware Travel Agency, 4001 Concord Pike, Wilmington, DE 19803

(☎ **302/479-0200**). To report lost or stolen traveler's checks call ☎ **800/ 221-7282.**

Area Codes   The area code for all of Delaware is 302. Some Brandywine Valley attractions lie over the Pennsylvania border and their area code is 610. Maryland introduced two new area codes in 1997 for a total of four: 301 and 240 in the western half of the state, and 410 and 443 in the eastern half, including Baltimore and Annapolis. Because there are now two area codes at work simultaneously in each region, you must dial the area code with every call, even if you're only calling the house next door.

Banks & ATM Networks   ATMs in both states generally use the following systems: Most, Cirrus, Plus, Novus, and Mac. In addition, you can use MasterCard or Visa to get a cash advance from most machines.

Car Rentals   See "Getting Around" earlier in this chapter.

Climate   See "When to Go" earlier in this chapter.

Embassies & Consulates   See chapter 4, "For Foreign Visitors."

Emergencies   Dial ☎ 911 for police or to report a fire or medical emergency.

Information   See "Visitor Information & Money" earlier in this chapter.

Newspapers/Magazines   The *Washington Post* and the *Baltimore Sun* are the major newspapers in Maryland. You'll find the *Philadelphia Inquirer* and the *News-Journal* (the Wilmington daily paper) in Delaware.

Police   Dial ☎ 911 or, in Baltimore, ☎ 311 for nonemergency situations that require police attention.

Taxes   State sales tax in Maryland is 5%. Delaware has no sales tax. Hotel tax in both states is 8%.

Time Zone   Maryland and Delaware are on eastern standard time. Daylight saving time is in effect from April through October.

Weather   For Baltimore weather call ☎ **410/936-1212;** for Wilmington call ☎ **302/429-9000.**

4 For Foreign Visitors

This chapter will provide some specifics about getting to the United States as economically and effortlessly as possible, plus some helpful information about how things are done in Maryland and Delaware—from receiving mail to making a local or long-distance telephone call.

1 Preparing for Your Trip

ENTRY REQUIREMENTS

Immigration laws are a hot political issue in the United States these days, and the following requirements may have changed somewhat by the time you plan your trip. Check at any U.S. embassy or consulate for current information and requirements.

DOCUMENT REGULATIONS Citizens of Canada and Bermuda may enter the United States without visas, but they will need to show proof of nationality, the most common and hassle-free form of which is a passport.

The U.S. State Department has a Visa Waiver Pilot Program allowing citizens of certain countries to enter the United States without a visa for stays of fewer than 90 days of holiday travel. At press time these included Andorra, Argentina, Australia, Austria, Belgium, Brunei, Denmark, Finland, France, Germany, Iceland, Ireland, Italy, Japan, Liechtenstein, Luxembourg, Monaco, the Netherlands, New Zealand, Norway, San Marino, Spain, Sweden, Switzerland, and the United Kingdom. (The program as applied to the United Kingdom refers to British citizens who have the "unrestricted right of permanent abode in the United Kingdom," that is, citizens from England, Scotland, Wales, Northern Ireland, the Channel islands, and the Isle of Man and not, for example, citizens of the British Commonwealth of Pakistan.)

Citizens from these countries need only a valid passport and a round-trip air or cruise ticket in their possession upon arrival. If they first enter the United States, they may then visit Mexico, Canada, Bermuda, and/or the Caribbean islands and return to the United States without needing a visa. Further information is available from any U.S. embassy or consulate.

Citizens of countries other than those specified above, or those traveling to the U.S. for reasons or length of time outside the restrictions of the Visa Waiver Program, or those who require waivers of inadmissibility, must have two documents:

- a valid passport, with an expiration date at least 6 months later than the scheduled end of the visit to the United States. (Some countries are exceptions to the 6-month validity rule. Contact any U.S. embassy or consulate for complete information.)
- a tourist visa, available from the nearest U.S. consulate. To obtain a visa, the traveler must submit a completed application form (either in person or by mail) with a 1¹/₂-inch square photo and the required application fee. There may also be an issuance fee, depending on the type of visa and other factors.

Usually you can obtain a visa right away or within 24 hours, but it may take longer during the summer rush period (June to August). If you cannot go in person, contact the nearest U.S. embassy or consulate for directions on applying by mail. Your travel agent or airline office may also be able to provide you with visa applications and instructions. The U.S. consulate or embassy that issues your visa will determine whether you will be issued a multiple- or single-entry visa. The Immigration and Naturalization Service officers at the port-of-entry in the U.S. will make an admission decision and determine your length of stay.

MEDICAL REQUIREMENTS   Inoculations are not needed to enter the United States unless you are coming from, or have stopped over in, areas known to be suffering from epidemics, particularly cholera or yellow fever.

If you have a disease requiring treatment with medications containing narcotics or drugs requiring a syringe, carry a valid signed prescription from your physician to allay suspicions that you are smuggling drugs.

CUSTOMS REQUIREMENTS   Every adult visitor may bring in free of duty: 1 liter of wine or hard liquor; 200 cigarettes or 100 cigars (but no cigars from Cuba) or 3 pounds of smoking tobacco; $100 worth of gifts. These exemptions are offered to travelers who spend at least 72 hours in the United States and who have not claimed them within the preceding 6 months. It is altogether forbidden to bring into the country foodstuffs (particularly cheese, fruit, cooked meats, and canned goods) and plants (vegetables, seeds, tropical plants, and so on). Foreign tourists may bring in or take out up to $10,000 in U.S. or foreign currency with no formalities; larger sums must be declared to customs on entering or leaving.

INSURANCE

There is no nationwide health system in the United States. Because the cost of medical care is extremely high, we strongly advise every traveler to secure health insurance coverage before setting out.

You may want to take out a comprehensive travel policy that covers (for a relatively low premium) sickness or injury costs (medical, surgical, and hospital); loss or theft of your baggage; trip-cancellation costs; guarantee of bail in case you are arrested; costs of accident, repatriation, or death. Such packages (for example, "Europe Assistance" in Europe) are sold by automobile clubs at attractive rates, as well as by insurance companies and travel agencies.

MONEY

CURRENCY & EXCHANGE   The American monetary system has a decimal base: one U.S. **dollar** ($1) = 100 **cents** (100¢). Dollar bills commonly come in $1 ("a buck"), $5, $10, $20, $50, and $100 denominations (the last two are not welcome when paying for small purchases and are not accepted in taxis or movie theaters).

There are six denominations of coins: 1¢ (one cent or a "penny"), 5¢ (five cents or a "nickel"), 10¢ (ten cents or a "dime"), 25¢ (twenty-five cents or a "quarter"), 50¢ (fifty cents or a "half-dollar"), and the rare $1 piece.

The foreign exchange bureaus so common in Europe are rare even in airports in the United States and nonexistent outside major cities. Try to avoid having to change foreign money or traveler's checks in currency other than U.S. dollars at a small-town branch or even a branch in a big city.

TRAVELER'S CHECKS   It's actually cheaper and faster to get cash at an automatic teller machine (ATM) than to fuss with traveler's checks. If you do bring them, traveler's checks denominated in U.S. dollars are readily accepted at most hotels, restaurants, and large stores.

CREDIT CARDS   The method of payment most widely used is the credit card: Visa (BarclayCard in Britain), MasterCard (EuroCard in Europe, Access in Britain, Chargex in Canada), American Express, Diners Club, Discover, and Carte Blanche. You can save yourself trouble by using "plastic money" rather than cash or traveler's checks in most hotels, restaurants, and retail stores (a growing number of food and liquor stores now accept credit cards).

SAFETY

GENERAL   While tourist areas are generally safe, crime is on the increase everywhere, and U.S. urban areas tend to be less safe than those in Europe or Japan. Visitors should always stay alert. This is particularly true of large U.S. cities. It is wise to ask the city's or area's tourist office if you're in doubt about which neighborhoods are safe. Avoid deserted areas, especially at night.

Remember also that hotels are open to the public, and in a large hotel, security may not be able to screen everyone entering. Always lock your room door—don't assume that once inside your hotel you are automatically safe and no longer need be aware of your surroundings.

Though again, tourist areas are relatively safe, property crime in particular has been on the rise in Baltimore in recent years. Avoid carrying valuables and excessive amounts of cash with you on the street; don't leave valuables in your car unattended; and in theaters, restaurants, and other public places, keep your possessions in sight.

DRIVING   Safety while driving is particularly important. Question your rental agency about personal safety, or ask for a brochure of traveler safety tips when you pick up your car. Obtain written directions, or a map with the route marked in red, from the agency showing how to get to your destination. Make sure you have enough gasoline in your tank to reach your intended destination so that you're not forced to look for a service station in an unfamiliar and possibly unsafe neighborhood. And, if possible, arrive and depart during daylight hours.

Recently more and more crime has involved cars and drivers. If you drive off a highway into a doubtful neighborhood, leave the area as quickly as possible. If you have an accident, even on the highway, stay in your car with the doors locked until you assess the situation or until the police arrive. If you are bumped from behind on the street or are involved in a minor accident with no injuries and the situation appears to be suspicious, motion to the other driver to follow you. *Never* get out of your car in such situations.

If you see someone on the road who indicates a need for help, *don't* stop. Take note of the location, drive on to a well-lighted area, and telephone the police by dialing ☎ **911.**

Park in well-lighted, well-traveled areas if possible. Always keep your car doors locked, whether attended or unattended. Look around you before you get out of your car, and never leave any packages or valuables in sight. If someone attempts to rob you or steal your car, do *not* try to resist the thief/carjacker—report the incident to the police department immediately.

2   Getting to & Around the U.S.

GETTING TO THE U.S.

British Airways (☎ **0181/759-5511** in the U.K., or 800/247-9297 in the U.S.) offers daily flights from London to both Baltimore–Washington International Airport (BWI) and Philadelphia International Airport. In addition, **Virgin Atlantic** (☎ **0293/747-747** in the U.K., or 800/862-8621 in the U.S.) also has scheduled daily flights from London to BWI.

Delta (☎ **800/221-1212**) and its international partners have scheduled flight routes from more than a dozen major European cities, including Shannon, Dublin, London, Berlin, Frankfurt, Paris, Rome, and Moscow to New York's John F. Kennedy International Airport (JFK). From JFK you can catch Delta connecting flights to both BWI and Philadelphia International Airport.

For passengers flying from Australia or New Zealand, either British Airways (BA) or Qantas goes from Sydney to London in 24 hours, where a connecting flight on either BA or Virgin Atlantic to the Baltimore–Philadelphia area (see above) can be made.

Air Canada (☎ **800/268-7240** in Canada, or 800/776-3000 in the U.S.) flies daily from Toronto's Pearson Airport to both BWI and Philadelphia International Airport. If you are coming from other major cities in Canada, Air Canada routes most flights through a connection at Toronto.

Travelers from overseas can take advantage of the **APEX (Advance Purchase Excursion) fares** offered by all the major international carriers.

The visitor arriving by air, no matter what the port of entry, should cultivate patience and resignation before setting foot on U.S. soil. Getting through Immigration control may take as long as 2 hours on some days, especially summer weekends. Add the time it takes to clear Customs and you'll see that you should make very generous allowances for delay in planning connections between international and domestic flights—an average of 2 to 3 hours at least.

In contrast, travelers arriving by car or by rail from Canada will find border-crossing formalities streamlined to the vanishing point. And air travelers from Canada, Bermuda, and some places in the Caribbean can sometimes go through Customs and Immigration at the point of departure, which is much quicker.

For further information about getting to Maryland and Delaware, see "Getting There," in chapter 3.

GETTING AROUND THE U.S.

BY AIR   Some large U.S. airlines offer travelers on their transatlantic or transpacific flights special discount tickets for any of their U.S. destinations (American Airline's Visit USA program and Delta's Discover America program, for example). They are not on sale in the United States and must, therefore, be purchased before you leave your foreign point of departure. This system is the best, easiest, and fastest way to see the United States at low cost. You should obtain information well in advance from your travel agent or the office of the airline concerned, since the conditions attached to these discount tickets can be changed without advance notice.

BY TRAIN   Long-distance trains in the United States are operated by Amtrak, the national rail passenger corporation. International visitors can buy a **USA Railpass,**

good for 15 or 30 days of unlimited travel on Amtrak, available through many foreign travel agents. Prices in 1998 for a 15-day pass were $260 off-peak, $375 peak; a 30-day pass costs $350 off-peak, $480 peak. (With a foreign passport, you can also buy passes at some Amtrak offices in the United States, including locations in Boston, Chicago, Los Angeles, Miami, New York, San Francisco, and Washington, D.C.) Reservations are generally required and should be made for each part of your trip as early as possible.

However, visitors should be aware of the limitations of long-distance rail travel in the United States. Though train service in the Northeast Corridor line between Boston and Washington, D.C. (this line includes Baltimore), is perhaps the best in the United States, service elsewhere is rarely up to European standards: Delays are common, routes are limited and often infrequently served, and fares are rarely significantly lower than discount airfares. Thus cross-country train travel should be approached with caution.

BY BUS   The cheapest form of public transportation in the United States is often by bus. **Greyhound,** the sole nationwide bus line, offers an **Ameripass** for unlimited travel for 7 days at $199, 15 days at $299, 30 days at $409, and 60 days at $599. Bus travel in the United States can be both slow and uncomfortable, so this option is not for everyone. In addition, bus stations are often located in undesirable neighborhoods.

BY CAR   The United States is a car culture, and the most cost-effective, convenient, and comfortable way to travel through the country is by car. The major cities in Maryland and Delaware lie along Amtrak's Northeast Corridor, so train travel is possible and relatively convenient to Baltimore and Wilmington. However, public transportation within the cities or to the suburban and rural areas is limited or nonexistent. For information on renting cars in the United States, see the "Getting Around" sections in individual city and region chapters and "Automobile Organizations" and "Automobile Rentals" in "Fast Facts: For the Foreign Traveler," below.

FAST FACTS: For the Foreign Traveler

Automobile Organizations   Auto clubs will supply maps, suggested routes, guidebooks, accident and bail-bond insurance, and emergency road service. The major auto club in the United States, with close to 1,000 offices nationwide, is the **American Automobile Association (AAA).** Members of some foreign auto clubs have reciprocal arrangements with AAA and enjoy its services at no charge. If you belong to an auto club in your home country, inquire about AAA reciprocity before you leave. You may be able to join AAA even if you're not a member of a reciprocal club; to inquire, call ☎ **800/222-4357.** In addition, some automobile-rental agencies now provide many of these same services. Inquire about their availability when you rent your car.

Automobile Rentals   To rent a car you need a major credit or charge card and a valid driver's license. Sometimes a passport or international driver's license is also required if your driver's license is in a language other than English. You usually need to be at least 25, although some companies do rent to younger people but may add a daily surcharge. Be sure to return your car with the same amount of gas you started out with; rental companies charge excessive prices for gasoline. Keep in mind that a separate motorcycle driver's license is required in most states. (See the "Getting Around" section in individual city and region chapters for car-rental companies.)

Business Hours   **Banks** are usually open weekdays from 9am to 3 or 4pm, until 6pm on Friday, and some are open Saturday morning. There's usually 24-hour access to the automatic teller machines (ATMs) at most banks and other outlets. Generally, **offices** are open weekdays from 9am to 5pm. **Stores** are generally open Monday through Saturday from 10am to 6pm, and some are open Sunday from noon to 5pm. Malls are open until 9pm Monday through Saturday. Most bars stay open until 2am.

Climate   See "When to Go," in chapter 3.

Currency   See "Money" in "Preparing for Your Trip," above.

Currency Exchange   You'll find currency exchange services in major airports with international service. Elsewhere, they may be quite difficult to come by. A very reliable choice is **Thomas Cook Currency Services** (☎ **800/287-7362**), which has been in business since 1841 and offers a wide range of services. It sells commission-free foreign traveler's checks, U.S. traveler's checks, drafts, and wire transfers; it also does check collections (including Eurochecks). The rates are competitive and the service is excellent. There are offices at Philadelphia International Airport, Dulles International Airport, and Ronald Reagan Washington National Airport.

Drinking Laws   You must be 21 to consume or purchase alcoholic beverages.

Electricity   The United States uses 110–120 volts A.C., 60 cycles, compared to 220–240 volts A.C., 50 cycles, as in most of Europe. In addition to a 100-volt transformer, small appliances of non-American manufacture, such as hair dryers and shavers, will require a plug adapter, with two flat, parallel pins.

Embassies & Consulates   All embassies are located in the national capital, Washington, D.C.; some consulates are located in major U.S. cities, and most nations have a mission to the United Nations in New York City. Travelers can obtain telephone numbers for their embassies and consulates by calling information in Washington, D.C. (☎ **202/555-1212**).

The embassy of **Australia** is at 1601 Massachusetts Ave. NW, Washington, DC 20036 (☎ **202/797-3000**). There is a consulate in New York City at the International Building, 630 Fifth Ave., Suite 420, New York, NY 10111 (☎ **212/408-8400**). Other Australian consulates are in Chicago, Honolulu, Houston, Los Angeles, and San Francisco.

The embassy of **Canada** is at 501 Pennsylvania Ave. NW, Washington, DC 20001 (☎ **202/682-1740**). There's a Canadian consulate in New York at 1251 Ave. of the Americas, New York, NY 10020 (☎ **212/596-1600**). Other Canadian consulates are in Atlanta, Buffalo (NY), Chicago, Cleveland, Dallas, Detroit, Los Angeles, Miami, Minneapolis, and Seattle.

The embassy of the **Republic of Ireland** is at 2234 Massachusetts Ave. NW, Washington, DC 20008 (☎ **202/462-3939**). There are Irish consulates in Boston, Chicago, New York, and San Francisco.

The embassy of **New Zealand** is at 37 Observatory Circle NW, Washington, DC 20008 (☎ **202/328-4800**). New Zealand consulates are in Chicago, New York, Los Angeles, Salt Lake City, San Francisco, San Diego, and Seattle.

The embassy of the **United Kingdom** is at 3100 Massachusetts Ave. NW, Washington, DC 20008 (☎ **202/462-1340**). There's a British consulate in New York at 845 Third Ave., New York, NY 10022 (☎ **212/745-0200**). Other British consulates are in Atlanta, Boston, Chicago, Cleveland, Dallas, Houston, Los Angeles, Miami, and Orlando.

Emergencies   Call ☎ **911** to report a fire, call the police, or get an ambulance. This is a toll-free call (no coins are required at a public telephone).

If you encounter traveler's problems, check the local telephone directory to find an office of the **Traveler's Aid Society,** a nationwide, nonprofit, social-service organization geared to helping travelers in distress. Their services might include reuniting families separated while traveling, providing food and/or shelter to people stranded without cash, or even emotional counseling. If you're in trouble, seek them out.

Gasoline (Petrol) One U.S. gallon equals 3.8 liters, while 1.2 U.S. gallons equal 1 Imperial gallon. There are usually several grades (and price levels) of gasoline available at most gas stations, and their names change from company to company. The unleaded ones with the highest octane rating are the most expensive. Note that the price is often lower if you pay in cash instead of by credit or charge card.

Holidays On the following legal national holidays, banks, government offices, post offices, and many stores, restaurants, and museums are closed: January 1 (New Year's Day); the third Monday in January (Martin Luther King Day); the third Monday in February (Presidents' Day, Washington's Birthday); the last Monday in May (Memorial Day); July 4 (Independence Day); the first Monday in September (Labor Day); the second Monday in October (Columbus Day); November 11 (Veterans Day/Armistice Day); the last Thursday in November (Thanksgiving Day); and December 25 (Christmas). Also, the Tuesday following the first Monday in November is Election Day and is a legal holiday in presidential election years.

Legal Aid If you are stopped for a minor infraction (for example, of the highway code, such as speeding), never attempt to pay the fine directly to a police officer; you may wind up arrested on the much more serious charge of attempted bribery. Pay fines by mail or directly into the hands of the clerk of the court. If accused of a more serious offense, it's wise to say and do nothing before consulting a lawyer. Under U.S. law, an arrested person is allowed one telephone call to a party of his or her choice. Call your embassy or consulate.

Mail If you want your mail to follow you on your vacation and you aren't sure of your address, your mail can be sent to you, in your name, c/o **General Delivery** at the main post office of the city or region where you expect to be. The addressee must pick it up in person and must produce proof of identity (driver's license, credit card, passport, etc.).

Mailboxes are blue with a blue-and-white logo and carry the inscription UNITED STATES POSTAL SERVICE. If your mail is addressed to a U.S. destination, don't forget to add the five-figure postal code, or ZIP (zone improvement plan) code, after the two-letter abbreviation of the state to which the mail is addressed (MD for Maryland, DE for Delaware).

Domestic **postage rates** are 20¢ for a postcard and 32¢ for a letter. Check with any local post office for current international postage rates.

Medical Emergencies For an ambulance, dial ☎ **911.**

Newspapers/Magazines National newspapers include the *New York Times, USA Today,* and the *Wall Street Journal.* National news weeklies include *Newsweek, Time,* and *U.S. News & World Report.* In Maryland and Delaware the major newspapers include the *Washington Post, Baltimore Sun,* and *Philadelphia Inquirer.*

Post Office See "Mail," above.

Safety See "Safety" in "Preparing for Your Trip," above.

Taxes In the United States there is no VAT (value-added tax) or other indirect tax at a national level. Every state, and each county and city in it, has the right to levy its own nonrefundable local tax on all purchases, including hotel and restaurant checks, airline tickets, and so on. Delaware has no state sales tax, and Maryland's sales tax is 5%. Hotel tax in both states is 8%.

Telephone, Telegraph, Telex & Fax   The telephone system in the United States is run by private corporations, so rates, especially for long-distance service and operator-assisted calls, can vary widely—even on calls made from public telephones. Local calls in the United States usually cost 25¢.

Generally, hotel surcharges on long-distance and local calls are astronomical. You're usually better off using a **public pay telephone,** which you'll find clearly marked in most public buildings and private establishments as well as on the street. Outside metropolitan areas, public telephones are more difficult to find. Stores and gas stations are your best bet.

Most **long-distance and international calls** can be dialed directly from any phone. For calls to Canada and other parts of the United States, dial 1 followed by the area code and the seven-digit number. For international calls, dial 011 followed by the country code, city code, and the telephone number of the person you wish to call.

Note that all calls to area code 800 and 888 are toll-free. However, calls to numbers in area codes 700 and 900 (chat lines, bulletin boards, dating services, etc.) can be very expensive—usually a charge of 95¢ to $3 or more per minute, and they sometimes have minimum charges that can run as high as $15 or more.

For **reversed-charge** or **collect calls,** and for **person-to-person calls,** dial 0 (zero, *not* the letter O) followed by the area code and number you want; an operator will then come on the line, and you should specify that you are calling collect, or person-to-person, or both. If your operator-assisted call is international, ask for the overseas operator.

For local **directory assistance** (information), dial 411; for **long-distance information,** dial 1, then the appropriate area code and 555-1212. For local calls in most parts of the country (Delaware included), you simply dial the seven-digit number of the person you wish to reach. However, in Maryland, you must dial the area code followed by the seven-digit number. (You do not need to dial 1 first.) Maryland has four area codes—301 and 240 in the western part of the state and 410 and 443 in the eastern part of the state (including Baltimore). Always ask for the area code if it's not offered (though it usually is), because within the two regions there is no geographical distinction between the two area codes.

Like the telephone system, **telegraph** and **telex** services are provided by private corporations such as ITT, MCI, and above all, Western Union. You can bring your telegram into the nearest Western Union office (there are hundreds across the country) or dictate it over the phone (a toll-free call, ☎ **800/325-6000**). You can also telegraph money, or have it telegraphed to you, very quickly over the Western Union system. (Note, however, that this service can be very expensive. The service charge can run as high as 15% to 25% of the amount sent.)

Most hotels have **fax** machines available for guest use (be sure to ask about the charge for use), and many hotel rooms are even wired for guests' fax machines. You'll probably also see signs for public faxes in the windows of local shops.

Telephone Directory   There are two kinds of telephone directories available to you. The general directory is the so-called **White Pages,** in which private and business subscribers are listed in alphabetical order. The inside front cover lists the emergency number for police, fire, and ambulance, and other vital numbers (like the Coast Guard, poison-control center, crime-victims hotline, and so on). The first few pages are devoted to community service numbers, including a guide to long-distance and international calling, complete with country codes and area codes.

The second directory, printed on yellow paper (hence its name, **Yellow Pages**), lists all local services, businesses, and industries by type of activity, with an index at the back. The listings cover not only such obvious items as automobile repairs by make of car, or drugstores (pharmacies), often by geographical location, but also restaurants by type of cuisine and geographical location, bookstores by special subject and/or language, places of worship by religious denomination, and other information that the tourist might otherwise not readily find. The Yellow Pages also include city plans or detailed area maps, often showing postal ZIP codes and public transportation routes.

Time   The United States is divided into six **time zones.** From east to west, these are: eastern standard time (EST); central standard time (CST); mountain standard time (MST); Pacific standard time (PST); Alaska standard time (AST); and Hawaii standard time (HST). Always keep changing time zones in mind if you're traveling (or even telephoning) long distances in the United States. For example, noon in New York City (EST) is 11am in Chicago (CST), 10am in Denver (MST), 9am in Los Angeles (PST), 8am in Anchorage (AST), and 7am in Honolulu (HST). Maryland and Delaware observe eastern standard time, 7 hours behind Greenwich mean time.

Daylight saving time is in effect from the first Sunday in April through the last Sunday in October (actually, the change is made at 2am on Sunday) except in Arizona, Hawaii, part of Indiana, and Puerto Rico. Daylight saving time moves the clock 1 hour ahead of standard time.

Tipping   This is part of the American way of life, on the principle that you must expect to pay for any service you get (many service personnel receive little direct salary and must depend on tips for their income). Here are some rules of thumb:

In **hotels,** tip bellhops $1 per piece and tip the chamber staff $1 per day. Tip the doorman or concierge only if he or she has provided you with some specific service (for example, calling a cab for you or obtaining difficult-to-get theater tickets).

In **restaurants, bars, and nightclubs,** tip the service staff 15% of the check, bartenders 10% to 15%, checkroom attendants $1 per garment, and valet parking attendants $1 per vehicle. Tip the doorman only if he has provided you with some specific service (such as calling a cab for you). Tipping is not expected in cafeterias and fast-food restaurants.

Tip **cab drivers** 15% of the fare.

As for **other service personnel,** tip porters at airports or railroad stations $1 per piece and tip hairdressers and barbers 15% to 20%.

Tipping ushers in cinemas, movies, and theaters and gas-station attendants is not expected.

Toilets   Foreign visitors often complain that public toilets are hard to find in most U.S. cities. True, there are none on the streets, but the visitor can usually find one in a bar, restaurant, hotel, museum, department store, or service station—and it will probably be clean (although the last-mentioned sometimes leaves much to be desired). Note, however, a growing practice in some restaurants and bars of displaying a notice that "toilets are for the use of patrons only." You can ignore this sign, or better yet, avoid arguments by paying for a cup of coffee or soft drink, which will qualify you as a patron. The cleanliness of toilets at railroad stations and bus depots may be more open to question. Some public places are equipped with pay toilets, which require you to insert one or more coins into a slot on the door before it will open.

Baltimore 5

Baltimore is uniquely American and even more so uniquely Maryland. You certainly wouldn't call Baltimore an international city. High-priced art galleries and other high cultural frills are noticeably absent; if Baltimoreans want these sort of things, they can drive to Washington, D.C. This town is unapologetically blue collar. Its culture is diverse but very much local, based on the Chesapeake, immigrant communities, the harbor and the dock workers, and neighborhood institutions like diners and old movie theaters.

Don't get me wrong—Baltimore isn't backward. In its way, it's a metropolitan town, filled with great restaurants, good theater, and fine museums (and crime and financial hardship as well). Visitors will enjoy Baltimore's traditional attractions, such as the fascinating National Aquarium and the truly unique American Visionary Art Museum, as well as its scruffier or more offbeat charms, like the Lexington Market and the funky antique and craft shops around Fells Point. Baltimore succeeds in mixing big city fun with its own ambience of gritty homespun friendliness. When you come out of the National Aquarium after spending an hour or two among sharks, piranha, and barracuda, your first instinct might be to say (just like a true Baltimorean), "Hey hon, let's go get some seafood and have a beer."

If you haven't been to Baltimore recently, you'll immediately notice some striking new additions to the city's night skyline: the sloping tentlike peaks of the Columbus Center, the more traditional coliseum shape of the Baltimore Ravens' new stadium, and a bright neon guitar over the Hard Rock Cafe at the Inner Harbor. And you can't underestimate the impact of Camden Yards, Baltimore's beautiful new ballpark, in revitalizing the downtown area. But during your stay, don't forget to look beyond that giant neon guitar to old Baltimore: the cobblestone streets of Fells Point, the Domino's Sugar sign shining across the harbor, the towering smokestacks of the Power Plant, and of course, the real source of Baltimore's charm, the people.

1 Orientation

ARRIVING

BY PLANE The **Baltimore–Washington International Airport,** Route 46 (☎ **800/I-FLY-BWI** or 410/859-7111), is 10 miles south of downtown Baltimore. To drive to downtown Baltimore from the

---
Impressions

We Baltimoreans let it all hang out—literally. When out-of-towners come here, they see things other cities try to hide, ban through local ordinance or vanquish through social pressure—tattooed midriffs, smiles with brown teeth, bellies the size of beach balls, hairdos from hell, rampant polyester, guys with long sideburns, women in white go-go boots.

—Dan Rodricks, *Evening Sun* (c. 1990)

---

airport, take I-195 west to Route 295 north, which will take you into downtown. Also, **SuperShuttle** (☎ **800/258-3826** or 410/859-0800) operates vans between the airport and all the major downtown hotels. Departures are scheduled every 30 minutes between 5:45am and 11:15pm, and the cost is $11 per person one-way or $17 round-trip.

Each day, hundreds of flights from both domestic and international points land at this airport. Some useful airline telephone numbers are **American** (☎ 800/ 433-7300); **Delta** (☎ 800/221-1212); **Continental** (☎ 800/525-0280); **Northwest** (☎ 800/225-2525); **Southwest** (☎ 800/435-9792); **TWA** (☎ 800/221-2000); **United** (☎ 800/241-2000); and **US Airways** (☎ 800/428-4322).

BY CAR   From the northeast and south, take I-95 to I-395 (exit 53), which goes straight to downtown. Traffic from the west approaches on I-70, which connects with I-695 (the Baltimore beltway), leading to I-95 north and into town. Coming from the northeast on I-95, you'll have to go through the Fort McHenry Tunnel to get to I-395. This eight-lane structure is the widest tunnel in the world and one of the largest public works developments in history; the toll per car is $1.

Once you arrive, you'll find numerous commercial lots and garages and indoor parking in many hotels. There's a public metered lot off Light Street next to Harborplace and street parking throughout the city, but the best bet for availability and safety are the hotel and commercial garages. Rates average about $3.50 an hour or $8 to $16 a day and $5 for Orioles or Ravens games. Most maps produced by the tourism office indicate public parking places.

BY TRAIN   Baltimore is a stop on **Amtrak's** Northeast Corridor, between Wilmington and Washington, D.C. Trains arrive at and depart from Baltimore's busy Pennsylvania Station, 1500 N. Charles St. (☎ **800/872-7245** or 410/ 291-4267), in the center of the city (north of the Inner Harbor), and **BWI Airport Rail** station (☎ **410/672-6169** or 410/672-4494), south of the city at the airport. In addition, the **Maryland Area Rail Commuter service (MARC)** provides rail service between downtown (Pennsylvania Station) and Washington, D.C., stopping at BWI Airport Rail station en route. Service is provided Monday through Friday from approximately 6am to 10pm, and the fare to the airport is $3 one-way. For more information call ☎ **800/325-RAIL.**

BY BUS   Regular bus service is provided to and from Baltimore via **Greyhound** (☎ **800/231-2222**) and **Trailways** (☎ **800/343-9999**). Buses arrive and depart from the **Baltimore Travel Plaza** (☎ **410/633-4611**), 5501 O'Donnell St., off I-95 at exit 57, just north of the Ft. McHenry Tunnel.

VISITOR INFORMATION

For advance information to help plan a visit, contact the **Baltimore Area Convention and Visitors Association (BACVA),** 100 Light St., 12th Floor, Baltimore, MD 21202 (☎ **800/343-3468** or 410/659-7300). Once you're in town, there are several visitor centers open daily for on-the-spot inquiries. These locations include a ground-floor walk-in office at Constellation Pier at the Inner Harbor, 300 W. Pratt St. (☎ **800/282-6632** or 410/837-4636); a kiosk in the main lobby of the Pennsylvania Railroad Station, 1525 N. Charles St.; and booths at the Baltimore–Washington International Airport at Pier C (main entrance) and Pier D (international terminal). In addition to general sightseeing brochures, all offices distribute copies of the *Baltimore Quick Guide,* a comprehensive magazine-style guide to what's happening in and around the city.

CITY LAYOUT

Baltimore is a sprawling mass of a city, fanning out and mostly north from the harbor to the south. But most visitors only see the downtown business and tourist districts, and there's a good reason why: North Baltimore is primarily residential, with a few college campuses and medical schools scattered about.

MAIN ARTERIES & STREETS   The Inner Harbor, the primary tourist destination, is bordered by Light Street on the west, Pratt Street on the north, and Key Highway to the south. Directly north of the Inner Harbor is Charles Center, the main downtown business area, a 33-acre complex incorporating apartments, office buildings, hotels, shops, landscaped plazas, and a theater, all connected by an overhead walkway. It is bounded by Liberty, Saratoga, Lombard, and Charles streets, the last of which divides Baltimore from east to west and is the major northbound thoroughfare.

The Baltimore Convention Center and Oriole Park at Camden Yards are directly west of the Inner Harbor along Pratt Street. Almost all downtown streets run only one way, with the important exceptions of Eutaw and Howard streets. The Jones Falls Expressway (I-83) runs roughly north–south from the harbor area to the northern suburbs, and is often the fastest way to get uptown.

FINDING AN ADDRESS   Charles Street is the main northbound artery through town and divides the city east to west. All addresses designated "East" are east of Charles Street; all designated "West" are west of Charles Street. Baltimore's numbered streets all run east to west, with the numbers increasing as you head north.

MAPS   For maps, brochures, and useful pamphlets to help you plan and enjoy your trip, contact the Baltimore Area Visitors Center, Constellation Pier, 300 W. Pratt St., Baltimore, MD 21201 (☎ **800/282-6632** or 410/837-4636).

NEIGHBORHOODS IN BRIEF

A word about safety: Outside the primary tourist destinations listed below, Baltimore's neighborhoods can change rapidly from safe to somewhat scary. So use caution and be sure you know where you're going. In particular, avoid the area surrounding Johns Hopkins Hospital and Medical School, just northeast of Fells Point and Little Italy, unless you have a medical emergency. (The hospital is not in the same location as Johns Hopkins University, the undergraduate institute, in north Baltimore, which is in a relatively safe neighborhood.)

Inner Harbor   Sooner or later, you'll wind up at the Inner Harbor at the city's southern edge. With its pavilions of boutiques, markets, and restaurants, and its modern museums, open-air concert decks, state-of-the-art convention center, and boats of all sizes, the Inner Harbor is a showplace of Baltimore at its best. Once a row of abandoned warehouses and factories, this waterfront area is now a successful urban restoration.

Mount Vernon/Charles Street   North of the Inner Harbor and Charles Center, along Charles Street, is an area known as Mount Vernon, dominated by a 178-foot monument dedicated to George Washington. Laid out in 1827, Mount Vernon was once the city's most fashionable residential district. It is still a delight, with its elegant town houses and four parklike squares. This is also the location of many of the city's oldest churches and cultural institutions, including the Peabody Conservatory of Music, one of the leading music schools in the world, and the Walters Art Gallery.

Little Italy   East of the Inner Harbor is one of Baltimore's most colorful and self-contained ethnic neighborhoods, Little Italy. You'll find about two dozen fine Italian restaurants here as well as some fine examples of neighborhood row houses, with their gleaming white marble front stoops that the residents still scrub daily. Here as in many of Baltimore's ethnic neighborhoods, the practice of window-screen painting is still carried on by craftspeople. Passersby can't see in, but window sitters can see out. Though you can walk from Little Italy to the Inner Harbor, it's best to call a cab or drive if you're out late.

Fells Point   Still farther east is Fells Point, the old seaport where Baltimore began. Fells Point today is an old-world area with brick-lined streets and more than 350 original residential structures reflecting the architecture of the American Federal period. Daytime visitors will find unique shops and boutiques, but Fells Point really comes to life at night, when its dozens of bars open for business.

2 Getting Around

BY PUBLIC TRANSPORTATION

BY RAIL & SUBWAY   Baltimore's Mass Transit Administration (MTA), operates **Light Rail,** a 27-mile system of above-ground rail lines reminiscent of the city's old trolleys. It travels on one line in a north–south direction from the suburb of Timonium to the north to Glen Burnie to the south. The key stop within the city is Camden Station, next to the Orioles' ballpark. Though it wasn't really made for tourists, the light rail is the ideal way to get to a game or to travel within the downtown area between Camden Yards and the Inner Harbor to Lexington Market and the cultural center or antique area around Mount Vernon Place.

Tickets are dispensed at machines at each stop. Trains run Monday through Saturday every 15 to 30 minutes between 5am and 11pm, and Sunday every 15 minutes between 11am and 7pm. Minimum fare is $1.35. For information call ☎ **800/543-9809** or 410/539-5000.

Baltimore's MTA also operates **Metro,** a subway system that connects the downtown area with the northwest suburbs. Trains run from Johns Hopkins University Hospital in east Baltimore through Charles Center and north to the suburb of Owings Mills. Service runs Monday through Friday from 5am to midnight and Saturday from 6am to midnight. The minimum subway fare is $1.35; for more information call ☎ **800/543-9809** or 410/539-5000.

BY BUS   The MTA operates a network of buses that connects all sections of the city. Service is daily, but hours vary. The base fare is $1.35 and exact change is necessary, or you can buy a day pass for $3. For information and schedules call ☎ **800/543-9809** or 410/539-5000.

BY TROLLEY   One of the best ways to tour Baltimore is via the **Baltimore Trolley,** a motorized trolley-style bus that is a replica of Baltimore's original cabled vehicles. The trolley ride, which is fully narrated, operates continuously, stopping at all major hotels and attractions. You can get on at any point along the route and ride the complete circuit, boarding and reboarding as many times as you wish, for an inclusive 1-day price of $12 for adults and $4.50 for children 5 to 12. These colorful trolleys operate daily, April through October from 10am to 4pm. For full information, call ☎ **410/752-2015.**

Ed Kane's Water Taxi & Trolley (☎ 800/658-8947 or 410/563-3901) connects several points on the Inner Harbor to Little Italy, City Hall, Mount Vernon, and other places of interest. The cost is $7 for adults and $3 for children under 10 for unlimited use of the trolley and the water taxi. Trolleys run mid-May through early September daily from 10am to 8pm, and mid-April through mid-May and September through mid-October Friday through Sunday from 10am to 8pm. You can buy tickets and catch the trolley at the ticket kiosk on the Light Street side of Harborplace.

BY CAR

Most car-rental agencies are located at Baltimore–Washington International Airport, including **Avis** (☎ 800/331-1212), **Budget** (☎ 410/276-7244), **Enterprise** (☎ 410/787-9210), and **Hertz** (☎ 410/850-7400). If you plan to stay in the harbor area, it is much easier to walk or take one of the water taxi services than to drive and park.

BY TAXI

All taxis in the city are metered; the three largest fleets are **Yellow Cab** (☎ 410/685-1212), **Sun Cab** (☎ 410/235-0300), and **Diamond Cab** (☎ 410/947-3333). For airport trips, call **BWI Shuttle Express** (☎ 410/859-0800).

BY WATER SHUTTLE

Water shuttle is a convenient and very pleasant way to hop between Baltimore's major waterside attractions and neighborhoods. Two companies operate water taxi service to the main harbor attractions. **Ed Kane's Water Taxi & Trolley** (☎ 800/658-8947 or 410/563-3901) runs a continual service between about a dozen Inner Harbor locations including Harborplace, Fells Point, Little Italy, and Ft. McHenry. The main stops at Harborplace are on the corner between the two pavilions and at Pier 1. Tell the mate where you want to go because not all taxis stop at every destination. The cost is $3.50 for adults and $2.25 for children under 10 for unlimited use of the water taxi for a full day. Tickets include a "Letter of Marque," a set of discount coupons for area restaurants, museums, and shops. Combined tickets for all-day use of the water taxi and trolley cost $7 for adults and $3 for children. Service operates from May through September, Monday through Thursday 10am to 11pm, Friday and Saturday 10am to midnight, and Sunday 10am to 9pm; April and October, Monday through Thursday 11am to 9pm, Friday 11am to midnight, Saturday 10am to midnight, and Sunday 10am to 9pm. Boats are at landings every 15 to 18 minutes. From November through March boats arrive at landings about every 45 minutes and operate daily from 11am to 6pm.

The **Harbor Shuttle** (☎ 410/675-2900) operates to pretty much the same destinations as Ed Kane's Water Taxi, and their stops are usually right next to each other. Adults can ride all day for $2.50 and children for $2. The shuttle runs from April through September, weekdays between 11am and 11pm and weekends between 10am and midnight. From October to March service is reduced according to demand.

The **Fort McHenry Shuttle** (☎ 410/685-4288) is a narrated shuttle service connecting Fort McHenry to the Inner Harbor. A round-trip ticket costs $5 for adults,

$3.75 for children under 12; a one-way ticket is $3 for adults, $2 for children under 12. The shuttle runs from May to September between 11am and 6pm daily. Departures are every half hour from Memorial Day to Labor Day and every hour during the rest of May and September.

ON FOOT

Because most of the major attractions are clustered around the Inner Harbor, walking is often the easiest way to get around. The trek from Charles Center to the Inner Harbor is made even easier by an elevated pedestrian walkway called **Skywalk.** Following an indoor-outdoor path, the well-posted route begins at Charles and Saratoga streets and ends at Harborplace, connecting commercial buildings, shops, theaters, pedestrian plazas, the Baltimore Convention Center, restaurants, and hotels along its safe and traffic-free route.

FAST FACTS: Baltimore

American Express The office is at 32 South St., Baltimore, MD 21202 (☎ **410/ 837-3100**).

Airport See "Arriving," earlier in this chapter.

Camera Repair Reliable downtown shops include the **Camera Doctor,** 133 S. Broadway (☎ **410/732-1717**) for repairs; and the **Ritz Camera Center,** 37 S. Charles St. (☎ **410/727-0220**) and 200 E. Pratt St. (☎ **410/685-0077**); and the **Dark Room,** 308 N. Charles St. (☎ **410/539-5639**) for 1-hour processing.

Car Rentals See "Getting Around," earlier in this chapter.

Climate See "When to Go," in chapter 3.

Emergencies Dial ☎ **911** for fire, police, or ambulance.

Eyeglass Repair Many national optical chains operate in the Baltimore area, including **Lens Crafters** (☎ **410/740-2278**) in the Columbia Mall and **Pearle Vision Center** (☎ **410/675-2275**) at Eastern Avenue and Conkling Street.

Hospitals City hospitals include **The Johns Hopkins Hospital,** 600 N. Wolfe St. (☎ **410/955-5000**); **University of Maryland Medical Center,** 22 S. Greene St. (☎ **410/328-8667**); and **Mercy Medical Center,** 301 St. Paul St. (☎ **410/ 332-9000**).

Information See "Visitor Information," earlier in this chapter.

Liquor Laws Restaurants, bars, hotels, and other places serving alcoholic beverages may be open from 6am to 2am except on Sunday and election days, when some opt to close. The minimum age for buying or consuming alcohol is 21.

Newspapers/Magazines The major daily newspaper is the *Baltimore Sun;* the *Washington Post* is also widely read. The leading monthly local magazine is *Baltimore.*

Pharmacies There are two downtown branches of **Rite Aid,** one at 200 E. Baltimore St. (☎ **410/727-4494**) and another at 201 N. Charles St. (☎ **410/ 539-1541**).

Police Dial ☎ **911.**

Post Office The main post office is at 900 E. Fayette St. (☎ **410/347-4605**). Hours are 8:30am to 5pm.

Safety Frequent patrols through the Inner Harbor and the other main tourist areas by both police and the Clean and Safe Team have cut down on the number of muggings, pickpocketings, or purse snatchings in these areas. But use common sense, as you would anywhere else: Walk only in well-lit, well-populated streets.

Taxes The state sales tax is 5%. The local hotel tax is an additional 8%.

Taxis See "Getting Around," earlier in this chapter.

Telegrams & Telex **Western Union,** 17 Commerce St. (☎ **800/227-5899** or 410/242-2011).

Transit Information Call Baltimore's **Mass Transit Administration (MTA)** at ☎ **410/539-5000.**

3 Accommodations

In recent years, new properties have sprung up, especially around the Inner Harbor, and the grand older properties have been restored and renovated. There are now more than 5,600 hotel rooms, most of them first class and deluxe. Thus it can be hard to find a double for under $100 during the week; happily, some hotels offer special weekend rates and inclusive weekend packages that represent savings of 35% to 50% off normal Sunday through Thursday tariffs. So don't be scared off by your first look at the room prices—try to time your visit for a weekend.

INNER HARBOR
VERY EXPENSIVE

✪ **Harbor Court Hotel.** 550 Light St., Baltimore, MD 21202. ☎ **800/824-0076** or 410/234-0550. Fax 410/659-5925. 203 rms, 25 suites. A/C MINIBAR TV TEL. $210–$250 double; $375–$2,000 suite. AE, CB, DC, MC, V. Self-parking $14; valet parking $18.

For one of the best locations overlooking the water, treat yourself to a stay at this lovely, intimate property with old-world charm. It features a distinctive brick facade, marble floors, crystal chandeliers, paneled walls, masterful artworks, and fine reproduction furniture. Over half the spacious guest rooms face the harbor, and each is outfitted with period-style furnishings and designer fabrics.

Dining/Entertainment: The choices include Brightons, an informal cafe; Hamptons, a 4-star restaurant serving American and French cuisine (see "Dining" section); and Explorer's, a cozy enclave with piano music nightly.

Services: Concierge, 24-hour room service, dry-cleaning and laundry service, newspaper delivery, twice-daily maid service, express checkout, valet parking.

Facilities: Indoor pool, health club, Jacuzzi, saunas, sundeck, racquetball/squash court, business center, conference rooms, beauty salon.

Harbor Inn Pier 5. 771 Eastern Ave. (at the end of Pier 5, behind the Columbus Center). Baltimore, MD 21202. ☎ **410/539-2000.** Fax 410/783-1469. 60 rms, 5 suites. A/C MINIBAR TV TEL. $225–$285 double; $500–$1,500 suite. AE, CB, DC, DISC, MC, V. Self-parking $8.50; valet parking $10.

The interior of this unassuming three-story brick building on the waterfront is like nothing else in the city. The hotel's new management has removed the old nautical fixings and made the hotel art deco from top to bottom. There are big, cushy purple, beige, and green chairs and sofas in the lobby, custom-designed furnishings throughout the hotel, and handmade comforters on all the beds. Like many of the city hotels, guest rooms have been designed with the business traveler in mind, with large desks, data ports, and in-room safes large enough to hold a laptop computer. But the rooms also have those luxuries that appeal to just about everyone: fresh fruit baskets at check-in, bottled water, plush bathrobes, umbrellas, and much more. All rooms offer water views (a harbor view room is better than the standard water view). Rooms on the second floor have balconies.

Dining/Entertainment: The Dish Cafe serves three meals daily; Lenny's Chophouse is open for lunch and dinner; and McCormick's & Schmick's is the hotel's fine-dining dinner option. In the evening you can stop by the Cobalt Lounge, the new martini lounge, for excellent harbor views, or Cohibar, the hotel's cigar bar.

Services: Concierge, 24-hour room service, dry-cleaning and laundry service, newspaper delivery, secretarial services, valet parking, courtesy car or limo, nightly turndown, twice-daily maid service, 1-hour shoe shine.

Facilities: Kitchenettes (in suites), video rentals, health club, business center, conference rooms, library.

✪ **Hyatt Regency Baltimore.** 300 Light St., Baltimore, MD 21202. ☎ **800/233-1234** or 410/528-1234. Fax 410/685-3362. 486 rms. A/C MINIBAR TV TEL. $190–$250 double. AE, CB, DC, DISC, MC, V. Self-parking $12; valet parking $15.

Located opposite the Light Street Pavilion of Harborplace, this Baltimore mainstay was the first large-scale conference hotel built on the harbor, and it is an architectural standout. The mirrored exterior reflects the passing boats and Harborplace, and a bank of rounded glass elevators, rising from the six-story Hyatt atrium, provides guests and nonguests with unsurpassed harbor views. All the guest rooms were remodeled in the spring of 1996 with dark woods and comforters, brass fixtures, live plants, and mirrored closets, and all offer wide windows and dramatic views of the water or the city. Guests have direct access to the convention center and Harborplace via the skywalk.

Dining/Entertainment: Choices include a recently remodeled and renamed rooftop (15th-floor) restaurant called Pisces (formerly Berry and Elliott's; see "Dining," later in this chapter); Bistro 500, an informal three-meal restaurant and cigar-friendly bar; and Perk's coffee bar in the atrium.

Services: Concierge, room service, dry-cleaning and laundry service, newspaper delivery, nightly turndown, express checkout, valet parking.

Facilities: Outdoor pool, health club with on-duty trainer, Jacuzzi, sauna, sundeck, tennis courts, jogging track, business center, conference rooms, gift shop.

Renaissance Harborplace Hotel. 202 E. Pratt St., Baltimore, MD 21202. ☎ **800/468-3571** or 410/547-1200. Fax 410/783-9676. 622 rms. A/C MINIBAR TV TEL. $199–$235 double; packages available. AE, CB, DC, DISC, MC, V. Self-parking $11; valet parking $14.

With Harborplace at its doorstep, fine views are a draw at this hotel, one of the largest in the waterfront area. It's part of the Gallery at Harborplace, a complex that includes an office tower, underground parking garage, and a four-level, glass-enclosed atrium of 75 shops and restaurants. The completely renovated guest rooms have contemporary decor and sweeping views of the harbor or cityscape.

Dining/Entertainment: Windows, an all-day restaurant/lounge, offers expansive views of the Inner Harbor (see "Dining," below); there is also a lobby bar for cocktails.

Services: Concierge, 24-hour room service, dry-cleaning and laundry service, newspaper delivery, nightly turndown, in-room massage, twice-daily maid service, baby-sitting, express checkout, valet parking.

Facilities: Indoor pool, health club, Jacuzzi, sauna, sundeck, business center, conference rooms, shopping at the Gallery.

Inner Harbor & Mount Vernon Accommodations & Dining

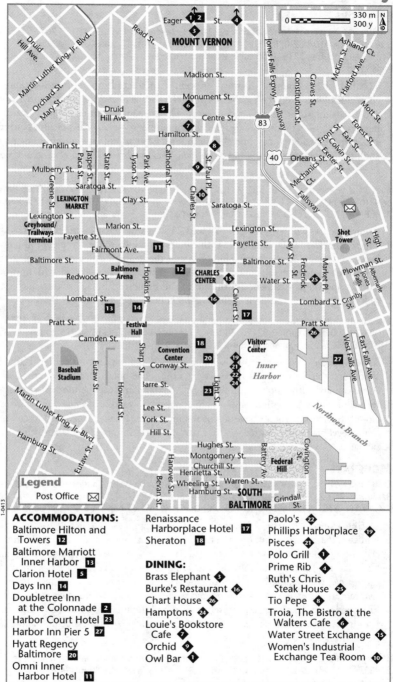

ACCOMMODATIONS:

Baltimore Hilton and
  Towers **12**
Baltimore Marriott
  Inner Harbor **13**
Clarion Hotel **5**
Days Inn **14**
Doubletree Inn
  at the Colonnade **2**
Harbor Court Hotel **23**
Harbor Inn Pier 5 **27**
Hyatt Regency
  Baltimore **20**
Omni Inner
  Harbor Hotel **11**

Renaissance
  Harborplace Hotel **17**
Sheraton **18**

DINING:

Brass Elephant **3**
Burke's Restaurant **16**
Chart House **26**
Hamptons **24**
Louie's Bookstore
  Cafe **7**
Orchid **9**
Owl Bar **1**

Paolo's **22**
Phillips Harborplace **19**
Pisces **21**
Polo Grill **1**
Prime Rib **4**
Ruth's Chris
  Steak House **25**
Tio Pepe **8**
Troia, The Bistro at the
  Walters Cafe **6**
Water Street Exchange **15**
Women's Industrial
  Exchange Tea Room **10**

EXPENSIVE

Baltimore Marriott Inner Harbor. 110 S. Eutaw St., Baltimore, MD 21202. ☎ **800/ 228-9290** or 410/962-0202. Fax 410/625-7832. 525 rms, 12 suites. A/C MINIBAR TV TEL. $129–$195 double; $230–$650 suite; weekend packages available. AE, CB, DC, DISC, MC, V. Parking $8.

This hotel has a dramatic 10-story, crescent-shaped facade and a great location—a couple of blocks from the Charles Center, Harborplace, and the convention center, and across the street from Camden Yards. The busy lobby centers around a cascading waterfall. Guest rooms are designed in contemporary style. Other facilities include a garden-themed restaurant and elegant lounge, game room, indoor swimming pool, and fitness center with sauna and whirlpool. There is also a video checkout and message system.

Omni Inner Harbor Hotel. 101 W. Fayette St., Baltimore, MD 21202. ☎ **800/THE-OMNI** or 410/752-1100. Fax 410/752-6832. 702 rms. A/C MINIBAR TV TEL. $125–$175 double. AE, CB, DC, MC, V. Self-parking $9; valet parking $15.

Comprised of two beige towers—27 and 23 floors in height—this property is the largest hotel in Maryland, popular with conventions and groups. In spite of its name, it is situated not on the Inner Harbor but in the heart of downtown opposite the Charles Center and the Baltimore Arena. Most bedrooms are L-shaped, with mirrored closets, traditional dark wood furnishings, and designer fabrics. Facilities include a grill room, cafe, bar, outdoor swimming pool, fitness center, and gift shop.

Sheraton Inner Harbor. 300 S. Charles St., Baltimore, MD 21201. ☎ **800/325-3535** or 410/962-8300. Fax 410/962-8211. 338 rms. A/C MINIBAR TV TEL. $149–$225 double. AE, CB, DC, DISC, MC, V. Self-parking $12; valet parking $19.

The Sheraton is conveniently near Harborplace, the convention center, Camden Yards, and the skywalk. Harbor views are a plus. The hotel's decor is accented with American art, with emphasis on works by Maryland artists. The modern rooms offer a choice of styles, with computer card access, light wood furnishings, and mirrored closets; the cheaper rooms have city or stadium views. Facilities include a restaurant, lobby-level piano bar, baseball-themed bar, indoor swimming pool, health club, and sauna.

MODERATE

Baltimore Hilton and Towers. 20 W. Baltimore St. (between Charles and Howard sts.), Baltimore, MD 21202. ☎ **800/333-3333** or 410/539-8400. Fax 410/625-1060. 440 rms. A/C TV TEL. $109–$159 double. AE, CB, DC, DISC, MC, V. Self-parking $12; valet parking $15.

Dating from 1928, this 19-story French Renaissance–style hotel, formerly the Radisson Plaza Lord Baltimore, is located in the heart of the city's theater and financial district. In recent years, it has changed hands and been renovated again and again, but it has managed to retain much of its original charm. The entrance is particularly impressive, with its marble columns, hand-carved artwork, brass fixtures, and massive central chandelier. Guest rooms, accessible by computer-card keys, are tastefully furnished with dark woods, mirrored closets, and floral fabrics. Concierge and valet laundry services are available. Facilities include a cafe, bar, fitness center, and business center.

Days Inn Inner Harbor. 100 Hopkins Place (between Lombard and Pratt sts.), Baltimore, MD 21202. ☎ **800/325-2525** or 410/576-1000. Fax 410/576-9437. 250 rms. A/C TV TEL. $79– $199 double. AE, CB, DC, DISC, MC, V. Parking $7.50.

This modern nine-story hotel is one of the Inner Harbor area's best bargains. It is conveniently situated between the arena and convention center. Guest rooms offer standard chain-motel furnishings, and amenities include an outdoor heated pool, a patio courtyard, and a full-service restaurant.

Holiday Inn Inner Harbor. 301 W. Lombard St., Baltimore, MD 21201. ☎ **800/HOLIDAY** or 410/685-3500. Fax 410/727-6169. 373 rms, 2 suites. A/C TV TEL. $139–$159 double; $275 suite. AE, DC, DISC, MC, V. Self-parking $6.

You know what you get from a Holiday Inn, and for good value and location, it's hard to beat this old-timer, the first major chain property in Baltimore. It has since added an executive tower with 175 rooms geared to business travelers and has been updated and renovated regularly. Guest rooms are decorated with traditional dark wood furniture including a desk and reclining chair, brass fixtures, watercolor art, and wide windows providing views of the city skyline. It is located between the Baltimore Arena and the convention center, a block away from Oriole Park and 3 blocks from Harborplace. Facilities include a restaurant and lounge, a health center with a glass-enclosed 50-foot indoor swimming pool, sauna, and exercise center, and a business center.

CHARLES STREET/MOUNT VERNON AREA

Clarion Hotel at Mt. Vernon Square. 612 Cathedral St., Baltimore, MD 21201. ☎ **800/ 292-5500** or 410/727-7101. Fax 410/789-3312. 104 rms. A/C TV TEL. $119–$219 double; weekend discounts available. AE, CB, DC, DISC, MC, V. Self-parking $8; valet parking $12.

This Mount Vernon–area hotel first opened in 1930. It later became an apartment building, reemerged in 1985 as the Peabody Court Hotel, and changed its name to the Latham in 1992 and finally the Clarion in 1995. The building has undergone a total renovation and rejuvenation, giving it a European-style ambience and luxury. As you step inside the lobby, dominated by a 6-foot, 500-pound Baccarat crystal chandelier, a sense of grandeur greets you. The public rooms feature period furniture, hand-loomed carpeting, and original art. Each of the guest rooms has period furniture, imported lamps, and a marble bathroom. Concierge, laundry and dry-cleaning service, and baby-sitting are available.

Doubletree Inn at the Colonnade. 4 W. University Pkwy., Baltimore, MD 21218. ☎ **800/ 222-TREE** or 410/235-5400. Fax 410/235-5572. 125 rms, 33 suites. $129–$159 double; $175–$250 suite; weekend packages available. AE, DC, DISC, MC, V. Self-parking $7; valet parking $9.

Situated 4 miles from the central business district and Inner Harbor, this hotel is a little off the beaten track, but it's a good option if you want to be close to Johns Hopkins University (across the street) and other northside attractions such as the Baltimore Museum of Art. Although the multicolumned entrance is unusually grandiose and the lobby is a bit overwhelming with its collection of original 18th-century European master paintings, a friendly atmosphere comes to the fore from the moment of check-in—guests receive complimentary chocolate chip cookies as a welcome. The rooms are very comfortable, with Biedermeier-inspired furnishings. Nightly turndown is provided. Facilities include a popular restaurant, the Polo Grill (see "Dining," below), an indoor glass-domed pool surrounded by Italian marble and Tivoli lights, two Jacuzzis, an exercise room, access to the university jogging track and tennis courts, and a business center. There is also a complimentary shuttle to the Inner Harbor.

FELLS POINT/LITTLE ITALY

✪ **Admiral Fell Inn.** 888 S. Broadway, Baltimore, MD 21231. ☎ **800/292-4667** or 410/ 522-7377. Fax 410/522-0707. 80 rms. A/C TV TEL. $155–$215 double. AE, DC, MC, V. Free self-parking; valet parking $6.

Fells Point & Little Italy Accommodations & Dining

ACCOMMODATIONS:
Admiral Fell Inn **1**
Inn at Henderson's Wharf **2**

DINING:
Adrian's Book Cafe **3**
Bertha's **4**
Chiapparelli's **5**
Da Mimmo **6**
Haussner's **7**
Obrycki's **8**
Piccolo's **9**
Sabatino's **10**
Vaccaro's **11**

Updated and expanded over the years, this charming inn sits just a block from the harbor in the heart of Fells Point. It is composed of seven buildings, built between 1790 and 1920 and blending Victorian and Federal-style architectures. Originally a boardinghouse for sailors, later a YMCA, and then a vinegar bottling plant, the inn was completely renovated in 1985 and again in 1995, and now includes an antique-filled lobby and library and three dining options—Savannah's, a fine-dining restaurant on the premises, and Sea Witch Restaurant and Raw Bar and The Point, nearby. The guest rooms are individually decorated, with modern bathrooms; many have canopied four-poster beds and are named after historical characters (for example, Carroll Room and Calvert Room). Some units are "attic" rooms and can be quite small; others are larger and are equipped with Jacuzzis. The inn also offers concierge service, complimentary van transport to the downtown area, and baby-sitting.

Inn at Henderson's Wharf. 1000 Fell St., Baltimore, MD 21231. ☎ **800/522-2088** or 410/522-7777. Fax 410/522-7087. 38 rms. A/C TV TEL. Apr–Nov $120–$160 double; Dec–Mar $95–$115 double. Rates include continental breakfast. AE, CB, DC, MC, V. Free parking.

Located on the waterfront at Fells Point, this inn occupies the ground floor of a former B&O railroad warehouse dating from the 1800s and restored in 1991; the rest of the structure has been converted into a condominium development. The guest rooms, which face the water or the central courtyard with English-style gardens, are decorated with period reproduction furniture, paneled or brick walls, floral quilted fabrics, nautical art, and brass fixtures. Room service and valet laundry service are

🎭 Family-Friendly Hotels

Despite all the city's family-oriented attractions, Baltimore's hotels are clearly designed with the business traveler in mind. Room rates near the harbor are expensive, and fewer and fewer hotels are offering discounted weekend rates. But there are still a few good options for those traveling with kids.

Holiday Inn Inner Harbor *(see p. 57)*   If you're willing to walk the meager 3 blocks to the harbor, and to sacrifice water views, you can save considerable money at this Baltimore mainstay. Rates are slightly discounted on weekends, and children under 12 stay for free and eat for free in the hotel restaurant. And if you're coming to see the Orioles play, you can't beat the location, only a block from Camden Yards.

Renaissance Harborplace Hotel *(see p. 54)*   Of the three hotel options right on the harbor, the Renaissance has the best offerings for families. If you plan your visit for a weekend, you can get a significant discount, especially if you opt for a room without a harbor view, and people under 17 stay free. The hotel also offers baby-sitting for an additional fee.

provided. Facilities include an exercise studio and a 220-slip marina, for those who prefer to arrive by boat.

4 Dining

"Crabtown" has always been well known for its excellent seafood restaurants, and the development of the Inner Harbor has provided an impetus and an ideal setting for even more eateries emphasizing the sea's bounty.

Baltimore is also home to a wide array of restaurants featuring regional and ethnic cuisines and traditional steak houses. In addition to the waterfront, you'll find clusters of restaurants downtown along Charles Street (known locally as "Restaurant Row") and in the older neighborhoods such as Little Italy and Fells Point.

INNER HARBOR AREA
VERY EXPENSIVE

✪ **Hamptons.** In the Harbor Court Hotel, 550 Light St. ☎ **410/234-0550.** Reservations required. Main courses $28–$38; brunch $25–$28. AE, CB, DC, DISC, MC, V. Tues–Thurs 5:30–10pm; Fri–Sat 5:30–11pm; brunch Sun 10:30am–3pm. AMERICAN/FRENCH.

Overlooking the Inner Harbor and the National Aquarium, this highly touted restaurant is the main dining room of the posh Harbor Court Hotel, and well worth a splurge for a special night out or sumptuous brunch. Specialties include pan-roasted lobster with herbs and garlic and crabmeat risotto; boneless breast of duck stuffed with a game bird and herb mousse and served with a confit of duck and an orange glaze with dried cranberries; grilled veal chop with garlic and spicy apple chutney; blackened and Cajun-spiced buffalo with mushroom and shallot marmalade; rack of lamb baked with rosemary and mustard with fresh mint sauce; and smoked squab with andouille sausage stuffing and Creole sauce.

EXPENSIVE

Chart House. 601 E. Pratt St. ☎ **410/539-6616.** Reservations recommended for dinner. Main courses $13.95–$34.95; lunch $6.95–$12.95. AE, CB, DC, DISC, MC, V. Mon–Sat 11:30am–2:30pm, Sun 1–10pm; Mon–Thurs 5–10:30pm, Fri 5–11:30pm, Sat 4–11:30pm. Shorter hrs. in winter. INTERNATIONAL/SEAFOOD.

(👨) Family-Friendly Restaurants

With all the seafood in Baltimore, finding an affordable family restaurant can sometimes be difficult. But the restaurants and food courts at the Inner Harbor are generally a good bet, and most seafood restaurants throughout town offer the traditional alternatives for children.

Phillips Harborplace *(see p. 62)*   Phillips is perhaps the city's most affordable place to get good seafood, even more so if you're traveling with the whole family. The Harborplace location is ideal for lunch or dinner after a day at the Aquarium or the Science Center, and the children's menu includes both seafood and traditional favorites such as burgers and fries and fried chicken.

Paolo's *(see p. 61)*   If you need a break from all those crab dishes, try this Italian restaurant at the Inner Harbor (not in Little Italy). It's a local chain, but the food and the location are exceptional, and the children's menu offers a change of pace: pan-fried chicken with pasta, pasta with marinara or meat sauce, and pizza.

Just east of Harborplace, this restaurant sits right on the water's edge next to the National Aquarium. Originally a warehouse for the nearby Power Plant, this building has been tastefully converted into a bilevel restaurant with an outside deck. The decor is appropriately nautical, with ship replicas and carvings, and photos of the sea and the old Baltimore waterfront. Lunch features super deli sandwiches (from crab salad to smoked turkey) and raw-bar selections. Dinner entrees include exotic fish such as mahimahi, mako, and yellowfin tuna, as well as baked stuffed flounder, crab imperial, crab cakes, and lobster tails; steaks and prime rib are also specialties. For dessert, don't miss the mud pie.

✪ Pisces. In the Hyatt Regency Hotel, 300 Light St., 15th floor. ☎ **410/528-1234.** Reservations required for dinner. Main courses $17.95–$24.95. AE, CB, DC, DISC, MC, V. Daily 4:30am–1am. INTERNATIONAL.

Overlooking the Inner Harbor, Camden Yards, and the downtown skyline, this two-tiered rooftop restaurant was voted "Baltimore's best view" by the readers of *Baltimore* magazine. Pisces was completely renovated and renamed (it was formerly Berry and Elliot's), and just reopened in fall of 1997. Menu specialties include Maryland crab cakes; salmon in pastry with spinach and Boursin cheese; roasted red snapper with sesame-soy marinade, plum tomatoes, pancetta, and basil; grilled medaillons of veal with a trio of mushrooms and rich cognac demiglace; lamb chops served atop a pink peppercorn sauce flavored with rosemary confetti; grilled petit filet mignon with rock lobster tail; and ribbon pasta tossed with roast chicken, asparagus, grilled peppers, tomatoes, and cream.

Ruth's Chris Steak House. 600 Water St. ☎ **410/783-0033.** Reservations required. Main courses $15.95–$30.95. AE, CB, DC, DISC, MC, V. Mon–Thurs 5–10pm, Fri–Sat 5–11pm, Sun 4–9pm. AMERICAN.

Located between South Frederick and Market streets on the first floor of the Brokerage, this restaurant is a favorite with the suit-and-tie crowd. Its dark wood furnishings, tiled floor, globe lanterns, and tree-size leafy plants contribute to its clubby atmosphere. This is a place to come for beef—there are six choices of steak on the menu, all butter-bathed and prepared to order, plus prime rib and filet mignon.

Alternatively, there is lobster, salmon, swordfish, and blackened tuna, as well as lamb chops and chicken.

Windows. In the Renaissance Harborplace Hotel, 202 E. Pratt St. ☎ **410/547-1200.** Reservations required. Main courses $15.95–$30.95; lunch $8.95–$14.95. AE, DC, DISC, MC, V. Daily 6:30am–11pm. AMERICAN.

Situated on the fifth floor of the Renaissance Harborplace Hotel, this restaurant not only offers sweeping views of the Inner Harbor but it has also earned serious culinary recognition. This isn't your average hotel restaurant. The chef uses fresh seasonal Maryland products and ingredients, many of which are grown right in the hotel's own in-house roof garden or come from individual specialist suppliers. Entrees at dinner include Indian-spiced roast chicken with stewed vegetables; grilled duck breast with Michigan sun-dried cherries and woodland mushrooms; seared scallops in a smoked salmon and tomato vodka cream sauce; and a variety of fresh-from-the-boat Maryland crab selections. Lunch offers salads, sandwiches, pastas, and light entrees. The hands-on Executive Chef Guy Reinbold is a personality in his own right, often quoted in *Bon Appétit* or *Gourmet,* and usually roaming the dining room to check on customer satisfaction firsthand.

MODERATE

Burke's Restaurant. 36 Light St. (at Lombard St.). ☎ **410/752-4189.** Reservations recommended for dinner. Main courses $6.95–$20.95; lunch $3–$10. AE, MC, V. Daily 7am–2am. INTERNATIONAL.

Located opposite Harborplace, this tavern-style restaurant has been a downtown fixture for more than 50 years. There are two rooms—one with a long, dark wood bar, ceiling fans, aged barrels, pewter tankards, and booth or stool seating; and another with a Tudor-style ceiling, wrought-iron chandeliers, framed prints depicting "Old Maryland" scenes, and traditional table seating. The menu here is extensive and the food particularly good. Crab cakes are a perennial standout. Dinner entrees include steaks, beef ribs, barbecued chicken, and seafood combination platters. The deep-fried onion rings are a house specialty. The Comedy Factory (see "Baltimore After Dark," below), above the restaurant, features live shows on Friday and Saturday nights.

Hard Rock Cafe. 601 E. Pratt St. ☎ **410/347-7625.** Main courses $5.99–$14.99. AE, MC, V. Sun–Thurs 11am–midnight, Fri–Sat 11am–1am. AMERICAN.

Repeat visitors to Baltimore will undoubtedly notice a new addition to the city's night skyline: a giant, lighted electric guitar perched atop the old and ill-fated Power Plant building. Nothing seems to be able to survive for long in this building, which has stood empty for the past few years. Nonetheless, the city welcomes this latest attempt, and the Hard Rock does seem to be faring better than its predecessors. The decor and atmosphere is typical Hard Rock: Photos and music memorabilia (including an outfit worn by Madonna) adorn the walls, and a classic-car-shaped bar, complete with fins, is the centerpiece of the restaurant. The menu features the usual, unremarkable fare served in large portions: salads, sandwiches, pasta dishes, and a good selection of milk shakes and smoothies.

✪ Paolo's. 301 Light St., Harborplace (on Level 1 of the Light Street Pavilion). ☎ **410/ 539-7060.** Reservations not accepted. Main courses $7.95–$17.95; lunch $4.95–$17.95. AE, CB, DC, DISC, MC, V. Mon–Fri 11am–midnight; Sat–Sun brunch 10:30am–3pm, dinner 3pm–midnight. ITALIAN/AMERICAN.

This informal, wide-windowed restaurant offers indoor and outdoor seating overlooking the harbor. Working out of an open kitchen, chefs prepare creative food at reasonable prices. Entrees include veal with saffron risotto, grilled rib-eye steak, clay pot–roasted chicken, osso bucco, quail charbroiled with spinach and egg fettuccine, and mixed grills. A variety of pastas are also served, as well as pizzas made in a wood-burning oven with a variety of traditional and exotic toppings.

Phillips Harborplace. Level 1, Light Street Pavilion, Harborplace. ☎ **410/685-6600.** Reservations not accepted. Main courses $11.95–$22.95; lunch $6.95–$10.95. AE, DC, DISC, MC, V. Daily 11am–1am. SEAFOOD.

Of the more than a dozen restaurants and sidewalk cafes in the festive Harborplace development, this is a standout, and the best place for good, reasonably priced seafood. It's a branch of the very successful establishment of the same name that has been an Ocean City, Maryland, landmark since 1956. Dinner is a feast of fresh seafood, featuring crab in many forms—soft-shell crabs, crab and lobster sauté, crab cakes, crab imperial, and all-you-can-eat portions of steamed crab. Other seafoods offered include salmon, swordfish, lobster, oysters, and mahimahi. Steaks and other meats are also available. There's a lively sing-along piano bar and entertainment at night.

Water Street Exchange. 110 Water St. ☎ **410/332-4060.** Reservations recommended. Main courses $5.95–$26.95. AE, CB, DC, DISC, MC, V. Mon 11:30am–3pm, Tues–Fri 11:30am–10pm, Sat 5:30–10pm. AMERICAN.

Resting on the site of an old wharf just a block north of Pratt Street and Harborplace, this multilevel Victorian-style restaurant has been beautifully restored with original brick walls, local artwork, brass fixtures, and a huge mahogany bar. The menu features light fare such as sandwiches, salads, omelets, and burgers, as well as dishes with an international flair, such as Cajun chicken Alfredo, jambalaya pasta, chicken Bernando (chicken fillet topped with broccoli and crab imperial), and traditional Maryland crab cakes. From March through October, there is also outdoor cafe seating on a brick-lined front courtyard.

Wharf Rat. 206 W. Pratt St. (at Hanover St. across from the convention center). ☎ **410/244-8900.** Main courses $11.75–$19.95; lunch $5.95–$9.95. AE, CB, DC, MC, V. Daily 11:30am–10pm. INTERNATIONAL.

The Wharf Rat offers several light entrees and sandwiches for dinner and lunch. Doubling also as a brew pub and bar, much of the restaurant's decor revolves around themes of brewing. There's lots of paraphernalia from traditional British, Scottish, and Irish beers and a glass wall in the dining room that allows diners to peek in on the beer making. The pub's Oliver Brewery offers a wide variety of ales and stouts, but our favorite was the porter. Sandwiches and pub fare include the standards: fish-and-chips, Reuben sandwiches, and the more avant-garde Wharf Club, a triple-decker sandwich with crabmeat, shrimp salad, bacon, and cheese. For dinner try the London broil or the Kensington Garden (chicken breast seasoned Cajun style and served with bell peppers, mushrooms, black olives, and white wine).

CHARLES STREET/MOUNT VERNON
VERY EXPENSIVE

Polo Grill. 4 W. University Pkwy. (in the Doubletree Inn at The Colonnade). ☎ **410/235-8200.** Reservations required. Main courses $16.95–$35.95. AE, CB, DC, DISC, MC, V. Mon–Thurs 6:30am–11pm, Fri 6:30am–midnight, Sat 7am–midnight, Sun 7am–10pm. AMERICAN.

It doesn't matter that this restaurant is 4 miles north of downtown—the movers and shakers of Baltimore gather here each evening from all directions. Often compared to New York's 21 Club or Washington's Jockey Club for atmosphere, this clubby restaurant is handsomely ensconced in the main dining room at the Doubletree Inn at The Colonnade, opposite Johns Hopkins University. The menu changes every day, but don't be surprised to find farm-raised emu or roast loin of elk featured, as well as signature dishes such as Panos and Paul's famous fried lobster tail with drawn butter and honey mustard sauce; penne pasta with blackened chicken; and Oriental-style barbecued salmon with soya butter on warm sesame spinach leaves. Fresh lobster by the pound and prime cut-to-order steaks are also popular.

✪ Prime Rib. 1101 N. Calvert St. (between Biddle and Chase sts.). ☎ **410/539-1804.** Reservations required. Main courses $16.95–$39. AE, CB, DC, MC, V. Mon–Sat 5pm–midnight, Sun 4–11pm. AMERICAN.

In the heart of the Mount Vernon district, this restaurant has been a standout for fine beef since 1965, often called "the shrine to prime" by locals. In addition to aged Midwestern beef, fresh Chesapeake Bay seafood is a specialty of the chef, who has won accolades from the prestigious Chaîne des Rôtisseurs. Most people start with the house trademark, Greenberg potato skins, named after a regular customer. Entrees include prime rib, steak, rack of lamb, veal chops, and such seafood dishes as blackened swordfish, crab cakes, and lobster tails. This restaurant is a favorite with the corporate crowd and those who like to be pampered—in a setting of self-fringed table lamps, leopard-spotted carpeting, and a pianist tinkling softly on the baby grand.

EXPENSIVE

Brass Elephant. 924 N. Charles St. ☎ **410/547-8480.** Reservations required. Main courses $13–$23; lunch $5.95–$10.95. AE, CB, DC, DISC, MC, V. Mon–Fri 11:30am–2pm; Mon–Thurs 5:30–9:30pm, Fri–Sat 5:30–10:30pm, Sun 5–9pm. NORTHERN ITALIAN/MEDITERRANEAN.

This trendy restaurant, nestled in the Mount Vernon district between Reade and Eager streets, is housed in a restored 1861 town house, originally the home of businessman Charles Stuart. The decor carries on the 19th-century tradition with an open fireplace, gold-leaf trim, chandeliers, and, as its name implies, lots of brass fixtures. Gentle shades of blue and classical background music add to the serene atmosphere. Lunch ranges from open-faced sandwiches and omelets to pastas and light entrees. Dinner choices include grilled salmon al pesto, veal portofino with roasted shallots and shiitake mushrooms, shrimp and scallops cioppino, medaillons of beef Marsala, and rack of lamb.

Orchid. 419 N. Charles St. ☎ **410/837-0080.** Reservations recommended for dinner. Main courses $16–$27.95; lunch $8.95–$13.95. AE, MC, V. Tues–Sat 11:30am–2:30pm; Tues–Thurs 5–10:30pm, Fri–Sat 5–11:30pm, Sun 4–9:30pm. INTERNATIONAL.

This restaurant, in a converted row house near Franklin Street, prepares classic French dishes with creative Asian accents. The decor is lovely, with a fireplace, crisp linens, brass chandeliers, and, of course, orchids on each table. The eclectic menu includes house favorites such as spicy tuna with fresh mango in a warm sesame sauce; mixed grill Escoffier, a combination of veal and beef tenderloins with lamb chops and three different sauces; and fillet of flounder "Orchid," with crispy almonds, ginger, pineapple, and lemon butter sauce.

Owl Bar. 1 E. Chase St. ☎ **410/347-0888.** Reservations recommended for dinner. Main courses $16–$28; lunch $5–$10. AE, DC, DISC, MC, V. Mon–Sat 11:30am–11pm or later, Sun 11am–11pm. ITALIAN/AMERICAN.

Housed in the once-revered Belvedere Hotel (now condominiums and offices) in classy Mount Vernon, this restaurant seeks to restore some of the luster and panache of turn-of-the-century Baltimore. The entrance is lined with photos that tell the story of Baltimore's great citizens and notable visitors, and the interior has all the trappings of yesteryear—brass rail bar, paneled walls, leather furnishings, and the famous blinking owls that gave the bar its name. Only the menu bows to contemporary tastes, with a brick oven that turns out such trendy creations as white pizza (made with all white cheeses), Peking pizza (made with Peking duck and hoisin sauce), and hickory-smoked vegetarian pizza (topped with hummus and fontina cheese). Specialty pastas are also appealing, from penne Granchio (jumbo lump crabmeat sautéed with artichoke hearts, plum tomatoes, and penne in a Pinot Grigio butter sauce), to farfalle (butterfly pasta in vodka tomato cream sauce and julienne of prosciutto). Other choices include osso bucco, Black Angus steaks, and free-range chicken stuffed with veal and fresh herbs.

The same management is also attempting to breathe life back into two other sections of the former hotel—the adjacent room known as Champagne Tony's, also featuring contemporary Italian cuisine, and the 13th-floor rooftop room, Champagne and Truffles, which offers desserts and cappuccino with piano music and panoramic views of the city.

Tío Pepe. 10 E. Franklin St. (just off Charles St.). ☎ **410/539-4675.** Reservations required. Main courses $15.75–$22.75; lunch $7.50–$16.75. AE, DC, DISC, MC, V. Mon–Fri 11:30am–2:30pm; Mon–Thurs 5–10:30pm, Fri 5–11pm, Sat 5–11:30pm, Sun 4–10:30pm. SPANISH.

This highly praised restaurant exudes a Spanish wine cellar atmosphere, with arched cavern-style entranceways, wrought-iron railings, and white stucco walls decorated with colorful ceramic plates. The menu emphasizes the Catalan region of Spain, offering dishes such as paella; rack of lamb; tournedos Tío Pepe (beef with sherry-wine sauce and mushrooms); chicken with tomatoes, green and red pimientos, and mushrooms; red snapper à la vasca (with green sauce, clams, mussels, asparagus, and boiled egg); fillet of sole with bananas and hollandaise sauce; and Spanish prawns flavored with brandy.

MODERATE

۞ Louie's Bookstore Cafe. 518 N. Charles St. (between Centre and Hamilton sts.). ☎ **410/962-1224.** Main courses $7.95–$16.95; lunch $3.95–$11.95. AE, MC, V. Mon 10am–midnight, Tues–Thurs 10am–12:30am, Fri 10am–1:30am, Sat 11:30am–1:30am, Sun 10:30am–midnight. INTERNATIONAL.

As its name implies, this cafe, on Restaurant Row, is a blend of bookstore and bistro. Staffed by artists and musicians, this unusual eatery is decorated with paintings by local talent and an eclectic blend of furniture, with chamber music emanating from the background. Dinner entrees include crab cake platter, vegetable stir-fry, hijiki and tofu, steaks, and "Chestertown Chicken," white meat marinated in a curry, garlic, and lemon sauce. Lunch features creative salads (such as artichoke and feta with spinach) and sandwiches. But the biggest attraction is their selection of coffee, tea, and desserts, made on the premises. There are regular book signings and readings, and live solo or duo classical music every night.

INEXPENSIVE

Troia, The Bistro at the Walters Cafe. 600 N. Charles St. ☎ **410/752-2887.** Reservations recommended. Main courses $5.95–$11.95. AE, MC, V. Tues and Sun 11:30am–3:30pm, Wed–Sat 11:30am–3:30pm and 5:30–10pm. REGIONAL ITALIAN.

Nestled on the lower level of the Walters Art Gallery, this restaurant is surrounded by corridors of great art and is a favorite with Baltimoreans for lunch or brunch. With such a creative atmosphere, it's no wonder that the constantly changing menu is very imaginative. Entrees range from salads and sandwiches to exotic quiches, pizza, and pastas, as well as traditional crab cakes, shaved honey-baked ham, and house specials of barbecued North Atlantic salmon and Moss's white meat loaf (made with herbed turkey).

✪ **Women's Industrial Exchange Tea Room.** 333 N. Charles St. ☎ **410/685-4388.** Main courses $3.95–$6.95. MC, V. Mon–Fri 7am–2:30pm; lunch counter 10:30am–2pm. Closed major holidays. AMERICAN.

Carrying on a 19th-century Baltimore tradition, this restaurant is in the back room of a craft shop/bakery run by the Women's Industrial Exchange, a foundation designed to help needy women and men of the city by consigning their handmade goods. It is housed in an 1815 building of fine Flemish bond work, wrought-iron railings, and marble steps. The restaurant setting is rich in Old Baltimore atmosphere, with historic wall murals, ceiling fans, fireplace, and motherly and grandmotherly waitresses. (In the movie *Sleepless in Seattle,* part of which was filmed here, waitress Miss Marguerite made her acting debut at age 92.) The menu is simple—homemade soups, salads, sandwiches, omelets, meat or fish platters, and luscious desserts (charlotte russe is a specialty). Afterward, take time to browse in the shop and examine the many samples of local handiwork. If you're in a hurry, there is also a lunch counter in the building's basement (entrance from Pleasant Street).

FELLS POINT/LITTLE ITALY
EXPENSIVE

Da Mimmo. 217 S. High St. ☎ **410/727-6876.** Reservations recommended. Main courses $15–$35; lunch $8–$12. AE, CB, DC, MC, V. Sun–Thurs 11:30am–11:30pm, Fri–Sat 11:30am–1am. GOURMET ITALIAN.

If you like music with your meal, head to this small candlelit Little Italy restaurant with piano entertainment nightly in the Roman-style lounge. The restaurant has recently been renovated, creating a dark, clublike atmosphere. It also added a cigar lounge. The varied menu features everything from chicken cacciatore, lobster tetrazzini, and filet mignon to their award-winning butterflied veal chops. Lunch is also available here, with sandwiches, pastas, and seafood dishes.

✪ **Haussner's.** 3244 Eastern Ave. ☎ **410/327-8365.** Reservations accepted only for lunch. Main courses $7.95–$24.95. AE, DC, DISC, MC, V. Tues–Sat 11am–10pm. INTERNATIONAL.

Established in 1926 by Bavarian-born William Henry Haussner, this landmark restaurant is firmly ensconced in the ethnic enclave of east Baltimore known as Highlandtown. The restaurant is still run today by the founder's widow, Frances, and family. This is not only a great place to go for good value and good food (the main dining room seats 500), it is also an art and antique gallery, with paintings, porcelains, sculptures, clocks, and figurines, collected over the years by the Haussners. Even the menu features sample paintings. Haussner's also houses what they claim is the world's largest ball of string.

The cuisine, however, is the pièce de résistance, with more than 100 entrees, all fresh and delicious daily. The menu, which changes daily, offers all kinds of meats and seafoods, including frog's legs, finnan haddie, lobster tails, sweetbreads, baked rabbit, Wiener schnitzel, roast loin of boar, and pig's knuckles. With its own bakery on the premises, Haussner's is also known for its desserts (more than 30 varieties, from strawberry pie and apple strudel to honey almond cake). Lighter choices include salads, omelets, and sandwiches.

✪ **Obrycki's.** 1727 E. Pratt St. ☎ **410/732-6399.** Reservations accepted only for "early-bird" meals, Mon–Fri noon–7pm and Sat–Sun noon–6pm. Main courses $14.95–$26.95; lunch/light fare $5.95–$12.50. AE, CB, DC, DISC, MC, V. Mon–Sat noon–11pm, Sun noon–9:30pm. Closed mid-Dec to mid-Mar. SEAFOOD.

Fells Point, the waterfront neighborhood where Baltimore began, is one of the city's best areas for seafood. Without a doubt, the benchmark of all the eateries here is Obrycki's, situated between South Broadway and South Register streets. Food connoisseurs Craig Claiborne and George Lang rave about this place. The decor is particularly charming, with stained-glass windows, brick archways, and wainscoting along the walls. But the big attraction is the fresh seafood, especially if you enjoy crabs. This is the quintessential crab house, where you can crack open steamed crabs in their shells and feast on the tender, succulent meat to your heart's content. There's crab soup, crab cocktail, crab balls, crab cakes, crab imperial, and soft-shell crabs. The rest of the menu is just as tempting—shrimp, lobster, scallops, haddock, flounder, and steaks. Among the lunchtime choices are seafood salads and sandwiches. The service is extremely attentive.

Sabatino's. 901 Fawn St. (at the corner of High St.). ☎ **410/727-9414.** Reservations recommended. Main courses $9.95–$23.95; lunch $5–$12. AE, DC, DISC, MC, V. Daily noon–3am. ITALIAN.

Both northern and southern Italian cuisine are featured at this Little Italy restaurant with a plain stucco facade and a colorful interior. This is a particularly good late-night dining spot, open every day until 3am. Dinner entrees include shrimp scampi, calamari marinara, beef pizzaiola, lobster fra diavolo, and two dozen pastas such as spaghetti with broccoli and anchovy sauce.

MODERATE

Bertha's. 734 S. Broadway. ☎ **410/327-5795.** Reservations accepted only for parties of 6 or more. Main courses $7.95–$19.95; lunch $4.95–$11.95. MC, V. Sun–Thurs 11:30am–11pm, Fri–Sat 11:30am–midnight. INTERNATIONAL/SEAFOOD.

Don't miss this Fells Point landmark, known for its mussels and music. The decor is a blend of yesteryear, with original brick walls, antique prints, old wine bottles, and nautical bric-a-brac. You'll also see musical instruments fashioned into chandeliers and wall hangings, a reminder that folk music or jazz is performed here on many weekend nights. Mussels headline the menu throughout the day, prepared in a dozen different ways, such as in garlic butter; in sour cream and scallions; or with anchovy, tomato, and garlic butter. Other specialties include shellfish royale, a medley of shrimp, oysters, scallops, mussels, and Smithfield ham in a cream sauce with sherry; and a hearty paella with chicken, shrimp, scallops, Spanish sausage, and of course, mussels (they're made to order, so allow 30 minutes' wait time). Lunch choices include salads, omelets, sandwiches, and burgers. Afternoon tea, Scottish style, is also served daily from 3 to 4:30pm except Sunday (reservations required).

Chiapparelli's. 237 S. High St. (at Fawn St.) ☎ **410/837-0309.** Reservations required. Main courses $10.95–$22.95; lunch $5.95–$14.95. AE, CB, DC, DISC, MC, V. Mon–Thurs 11am–10:30pm, Fri–Sat 11am–midnight, Sun 11:30am–10pm. SOUTHERN ITALIAN.

In the heart of Little Italy, this restaurant is a longtime favorite. Southern Italian dishes are the trademark here, with special plaudits for Mom Chiapparelli's ravioli (stuffed with spinach and ricotta). Dinner is the main event, and veal is the star of the menu, cooked at least a dozen different ways, along with tasty chicken dishes and such classics as lobster fra diavolo, shrimp parmigiana, and steak Italiana.

Piccolo's. 1629 Thames St. ☎ **410/522-6600.** Reservations recommended for dinner. Main courses $8.95–$19.95; lunch $6.95–$12.95. AE, CB, DC, DISC, MC, V. Mon–Thurs 11:30am–10pm, Fri–Sat 11:30am–11pm, Sun 10:30am–10pm. TUSCAN/ITALIAN.

Located at the foot of Broadway on the waterfront in Fells Point, this wide-windowed restaurant offers great water views and a choice of indoor or outdoor seating, conveying a little bit of the flavor of Venice minus the gondolas. The menu offers an array of Americanized pastas and pizzas with varied toppings and accompaniments. Entrees at dinner range from standard veal and beef dishes to house specialties such as Pollo alla Piccolo (chicken stuffed with spinach, mozzarella, and prosciutto) or sea scallops Conca d'Oro (a sauté of scallops with spinach, sun-dried tomatoes, pine nuts, and scallions). The lunch menu also offers salads and sandwiches.

INEXPENSIVE

Adrian's Book Cafe. 714 S. Broadway. ☎ **410/732-1048.** All items $3.95–$6.95. AE, DISC, MC, V. Sun–Thurs 11am–11pm, Fri–Sat 11am–midnight. CAFE.

Situated in the heart of Fells Point, this ground-floor bookstore and upstairs cafe provides a bit of tranquillity amid the bustle of Broadway. It is named after New York artist Adrian Rappin, whose paintings line the walls. The menu changes daily and features primarily vegetarian fare, including pastas, salads, sandwiches, quiches, chilis, and desserts, all made fresh on the premises. Book readings and signings, art shows, and live acoustic music are scheduled several times a week.

✪ **Vaccaro's.** 222 Albemarle St. ☎ **410/685-4905.** Desserts $3.75–$7.50. AE, MC, V. Mon–Wed 7:30am–10pm; Thurs, Fri, and Sun 7:30am–11pm; Sat 7:30am–1am. ITALIAN/DESSERTS.

Vaccaro's is a Baltimore tradition. We never visit the city without stopping by for the best dessert and coffee in town. The place is famous for its cannoli, but the rum cake and tiramisù are also excellent. And if you just can't decide when you see the menu, you can get a sampler plate and try a little of everything. There's also a second location at the Light Street Pavilion in Harborplace.

5 Exploring the Inner Harbor

Although much of Baltimore's business activity takes place along Charles Street, the focal point of the city for visitors is the Inner Harbor, home of the Baltimore Convention Center and Festival Hall Exhibit Center, the Harborplace shopping pavilions, the National Aquarium and other museums, Oriole Park at Camden Yards (and by fall 1998 the new Baltimore Ravens stadium), and the Pier 6 Concert Pavilion.

But first and foremost, the Inner Harbor is a deep-water port. Boats from all over the world dock here, and it's not unusual on summer weekends for the harbor to be overrun with the white dress uniforms of sailors from here or across the seas. It's easy to get caught up in all the sites and shopping, but don't forget to stop and enjoy the people, the bustle of the harbor, and the water.

Note: At press time, the **Baltimore City Life Museums** were closed to the public with no indication of when or if they would reopen. I've included an abbreviated review below, should the museums reopen during the life of the book; however, be sure to call ahead before you attempt a visit.

✪ **National Aquarium in Baltimore.** 501 E. Pratt St., on the harbor. ☎ **410/576-3800.** Admission $11.95 adults, $10.50 seniors, $7.50 ages 3–11. July–Aug daily 9am–8pm; Mar–June and Sept–Oct Sat–Thurs 9am–5pm, Fri 9am–8pm; Nov–Feb Sat–Thurs 10am–5pm, Fri 10am–8pm.

A spectacular seven-level glass-and-steel structure, the Aquarium is the centerpiece of the Inner Harbor and without a doubt the biggest attraction in Baltimore. It contains more than 10,000 specimens of mammals, fish, rare birds, reptiles, and amphibians. All the creatures are on view in settings that re-create their natural habitats, including a South American rain forest reproduction, a 335,000-gallon Atlantic coral reef exhibit that gives a "diver's eye" view of thousands of tropical fish, and a 225,000-

gallon Open Ocean Exhibit that showcases species of sharks. In addition, the Marine Mammal Pavilion is home to Atlantic bottlenose dolphins, housed in a 1.2-million-gallon complex of four pools, surrounded by the world's largest acrylic windows and a 1,300-seat amphitheater. Visitors not only have an opportunity for close-up observation of dolphin behavior but they can also attend an ongoing program of 20-minute educational talks, presented by Aquarium trainers. In addition, there are nature films, a gallery of exhibits, an aquatic education resource center, and an animal care and research complex. The Aquarium does sell out, and crowds can cause delays in getting in and through the complex. Consider calling ahead for advanced, timed tickets and/or visiting at nonpeak times—weekdays before 11am or after 3pm.

✪ **American Visionary Art Museum.** 800 Key Hwy. ☎ **410/244-1900.** Admission $6 adults, $4 seniors and children. Tues–Sun 10am–6pm. Closed Thanksgiving and Dec 25. Take Light St. south, turn left onto Key Hwy. (at the Maryland Science Center); museum is about 3 blocks on right.

This unique new museum, easily identified by "Whirligig," a 55-foot, multicolored, wind-powered sculpture at the front of the building, houses the finest collection of visionary art in the country. Visionary art, the museum says, is "art produced by self-taught individuals usually without formal training, whose works arise from an innate personal vision that revels foremost in the creative act itself." The works here are often abstract, made from unusual media, and quite amazing (for example, we saw a series of sculptures made from wooden matches).

The seven indoor galleries display several changing thematic exhibitions each year. Outside the main building there's a central sculpture garden (home of the "Whirligig"), a wildflower sculpture garden, and a tall sculpture barn. Some of the museum's exhibits contain works not suitable for young children, but they are clearly marked as such. The restaurant, the Joy America Cafe, serves dishes that are beautifully displayed and well prepared, and the museum shop carries some truly unusual visionary gifts.

✪ **Babe Ruth Birthplace and Museum/Baltimore Orioles Museum.** 216 Emory St. ☎ **410/727-1539.** Admission $5 adults, $3 seniors, $2 ages 5–16. Apr–Oct daily 10am–5pm (until 7pm on Orioles home game days); Nov–Mar daily 10am–4pm. Closed Thanksgiving, Dec 25, and Jan 1. Take the light rail to Camden Yards; walk 2 blocks west on Pratt St., then south on Emory St.

Baseball fans will want to make a pilgrimage to the house where the game's greatest player was born on February 6, 1895. Located 2 blocks west of the Orioles' playing fields at Camden Yards, this restored house and the adjoining museum contain personal mementos of George Herman ("Babe") Ruth, the Sultan of Swat. The exhibits focus on the Baltimore Orioles and Maryland baseball as well as the great Babe. You can reach out and touch the Babe's own hats, bats, and gloves. There's also an audiovisual presentation on the Babe, World Series highlights, the Orioles, and more.

Baltimore and Ohio (B&O) Railroad Museum. 901 W. Pratt St. ☎ **410/752-2490.** Admission $6.50 adults, $5.50 seniors, $4 ages 3–12; train rides $2 per person. Museum daily 10am–5pm; train rides Sat–Sun at 11:30am, 12:30pm, 2:30pm, 3:30pm. Closed Thanksgiving and Dec 25. Bus: 31.

A trailblazer in American railroading, this city is also the setting of a fascinating railroad museum, situated 10 blocks west of the Inner Harbor. Often called a railroad university, this museum has hundreds of exhibits, from double-decker stagecoaches on iron wheels and early diesels to steam locomotives and the 1830 Mount Clare Station, the nation's first passenger and freight station. There's also an 1844 roundhouse with the original B&O tracks and turntable. Peter Cooper built and tested his famous

Baltimore Attractions

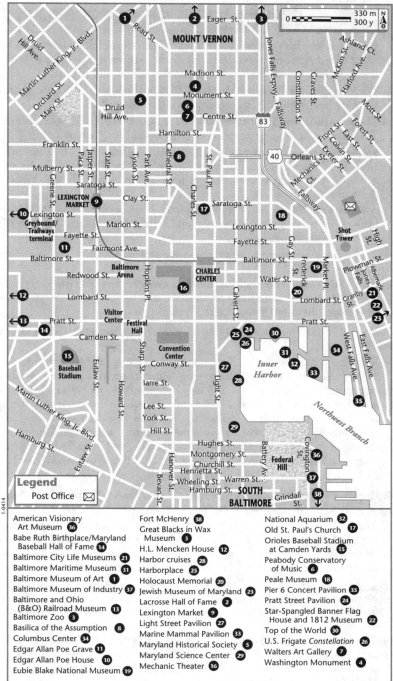

Legend
Post Office ⊠

American Visionary
  Art Museum 36
Babe Ruth Birthplace/Maryland
  Baseball Hall of Fame 14
Baltimore City Life Museums 21
Baltimore Maritime Museum 31
Baltimore Museum of Art 1
Baltimore Museum of Industry 37
Baltimore and Ohio
  (B&O) Railroad Museum 13
Baltimore Zoo 3
Basilica of the Assumption 8
Columbus Center 34
Edgar Allan Poe Grave 11
Edgar Allan Poe House 10
Eubie Blake National Museum 19

Fort McHenry 38
Great Blacks in Wax
  Museum 3
H.L. Mencken House 12
Harbor cruises 28
Harborplace 25
Holocaust Memorial 20
Jewish Museum of Maryland 23
Lacrosse Hall of Fame 2
Lexington Market 9
Light Street Pavilion 27
Marine Mammal Pavilion 33
Maryland Historical Society 5
Maryland Science Center 29
Mechanic Theater 16

National Aquarium 32
Old St. Paul's Church 17
Orioles Baseball Stadium
  at Camden Yards 15
Peabody Conservatory
  of Music 6
Peale Museum 18
Pier 6 Concert Pavilion 35
Pratt Street Pavilion 24
Star-Spangled Banner Flag
  House and 1812 Museum 22
Top of the World 30
U.S. Frigate Constellation 26
Walters Art Gallery 7
Washington Monument 4

69

⭐ Frommer's Favorite Baltimore Experiences

Cannoli at Vaccaro's. All the desserts are scrumptious here, but the cannoli is tradition. Skip dessert wherever you're having dinner and come here. If you can't make it to Little Italy, you can stop by the shop at the Light Street Pavilion.

The View from the Elevator at the Hyatt. Short of a harborside room in the Hyatt, this is the best view in the city, especially at night. And it's free.

The Seventh-Inning Stretch. There's nothing like a crowd of 45,000 in Camden Yards uniting for a rousing rendition of "Thank God I'm a Country Boy."

Spring in Sherwood Garden. This little community garden in north Baltimore is out of the way and hard to find, but it's an oasis in May when all the tulips are blooming. And the trip there will take you through lovely residential neighborhoods that tourists seldom see.

A Water Taxi Ride to Fells Point/Little Italy. It's an inexpensive way to see the harbor from the water and, if you're staying in the Inner Harbor, a great way to avoid the hassle of parking in Fells Point or Little Italy.

Tom Thumb on this site, and Samuel Morse strung his first telegraph wires through this depot. On weekends a steam train will also chug you along on a 150-year round-trip through the annals of American train travel.

Baltimore City Life Museums. 800 E. Lombard St. ☎ **410/396-3523.** Call ahead for admission and hrs.

When this book went to press, all six of the Baltimore City Life Museums were closed to the public, and we were unable to get information on when or if they would be reopened. However, visitors can still tour **Brewer's Park,** the site of a 1783 brewery on Museum Row, northeast of the Inner Harbor. An outdoor interpretive display shows the position of the original buildings, from the warehouse and malt houses to the brewer's houses, kitchen, and privy. Also clustered together on Museum Row are four of the now closed museums: Carroll Mansion, the Center for Urban Archaeology, the 1840 House, and the Shot Tower. The other two museums, the H. L. Mencken House and the Peale Museum, are located in Mt. Vernon.

Baltimore Maritime Museum. Pier 4, Pratt St. ☎ **410/396-3453.** Admission $5.50 adults, $4.50 seniors, $3 ages 5–12. Daily 11am–6pm; shorter hrs. in winter.

This outdoor complex is the home of the U.S. Coast Guard cutter *Taney,* the last ship still afloat that fought in Pearl Harbor; the submarine USS *Torsk,* which sank the last enemy ship in World War II; and the lightship *Chesapeake,* a floating lighthouse built in 1930. The vessels are moored to the dock and are open to visitors.

Columbus Center. 701 E. Pratt St., piers 5 and 6. ☎ **410/576-5700** or 410/576-5772. Admission $7 adults, $6 seniors, $5 ages 4–11. Not open for walk-in visitors. Open for group tours by appointment; arrangements can be made for individuals to visit during scheduled group tours.

This strikingly futuristic $160 million building houses the highly touted new national center for marine biotechnology research. This is not just a new and improved science center; scientists and students actually conduct research here. The center's Hall of Exploration, 23,000 square feet of exhibition space spread across three floors, allows the public to observe and experience this important work. There are approximately 50 exhibits, ranging from *Shark Attack!,* a video presentation of an attack from the shark's perspective, to an electronic DNA map, which tells you which human characteristics are associated with which genes. In addition, you can don a lab coat and participate in the numerous activities, demonstrations, and experiments that take place in the exploration and microscopy labs. The Real Science Store on the first floor is accessible to the general public without paid entry into the center and features a fun selection of gifts, books, games, and toys with a science focus.

Note: At press time, the Hall of Exploration had just closed its doors to walk-in, individual visitors, and is currently open only for group tours, but if you're in town and would like to visit, call ahead and the staff can usually arrange for you to join a tour. The center does plan to reopen for the general public in the near future, though no specific date is available.

◆ Fort McHenry National Monument and Historic Shrine. E. Fort Ave. ☎ **410/ 962-4290.** Admission $2; free for age 62 and over and under age 17. Daily 8am–4:45pm. Closed Jan 1 and Dec 25.

The sight of our flag flying over this star-shaped fort during the 1814 Battle of Baltimore inspired Francis Scott Key to write the words of the "Star-Spangled Banner." The American forces were successful against the British, and the fort never again came under attack. It remained an active military base for many years, however, until 1925, when it became a national park. To assist visitors in touring the fort, there are historical and military exhibits, a 15-minute film shown every half hour, and explanatory maps. During the summer months, guided activities are regularly scheduled.

Holocaust Memorial. Corner of Water, Gay, and Lombard sts. ☎ **410/752-2630.** Free admission. Daily 24 hrs.

Nestled in the heart of downtown near the Inner Harbor, this open-air memorial center and sculpture stand as a stark reminder of the six million Jews murdered by the Nazis in Europe between 1933 and 1945.

Jewish Museum of Maryland. 15 Lloyd St. ☎ **410/732-6400.** Admission $3. Sun and Tues–Thurs noon–4pm. Travel east on Pratt St.; turn left on Central St., left on Lombard St., and then right onto Lloyd St.

For insight into Baltimore and Maryland's Jewish history, stop by this museum, located a couple of blocks north of East Pratt Street and Little Italy. It consists of two restored 19th-century synagogues—the Lloyd Street Synagogue, built in 1845 and the oldest in Maryland, and the B'nai Israel Synagogue, built in 1876 and still in active use as Baltimore's only downtown synagogue. In 1997 the museum underwent an extensive construction project that almost doubled its size, adding a second exhibit gallery, a visitors' orientation center, a larger museum shop, and a new permanent children's exhibit, "The Golden Land: A Family Learning Center."

Maryland Science Center. 601 Light St., on the harbor. ☎ **410/685-5225.** Admission $9 adults, $7 seniors and ages 4–17, free under age 4; NightMAX movies $6. Mon–Fri 10am–5pm, Sat–Sun 10am–6pm, with extended hrs. in summer.

Situated on the edge of the Inner Harbor, this center features hundreds of hands-on activities, live demonstrations, and interactive displays ranging from a simulated space station control center to experiments revealing the properties of sight, sound, magnetism, light, and mechanics. Changing temporary exhibits, such as the recent exhibition exploring the real and not-so-real science of *Star Trek,* enhance the center's permanent displays. In addition, film presentations in the five-story IMAX movie theater and scientific shows in the Davis Planetarium are scheduled several times daily and are included in the admission price. Special IMAX double features, called NightMAX, are presented on Friday and Saturday evenings.

A Day at the Ballpark

I'm not going to mince words here: Oriole Park at Camden Yards is the most beautiful stadium in baseball today. And I'm not just saying that because I'm from Maryland, I'm a huge Orioles fan, and I think Cal Ripken Jr. is just an all-around great guy. Okay, so I might be a little biased, but Camden Yards is so successful that it's inspired other cities, like Cleveland and Denver, to build similar parks. And I even know a few Yankees fans who like this place.

So what's so great about it? Every ballpark has it's trademark feature. At Camden Yards it's the B&O Warehouse, the longest building on the east coast at 1,016 feet long by 51 feet wide. It stands behind right field on the other side of Eutaw Street, and just as every player in Fenway Park tries to sock one over the Green Monster, everyone here tries to hit the warehouse. At press time, no one has done it in a regular season game, though Ken Griffey Jr. hit it once during the All-Star Home Run Game. (There used to be a plaque marking the spot where the ball struck the warehouse, but apparently some Yankees fans stole it.) Other players have come close. Fans walking down Eutaw Street on their way to the seats can look for the bronze baseballs imprinted in the street marking all 15 home runs that made it outside the field and onto the street.

But what makes Camden Yards special isn't just the warehouse. This was the first park to be built in Retro style. Every detail makes the place feel like a traditional old-fashioned ballpark, from the exterior brick facade to the 1912-style press box. When you enter the stadium, you're greeted by friendly ushers in black caps and sweaters, white button-down shirts, and orange bow ties. The builders even paid homage to other all-time favorite ballparks, adding a miniature version of the Green Monster in center field and attempting to cover the wall with ivy, a nod to Wrigley Field. (Baltimore's hot, steamy summers aren't exactly conducive to ivy, but it's slowly progressing.)

And the stadium is not without it's modern touches and improvements. Some were even made at the suggestion of fans, like the tiered bull pens in left-center field, which make it possible for spectators to watch the pitchers from both teams as they warm up. Even the food is better at Camden Yards: The wieners are hot and the beer is cold. And if you're not a fan of hot dogs and the typical draft beer served at baseball games, you can buy bottled imports, domestics, and microbrews (poured into a plastic cup before you return to your seat) to wash down one of Boog's famous barbecue sandwiches.

But all of these special little details would come to naught if it weren't for the fans. We Orioles fans are notoriously loyal, friendly, and exuberant. No matter the score, at the seventh-inning stretch we all stand up to stomp, clap, and belt out "Thank God I'm a Country Boy." I've seen the wave go around the stadium five or six times in a row. We'll rarely boo or curse; when one of our boys strikes out, you're more likely to hear from us a collective sigh of disappointment. And we're even nice to the visiting teams and fans . . . usually. You might not want to wear a Yankees cap; we're still stinging a little from the 1996 pennant race.

—Denise Hawkins Coursey

Star-Spangled Banner Flag House and 1812 Museum. 844 E. Pratt St. (at the corner of Albemarle St., 2 blocks from the Columbus Center). ☎ **410/837-1793.** Admission $4 adults, $3 seniors, $2 children. Tues–Sat 10am–4pm. Closed major holidays.

A national historic landmark, this Federal-style house (1793) was once the home of Mary Pickersgill, the seamstress who made the 30-by-42-foot red, white, and blue Fort McHenry flag that inspired Francis Scott Key to write the poem that was to become our national anthem. It is full of period furnishings and a collection of Early American art. Adjacent to the house is a museum of 1812 military artifacts commemorating the defense of Baltimore. Outside is an unusual garden featuring a map of the continental United States made of stones native to each state.

Top of the World. 401 E. Pratt St., on the harbor. ☎ 410/837-4515. Admission $2.50 adults, $1.50 seniors and ages 5–15. Mon–Sat 10am–5pm, Sun 11am–5pm.

For a sweeping overview of the whole harbor and city, head for this sky-high observatory on the 27th floor of the World Trade Center, the world's tallest pentagonal building, next to Harborplace. In addition to looking at the cityscapes below, you can acquire a bit of background about Baltimore from the sky-high exhibits, hands-on displays, and multimedia presentations. Try to visit during some of their annual special events, such as Saturday Sunsets, featuring live jazz and refreshments.

6 More Attractions in the Charles Street/ Mount Vernon Area

Baltimore Museum of Art. Art Museum Dr., N. Charles St., and 31st St. ☎ **410/396-7100.** Admission $6 adults, $4 seniors and students with I.D., free for age 18 and under. Wed–Fri 11am–5pm, Sat–Sun 11am–6pm; first Thurs every month 5–9pm. Bus: 3 or 11. Take Howard St. north; bear right onto Art Museum Dr., about 3 miles north of the harbor.

Located on the northern edge of the city near Johns Hopkins University, this is the largest museum in Maryland, with two outdoor sculpture gardens and exhibits of art from all periods. The Impressionist collection is particularly impressive. In late 1994 the museum added a $10 million modern art wing that houses a diverse 16-gallery collection of 20th-century art, including the largest ensemble of paintings by Andy Warhol outside of the Andy Warhol Museum in Pittsburgh, as well as the works of more than 75 other American and European artists of the post-1945 period.

Baltimore Zoo. Greenspring Ave., Druid Hill Park. ☎ **410/396-7102.** Admission $7.50 adults, $4 seniors and ages 2–15. Daily 10am–4pm.

The third oldest zoo in the United States, this is a natural expanse of 150 acres of grassy slopes, tree-topped hills, and mountain caves. It provides an agreeable habitat to more than 1,200 animals, birds, and reptiles from seven continents, from bears to black-footed penguins, and their newest additions, wallabies and snow leopards. For young visitors, there's also an 8-acre interactive children's zoo. To get there, take the Druid Hill Lake Drive exit on I-83 and then follow the signs for the zoo.

✪ Basilica of the National Shrine of the Assumption of the Blessed Virgin Mary. Cathedral and Mulberry sts. ☎ **410/727-3564.** Free admission, but donations welcome. Mon–Fri 7am–5pm, Sat–Sun 7am–6:30pm. Take Charles St. north; turn left on Franklin St. and left again onto Cathedral St.

Begun in 1806, this was the first metropolitan cathedral in the United States, and the mother church for Baltimore's Catholic population. A fine example of neoclassical architecture, it was designed by Benjamin Henry Latrobe, the same architect who designed the nation's capitol. Highlights include a grand organ dating from 1821, a high altar built in 1822, stained-glass windows installed between 1943 and 1947, and paintings that were gifts from European kings. The remains of Bishop John Carroll, America's first Catholic bishop, are also interred here. Guided tours are conducted every Sunday at noon or by appointment. Masses are held weekdays at 7:30am and 12:10pm, Saturday at 7:30am and 5:30pm, and Sunday at 7:30am, 9am, 10:45am, 4pm, and 5:30pm.

Edgar Allan Poe's Grave Site and Memorial. Westminster Cemetery on the southeast corner of Fayette and Greene sts. ☎ **410/706-2072.** Daily 8am–dusk. Closed major holidays.

There are three very modest memorials at the poet Poe's grave, and most visitors agree that the writer who brought us "The Raven," "The Tell-Tale Heart," and "The Masque of the Red Death" deserves better. Perhaps appropriately, Poe's grave has been the site of much mystery and some havoc. More than a decade after the poet died and was placed in an unmarked grave in 1849, his relatives undertook to give him a pleasant and appropriate grave marker. A 3-foot-high stone was carved of Italian marble and inscribed in Latin with "Here, at last, he is happy. Edgar Allan Poe, died Oct. 7, 1849." But before it could be installed, the stone was shattered to pieces when a train derailed, crashed through the monument yard, and destroyed it. In the century since, the site has been adorned with three newer monuments: the main memorial grave, which features a bas-relief bust of Poe; a small grave stone adorned with a raven at Poe's original burial lot; and a plaque placed by the French, who through their poet Baudelaire enjoy some of the best translations of Poe's works.

Edgar Allan Poe House. 203 N. Amity St. ☎ **410/396-7932.** Admission $3 adults, $1 under age 13. Apr–July and Oct to mid-Dec Wed–Sat noon–3:45pm; Aug–Sept Sat noon–4pm. Closed mid-Dec to Mar.

The tiny house where Edgar Allan Poe wrote many of his great works is located in the heart of Baltimore. Poe lived here for 3 years (1832–35) while courting his cousin, whom he later married. The building contains Poe memorabilia, plus period furniture, ever-changing exhibits, and a video presentation of leading Poe works.

✪ Great Blacks in Wax Museum. 1601–03 E. North Ave. ☎ **410/563-3404.** Admission $5.75 adults, $5.25 seniors and college students, $3.75 ages 12–17, $3.25 ages 2–11. Jan 15–Oct 15, Tues–Sat 9am–6pm, Sun noon–6pm; Oct 16–Jan 14, Tues–Sat 9am–5pm, Sun noon–5pm. Closed Mon except during Black History Month (Feb), July, and Aug.

Nestled in the northeast corner of the city, this is the nation's first and only wax museum dedicated to famous black heroes and historical legends. Displays are in chronological order, and each highlights a period in African-American history, from ancient Africa to slavery and the Civil War to the civil rights era. The people portrayed include black inventors, pilots, religious and education leaders, scientists, and more.

Lacrosse Hall of Fame Museum. 113 W. University Pkwy. ☎ **410/235-6882.** Admission $2 adults, $1 students. Call for hrs.

Located in the Johns Hopkins University milieu, this unique museum presents 350 years in the history of lacrosse, America's oldest sport. The displays include rare photographs and photomurals of men and women at play, art, vintage equipment and uniforms, sculptures, trophies, memorabilia, a trivia game, and an audiovisual show. Among the renovations are a separate Hall of Fame room and an interactive computer kiosk giving access to data on the Hall of Famers. At press time, new hours of operation had not been determined, and the admission price may change, so call before you visit.

Maryland Historical Society. 201 W. Monument St. ☎ **410/685-3750.** Admission $4 adults, $2.50 seniors, $3 ages 5–17. Tues–Fri 10am–5pm, Sat 9am–5pm, Sun 1–5pm.

Nestled beside Mount Vernon and Antique Row between Park Avenue and Howard Street, this society was established in 1844. It houses many of the city's treasures, such as the original "Star-Spangled Banner" manuscript and silver from America's largest 19th-century silver collection, as well as more than 3,000 maps, 4,500 prints, 45,000 relics and artifacts, 55,000 books, and 200,000 photographs, all depicting Maryland in permanent and changing exhibits. In addition, there are antique dolls, toys, furniture, and clocks.

Old St. Paul's Church. Charles and Saratoga sts. ☎ **410/685-3404.** Free admission, but donations welcome. Mon, Wed, and Fri 11:30am–1pm, Sun 8:30am–12:30pm.

Opened in 1856, this church is the sixth of a parish dating from 1692 and the mother church for the Episcopal diocese of the city of Baltimore. Designed by Richard Upjohn in the basilica style, it is noted for its Tiffany windows and inlaid mosaic work including marble reliefs of Moses and Christ dating from 1812. Don't miss a chance to hear the church bells ring; they are part of a carillon given by the people of Baltimore to the church. The choir of men and boys, one of the best in North America, sings every Sunday (September to May) at 10:30am.

✪ **Walters Art Gallery.** 600 N. Charles St. ☎ **410/547-9000.** Admission $6 adults, $4 seniors, free for age 18 and under, free before noon on Sat. Tues, Wed, and Fri 10am–4pm, Thurs 10am–8pm, Sat–Sun 11am–5pm. Bus: 3, 11, and 22; light rail to Centre St.; or take Charles St. north to the Washington Monument.

Designed in an Italianate palazzo style, this museum houses more than 30,000 works of art, spanning some 5,000 years. The collection includes Asian, Egyptian, Greek, Roman, Byzantine, medieval, Renaissance, baroque, romantic, Impressionist, and art nouveau works. In addition, there are exhibits of historic jewelry, medieval armor, and illuminated manuscripts.

Washington Monument and Museum. Mount Vernon Place. ☎ **420/396-0929.** Donation $1 per person. Wed–Sun 10am–4pm. Take Charles St. north to the monument.

This monument, 178 feet tall, stands as the country's first major architectural memorial to George Washington. Begun in 1815, it was designed by Robert Mills, who also designed the Washington Monument (begun in 1848) in Washington, D.C. To learn the whole story, step inside this building and have a look at the exhibit *The Making of a Monument.* The physically fit can also climb the 228 steps to the top of the tower and see why this spot is often called the best view in Baltimore.

7 Organized Tours & Cruises

WALKING & TROLLEY TOURS

One of the best ways to get acquainted with the city is to hop aboard a **Baltimore Trolley** (☎ 410/880-0999). These colorful motorized trolleys really provide two services: a narrated tour of major Baltimore sights and a means of transportation between them. You can stay on board and enjoy the complete 2-hour tour, or you can get off at one stop, linger a while, and then reboard at your leisure. One ticket entitles you to reboarding privileges throughout the day, at a total of 20 different stops. You can start your tour at any of the trolley boarding points, clearly posted, all over the city. Tickets cost $12 for adults and $4.50 for children 12 and under and are available from the trolley driver, at certain hotels, and at the Inner Harbor ticket kiosk on Light Street.

Baltimore Heritage Walking Tours (☎ 410/624-2585) offers 2-hour guided walking tours of the city's unique neighborhoods and historic areas. Tours cost $10 per person and begin at various sites. Itineraries change monthly, so phone ahead to see what will be covered at the time of your visit. Reservations are necessary.

A number of organizations offer specialized tours, concentrating on specific neighborhoods or sites. **Concierge Plus, Inc.** (☎ 410/547-0479) provides **Little Italy** and **Hollywood on the Harbor** walking tours, which give interesting and fun perspectives on the city. The Little Italy excursion takes you on a lunch tour, coupling good food with insight into the history of the neighborhood. The **Hollywood on the Harbor** tour, which won a 1997 Maryland Tourism best new tour award, explores Fells Point, pointing out sites used in the filming of *Homicide, Sleepless in Seattle,* and other movies and shows filmed in Baltimore. Tours are offered on weekends year-round at 11:30am. The Little Italy tour costs $35 per person; the Hollywood on the Harbor tour costs $25 per person. Both tours include lunch.

Baseball fans should not miss a tour of ✪ **Oriole Park at Camden Yards.** Well-informed tour guides fill you in on such important facts as where Eddie Murray hit his 500th home run, why there are no bat racks in the dugout, and how many miles of beer lines run under the stadium seats. Best of all, you get to go to all those places the average fan can't usually see: the dugouts, the umpires' tunnel, and the press box. Tickets cost $5 for adults and $4 for seniors and children and can be purchased at the Orioles Ticket Office at the ballpark. During baseball season, tours are conducted weekdays from 11am to 2pm on the hour, Saturday from 10:30am to 2pm on the half hour, and Sunday from 12:30 to 2pm on the half hour. Call ☎ 410/547-6234 for the off-season tour schedule and other information.

CRUISES & BOATING TOURS

Baltimore Patriot. Constellation Dock, Pratt St. ☎ 410/685-4288. $6.60 adults, $3.30 under age 12. Three cruises daily Apr, May, Sept, and Oct; June–Aug hourly departures 11am–4pm daily.

Maryland Tours operates this 300-passenger, two-deck boat on a 16-mile, 1 1/2-hour narrated route around the Inner Harbor and Patapsco River.

✪ *Bay Lady/Lady Baltimore.* 301 Light St. ☎ 410/727-3113. Lunch $25; dinner $38.50; moonlight cruise $21.50; Sunday brunch $29.95; crab feast $48. Lunch daily noon (boarding 11:30am); dinner Mon–Sat 7pm (boarding 6:30pm); dinner Sun 5pm (boarding 4:30pm); moonlight cruise Fri–Sat 11:30pm (boarding 11pm).

Harbor Cruises operates three different cruises on board these two 450-passenger, three-deck luxury ships, all departing from the Light Street dock next to Harborplace. The program includes a 2-hour lunch, a 3-hour dinner, and a 2 1/2-hour moonlight excursion. The prices for the lunch and dinner trips include a narrated tour, seated meal, and entertainment. Special theme cruises, such as Sunday afternoon bull roasts, Friday lobster or crab nights, and holiday observances, are also held throughout the year. In addition, on selected dates there are cruises to Annapolis, St. Michaels, and along the C&D Canal for fall foliage.

Clipper City. 720 Light St. ☎ 410/539-6277. Afternoon sail $12 adults, $2 under age 12; calypso and reggae sail $20 adults; Sun brunch $30 adults. Afternoon sail Mon–Sat noon and 3pm, Sun 3pm and 6pm; calypso and reggae sail Fri–Sat 8pm; Sun brunch 11am.

This sleek 149-passenger topsail schooner is a replica of an 1854 vessel and one of the largest tall ships licensed in the United States to carry passengers. It offers 2-hour afternoon excursions, 3-hour evening trips with live calypso and reggae music, and 3-hour Sunday champagne brunch sails, all departing from the dock next to the Maryland Science Center.

Nighthawk. 1715 Thames St. ☎ 410/276-7447. Moonlight sail $32.50 per person; murder-mystery cruises $45 per person. May–Sept, moonlight sail Wed and Fri–Sat 7:30pm; call for murder-mystery cruise schedule.

Sailing from Fells Point, this 82-foot, 49-passenger windjammer offers 3-hour excursions into the waters of the Inner Harbor and Patapsco River. The schedule includes moonlight sails with buffet dinner and live music. "Murder-mystery" cruises are offered occasionally. The ship is also available for private charters.

8 Spectator Sports & Outdoor Activities

BASEBALL From April to October, when the **Baltimore Orioles** play ball, the city catches "Oriole fever"—everyone wants to go to the games and everyone talks about the results. If there's a home game during your visit, do whatever you have to do to get a ticket: It's a real Baltimore experience. The team plays at Oriole Park at Camden Yards, 333 W. Camden St. (☎ **410/685-9800**). Afternoon games are usually at 1:35pm and evening games are slated for 7:35pm. Ticket prices range from $7 to $30.

FOOTBALL The **Baltimore Ravens** are tentatively scheduled to begin playing in the new stadium, right next door to Camden Yards, in August 1998. There will only be 5,000 seats sold on a per game basis (the rest will be for season ticket holders). Ticket prices will average about $35 and range from $17 to $75. For information or tickets call ☎ **888/919-9797** or 410/261-RAVE.

HORSE RACING Maryland's oldest thoroughbred track and the site of the annual Preakness Stakes is **Pimlico Race Course,** Park Heights and Belvedere Avenues (☎ **410/542-9400**), about 5 miles from the Inner Harbor on the city's northwest side. The full racing season extends from mid-March to mid-June and early September to early October. The highlight is of course the Preakness, the middle jewel in racing's Triple Crown, held on the third Saturday in May. Post time is noon to 1pm, and normal admission charges are $3 for the grandstand and $5 for the clubhouse, plus $1 to $3 per car for parking. Pimlico is also the home of the National Jockey's Hall of Fame, open from 9 to 11am during the racing season, free of charge.

9 Shopping

Baltimore's prime shopping locale is the Inner Harbor. **Harborplace,** Pratt and Light streets (☎ **410/332-4191**), the two glass-enclosed bilevel shopping malls on the waterfront, features more than 135 shops, food and craft vendors, restaurants, and cafes. It is divided into two pavilions. The Light Street Pavilion functions primarily as a large food court, with some retail shops on the second floor. If you can't make it to Little Italy, you can sample some of Vaccaro's desserts here or grab a quick crab cake from Phillips or one of the many other seafood vendors. The Pratt Street Pavilion contains most of the retail stores, which are mainly those you'd find at a suburban mall. From April through September free concerts are staged in the amphitheater in front of the pavilions. Open Monday through Saturday from 10am to 9pm and Sunday from 10am to 6pm.

The Pratt Street Pavilion is connected via skywalk to a full-scale mall, **The Gallery,** in the Renaissance Harbor Hotel (☎ **410/332-4191**). Opened in 1987, this four-story atrium trimmed in brass and mahogany contains more than 75 fine shops, including Banana Republic, Brooks Brothers, Ann Taylor, and the Disney Store. Open Monday through Saturday from 10am to 10pm and Sunday from noon to 6pm.

In addition, there are hundreds of fine individual shops scattered throughout Baltimore. Certain parts of the city are known for specific types of shopping, such as Antique Row along North Howard and West Read streets, featuring more than 40 independently owned antique shops. Fells Point is rich in antique, art, souvenir, and craft shops.

SHOPPING A TO Z
ANTIQUES & COLLECTIBLES
Harris Auction Galleries. 875 N. Howard St. ☎ **410/728-7040.**

Try this shop for small pieces of art and collectibles including watches, plates, prints, paintings, jars, jugs, and Oriental pieces. Auctions are often held on Sunday here; check in advance. Open weekdays from 9am to 5pm, Saturday from 10:30am to 2pm.

L.A. Herstein and Co. 877 N. Howard St. ☎ **410/728-3856.**

The specialty of this shop is antique Tiffany lamps and shades, including repairs and parts replacements. Open Monday and Tuesday from 11am to 4pm, Friday and Saturday from 10am to 5pm.

ARTS & CRAFTS
Angeline's Art Gallery & Boutique. 1631 Thames St. ☎ **410/522-7909.**

Located in the Brown's Wharf complex of shops at Fells Point, this shop specializes in original paintings and drawings by local and national artists, especially Baltimore and Fells Point scenes. There are also batiks, prints, ceramics, exotic jewelry, curios, and sculpture. Open Sunday through Thursday from 11am to 6pm and Friday and Saturday from 11am to 11pm.

Art Gallery of Fells Point. 1716 Thames St. ☎ **410/327-1272.**

A cooperative gallery featuring works by Maryland and regional artists, this shop is located in the heart of the Fells Point district. Art for sale includes oil paintings, watercolors, drawings, sculpture, photography, pastels, fibers, and jewelry. Open Tuesday through Sunday from noon to 5pm.

A People United. 516 N. Charles St. ☎ **410/727-4470.**

More than an average commercial enterprise, this nonprofit shop features a variety of goods made by women who are part of development cooperatives in India, Nepal, Thailand, Guatemala, Kenya, and other lands. You'll find a colorful selection of exotic clothing, jewelry, and accessories. Open Monday through Saturday from 11am to 6pm and Sunday from noon to 5pm.

✪ **Women's Industrial Exchange.** 333 N. Charles St. ☎ **410/685-4388.**

Founded in 1882, this enterprise aims to help the needy women and men of the city by selling their handiwork and employing them in the shop and adjacent restaurant (see "Dining," above). The crafts offered are often one-of-a-kind, from knitwear, quilts, afghans, and needlepoint, to jewelry, original photo cards, woodwork, dolls, tableware, and baked goods. Open weekdays from 9am to 3pm.

GIFTS & SOUVENIRS
Brassworks Company. 1641 Thames St. ☎ **410/327-7280.**

This Fells Point shop stocks a large selection of fine quality gifts, accessories, and decorative furnishings, from brass and copper items to lamps, candlesticks, and door and furniture hardware. Open weekdays from 8:30am to 5:30pm, Saturday from 10am to 6pm, Sunday from noon to 6pm.

Gift Ahoy. 1625 Thames St. ☎ **410/558-1933.**

This shop specializes in gifts and souvenirs that have the colors, symbols, and motifs of the City of Baltimore, State of Maryland, and Chesapeake Bay area, including the game Chesapeakeopoly. In addition, there are home furnishings, apparel, and art with a nautical theme. It's located at Brown's Wharf in Fells Point. Open May through September, Sunday through Thursday from 10am to 6pm and Friday and Saturday from 10am to 9pm.

Grrreat Bears and Childhood Delights. 1643 Thames St. ☎ **410/276-4429.**

This Fells Point shop is a treasure trove of teddy bears and related playthings—stuffed animals, dolls, puppets, toys, puzzles, tractors, trucks, books for the young and young at heart, and collectible miniatures. Open Sunday through Tuesday from 9:30am to 5pm, Wednesday through Saturday from 9:30am to 9:30pm.

MARKETS

Baltimore Farmers' Market. Holiday and Saratoga sts. ☎ **410/752-8632.**

For a look at Old Baltimore, stop to see this weekly outdoor gathering, a great source for crafts, herbs, jams, jellies, baked goods, and smoked meats, as well as local produce and flowers. Open from late June through December, Sunday from 8am until sold out.

Broadway Market. S. Broadway between Fleet and Lancaster sts. No phone.

Smell and taste the flavors of Baltimore's original seaport at this 200-year-old market, tucked in the heart of Fells Point. The market area consists of two large covered buildings, each staffed by local vendors selling fresh produce, flowers, crafts, and an assortment of ethnic and raw bar foods, ideal for snacking, a quick lunch, or a picnic. Open daily from 8am to 6pm.

✪ Lexington Market. 400 W. Lexington St. ☎ **410/685-6169.**

Established in 1782, this Baltimore landmark claims to be the oldest continuously operating market in the United States. It houses more than 140 merchants, selling prepared ethnic foods (for eat-in or take-away), fresh seafood, produce, meats, baked goods, sweets, and more. It's a real slice of Baltimore, well worth a visit for the aromas, flavors, sounds, and sights, as well as good shopping. Open Monday through Saturday from 8:30am to 6pm.

10 Baltimore After Dark

Baltimore shares its nightlife with Washington, D.C., and vice versa; the two cities comprise one metropolitan area, a fact Marylanders live with and fully enjoy, but outsiders don't always pick up on. What does this mean to the average tourist looking for something to do on Friday night? Big bands and artists don't play both cities (in fact, they usually play in Washington); Broadway musicals can be seen in either the Kennedy Center in Washington or the Mechanic in Baltimore; and there are twice as many smaller venues for live music or theater.

In fact, most local papers list happenings in both cities, so you don't even have to look very hard. Check the arts and entertainment sections of the *Baltimore Sun* and the *Washington Post*. The *City Paper*, a free Baltimore weekly, will tell you what's going on in the local bars and clubs, including those in D.C.

For tickets to most shows and performances you can contact individual box offices or **TicketMaster** at ☎ **410/481-SEAT.** You can also try **Baltimore Tickets** (☎ **410/752-TICS**) at the visitor center at the Inner Harbor.

THE CLUB & MUSIC SCENE

D.C.'s club scene tends to overshadow Baltimore's, but Baltimore still has a nice variety of small live-performance venues. The disappearance of the rock club

Hammerjack's (which hosted just about every rock band whose first album wasn't a smash hit and many whose were) and its subsequent replacement with the Camden Yards/Raven's Stadium parking lot has been something of a mixed bag for rock fans; not as many big-name bands come to Baltimore, but when they do you get to see them in the far more intimate (read smaller) setting at Bohager's.

ROCK, JAZZ & BLUES

✪ **Bohager's.** 515 S. Eden St. (at Fleet St. in Fells Point). ☎ **410/563-7220.** Cover dependent on talent; no cover on Fri and Sat.

Now that Hammerjack's is no more, Bohager's is the only small venue in town where you can hear reasonably big-name rock performers. David Byrne, Smash Mouth, Veruca Salt, and Local H recently made appearances here.

Buddies Pub & Jazz Club. 313 N. Charles St. ☎ **410/332-4200.** No cover.

This informal and lively place is known for its live jazz sessions on Wednesday through Saturday, with open mike night on Thursday. House drummer Bing Miller heads a trio that performs regularly. Music starts around 9pm and continues to 1:30am.

Cat's Eye Pub. 1730 Thames St., Fells Point. ☎ **410/276-9866.** Usually no cover.

A Fells Point bar with an Irish pub feel, Cat's Eye sports flags from around the world, exposed brick walls, wood floors, and a back room with chess boards and game tables. There's also live music nightly ranging from traditional Irish music to blues, bluegrass, zydeco, and jazz.

Eight by Ten. 10 E. Cross St. ☎ **410/625-2001.** Cover dependent on talent.

The emphasis at this Fells Point establishment is on blues, but rock groups also play here regularly, and there's an occasional jazz performance too.

The Horse You Came In On. 1626 Thames St., Fells Point. ☎ **410/327-8111.** No cover.

This Fells Point watering hole is popular with both the local college and postcollege crowds. It features live rock or acoustic rock music nightly.

FOLK

Mick O'Shea's Irish Pub. 328 N. Charles St. ☎ **410/539-7504.** No cover.

If you're in a St. Patrick's Day mood on any weekend, come to this pub in the heart of the city for traditional Irish music. There's live music Thursday through Saturday from 7 to 9pm.

DANCE CLUBS

Baja Beach Club. 55 Market Place (at E. Lombard St.). ☎ **410/727-0468.** No cover.

Located at the Brokerage, opposite Harborplace, this club presents progressive deejay dance music Wednesday through Sunday from 8pm to 2am.

Hurricane's. 7032 Elm Rd. (in the Sheraton International Hotel at BWI). ☎ **410/859-3300.** Cover $2–$3.

Hurricane's is quite popular with the Baltimore area's suburban dance crowd. Facilities include pop music, two bars, and two beer coolers, where you can skip the lines at the bars and just buy a beer.

COMEDY CLUBS

Comedy Factory. 36 Light St. (at Lombard St.). ☎ **410/752-4189.** Cover $10.

Located above Burke's Restaurant, this club presents live comedy acts Friday and Saturday at 8:30 and 10:30pm and offers half-price admission with a hotel key.

THE BAR & COFFEEHOUSE SCENE

Baltimore has two distinct bar scenes: sports bars, where fans who couldn't get tickets gather to watch the game or to discuss the results, and the Fells Point scene, which includes some bars that have music (they're listed above). Sports fans can stroll into any of a dozen bars in the vicinity of Camden Yards for lively game conversation, but try **Downtowne Sports** (☎ 410/659-5844), 200 W. Pratt St.; **Pickles Pub** (☎ 410/752-1784), 520 Washington Blvd.; or **Orioles Bar** (☎ 410/962-8300) in the Sheraton Inner Harbor. Fells Point, with its old-world charm and combination of cozy pubs in historic row houses and hip clubs in old industrial buildings, is the focal point of Baltimore's nightlife and a favorite among the local college students and young professionals.

BARS, BILLIARDS & BREW PUBS

✪ **Baltimore Brewing Company.** 104 Albemarle St. (between Little Italy and the Inner Harbor). ☎ **410/837-5000.** No cover.

The home of DeGroen's beer, this microbrewery is part German restaurant, part beer hall. Its large drinking area is lined with sturdy picnic tables and wicker bottom chairs. On the side is one very long, copper-lined bar where the staff serves up DeGroen's five main beers on draft. You can even purchase any of the beers to go in growlers.

Edgar's Billiards Club and Bar. 1 E. Pratt St., on the Skywalk. ☎ **410/752-8080.** No cover.

This upscale day-and-night club offers 16 full-size pool tables as well as smoking and nonsmoking areas and a fine selection of cigars.

John Steven, Ltd. 1800 Thames St. ☎ **410/327-5561.** No cover.

When you enter this establishment on the eastern edge of the Fells Point bar district, you'll be assaulted by the fragrant smell of steamed shrimp. That's what we like about John Steven—it's a great place to sit down and have a beer and a pound or so of the little swimmers, medium, large, or jumbo.

Wharf Rat. 206 W. Pratt St. (at Hanover St. across from the convention center). ☎ **410/244-8900.** No cover.

This small Baltimore favorite is a frequent stop for conventioneers looking to have a drink. It has a pool table and a dining area adorned with the paraphernalia of traditional English, Scottish, and Irish beers. It's also a brew pub, so you can sip an Oliver ale or stout and look in on the brewery through the large windows in the dining area. We recommend the Oliver porter. For information on eating here, see the listing in "Dining," above.

COFFEEHOUSES

If you are looking for a more refined way to spend your evening, you might try out Baltimore's newly emergent coffeehouse scene, where you can sip an espresso, grab a light bite to eat, and feel, if you choose, just a bit intellectual.

Adrian's Book Cafe. 714 S. Broadway, Fells Point. ☎ **410/732-1048.**

Adrian's has perhaps the quintessential coffeehouse atmosphere, set in a narrow Fells Point row house. Here you can drink java in a cozy room lined with books about everything from Socrates to Che Guevara.

Donna's. 2 W. Madison St. (1 block from Mt. Vernon's Washington Monument), Mt. Vernon. ☎ **410/385-0180.**

Donna's offers an upscale coffeehouse environment with a wide variety of both coffees and light cuisine.

✪ **Louie's Bookstore Cafe.** 518 N. Charles St. ☎ **410/962-1224.** No cover.

This bookshop/bar/cafe presents live classical music every night until at least midnight, featuring local artists playing the lute, guitar, piano, or violin.

MOVIES

Charles Theater. 1711 N. Charles St. ☎ **410/727-3456.**

The Charles is Baltimore's aging movie palace. Although most of the charm of this near-500-seat theater is buried beneath its 1960s/'70s interior decor, it is still quite popular with local film fans. It shows first-run and lesser-known art films nightly.

IMAX Theater/Maryland Science Center. 601 Light St., on the harbor. ☎ **410/685-5225.**

If you don't make it to the Science Center during the day, you can still enjoy the double features presented each weekend on the theater's 5-story-high, 75-foot-wide screen. Admission to the "NightMAX" shows is $6. Call for show times.

✪ **The Senator.** 5904 York Rd. ☎ **410/435-1118.**

This 1930s 900-seat, art-deco movie house was rated as one of the four best motion picture theaters in the country by *USA Today.* It has hosted the world premieres of such Baltimore-based flicks as *Serial Mom, Diner,* and *Avalon.* The Senator's regular programs include high-quality first-run films, classics, and art films, and also occasional live musical performances.

THE PERFORMING ARTS

Because of its proximity to the nation's capital and all the cultural offerings there, Baltimore's performing arts scene tends to get overlooked, or at least overshadowed. And the city's deserved reputation as a blue-collar town is a bit incongruous with the idea of a great center for the arts. But the fact is, when you start counting theaters, large venues, and well-respected performances, Baltimore can give Washington a run for its money.

All the large venues lie within a few blocks of Charles Street and span about 20 blocks beginning at the harbor. The **Baltimore Arena** (☎ **410/347-2000**), the city's largest hall with a capacity of 16,000, is the setting for an ever-changing program of entertainment and sports events, including concerts, plays, circuses, ice shows, and soccer and hockey matches. Nearby the **Pier Six Concert Pavilion** (☎ **410/ 837-4636**), on the harbor, presents the top names of the music industry in live concerts from May through September.

The setting for most of the touring Broadway musicals and dramas to come to Baltimore is the **Morris A. Mechanic Theater** (☎ **410/625-1400**), at Baltimore and Charles streets, a block from the harbor. Performances of the Baltimore Symphony Orchestra are held at the ✪ **Joseph Meyerhoff Symphony Hall** (☎ **410/ 783-8000**). The **Lyric Opera House** (☎ **410/685-0692**) presents performances of the Baltimore Opera Company from October through May. The **Peabody Conservatory of Music** (☎ **410/659-8124**) hosts a variety of classical music and opera performances. The primary venue for theater is **Center Stage** (☎ **410/332-0033**), though several smaller companies operate out of Fells Point (see "Theater," below.)

OPERA & CLASSICAL MUSIC

The world-class ✪ **Baltimore Symphony Orchestra** (☎ **800/442-1198** or 410/ 783-8000) performs almost nightly at the Joseph Meyerhoff Symphony Hall from September through June. Each season brings several new and diverse series ranging from traditional classics to pops to the "Classically Black" series, showcasing the works of African-American and African-British composers and performers. New director David Yuri Temirkanov is set to take over in 1999, replacing the veteran David Zinman. Tickets range from $13 to $60. In addition, the **Peabody Symphony Orchestra** (☎ 410/659-8124), directed by Harima Terimurai, performs regularly at the Peabody Institute of Johns Hopkins University in Friedberg Hall. Ticket prices range from free to $24.

The **Baltimore Opera Company** has been a tradition in the city for almost 50 years. Performances are held in the **Lyric Opera House** (☎ 410/727-6000), 140 W. Mt. Royal Ave. Ticket prices range from $22 to $100. Contact the Lyric for schedule information and tickets.

THEATER

Recognized as Maryland's resident professional theater and the state theater of Maryland, ✪ **Center Stage** (☎ 410/332-0033), 700 N. Calvert St., provides an intimate setting for first-rate repertory and original shows, from cabaret-style musicals, comedies, and classics, to modern and contemporary masterworks. Recent productions have included *Romeo and Juliet, HMS Pinafore,* and two original plays by Maryland natives. Tickets range from $10 to $38.

In Fells Point, two reliable theaters enhance the city's offerings. **Fells Point Corner Theater** (☎ 410/276-7837), 251 S. Ann St., hosts eight productions a year, primarily contemporary and historic dramas, including *Arcadia* by Tom Stoppard and *Cryptogram* by David Mamet. **Vagabond Players** (☎ 410/563-9135), 806 S. Broadway, presents a variety of classics, contemporary comedies, and dramas. Tickets at both theaters run about $10.

The city's prominent black theater company **Arena Players** (☎ 410/728-6500), 802 McCulloh St. (just west of Mount Vernon), presents contemporary plays and romantic comedies. Tickets cost $12 to $15.

6

Annapolis &
Southern Maryland

Annapolis never ceases to amaze us. It is a town steeped in history and tradition—from the Senate chamber where Congress ratified the treaty that ended the Revolutionary War to noon formation at the United States Naval Academy. More than 1,500 historic buildings are next to the narrow brick-lined streets and alleys (there are more colonial buildings in Annapolis than any other place in the country), and men and women wearing tricornes, knickers, petticoats, and aprons show visitors around town. And yet, amid all this history, business goes on as usual—the business of running the state, training young naval officers, educating students in the classics at St. John's, and shipping, sailing, and trading at City Dock—just as it has for 300 years.

1 Orientation

ARRIVING

BY PLANE   Annapolis is served by **Baltimore–Washington International Airport** (☎ **800/I-FLY-BWI** or 410/859-7111), located approximately 20 miles northwest of the city. Minibus transfer services between the airport and the major hotels of Annapolis and the Naval Academy are operated by **BWI Shuttle Express** (☎ **410/859-0800**). Reservations are required at least 2 hours in advance. The fare is $19 one-way and $29 round-trip. Transfer by taxi is approximately $35 one-way. Contact **BWI Taxi Service** at ☎ **410/859-1100**.

BY CAR   From Baltimore and points north, take I-695 (the Baltimore beltway) to I-97 south and Route 50 east. Rowe Boulevard from Route 50 will take you into the city. From Washington, D.C., take Route 50 east off the Washington beltway (I-495) to Rowe Boulevard.

It's best to walk the historic district because parking is generally difficult. **Parking garages** are located next to the visitor center off Northwest Street, on Duke of Gloucester Street behind City Hall, on Washington Street, and on South Street. You can also park at the Navy/Marine Corps Stadium (off Rowe Boulevard at Taylor Avenue) and ride the Annapolis Trolley into the historic district. Trolleys depart every 15 minutes; it's free on weekends and costs 75¢ during the week.

BY BUS   Greyhound (☎ **800/231-2222**) offers service from the eastern seaboard; buses depart from and arrive at the Navy/Marine

Corps Stadium on Rowe Boulevard. **Baltimore MTA** (☎ **410/539-5000**) provides weekday service to and from Baltimore; buses stop at College Avenue by the State Buildings and the Navy Marine Corps Stadium. Commuter service from Washington is provided by **Washington MTA** (☎ **800/543-9809**), from the New Carrollton Metro Station to the Loews Hotel and the Navy Marine Corps Stadium. **Dillon's Bus Service** (☎ **800/673-8435** or 410/647-2321) offers weekday direct service to and from D.C. with buses stopping at the Navy/Marine Corps Stadium, Harry S. Truman Park, and several other places downtown.

VISITOR INFORMATION

The **Annapolis and Anne Arundel Conference and Visitors Bureau** (☎ **410/ 280-0445** or 410/268-TOUR) runs a very helpful visitor center at 26 West St., just west of Church Circle, with maps and brochures on just about everything. Bus and walking tours (see "Organized Tours & Cruises," below) leave from this office daily; they also have a gift shop and offer reservation service. It's open daily from 9am to 5pm. The bureau also runs an information booth at City Dock during the summer. Be sure to pick up a free copy of *Destination Annapolis,* a magazine produced by the visitors bureau with a good map of the downtown area. At most restaurants and hotels you can also pick up a copy of *Inside Annapolis,* a free bimonthly magazine listing local events as well as area businesses.

CITY LAYOUT

The city layout is based on two central circles: State Circle and Church Circle. All other streets radiate from these two points. The U.S. Naval Academy is in its own enclave, east of State Circle. City Dock is east of both circles, at the end of Main Street off Church Circle.

2 Getting Around

BY PUBLIC TRANSPORTATION

BY SHUTTLE For visitors and locals, **Annapolis Transit** (☎ **410/263-7964** on weekdays and 410/263-7994 on weekends) operates the Annapolis Trolley, a shuttle-bus service using gasoline-powered trolleys between the historic/business district and the parking area of the Navy/Marine Corps Stadium. Shuttles operate Monday through Friday from 6:30am to 8pm, Saturday and Sunday from 10am to 6pm (extended until 8pm during the summer); trolleys depart approximately every 15 minutes. The one-way fare is 75¢.

BY BUS From Monday through Saturday, **Annapolis Transit** also runs commuter bus service from the historic district to other parts of the city such as the Annapolis Mall or Eastport. Base fare is 75¢ and exact change is required. Buses run every half hour, starting at 5:30am and continuing to 6:30pm.

BY CAR

RENTALS Car-rental firms represented in Annapolis include **Budget,** 2002 West St. (☎ **410/266-5030**); **Discount,** 1032 West St. (☎ **410/269-6645**); and **Enterprise,** 1023 Spa Rd. (☎ **410/268-7751**).

PARKING True to its 18th-century style, midtown Annapolis is very compact, with lots of narrow streets; consequently, parking in the historic district is limited. Visitors are encouraged to leave their cars in a park-and-ride lot, located on the edge of town off Rowe Boulevard just west of the Navy/Marine Corps Stadium, and take the Annapolis Trolley into town. Other parking garages are located behind the visitor

A Field Guide to Annapolis Architecture

With 350 years of historic homes and buildings representing at least eight different architectural styles, downtown Annapolis can turn even the least architecturally and historically minded visitor into a reasonably well-informed student, able, at the very least, to identify and distinguish between Georgian and Federal buildings. Of course, if, like us, you know almost nothing about architecture to begin with, just strolling down the brick-lined streets and carefully studying the brightly colored homes is not going to do it. Fortunately, the Historic Annapolis Foundation created the Historic Marker Program just for us uninformed visitors. The marker program identifies buildings of either historic or architectural interest and encourages their restoration and maintenance—not an unusual program for a historic town. But in Annapolis, the octagonal plaques, emblazoned with the 400-year-old Liberty Tree, are color-coded according to architectural style, making them particularly helpful to visitors and locals alike. So, you can tell at a glance the style and time period of a building.

The Historic Annapolis Foundation publishes a brochure, "Three Centuries of Architecture in Annapolis," that gives a brief history of architecture in the city and, more importantly, explains the color-coding system. However, these brochures are difficult to come by, so listed below are the colors used on the plaques and a brief explanation of the architecture and time period they represent. As you explore the town, you may notice some plaques that have two colors, one on the border and another on the interior. This indicates that the building has elements of both styles.

- Dark Green: 17th-Century Vernacular (1684–1700). These structures are generally simple utilitarian homes with wooden frames and few, if any, decorative features. Small windows and a single, central chimney are common.

center off Northwest Street, on Duke of Gloucester Street behind City Hall, on Washington Street, and on South Street.

BY TAXI

If you need transportation once you are in town, call **Arundel and Colonial Cab** (☎ 410/263-2555 or 410/263-4200), **Capital City Cab** (☎ 410/267-0000), or **Yellow Checker Cab** (☎ 410/268-3737).

BY WATER TAXI

From late May through Labor Day, the **Jiffy Water Taxi** (☎ 410/263-0033) operates from the City Dock to restaurants and other destinations along Spa and Back Creeks. It's a handy way to avoid Annapolis auto traffic and a pleasant sightseeing experience as well. The fare ranges from $1 to $4, depending on destination. Hours are Monday through Thursday from 9:30am to midnight, Friday from 9:30am to 1am, Saturday from 9am to 1am, and Sunday from 9am to midnight. Service is limited in early May and in September and October.

FAST FACTS: Annapolis

Airport   See "Arriving," earlier in this chapter.

American Express   The office is in the Annapolis Mall on Bestgate Road (☎ 800/788-3559 or 410/224-4200).

- Brick Red: 18th-Century Vernacular (1700–84). Like 17th-century vernacular, these buildings are also simple and unadorned and they were often designed by their owners. They're generally two-story homes with steeply pitched roofs and small windows with many panes.
- Bronze: Georgian (1735–90). The primary feature of Georgian architecture inside and out is symmetry. Houses in this style should be quite easy to find—there are over 60 examples in the historic district and they tend to be the larger buildings in town. This architectural style was popular with the wealthiest citizens; see the William Paca House for a fine example.
- Blue: Federal (1784–1840). This style also stresses symmetry, but in Annapolis the houses tend to be more modest brick or frame structures. Many are row houses with steep roofs, small window panes, and prominent chimneys on either side.
- Light Green: Greek Revival (1820–60). Buildings of this style are characterized by low roofs, columns or pilasters, and a cornice. There are only a handful of buildings of this style in Annapolis.
- Purple: Victorian (1837–1901). This period includes French Second Empire, Italianate Bracketed, and Queen Anne styles, which exhibit elaborate ornamentation on doors and porches, mansard roofs, and large, sometimes bay, windows.
- Gray: 19th/20th-Century Vernacular (1837–1930). Like earlier vernacular structures, buildings of this period and style are simple in design, but they do exhibit some ornamentation on doors, window moldings, or porches.
- Yellow: 20th-Century Distinctive (1901–). This is a catch-all category for newer buildings of architectural interest. They reflect a number of earlier styles but use modern materials and often have large single-pane windows, asphalt roofing, and metal detailing.

Area Code   The area codes in Annapolis are 410 and 443.

Camera Repair   Convenient downtown shops are **A.L. Goodies' One-Hour Photo,** 112 Main St. (☎ **410/263-6919**), and **Ritz Camera,** 138 Main St. (☎ **410/263-6050**).

Car Rentals   See "Getting Around," earlier in this chapter.

Emergencies   Dial ☎ **911** for fire, police, or ambulance.

Eyeglass Repair   Several national optical chains operate in the Annapolis area, including **Sterling Optical** (☎ **410/266-9171**) in the Annapolis Mall and **Visionworks** (☎ **301/261-8337**) in the shopping center across from the Annapolis Mall.

Hospitals   **Anne Arundel Medical Center** is at Franklin and Cathedral streets (☎ **410/267-1000**).

Information   See "Visitor Information," earlier in this chapter.

Liquor Laws   Places serving alcoholic beverages may be open from 6am to 2am, except on Sunday and election days. The minimum age for buying or consuming alcohol is 21.

Newspapers/Magazines   Local daily newspapers include the *Annapolis Capital* and the *Anne Arundel County Sun*. The *Baltimore Sun* and the *Washington Post* are also widely available. The leading monthly magazine is *Annapolis*.

Pharmacies   A downtown branch of the national chain **Rite Aid** is located at 179 Main St. (☎ **410/268-0583**).

Police   For nonemergency police assistance, dial ☎ **311.** For emergencies, dial ☎ **911.**

Post Office   The main branch is at Church Circle and North West Street (☎ **410/263-9292**). Open Monday through Friday from 8:30am to 5pm.

Taxes   The local sales tax is 5%; the local hotel tax is an additional 8%.

Taxis   See "Getting Around," above.

Transit Information   Call the **Annapolis Department of Public Transportation** (☎ **410/263-7964**).

3 Accommodations

The main accommodation choices in Annapolis are concentrated in or near the downtown area. Consequently, most hotels and inns are within walking distance of the major attractions, shopping, and restaurants. Convenience is costly, however, and except for a few motels on the outskirts of town, it is hard to find a double-occupancy room in Annapolis under $100, and even more of a coup to find one under $75. To lessen the dent in your wallet, many properties offer packages at specially reduced rates; be sure to ask whether a package rate applies at the time you intend to visit.

EXPENSIVE

Annapolis Marriott Waterfront. 80 Compromise St., Annapolis, MD 21401. ☎ **800/ 228-9290** or 410/268-7555. Fax 410/269-5864. 150 rms, 1 suite. A/C TV TEL. $120–$249 double; $450 suite. AE, CB, DC, DISC, MC, V. Valet parking $12.

The only waterfront hotel in Annapolis, this modern six-story property enjoys an ideal location, beside the City Dock overlooking the Chesapeake Bay. Recently refurbished, the guest rooms are decorated in contemporary style, enhanced by floor-to-ceiling windows. Most of the rooms have balconies facing the harbor, and the rest overlook the historic district. The lobby is also newly renovated and there is an impressive collection of historical photographs and ship models in an adjacent gallery that is open to the public.

    Dining/Entertainment: For meals or cocktails with a tropical island ambience, try Pusser's Landing (see "Dining," later in this chapter), an indoor and outdoor restaurant and lounge.

    Services: Concierge, room service, dry cleaning, nightly turndown, express checkout, valet parking, free coffee in lobby.

    Facilities: Spectravision movie channels, exercise room and access to nearby health club, sundeck, 300-foot boardwalk, boat-docking slips.

✪ **Loews Annapolis Hotel.** 126 West St., Annapolis, MD 21401. ☎ **800/223-0888** or 410/ 263-7777. Fax 410/263-0084. 210 rms, 7 suites. A/C MINIBAR TV TEL. $115–$165 double; $200–$300 suite; weekends $135–$185 double. AE, DC, MC, V. Self-parking $7; valet parking $10.

With a handsome red-brick facade and a tree-shaded courtyard entrance, this modern six-story hotel near Church Circle in the heart of the historic district blends remarkably well with the surrounding historic buildings. Recently renovated, it has a spacious lobby and skylit public areas including a unique conference center that was formerly the Washington/Baltimore and Annapolis Power Substation. Guest rooms, furnished in dark woods, quilted plaid prints, and nautical art, offer views of the city skyline and historic area.

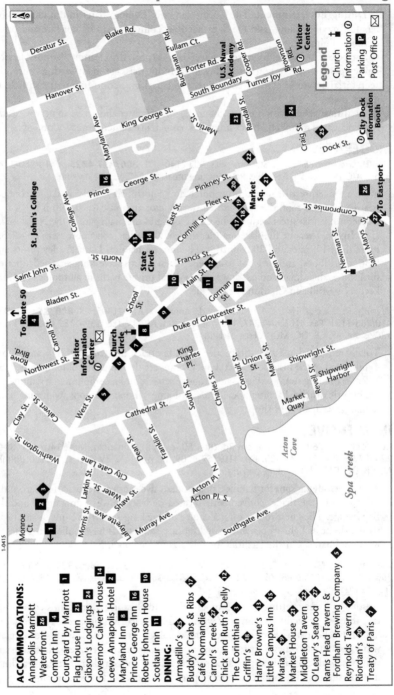

Annapolis Accommodations & Dining

Legend
- ♱ Church
- ⓘ Information
- Ⓟ Parking
- ⊠ Post Office

ACCOMMODATIONS:
- Annapolis Marriott Waterfront **26**
- Comfort Inn **4**
- Courtyard by Marriott **1**
- Flag House Inn **23**
- Gibson's Lodgings **24**
- Governor Calvert House **14**
- Loews Annapolis Hotel **2**
- Maryland Inn **8**
- Prince George Inn **16**
- Robert Johnson House **10**
- Scotlaur Inn **11**

DINING:
- Armadillo's **25**
- Buddy's Crabs & Ribs **17**
- Café Normandie **9**
- Carrol's Creek **22**
- Chick and Ruth's Delly **12**
- The Corinthian **3**
- Griffin's **18**
- Harry Browne's **13**
- Little Campus Inn **15**
- Maria's **21**
- Market House **24**
- Middleton Tavern **22**
- O'Leary's Seafood **27**
- Rams Head Tavern & Fordham Brewing Company **5**
- Reynolds Tavern **6**
- Riordan's **20**
- Treaty of Paris **7**

89

Dining/Entertainment: The Corinthian (see "Dining," later in this chapter) offers full-service dining, and the Weather Rail Lounge serves lighter fare and offers outdoor dining.

Services: Concierge, room service (6:30am–11pm), dry cleaning, laundry service, newspaper delivery, nightly turndown, in-room massage, baby-sitting, business/secretarial services, express checkout, valet parking, complimentary shuttle to downtown.

Facilities: Spectravision movie channels, fitness center and access to nearby Merrit Athletic, game room, children's programs, conference center, beauty salon, gift shop.

MODERATE

Flag House Inn. 26 Randall St., Annapolis, MD 21401. ☎ **800/437-4825** or 410/280-2721. 5 rms. A/C TV. $85–$130 double. Rates include breakfast. MC, V. Free parking.

With a gingerbread-trimmed front porch and colorful state and city flags flying beneath a mansard roof, this lovely three-story Victorian house (ca. 1858) is nestled on a quiet residential street between the City Dock and the main gate of the Naval Academy. Inside, over the fireplace mantle, there is also a flag collection, with flags from more than 40 states and 20 countries. The interior features Laura Ashley prints and fabrics, antiques, and original paintings. Guest rooms have king-size beds, period furnishings, handmade quilts, down pillows, and private baths in all rooms. The innkeepers are Bill and Charlotte Schmickle.

Wyndham Garden Hotel. 173 Jennifer Rd., Annapolis, MD 21401. ☎ **800/351-9209** or 410/266-3131. Fax 410/266-6247. 190 rms, 7 suites. A/C TV TEL. $89–$139 double; $129–$209 suite. AE, CB, DC, MC, V. Free parking.

Totally renovated in 1995, this modern six-story brick-fronted hotel is located about 4 miles west of the historic district. Guest rooms are decorated in contemporary style. There is evening room service, valet laundry service, and a complimentary shuttle to the historic district. Facilities include a cafe, lounge, indoor/outdoor swimming pool, sauna, Jacuzzi, and gift shop.

INEXPENSIVE

Comfort Inn. 76 Old Mill Bottom Rd. (Rte. 50, exit 28), Annapolis, MD 21401. ☎ **800/221-5150** or 410/757-8500. Fax 410/757-4009. 60 rms. A/C TV TEL. $60–$120 double. AE, CB, DC, DISC, MC, V. Free parking.

A favorite lodging spot for families, this modern two-story motel is set back from the main road in the shade, conveniently located midway between downtown and the Bay Bridge. The guest rooms offer a choice of one king-size or two queen-size beds, with a decor of light woods and pastel fabrics; some units have pullout couches or whirlpool baths. On-site facilities include an outdoor pool.

Courtyard by Marriott. 2559 Riva Rd., Annapolis, MD 21401. ☎ **800/321-2211** or 410/266-1555. Fax 410/266-6376. 149 rms. A/C TV TEL. $69–$99 double. AE, DC, DISC, MC, V. Free parking.

Nestled in a quiet setting about 5 miles west of the historic district, this contemporary three-story facility is a favorite with business executives on weekdays and families on weekends. The rooms follow the usual Courtyard plan, with sliding glass windows and balconies or patios facing a central landscaped terrace. Guest units are spacious, with a separate sitting area, sofa, desk, and coffeemaking fixtures. Facilities include a restaurant, indoor swimming pool, whirlpool, and exercise room.

Gibson's Lodgings. 110–114 Prince George St., Annapolis, MD 21401. ☎ **410/268-5555.** 18 rms (7 with bath, 4 with shower only), 2 suites. A/C TV TEL. $68–$85 with shared bath, $78–$98 with bath, $113–$125 suite. Rates include continental breakfast. AE, MC, V. Free parking.

> ### 🎈 Family-Friendly Hotels
>
> **Courtyard by Marriott** *(see p. 90)*   For families on a budget, the Courtyard by Marriott, 5 miles west of the historic district, is a fine choice. Children stay free with their parents, the guest rooms are quite spacious, and the indoor swimming pool will help keep kids entertained whether you're visiting in June or January.
>
> **Loews Annapolis Hotel** *(see p. 88)*   This is *the* place to stay with your family in the historic district. The hotel provides board games, video games, and movies, as well as Welcome Kits for children under 10. The front desk can even arrange baby-sitting and a special "Back of the House" tour of the hotel.

Operated by Claude and Jeanne Schrift, this three-building complex (consisting of two restored town houses and a modern three-story annex) is an ideal spot if you want to be within walking distance of the harbor, the historic district, and the Naval Academy. The main building, the Patterson House (dating from 1760), is a Federal–Georgian house with a Victorian facade. It has six rooms, sharing three bathrooms, and two parlors where breakfast is served each morning. The adjacent Berman House, a tri-gable variation of a 19th-century stucco Homestead-style dwelling, has eight guest rooms with four shared baths and one room with private bath. The annex (or Lauer House), constructed in 1988 of brick to blend in with the older buildings, has two suites and four guest rooms, all with private bath, plus meeting and seminar rooms. A central garden and courtyard serve as a common ground for all three buildings.

Scotlaur Inn. 165 Main St., Annapolis, MD 21401. ☎ **410/268-5665.** 10 rms. A/C TV TEL. $55–$75 double. Rates include breakfast. MC, V. Parking in adjacent public garage.

One of the best values in town, this inn is housed in a three-story brick building in the heart of the historic district. The ground floor belongs to Chick and Ruth's Delly (see "Dining," later in this chapter), an Annapolis tradition for good food at reasonable prices. Both the eatery and the inn are owned by the Levitt family, who are full of enthusiasm and offer a warm welcome. The guest rooms are handsomely furnished in a turn-of-the-century style but require walking up one or two flights of stairs (no elevator).

HISTORIC INNS

Thanks to the efforts of a local preservationist and developer, Paul Pearson, five of Annapolis's most historic buildings were purchased and saved from destruction more than 20 years ago. With the guidance and encouragement of the nonprofit group Historic Annapolis, Pearson has since turned the properties into three elegant inns. Clustered around Annapolis's two key city circles, these landmark buildings are now collectively known as the **Historic Inns of Annapolis.** To reserve a room at any one of the locations, contact the central office of the Historic Inns of Annapolis, 58 State Circle (☎ **800/847-8882** or 410/263-2641).

Governor Calvert House. 58 State Circle. ☎ **800/847-8882** or 410/263-2641. Fax 410/268-3613. 55 rms. A/C TV TEL. $105–$195 double. AE, CB, DC, DISC, MC, V. Valet parking $12.

Both a conference center and a hotel, this lodging is composed of several restored and integrated colonial and Victorian residences. One of the public rooms, which dates from 1727, contains an original hypocaust (a warm-air heating system), now covered with a huge sheet of tempered glass and used as a museum display area. The bedrooms are furnished with antiques. Facilities include underground parking and a sunny ground-floor atrium.

Maryland Inn. 16 Church Circle. ☎ **800/847-8882** or 410/263-2641. Fax 410/268-3813. 44 rms. A/C TV TEL. $105–$195 double. AE, CB, DC, DISC, MC, V. Valet parking $12.

Wedged into a busy triangular intersection, this impressive flatiron-shaped structure was built on "Drummer's Lot" (so named because the town drummer announced the daily news on this spot) and has been operating as an inn since the 1770s. It has been carefully restored and is now decorated in period furnishings including antique fireplaces, rush-seated chairs, lantern fixtures, country hunt prints, and Queen Anne and Louis XIV pieces. Facilities include the Treaty of Paris restaurant (see "Dining," later in this chapter) and a tavern.

Robert Johnson House. 23 State Circle. ☎ **800/847-8882** or 410/263-2641. Fax 410/ 268-3813. 30 rms. A/C TV TEL. $105–$195 double. AE, CB, DC, DISC, MC, V. Valet parking $12.

Located between School and Francis streets and overlooking the governor's mansion and the Maryland State House, this lodging consists of three adjoining Georgian homes, dating from 1773. The artfully restored and furnished guest rooms are individually decorated with four-poster beds and antiques; each unit also has a private bath.

4 Dining

Annapolis is well known for its excellent restaurants, from colonial dining rooms and taverns to romantic bistros and waterside seafood houses. Many choice dining spots are also located in the city's hotels and restored inns. For families and travelers on the go, Annapolis is home to Restaurant Park, a fast-food and family-style complex of eateries located at the intersection of Routes 50, 301, and 450, about 4 miles from downtown, opposite the Annapolis Shopping Plaza.

EXPENSIVE

Corinthian. 126 West St. ☎ **410/263-1299.** Reservations required. Main courses $19.95–$27.95; lunch $5.95–$16.95. AE, CB, DC, DISC, MC, V. Mon–Sat 11am–2pm and 5–10pm, Sun 9am–2pm and 5–10pm. INTERNATIONAL.

The main dining room of the Loews Hotel, this restaurant draws people to Annapolis in its own right, having won *Wine Spectator's* Award for Excellence 3 years' running. Floor-to-ceiling windows, indirect lighting, fish and waterfowl art, and a colorful assortment of plants and dried flowers create an elegant and subdued atmosphere. New chef Greg Sharpe creates such dishes as lemon-baked crab cakes with angel-hair pasta; jumbo shrimp and scallops with penne in lobster sauce; pan-seared lamb chops with rosemary goat cheese polenta; and various cuts of dry-aged steaks and prime rib. Four-course fixed-price dinners offer particularly good value.

Harry Browne's. 66 State Circle. ☎ **410/263-4332.** Reservations recommended for dinner. Main courses $15.95–$21.95; lunch $5.95–$13.95. DISC, MC, V. Mon–Thurs 11am–3pm and 5:30–10pm, Fri–Sat 11am–3pm and 5:30–11pm, Sun 10am–3pm and 3:30–9pm. INTERNATIONAL.

A favorite haunt of legislators, this midtown eatery exudes an old-Maryland ambience, with nautical chandeliers, globe lights, and large framed mirrors. For a change of pace, there is also an art deco cocktail lounge upstairs and an outdoor brick-floored courtyard cafe. Dinner entrees range from blackened swordfish, crab cakes, and grilled salmon to seared duck in cherry-and-port sauce, rack of lamb, and a variety of steaks. Lunch includes an interesting array of salads, quiches, croissant sandwiches, pizzas, and burgers.

Middleton Tavern. 2 Market Space and Randall St. ☎ **410/263-3323.** Reservations not accepted. Main courses $11.95–$33.95; lunch $4.95–$9.95. AE, DISC, MC, V. Mon–Fri 11am–2am, Sat–Sun 10am–2am. AMERICAN.

🙂 Family-Friendly Restaurants

Buddy's Crabs & Ribs *(see p. 95)* This is a favorite among local kids and their parents for its extensive menu (for children and adults), good food, and reasonable prices. You can get everything from steamed blue crabs and barbecue baby-back ribs to fried shrimp, a variety of chicken dishes, and the ever-popular burgers and fries.

Chick and Ruth's Delly *(see p. 96)* A long-standing Annapolis favorite, Chick and Ruth's has something to please everyone, which is why this fun little deli is often overflowing with people. There's a children's menu for breakfast and one for lunch and dinner. Most kids (and many adults) will also want to save room for one of the fabulous ice-cream sundaes, milk shakes, or specialty desserts.

Corinthian *(see p. 92)* For more upscale dining, try the Corinthian in the Loews Annapolis Hotel. Parents can enjoy prime rib, pecan-encrusted salmon, or pan-seared lamb chops, while children can choose from chicken strips, the catch of the day, or a burger, all with veggies, soup or salad, and fries.

Established in 1750 by Horatio Middleton as an inn for seafaring men, this restaurant has had many prominent patrons, including George Washington, Thomas Jefferson, and Benjamin Franklin. Today, restored and expanded, this City Dock landmark offers dinner entrees such as crab cakes, chargrilled swordfish, lobster Luicci (lightly breaded lobster tails broiled in herbs and butter), and fillet of sole (stuffed with crab, spinach, and mushrooms), as well as T-bone steaks, pizzas, pastas, fajitas, and chateaubriand for two.

Treaty of Paris. 16 Church Circle. ☎ **410/263-2641.** Reservations recommended for dinner. Main courses $16.95–$34.95; lunch $5.95–$11.95. AE, CB, DC, DISC, MC, V. Mon–Fri 7am–3pm and 6–9:30pm, Sat 8am–3pm and 6–9:30pm, Sun 8am–2pm and 6–9:30pm. AMERICAN.

Centrally located in the Maryland Inn, this cozy dining room exudes an 18th-century ambience with a decor of brick walls, colonial-style furnishings, and an open fireplace, all enhanced by the glow of candlelight. The eclectic menu offers such dishes as sautéed rockfish, veal sweetbreads, smoked breast of duck, crab imperial, veal Oscar, blackened steaks, and beef Wellington. The restaurant also offers a popular Sunday brunch.

MODERATE

Café Normandie. 185 Main St. ☎ **410/263-3382.** Reservations recommended for dinner. Main courses $13.95–$20.95; lunch $4.95–$9.95; breakfast $1–$8.95. AE, DC, DISC, MC, V. Sun–Thurs 8am–10pm, Fri–Sat 8am–10:30pm. FRENCH.

This simple shop front establishment in the heart of Annapolis's historic district is the next best thing to an authentic French country restaurant. It serves meals throughout the day but is especially good for dinner. Specialties include home-style and regional dishes such as shrimp Provençal, trout amandine, beef bourguignon, duck with raspberry sauce, bouillabaisse, and an assortment of crepes. On many evenings, there are early-bird specials from 5 to 6:30pm; check in advance.

Carrol's Creek. 410 Severn Ave. ☎ **410/263-8102.** Reservations accepted only for indoor weekday lunches and dinners; priority seating on weekends. Main courses $13.95–$23.95; lunch $4.95–$10.95. AE, DC, DISC, MC, V. Mon–Sat 11:30am–10pm, Sun 10am–10pm. AMERICAN.

Sitting on the harbor in the Eastport section of the city, this festive red-trimmed restaurant offers some of the best views of the water and the Annapolis skyline.

Seating is available in a wide-windowed setting indoors or on an umbrella-shaded outdoor porch. The menu features such creative choices as Mediterranean flounder, baked on wilted spinach and topped with tomatoes, onions, black olives, and herbs; shrimp and scallops tequila, with mixed peppers and garnished with jalapeño cornbread; Southwestern blackened prime rib; and pastas such as wild mushrooms with sun-dried tomato linguine.

Maria's. 12 Market Space, City Dock. ☎ **410/268-2122.** Reservations recommended for dinner. Main courses $10.95–$20.95; lunch $4.95–$13.95. AE, MC, V. Mon–Thurs 11am–2:30pm and 4–10pm, Fri–Sat 11am–2:30pm and 4–11pm, Sun 11am–2:30pm and 4:30–10pm. SICILIAN.

Operated by Mama Maria and Pietro Priola, this restaurant is known for its authentic Italian cuisine. There is seating downstairs and upstairs, with the upper rooms providing a slightly more formal setting overlooking the dock area. Specialties of the house include home-baked stuffed pasta, deep-dish Sicilian pizzas, and standard thin-crust pizzas, as well as veal saltimbocca, chicken cacciatore, and a variety of traditional beef and seafood choices. Lunch offers part-portions of dinner items or a selection of sandwiches, subs, salads, and burgers.

✪ **O'Leary's Seafood.** 310 3rd St. ☎ **410/263-0884.** Reservations not accepted. Main courses $10.95–$21.95. DC, MC, V. Mon–Thurs 5:30–10pm, Fri–Sat 5–11pm, Sun 5–10pm. SEAFOOD.

Located in the Eastport section of Annapolis, just over the Spa Creek Bridge, this spot has been synonymous with fine seafood for almost half a century. It is close to the water, but its paned windows really offer no sea views. The modern decor includes a timbered ceiling, light woods, potted palms, and table accessories made by the local pottery. The menu emphasizes fresh seafood, with the day's selections always posted on the blackboard. Each dish is prepared to order, either mesquite grilled, sautéed, poached, baked, or blackened. In addition, you'll usually find blackened gulf shrimp served with cucumber–and–sour cream sauce; mussels marinara; lump crabmeat baked in a cognac cream sauce with almonds; and backfin crab cakes. For meat eaters, there is mesquite-grilled strip steak and chicken au poivre or chicken marinated in raspberry vinaigrette and topped with raspberry butter.

Pusser's Landing. 80 Compromise St. ☎ **410/626-0004** or 410/268-7555. Reservations recommended for dinner. Main courses $8.95–$23.95; lunch $5.95–$13.95. AE, DC, DISC, MC, V. Daily 6:30am–midnight. BRITISH/WEST INDIAN.

With a Virgin Islands decor and nautical ambience, this restaurant is named after British Navy Pusser's Rum, a blend of five West Indian rums. Patrons of this restaurant today can taste the brew in a variety of cocktails while dining outdoors along the waterfront or in an indoor fireside setting. The menu offers West Indies dishes with a British influence, such as Pusser's Chicken Roti, which is the islands' equivalent of a burrito, with chicken, potato, and onion stewed in a light curry sauce and wrapped in a shell of soft pastry; charcoal-grilled Jamaican jerk beef; as well as traditional shepherd's pie, fish-and-chips, and Cumberland sausage on a bed of mashed potatoes. Steaks and fresh seafood are also available. Lunch offers hot and cold sandwiches and build-your-own burger combinations.

✪ **Rams Head Tavern & Fordham Brewing Company.** 33 West St. ☎ **410/268-4545.** Reservations recommended for dinner. Main courses $5.95–$24.95; lunch $5.95–$10.95. Mon–Sat 11am–2am, Sun 10am–2am. AE, MC, V. INTERNATIONAL.

This informal shopfront pub/restaurant prides itself on serving more than 170 different beers from around the world, including, of course, the entire selection from its own microbrewery, the Fordham Brewing Company. As a restaurant, it offers several different settings, ranging from cozy little rooms with brick walls and working fireplaces and/or views of the microbrewery to a wisteria-covered outdoor patio. The menu is the same all day, but smaller "lunch" portions of their entrees are offered for a lower price. The Catfish Po' Boy, a catfish fillet covered in blue cornmeal and deep-fried, is excellent, as is the Jamaican Jerk Rasta Pasta, jerk chicken with tricolored fettuccine, though it's very spicy. But the menu also includes more traditional regional fare, such as jumbo lump crab cakes and grilled tuna steak, lots of burgers and sandwiches, and a large selection of appetizers (we like the Pink House Dip, which is artichoke, spinach, and cream cheese). For our money, this is one of the best casual dining spots in the area.

Reynolds Tavern. 7 Church Circle (at Franklin St.). ☎ **888/626-0381** or 410/626-0380. Reservations recommended for dinner. Main courses $12.95–$24.95. AE, MC, V. Mon–Thurs 6–9pm, Fri–Sat 6–10pm, Sun 5:30–8:30pm. AMERICAN.

Tucked on the edge of the historic area, this restaurant is housed in one of the city's most historic sites. Built by William Reynolds in 1747, it first served as a hat business, then a tavern called the Beaver and Lac'd Hat, later a boardinghouse, and finally it became a public library. Since restored, it still exudes a colonial charm, with period furniture, stenciled walls, and lantern lights. In warm weather, there is also outdoor seating on a brick-walled courtyard terrace sheltered by boughs of 100-year-old magnolias and great Persian walnut trees and enhanced by the aromas of an adjacent herb garden.

The signature dish is the house-smoked Reynolds Seafood Trio, a combination platter of crab cake and two other seafood items, according to season. Otherwise the menu changes seasonally but often includes grilled honey-barbecued gulf shrimp, blackened pan-fried catfish, or rack of lamb au jus. A fixed-price option is available Sunday through Thursday. For $23.95, you get an appetizer, salad, entree, and dessert from the regular menu.

MODERATE/INEXPENSIVE

Armadillo's. 132 Dock St., on the City Dock. ☎ **410/268-6680.** Reservations accepted for parties of 6 or more. Main courses $6.95–$15.95. AE, MC, V. Mon–Fri 11am–11pm, Sat 8am–1:30am, Sun 8am–10pm. MEXICAN/AMERICAN/SEAFOOD.

With a decor of Native American art and pottery, this busy two-story restaurant adds a south-of-the-border ambience to the waterfront area. The menu offers tacos, burritos, enchiladas, empanadas, tostadas, and chimichangas, as well as burgers, steaks, and seafood platters. For dessert, try the bananas sautéed with brandy and brown-sugar sauce.

Buddy's Crabs & Ribs. 100 Main St. ☎ **410/626-1100** or 410/268-0771. Reservations not accepted. Main courses $8.95–$16.95; fast-food items $3.95–$7.95; lunch buffet $6.95. AE, CB, DC, DISC, MC, V. Sun–Thurs 11am–10pm, Fri–Sat 11am–11pm. AMERICAN.

Housed in a converted old building with a decor that includes an original tin ceiling, lots of leafy plants, big-screen TVs, and ceiling fans, this busy and casual restaurant is on the second floor overlooking the City Dock and Main Street. As the name implies, crabs are an important part of the menu, with all-you-can-eat steamed blue crab specials, as well as crab cakes and soft-shell crabs. Other favorites include barbecued baby-back ribs, fried shrimp, flounder amandine, and a variety of steaks, chicken dishes, sandwiches, burgers, and salads. The same menu is used at lunchtime, when a buffet is also available.

Griffin's. 22–24 Market Space, City Dock. ☎ **410/268-2576.** Reservations accepted Mon–Thurs only. Main courses $8.95–$19.95; lunch $4.95–$7.95. AE, DC, DISC, MC, V. Daily 11am–2am. AMERICAN.

Service is swift and attentive at this busy restaurant, almost in keeping with the rhythm of the rock music that blares in the background. It has a long turn-of-the-century-style bar, specializing in microbrews, and two dining areas with high vaulted ceilings, exposed brick walls, tile and marble flooring, mounted animal heads, and a unique collection of framed feathered masks, all surrounding several dozen small and tightly packed tables. The menu changes regularly, but you're likely to find such specialty dishes as Tuna Randell, a fillet coated with Cajun spices and grilled with bell peppers; filet mignon Muñoz, charcoal grilled with house port wine sauce; Charleston Porterhouse pork chops, marinated in juniper berries, peppercorns, and grilled; and Griffin's Penne Pasta, with chicken, broccoli, and sun-dried tomatoes.

Little Campus Inn. 61–63 Maryland Ave. ☎ **410/263-9250.** Reservations recommended for dinner. Main courses $7.95–$16.95; lunch $3.95–$7.95. AE, MC, V. Mon–Thurs 5–10:30pm, Fri–Sat 5–11pm. AMERICAN.

This midtown restaurant has been a favorite since 1923. The second generation of the Nichols family now runs the homey eatery, known for its hearty home-style food and decor of original brick, dark woods, and murals of early Annapolis. Lunch includes fried chicken, omelets, and breaded veal steak. Dinner selections include beef or lamb shish kebab; spaghetti with meatballs; chicken Kiev; baked, smoked, or fresh ham; shrimp and oyster gumbo; and seafood samplers (crab, lobster, scallops, shrimp, crab claws, fish fillet, and clams casino).

Riordan's. 26 Market Space. ☎ **410/263-5449.** Reservations accepted only on Fri and Sat. Main courses $11.95–$19.95; lunch $5.95–$8.95. AE, DC, DISC, MC, V. Mon–Sat 11am–2am, Sun 10am–2am. AMERICAN.

An Irish ambience prevails at this Early American tavern, as evidenced by an illuminated shamrock at the entrance and an Irish flag on the ceiling. The eclectic decor also includes Tiffany lamps, ceiling fans, vintage pictures and posters, and colorful stained glass. Light choices (overstuffed sandwiches, burgers, pastas, and salads) are available throughout the day. The regular dinner menu includes crab-stuffed flounder, prime rib, steamed shrimp, grilled marinated chicken, pasta, and steaks.

INEXPENSIVE

✪ Chick and Ruth's Delly. 165 Main St. ☎ **410/269-6737.** Main courses and lunch $2.95–$7.95. No credit cards. Daily 24 hrs. AMERICAN.

To sample an Annapolis tradition, stop in at this ma-and-pa establishment that has been run by the Levitt family for more than 30 years. This small storefront deli/restaurant, decorated in true diner fashion with orange as the dominant color, is famous for its 50 or so sandwiches named after either local and national political figures or local attractions, such as the Paris Glendenning (baked potato stuffed with broccoli and cheese), the Barbara Mikulski (open-faced tuna with melted cheese on a bagel), the Kathleen Kennedy Townsend (kosher hot dog, raw onion, and relish), the Main Street (corned beef and coleslaw), and even the Bill Clinton (turkey breast, lettuce, and tomato on whole wheat). Platters, pizzas, salads, sundaes, and milk shakes are also available.

Market House. City Dock. ☎ **410/269-0941.** All items $2–$8. No credit cards. Daily 9am–6pm, but individual shops may vary. DELI/FAST FOOD.

Originally a central farmers' produce station built in 1784 and rebuilt in 1858, this place still retains much of the flavor of a market, with open stalls and a variety of foods, although the wares now fall mostly into the fast-food category. Stroll around and order your pick of raw bar items, sandwiches, deli food, pizza, desserts, cheeses, salad bar, breads and pastries, espresso, and more. It's the ideal spot to grab a quick meal, browse, or stock up for a picnic.

5 Attractions

The entire midcity area of Annapolis is a National Historic District, with more than 1,500 restored and preserved buildings. Since the streets are narrow and parking is difficult, the ideal way to see the sights is on foot. Several guided walking tours are described below; self-guided walking tour maps are also available free of charge from the visitor center.

Plan to spend some time around the City Dock along the Annapolis waterfront. This is a yachting hub, with hundreds of craft of all sizes in port. Various sightseeing cruises of the harbor are available in spring, summer, and fall. The City Dock is also home to fine seafood restaurants, lively bars, specialty shops, galleries, and a summer theater.

✪ **U.S. Naval Academy.** 52 King George St. (at Randall St.; enter via Gate 1 at this intersection). ☎ **410/263-6933.** Free admission to grounds; visitor center (including guided walking tour) $5.50 adults, $4.50 seniors, $3.50 students. Mar–Nov daily 9am–5pm, Dec–Feb daily 9am–4pm. Closed Jan 1, Thanksgiving, and Dec 25.

Founded in 1845, this national historic site is the U.S. Navy's undergraduate professional college, spread over 338 acres along the Chesapeake Bay and Severn River on the eastern edge of town. To acclimate yourself and join a guided tour (see "Organized Tours & Cruises," later in this chapter), step into the Armel–Leftwich Visitor Center at the Halsey Field House, just inside Gate 1. Here you can view a 12-minute orientation film and browse among the exhibits on the life of a midshipman. Among the attractions are the chapel and crypt of John Paul Jones and the U.S. Naval Academy Museum in Preble Hall, which contains fascinating collections of nautical relics, paintings, ship models, and other historic items.

Try to plan your trip to coincide with noon formation (held in Tecumseh Court at 12:05pm Monday through Saturday and at 12:30pm on Sunday), when all the midshipmen line up and are accounted for before marching in for the noon meal. Commissioning Week, usually surrounding the last Wednesday in May, is a colorful time of full-dress parades; it is also a busy period for Annapolis hotels, as relatives and friends of the midshipmen pour into the city.

Banneker–Douglass Museum. 84 Franklin St. (off the south side of Church Circle). ☎ **410/974-2893.** Free admission. Tues–Fri 10am–3pm, Sat noon–4pm.

Named after two prominent local black residents, Benjamin Banneker and Frederick Douglass, this museum presents arts and crafts, exhibits, lectures, and films, all designed to portray the historical life and cultural experiences of African-Americans in Maryland. The site was formerly the Old Mount Moriah African Methodist Episcopal Church.

Charles Carroll House. 107 Duke of Gloucester St. (behind St. Mary's Church at Spa Creek). ☎ **410/263-1737.** Admission $4 adults, $3.50 seniors, $2 ages 12–17, free under age 12. Mar–Dec Fri noon–4pm, Sat 10am–2pm, Sun noon–4pm; Tues–Thurs tours by appointment. Closed Easter, Thanksgiving, Dec 24, and Dec 25.

Built in 1721 and 1722 and enlarged in 1770, this is the birthplace and dwelling of Charles Carroll of Carrollton, the only Roman Catholic to sign the Declaration of Independence. It sits on high ground overlooking Spa Creek, a block from City Dock. Visitors can tour the house plus the 18th-century terraced boxwood gardens and a 19th-century wine cellar.

> ⭐ **Frommer's Favorite Annapolis Experiences**
>
> **Noon Formation at the Naval Academy.** Don't miss this impressive daily ritual, when all present midshipmen, usually about a third of the battalion of 4,000, suit up, assemble, and march in for their noon meal.
>
> **Milkshakes at Chick and Ruth's Delly.** Actually anything on the menu at this homey, busy little diner is a treat, but we highly recommend the thick, chocolate milk shakes.
>
> **Sailing, Sailing, Sailing.** A trip to Annapolis is not complete without a view of the city from the water, the dome of the State House rising majestically above the harbor. Of course, sailing into the harbor is the ideal, but a trip on one of the many sightseeing boats is a good alternative.

Hammond–Harwood House. 19 Maryland Ave. (northeast of State Circle, at the corner of King George St.). ☎ **410/269-1714.** Admission $4 adults, $3 ages 6–18. Mon–Sat 10am–4pm, Sun noon–4pm. Closed Jan 1, Thanksgiving, and Dec 25.

Built in 1774, this house is one of the finest examples of Georgian architecture in the United States. It is also an outstanding example of the Maryland five-part plan that connects the central section by hyphens to semioctagonal wings. Famous for its center doorway of tall Ionic columns, the interior is a showcase of decorative arts and paintings as well as ornamentation and wood carvings. The house is named for its first and last owners: Mathias Hammond, a Maryland member of the Provincial Assembly, and the Harwood family, who owned the house before it became a museum. The newest addition to the museum is a photo exhibit documenting the house from the 1920s to the present.

✪ **London Town House and Gardens.** 839 Londontown Rd., Edgewater, MD. ☎ **410/222-1919.** Admission $6 adults, $4 seniors, $3 ages 7–12. Mar–Dec Mon–Sat 10am–4pm, Sun noon–4pm; Jan–Feb gardens Mon–Sat 10am–4pm, Sun noon–4pm; house tours by appointment. Take Rte. 50 to Rte. 655 (exit 22), then take Rte. 2 south, over the South River Bridge. Turn left on Mayo Rd., then left on Londontown Rd.

Just south of Annapolis, across the South River, stands the 1760s Georgian home of William Brown, the only remaining structure from what was once a bustling trade town called London Town that rivaled Annapolis in size and importance. The London Town Foundation, in conjunction with Anne Arundel County, has undertaken the enormous archaeological task of unearthing the 23 acres around the William Brown House and rebuilding the lost town. In the meantime, they've opened the house, the 8-acre woodland gardens, and the dig sites to the public. On Tuesday, Thursday, and alternate Wednesdays in the summer, fall, and spring, when archaeologists are on-site, visitors can participate in the digging, as well as tour the gardens and the house. During my recent visit, two dig sites were open: the trash site at the carpenter's shop and the cellar of Rumney's Tavern. The house, like the archaeological sites, is quite open and accessible; the foundation wishes to educate the public not only about the social history of the town and times but also about the process of restoration and excavation. So don't expect a du Pont estate; this is a work in progress, exposed water-damaged walls and all.

✪ **Maryland State House.** State Circle. ☎ **410/974-3400.** Free admission. Daily 9am–5pm. Closed Jan 1, Thanksgiving, and Dec 25.

Located in the center of Annapolis, this is the oldest U.S. state capitol in continuous legislative use (built between 1772 and 1779). The building also served as the

Annapolis Attractions

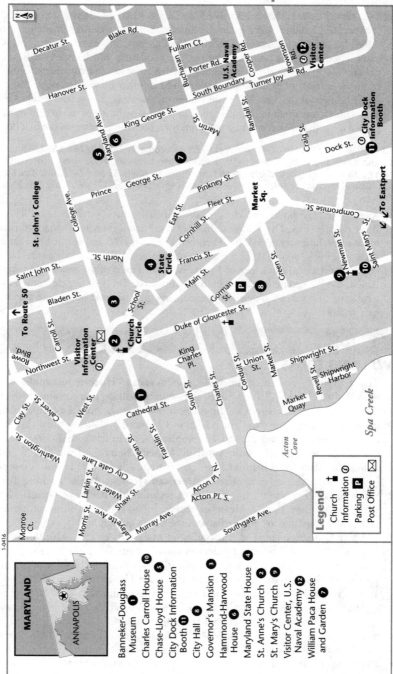

Legend

Church ✝
Information ⓘ
Parking 🅿
Post Office ✉

MARYLAND
ANNAPOLIS

Banneker-Douglass Museum ❶
Charles Carroll House ❿
Chase-Lloyd House ❺
City Dock Information Booth ⓫
City Hall ❽
Governor's Mansion ❸
Hammond-Harwood House ❻
Maryland State House ❹
St. Anne's Church ❷
St. Mary's Church ❾
Visitor Center, U.S. Naval Academy ⓬
William Paca House and Garden ❼

U.S. capital from November 26, 1783, to August 13, 1784. As you step inside the Old Senate Chamber, you'll be in the historic spot where George Washington resigned his commission as commander-in-chief of the Continental armies. This was also the setting for the ratification of the Treaty of Paris, which ended the Revolutionary War. The dome of this building, the largest of its kind constructed entirely of wood, is made of cypress beams and is held together by wooden pegs. You can stroll throughout the State House on your own, examining the various exhibits that depict life in Annapolis in colonial times, or you can make use of the free 30-minute guided tours that depart at 11am and 3pm from the visitor center on the first floor.

✪ **William Paca House and Garden.** 186 Prince George St. ☎ **410/263-5553.** Admission to tour house $4 adults, $2 ages 6–18; to tour garden $3 adults, $1.50 ages 6–18; combination package covering both the house and the garden $6 adults, $3 ages 6–18. Mar–Dec Mon–Sat 10am–4pm, Sun noon–4pm; Jan–Feb Fri–Sun 10am–4pm. Closed Thanksgiving, Dec 24, and Dec 25.

Among the great historic residences in Annapolis is this former home of William Paca, a signer of the Declaration of Independence and a governor of Maryland during the Revolutionary period. Built between 1763 and 1765 and restored by Historic Annapolis from 1965 to 1976, it is a five-part structure, with a stalwart central block, hyphens and wings, and a total of 37 rooms. Guided tours of the house are available. Behind the Paca estate is a 2-acre pleasure garden consisting of five elegant terraces, a fish-shaped pond, a Chinese Chippendale bridge, a summer house, and a wilderness garden.

6 Organized Tours & Cruises

WALKING TOURS

To see all that is best about Annapolis, plan to take a **"Historic Annapolis Walk with Walter Cronkite,"** a self-guided audiocassette walking tour narrated by the famous TV news broadcaster. The Historic Annapolis Foundation is the sponsor of this comprehensive walking tour, which takes in 19 historic and architectural sites with a 45-minute commentary that can be completed at a leisurely pace in 1 1/2 hours. It is available only at the Historic Annapolis Museum Store, 77 Main St. (☎ **410/ 268-5576**), daily from 10am to 5pm. Cost per rental is $5. The Historic Annapolis Foundation also offers an **African-American Heritage Audio Walking Tour,** which covers 15 sites in the historic district, including the Banneker–Douglass Museum, the Matthew Henson Memorial, and St. John's College. Tours take approximately 1 1/2 hours and are also available at the Museum Store.

Three Centuries Tours of Annapolis, 48 Maryland Ave. (☎ **410/263-5401**), is known for its well-informed guides in colonial costume. Their historic district tours, which cover the highlights of the historic district and the Naval Academy and provide admission to the William Paca Garden, are 2 hours in length and are operated on a turn-up-and-go basis, with no reservations required.

Tours are operated daily, April 1 through October 31 at 10:30am, departing from the visitor center at 26 West St. and at 1:30pm from the City Dock information booth. From November 1 through March 31, there is an afternoon tour on Saturday only, at 2:30pm, departing from Gibson's Lodgings. The price is $8 for adults and $3 for students. (If you take a morning tour, the guides try to get you to the Naval Academy in time for the noon meal formation.) Three Centuries Tours also offers preplanned and tailor-made tours by reservation, focusing on such topics as colonial life (for young visitors), historic mansions, and bay cruises.

The **U.S. Naval Academy Walking Tours** depart from the Armel–Leftwich Visitor Center of the U.S. Naval Academy, Gate 1, King George and Randall streets (☎ **410/263-6933**), every day of the year except January 1, Thanksgiving, and December 25. From June through Labor Day, tours depart every half hour Monday through Saturday from 9:30am to 3:30pm and Sunday from 12:30 to 3:30pm; from September through November and March through Memorial Day, tours are hourly Monday through Friday from 10am to 3pm, and every half hour Saturday from 10am to 3:30pm and Sunday from 12:30 to 3:30pm; and from December through February tours are Monday through Saturday at 11am and 1pm and Sunday at 12:30pm and 2:30pm. The price is $5.50 for adults, $4.50 for seniors, and $3.50 for students.

BUS TOURS

A great way to get acquainted with the city and some of the outlying areas is the bus tour operated by **Discover Annapolis Tours,** 31 Decatur Ave. (☎ **410/626-6000**). This air-conditioned, 25-passenger minibus takes visitors past the highlights of the historic district—the State House, the Chase–Lloyd House, the Hammond–Harwood House, and St. Johns College, to name a few—as well as to some areas the walking tours don't cover—Eastport, the Charles Carroll House, and the Severn River Scenic Overlook. The narrated tours last about an hour and provide more than just the history of the town. Matt Grubbs, your guide and driver, also gives his visitors some hints on how to see the town. Tours are operated year-round, departing from the lot behind the visitor center at 26 West St. at 11:30am, 1:30pm, and 3:30pm daily in spring through fall, weekends only in winter. Cost is $9 for adults and $3 for children 12 and under.

CRUISES & BOATING TOURS

To see the sights of Annapolis from the water, **Chesapeake Marine Tours,** Slip 20, City Dock (☎ **410/268-7600**), operates a variety of cruises along Annapolis Harbor and beyond. Choices include the *Harbor Queen,* a 297-passenger double-deck vessel offering a 40-minute narrated cruise that covers the highlights of Annapolis Harbor, U.S. Naval Academy, and the Severn River; *Miss Anne,* a 24-passenger covered one-deck launch that provides a 40-minute narrated tour focusing on the residential waterfront along Spa Creek and the Naval Academy shore; *Providence,* a 149-passenger double-deck boat that offers 90-minute narrated Severn River cruises, as well as luncheon cruises, around Annapolis Harbor, along the U.S. Naval Academy grounds, and through the Severn River; and *Annapolitan II,* a 102-passenger double-deck boat that provides a full-day cruise on the bay (7^1/$_2$ hours, advance reservations advised), departing from Annapolis and cruising to St. Michaels on the Eastern Shore. In addition, two "adventure cruises" are operated aboard the 48-passenger *Rebecca:* the Thomas Point Lighthouse Cruise, a 90-minute trip on the Severn River to the lighthouse, and the Creeks of Annapolis Cruise, a 75-minute tour of Spa and Back Creeks. Tours range from $6 to $35 for adults and $3 to $20 for children 11 and under. Sailings are daily from Memorial Day through Labor Day, with abbreviated schedules in the spring and fall.

7 Outdoor Activities

With the Chesapeake Bay and Severn River at its doorstep, Annapolis is considered the pleasure-boating capital of the eastern United States. The city offers many opportunities to enjoy sailing and water sports, as well as other outdoor activities.

BICYCLING   Though the streets of Annapolis are often a bit too crowded for a leisurely biking excursion, just outside the city there are several pleasant parks and paths for cycling. A good place to bike is the **Baltimore and Annapolis Trail** (☎ **410/222-6244**), a smooth 13.3-mile-long asphalt route that runs from Annapolis into the suburbs. Formerly a rail corridor, it's considered a "community sidewalk" by the locals and is ideal for biking, walking, jogging, in-line skating, or just meandering. It begins at Ritchie Highway, just outside of Annapolis at the Route 50 interchange, and ends on Dorsey Road at Route 648 in Glen Burnie. It's open daily from sunrise to sunset.

Just outside the city, on the South River and Harness Creek, **Quiet Waters Park** (☎ **410/222-1777**) has 6 miles of biking/hiking trails with an overlook along the South River. You can even rent bicycles at the visitor center from spring through fall. The park is open from 7am to dusk, 6 days a week (it's closed on Tuesday), and there's a $4-per-vehicle entrance fee.

SAILING SCHOOLS & SAILING TRIPS   Learn to sail at the oldest and largest sailing school in America: the **Annapolis Sailing School,** 601 Sixth St., P.O. Box 3334, Annapolis, MD 21403 (☎ **800/638-9192**). With more than 120 boats and a huge support staff, this facility offers a wide range of instructional programs for novice and veteran sailors, including their brand-new KidShip program for children ages 5 to 15. Courses range from a weekend beginner's course for $225 to a 5-day advanced course in preparation for bareboat (skipperless) charters, from $700 and up. If you're on a short visit, you can also sign up for their "Sailing Sample" package, a 2-hour course for just $25.

Womanship, 410 Severn Ave., Annapolis, MD 21403 (☎ **410/267-6661**), is a sailing program designed for women by women. Instruction is geared to all levels, from novice to advanced, in either daytime or live-aboard settings. Course duration ranges from 2 to 7 days, priced from $298 to $1,050. There are also courses for mothers and daughters, families, and youths (ages 10 to 17).

There are many sailing schools in the area, so call around to find the best rate and a schedule that suits your needs. Some others in the area are **Chesapeake Sailing School** (☎ **800/966-0032** or 410/269-1594) and **AYS Charters and Sailing School** (☎ **800/638-9192** or 410/267-7205).

If you prefer to sit back and let a captain and crew take you out for a sailboat ride, you can board the 36-foot sloop **Beginagain,** 1056 Eaglewood Rd., Annapolis (☎ **800/295-1422** or 410/626-1422), departing from the City Dock. The *Beginagain* can carry only six passengers, so it has an intimate feel. Operating from May through September, this vessel offers 3-hour trips, departing daily at 9am, 1pm, and 6pm (May through July) or 5pm (August and September). Cost is $50 per passenger.

The 74-foot classic wooden yacht **Schooner Woodwind** and her brand-new (in 1998) sister ship the **Woodwind II,** 301 Fourth St., Annapolis (☎ **410/267-6333**), depart from the Marriott Hotel side of the City Dock for 2-hour sailing trips. Departures are at 11am, 1:30pm, 4pm, and 6:30pm on Tuesday through Sunday and on Monday at 6:30pm from late May through August; at noon, 3pm, and 5:30pm Tuesday through Sunday in early May and September; and at noon and 3pm in April, October, and November. The sunset cruises, which depart daily at 6:30pm or 5:30pm depending on the season, have a different theme each day, such as beer-tasting on Tuesday and ecotours on Thursday. Cost is $22 to $25 for adults and $12 to $15 for children under 12. Day-sail rentals and lessons are also available. A half-day lesson for up to four people costs $250, and rentals are $140 for a half day and $200 for the whole day. Three-day windjammer cruises are also available, as are "boat and breakfast" overnight accommodations on board the vessel.

WATER-SPORT RENTALS   To rent a sailboat, you can contact most of the sailing schools in the area, including all the ones listed above. For speedboats, contact **Suntime Boat Rentals,** 2822 Solomons Island Rd., Route 2, Edgewater (☎ **410/ 266-6020**). This company rents 17¹/₂-foot boats with 90- to 115-horsepower engines from $56 to $65 an hour or $325 to $375 per day; and 19-foot boats with 195-horsepower engines from $75 an hour or $435 a day. WaveRunners are also available from $50 per half hour or $70 per hour.

8 Shopping

Annapolis is a good shopping and browsing town. The historic district is lined with boutiques and shops of international and local appeal. Most stores in the historic district are open at least Monday through Saturday from 11am to 5 or 6pm and Sunday from noon to 5pm. Many stay open until 8 or 9pm on Friday and Saturday and several open at 10am or earlier during the week. Any notable exceptions are listed below.

ANTIQUES

Walnut Leaf Antiques and Appraisals. 62 Maryland Ave. ☎ **800/224-7355** or 410/ 263-4885.

This shop specializes in period and oak furniture, European and Oriental porcelain, cut glass, vintage costume jewelry, nautical and optical antiques, and 20th-century collectibles. Open daily from noon to 5pm.

ART

Annapolis Marine Art Gallery. 110 Dock St. ☎ **410/263-4100.**

Overlooking the City Dock, this gallery is devoted to marine and seabird art by living artists. It offers original paintings, graphics, ship models, scrimshaw, and sculptures.

Gallery on the Circle. 18 State Circle (between School and Franklin sts.). ☎ **410/268-4566.**

The Maryland Federation of Art, a member's nonprofit cooperative organization, operates this gallery, exhibiting traditional and contemporary original art in all media. It is housed in the storage loft of an old general store; the 1840s building has brick walls and beamed ceilings. Closed Monday.

League of Maryland Craftsmen. 54 Annapolis Ave. ☎ **410/626-1277.**

This gallery displays and sells the work of more than 100 Maryland artists, including paintings in oil, watercolor, and acrylic, as well as etchings, drawings, photographs, sculpture, and wood carvings. There are also works in fiber-silk, stained glass, porcelain, and pottery. A new branch of the shop opened in Frederick in the summer of 1997 (see "Frederick" in chapter 9). Closed Tuesday.

Main Street Gallery. 109 Main St. ☎ **410/280-2787.**

Situated near the City Dock, this is a cooperative effort by more than 50 Maryland artists who have pooled their energy, resources, and talents to create an innovative exhibition space and retail gallery. Open Sunday, Monday, Wednesday, and Thursday from 10am to 6pm, Friday and Saturday from 10am to 8pm.

Whitehall Gallery. 57 West St. ☎ **410/269-6161.**

This gallery specializes in antique prints and maps, nautical and duck art, Annapolis waterfront scenes, and prints of herbs and flowers. Open weekdays from 9am to 5pm, Saturday from 11am to 4pm.

BOOKS
Briarwood Bookshop. 88 Maryland Ave. ☎ **410/268-1440.**

This shop specializes in second-hand and old books, with many scholarly and hard-to-find items. There's also a good selection of Maryland-related and naval history volumes and old prints.

CLOTHING
✪ **Avoca Handweavers.** 141–143 Main St. ☎ **800/981-9039** or 410/263-1485.

This is the American branch of the Irish company founded in 1723. Soft and colorful Irish tweeds are the specialty here, with a wide selection of capes, coats, caps, suits, shawls, and sweaters, as well as Irish books, jewelry, glassware, and pottery. Open Monday through Saturday from 10am to 8pm, Sunday from 11am to 5pm.

CRAFTS & COLLECTIBLES
Annapolis Country Store. 53 Maryland Ave. ☎ **410/269-6773.**

Claiming to be the oldest and largest wicker shop in Maryland, this shop also stocks pottery, mugs, candles, cards, jams, kitchen accessories, and Classic Pooh collectibles.

✪ **Annapolis Pottery.** 40 State Circle. ☎ **410/268-6153.**

As its name implies, this is a real working pottery as well as a shop. Potters work at the wheel almost every day, and visitors are invited to watch and ask questions. The handmade items include vases, dishes, and plates, as well as one-of-a-kind pieces. Many pieces can be personalized with names or logos on request.

The Nature Company. 134 Main St. ☎ **410/268-3909.**

A branch of the environmentally conscious enterprise that began in California, this shop specializes in the arts and crafts of indigenous peoples, as well as products developed to support the sustainable use of natural resources. The items on sale include rain forest shampoos and aloe moisture soaps, audiocassettes of environmental sounds, books on the environment, Native American arts and crafts, Earth Day symbols, and recycled paper products.

GIFTS & SOUVENIRS
Christmas Spirit. 180 Main St. ☎ **410/268-2600.**

It's Christmas every day at this festive shop in the heart of the historic district. The wares include lights and hand-crafted ornaments from around the world, angel tree tops, tree skirts, vintage Victorian decorations, candles, nutcrackers, character Santas, gift wrap, cards, and more. Open daily from 10am to 6pm.

Gift Horse. 77 Maryland Ave. ☎ **410/263-3737.**

This is an emporium of unusual gift items, from glass, brass, pewter, and armetale (an alloy composed of 10 metals, similar to pewter), to oil lamps, figurines, prisms, mobiles, and paperweights.

Pewter Chalice. 168 Main St. ☎ **410/268-6246.**

If you are fond of pewter and armetale, this is a great spot to browse or shop. You'll find pewter goblets, bowls, tankards, candelabra, pitchers, flagons, plates, teapots, candlesticks, cutlery, flasks, inkwells, jewelry boxes, vases, and much more.

MALLS & MARKETS
Annapolis Harbour Center. 2512A Solomons Island Rd. ☎ **410/266-5857.**

One of the area's newest shopping clusters, positioned west of downtown at the junction of Routes 2 and 665, this mall is laid out like a maritime village, with more than

40 different shops, services, and fast-food eateries, as well as nine movie theaters. Open Monday through Saturday from 10am to 9pm and Sunday from noon to 5pm.

Annapolis Mall. Defense Hwy. and Rte. 178. ☎ **410/266-5432.**

If shopping on a big scale interests you, then head to this mall, situated off Route 50 between West Street and Bestgate Road. There are three department stores (Hechts, J.C. Penney, and Montgomery Ward) as well as more than 125 specialty shops. Open Monday through Saturday from 10am to 9:30pm and Sunday from 11am to 6pm.

Maritime & Naval Items. Peppers. 133 Main St. ☎ **410/267-8722.**

This place offers a large selection of officially licensed navy clothing, from sweatshirts, T-shirts, and sweaters to hats and accessories. Open Monday through Saturday from 10am to 6pm, Sunday from noon to 5pm.

Pennsylvania Dutch Farmers Market. 2472 Solomons Island Rd. ☎ **410/573-0770.**

Situated opposite the string of shops at Annapolis Harbour Center (see above), this market is an attraction in itself, run by Amish and Mennonite families from Lancaster County, Pennsylvania. The wares range from traditional sausages and pickled products to chemically free vegetables and fruits, as well as homemade jams, fudge, candies, cakes, pies, and soft pretzels, all ideal for a picnic or snack. There is also a section devoted to crafts such as handmade quilts. Open Thursday 10am to 6pm, Friday 9am to 6pm, and Saturday 9am to 3pm.

Ship and Soldier Shop. 58 Maryland Ave. ☎ **410/268-1141.**

This is a good source for metal models and miniatures of the army, navy, and marines (and the Royal Canadian Mounted Police), as well as models of cars, ships, trains, and planes. Closed Monday.

Sign O' the Whale. 99 Main St. ☎ **410/268-2161.**

Situated at Green Street across from the City Dock, this eclectic shop offers an assortment of naval and nautical crafts, as well as Chesapeake Bay–related art, glass sailboats, scrimshaw, ceramics, sculpture, and apparel.

9 Annapolis After Dark

Annapolis is a town of small venues: Most local bars feature live music on weekends— everything from pop to classic rock to blues and funk—and there are a few good local theater companies. But I'm afraid if you're looking for Broadway musicals or nationally acclaimed symphonies, you'll have to trek to the Kennedy Center or the Mechanic Theater in Washington, D.C., or Baltimore, either of which is a perfectly viable and inviting option, since they're both only about a half hour away.

For up-to-date weekly listings of concerts and other entertainment events in the Annapolis area, check the "Entertainment" section of the *Capital* newspaper on Friday. *Inside Annapolis,* a bimonthly publication distributed free throughout the city, also gives a summary of entertainment venues and upcoming events and other information of use to visitors. The visitors bureau also publishes seasonal events calendars; you can pick these up at the visitors center on West Street.

BARS & CLUBS

ACME. 163 Main St. ☎ **410/280-6486.** No cover.

I'm almost afraid to mention it, but, yes, this is a place where Naval Academy midshipmen frequently go to party. ACME is also quite popular with all sorts of other overly indulgent college types and is a good place to occasionally catch local up-and-coming alternative rock and acoustic bands.

Armadillo's. 132 Dock St. ☎ **410/268-6680.** Cover $2–$4.

This place offers a variety of live entertainment—jazz, blues, funk, classic rock, acoustic rock, and oldies. Music usually starts at 9:30pm daily.

✪ King of France Tavern. 16 Church Circle. ☎ **410/269-0990.** Cover $3–$10, depending on the music.

The colonial kitchens of the Maryland Inn serve as the setting for this club, which is known for its jazz, as well as occasional programs of folk, classical, chamber music, and big bands. The Charlie Byrd jazz trio often plays here on Friday through Sunday nights. Music starts at 8 or 8:30pm.

McGarvey's Saloon. 8 Market Space. ☎ **410/263-5700.** No cover.

McGarvey's, O'Brien's, and Riordan's, three bars near the City Dock, make up arguably the most happening area of Annapolis at night. McGarvey's doesn't usually have live music, but it's still a great place for seafood and beer.

O'Brien's Oyster Bar and Grill. 113 Main St. ☎ **410/268-6288.** Cover $2.

Situated across from the City Dock, O'Brien's is Annapolis's best rock venue. It features live rock music on Friday and Saturday nights and live acoustic rock the rest of the week. Music begins nightly at around 9:30 or 10pm.

Pusser's Landing. 80 Compromise St. (in the Marriott Waterfront Hotel). ☎ **410/626-0004.** No cover.

This elegant bar is set on the harbor at the Marriott Waterfront. It offers a good place to socialize and have a couple of drinks, without all of the racket of the rowdier bars on the City Dock down toward the Market Place.

Rams Head Tavern. 33 West St. ☎ **410/268-4545.** No cover.

Set in an old town house on West Street between the Loews Annapolis Hotel and Church Circle, Rams Head is the home of the Fordham Brewing Company and, needless to say, a great place to grab a beer. Because there is a restaurant at the tavern, the clientele tends to range in age from 21 to 60 and up. There are two barrooms, one upstairs with a vaulted ceiling and the other in the cozy brick-lined basement. Live jazz, blues, and acoustic rock are featured Monday through Thursday.

Riordan's Saloon. 26 Market Space. ☎ **301/261-1524.** No cover.

Popular with the postcollege crowd, Riordan's is a little more upscale than its neighbors, McGarvey's and O'Brien's, but it isn't at all stuffy. It offers live music (usually acoustic rock) 4 nights a week.

THE PERFORMING ARTS

The town's largest venue, the **✪ Maryland Hall for the Creative Arts,** 801 Chase St. (☎ **410/263-5544**), presents performances by the Annapolis Symphony Orchestra, Annapolis Chorale, Annapolis Chamber Orchestra, and the Ballet Theater of Annapolis, as well as one-person shows. Performances are nightly at 7 or 8pm and tickets range in price from $10 to $30. In 1997 the hall instituted a summer concert series (made possible because of the newly installed air-conditioning system), featuring the U.S. Naval Academy Band.

Summer is a great time for the performing arts in Annapolis; there are several free outdoor concert series and theater productions. The **Naval Academy Summer Serenade** (☎ **410/203-1262**), held weekly at the City Dock, features the Next Wave, the Electric Brigade, and the full concert band. Concerts are free, but you have to bring your own seating. Quiet Waters Park, south of Annapolis on the South River, also hosts a summer concert series (free for walk-ins, but admission charged for cars). Call ☎ **410/222-1777** for more information.

Since 1966 the **Annapolis Summer Garden Theatre,** 143 Compromise St. at Main Street across from the City Dock (☎ **410/268-9212**), has been staging musical and theater performances at reasonable prices every summer. Recent performances included *Anything Goes* and *L'il Abner.* Shows are daily at 8:30pm. Reservations by phone are encouraged, and tickets cost $8 for shows Monday through Wednesday and $10 Thursday through Saturday.

Year-round the **Chesapeake Music Hall** at 339 Busch's Frontage Rd. (☎ **800/ 406-0306** or 410/626-7515) offers a program of Broadway-style musicals and comedies, as well as Murder Mystery Dinner Theater, country line dancing, and jazz nights. The price includes a dinner or brunch buffet. Tickets range from $26.95 to $29.95, and performances are held Thursday, Friday, and Saturday at 8pm (dinner buffet at 6:30pm) and Sun at 2:30pm (brunch buffet at 1pm). **Colonial Players Theater,** 108 East St. (☎ **410/268-7373**), also offers year-round theater in a 180-seat theater-in-the-round setting. The company performs five plays each year. Shows are Thursday through Saturday at 8pm and Sunday at 2:30 or 7:30pm, and ticket prices range from $8 to $11.

10 Solomons & Calvert County

For over a hundred years Calvert County has been the Chesapeake playground of citizens of Baltimore, Western Maryland, and Washington, D.C. Lately, the town of Solomons, with its mixture of history, outdoor fun, and marine sports, has become the center of this scene.

Solomons, often mistakenly called "Solomons Island" after the island that makes up its center, is a town dominated by water. It's composed of an island and the end of two peninsulas formed by the Patuxent River, Back Creek, and Mill Creek (the Patuxent's mouth into the Chesapeake is visible from the town's southern end). The island is connected to land by a bridge so short that if you blink you'll miss it, but this in no way detracts from the feeling that you are surrounded by water. A walk through town will take you past numerous sailboats, yachts, and charter fishing boats, as well as old and modern watermen's homes, the century-old Drum Point Lighthouse, and Solomons's wide public pier, the place to see beautiful sunsets over the Patuxent.

What about the rest of Calvert County? Well, it offers excellent hiking, fossil-hunting, easy access to the historical sites of St. Mary's County, and some of the premier charter fishing on the Chesapeake.

ESSENTIALS

GETTING THERE   Solomons is at the southern tip of the peninsula of Calvert County. Maryland Routes 2 and 4 merge together and run north–south across the county, giving access to all the sights. To reach Solomons from Washington, D.C., and points south take I-95 to the exit for Route 4 south and follow Route 4 all the way to Solomons. From Annapolis and points north take the exit for Route 2 south off U.S. 50 and follow Route 2 to Solomons.

VISITOR INFORMATION   Calvert County can provide a wealth of information on the area before you make your trip. Write to Calvert County Department of Economic Development, Courthouse, Prince Frederick, Maryland 20678, or call ☎ **800/331-9771** or 410/535-4583. Once you're there you can stop by the information center just outside Solomons at the base of the Governor Thomas Johnson Bridge on Route 2–4.

ATTRACTIONS

Calvert County offers a great combination of worthwhile attractions, relaxing scenery, and loads of outdoor fun. And it would be a shame to be so close to St. Mary's County's historic sites and miss them, so be sure to check them out in the next section.

✪ Battle Creek Cypress Swamp Sanctuary. Grays Rd., Prince Frederick. ☎ **410/535-5327.** Free admission. Apr–Sept Tues–Sat 10am–5pm, Sun 1–5pm; Oct–Mar Tues–Sat 10am–4:30pm, Sun 1–4:30pm. Take Rte. 506 west from Rte. 2–4, then turn left onto Grays Rd.; the Sanctuary is ¹/₄ mile on the right.

In 1957 the Nature Conservancy bought this 100-acre parcel of land as a sanctuary on the northernmost limit of the natural range of the great bald cypress trees that once dominated the swamps of the southern states. A quarter-mile elevated boardwalk trail allows visitors to explore this primeval environment of ferns, flowers, and ancient cypress trees. You might also spot frogs, turtles, crayfish, and raccoons, if you are quiet and lucky. Inside the visitors center are exhibits on the natural and historical heritage of the swamp area, including an interesting display on animal tracks and a rare albino turtle.

Calvert Cliffs Nuclear Power Plant Visitor Center. 1650 Calvert Cliffs Pkwy. (just off of Rte. 2–4 south of Prince Frederick). ☎ **410/495-4673.** Free admission. Daily 10am–4pm.

This, Maryland's first nuclear power plant, is in many ways an ideal corporate citizen of Calvert County, regularly donating considerable funds for county improvements. However, the visitors center, housed in a 19th-century tobacco barn, is a little strange. Placed on the edge of a hill above the plant, it offers a few exhibits on energy consumption, nuclear power, and the history of the site, as well as an overlook with views of the plant and, a short ways off shore in the Chesapeake Bay, the turning and twisting waters being sucked and expelled from its cooling system.

✪ Calvert Marine Museum and Drum Point Lighthouse. Rte. 2, Solomons Island Rd., Solomons. ☎ **410/326-2042.** Admission $4 adults, $3 age 55 and over, $2 ages 5–12. Daily 10am–5pm.

This gem of a small museum explores the area's relationship to the sea. Visitors are treated to exhibits on marine paleontology and local fossils from Calvert Cliffs (see "Other Outdoor Activities," below), including the jaws of now extinct varieties of the Great White Shark, and an estuary aquarium showing examples of life in the Patuxent, with occasional opportunities to touch friendly turtles and horseshoe crabs. You'll also find various exhibits on local maritime history, from the British fleet's defeat of the American Flotilla during the Revolutionary War to modern recreational boating. Children will love the Discovery Room, filled with hands-on activities.

Outside you'll find two playful river otters who love to charm visitors, and the picturesque Drum Point Lighthouse, which you can tour if you're willing to brave the very steep stairs. Drum Point is one of the three remaining screwpile lighthouses (they look like hexagonal cottages mounted on metal poles) that served on the Chesapeake around the turn of the century. The other two are Thomas Point Lighthouse, in the bay near Annapolis, and Hooper Straight Lighthouse now housed at the Chesapeake Bay Maritime Museum in St. Michaels—see chapter 7. The museum also offers harbor cruises aboard the bugeye *Wm. B. Tennison* (see "Charter Fishing & Cruises," below).

CHARTER FISHING & CRUISES

One of Calvert County's biggest draws is its large fleet of charter fishing boats. Rockfish (striped bass or stripers if you're from north of the Chesapeake) are frequently the main quarry, but bluefish, Spanish mackerel, white perch, spot, croaker, floun-der, sea trout, and black drum are also sought, depending on the time of year. It's best to check with your prospective charter boat captain to find out what is in sea-son before you plan your trip.

Charter fishing in the area is organized in two ways: through loose affiliations of charter captains and through organized charter operations. It's easy to charter a boat through either of these systems. In the case of an organized charter operation such as **Bunky's Charter Boats** (see below), you call their office and they will supply a boat. If all of their boats are full, they will contact a local charter captain from out-side their fleet and have him run the charter for them.

It works a little differently with captains' associations. In this case you call a con-tact person for the association, usually one of the captains. If that captain has an opening, he will offer to take you out on his boat. If he doesn't have an opening, he will either arrange for another captain to take you out or give you the names and telephone numbers of captains in the association who might be available. It's that easy.

When you are ready to make your fishing trip, there are a few important things to remember. First, ask the captain what you will need to bring. Most charters in-clude fishing gear; some supply bait free of charge and some do not. You'll always need something to bring the fish home in, so don't forget the cooler. And remember that the mates on charter boats work for cash tips, which should usually be at least 15%.

SOLOMONS

Bunky's Charter Boats, Inc. 14448 Solomons Island Rd. S., Solomons. ☎ **410/326-3241.**

Bunky's is operated out of a well-stocked bait-and-tackle shop right across from the walking pier on Solomons Island. They have a fleet of 10 charter boats, including one 48-foot headboat, the *Mar-Chelle*. Charter rates for up to six passengers on all boats except the *Mar-Chelle* are $260 per half day (6 hours) and $360 per full day (8 hours). There's a per-person charge of $40 for extra people. Rates for six people on the *Mar-Chelle* are $300 per half day and $400 per full day; again, extra passengers are $40 more each. Nonfishing cruises on the *Mar-Chelle* are available for $125 per hour with a 2-hour minimum. Bunky's also rents 16-foot power skiffs for those who want to go it on there own, but remember you need a license to fish if you are not on a charter boat.

***Fin Finder* Charters and the Solomons Charter Captains Association.** P.O. Box 831, Solomons, MD 20688. ☎ **800/831-2702.**

Capt. Sonney Forest is your contact for the Solomons Charter Captains Association (SCCA). The association runs many of their 25 boats out of the Calvert Marina Charter Dock on Dowell Road (☎ **410/326-4251**), where Captain Forest is the dock master. Eight of the SCCA's boats can carry more than six people; some can carry as many as 30. Standard association rates for up to six people are $400 per 8-hour day and $40 extra per person for additional passengers.

The *Fin Finder*, a 46-foot Chesapeake-style boat, is Captain Forest's own charter boat. It carries up to 30 passengers. In addition to standard daily charters, Captain Forest also offers cruise tours and special package trips including an overnight fish-ing excursion to Crisfield, across the bay (see chapter 7).

CHESAPEAKE BEACH

Chesapeake Beach boasts the largest fleet on the bay, with over 35 boats. Besides that, it isn't much of a town. To get there from Annapolis, take Route 2 south to Route 260 west, which ends just north of the harbor at Route 261. From

Washington, D.C., take Route 4 west to Route 260 west and follow the directions above. Once you reach the Chesapeake Beach harbor, directions are simple. On the north side of the harbor is a water slide; everything else is on the south side. Rod-N-Reel and the Chesapeake Beach Railway Museum are on the south side of the harbor and on the bayside of Route 261. Seaside Charters is on the inland side of Route 261, just behind Abner's Crab House.

Rod-N-Reel Charter Fishing. P.O. Box 99, Chesapeake Beach, MD 20732. ☎ **800/ 233-2080** or 310/855-8450.

Rod-N-Reel is the largest single charter fishing operation in Maryland's share of the Chesapeake, with over 25 boats, including two headboats: the 65-foot *Tom Hooker* and the 55-foot *Bounty Hunter*. Charter rates for up to six people are $295 per 6-hour trip (these are scheduled 6am to noon and 1 to 7pm) and $415 per 8-hour trip (departing anytime between 6am and 9am, your choice). As usual it is $40 per person extra for over six people.

Seaside Charters. Harbor Rd., Chesapeake Beach. ☎ **301/855-4665.**

Seaside Charters is an association of charter captains with 15 boats and some of the best rates in the area. Straight-shooting Captain Russ Mogel will generally be your contact when you call. Rates are $275 per half day (6 hours) and $350 per full day (8 hours). Captain Mogel's own charter boat, the *Mary Lou II,* is a 38-foot custom-built sportfishing vessel. Captain Mogel likes to limit his passengers to six so they all have plenty of room. The *Mary Lou II* also offers evening outings and night fishing. (Captain Mogel's direct number is ☎ **301/855-0784**.)

OTHER OUTDOOR ACTIVITIES

HIKING & BIRD WATCHING   Calvert County's unique topography of rolling hills and tidal marsh estuary gives it some truly wonderful areas for communing with nature.

For those who prefer seeing flora and fauna to taking a stout walk, **Battle Creek Cypress Swamp Sanctuary's** half-mile nature loop (see "Attractions," above) is a great option.

If you're up for a brisk 2-mile hike, ✪ **Calvert Cliffs State Park** has long been one of Maryland's favorite outdoor destinations. A winding trail follows a trickling brook as it travels down from the hills to a lush, beautiful tidal marsh. However, it's at the end of the trail where the park holds its real surprises. There the tidal marsh opens across a small beach into the Chesapeake Bay and to either side stand the 30-foot-tall eroding hillsides known as Calvert Cliffs.

These multicolored cliffs, first noted by English explorer John Smith, expose several layers of sediment that were once at the bottom of a prehistoric ocean. As the winds and water of the bay erode them they yield ancient secrets—fossils. Because of recent landslides the state park has restricted access to the bottoms of the cliffs. However, they do allow **fossil hunting** on the beach and usually provide a number of wire sieves to make your search easier. Typical finds include fossilized shells and crustaceans and the occasional prehistoric shark's tooth, but dinosaur bones are not unheard of (for more on Calvert Cliff's paleontology, see the Calvert Maritime Museum listing above). So enjoy the hunt and the scenery.

Flag Ponds Nature Park, Route 2–4 (☎ **410/586-1477** or 410/535-5327), has several trails offering access to the forested heights of Calvert Cliffs, sandy beaches, and freshwater ponds with observation platforms for spotting waterfowl.

SPORT FISHING   Although charter fishing is this area's forte, there are also several choice locations for sport fishing, including **Bay Front Park,** Chesapeake Beach

(☎ **410/257-2230**); the fishing pier at **Flag Ponds Nature Park,** Route 2–4 (☎ **410/586-1477**); and **Solomons Fishing Pier,** located under the Governor Thomas Johnson Bridge (Route 4) in Solomons.

Bait and tackle are available at **Bunky's Charter Boats, Inc.,** 14448 Solomons Rd. South, Solomons (☎ **410/326-3241**); and **Rod-N-Reel,** Harbor Road and the Bay, Chesapeake Beach (☎ **301/855-8450**).

SWIMMING Both **Flag Ponds Nature Park** (Route 2–4) and Chesapeake Beach's **Bay Front Park** offer pleasant unguarded beaches for bay swimming. Remember that whenever swimming in the Chesapeake you should be wary of the dreaded sea nettles, small jellyfish-like stinging creatures, far too common in the bay.

WHERE TO STAY

Back Creek Inn Bed & Breakfast. Alex and Calvert sts., P.O. Box 520, Solomons, MD 20688. ☎ **410/326-2022.** Fax 410/326-2946. 7 rms, 2 suites, 1 cottage. A/C. Apr–Oct $95 double, $125 suite, $145 cottage; Nov–Mar $75–$85 double, $100 suite, $125 cottage. Rates include breakfast. AE, MC, V. Free parking.

Housed in a blue 1880 waterman's house, this inn offers travelers a relaxing stay in a serene and lovely setting. The home is decorated with antiques, handmade quilts, fresh flowers from the inn's well-kept garden, and original paintings by innkeeper Carol Pennock. From its cozy sitting room you can watch boats drift by in the waters of Back Creek just past the patio and garden. The Lavender Room is a small cottage located behind the house and has its own private screened porch with a pleasant view of Back Creek. The Tansy, Chamomile, and Peppermint rooms also enjoy water views. The inn has Garden Tea on Wednesday from 3 to 5pm. The full breakfast, which often includes fresh baked goods, is quite good. In warm months there is a Jacuzzi in the rear garden for guest use. There is no smoking at the inn. Children under 12 are not allowed.

Comfort Inn Beacon Marina. Lore Rd., P.O. Box 869, Solomons, MD 20688. ☎ **800/228-5150** or 410/326-6303. 60 rms. A/C TV TEL. $71–$140 double. AE, DC, DISC, MC, V. Free parking.

This well-maintained but slightly older blue-shingled two-story hotel is geared toward nautical enthusiasts as well as average travelers. The hotel complex includes a 146-slip marina, with 48 covered slips and a complete yacht-servicing yard. The rooms are very clean and comfortable, and although the windows are not huge, they do open to let in the pleasant breeze off Back Creek. Ten of the rooms have full-size private Jacuzzis. The interior of the hotel has recently been redone with contemporary carpeting and fixtures, and the hotel is in the process of updating bathrooms with more modern fixtures. Facilities include an outdoor pool and hot tub, a private picnic area with grills, and a waterfront restaurant.

Holiday Inn Select Solomons. 155 Holiday Dr., P.O. Box 1099, Solomons, MD 20688. ☎ **800/356-2009** or 410/326-6311. Fax 410/326-1069. 326 rms. AC TV TEL. $99–$164 double. AE, DC, DISC, MC, V. Free parking.

By far the biggest hotel in Solomons, this contemporary complex boasts a marina, a health club, an outdoor pool, tennis and volleyball courts, a large courtyard and patio, and a dockside bar. There are many rooms with good views, most of which are on the second floor or above and are on the southern sides of the ends of the hotel's guest wings. Other facilities include a business center, two ballrooms for conferences, and a waterfront restaurant.

Solomons Victorian Inn. 125 Charles St., P.O. Box 759, Solomons, MD 20688. ☎ **410/326-4811.** 5 rms, 3 suites. A/C. $90–$165 double. Rates include breakfast. MC, V. Free parking.

Known locally as the Davis House, this late Victorian structure was built by Solomons shipbuilder Clarence Davis, who would later build President Kennedy's yacht, the *Manitou*. All but one of the rooms enjoy a view of either Back Creek Harbor or the Patuxent River. The inn is decorated in antiques and reproductions and has four public spaces: a formal living room, a sitting room, a library, and a beautiful glassed-in porch where breakfast is served. Try to get the impressive Solomons Sunset suite, which features a king-size bed, a microwave and galley area, a whirlpool tub, and great views of the harbor on two sides. As of this printing, innkeepers Helen and Richard Bauer are putting the finishing touches on two new suites, both of which will have whirlpool tubs and excellent views of the harbor. Minimum 2-night stays apply on certain holiday and event weekends. No children under 13 years are permitted.

Tidewater Treasures. 7315 Bayside Rd. (off Rte. 261, just south of Chesapeake Beach Harbor), Chesapeake Beach, MD 20732. ☎ **410/257-0785.** 4 rms with shared baths. A/C. $84–$109 double. Rates include full or continental breakfast. No credit cards. Free parking.

This small, homey, contemporary bed-and-breakfast is the only accommodation available in Chesapeake Beach, and as such it is a great launching point for charter fishing and other explorations in Calvert County. Innkeepers Bob and Sharon Oldham are animal lovers and it shows. In addition to the friendly animals in residence—a dog, two cats, and a talkative umbrella cockatoo named Sydney—the inn looks over a beautiful tidal marsh full of wildlife. On the bayside of the inn is a large porch where breakfast is sometimes served in summer. A public but secluded beach is nearby. As the inn is quite small, the four rooms share two bathrooms; however, for a slightly increased rate bathrooms can be made private for the two larger rooms (both of which have bay views). Both bayside rooms have queen-size beds; the other rooms have double beds, making them suitable for children.

WHERE TO DINE

C.D. Cafe, Inc. Avondale Center, 14350 Solomons Island Rd., Solomons. ☎ **410/326-3877.** Reservations not accepted. Main courses $6.95–$17.95; lunch $5.95–$10.95. MC, V. Mon–Sat 9am–2:30pm, Tues–Sat 5:30–9pm, Sun 9am–3pm and 5:30–8:30pm. CONTINENTAL.

Almost every local we talked with recommended the C.D. Cafe for lunch. After eating there, it is easy to see why. This tiny and relaxed restaurant, located in the green-awninged Avondale shopping center just off Solomons Island, offers a nice range of continental dishes from smoked salmon cakes to a really spicy Cajun shepherd's pie. They open every morning at 9am for newspaper reading, coffee, and pastries. Lunch starts Monday through Saturday at 11:30am and Sunday at 11am.

Lighthouse Inn. Patuxent Ave., Solomons. ☎ **410/326-2444.** Reservations strongly recommended. Main courses $11.95–$26.95. AE, DISC, MC, V. Mon–Fri 5–9pm, Sat 5–9pm, Sun 1–7pm. SEAFOOD.

Fine dining overlooking a picturesque harbor is what you get at this popular restaurant near the heart of Solomons Island. The dining room is divided into a floor area and a loft, both offering a sweeping view of Back Creek Harbor out floor-to-ceiling windows. The bar is a replica of a Chesapeake Bay–style log canoe. Dinner specials include the likes of grilled swordfish in a spicy Cajun sauce, but our favorite remains the excellent lightly broiled crab cakes.

Smokey Joe's. Rte. 261 and Mears Ave., Chesapeake Beach. ☎ **410/257-2427.** Reservations not accepted. Main courses $9.95–$16.95. AE, MC, V. Sun–Thurs 11am–10pm, Fri–Sat 11am–midnight. AMERICAN.

Smokey Joe's is a favorite of Chesapeake Beach charter captains because of its excellent barbecue and location on the charter dock next to Rod-N-Reel. This very casual bar/restaurant has several window-side tables where you can watch the charter boats sway in their moorings. In short it's a great place to stop for a beer and a sandwich after a day on the bay. My favorite is the barbecued chicken sandwich with ham and Swiss cheese—*mmm good.*

Stoney's Seafood House. Oyster House Rd., Broomes Island. ☎ **410/586-1888.** Reservations accepted for large parties only. Main courses $3.95–$15.95. AE, DISC, MC, V. Feb 14–Oct 31 Sun–Thurs 11am–9pm, Fri–Sat 11:30am–10pm. SEAFOOD.

Take Road 264 west off Route 2–4 to get to this great little seafood house in the small community of Broomes Island. It has a large porch for outdoor dining and sits right on the water, within view of the towering Governor Thomas Johnson Bridge crossing the Patuxent in the distance. But people don't come here for the view—they come for the crab cakes. Stoney's, like every other seafood place in Maryland, purports to have the "best crab cakes in the world"; the difference is that Stoney's may be right. They make a fine filet mignon sandwich as well. If you happen to be visiting in the winter, Stoney's has another location in Prince Frederick, open year-round.

11 St. Mary's County

It's a long way to St. Mary's County from any of the surrounding metropolitan areas, approximately 80 miles from Annapolis, but for history buffs and anglers it's well worth the trip. With the Potomac River on one side and the Chesapeake Bay and the Patuxent River on the other, this lush peninsula is today a great place for fishermen, and it suited the first settlers of Maryland in 1634 as well. Today's St. Mary's City is the site of a "living museum," re-creating life in Maryland's first capital.

But aside from the water and the reconstructed colonial town, St. Mary's County doesn't have much to offer tourists, so if you decide to visit, stay in Solomons, which is about 30 minutes from St. Mary's City, and drive over for the day. (See "Solomons & Calvert County," above.)

ESSENTIALS

GETTING THERE   Maryland Routes 5 and 235 run the length of St. Mary's County, providing access to all the major sites of interest. You can get to Route 5 from I-495 (the Washington beltway). From Annapolis, take Route 2 south to Solomons, then Route 4 across the Governor Thomas Johnson Bridge; it will intersect with Route 235 a few miles past the bridge.

VISITOR INFORMATION   To obtain information before you set out, contact **St. Mary's County Division of Tourism,** P.O. Box 653, Leonardtown, MD 20650 (☎ **800/327-9023** or 301/475-4404). You can also stop by the **St. Mary's County Chamber of Commerce Visitor Information Center** at 6260 Waldorf–Leonardtown Rd. (Route 5), Mechanicsville, MD (☎ **301/884-5555**).

HISTORIC ST. MARY'S CITY: MARYLAND'S FIRST CAPITAL

After you have seen the current capital of Maryland, you really should have a look at the state's first capital, ✪ **Historic St. Mary's City,** off Route 5 (☎ **800/ SMC-1634** or 301/862-0990), a National Historic Landmark and one of the country's best-preserved archaeological sites. When you arrive in St. Mary's City (known originally as *St. Marie's Citty*), don't expect a panorama of colonial buildings like Annapolis. Don't even expect to find a city in the form we know it.

This secluded corner of Maryland is almost exactly as it was in 1634, the year *The Ark* and *The Dove* arrived from England with the first 140 colonists under a royal charter from Lord Baltimore. Today's Historic St. Mary's City is a "living history" outdoor museum spread out over 850 acres of tidewater landscape. Thanks to years of archaeological excavations, the town has been authentically reassembled to show a typical tobacco farm plantation, the first State House, a primitive tavern, and other sites. There's also a waterfront preserve and woodland nature trails.

A tour of St. Mary's City starts at the visitor center. You'll see a 5-minute introductory audiovisual presentation and exhibits on life here more than 350 years ago. Plan to spend at least 2 hours outside to explore the Town Center, the Woodland Indian Loghouse, and other buildings, and to see the *Maryland Dove,* a replica of Lord Baltimore's square-rigged ship. In addition to the sites and exhibits, the site hosts a regular program of demonstrations, such as cargo handling on the *Dove,* and living history performances (don't miss "The Many Trials of John Halfhead," a performance depicting a day in the local courtroom).

The facilities include a cafe, Farthing's Kitchen (where you can get sandwiches, soups, and snacks), and a gift shop. Admission is $6.50 for adults, $6 for seniors and students, and $3.50 for ages 6 to 12. It's open from mid-March to the end of November, Wednesday through Sunday from 10am to 5pm.

OTHER HISTORIC SITES

After visiting St. Mary's City, jump forward a century or so and tour the ✪ **Sotterley Plantation** (☎ **800/681-0850** or 301/373-2280), a 1710 tidewater plantation on the Patuxent River on Route 245, off Route 235 in Hollywood, Maryland. The manor house, constructed in 1717 and expanded about 10 years later, is a rare surviving example of post-in-ground construction, once common in this region. Visitors can tour the first floor of the house and admire the fine woodwork of Richard Boulton, an indentured servant, including shell alcoves in the dining room and the Chinese Chippendale staircase. Also open to visitors are the formal gardens and several surviving outbuildings—the Customs Warehouse, a brick necessary, the smokehouse, the corn crib, and one of the few remaining slave quarters open to the public. Admission is around $7. At press time hours were Tuesday through Sunday from 10am to 4pm from May to October. But recently the plantation has come under financial difficulty, so hours and admission charges may vary. It's best to call ahead.

For true Civil War buffs, one of the lesser-known and least-visited war sites, **Ft. Lincoln,** is inside Point Lookout State Park (see "Outdoor Activities at Point Lookout State Park," below). In 1862, the U.S. government leased the parkland and built a hospital and later a prison camp for Confederate soldiers. By the end of the war 52,000 Confederate soldiers had passed through this camp, where more than 3,500 of them died, ironically within sight of Virginia across the Potomac. Today, the fort is open to the public during park hours, if you can find it. Go to the beach picnic area and walk north along the water until you find the trail. There are no rangers or reenactors, just a few signs and the lonely remains of the fort.

OUTDOOR ACTIVITIES AT POINT LOOKOUT STATE PARK

Located at the tip of St. Mary's County, at the confluence of the Potomac River and the Chesapeake Bay, **Point Lookout State Park** (☎ **301/872-5688**) is the county's summer playground and a haven for anglers across the state. The park encompasses approximately 1,046 acres and offers everything from a beach picnic area and camping to a fishing pier, boat launch facilities, and cruises to Smith Island. Route 5 will take you into the park, and the visitor center inside the camping area will supply you with information on ranger programs, boat rentals, camping, and other activities.

Visitors interested in **fishing** can cast their lines just about anywhere during the day except the beach swimming area. Favorite areas are the pier on the bayside and at the point, on either the bay or river side. Campers can also fish at designated piers within the camping facility. A fishing license is required unless you're fishing from the Potomac shoreline. Rowboat, canoe, and motorboat rentals are available at the camp store off Route 5 near the boat launch. You can also catch a ride to Smith Island on the *Capt. Tyler* (☎ **410/425-2771**) from here. Boats depart at 10am Wednesday through Sunday and return to Point Lookout at 4pm. For more information on Smith Island, see "Crisfield & Smith Island," in chapter 7.

The park offers 143 wooded **campsites** (26 of these with full hookups). Prices range from $15 to $21 per site, depending on hookup services, and reservation service is available for an extra charge (☎ **301/872-5688**). The camp office, at the entrance to the camping area, is open from 8am to 11pm. Day-use facilities with a guarded beach for **swimming** and **picnicking** are on the Potomac side of the park, past the fishing pier. Entrance fee at the park is free except on weekends and holidays May through September, when it costs $3 per person.

7

The Eastern Shore

When you hear the words *Chesapeake Bay,* a lot of what comes to mind is Maryland's Eastern Shore, a region of beautiful waterways and wetlands, flocks of wildfowl, log canoes under sail, cottage-style screwpile lighthouses, quaint towns, hardworking watermen, and, of course, seafood. If all this is what you are coming for, then the Eastern Shore really delivers.

There's a surprisingly wide variety of settings in which to soak up the salty charm that is the Chesapeake. The region's collection of bay-side communities includes everything from the small historic towns of Chestertown and Chesapeake City in the rolling highlands of the north bay to Talbot County's Easton–Oxford–St. Michaels trio, the epicenter of the shore's ambience, to the fishing and crabbing harbors of the southern bay. Since St. Michaels has been almost completely transformed from small village to major tourist attraction, interest in the less-visited working seafood harbors of Cambridge, Crisfield, and Smith Island to the south has increased. Crisfield has just begun offering guided walking tours of the city and the harbor, giving visitors a chance to see the workings of the seafood industry and of modern watermen. So if you're planning a trip to the Eastern Shore, you should select your destination carefully. Because even though all these towns share one great common denominator—the Chesapeake Bay—in many ways places like Crisfield, St. Michaels, and Chestertown are worlds apart.

1 Talbot County: Easton, St. Michaels & Oxford

40 miles SE of Annapolis, 60 miles SE of Baltimore, 110 miles SW of Wilmington

Talbot County is the best destination for first-time visitors to the Eastern Shore. It's got all the bayside small-town charm of other places along the bay and all the creature comforts of a tourist destination—a variety of hotels, inns, and bed-and-breakfasts, and lots of restaurants to choose from (of course, nearly all serve the same fare—crab, crab, and more crab). The three main destinations in Talbot County—Easton, St. Michaels, and Oxford—are close together, but each has its own distinct flavor. So it's best to stay in

Maryland's Eastern Shore

MARYLAND
Eastern Shore Area

ANNAPOLIS

❶ Easton
❷ St. Michaels
❸ Oxford
❹ Chestertown
❺ Chesapeake City
❻ Cambridge
❼ Crisfield

A hundred years ain't a very long time on the Eastern Shore!
                            —local citizens, as quoted in *Maryland in Focus*

the town that appeals to you most in terms of atmosphere and amenities, and travel out to other attractions, restaurants, or towns of interest.

Easton, the largest of the Talbot County trio, is today a quiet little working community. The many coves of the Miles and the Tred Avon rivers jut in and surround the city, and yet, when walking through Easton's historic district the feeling of being near water is noticeably absent. Despite its size, Easton has relatively few options for accommodations. However, its motor inns and hotels offer clean, comfortable, and affordable alternatives to the pricier inns of St. Michaels and Oxford.

We like to picture Easton as the inner core or heart of the area, with two arms stretching out toward the Chesapeake. The upper (and longer) arm takes you to the village of St. Michaels on the Miles River and to Tilghman Island, dangling right on the Chesapeake. The lower arm goes straight to Oxford, a sheltered town nestled along the shores of the Tred Avon River.

One of the oldest settlements along the Chesapeake, St. Michaels flourished in colonial times as a shipbuilding center, the birthplace of the illustrious *Baltimore* clipper. Today it is an aesthetic delight. There are no billboards or fast-food chains, but you will find bed-and-breakfasts on all the quiet tree-lined streets, boutiques and specialty shops lining the main street through town, and a sparkling clean harbor that attracts at least 20,000 boats a year. If you travel another 15 miles down Route 33, you'll come to Tilghman Island, an enclave with great seafaring atmosphere and an important base for fishermen of oysters, crabs, clams, and fin fish.

Oxford, also one of the oldest towns in Maryland, is the sleepiest of the three Talbot County destinations, with only two hotels and three restaurants. The most scenic way to get here is via the Oxford–Bellevue Ferry, the oldest privately operated ferry in the country, across the Tred Avon River. The appeal of Oxford is its quiet, secluded streets; the town's vehement opposition to all things commercial and touristy; and the crab cakes at the Robert Morris Inn.

ESSENTIALS

GETTING THERE   The best way to get to the Easton area is by car, via Route 50 from all directions.

Easton Municipal Airport (☎ 410/822-8560), about 3 miles north of the city on Route 50, services local charter planes. **US Airways** (☎ 800/428-4322) operates scheduled commuter flights into **Salisbury/Wicomico County Airport** (☎ 410/548-4827), in Salisbury, 60 miles southwest of Easton.

Greyhound (☎ 800/231-2222) offers regular bus service into its depot at the junction of Routes 50 and 309.

VISITOR INFORMATION   For maps, brochures, and complete lodging and restaurant information about Easton and environs, contact the **Talbot County Conference and Visitors Bureau,** Tred Avon Square, Marlborough Ave., P.O. Box 1366, Easton, MD 21601 (☎ 410/822-4606), just north of the historic district at the junction of Route 322.

GETTING AROUND   The only way to get around Talbot County is by car. Route 33 from Easton will take you to St. Michaels and Tilghman Island, and Route 333 goes to Oxford. The shortest and most scenic route from Oxford to St. Michaels is

And just in case.

We're here with American Express® Travelers Cheques
and Cheques *for Two*.® They're the safest way to carry
money on your vacation and the surest way to get a
refund, practically anywhere, anytime.

Another way we help you...

do more

AMERICAN
EXPRESS

**Travelers
Cheques**

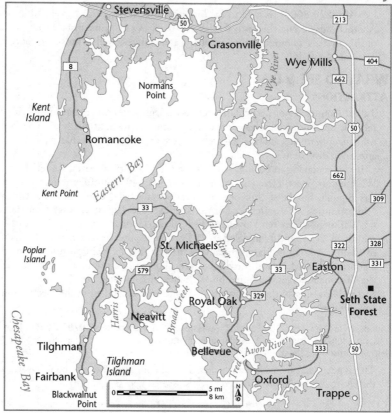

via the **Oxford–Bellevue Ferry** (☎ **410/745-9023**) across the Tred Avon River. Established in 1683, this is the country's oldest privately operated ferry. The trip is only a mile long and takes about 7 minutes. You can catch the ferry either from Bellevue, off Routes 33 and 329, near St. Michaels, or at Oxford (off Route 333). The ferry operates daily from March through mid-December, with continuous service every 20 minutes. From June 1 to Labor Day, the ferry runs Monday through Friday from 7am to 9pm and weekends from 9am to 9pm; the rest of the operating year it runs Monday through Friday from 7am to sunset and weekends from 9am to sunset. Rates for a car and two persons are $4.50 one-way and $7 round-trip; extra car passenger, 50¢; walk-on passengers, $1.

If you don't bring your own car to the Easton area, you can rent one from **Avis,** Easton Municipal Airport (☎ **410/822-5040**); or **Hertz,** Goldsborough Road and Route 50 (☎ **410/822-1676**). For local cab service, try **Scotty's Taxi** (☎ **410/ 822-1475**).

SPECIAL EVENTS The ✪ **Waterfowl Festival,** held the second week in November in Easton, is one of two big events in Talbot County. This 3-day festival brings together waterfowl enthusiasts of all kinds: carvers, painters, sculptors, collectors, and photographers. It features not only displays of waterfowl art but duck-calling contests, auctions, and dog trials. For information call ☎ **410/832-4567.** The other major event in the county, the ✪ **Mid-Atlantic Maritime Festival**

(☎ 401/820-8606), is held in St. Michaels annually the third weekend in May. Another 3-day event, this festival celebrates the area's maritime history with displays of ship models, photographs, nautical arts and crafts, as well as music, seafood, and a parade of tall ships.

WHAT TO SEE & DO
ATTRACTIONS

Talbot County is not particularly rich in museums and other attractions—it's the relaxed, small-town atmosphere and the presence of water at nearly every turn that draw people to this enclave. However, there are a few places that make pleasant afternoon diversions.

If you're staying in Easton, stroll around the **historic district,** centered around Washington Street. Here you will find more than 40 beautifully restored and preserved public buildings, churches, and private homes, all dating back to the 18th and 19th centuries. The centerpiece of the district is the **Talbot County Courthouse,** on Washington between Dover and Federal streets. First built from 1710 to 1712, rebuilt in 1791, and remodeled in 1958, this impressive structure is the symbol of Easton. Among its claims to fame is the fact that its main portion was used as a subcapital of Maryland for the Eastern Shore. In addition, a document called the "Talbot Reserves," adopted on the courthouse grounds in May 1774, was the first public airing of the sentiments that were later embodied in the Declaration of Independence.

Academy of the Arts. 106 South St. (at Harrison St.), Easton. ☎ **410/822-0455.** Free admission. Mon–Sat 10am–4pm. Closed Aug. From Rte. 50, turn on Dover St. going west and then left on Harrison St.; the academy will be 1 block up on the corner.

This is a regional arts center, with changing exhibitions of interest about the area and the entire Eastern Shore. Concerts are also staged here periodically.

○ **Chesapeake Bay Maritime Museum.** Mill St., Navy Point, St. Michaels. ☎ **410/745-2916.** Admission $7.50 adults, $6.50 seniors, $3 ages 6–17, free under age 6. Mid-June to Sept daily 9am–7pm, Oct–Dec daily 9am–5pm, Jan–Feb daily 10am–4pm, Mar to mid-June daily 9am–5pm. Closed Jan 1, Thanksgiving, and Dec 25. Take Rte. 33 into St. Michaels; turn right at Mill St. and follow signs to the museum.

Dedicated to the preservation of maritime history and specifically to the Chesapeake Bay area, this waterside museum is the setting for the largest collection of Chesapeake Bay watercraft in existence (76 boats), located on 18 acres of land occupying 23 buildings, eight of which are open to the public. The comprehensive collection is comprised of many floating exhibits, including a skipjack and a restored log-bottom bugeye, as well as crabbing skiffs, workboats, and log canoes. Some of the other highlights include an authentic 1879 screwpile lighthouse, a working boatyard, an extensive waterfowl decoy collection, and a 4,000-volume library—a resource that James Michener relied upon when writing his best-seller *Chesapeake.* The Steamboat Building, opened in 1993, focuses on steam and mechanical propulsion on Chesapeake Bay.

○ **Historical Society of Talbot County.** 25 S. Washington St., Easton. ☎ **410/822-0773.** Museum $3 adults, $2 ages 6–12; guided tour of houses $3 adults, $2 ages 6–17; combined museum and house tour $5 adults. Year-round Tues–Sat 10am–4pm, April–Dec Sun noon–3pm. From Rte. 50 south, turn right onto Goldsborough St., then left onto Washington St.; the entrance is 2 blocks down on the right.

This society maintains eight historic buildings, five of which are open to the public. A focal point of the historic district, the historic sites include an 1850s commercial building, now the headquarters of the society and site of a modern museum; the 1795 Joseph Neall House and the 1810 Joseph Neall House, both restored homes of Quaker cabinetmaker brothers; the partially restored 1670 Wenlocke Christison House, known locally as "The Ending of Controversie" House; and the 1810 Tharpe House, which now serves as a museum shop and library. The buildings surround a lovely Federal-style garden, also open to visitors.

Orrell's Biscuits. 14124 Old Wye Mill Rd. (Rte. 662), Wye Mills, MD 21679. ☎ **410/ 820-8090.** Free admission. Open Tues–Thurs; phone for hrs. From Easton, take Rte. 662 north approximately 12 miles; the bakery is next to the Old Wye Church.

The tiny community of Wye Mills is the home of a family enterprise producing a unique Eastern Shore biscuit that has been a tradition for more than 300 years. With their kitchen as a bakery, the Orrell family produces hundreds of biscuits every day. Following an original recipe without baking powder or soda, the Orrells and their staff shape each specimen by hand into the size of a walnut, producing a crusty biscuit with a soft center. Visitors are welcome to watch the baking process, sample the results, and purchase at the source. The biscuits are also on sale throughout Maryland and can be ordered by mail.

Third Haven Friends Meeting House. 405 S. Washington St., Easton. ☎ **410/822-0293.** Free admission, but donations welcome. Daily 9am–5pm.

Located in a tree-shaded residential area on the banks of the Tred Avon Creek, three quarters of a mile south of downtown, this structure is believed to be the oldest frame building dedicated to religious meetings in the United States and the oldest known building in Maryland. Made of pine and oak, and originally paid for in tobacco, it has been used continuously since the late 17th century. William Penn is said to have worshipped here. The building has recently been restored under the auspices of the Maryland Historical Trust.

Wye Mill. Rte. 662, off Rte. 50, Wye Mills. ☎ **410/827-6909.** Free admission, but suggested donation is $2. Mid-Apr to mid-Nov Mon–Fri 10am–1pm, Sat–Sun 11am–4pm. Follow Rte. 662, 12 miles north of Easton.

The nearby town of Wye Mills is the site of this mill dating from the 17th century. Though the town is named for two mills, only one of these structures survives today. Owned and maintained by a nonprofit group known as Preservation Maryland, the mill is the earliest industrial-commercial building in continuous use in the state. In Revolutionary days, flour from this mill was produced for George Washington's troops at Valley Forge. Visitors today can see the mill in operation and sample some of the flour—whole wheat or cornmeal.

While in Wye Mills, stop to see the huge tree that dominates the town—the **Wye Oak,** the largest white oak in the United States and Maryland's official state tree. Measuring 4¹/₂ feet above its base, the Wye Oak is 37 feet in circumference and 95 feet high, with a crown spanning 165 feet, shading an area of almost half an acre. The tree is believed to be more than 450 years old.

ORGANIZED TOURS

Historical walking tours of Easton's downtown area are conducted year-round by members of the Historical Society of Talbot County, 25 Washington St., Easton (☎ 410/822-0773). Tours last about an hour and begin daily at 11:30am and 1:30pm. Cost is $2 for adults and 50¢ for ages 6 to 17.

For those who would like to see the highlights of the area by boat, **Patriot Cruises,** P.O. Box 1206, St. Michaels (☎ 410/745-3100), offers 1-hour narrated cruises on board the *Patriot*, a 65-foot, two-deck vessel with indoor and outdoor seating. The

Excursions in the Countryside

The Eastern Shore isn't all crabs and watermen; a large part of the region's appeal is its unspoiled and attractive scenery. That's why cyclists love it here—that and the reasonably flat terrain. And that's why whether you're staying in Easton, Oxford, or St. Michaels, there is no excuse for not hopping in a car or on a bike and soaking up some of the charm of the countryside—its open farmland, tiny towns, wildfowl, tidal marshes, and glistening waterways. Here are a few of the highlights.

- The **Easton–Oxford–St. Michaels circuit** is a 30-mile loop that connects the area's three main travel destinations. Whether you're shopping or just trying to tour the area thoroughly, you are likely to be traveling a stretch of this scenic route. It is made up of three legs. Route 33 between St. Michaels and Easton is the most functional and least interesting, although it does offer an occasional glimpse of the Miles River. Route 333 between Easton and Oxford is very pleasant, but don't drive too slowly or you'll upset the locals. In late fall the cornfields along this road frequently sport dozens of Canada geese who feed themselves on what the farmers missed. The third leg is, of course, the most interesting because it involves leaving the quiet town of Oxford on the Oxford–Bellevue Ferry (see "Getting Around," above) and crossing the lovely Tred Avon River. After you and your vehicle safely land in Bellevue, you complete the circuit by taking a right on Ferry Neck Road and following it until it meets up with Bellevue Road. Then follow Bellevue Road until it intersects with Royal Oak Road in the village of Royal Oak and take a left. Royal Oak Road will return you to Route 33 and back to St. Michaels.
- No trip to the area would be complete without making the short jaunt west on Route 33 from St. Michaels to its terminus on **Tilghman Island,** where you can

cruise plies the waters of the Miles River and the shoreline off St. Michaels, passing historic homes, waterfowl, and watermen harvesting blue crabs, clams, and oysters. Operating from April through October, the trip costs $9 for adults and $4 for children under 12. The boat sails from the dock next to the Chesapeake Bay Maritime Museum at 11am, 12:30pm, 2:30pm, and 4pm.

OUTDOOR ACTIVITIES

BICYCLING　**St. Michaels Town Dock Marina,** 305 Mulberry St., St. Michaels (☎ 410/745-2400), rents bikes for $3 an hour, $5 for 2 hours, or $14 for a full day. Open April through November. You can also get three-speeds and tandems bikes at **Oxford Mews,** 105 S. Morris St., Oxford (☎ 410/820-8222), every day except Wednesday, from $3.50 an hour with a $7 minimum; $14 a day.

FISHING　Fishing excursions along the Chesapeake are the specialty of **Harrison's Sport Fishing Center,** 21551 Chesapeake House Dr., Tilghman Island (☎ 410/886-2121 or 410/886-2109), a family enterprise more than 100 years old. Complete fishing packages are available from $175 per person per day, including all fishing, tackle, boat transport, a room at the nautically themed Harrison's Chesapeake House Country Inn, and meals (a boxed lunch, plus a huge fisherman's breakfast and dinner at the Harrison's Chesapeake House restaurant). Depending on the time of year, the catch often includes rockfish (striped bass or stripers), sea trout, blues, croakers, spot, or perch. **Albright's Sportsman's Travel Service** (☎ 800/474-5502) can also help you plan your fishing trip.

see the Chesapeake Bay in all its glory. On your way you'll pass numerous farms, occasional vacation homes and secluded estates, and from time to time flashes of the eastern bay behind the tall pines of the area. Near the end you'll cross the tiny Knapp Narrows and enter the little fishing town of Tilghman for which Tilghman Island is named. Go straight through Tilghman, after which Route 33 becomes Black Walnut Road and the open bay appears on your right. A sunset here is well worth the trip. Unfortunately when you get ready to leave you'll have to make a U-turn just outside the gates of the private property on Black Walnut Point.

- The tiny town of **Wye Mills** is home to three historical features that have stood well against the tests of time: Old Wye Church, the Wye Mill, and the Wye Oak. Reach them by meandering up Route 662 north from Easton. Old Wye Church, an Anglican church, has stood in a grove of oak trees since 1721. Possibly as old, the Wye Mill ground flour for Washington's troops at Valley Forge in 1778. Its stones, driven by a waterwheel, still grind today. Nearby, the Wye Oak, Maryland's state tree, has stood its ground for over 450 years, since before Europeans even saw the Chesapeake. Old Wye Church is still a working church and is not open to the general public except for services. Wye Mill is open weekends April 1 to October 1 from 11am to 4pm. Wye Oak is visible from Route 662, we hope, always.

- For those who have the wandering bug, just because you are staying in Talbot County doesn't mean you're trapped here. Just bop down Route 50 south across the Choptank River and past the port of Cambridge to the **Spocott Windmill** or **Blackwater National Wildlife Refuge** (see "Blackwater National Wildlife Refuge," below) because Dorchester County is beautiful, too.

GOLF There's plenty of room to swing at the **Hog Neck Golf Course,** 10142 Old Cordova Rd., Easton (☎ **410/822-6079**), rated among the top 25 public courses in the United States by *Golf Digest.* Situated north of town off Route 50, between Route 309 and Rabbit Hill Road, it offers a par-72, 18-hole championship course and a par-32, 9-hole executive course. Rates for nonresidents are typically $30 to $49 for 18 holes, including cart rental. Facilities also include a driving range, putting green, and pro shop. Open February to December, weekdays from 7am to sunset, and weekends from 8am to sunset.

HUNTING Maryland's Eastern Shore is considered by many to be the finest duck- and goose-hunting region on the Atlantic flyway. Every year, more than 500,000 migratory game birds winter on the fields, marshes, rivers, tidal flats, and waters of Maryland. More than 20 local organizations conduct regular guided waterfowl hunts for Canada geese (late November through late January), ducks (late November through mid-January), and sea ducks (early October through mid-January). Some quail and pheasant hunting is also available. **Albright's Sportsman's Travel Service,** 36 Dover St., Easton, MD 21601 (☎ **800/474-5502** or 410/820-8811), can help plan any sort of hunting or fishing trip you have in mind.

WATER SPORTS Much of the focus of outdoor life in the Easton–St. Michaels–Oxford area is in and around the water. Whether you have your own boat or not, you'll always find lots of activity at **St. Michaels Town Dock Marina,** 305 Mulberry St., St. Michaels (☎ **410/745-2400**). You can rent runabouts with outboard engines for $99 for 3 hours or $169 for 8 hours. Some larger boat rentals are also available. If you have your own craft, you can also dock it here. Overnight dockage charges are $1.50 per foot on weekdays and $2 per foot on weekends. Some smaller slips are also available, as is hourly dockage, with a $5 per hour minimum.

St. Michaels Harbour Inn and Marina Aqua Center, 101 N. Harbor Rd., St. Michaels (☎ 410/745-9001), also offers water-sports rentals. You can rent canoes by the hour for $10 or by the day for $35 and aquabikes for $12 per hour.

SHOPPING

The Easton–St. Michaels–Oxford area is full of craft, antique, and specialty shops. Talbot St. in St. Michaels, lined with shops for about 6 blocks, is in general the best place for shopping. Most shops in the area are open weekdays from 10am to 6pm; many are open weekends, but expect reduced hours in winter.

Easton

Albright's Gun Shop. 36 Dover St., Easton. ☎ **800/474-5502** or 410/820-8811.

Located across from the Tidewater Inn, this shop stocks guns and accessories, bow-hunting supplies, sport clothing and watches, canvas goods, and fishing tackle. It is also the home of Albright's Sportsman's Travel Service (see "Hunting," above). Custom repair and gunsmithing are done on the premises. Open weekdays from 9am to 5:30pm, Saturday from 9am to 3:30pm, Sunday from 11am to 3pm, with extended hours in the waterfowl season.

✪ **Cherry's.** 26 W. Dover St., Easton. ☎ **410/822-4750.**

Since 1926, this store has been a favored spot for ladies' and men's quality sportswear, outdoor wear, and casual shoes.

Country Treasures. 200 Main St., Preston. ☎ **410/673-2603.**

Located in Preston, west of Easton on Route 331, this shop is a favorite for antique-seekers, stocking a great variety of home furnishings, from quilts to rolltop desks.

Crackerjacks. 7 S. Washington St., Easton. ☎ **410/822-7716.**

This children's store stocks all sorts of books, toys, games, dolls, stuffed animals, pinwheels, crafts, and more.

Heavenly Miniatures. 24 N. Harrison St., Easton. ☎ **410/822-1519.**

Small is beautiful in this tiny shop, which offers miniature dolls, dollhouses, doll furniture, animals, and more. Open May through October, Tuesday through Sunday from 10am to 5pm; and November through April, Tuesday through Saturday from 10am to 5pm.

Rowen's Stationery and Bookstore. 14 N. Harrison St. and 8–19 Washington St., Easton. ☎ **410/822-2095.**

This is both a bookstore and a stationery store, with two entrances. It stocks a variety of books about the Eastern Shore, Chesapeake Bay, state of Maryland, sailing and nautical topics, wetlands, waterfowl, bird watching, and decoys. It also sells stationery, artist's supplies, kites, prints, housewares, kitchen gadgets, gifts, and souvenirs with crab-design motifs.

St. Michaels

Harbour Dasher. 100 S. Talbot St., St. Michaels. ☎ **410/745-3354.**

This specialty shop for men features traditional and contemporary sportswear, accessories, and gifts.

Hodgepodge. 308 S. Talbot St., St. Michaels. ☎ **410/745-3062.**

Antiques, as well as a great variety of fabrics, accessories, baskets, decoys, afghans, and more, fill this shop.

✪ **The Mind's Eye.** 100 S. Talbot St. ☎ **410/745-2023.**

Don't miss this unique gift gallery, filled with folk art and crafts: wood carvings, pottery and glassware, jewelry, cards, and wall hangings.

St. Michaels Candy Company. 216 S. Talbot St., St. Michaels. ☎ **410/745-6060.**

For those with a sweet tooth, here is a shop stocked with handmade chocolates, truffles, novelty candies, gourmet ice cream, yogurt, and unique gift items such as chocolate crabs and oysters, cookbooks, beer-making kits, and kitchen accessories.

Oxford

✪ **Bellevue Store.** 5592 Poplar Lane, Royal Oak. ☎ **410/745-5282.**

It's worth taking the Oxford–Bellevue Ferry just to get to this antique/art/gift shop. The large front room is full of primitive antiques, but a smaller room in the back houses books of regional interest, handmade paper, sculptures, and wall hangings.

Crockett Bros. Boatyard, Inc. 202 Bank St., Oxford. ☎ **410/226-5113.**

A wide selection of seafaring clothes and collectibles makes this one of the best-stocked chandleries on the Eastern Shore. The wares range from nautical necessities and yachting apparel to gifts and games.

Silent Poetry. 201 Tilghman St., Oxford. ☎ **410/226-5120.**

Inspired by a 4th-century Greek poet who declared that art is "silent poetry," this shop stocks an assortment of original paintings by regional artists, limited-edition etchings and prints, and decoys and carvings by local craftspersons. In addition, there are fragrances, candles, linens, china, scrimshaw, potpourri, books, seasonal decorations and one-of-a-kind gift wrap, plus herbs and seasonings.

WHERE TO STAY

The Easton–St. Michaels–Oxford area offers a range of modern and old-world accommodations. It is also possible to explore Talbot County from a base on Kent Island, north of Easton at the end of the Bay Bridge. Most accommodations fall into the moderate category, although suites and luxury rooms can be very expensive. Rates on weekends are often subject to surcharges; summer prices are usually the highest. Top rates can also apply at many places during waterfowl hunting season (October through January).

EASTON

Comfort Inn. 8523 Ocean Gateway (Rte. 50), Easton, MD 21601. ☎ **800/228-5150** or 410/ 820-8333. Fax 410/820-8436. 84 rms. A/C TV TEL. $67–$90 double. Rates include continental breakfast. AE, CB, DC, MC, V. Free parking.

This two-story hacienda-style property is one of the newest lodgings in this area. Set back from busy Route 50 and surrounded by trees, it has a bright and airy lobby with lots of light woods and plants. The guest rooms, many of which surround a central courtyard, are furnished with pastel tones and waterfowl art. Facilities include an outdoor swimming pool and a small restaurant.

Days Inn. 7018 Ocean Gateway (Rte. 50), Easton, MD 21601. ☎ **800/325-2525** or 410/ 822-4600. Fax 410/820-9723. 80 rms. A/C TV TEL. $49–$79 double. Rates include continental breakfast. AE, CB, DC, DISC, MC, V. Free parking.

Set back from the main road in a shady setting between Easton and Oxford, this motel is a favorite with families. The guest rooms offer a well-maintained contemporary decor with coffeemakers, standard furnishings, and a choice of bed sizes. Facilities include an outdoor swimming pool.

✪ **Tidewater Inn.** 101 E. Dover St., P.O. Box 359, Easton, MD 21601. ☎ **800/237-8775** or 410/822-1300. Fax 410/820-8847. 114 rms, 8 suites. A/C TV TEL. $129–$160 double; $215–$295 suite. AE, CB, DC, MC, V. Free valet parking.

If you want to stay right in the heart of Easton, this four-story brick-fronted inn is the ideal place. Built in 1949 in the tradition of old public houses of colonial days, its decor features dark woods, arched doorways, hurricane lamps, electric candles, flagstone floors, open fireplaces, and paintings of 18th-century Easton. Bedrooms are furnished with reproduction pieces. Amenities include a swimming pool, valet service, entertainment on Saturday evening, a hunting-themed restaurant, and a wildfowl-themed bar.

St. Michaels

✪ **Hambleton Inn.** 202 Cherry St., St. Michaels, MD 21663. ☎ **410/745-3350.** Fax 410/745-5709. 5 rms. A/C. $115–$245 double. Rates include breakfast. MC, V. Free parking.

A turn-of-the-century atmosphere prevails at this bed-and-breakfast inn facing the harbor. Innkeepers Steve and Kimberly Furman took over the inn in 1995, updated the guest rooms, and gave the exterior a face-lift. All rooms have a view of the waterfront, private bath, and antique furnishings; some also have working fireplaces. An enclosed porch is available for guests as a relaxing lookout from which to watch the boats go by. Guests can also use the new dock facilities and complimentary bicycles.

Inn at Perry Cabin. 308 Watkins Lane, St. Michaels, MD 21663. ☎ **800/722-2949** or 410/745-2200. Fax 410/745-3348. 20 rms, 19 suites. A/C TV TEL. $195–$395 single or double; $435–$595 suite. Rates include breakfast and afternoon tea. AE, CB, DC, MC, V. Free parking.

Acquired by Sir Bernard Ashley of Laura Ashley Enterprises in 1990, this proper English country inn set on the Miles River aims for the highest luxury standards and charges accordingly. No expense has been spared in the appointments or decor that, not surprisingly, showcase Laura Ashley designs and furnishings. Pampering sets this place apart—from a full-time concierge to turndown services, fresh flowers in every room, morning newspaper at your door, and a complete afternoon tea in the drawing room each day. Perry Cabin served as a private home and a riding academy before first opening its doors as an inn in 1980. Facilities include a restaurant, outdoor terrace, rose and herb garden, boat docking, indoor heated swimming pool, and fitness center. There's also access to golf, fishing, horseback riding, hunting, and a helicopter pad.

St. Michaels Harbour Inn. 101 N. Harbor Rd., St. Michaels, MD 21663. ☎ **800/955-9001** or 410/745-9001. Fax 410/745-9150. 8 rms, 38 suites. A/C TV TEL. $99–$409 double or suite. AE, CB, DC, DISC, MC, V. Free parking.

It's hard to beat this inn for views of the water and boats. Situated right along the marina, this modern hotel offers rooms and suites, all with sweeping views of the water and most with private balconies or terraces. Each room has contemporary furnishings with maritime-themed art, standard accessories, and a coffeemaker. The suites also have kitchenettes, wet bars, and sitting rooms. Other amenities include short-term berthing for guest boats on a 60-slip marina, an outdoor swimming pool, an exercise room, bike and water-sports rentals, a guest laundry, a poolside bar, and a nautical-style restaurant overlooking the harbor. The restaurant is particularly romantic at dinner as the sun sets over the marina.

○ Wades Point Inn on the Bay. Wades Point Rd., McDaniel, St. Michaels, MD 21663. ☎ **410/745-2500.** Fax 410/745-3444. 23 rms (16 with private bath, 7 with shared bath). $95–$145 in main house, $150–$195 in adjoining building, single or double. Rates include continental breakfast. MC, V. Free parking. Five miles west of St. Michaels, off Rte. 33.

A long country road leads to this grand old house set on a curve of land overlooking Chesapeake Bay. Surrounded by a sprawling lawn and 120 acres of fields, woodlands, and nature trails, this inn offers seclusion, peace, and some of the best sunset views you'll ever see. The inn was built in the early 19th century by Thomas Kemp, a shipbuilder credited with creating the *Baltimore Clipper* ships. It is now owned by caring and cordial innkeepers Betsy and John Feiler.

The main house today offers varied guest rooms (with private or shared baths), all furnished with antiques and cooled by the cross-ventilation of bay breezes, ceiling fans, and screened porches. For modern comforts mixed with reproduction furnishings and decor, request a room in the newer adjacent Kemp Building. Its 12 rooms all have private baths and air-conditioning, and most have private porches or balconies; four have kitchenettes. Breakfast is served in a bright wicker-filled room in the main house overlooking the bay. A 2-night stay is required for weekends and holidays. Discounts available for stays of 3 days or more.

OXFORD

Oxford Inn. 504 S. Morris St., P.O. Box 627, Oxford, MD 21654. ☎ **410/226-5220.** 10 rms (6 with private bath, 4 share 2 baths), 1 suite. A/C. $80–$140 double; $200 suite. Rates include continental breakfast. DISC, MC, V. Free parking.

Surrounded by a white picket fence, this three-story Victorian house sits beside Town Creek. The guest rooms are individually furnished with antiques, quilts, armoires, dressing tables, and wicker or oak furniture. Many of the rooms have window seats and/or views of the water; six have private baths. Facilities include a nautically themed restaurant called Pope's Tavern, with indoor and outdoor seating; and a second-floor sitting room with bay windows overlooking the water and a telephone, TV, and VCR for guest use. The innkeepers are the Schmitt family.

○ Robert Morris Inn. 314 N. Morris St. and The Strand, P.O. Box 70, Oxford, MD 21654. ☎ **410/226-5111.** Fax 410/226-5744. 35 units. A/C. Apr–Nov $100–$240; Dec–Mar $60–$120. Rates include continental breakfast. AE, MC, V. Open selected weekends only Dec–Mar. Free parking.

This historic inn overlooking the Tred Avon River was once the home of Robert Morris Jr., a financier of the American Revolution. Built in 1710 by ships' carpenters, the inn retains much of the original flooring and staircase. The Robert Morris offers a simple, relaxed setting, ideal for intimate weekend getaways. The decor is country-romantic with antiques and reproductions. Bathrooms are the inn's specialty—many rooms have large, footed tubs with movable faucets and come complete with bubble bath. Though some of the rooms themselves are small, many have separate sitting rooms, river views, and, of course, large bathrooms. There are also rooms with private porches at the Sandaway, a nearby lodge situated on a private beach. The inn's restaurant reputedly has the best crab cakes on the Eastern Shore (see "Where to Dine," below). Just across the Strand is the Oxford–Bellevue Ferry, which makes several trips daily (in-season) to nearby St. Michaels.

How to Eat a Crab

"There is a saying in Baltimore," H. L. Mencken once wrote, "that crabs may be prepared in fifty ways and that all of them are good." This may well be true, but out of the 50, every seafood restaurant in the state (and in Delaware, too) will usually have these three mainstays: steamed hard crabs, soft-shell crabs, and crab cakes. Before we explain the logistics of eating these three variations of our favorite shellfish, here are a few things every crab consumer should know:

Old Bay is that red, powdery stuff that covers all the steamed crabs you find in Maryland and Delaware. It's *the* spice used in preparing pretty much all crab dishes in these parts, but it's used particularly generously on steamed crabs. You'll also find Old Bay on french fries and even potato chips.

Soft-shell crabs are crabs harvested while molting, so their shells are soft enough to be eaten whole.

Finally, crabs are **in season** from about March through October, and the best time for them is July through September. Any off-season crabs you eat will probably be imported (and inferior, of course).

Now to business. **Crab cakes** are no more difficult to eat than a hamburger. They're served either plain or as a sandwich, and can be topped with tartar sauce, mayo, ketchup, or whatever condiment you wish.

Soft-shell crabs are just as easy to consume, if you don't think about what you're eating. They are most often deep-fried and served as a sandwich. And you just eat the whole thing. We must admit, we've never been able to try them, but everyone we know who has loves them.

But what everyone really needs to know is how to eat a **steamed hard crab.** First of all, remember that this can be a messy operation; do not for any reason wear

KENT ISLAND

Kent Manor Inn. 500 Kent Manor Dr., Stevensville, MD 21666. ☎ **800/820-4511** or 410/643-5757. 24 rms. A/C TV TEL. $130–$175 double. AE, DC, DISC, MC, V. Free parking. Off Rte. 8, exit 37 of Rte. 50/301.

Dating from 1820, this sprawling three-story Victorian-style inn exudes a southern plantation atmosphere, sitting on 226 acres of Kent Island farmland rimmed by a mile of Thompson Creek waterfront. The public areas are rich in antiques, original Italian marble fireplaces, and brass fixtures. Guest rooms, including some ground-floor units, have Victorian reproduction furniture, four-poster beds, and frilly fabrics, and most have verandas that overlook Thompson Creek. Facilities include a restaurant with a country manor ambience (see "Where to Dine," below), a bar, and access to a nearby golf course.

Sleep Inn. 101 VFW Ave., Grasonville, MD 21638. ☎ **800/62-SLEEP** or 410/827-8921. Fax 401/827-8801. 50 rms. A/C TV TEL. $59.95–$99.95 double. Rates include continental breakfast. AE, CB, DC, DISC, MC, V. Free parking.

This two-story hotel for bargain-hunters is new in the area. Set back from Route 50/301 (accessible by exits 44A and 44B), it offers guest rooms with standard furnishings plus a refrigerator. An outdoor swimming pool and restaurants are nearby.

WHERE TO DINE

Seafood-lovers, rejoice. Talbot County is prime crab, oyster, and fish country. Crab in all forms is the main attraction—whether crab claws, soft-shell crabs, or just the

light-colored or expensive clothing. Second, the beverage of choice when sitting down to a bushel of crabs with a group of friends is beer—some red-blooded American lager is preferred among the locals, but any kind will do. That said, here's how you get the meat out of that pesky shell:

1. Flip the crab so that the underside (the white side) is facing up. Remove all the legs and claws by grasping each firmly at the first joint (the one closest to the torso), breaking the joint, and then gently pulling away. If you're lucky, or talented, you'll be able to remove a lot of the inner meat with each leg.

2. Remove the meat from the claws by first breaking each claw arm in half at the middle joint. For the lower half of the arm, use a knife handle or hammer to crack the shell and then remove the meat. To get the meat from the claw itself, break off the movable pincher with your hand (be careful, it can be sharp), and pull gently, like when you removed the legs; once again, with luck or talent you should be able to pull the meat out of the shell. If not, use the knife handle or hammer to crack/smash the shell and remove the claw meat.

3. To extract the meat from the main body, pry off the apron (the plate on the underside of the crab) with a knife or your fingers, and discard. Then, using a knife point, lift off the top shell (this will reveal some unpleasant-looking crab stuff, so be brave) and discard it. Scrape away the yellowish "mustard," intestines, and other unpleasantries with a knife. You're almost to the meat.

4. Hold both sides of what is left of your crab in your hands and break it in half. Use a knife to break through the brittle white membrane that houses the meat in each half. Then, pick out the meat with your fingers or the end of a knife and enjoy.

plain hard-shell variety. You'll find it served as plump crab cakes, thick crab chowder, and rich crab imperial in a creamy sauce. Come and have your fill; here the crab is plentiful and the price is right.

EASTON

Legal Spirits. 42 E. Dover St., Easton. ☎ **410/820-0033.** Reservations recommended for dinner. Main courses $9.95–$18.95; lunch $4.95–$10.95. AE, MC, V. Mon–Thurs 11:30am–10pm, Fri–Sat 11:30am–11pm, Sun noon–9pm. AMERICAN.

Housed in the historic Avalon Theater complex dating from 1921, this tavern-style restaurant has a turn-of-the-century atmosphere. With a tin ceiling, stained-glass windows, and brass fixtures, it harks back to an era synonymous with silent movies, vaudeville, and art deco. The eclectic menu features Maryland seafood favorites from crab cakes to fried oysters, as well as steaks, pastas, and vegetarian choices such as wild mushroom stroganoff or vegetable tartare. Local favorites are waterfowl fried noodles, with boneless duck breast and fresh berry sauce, and shrimp and mussel stir-fry. Lunch items range from salads and sandwiches to burgers and soups.

Peach Blossoms. 6 N. Washington St., Easton. ☎ **410/822-5220.** Reservations required. Main courses $17.95–$19.95; lunch $6.95–$8.95. MC, V. Wed–Fri 11:30am–2pm and 5:30–9pm, Sat 5:30–9pm. INTERNATIONAL.

Situated in the heart of Easton's historic district opposite the Talbot County Courthouse, this is a bright bistro-style restaurant and wine bar, with a decor of leafy plants and light cane furniture. Everything is made on the premises, from tangy salad dressings to breads, pastries, and desserts. The menu changes daily, but lunch usually features salads, sandwiches, omelets, and pastas. Dinner selections include imaginative and colorfully presented dishes such as molasses-glazed duck with green chili cornbread stuffing, grilled grouper with citrus salsa, and veal medaillons with balsamic glaze and hazelnuts.

Rustic Inn. Talbottown Shopping Center, Easton. ☎ **410/820-8212.** Reservations recommended for dinner. Main courses $10.95–$21.95; lunch $4.95–$19.95. AE, MC, V. Tues–Fri 11:30am–2pm and 5–10pm, Sat–Mon 5–10pm. INTERNATIONAL.

Established in 1984, this eatery is situated in the midst of a string of shops. Although it can easily be overlooked, it is a hideaway well worth finding, especially for families. The decor features early farm implements, fishing gear, tobacco-growing tools, and old newspapers, all surrounding a wood-burning fireplace. Entrees include surf-and-turf, lobster tails, crab-and-oyster imperial, veal (Marsala, piccata, or scaloppini with sherry and mushrooms), chicken Divan, steak béarnaise, and "salty strip" (strip steak covered with freshly shucked sautéed oysters and mushrooms).

Yesteryears. Easton Plaza, Marlborough Ave., Easton. ☎ **410/822-2433.** Reservations recommended on weekends. Main courses $9.95–$17.95; lunch $3.95–$8.95. AE, MC, V. Mon–Sat 11am–11pm. AMERICAN.

Don't judge this restaurant by its nondescript concrete exterior, wedged in a busy shopping center. Step inside and savor the decor designed to convey the ambience of Washington Street at the turn of the century. The fittings incorporate genuine town memorabilia, from timbers salvaged from the old Dover Bridge to mirrors from the 19th-century Brick Hotel. The menu presents American food with an Eastern Shore accent, including chicken pot pie, crab cakes, prime rib, steaks, and barbecued baby-back ribs. In addition, there are several international favorites, including Italian pastas and teriyaki and cordon bleu dishes. There is also a large selection of salads, burgers, raw bar items, and tavern-style overstuffed sandwiches, such as "The Virginian" (hot ham and crab imperial with melted cheddar).

St. Michaels & Tilghman Island

Crab Claw. Navy Point, Mill St., St. Michaels. ☎ **410/745-2900.** Reservations not accepted. Main courses $8.95–$19.95. No credit cards. Mid-Mar to mid-Dec daily 11am–10pm. SEAFOOD.

There is no air-conditioning, just ceiling fans and lots of bay breezes, in this casual indoor-outdoor eatery on the lower end of the waterfront. The emphasis on the all-day menu is on crabs served in all styles—you'll find backfin crab cake, crab chowder, soft crab, "crab dogs" (on a stick), and crab imperial. Other seafood and fried chicken are also available.

Harrison's Chesapeake House. 21551 Chesapeake House Dr., Tilghman Island. ☎ **410/886-2121.** Reservations recommended for dinner. Main courses $10.95–$19.95; lunch $1.95–$12.95. MC, V. Daily 6am–9pm. SEAFOOD.

A tradition on the Eastern Shore dating from 1856, this nautically themed waterfront restaurant has been run by four generations of the Harrison family. The two dining rooms offer great views of the bay and fishing fleet. The menu includes all types of Chesapeake Bay seafood—prepared broiled, fried, au gratin, or sautéed. There is also pan-fried chicken, prime rib, and steaks. All dishes are cooked to order and served family style with lots of vegetables. Be sure to try the mashed potatoes topped with stewed tomatoes.

Higgins' Crab House. 1216 S. Talbot St., St. Michaels. ☎ **410/745-5151.** Reservations recommended for dinner. Main courses $9.95–$22.95; lunch $4.95–$7.95. AE, DC, DISC, MC, V. Mon–Fri 11:30am–9:30pm, Sat–Sun 11:30am–10pm (hrs. vary in winter). SEAFOOD.

Although not perched right on the water, this restaurant's decor is thoroughly nautical. There is seating both indoors and out. Lunch choices include sandwiches, burgers, seafood salads, and soups (crab vegetable and cream of crab are local favorites). Crab is the main feature at dinner; selections include an all-you-can-eat crab feast, hard crab of all sizes (available April 15 to November 15 only), soft-shell crabs, king crab legs, crab imperial, surf-and-turf, and crab cakes. Different varieties of shrimp, scallops, and steaks and barbecued baby-back ribs are also on the menu, as well as a Maryland favorite, fried chicken. It is situated on the approach to St. Michaels from Easton on Route 33.

Morsels. 205 N. Talbot St., St. Michaels. ☎ **410/745-2911.** Reservations recommended for dinner. Main courses $14–$23; lunch $5–$9. MC, V. Sun–Mon and Thurs–Sat 11am–3pm and 5:30–10pm (hrs. vary in winter). INTERNATIONAL.

The pink-and-white facade of this informal Victorian shopfront restaurant stands out along the main thoroughfare, as does its menu. Selections change seasonally but often include such treats as Moroccan chicken-and-almond pie; steak Eva (a grilled filet topped with mushrooms and béarnaise sauce); Basque seafood pasta (sautéed seafood in a roasted pepper sauce on spinach linguine); and a paella of chicken, shrimp, sausage, and mussels with Spanish beans and rice in a spicy tomato-pepper sauce.

St. Michaels Crab House. 305 Mulberry St., St. Michaels. ☎ **410/745-3737.** Reservations recommended for dinner. Main courses $9.95–$16.95; lunch $5.25–$11.95. DISC, MC, V. Apr–Oct Mon–Sat 11am–11pm, Sun 11am–10pm. SEAFOOD.

Located on the marina, this restaurant emphasizes casual dining, with a choice of indoor (air-conditioned) seating amid a nautical decor or a large outdoor area lined with picnic tables and umbrellas. The building itself dates from the 1830s, when it was an oyster-shucking shed; the patio bricks outside were kilned in St. Michaels during the late 1800s. The menu features all-you-can-eat steamed crabs and other crab dishes, from crab cakes and crab imperial to soft-shell crabs and snow crab legs. Other seafood choices include stuffed flounder, fried shrimp, and fried oysters. For landlubbers, there are steaks and barbecued or grilled chicken. Appetizers include an extensive raw bar. Lunch items range from soups and salads to sandwiches and burgers.

Town Dock Restaurant. 125 Mulberry St., St. Michaels. ☎ **410/745-5577.** Reservations recommended for dinner. Main courses $15–$23; lunch $7–$12. AE, DC, DISC, MC, V. Daily 11am–9pm. AMERICAN.

Sitting on high ground overlooking the harbor, this spot dates from the mid-19th century when it was known as the White Manor House and later as the Longfellow Inn. There are two dining levels inside; meals are also served on an adjacent deck overlooking the water. The chef/owner, Michael Rork, formerly chef of the highly touted Hamptons restaurant of the Harbor Court Hotel in Baltimore, endeavors to present a "new Eastern Shore" cuisine, with choices such as chicken Chesapeake (grilled breast with crab imperial and saffron glaze), vegetable stew (a blend of seasonal vegetables in broth, served over orzo), and fishermen's crepes. There are also traditional crab cakes, fried oysters, and daily beef and veal specials. Lunch choices include stews, salads, sandwiches, quiches, and seafood platters.

208 Talbot. 208 N. Talbot St., St. Michaels. ☎ **410/745-3838.** Reservations required. Main courses $19–$25; fixed-price 5-course dinner $43; lunch $8.50–$12.50. DISC, MC, V. Wed–Fri noon–2pm and 5–10pm, Sat 5–10pm, Sun 11am–2pm and 5–9pm. AMERICAN.

This restaurant is on a busy main thoroughfare at the end of town and offers no water views—but still the food draws a crowd every night. The menu emphasizes indigenous Eastern Shore seafood, produce, and herbs. Entrees change often but usually include pan-seared rockfish with wild mushrooms and oyster cream sauce; grilled Atlantic salmon with smoked salmon dill cream and red lentils; roasted free-range chicken with garlic mashed potatoes and minted peas; and rack of lamb and steaks. The decor is relaxing, with exposed brick walls, crisp white linens, botanical and waterfowl prints, and an oyster plate collection. Dinner on Saturday night is on a fixed-price basis.

OXFORD

✪ **Robert Morris Inn.** 314 N. Morris St. and The Strand, P.O. Box 70, Oxford. ☎ **410/226-5111.** Reservations not accepted. Main courses $14.95–$29.95; lunch $4.95–$12.95. AE, MC, V. Mid-Mar to Nov daily 8am–10am, noon–3pm, and 6–9pm. Closed Dec to mid-Mar. AMERICAN/SEAFOOD.

Crab is the specialty here; the crab cakes were rated by James Michener as the best on the Eastern Shore, and they make our list of the bests, too. Dating from the early 18th century, the dining room and tavern of this old inn (see "Where to Stay," above) are attractions in themselves, featuring original woodwork, slate floors, and fireplaces. The murals of the four seasons were made from wallpaper of 140 years ago, which was printed on a screw-type press using 1,600 woodcut blocks carved from orange-wood. Some of the exceptional dishes are crab Norfolk (crab sautéed with butter and sherry), crab imperial, and baked seafood au gratin cakes (crab and shrimp with Monterey Jack cheese, cheddar, and seasonings). Lunch items range from sandwiches and salads to omelets, burgers, seafood platters, and hot entrees. Jackets are required for men in the main dining room except from Memorial Day to Labor Day.

Schooner's Landing. Foot of Tilghman St., Oxford. ☎ **410/226-0160.** Reservations accepted only for parties of 5 or more. Main courses $10.95–$19.95; lunch $3.95–$5.95. MC, V. Sun–Mon and Wed–Thurs 11:30am–9pm, Fri–Sat 11:30am–10pm (hrs. vary in winter). SEAFOOD.

Situated right on the marina, this informal spot is known for its wide-windowed views of the water, with seating both indoors and on a deck. The menu changes daily, depending on the latest catch, but usually includes hot steamed crabs in season, seafood pasta, crab cakes, crab imperial, jumbo shrimp scampi, soft-shell clams and crabs, mussels, and fried oysters, as well as steaks, prime rib, and barbecued or broiled breast of corn-fed chicken.

KENT ISLAND

Harris Crab House. Kent Narrows Way N., Grasonville. ☎ **410/827-9500.** Reservations not accepted. Main courses $7.95–$17.95; lunch $1.95–$7.95. MC, V. Daily 11am–10pm. Off Rte. 50 at exit 42. SEAFOOD.

This informal indoor-outdoor restaurant overlooks the Mears Point Marina. Heaping platters of fresh seafood are the specialty here, including crabs by the dozen; all-you-can-eat shrimp and crab; and various broiled, steamed, or fried combinations of hard and soft crabs, crab cakes, hard- and soft-shell clams, oysters, and scallops. In addition, the menu offers barbecued chicken and ribs. Lighter items, such as sandwiches and burgers, are popular at lunchtime. Get here early.

Kent Manor Restaurant. 500 Kent Manor Dr., Stevensville. ☎ **410/643-7716.** Reservations required. Main courses $19–$32; lunch $8–$13. AE, CB, DC, DISC, MC, V. Daily 11:30am–2:30pm and 5–9pm. Off Rte. 8, exit 37 of Rte. 50/301. INTERNATIONAL.

Overlooking more than 200 acres of farmland and waterfront on the east side of Kent Island, this historic manor house restaurant is an attraction in itself. It offers a choice of settings including four cozy candlelit Victorian dining rooms and an enclosed water-view solarium. Specialties of the house include local crab dishes, Black Angus steaks, veal California (a cutlet with artichoke hearts, sun-dried tomatoes, and pro-sciutto), seafood scampi, and roast quail stuffed with apples, raisins, and pine nuts with an apple brandy glaze.

2 Blackwater National Wildlife Refuge

84 miles SE of Baltimore, 101 miles SE of Washington, D.C., 111 miles SW of Wilmington

Over 17,000 acres of rich tidal marsh and woodland make up Blackwater National Wildlife Refuge. Even though only a fraction of this is made open to the public, it is still one of the hot spots for bird watchers on the Atlantic Flyway and the most popular refuge on the Delmarva Peninsula with tourists. Although set up in 1933 as a sanctuary for ducks, which had been greatly depleted by overhunting, currently the refuge's most numerous resident is the Canada goose. By peak season (usually November) more than 33,000 Canada geese have arrived in V-formations, covering the river's waters with fluttering masses of brown, white, and black. They are joined by as many as 15,000 ducks, numerous mute and tundra swan, and the ever-present herons. But peak season isn't the only time to visit this treasure. Many of the wild-fowl arrive early and leave late. And the refuge is home to many year-round residents, including the endangered peregrine falcon, Delmarva fox squirrel, and bald eagle.

JUST THE FACTS

GETTING THERE   From Route 50, take Route 16 southwest out of Cambridge, then turn south (left) on Route 335. Turn right onto Key Wallace Drive to get to the visitor center, auto tour, trails, and observation site.

VISITOR CENTER   The visitor center is located off Key Wallace Drive. It's open year-round Monday through Friday from 8am to 4pm, plus weekends in fall, winter, and spring from 9am to 5pm. For information write to Refuge Manager, Blackwater National Wildlife Refuge, 2145 Key Wallace Dr., Cambridge, MD 21613, or call ☎ **410/228-2677.**

FEES & REGULATIONS   Admission is $3 per vehicle and $1 for pedestrians or bicyclists. Regulations are the same as most national parks in terms of respecting the environment and wildlife. Pets are not permitted. For boating and fishing regulations, see "Other Outdoor Activities," below.

SEASONS   The Wildlife Drive and all outdoor facilities are open year-round, daily, from dawn to dusk. The best time to visit is from mid-October through mid-March, when the number of migratory waterfowl is at its peak. Crowds of people are also at their peak, but it's never unbearably crowded. If you're interested in boating or fishing, you must visit between April 1 and October 1; these activities are prohibited during peak migration. However, summer is peak season for mosquitoes, flies, and other biting insects, so come prepared with insect repellent and protective clothing. Insects are also a problem on dry land, particularly on the walking trails, so even if you're not fishing or boating, bring the bug spray and wear long sleeves.

SEEING THE BIRDS & WILDLIFE

Blackwater is the largest refuge on the Delmarva Peninsula, but very little of the over 17,000 acres is accessible by car or even on foot. That's because most of the refuge is under water much of the year, and unfortunately boating is prohibited during migration season. But the park service has done a good job of making use of its dry land, providing a paved 5-mile auto/bike tour, an observation site, and two short hiking trails. And frankly, there are so many birds here during migration that you couldn't possibly drive into the refuge without seeing huge flocks of Canada geese, ducks, and tundra swan. But the birds do keep their distance, so a good set of at least 10× binoculars is recommended gear.

THE WILDLIFE DRIVE

The park calls this paved loop the Wildlife Drive, but cyclists are also welcome on this easy, flat, 5-mile ride. Before you begin your tour, stop by the visitor center to pick up a map. The center also offers plenty of free literature on the wildlife, as well as several displays and a short video on ecology; so even if you're a novice bird watcher, you'll be able to identify some of the birds and other wildlife you'll see. When you finish stocking up on brochures and information, continue down Key Wallace Drive to the entrance to the driving tour, where you'll pay the park entrance fee at the self-pay station. The tour will take you by at least eight pools, the Little Blackwater River and the Blackwater River, and through wooded areas and marshes. You can stop anywhere along the driving route; the road is wide, offering plenty of space, and there are some designated pull-off spots.

The first official stop, with a parking area, is the **Marsh Edge Trail.** This one-third-mile, mostly boardwalk trail takes you through a mature pine forest to a typical Eastern Shore marsh, showing the range of vegetation on the refuge. The outer edge of the trail borders the Little Blackwater River, with some outstanding vistas and places to view the park's osprey nesting platforms. Continue south from the parking area to the observation site, which offers perhaps the best vantage point for viewing waterfowl in the park. If it's too crowded, consider skipping it the first time through and dropping by again later. Your entrance fee is good all day.

You'll have to backtrack to return to the driving tour. As soon as you're on the main route again, begin watching for the elusive and endangered **Delmarva fox squirrel.** During our recent visit, one ran out right in front of our car. They're beautiful creatures, large and silver-haired; spotting one will be the highlight of your trip.

The next official stop is the **Woods Trail,** a half-mile hike through a forest of pine and mixed hardwoods. This trail is often flooded, so ask about it at the visitor center. When you leave the parking lot at the Woods Trail, you'll enter the main marshland viewing area, overlooking five pools and the beautiful Blackwater River. There are no trails or observation towers, but you can park anywhere along the route, and you'll probably want to stop several times along the way.

After driving through this section, you can exit back onto Key Wallace Drive, but we suggest you continue to the next set of pools. Fewer visitors venture to this area, and its the best place in the park to spot **bald eagles.** The tour ends at Route 335. You can make a right and travel the short distance back to Key Wallace Drive, stop by the visitor center to report any unusual sightings, or even drive through the tour again if your schedule permits.

THE BIRDS & WILDLIFE: WHAT YOU'LL SEE DURING YOUR VISIT

The refuge provides a brochure that includes a "Wildlife Calendar," listing which birds and mammals can be seen each month. Here's a quick overview.

Of course, most people visit to view the migratory waterfowl. The migration season runs from mid-October through mid-March, but November is the absolute peak, with some 33,000 geese and over 15,000 ducks. If you visit during then you'll mostly likely see tundra swan, Canada and snow geese, and over 20 duck species, including mallards, black ducks, blue-winged and green-winged teal, widgeon, and pintails. Golden eagles are sometimes spied in winter, and bald eagle numbers increase with the migrant population. Most of these birds will travel north in the spring, but some stay throughout the summer to raise their young.

But ducks and geese are not the only birds on the refuge. In February and early March, northbound migrants such as killdeer, robins, bluebirds, and red-winged blackbirds pass through, and in April and May the majority of migrant marsh birds and songbirds return. During the summer months you may catch a glimpse of ospreys, warblers, vireos, orioles, and flycatchers. The refuge is also home to year-round populations of towhees, woodpeckers, bobwhite, woodcocks, great blue herons, and bald eagles.

Several types of mammals also make their homes in the refuge, including the endangered Delmarva fox squirrel. You may also see gray squirrels, raccoons, otters, opossums, skunks, and white-tailed deer. Muskrats, nutria, sika deer, and the red fox also live on the refuge but are more elusive and seldom seen.

OTHER OUTDOOR ACTIVITIES

BIKING   The 5-mile Wildlife Drive, described above, is open to cyclists whenever the park is open. The area surrounding the refuge to the south and east is also quite scenic, and the roads are flat and relatively untrafficked, making for some good biking. However, it is easy to get lost in the section of Dorchester County; the roads are not well marked, and the towns, really villages, are few and far between. Get a good map of the county and bring all the provisions you'll need because you won't find many places to stop along the way. For maps and information, write or call **Dorchester County Tourism** at 203 Sunburst Hwy., Cambridge, MD 21613 (☎ **800/522-TOUR** or 410/228-1000).

BOATING & FISHING   Although the refuge is a great place for boating and a fair place for fishing, these activities are only permitted from April 1 to October 1, which roughly corresponds to bug season. So bring your bug spray and wear appropriate clothing—long sleeves and pants. If you can handle the insects, the scenery is excellent. Launching is prohibited on the refuge, but a public ramp is available just south of the refuge on Shorter Wharf Road (turn right off Key Wallace Drive after crossing the Key Wallace Bridge).

You are allowed to fish or crab in the refuge from a boat but not from the shoreline or the Wildlife Drive. A valid state sport fishing license is required for fishing in the Blackwater and Little Blackwater rivers. All state fishing regulations apply on the refuge. The refuge is not known for great fishing, but the species that inhabit the waters include largemouth bass, rockfish (striped bass), white and yellow perch, black crappie, bullhead and channel catfish, carp, bluegill, and pickerel.

BASING YOURSELF IN CAMBRIDGE

Maryland's second largest deep-water port, Cambridge is an authentic functioning bay town on the Choptank River, and as such doesn't offer a lot of services for the casual tourist. However, Cambridge is the closest place to stay and eat for wildlife-lovers planning a visit to the Blackwater National Wildlife Refuge. And the wide, beautiful Choptank makes for what we think is one of the loveliest harbors on the Eastern Shore. Perhaps because the town still doesn't have a lot of amenities for visitors, the harbor remains underutilized and quiet.

You can also plan a visit to Blackwater from a base in Talbot County or even from Crisfield or Princess Anne. See the corresponding sections in this chapter for more details.

ESSENTIALS

GETTING THERE   Other than by private boat, traveling by car is the only way to get to Cambridge. From Washington, D.C., and most other points inland, take

Impressions

*It was simply there, the indefinable river, now broad, now narrow, in this age
turbulent, in that asleep, becoming a formidable stream and then a spacious bay and
then the ocean itself, an unbroken chain with all parts so interrelated that it will exist
forever.*

—James Michener, on the Choptank River, *Chesapeake*

Route 50 across the Bay Bridge and follow it south all the way to Cambridge. From
Wilmington and points north, follow Route 40 west and then turn on Route
301 south; take 301 until it intersects with Route 50 and then follow 50 south to
Cambridge.

VISITOR INFORMATION   For a map and travel brochures about Cambridge
and the surrounding area, contact **Dorchester County Tourism** at 203 Sunburst
Hwy., Cambridge, MD 21613, or call ☎ **800/522-TOUR** or 410/228-1000.

GETTING AROUND   The best ways to see the area sights are by car, bicycle, and
on foot. Cambridge itself is somewhat sprawling and therefore crosstown trips are best
made in a car. The area around Cambridge is mostly flat and well suited for cyclists.
To help you get around, county maps including a blowup of Cambridge are available from Dorchester County Tourism.

WHERE TO STAY

Although there is a sea of cheap motels on Route 50 in Cambridge, they are a notor-
ious lot. The two cozy accommodations listed below, however, offer a safe harbor.

Cambridge House. 112 High St., Cambridge, MD 21613. ☎ 410/221-7700. 6 rms. A/C.
$120 double. Rates include breakfast and high tea at 3pm. AE, MC, V. Free parking.

This is Cambridge's elegant contribution to the world of Eastern Shore B&Bs. Located in a Queen Anne–style sea captain's mansion on historic High Street, 1 block
from Long Wharf, this inn offers travelers a place to rest in comfort and style whether
they intend to visit the local sites or drive north to tour Talbot County. The inn features queen- and king-size beds as well as fireplaces in many rooms. Chef and innkeeper Stuart Schefers prepares the formal breakfasts, which are served in the dining
room or on the wraparound front porch.

Commodore's Cottage Bed & Breakfast. 215 Glenburn Ave., Cambridge, MD 21613.
☎ 410/228-6938. 2 cottages. A/C TV TEL. $75–$85 double. Rates include continental breakfast. MC, V. Free parking.

Taking one of these two unassuming brick cottages is perhaps the most relaxing way
to stay in the Cambridge area. They are located on the garden grounds of the
Brannock Maritime Museum. Both have their own full furnished kitchens, living/
dining room areas, and bedrooms. The decor is amazingly homey and comfortable
(there are even old *Reader's Digests* in the magazine rack beside the couch). Because
the two cottages are on opposite sides of the garden lawn, you really feel you can come
and go as you please. Gracious hosts Earl and Shirley Brannock provide a continental breakfast in the cottages each morning and make sure you feel you're at a home
away from home.

WHERE TO DINE

McGuigan's Pub. 411 Muse St. ☎ **410/228-7110.** Main courses $5.95–$17.95; lunch
$4.95–$9.50. AE, DISC, MC, V. Mon–Thurs 11am–9pm, Fri–Sat 11am–10pm. Pub open until
1am. INTERNATIONAL.

This Scottish pub with an Irish name is the best place to grab a bite in downtown Cambridge. Housed in a restored late-Victorian residence, the restaurant is divided into a pub section featuring music, a dart board, and a bar, and a more formal dining section with large windows looking out to Muse Street. Pub food, which includes beef cottage pie, fish-and-chips, and Mississippi (BBQ and onion) burgers, is served all day but is supplemented with a small dinner menu in the evening. Dinner entrees range from seafood crepes to braised lamb gigot chops. But don't eat too much; their Scottish trifle dessert is great. There's Guinness on draft in the pub.

✪ **Suicide Bridge Seafood House.** 6304 Suicide Bridge Rd., Hurloch, MD. ☎ **410/ 943-4689.** Reservations will get you seating preference over walk-in patrons. Main courses $9.95–$19.95; lobster and market-price dishes may be more. Tues–Wed 11am–9pm, Thurs–Sat 11am–10pm, Sun noon–9pm. SEAFOOD.

This local favorite with a strange name is really off the beaten path but worth the drive. A marina-style restaurant with wide windows overlooking Cabin Creek, Suicide Bridge has developed its following for a reason: The food is great. Even the salads are good—simple but good. Their variety of seafood dishes includes a few fancy items, such as scallop linguine. But most significant are their large lumpmeat crab cakes, truly flavorful without a lot of overpowering spices or extravagant presentation. They are just, once again I say it, good. Tuesday through Thursday the restaurant offers cut rates on steaks; they also offer a pound of shrimp and all-you-can-eat ribs for $11.95.

A BRIEF LOOK AT CAMBRIDGE'S MARITIME PAST & PRESENT

If you spend any time exploring Cambridge, you will invariably end up at **Long Wharf,** the town's marina and harbor, offering excellent views of the Choptank and the towering Route 50 bridge. The wharf is the starting point for cruises aboard the town's own skipjack, the ✪ *Nathan of Dorchester.* This traditional Chesapeake Bay–style oyster sailboat offers harbor cruises on some but not all summer weekends, evening sunset cruises, and special-event cruises. A trip aboard the *Nathan* is a great way to get acquainted with the city's past: oystering, shipbuilding, local heroes. Cruise prices range from $15 for sunset cruises to $25 for special events. For information and reservations call ☎ **410/228-1000** or 410/228-7141. When you leave the wharf, or sometime before your trip ends, be sure to make the drive out Water Street and Hambrooks Avenue to Riverside Drive for some more excellent river views.

Once you've learned the basics of Cambridge history, you may want to stop by one or both of the two small maritime museums for a more in-depth look. The **Richardson Maritime Museum,** 401 High St. (☎ **410/221-1871**), was named after master boatbuilder and local wonder Jim Richardson, who built the replica of the 17th-century *Dove* that now rests in St. Mary's City (see "St. Mary's County" in chapter 6). The museum has a nice collection of boat and boatbuilding memorabilia, from models of pungies, bugeyes, and skipjacks to the remains of a Native American log canoe. It's open Wednesday, Saturday, and Sunday from 1 to 4pm or by appointment. Across town the privately owned **Brannock Maritime Museum,** 210 Talbot Ave. (☎ **410/228-6938**), offers a glimpse of the area's history through photographs of and displays on local whaling ships, steamboats, and even the commanders of Maryland's old police navy. Open weekends 1:30 to 4pm and by appointment.

If you have the wandering bug, hop in your car or on your bike and travel about 6 miles west of Cambridge on Route 343. Among the fields and flatlands of Dorchester County sits one of shipbuilder Jim Richardson's little wonders, the **Spocott Windmill,** a working post-type windmill just like the ones that dotted this landscape in the 1800s. Next to the windmill there is an authentic miller's house that dates from around the turn of the 19th century. The site is open all the time, though a small gift shop on the premises keeps irregular hours. A small donation is requested.

3 Chestertown

55 miles E of Baltimore, 70 miles NE of Washington, D.C., 50 miles SW of Wilmington

By far the sleepiest of the Eastern Shore towns, Chestertown, founded in 1706 and perched on a hillside overlooking the Chester River, exudes historic charm and beauty and little else. As you walk down Water Street and High Street you are surrounded by lovely and ornate brick homes, many of which date from the mid-1700s, all reminding you that this was once a great port that rivaled Annapolis. Now, however, it is a quiet and welcome retreat for vacationers seeking to avoid other tourists. The area offers limited shopping (unless you drive south to Talbot County), lots of scenery, and a place to get away from it all. Chestertown is also home to Washington College, one of America's oldest colleges, established in 1782.

ESSENTIALS

GETTING THERE The only way to get to Chestertown is by car. From Easton, follow U.S. Route 50 north to Route 213 and then follow Route 213 north into Chestertown. From I-95 and U.S. Route 40, take the Elkton exit and follow Route 213 south into Chestertown.

VISITOR INFORMATION For a map and travel brochures about Chestertown and the surrounding area, contact the **Kent County Chamber of Commerce,** P.O. Box 146, 400 S. Cross St., Chestertown, MD 21620 (☎ **410/778-0416**). The office on Cross Street is officially open for walk-in visitors Monday through Friday from 9am to 4pm, but it's best to stop by in the morning or call ahead since the office occasionally closes for meetings in the afternoon.

GETTING AROUND Since there is no public transportation in Chestertown, touring by car is the best way to see the area sights. High Street is Chestertown's main thoroughfare. To help you get your bearings, a self-guided driving tour and walking tour brochure is available from the Kent County Chamber of Commerce.

SPECIAL EVENTS On Memorial Day weekend (Sunday) each year, Chestertown celebrates and reenacts one of its contributions to the cause of independence, the **Chestertown Tea Party.** On May 23, 1774, after hearing of the closing of the port of Boston, citizens of Chestertown boarded a British ship in the harbor and tossed its tea overboard. The festival includes a reenactment, boat rides, colonial parades with costumed participants, crafts, buggy rides, and ragtime bands. For information call the chamber of commerce at ☎ **410/778-0416.**

WHAT TO SEE & DO

The focal point of Chestertown is **High Street,** a wide thoroughfare lined with brick town houses. Notable buildings include the Georgian-style **Courthouse,** built in 1860; the **White Swan Tavern,** 231 High St., established in 1733; and the **"Rock of Ages" House,** 532 High St., an unusual 18th-century house built entirely of massive angular stones.

Water Street, hugging the Chester River, is the setting for the **Customs House** (ca. 1746), noted for its Flemish bond brickwork, and **"Wide Hall,"** one of the town's most elaborate merchant's houses (ca. 1770). The amazing thing about Chestertown's intricate architecture is that it is all so personalized; you get a feeling that each time an 18th-century resident decided to build a house they were trying to outdo their neighbors. More than two dozen buildings throughout the town are identified with plaques and described in the leaflet "A Walking Tour of Old Chester Town," available free from the chamber of commerce. If you happen to be in town on a Saturday morning, don't miss the **Chestertown Farmers' Market** at Chestertown Park from 9am to noon.

The area around the city is also worth exploring. About 15 miles southwest of town via Route 20 is **Rock Hall,** a boating and fishing center where the Chester River meets the Chesapeake Bay. The sunset from Rock Hall's tiny public beach is quite pretty. At night the twinkling lights of the Bay Bridge are visible across the bay to the south.

About halfway between Chestertown and Rock Hall, off Route 20, is historic **St. Paul's Church** (☎ 410/778-3180), erected in 1713, making it one of the oldest continually used churches in Maryland. Among the notables buried in the church's oak tree–shaded graveyard is actress Tallulah Bankhead. The church is open daily from 9am to 5pm; there is no admission charge, but donations are welcome.

Just south of Rock Hall, the little-known ✪ **Eastern Neck National Wildlife Refuge** is a boon to bird watchers and nature lovers alike. Like its larger cousin, Blackwater National Wildlife Refuge to the south, this wooded island is a winter haven for migratory birds, from Canada geese to the large tundra swan. It also offers a few pleasant nature trails (though bring your bug spray in late spring and summer). In spring and fall bald eagle sightings are not uncommon.

SHOPPING

Chester River Knitting Company. 113 S. Cross St. ☎ **800/881-0045** or 410/778-0374.

Step inside this little shop and watch knitters Bill and Beth Ruckelshaus at work, producing hand-framed cotton, wool, and cashmere sweaters. Making use of wool from local farms, many of the sweaters bear distinctive designs, such as a crab or waterfowl motif or nautical symbols. Sweaters can be knit to order. Unique straw hats are also for sale. Open Tuesday through Saturday 10am to 5pm.

✪ **Compleat Bookseller.** 301 High St. ☎ **410/778-1480.**

For my money this is the best bookstore on the Eastern Shore, possibly because of its proximity to Washington College. This shop, located on the corner of High and Cross streets, has a great collection of classics, literature, and best-sellers. But, most importantly, it offers numerous books of local interest, from histories of the Oyster Wars to coffee-table books about life on the Eastern Shore. Open Monday through Thursday 9:30am to 5:30pm, Friday 9:30am to 7pm, Saturday 9am to 5pm, and Sunday 11am to 4pm.

Dixon's Auction Sales. Rtes. 544 and 290, Crumpton. ☎ **410/928-3006.**

Located about 10 miles northeast of Chestertown, this unique auction complex has put Crumpton on the map. Weekly outdoor furniture auctions are spread over 15 acres. Bidders stand beside items they like, and Jesse Dixon swings by on a golf cart to lead the fast-paced auctioneer's chant. Inside a large barnlike structure, smaller items are up for auction. You might find rare antiques, a box full of brass doorknobs, 19th-century whaling harpoons, musical instruments, or records. Amish-made baked goods, smoked meat, cheese, and other foods are also for sale at an indoor lunch counter. Open every Wednesday from 9am to 6pm or later.

Village House. 103 S. Cross St. ☎ **410/778-5766.**

Wooden bird cages, needlepoint pillows, hand-painted plates and pottery, decorative candle holders, handmade wreaths, and lanterns fill this shop. In addition, there are household and garden accessories, and brass and cast-stone animal figurines. Open Monday through Saturday from 10am to 5pm.

WHERE TO STAY

✪ **Brampton Inn.** 25227 Chestertown Rd., Chestertown, MD 21620. ☎ **410/778-1860.** 8 rms, 2 suites. A/C. $95–$155 single or double; $115–$145 suite. Rates include breakfast. AE, MC, V. Free parking.

A curving tree-lined driveway leads to this three-story red-brick inn, just over a mile southwest of town (off Route 20). Built in 1860 and listed on the National Register of Historic Places, it sits on 35 acres surrounded by gentle hills and farmland. Guests enjoy the use of two gracious sitting rooms, a wide front porch, and extensive spruce-shaded grounds with lawn furniture. Rooms are furnished with authentic period antiques and canopy or four-poster beds; all have private baths and eight of the rooms have fireplaces. The suites have a sitting room and private TV. A cottage suite is accessible to handicapped visitors. A 2-night minimum stay is required on weekends and a 3-night minimum on holiday weekends.

✪ **Imperial Hotel.** 208 High St., Chestertown, MD 21620. ☎ **410/778-5000.** Fax 410/778-9662. 11 rms, 2 suites. A/C TV TEL. $125 double; $200–$300 suite. Rates include continental breakfast. AE, DC, DISC, MC, V. Free parking.

With a fanciful gingerbread-trimmed triple-porch facade, this three-story brick building is a focal point along the main street of this historic town. The interior includes a Victorian-style restaurant (see "Where to Dine," below), parlor and lounge/bar, cellar-level coffee/bakery/wine shop, and courtyard garden with a gallery displaying monthly exhibits of local and national art. Guest rooms are furnished with brass beds, period antiques, armoires, and colorful wallpapers. One suite is on the third floor with a private porch, parlor, and kitchen; the other occupies the top floor of an adjacent 18th-century carriage house. The innkeepers are Barbara and Bob Lavelle.

Inn at Mitchell House. 8796 Maryland Pkwy., Chestertown, MD 21620. ☎ **410/778-6500.** 6 rms. $75–$110 double. Rates include breakfast. MC, V. Free parking.

If you are looking for a quiet old-world retreat surrounded by remote farmland and habitats for birds, migrating geese, white-tailed deer, and red fox, try this three-story 1743 manor house with a screened-in porch. Nestled on 10 acres overlooking Stoneybrook Pond, it sits almost midway between Chestertown and Rock Hall off Routes 21 and 445; Tolchester marina is half a mile away. The guest rooms, named after historic people or places associated with the area, are furnished with four-poster beds, hook rugs, antiques, decorative wall coverings, and framed old prints. Most rooms have a fireplace or sitting area; all have private baths. On Friday and Saturday nights, dinner is also available to guests in the dining room (reservations are required 24 hours in advance). The innkeepers are Jim and Tracy Stone.

Lauretum Inn. 954 High St. (Rte. 20), Chestertown, MD 21620. ☎ **800/742-3236** or 410/778-3236. 3 rms, 2 suites. $60–$65 with shared bath, $90 with private bath, single or double; $95–$100 suite. Rates include continental breakfast. DISC, MC, V. Free parking.

Sitting amid 6 acres on a shady knoll about a mile outside of town, this three-story 19th-century Queen Anne Victorian (listed on the National Register of Historic places) was named Lauretum, meaning "Laurel Grove" in Latin, by its first owner, Sen. George Vickers. Highlights of the interior include a formal parlor with painted ceiling medallion and fireplace, reading room, screened porch, and sweeping central staircase. Guests enjoy use of antique-filled sitting rooms and a screened-in porch. Two rooms share a bath; one room and the two suites have private baths. There is a 2-night minimum stay on weekends and 3-night minimum on holiday weekends. The innkeepers are Peg and Bill Sites.

WHERE TO DINE

A Feast of Reason. High St. across from the Imperial Hotel. ☎ **410/778-3828.** Sandwiches $4–$4.50. No credit cards. Tues–Fri 10am–6pm, Sat 10am–4pm.

This airy little sandwich shop is a favorite of the college crowd and a great place to grab a bite while touring the historic district. It specializes in truly tasty gourmet sandwiches but also offers soups and salads. Both vegetarian and nonvegetarian options abound.

✪ **Imperial Hotel.** 208 High St. ☎ **410/778-5000.** Reservations required. Main courses $18.50–$24; lunch $6–$12. AE, DC, DISC, MC, V. Fri–Sat 11:45am–2pm; Tues–Sat 5:30–9:30pm, Sun noon–3pm. AMERICAN.

Housed in the center of the historic district, this inn offers fine cuisine and an elegant ambience reminiscent of bygone days. It has two intimate Victorian-themed dining rooms: the Hubbard Room, dominated by hunt-green tones and tallyho prints, and the Leighton Room, with a rich claret-colored motif. Seating is also available on the outdoor garden patio in the summer months (with live jazz on Friday evening). The menu changes seasonally, but house favorites often include pan-seared fillet of salmon with sautéed shrimp, bell peppers, onions, and tomatoes; grilled marinated leg of lamb with rosemary, mustard, and garlic butter; and roast fillet of monkfish with leek and watercress. Lunch items range from sandwiches and salads to pastas and quiches.

Old Wharf Inn. Foot of Cannon St. ☎ **410/778-3566.** Reservations accepted for parties of 5 or more. Main courses $7.95–$17.95; lunch $2.95–$12.95. AE, MC, V. Mon–Sat 11am–9pm, Sun 10am–9pm. AMERICAN/SEAFOOD.

Locals come here for good value and good views of the Chester River, though the food is less than spectacular. The restaurant has an informal "Old Chesapeake" atmosphere, with captain's chairs, ceiling fans, a row of paned windows overlooking the water, and ships' wheels adapted into lighting fixtures. The menu features Eastern Shore traditions such as fried chicken, Smithfield ham, crab cakes, fried oysters, and a half-dozen kinds of shrimp dishes (from fried and coconut battered to barbecued, stuffed, or Alfredo style). Specials on Tuesday and Thursday nights offer all-you-can-eat steamed shrimp. On Friday there is a prime rib, seafood, and pasta buffet.

4 Chesapeake City

54 miles NE of Baltimore, 40 miles SW of Wilmington, 25 miles NE of Chestertown

Nestled on the sides of the Chesapeake and Delaware (C&D) Canal, halfway between the bays, this village on the northern edge of Maryland's Eastern Shore offers a unique escape from the nearby bustle of the Northern Delaware suburbs. Originally known as Bohemia Village because of its proximity to the Bohemia River, the town dates from the 1780s, but its real birth came with the creation of the C&D Canal in 1804. Its homes still quietly reflect its Victorian heyday, when the canal was privately owned and casino riverboats cruised its placid waters. Now the town and its tiny harbor are a favorite overnight destination for Philadelphia-area recreational boaters, who sail here for relaxation, small-town atmosphere, and a little shopping.

ESSENTIALS

GETTING THERE If you're driving from Easton and other points on the southern Eastern Shore, take Route 301 northeast to Route 213, which leads directly into

Chesapeake City. From I-95 or U.S. Route 40, take the Elkton exit and follow Route 213 south. Of course, you can also sail into town along the canal if you have a launch.

VISITOR INFORMATION　For travel brochures about the Chesapeake City area, contact the **Cecil County Office of Economic Development,** Tourism Department, 129 E. Main St., Room 324, Elkton, MD 21921 (☎ **800/232-4595** or 410/ 996-5300).

GETTING AROUND　Although the downtown area of Chesapeake City lends itself to walking, the best way to see the surrounding sights is by car. There is no public transportation.

ORIENTATION　The C&D Canal divides the city into a north and south side. The main commercial and historic area is on the south side of the canal. It is a very walkable area, with one main street, Bohemia Avenue, where most of the shops and businesses are located. Pick up a copy of "Canal Town," a handy folder with a map, available free in all of the shops and public areas.

WHAT TO SEE & DO

To learn more about the town's focal point, head to the **C&D Canal Museum,** 815 Bethel Rd. (☎ **410/885-5622**). Located on the waterfront at Second Street, it features an enormous waterwheel once used to feed a lock on the canal and a series of exhibits on the canal's history and operation. The museum's grounds now house a reconstructed 30-foot-tall lighthouse (really more like a beacon). The museum is open Monday through Saturday from 8:15am to 4:15pm and closed all federal holidays. Admission is free.

To soak up the ambience of this canal-side city, spend some time in **Pell Gardens,** a grassy setting next to the museum, overlooking Back Creek on Rees Wharf at the end of Bohemia Street. Sit and relax in the gazebo or on one of the many wooden and iron benches.

A good way to get an overview of the surrounding area is to take a 3-hour **horse country tour,** operated by a local agency, Hill Holidays Travel, 103 Bohemia Ave., Chesapeake City, MD 21915 (☎ **800/874-4558** or 410/885-2797). The laid-back tour directors try to accommodate their customers' interests, but sites on the tour always include at least one of the leading horse farms in the area and a short walking tour of Chesapeake City. You might also get to see a 17th-century frontier tobacco plantation and one of the three area's historic churches—St. Augustine, St. Stephens, and Old Bohemia. Tours run from mid-March through October, departing on Tuesday and Thursday at 9am, and on Tuesday, Thursday, and Sunday at 1pm. Prices range from $15 to $20 per person and reservations are required. All tours depart from the Hill Holidays Travel Center. The agency can also arrange for sightseeing cruises on the canal ($5 to $20 per person, depending on the departure time and routing).

SHOPPING

Chesapeake City is a neat little shopping town, especially for arts and crafts.

Back Creek General Store. 100 Bohemia Ave. ☎ **410/885-5377.**

Housed in a historic 1861 building, this shop features a variety of arts and crafts, including throw rugs, pottery, pewter, music boxes, prints, candles, soaps, scents, and books on the Eastern Shore and its birds. Open Monday and Tuesday from 11am to 5pm, Wednesday, Thursday and Sunday from 11am to 8pm, and Friday and Saturday from 11am to 9pm.

Black Swan Antiques. Third and Bohemia aves. ☎ **410/885-5888.**

The best of the local antique stores, the Black Swan isn't large, but it does have some nice furniture and country accessories, as well as a few very fine old tool kits, and, during my visit, a great collection of model sailboats and yachts. Open weekends from noon to 5pm.

Canal Artworks. 17 Bohemia Ave. ☎ **410/885-5083.**

Located in the Riley House, a building dating from 1831 next to the Bayard House, this shop/studio displays paintings of the Chesapeake City area by local artist Jon deVos, who can often be seen at work. Original prints, limited-edition prints, and note cards are for sale. Open Friday, Saturday, and Sunday from 11:30am to 8pm and by appointment.

Maren's. 200 Bohemia Ave. ☎ **410/885-2475.**

Horse-themed jewelry draws many people to this store, as does a wide array of local folk and wildlife art. There is also a Christmas Corner for Yuletide shopping year-round and a Dickens Room for collectors. Open daily from 10am to 5pm or later.

WHERE TO STAY

Blue Max Inn. 300 Bohemia Ave., Chesapeake City, MD 21915. ☎ **410/885-2781.** Fax 410/885-2809. 7 rms. A/C TV TEL. $80–$105 double. DISC, MC, V. Free parking.

Built in 1844, this house was once occupied by author Jack Hunter while he was writing his book *The Blue Max.* True to its name, this house has been furnished with an emphasis on blue-and-white decor, both inside and outside. The bedrooms are modern and large. Guests enjoy use of a cozy parlor with a fireplace, dining room, and first- and second-floor porches overlooking the heart of the historic district. Innkeeper Philip Braeunig Jr. has recently added some pleasant touches to the inn's garden, including a miniature waterfall.

✪ Inn at the Canal. 104 Bohemia Ave., P.O. Box 187, Chesapeake City, MD 21915. ☎ **410/885-5995.** Fax 410/885-3585. 6 rms, 1 suite. A/C TV TEL. $75–$110 double; $130 suite. Rates include breakfast and afternoon refreshments. AE, CB, DC, DISC, MC, V. Free parking.

Situated on Back Creek Basin, a block from the C&D Canal in the heart of the historic district, this three-story Victorian house dates from 1870 and is known locally as the Brady–Rees House. Innkeepers Mary and Al Ioppolo have sought to preserve the house's 19th-century atmosphere by furnishing it with antiques and family heirlooms including a large collection of old baking and cooking implements on the fireplace wall of the kitchen. The guest rooms are individually decorated with antiques and quilts. Half of the bedrooms have views of the water. Guests enjoy use of the turn-of-the-century dining room, guest parlor, and two wicker-filled porches where you can sit and watch the boats breeze by on the canal. In the old milking room of the house, the Ioppolos run a fine little antique store, Inntiques, specializing in restored furniture and tools; inn guests get a discount.

WHERE TO DINE

✪ Bayard House. 11 Bohemia Ave. ☎ **410/885-5040.** Reservations recommended for dinner. Main courses $16.95–$24.95; lunch $8.95–$12.95. AE, DISC, MC, V. Mon–Fri 11:30am–3pm and 5–9pm, Sat 11:30am–3pm and 5–10pm, Sun noon–9pm. AMERICAN.

Few people come to Chesapeake City without stopping for a meal at this highly acclaimed restaurant, perched right beside the canal and considered to be the oldest building in Chesapeake City. It dates from the early 1780s when Samuel Bayard built a manor home on this site. Two dining areas are offered: a glass-enclosed dining room with wide windows overlooking the water and an outdoor canal-side patio fanned by gentle breezes. Featured dishes include tournedos Baltimore (twin petit filet mignons, one topped with a crab cake and the other with a lobster cake, served with Madeira-cream and seafood-champagne sauces) and grilled Jamaican jerk pork loin and chicken (boneless pork and breast of chicken in hot jerk seasoning with a citrus salsa). For us, however, the best part of the dinner was the appetizer—the New Age Crab Cake, a delicious crab cake in a slightly spicy blue-corn breading. It's Eastern Shore meets the Rio Grande.

Schaefer's Canal House. 208 Bank St. ☎ **410/885-2200.** Reservations recommended. Main courses $18–$32; lunch $6–$12; brunch $14.95. AE, MC, V. Mon–Sat 8am–10pm, Sun 8am–9pm; brunch Sun 11am–3pm. AMERICAN.

First opened in 1908 as a general store, this wide-windowed restaurant sits on the north side of the canal facing Chesapeake City's historic district. From June through August, seating is available on the dockside terrace. The menu offers a variety of meat and seafood dishes such as prime rib, breast of capon in lemon-lime champagne sauce, crab cakes, fried shrimp amandine, crab-stuffed flounder, and surf-and-turf, as well as a vegetarian stir-fry. On Thursday night there's a seafood buffet for $18.95.

5 Crisfield & Smith Island

138 miles SE of Baltimore, 54 miles SW of Ocean City, 135 miles S of Wilmington

The small town of Crisfield, on the extreme southern end of the Eastern Shore, was once to Chesapeake Bay seafood what Chicago is to meat packing—that is to say, huge. Millions of oysters came through the town, their empty shells piling and piling to eventually create a new shoreline. Crisfield was the "seafood capital of the world."

Since then, economic winds have changed, and like many once great industrial towns Crisfield has shrunk considerably. However, the heart of the town is still seafood. Every day its plants ship out their daily harvest of crabs and oysters to cities around the world. The town's harbor and seafood processing area are now built almost entirely on the remains of those oyster shells of the past—its treeless alleys sport crumbling shell where dirt would normally be. When you come today to Crisfield or its nearby neighbor Smith Island, you come for two reasons: to learn about the lives of the watermen and the seafood industry, and to eat the seafood.

ESSENTIALS

GETTING THERE   Crisfield is accessible by car via Routes 413 and 13.

VISITOR INFORMATION   For brochures, maps, and all sorts of helpful information about Crisfield and the surrounding countryside, contact the **Somerset County Tourism Office,** 11440 Ocean Hwy. (Route 13), P.O. Box 243, Princess Anne, MD 21853 (☎ 800/521-9189 or 410/651-2968); or the **Crisfield Chamber of Commerce,** J. Millard Tawes Museum, Somers Cove Marina, P.O. Box 292, Crisfield, MD 21817 (☎ **800/782-3913** or 410/968-2500). In Crisfield, you can stop by the chamber office and museum for brochures and information from the helpful staff.

SPECIAL EVENTS   Crisfield's two biggest events in order of significance are the ✪ **National Hard Crab Derby and Fair** and the **J. Millard Tawes Crab and Clam Bake** (for information on both events contact the Crisfield Chamber of Commerce, above). The Hard Crab Derby and Fair is a 3-day event, with a crab-cooking contest, crab-picking contest, country music, and of course the hard crab race. It's held Labor Day weekend every year, and admission is $3. Make hotel reservations well in advance. The Crab and Clam Bake, held annually from 1 to 5pm on the third Wednesday in July, is an outdoor all-you-can-eat affair featuring crabs, clams, fish, corn on the cob, and watermelon, not to mention a lot of local politicians; the cost is usually around $30 per person.

WHAT TO SEE & DO

The **J. Millard Tawes Museum,** 3 Ninth St. (☎ **410/968-2501**), on the Somers Cove Marina, was founded in 1982 to honor a Crisfield-born former governor of Maryland. It also currently houses the chamber of commerce offices. The exhibits here will give you useful background about the history of Crisfield and the development of the city's seafood industry. The museum offers an escorted **walking tour** of the port, which is really the best way to see the town. The tour takes you into the Metompkin Bay Oyster Co. seafood processing area, where you'll see soft-shell crabs in pealing bins and hundreds of pounds of hard-shell crabs being picked by lightning-fast workers. The museum also plans to begin offering a minibus tour in 1999 that will take visitors past the homes of former seafood barons and former Maryland governor J. Millard Tawes and the old workshop of the Ward brothers, local master carvers. Open daily May through October from 9am to 4:30pm and Monday through Friday November through April from 9am to 4:30pm. Admission to the museum is $1 for adults and 50¢ for children. The walking tour costs $2.50 for adults; it's free for children under 12.

About 15 miles north of Crisfield on Route 13 is **Princess Anne,** a well-preserved colonial town created in 1733. Its highlight is the **Teackle Mansion** (☎ **410/651-1705**), built in 1801 and patterned after a Scottish manor house. This was the residence of Littleton Dennis Teackle, an associate of Thomas Jefferson and one of the principal transoceanic shipping magnates of the 18th century. He is also credited with establishing Maryland's first public school system and the first public commercial bank on the American continent. With two entrances, one fronting the Manokin River (which is now obscured by trees) and one facing the town, this grand house measures nearly 200 feet in length and is symmetrically balanced throughout. Though the mansion has lately suffered through some financial hard times and could use a few repairs and new paint on its shutters, it is still quite a sight to see. It's open for guided tours year-round on Sunday from 2 to 4pm and from March to mid-December also on Wednesday from 1 to 3pm and Saturday from 11am to 3pm. Some of the things you'll see are elaborate plaster ceilings, mirrored windows, a 7-foot fireplace, a beehive oven, American Chippendale furniture, Della Robbia (fruit-designed) ceilings, a Tudor–Gothic pipe organ, an 1806 silk world map, and a 1712 family Bible. The admission and tour charge is $2 per person. For more information call ☎ **410/651-3020** or 410/651-2238.

OUTDOOR ACTIVITIES

The **Somers Cove Marina,** 715 Broadway, Crisfield (☎ **410/968-0925**), a $30 million development built on the site of a farm started in 1663 by Benjamin Somers, is one of the largest facilities of its kind in Maryland. The marina is ultramodern, able to accommodate all types of vessels, from 10 feet to 150 feet. There are boat ramps, deluxe tiled showers, a laundry room, a swimming pool, boat storage, electricity and water, a fuel dock, and 485 boat slips.

Head boats leave from the marina and from the nearby town dock each day, taking passengers on **fishing trips** in pursuit of flounder, trout, spot, drum, and blues. For further information, walk along the waterfront and talk with the various boatmen on duty or call any of the following: **Capt. Curtis Johns** (☎ **410/623-2035**);

Capt. Joe Asanovich (☎ 410/957-2562); Capt. George Ray and Sons (☎ 410/ 968-3307, 410/827-4592, or 410/643-8964); Capt. Keith Ward (☎ 800/ 791-1470 or 410/968-0074); and Capt. Lionel Daugherty (☎ 410/968-0947). Prices start at around $30 per person.

Unique **Janes Island State Park,** 26280 Alfred Lawson Dr., Crisfield, MD 21817 (☎ 410/968-1565), gives nature lovers and outdoor enthusiasts a place to **hike, camp, canoe,** and **powerboat.** Sitting on the edge of the Tangier Sound, Janes Island has excellent scenery, beautiful sunsets, and a winding canoe/boat trail, the only way to see the island portion of the park. The park rents canoes and rowboats for $3.15 per hour or $15.75 per day and small motorboats for $8.40 per hour.

SHOPPING

Besides crab, this area's other claim to fame is the **Carvel Hall Factory Outlet,** Route 413, Crisfield (☎ 410/968-0500). Carvel Hall was started in 1895 when a young blacksmith hammered out his first seafood-harvesting tools on a borrowed anvil. Today discounts of up to 50% are given on brand-name cutlery, made entirely in this Crisfield plant, plus hundreds of other nationally known gift items such as glassware, pewter, sterling silver, plated hollowware, brass, and crystal. Open daily from 10am to 6pm (closed major holidays).

WHERE TO STAY

Choosing where to stay is easy in Crisfield. There are only three motels in town, all in the moderate category with basic accommodations. The best choice, however, is a little ways out of town at a nearby country inn in Princess Anne.

Paddlewheel Motel. 701 W. Main St., Crisfield, MD 21817. ☎ **410/968-2220.** Fax 410/ 425-2771. 19 rms. A/C TV. $35–$80 double. MC, V. Free parking.

Located in the heart of town, this modern two-story motel is within walking distance of the City Dock and waterfront. It offers rooms equipped with two double beds and standard furnishings. A continental breakfast is provided. The Paddlewheel is open April through December.

Pines Motel. N. Somerset Ave., P.O. Box 106, Crisfield, MD 21817. ☎ **410/968-0900.** 40 rms. A/C TV. $45–$80 double. No credit cards. Free parking.

For more than 30 years, this motel has offered fine lodging in a quiet residential setting amid tall pine trees. The modern ground-level units all have contemporary furnishings, two double beds, wall-to-wall carpeting, and views of the adjacent outdoor swimming pool and picnic area. Twelve rooms with kitchenettes are available for $15 extra. Open year-round.

Somers Cove Motel. R.R. Norris Dr., P.O. Box 387, Crisfield, MD 21817. ☎ **800/827-6637** or 410/968-1900. 40 rms. A/C TV TEL. $45–$80 double. MC, V.

Views of the water add to the setting of this modern two-story facility, opened in 1979. The motel offers rooms with one or two double beds; each room also has a balcony or patio. Guest amenities include an outdoor heated swimming pool, patios, picnic tables, barbecue grills, boat-docking facilities, and ramps. Open year-round. Seven rooms with kitchenettes are available for $10 extra per room.

✪ **Waterloo Country Inn.** 28822 Mt. Vernon Rd., Princess Anne, MD 21853. ☎ **410/ 651-0883.** Fax 410/651-5592. 3 rms, 2 suites. A/C TV TEL. Apr to mid-Oct $125–$225 double; mid-Oct to Dec $105–$205 double. Rates include breakfast. AE, MC, V. Free parking.

The Waterloo Country Inn, set in a dignified brick manor house built in the Federal style in 1775, is easily one of the most elegant and charming accommodations on the Delmarva Peninsula. Surrounded by farmland and overlooking a tidal pond on Monie Creek near Princess Anne, this small inn's amenities are gracious and numerous. Most of the rooms have dark hardwood floors and are decorated with antiques and sophisticated artwork. All rooms have full baths. The Chesapeake Suite on the third floor features a Jacuzzi for two. The Manokin Room on the first floor is fully wheelchair accessible. Dinner can be arranged for guests—locals claim that the Waterloo offers the best fine dining in the area. Bicycles and canoes are available for exploring the quiet country roads as well as the gentle waters of the Monie. Situated about 30 minutes from Crisfield, the Waterloo is a great place from which to stage a visit to Crisfield, Salisbury, or the surrounding wildlife areas. However, if you're looking for a little seclusion, there is no reason to leave Waterloo and Princess Anne at all.

WHERE TO DINE

The focus of attention here is seafood and plenty of it. This is the place to have your fill of crab, from crab omelets for breakfast, to crab soup and crab sandwiches for lunch, to crab cooked in a dozen different ways for dinner. Most restaurants in town serve an inexpensive breakfast starting between 5:30 and 6am to cater to the resident and visiting fishermen.

Original Captain's Galley. 1021 W. Main St. ☎ **410/968-3313.** Reservations recommended for dinner. Main courses $6.95–$18.95; lunch $2.95–$7.95. MC, V. Summer daily 8am–11pm; winter daily 11am–9pm. SEAFOOD.

Overlooking the City Dock, this contemporary-style, wide-windowed restaurant is the ideal place to watch the boats moving in and out of the harbor. The dinner entrees include crab cakes, crab imperial, crab au gratin, and a gargantuan "seafood feast" (soft crab, crab cake, fish fillet, scallops, shrimp, and oysters), as well as steaks and fried chicken. Lunch choices are mainly sandwiches, such as crab cake, oyster fritter, crab imperial, soft crab, shrimp or tuna salad, and assorted meats.

✪ **Watermen's Inn.** Ninth and Main sts. ☎ **410/968-2119.** Reservations recommended for dinner. Main courses $7.95–$18.95; lunch $2.95–$8.95. AE, DISC, MC, V. Tues–Thurs 11am–9pm, Fri–Sat 11am–10pm, Sun 8am–9pm. AMERICAN.

Although this eatery does not boast water views, the food here is the prime attraction—a little out of the ordinary, with an ever-changing menu of cooked-to-order dishes. Dinnertime choices focus on baked stuffed jumbo soft crabs, crab cakes, baked stuffed flounder, jumbo fantail shrimp, crab au gratin, fried chicken, imported baby-back ribs, charbroiled steaks, vegetarian plates, and a signature cream of crab soup.

AN EXCURSION TO SMITH ISLAND

Located 13 miles west of Crisfield in the midst of Chesapeake Bay's Tangier Sound, Smith Island is Maryland's only inhabited offshore island. In many ways, it is a world set apart—there are no sidewalks, beaches, convenience stores, boat rentals, movie theaters, liquor stores, bars, fast-food chains, boutiques, Laundromats, or taxi cabs. The people make their living primarily from the sea, by crabbing and oystering.

Many Smith Islanders are the direct descendants of British colonists who first settled the island in the early 1700s. To this day, because of their separation from the mainland, they speak with a distinctive accent and speech pattern, said by some to be a holdover of the Elizabethan/Cornwall dialect. Lately the Smith Island way of life has been somewhat threatened by "summer people," who buy up family homesteads to be used as vacation homes. Despite this, visitors who take the lovely boat trip across the Tangier Sound are always surprised by the tranquillity of this island.

ESSENTIALS

GETTING THERE   Follow the directions above to Crisfield. From Crisfield you must either take one of the passenger ferryboats that depart from the City Dock or from Somers Cove Marina or take your own boat.

Regardless of which ferryboat you take, the trip takes approximately 35 minutes to 1 hour, depending on the route and time of year. The price of the trip averages from $20 to $25 round-trip. All boats usually depart Crisfield around noon and return from the island around 5pm. The *Captain Tyler II* departs from the Somers Cove Marina and docks in Ewell; it offers the most complete touring package, with an optional family-style lunch at the Bayside Inn in Ewell and a short narrated bus tour. Contact **Capt. Alan Tyler** (☎ **410/425-2771**) for exact schedules and reservations. Captain Tyler also operates ferry service from Point Lookout State Park in Southern Maryland. See chapter 6 for details.

Capt. Otis Ray Tyler (☎ **410/968-3206**) operates the *Island Belle II* and the *Island Princess,* which depart from the City Dock and dock in Ewell. His trip also offers an optional family-style lunch at the Harbor Side Restaurant. To catch a ferry to someplace on Smith Island besides Ewell, you have to travel with **Capts. Terry and Larry Laird** (☎ **410/425-5931** or 410/425-4471) on the *Captain Jason I* or *II.* Both boats depart from the City Dock and dock at Ewell and Tylerton (in the summer). In addition to these organized ferries, if you're feeling adventurous, you can usually stroll by the City Dock, talk to the captains there, and arrange transportation to and from the island with one of the watermen, usually for a little less than the ferryboats charge.

If you bring your own boat, be warned, there is no marina. The only gas dock is at the Smith Island Harbor in Ewell, open 8am to 5pm Monday through Saturday. Overnight docking is available for boats with a draft of under 3 feet. Contact Ruke's Store (☎ **410/425-2311**) or Charlie's Store (☎ **410/425-2111**). Before you set out, be sure to contact the **Somerset County Tourism Office** (☎ **800/521-9189**), or talk to some watermen at the City Dock, for directions into the harbor and information on water depth and tides.

VISITOR INFORMATION   You can pick up information about Smith Island in Crisfield at the **Crisfield Chamber of Commerce,** J. Millard Tawes Museum, Somers Cove Marina, P.O. Box 292, Crisfield, MD 21817 (☎ **800/782-3913** or 410/968-2500). Before your trip you can also contact the **Somerset County Tourism Office** (☎ **800/521-9189**), which publishes a very useful self-guided walking tour pamphlet with information on how to get to the island, tips on how to be a good visitor, and maps of each of the three towns and their points of interest.

Once you are on the island, be sure to stop by the new **Smith Island Center** (☎ **410/425-3351**) in Ewell for helpful information, displays, and a video giving the historical background on the island and its people (not to mention an air-conditioned place to avoid the summer heat). The center is open April through October, Thursday through Sunday from 11am to 4pm, and it's located on Smith Island Road, just down the road from the County Dock (where you will be dropped off if you take one of the ferries to the island) and the Bayside Inn.

GETTING AROUND   Unless you purchase a package that includes a bus tour of the island with your boat trip over, the only way to get around the island is on foot or on your own bicycle. No car rentals or bike rentals are available on the island and the ferries are passenger only, so you can't bring your car. You can, however, bring bicycles on the ferry.

ORIENTATION There are three towns on Smith Island, each with a working harbor. The island's largest town is **Ewell**, sometimes referred to as the "capital" of Smith Island. It is the most visited destination and home of the majority of the island's seafood-packing houses; it is still tiny. The other two towns are **Rhodes Point**, situated a mile south of Ewell and the island's center for boat repair, and **Tylerton**, Smith Island's most remote town (accessible only by boat from Ewell and Crisfield) and home to some of its more interesting architecture.

PREPARING FOR THE VISIT

Spending an afternoon on Smith Island can be an interesting but daunting experience. The idea of Smith Island as a quaint island community, with a deep history and strong ties to the sea, isolated from all the bustle of modern life on the mainland, is certainly appealing. But there are some realities visitors must keep in mind if they are going to have an enjoyable visit. First of all, even Ewell, the "capital" of Smith Island, is, as we said before, tiny. There are few amenities and only two small stores. In the summer, the heat and the insects—mosquitoes and biting flies—are significant problems. Luckily the new Smith Island Center provides rest rooms, water, and an air-conditioned respite from heat and insects. But, still, come prepared with water, sunscreen, insect repellent (the locals suggest Avon's Skin-So-Soft), lightweight clothing, and a hat.

Second, when you arrive on the island you may find yourself wondering why you came at all because, well, the Smith Island experience can be a bit unnerving. The Smith Islanders are friendly but a bit aloof, and they keep tight control over the tourist trade. All the ferries arrive and depart at the same time, so if you take one of them, you will probably be arriving with 30 or 40 other tourists (or more). You will all have lunch together, usually seated at large tables with 10 or 12 of your fellow passengers; you will all stroll the streets of Ewell at the same time; and then you will all leave, thus interrupting the lives of the islanders for an intentionally short amount of time each afternoon.

That said, let us remind you why you came here: to see exactly what an isolated, small island community is like. So come prepared, both physically and mentally, and you should have an enjoyable quiet afternoon in an intriguing setting.

SEEING THE ISLAND

In Ewell, be sure to stop by the Smith Island Visitor Center. It's a great place to learn about Smith Island history and culture and to brush up on island lingo. (That way when you hear an islander say, "She ain't pretty none, she's ugly," you'll know the speaker is actually paying the lass in question a compliment.) When you leave the visitor center, take a right on Caleb Jones Road and you'll soon come to the Middleton House, a former private residence now used as the interpretive center and headquarters for the Martin National Wildlife Refuge. The refuge is just across the narrow strait to the north of Smith Island, but it is not open to the public. The headquarters is seldom staffed and there is not much to see here, but you can just stroll in and look at the displays on the wildlife found in the refuge.

Other than the visitor center and the refuge headquarters, there's very little to do except meander through the streets by the islanders' homes, churches, and public buildings, meet and talk with the locals, and take in the peaceful environment. Before you catch the boat home, try to get a piece of Smith Island cake. If you don't have lunch at Bayside Inn or Harbor Side Restaurant, stop by Ruke's Store, across from the Smith Island Visitor Center.

8 Maryland's Atlantic Coast

aryland has over 3,000 miles of shoreline, but in summer it seems the only important ones are the 15 or so miles of accessible beach along the Atlantic coast, at least judging by the number of people crossing the Bay Bridge to get there. Indeed, if you decide to visit Ocean City (O.C. as the natives call it) any summer weekend, you may be joining what feels like the entire population of the Baltimore/Washington metro area.

The Atlantic shoreline is actually about 35 miles long and consists of two barrier islands—Ocean City on the north and Assateague Island on the south—which together offer visitors two of the most diametrically opposed beach scenes on the planet. Ocean City, a bustling tourist mecca, is 10 miles of beach lined with high-rise hotels, condos, restaurants, bars, minigolf courses, and even a few amusement parks. The 10-lane Coastal Highway runs the length of the island and across the Delaware border, giving visitors access to every nook and cranny of beach. From the pier on the southern tip of O.C., past the Ferris wheel and roller coaster, you can see across the narrow strait to Assateague, where wild ponies and sica deer have the run of the island and the humans who visit are generally restricted to about a 4-mile stretch of beach. The only accommodations here are state-run campsites, the road ends at the last site, and there's not so much as a gas station on the island.

So whether you enjoy wild beaches or wild beach parties, you're sure to find what you're looking for on one of these two islands. If, however, you prefer a more moderate beach setting, quiet but with all the modern conveniences, travel up the coast to Delaware's resorts, and check out chapter 13, "The Delaware Beaches."

1 The Great Outdoors on the Atlantic Coast

Like all beach towns, Ocean City is thought of as a place to, well, lie around on the beach and maybe eat some fresh seafood. But the fact is, the coastal region offers tons of ways to commune with nature, besides having dinner with 20 or 30 of your favorite crustaceans.

Opportunities for anglers abound; you can fish from just about anywhere—fishing piers, the beach, small crafts, charter boats, and even from the Route 50 bridge. Catch varies with the season, but croaker, spot, and flounder run the bay most of the summer and into early fall. Shark fishing in the Atlantic picks up in May and peaks in mid-June, followed by tuna, which peak in mid-July and run through fall. White marlin start roaming the waters by late July. Rockfish have seen a resurgence in recent years, and bluefish, sea trout, and tautog are plentiful throughout the season.

All the charter fishing boats—and there are many—operate out of O.C, so if you're looking for offshore big-game fishing, check out the Ocean City marinas. Surf fishing is best at Assateague, simply because you don't have to compete with as many beachgoers for a patch of sand and there are very few restrictions on when and where you can fish. Assateague also has good facilities for shoreline crabbing and clamming, especially if you're taking the whole family. The facility at Old Ferry Landing even has crabs painted on the boardwalk area to indicate the legal size limit.

Assateague and the waters off the island offer some interesting options for the adventuresome traveler. The Maryland end of Chincoteague Bay is ideal for canoeing and sea kayaking. There are even some canoe-in backcountry campsites on the bayside of the island. If you prefer to stay on dry land, you can explore the "untamed" sections of the island—that is, those sections not accessible by car—in an off-road vehicle (ORV). ORV trails run along the beach from the national park campground to the Virginia border. Backcountry camping is available on the oceanside of the island also, and this is a great way for surf fishermen to really get away from the beach crowds.

Golf courses have been popping up all over the coastal region (inland, not actually on the islands). So O.C. has built quite a name for itself as a haven for golfers. At least half a dozen area courses welcome visitors and many hotels offer golf packages. Ocean City Golf Getaway (☎ **800/4-OC-GOLF**) can make arrangements and schedule tee times for visitors at most courses.

Those are the highlights of the outdoor activities on Maryland's Atlantic coast, but remember that Delaware's beaches are quite close and offer a lot of the same and a few different or better outdoor options. Rehoboth Bay is a great place for birding and sea kayaking as well as fishing, and there are better, safer bike routes across the border. So look over chapter 13 before you set out.

2 Ocean City

144 miles SE of Baltimore, 153 miles W of Washington, D.C., 27 miles S of Dewey Beach

The narrow peninsula known as Ocean City is Maryland's star attraction along the Atlantic. A 10-mile strip of white sandy beach, Ocean City is a lively and well-developed vacationland, sandwiched between the "quiet" Delaware resorts of Fenwick Island and Bethany Beach to the north and the equally tranquil Assateague Island to the south.

In addition to its seafront side to the east, Ocean City is rimmed on its west by a series of picturesque bays with memorable names like Assawoman, Montego, Isle of Wight, and Sinepuxent. Ocean City's wide expanse of free beach is complemented by a 3-mile-long boardwalk lined with hotels, restaurants, shops, and amusements. It's no wonder that the city's small resident population of 7,500 easily swells to more than 250,000 on July and August weekends.

The beach itself has been developed to a 145-block length. The lower section, which was the original Ocean City, is home to the boardwalk, the amusement parks, and most of the older hotels. The upper section, from about 40th Street to 145th Street, is dominated by modern motels and rows of towering condominiums.

ESSENTIALS
GETTING THERE

From the west, use Route 50. Two bridges connect Ocean City to the mainland; use the Route 50 bridge, which enters the city near First Street, for addresses south of 45th Street; use the Route 90 bridge, which enters the city at 62nd Street, for addresses north of 45th. From the Delaware resorts to the north, follow Route 1 into Ocean City. From farther north, take either Route 13 or Route 113 to Route 50. From points south, take Route 13 to Route 113 north to Route 50.

The **Salisbury/Ocean City Regional Airport** (☎ 410/548-4827), 30 minutes west of Ocean City, off Walston Switch Road, handles regularly scheduled commuter flights to and from Baltimore, Washington, and Philadelphia via **US Airways Express** (☎ 800/428-4322). **Airport Chauffeur** (☎ 410/548-9075) offers car service from the airport to anywhere in Ocean City for a flat rate of $40. Private planes can fly into **Ocean City Municipal Airport** (☎ 410/213-2471), located 3 miles west of town off Route 611.

Carolina Trailways has daily services into Ocean City from points north and south, with nonstop buses from Baltimore, Washington, D.C., and Salisbury. All buses stop at the station at Second Street and Philadelphia Avenue (☎ 410/289-9307).

VISITOR INFORMATION

Ocean City has a very active and enthusiastic **Visitors Information Center** that stocks all kinds of helpful information, maps, and brochures. It is located right in the heart of town in the **Ocean City Convention and Visitors Bureau,** 4001 Coastal Hwy., between 39th and 41st streets, Ocean City, MD 21842 (☎ 800/OC-OCEAN or 410/289-8181), and is open daily all year, with extended evening hours on summer weekends. If you're heading into town from Route 50, stop at the **Ocean City Chamber of Commerce Information Center** at the intersection of Route 707 and Route 50 just before crossing the bridge into Ocean City. It's a great place to pick up information and brochures as well as discount coupons for everything from restaurants and shops to miniature golf and biplane rides.

GETTING AROUND

BY BUS   During peak season, when parking can be difficult, the bus is the fastest and most convenient way to get around. Buses run 24 hours a day year-round and follow one route from the Delaware border south along Coastal Highway (Route 1) to South Division Street and return north along Baltimore Street and Coastal Highway. In the summer months, buses run every 10 minutes; from October 20 through Memorial Day they run every half hour. The fare is $1 for a 24-hour period and exact change is required. For more information, contact the **Ocean City Municipal Bus Service,** 66th Street, bay side (☎ 410/723-1607).

BY BOARDWALK TRAIN   Starting at South First Street, a tram-type train runs along the 3-mile boardwalk every 20 minutes up to 27th Street. The trip lasts about a half hour and is an ideal way to familiarize yourself with the hotels, restaurants, and shops along the boardwalk. You can disembark at any point by raising your hand to signal the conductor. The fare is $1.50, payable as you board the train at the starting point. If there is room, the tram will also pick up new passengers along the route, but the fare remains the same. The train runs weekends from Easter through the first weekend of October and daily from Labor Day until Sunfest (the third weekend in September).

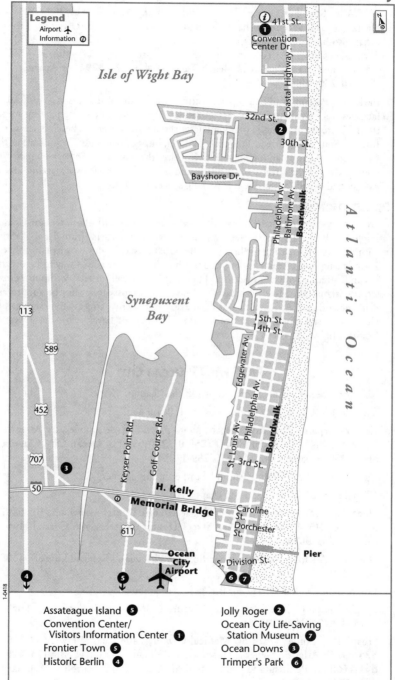

Legend
Airport ✈
Information ⓘ

Isle of Wight Bay

Atlantic Ocean

Synepuxent Bay

ⓘ 41st St.
❶ Convention Center Dr.

32nd St.
❷ 30th St.

Coastal Highway

Bayshore Dr.

Philadelphia Av.
Baltimore Av.
Boardwalk

15th St.
14th St.

Edgewater Av.
Philadelphia Av.

St. Louis Av.
Philadelphia Av.
3rd St.

Boardwalk

113
589
452
707
50 ❸

Keyser Point Rd.
Golf Course Rd.

H. Kelly
ⓘ Memorial Bridge

611

Caroline St.
Dorchester St.

Ocean City Airport ✈

S. Division St.
❻ ❼

Pier

1-0418
❹ ↓
❺ ↓

Assateague Island ❺	Jolly Roger ❷
Convention Center/ Visitors Information Center ❶	Ocean City Life-Saving Station Museum ❼
Frontier Town ❺	Ocean Downs ❸
Historic Berlin ❹	Trimper's Park ❻

BY CAR Rental cars are available at both airports. **Avis** (☎ **410/289-6121**) and **Hertz** (☎ **410/546-4800**) have offices at Salisbury/Ocean City Regional Airport. Hertz also has an office at Ocean City Municipal Airport (☎ **410/213-2400**). In downtown Ocean City contact **Thrifty,** 5601 Coastal Hwy. (☎ **410/524-4222**).

If you need a taxi, call **AAA Beach Taxi** (☎ **410/524-8294**) or **Atlantic Taxi** (☎ **410/250-5300**).

Parking Parking is difficult, particularly at the height of the season. Most public facilities, such as shopping centers and restaurants, offer ample free parking to patrons. There are also public parking lots in certain areas near the beach, such as the Inlet on South First Street. Free daily parking, but not overnight, is available at the Convention Center parking lot at 39th Street. Otherwise, you can park by meter 24 hours a day on the streets. Most hotels and motels have their own parking lots or garages and usually allow one free parking space per room.

ORIENTATION

Ocean City stretches for 10 miles, with one main north–south thoroughfare, Coastal Highway (Route 1). Cross streets are designated by numbers (from 1st to 145th), with numbers decreasing to the south. Because Coastal Highway runs not only the 10-mile length of Ocean City but also north into Delaware all the way to Lewes and beyond, street addresses on Coastal Highway are virtually useless without a cross-street designation. Most businesses will give you a cross street, but be sure to ask if it's not offered. Attractions and businesses on the cross streets are designated as either oceanside, for those east of Coastal Highway, or bayside, for those west of Coastal Highway.

FAST FACTS: Ocean City

Airports See "Getting There," earlier in this chapter.

Area Code Ocean City's area codes are 410 and 443.

Camera Repair For camera repair, photo processing, or supplies, try **Atlantic Color Lab,** 11511 Coastal Hwy. (☎ **410/723-4687**); or **Ocean City Camera Shop,** 3308 Coastal Hwy. (☎ **410/289-1135**).

Car Rentals See "Getting Around," earlier in this chapter.

Climate See "When to Go," in chapter 2.

Dentists Emergency work is provided at **Atlantic Dental Associates,** 105 58th St. (☎ **410/524-0500**); or **43rd Street Dental Center,** 4306 Coastal Hwy. (☎ **410/289-8828**).

Doctors Ask for a recommendation from the **Physician's Referral Line** (☎ **410/543-7090**).

Emergencies Dial ☎ **911** for fire, police, or ambulance.

Eyeglass Repair The local choice is **Accurate Optical,** 94th and Coastal Highway (☎ **410/524-0220**).

Hospitals Contact **75th St. Medical Center,** 7408 Coastal Hwy. (☎ **410/524-0075**); **Atlantic General Hospital,** 9733 Hathaway Dr., Berlin (☎ **410/641-1100**); or **Peninsula Regional Medical Center,** 100 E. Carroll St., Salisbury (☎ **410/546-6400**).

Information See "Visitor Information," earlier in this chapter.

Library   The Ocean City branch of the **Worcester County Library** is at 14th Street and Philadelphia Avenue (☎ **410/289-7297**).

Newspapers/Magazines   The *Daily Times* is the daily newspaper of Ocean City. The *Baltimore Sun* publishes "O.C. Tab," a supplement covering Ocean City events, weekly from April through October and on the first Sunday of each month during the rest of the year.

Pharmacies   Try **Bailey's,** 8th Street and Philadelphia Avenue (☎ **410/289-8191**); or **CVS Pharmacy,** 11905 Coastal Hwy. at 120th Street (☎ **410/524-5101**).

Police   Dial ☎ **911** or **410/641-3101** for state police or ☎ **410/289-7556** for beach patrol.

Post Office   The main post office is at 5th Street and Philadelphia Avenue (☎ **410/289-7819**). On the north end of town, the office is located at 120th and Montego Bay (☎ **410/524-6039**).

Radio   The local radio stations include WOCQ-104 FM and WKHI-99.9 FM for general programming, and WETT-96 FM for rock.

Taxes   The state sales tax is 5%; the county tax is 3%.

Taxis   See "Getting Around," earlier in this chapter.

Transit Information   Dial ☎ **410/723-1607.**

Weather   Dial ☎ **410/742-8400.**

EXPLORING OCEAN CITY
MUSEUMS & ATTRACTIONS

Ocean City Life-Saving Station Museum. Boardwalk at the Inlet (P.O. Box 603). ☎ **410/ 289-4991.** Admission $2 adults, $1 under age 12. June–Sept daily 11am–10pm, May and Oct daily 11am–4pm, Nov–Apr Sat–Sun noon–4pm.

Perched on the southern tip of the boardwalk in a meticulously restored 1891 life-saving station, this museum focuses on the history of the U.S. Life-Saving Service in Maryland, Delaware, and Virginia and includes some rare life-saving artifacts, including a life car and a restored surf rescue boat. In addition, there are displays of dollhouse models depicting Ocean City in its early years; a pictorial history of the significant hurricanes and storms that have hit the mid-Atlantic coast; saltwater aquariums with indigenous sea life; a mermaid exhibit; and a unique collection of sands from around the world.

✪ Ward Museum of Wildfowl Art. 909 S. Schumaker Dr. Salisbury, MD 21801. ☎ **410/ 742-4988.** Admission $7 adults, $5 seniors, $3 students; Sunday $8.50 family. Mon–Sat 10am–5pm, Sun noon–5pm. From Rte. 50 turn onto Rte. 13 south; turn left onto College Ave., which will veer left and become Beaglin Park Dr.; the museum is on the right.

Named for Lem and Steve Ward, the brothers from Crisfield who turned decoy carving into an art form, this museum houses the world's largest collection of contemporary and classic wildfowl art. The building sits on the edge of Shumaker Pond in the midst of a wildfowl sanctuary and habitat, so the flock of resident Canada geese and ducks will set the stage for your visit. The newly constructed 30,000-square-foot structure houses works of the Ward brothers as well as several galleries tracing the history of decoy making, from Native American reed figures to the most recent winners of the Ward World Championship Carving Competition, held each spring in Ocean City. Frankly, most of the works are just amazing. Be sure to ask a member of the knowledgeable staff to show you the difference between those that use inserted feathers and those made of solid wood; it will bring some of the works into an entirely new light. If you're visiting for an extended time, the museum has regularly scheduled programs for children and workshops on carving for adults. Even the gift shop is exceptional, with everything from fishing gear to luggage, as well as the usual gift sundries.

Wheels of Yesterday. 12708 Ocean Gateway (Rte. 50). ☎ **410/213-7329.** Admission $4. June–Sept daily 9am–9pm, Oct–May 9am–5pm. Take the Rte. 50 bridge out of Ocean City. Museum is on the left, across from the shopping outlets.

Car enthusiasts will enjoy strolling through this new museum, founded in spring 1997. Curator Jack Jarvis will lead you through the collection of more than 30 classic cars and exhibits, most of which are part of the private collection of Granville D. Trimper, owner of many of the rides and amusements at Ocean City's pier. Favorites include a 1928 seven-passenger Lincoln, several Model T Fords, "Jack Benny's" Overland, a 1934 race car, a Model T fire engine complete with Dalmatian and firefighter, and a replica of a 1950s service station.

ESPECIALLY FOR KIDS: AMUSEMENT PARKS, MINIATURE GOLF & WATER SLIDES

Ocean City claims to be the number one family resort on the East Coast and is home to several amusement parks and child-oriented activities. **Trimper's Rides and Amusement Park,** on the Boardwalk near the Inlet, between South Division and South First streets (☎ **410/289-8617**), was established in 1887 and is the granddaddy of Ocean City's amusement areas. It has more than 100 rides and attractions for the whole family, including a water flume and a 1902 merry-go-round with all hand-carved animals. Most rides average $1.50, but a wristband, costing $9.50, allows unlimited rides between noon and 6pm on weekends and 1 and 6pm on weekdays. The park is open daily, May through September, from noon or 1pm to midnight, and weekends from February to April and October to November. Weekend hours vary outside the summer season.

Jolly Roger, 30th Street and Coastal Highway (☎ **410/289-3477**), is home to **SpeedWorld,** the largest go-kart racing complex of its kind in the United States, as well as two 18-hole miniature golf courses, a water park, and more than 30 rides and other attractions. The go-kart tracks have varying minimum height requirements for children. Each attraction is individually priced. SpeedWorld go-kart rides cost from $3.50 to $5; miniature golf is $4.50 to $5; the water park is $15 per half day or $21 a day; and other individual rides are $1.20 to $2.40 each. The entire park is open daily Memorial Day through Labor Day; SpeedWorld is open noon to midnight; park rides run from 2pm to midnight; the minigolf is open 10am to midnight. SpeedWorld and the miniature golf courses are also open March through May and September through November, with reduced hours.

Pier Rides, on the Pier near the Inlet (☎ **410/289-3031**), is home to Ocean City's largest Ferris wheel and more than 50 other rides and attractions including a water park and fishing pier. All rides and attractions are individually priced. Tickets are priced at 30¢, and each ride requires four to nine tickets to enter. Pier Rides is open May through September 1 from noon to midnight on weekends and from 1pm to midnight on weekdays. It's also open weekends in September and from Easter until May; hours vary, so call ahead.

SHOPPING THE OUTLETS & THE BOARDWALK

The shopping in Ocean City may not be high class—you won't find many one-of-a-kind antiques, art, or jewelry—but it certainly is, well, big. With the shop-lined

Minigolf Mania

Ocean City may have the highest concentration of minigolf courses of any barrier island on earth. Here's a rundown of the four best courses on the island:

Old Pro Underwater Golf, 68th Street and Coastal Highway. There are eight different Old Pro Golf courses at four locations on Ocean City. All of them are good; two made our best list. Underwater Golf is the newest of the Old Pro courses and for our money the best minigolf in O.C. Although it's not actually under water, the course is under roof, entirely enclosed in a hangarlike barn that makes it one of the most fun places to be in O.C. when it's raining. As if this weren't enough, the wonderful sets and props include a sunken submarine that you play in and on and a hanging plaster killer whale. The holes, while not always difficult, are well thought out and fun; most include hills and curves, and many include shoots that drop your ball into (sometimes easy, sometimes not so easy) locations on lower greens. Large windows on one side of the barn open to let in a cool breeze.

Garden of Eden Miniature Golf, 18th Street and Coastal Highway. If you're looking for a slightly more challenging course in a slightly less childish setting, give Garden of Eden a try. There are no giant plaster whales or gorillas here, just a man-made waterfall and pond, and well-kept flowers and shrubbery surrounding a fun and interesting brick-lined course. Many holes offer more than one route to the cup, some involving chutes and one a loop. So put on your thinking cap and tee up.

Jungle Golf, next to Jolly Roger Park, 30th Street and Coastal Highway. Maybe you like fake animals on your golf course; if you do, this one's for you. Plastic lions and a rhinoceros look on as you negotiate 18 holes that wrap around and climb the sides of a series of man-made waterfalls. Although this course has one lame hole early on (in essence a flat, straight 10-foot putt), most are fun, and there are a few challenging and very steep holes on the back nine that ensure you end your round with a thrill. Since this is part of the Jolly Roger Park, when you're done you can go hit the go-karts.

Old Pro Castle Golf, 28th Street and Coastal Highway. A perennial favorite at Ocean City, Castle Golf at first glance looks flat and somewhat hokey, but that's what makes it fun! This course centers around a large, boxy, painted castlelike structure covered with plaster knights and other props suggesting the medieval. The holes are flat but well maintained and include lots of mechanized moving obstacles that spice up the game. The back nine holes take you into the castle structure and up onto its ramparts where the wood-lined greens play very differently from those on the ground. The castle also contains some wonderfully campy fake torture equipment. Although nowhere near as impressive as the more modern Underwater Golf, Castle Golf is an oldie-but-goodie.

boardwalk, the outlet center, and the dozens of strip malls along Coastal Highway, visitors will never be without a place to spend.

If you enter town from the Route 50 bridge, you can't miss the sprawling **Ocean City Factory Outlets** (☎ **800/625-6696**), a half mile from the bridge, on the mainland at the intersection of Golf Course Road. This large strip-mall complex is home to 40 brand-name outlet stores, including Ann Taylor, Bass, Jockey, Levi's, Mikasa, Nine West, OshKosh, Reebok, and Tommy Hilfiger. Parking is free and relatively plentiful, though, like the rest of Ocean City, it can be difficult during peak season.

The other outlet center in the area is in Rehoboth, Delaware. It's considerably bigger and, of course, you get to save the 5% state sales tax. So if you're a serious outlet shopper, you may want to consider the short trip north. See "Shopping" in chapter 13 for more information.

But perhaps the most popular and populated shopping destination is the Boardwalk—27 blocks of souvenir shops, candy stores, restaurants and snack shacks, and, of course, T-shirt shops. You'll find much of the same merchandise in all the T-shirt and souvenir shops, but there are a couple places worth visiting. **Ocean Gallery World Center** (☎ 410/289-5300) at 2nd Street is a standout along the boardwalk, with its mosaic-like facade of art from around the world. Its three stories are chock-full of art posters, prints, and original oil paintings, all offered for sale at closeout prices. The **Kite Loft** at 5th Street and Boardwalk (☎ 410/289-6852) has a large selection of kites, flags, windsocks, and toys.

GETTING OUTSIDE
GOLF

In recent years, the Ocean City area has blossomed as a golfing destination, frequently referred to as "The Myrtle Beach of the mid-Atlantic." The following courses welcome visitors and can be contacted individually or through a golfing association known as **Ocean City Golf Getaway,** 6101 Coastal Hwy., Ocean City, MD 21842 (☎ 800/4-OC-GOLF or 410/723-5207).

All courses listed below use a multitiered system for greens fees, which means they vary greatly even from morning to afternoon to evening. However, fees generally range from $20 to $72, with cheaper rates in the off-season and on summer afternoons. (Consider starting a round at about 4pm; the rates don't usually increase in the early evenings and the temperatures have started to drop.) All courses are open year-round from dawn to dusk.

Bay Club. 9122 Libertytown Rd., Berlin. ☎ 800/BAY-CLUB or 410/641-4081.

This course, less than 10 miles from the Boardwalk, offers traditional links and modern design in one 18-hole, par-72 championship course. Facilities include a clubhouse, driving range, practice green, club rentals, and lessons. There are plans to open a new 18-hole east course in spring of 1998.

Beach Club Golf Links. 9715 Deer Park Dr., Berlin. ☎ 800/435-9223 or 410/641-GOLF.

Reserving tee times is recommended at this semiprivate club that boasts two 18-hole, par-72 championship courses. It has a clubhouse, pro shop, club rentals, driving range, and putting green.

Eagle's Landing Golf Course. 12367 Eagle's Nest Rd., Berlin. ☎ 800/283-3846 or 410/213-7277.

Overlooking Sinepuxent Bay on a certified Audubon Sanctuary less than 4 miles from downtown, this public resort course features an 18-hole, par-72 municipal championship course, driving range, club rentals, lessons, pro shop, practice facilities, and clubhouse restaurant. Reservations are recommended.

Ocean City Golf & Yacht Club. 11401 Country Club Dr., Berlin. ☎ 800/442-3570 or 410/641-1779.

Founded in 1959, this club has two USGA-rated 18-hole championship courses, a seaside par-73 and a bayside par-72. There is a clubhouse, bar, and pro shop.

Pine Shore Golf. 11285 Beauchamp Rd., Berlin. ☎ 410/641-5100.

This public course, designed and built by Alan Janis, includes a 27-hole executive golf course, putting green, practice range, pro shop, and clubhouse with snack bar. All three nine-hole courses have been renovated in the last 2 years. Most recently new stone cart paths and renovated bunkers were added to the Pines course. Reservations are not accepted.

River Run. 11605 Masters Lane, Berlin. ☎ **800/733-RRUN** or 410/641-7200.

A Gary Player 18-hole signature course, par-71 River Run is a favorite in the area. It's a spikeless golf facility, so make sure to bring soft-soled footwear. Facilities include gas golf carts, pro shop, locker room, beverage carts, PGA golf pros, and driving range and putting greens. Reserving your tee time is recommended.

Rum Pointe Seaside Golf Links. 7000 Rum Pointe Lane, Berlin. ☎ **888/809-4653** or 410/629-1414. Open year-round, dawn–dusk.

This 18-hole par-72 championship course, impressively designed by the father/son team of P. B. and Pete Dye, opened in spring 1997, making it the newest addition to the family of Ocean City golf courses. Seventeen of the 18 holes sport views of the Sinepuxent Bay and nearby Assateague Island. Course facilities include a pro shop, driving range and practice facilities, PGA golf pro, clubhouse with full-service restaurant, and beverage cart. Reserving your tee time is recommended.

BAY CRUISING/FISHING

Since Ocean City is surrounded by the waters of the Atlantic Ocean and four different bays, sightseeing by boat is especially popular, as is fishing. From Memorial Day through September, most vessels double as fishing boats by day and sightseeing boats in the evening, but a few specialize in sightseeing or fishing only. The fishing departures usually run from April to October.

Angler. Talbot St., on the bay. ☎ **410/289-7424.** Fishing $30 adults, $15 under age 12; $5 rod rental. Departure daily 7:30am. Sightseeing $8 adults, $4 under age 12. Departures daily 7 and 9pm. Nature cruises $12 per person. Departure daily 4pm.

This 97-passenger vessel offers 7-hour headboat fishing excursions and 1-hour sightseeing cruises that go through the Inlet and north along the ocean coast. In addition, there are 2-hour nature cruises each afternoon.

Bay Queen. Ocean City Fishing Center, Shantytown Pier, West Ocean City. ☎ **410/213-0926.** Sightseeing $7 adults, $4 under age 12. Departures daily 10:30am, 12:30pm, 2pm, 3:30pm, and 7pm.

This 60-passenger boat offers day and night cruises covering the harbor as far south as Assateague Island.

Captain Bunting. 307 Dorchester, on the bay. ☎ **410/289-6720.** Fishing $20 adults, $14 under age 13; rod rental included. Departures daily 8am and 1pm. Sightseeing $6 adults, $3 under age 13. Departure daily 7:30pm.

This 88-passenger boat offers half-day (4-hour) headboat fishing trips and 1-hour evening cruises through the inlet and north along the ocean coast as far as 65th Street.

Judith M. Bahia Marina, between 21st and 22nd sts., on the bay. ☎ **410/289-7438.** Fishing $22 adults, $18 under age 12. Departures daily 8am and 1:30pm. Sightseeing $7 adults, $5 under age 12. Departure daily 7:30pm.

Four-hour deep-sea fishing is available to 80 people each day, followed by scenic ocean cruises for up to 150 passengers each evening, on this new vessel, equipped with all electronics, snack bar, and air-conditioning.

Miss Ocean City. Rte. 50 and Shantytown Rd., Shantytown Pier. ☎ **800/631-4848** or 410/ 213-0489. Daytime fishing $20 adults, $15 under age 12; rod rental included. Evening fishing $25 adults, $18 under age 12; rod rental included. Departures daily 8am and 1pm; evenings in season.

Four-hour headboat fishing is available each morning, afternoon, and some evenings on board this 150-passenger vessel.

O.C. Princess. Shantytown Pier (at Rte. 50 Bridge), West Ocean City. ☎ **410/213-0926.** Fishing $30 adults, $15 under age 12. Departure daily 7am. Sightseeing $18 adults, $10 under age 12. Departure daily 4pm.

One of the newest vessels to ply the waters around Ocean City, this 90-foot, 150-passenger party boat offers 7-hour daytime fishing trips and 3-hour evening nature cruises, with opportunities to observe marine life, from dolphins and whales to sea turtles, pelicans, and seabirds.

Sea Rocket. S. Division St. (next to coast guard station). ☎ **410/289-5887.** $8 adults, $5 ages 7–10, free under age 7 with an adult. Departures mid-June to early Sept 10am, 11am, noon, 2pm, 4pm, and 6pm; mid-May to mid-June and mid- to late Sept daily 11am, 1pm, and 3pm.

For sightseeing at top speed and splash, this 70-foot, 150-passenger open-top speedboat zooms along the waters of Ocean City and through the Assateague Island channel. It's a fun ride for kids. The trip lasts about 50 minutes.

Therapy. Ocean City Fishing Center, Shantytown Marina, West Ocean City. ☎ **410/ 213-0018.** Sightseeing $35 per person. Departures daily 9am, 1pm, and 5:30pm.

Cruise in bay and ocean waters for 3 hours aboard a 38-foot sailboat, accommodating a maximum of six persons. The route passes by Assateague Island with a chance to see dolphins, wild ponies, shorebirds, and other wildlife. Reservations are necessary.

Tortuga. Bahia Marina, between 21st and 22nd sts., on the bay. ☎ **410/289-7438.** Fishing $18 adults, $14 under age 12; $5 rod rental. Departures daily 7am, noon, and 5pm.

This 30-passenger boat offers 4-hour bay bottom-fishing trips for flounder in spring, summer, and fall.

HITTING THE BEACHES

SWIMMING   The entire 10-mile stretch of Ocean City beach is open to the public from 6am to 10pm daily, free of charge. Lifeguards are on duty from 10am to 5:30pm all summer. Beach chairs are provided at certain locations on a first-come first-served basis. These chairs must be used within 1 block of where they are assigned and kept.

SURFING   Two stretches of beach are designated as "surf beaches" each day and are announced on local radio stations, in the local newspaper, and on signs posted on the beach. Some surf shops in the area are **Quiet Storm,** 74th Street (☎ 410/ 723-1313); **Endless Summer,** 38th Street (☎ 410/289-3272) or 118th Street (☎ 410/524-7873); and **Ocean Atlantic,** 35th Street (☎ 410/289-3808).

OTHER OUTDOOR ACTIVITIES

BICYCLING   Bicycling is a good way to get around Ocean City and avoid traffic and parking problems. Cyclists on Coastal Highway share a lane with the buses. A headlight and rear reflector are required on all bicycles on the road after dark. Boardwalk biking is allowed between 5 and 10am during the summer, with extended hours in the off-season. Rental rates vary according to the type of bike, but you can expect to pay between $4 and $6 an hour for a two-wheeler, $10 an hour for a tandem, and $15 an hour for a tri-tandem. Two of the best sources are **Continental Cycle,** 73rd and Coastal Highway (☎ 410/524-1313); and **Mike's Bikes,** 1st Street (☎ 410/289-4637).

FISHING   Surf fishing is permitted on all the public beaches of Ocean City. However, between 9am and 6pm you cannot fish within 50 yards of swimmers or of anyone on the beach, which, in peak season, can be nearly impossible. Public fishing piers are located at Inlet Park, as well as bayside at the Third Street Pier, Ninth Street Pier, Convention Center Pier (at 40th Street), and Northside Park (at 125th Street). Fishing supplies and tackle can be found at **Bahia Marina Inc.,** 22nd Street and the bay (☎ **410/289-7438**); **Blue Marlin Tackle Co.,** Ocean City Fishing Center (☎ **410/213-0090**); and **Pauls Hook Line and Sinker,** Shanty Town Marina (☎ **410/289-1318**). For general fishing information call the **Fishing Information Hotline** at ☎ **410/524-6550.**

HORSE RACING   **Ocean Downs,** Route 50 at Route 589 (☎ **410/641-0600**), located 4 miles west of Ocean City, features harness racing under the stars with 12 races slated each night. On Monday, Wednesday, and Thursday in season, and on all nights during spring and fall, there is simulcast TV racing from other tracks. Grandstand admission and parking are free. Clubhouse admission is extra and the rates are subject to change. It's open from early July to early September. Race dates vary; post time is usually 7:30pm but may vary (call to check).

WATER SPORTS   From April through October, O.C. is a hotbed of all types of water activity, including sailing, parasailing, windsurfing, jet-skiing, powerboating, waterskiing, and more. Prices depend on type of equipment and duration of rental, but many boats can be rented from $30 to $70 an hour. Water skis and smaller equipment start at about $10 an hour, jet skis at $50 an hour. For full information, contact one of the following: **Advanced Marina Boat Rentals,** 122 66th St. and the bay (☎ **410/723-2124**); **Bahia Marina,** on the bay between 21st and 22nd streets (☎ **410/289-7438**); or **Bay Sports,** 22nd Street and the bay (☎ **410/289-2144**).

WHERE TO STAY IN DOWNTOWN OCEAN CITY

More than in any other part of Maryland, the lodgings in Ocean City depend on a short "high season." Summer (June through August) commands the highest rates, often with supplements on weekend nights as well. In many cases, minimum stays of 2 or 3 nights may apply, so check the rates in advance. Reservations are a must.

In almost all cases, the larger hotels offer money-saving package plans, particularly in the late spring or early autumn seasons, when Ocean City can be equally as lovely as in the peak of summer (and a lot less crowded). Although it is a great treat to overlook the ocean, rooms with partial or no views of the water often cost considerably less than those with oceanfront views.

EXPENSIVE

Carousel. 11700 Coastal Hwy., Ocean City, MD 21842. ☎ **800/641-0011** or 410/524-1000. Fax 410/524-1286. 271 rms, 190 condo units. A/C TV TEL. June–Aug $89–$229, Sept–May $49–$149 double; June–Aug $189–$289, Sept–May $99–$209 condo. AE, CB, DC, DISC, MC, V. Free parking.

Situated on the oceanfront between 117th and 118th streets, this hotel was considered a daring venture when it was launched in 1962 by Bobby Baker, a confidant of Lyndon Johnson. It was built on the northern end of the beach amid the sand dunes, a full 5 miles away from the rest of the Ocean City action. It proved to be a trendsetter, however, spurring the development of many other hotel/condo complexes. Today it is most famous as the hotel with a year-round ice-skating rink, the only one in the area. In addition, there is an indoor heated swimming pool, weight room, saunas, whirlpool, basketball and tennis courts, game room, and the largest deck on the beach. Guest rooms, located in a four-story hotel tower and a 22-story condo tower, all have balconies overlooking the beach and most have kitchenettes. There is also a restaurant, two lounges, a cafe, and a deli.

✪ Coconut Malorie Resort. 200 59th St., Ocean City, MD 21842. ☎ **800/767-6060** or 410/723-6100. Fax 410/524-9327. 85 suites. A/C TV TEL. June–Aug $159–$350, Sept–May $69–$199 double. AE, DC, DISC, MC, V. Free parking.

With a British colonial name and ambience, this hotel stands out on the bayfront. The palatial lobby features a waterfall, brass chandeliers, marble floors, palm trees, tropical foliage, and an eager staff attending to guests. The guest rooms are equally distinctive—all decorated with a Caribbean flavor, including a collection of Haitian art. Each unit is a suite, comprised of a bedroom (often dominated by a four-poster bed), a marble bathroom with whirlpool Jacuzzi tub, lighted makeup/shaving mirror, and hair dryer, and a sitting and dining area, with a private balcony, kitchen, wet bar, refrigerator, microwave oven, and coffee- and teamaker. Facilities include an outdoor swimming pool and sundeck and a full-time concierge desk. This hotel is also connected by footbridge (and by the same ownership) to Fager's Island restaurant and lounge (see "Dining," below).

✪ Dunes Manor. 2800 Baltimore Ave., Ocean City, MD 21842. ☎ **800/523-2888** or 410/289-1100. Fax 410/289-4905. 160 rms, 10 suites. A/C TV TEL. $45–$209 double; $85–$280 suite (depending on the season). AE, CB, DC, DISC, MC, V. Free parking.

The Dunes Manor is situated on its own stretch of beach just north of the boardwalk at 28th Street. The 11-story property is enhanced by a grand open porch (with rockers), rooftop cupolas, and a private miniboardwalk facing the ocean, not to mention the pink-and-white Victorian facade. Each of the bedrooms and suites has an oceanfront view, a balcony, two double beds, a decor of light woods and floral fabrics, and a refrigerator. The guest amenities include an indoor/outdoor pool, Jacuzzi, exercise room, sundeck, and Victorian-style restaurant and lounge. Tea and crumpets are served in the lobby each afternoon. The hotel provides free shuttle service with advance notice to and from the Ocean City bus terminal and Salisbury/Ocean City Regional Airport.

✪ Lighthouse Club Hotel. Fager's Island, 56th St. (on the bay), Ocean City, MD 21842. ☎ **800/767-6060** or 410/723-6100. Fax 410/526-3928. 23 suites. A/C TV TEL. June–Aug $199–$269, Sept–May $179–$239 suite. Rates include continental breakfast. AE, DC, DISC, MC, V. Free parking.

Overlooking the Isle of Wight Bay and boasting an octagonal lighthouse exterior, this three-story inn sits on a patch of wetlands surrounded by water. The library-style reception area has a homey atmosphere and the guest rooms are equally welcoming. Each unit is a suite, comprised of a marble bathroom with Jacuzzi tub, hair dryer, and lighted makeup mirror and a large combined sitting area and bedroom, decorated with light woods and rattan furnishings, white linens, and brass fixtures. Eight of the units have gas fireplaces, double Jacuzzis, and balconies, and all are equipped with wet bar, refrigerator, ice maker, and coffee- and teamaker. Services include in-room continental breakfast, evening turndown, and VCR rentals. The only drawback to this luxurious, romantic inn is its open airy design: The cathedral ceiling allows noise from the lobby to drift up to the guest rooms. There's an outdoor swimming pool and footbridge access to Fager's Island restaurant (see "Dining," below).

Princess Royale Resort. Oceanfront (at 91st St.), Ocean City, MD 21842. ☎ **800/4-ROYALE** or 410/524-7777. Fax 410/524-7787. 310 one-bedroom suites, 30 two- and three-bedroom suites. A/C TV TEL. June–Aug $139–$269 one-bedroom suite, $150–$265 two-bedroom suite, $225–$315 three-bedroom suite; Sept–May $79–$189 one-bedroom suite, $159–$199 two-bedroom suite, $179–$219 three-bedroom suite. *Note:* From mid-June to Labor Day special inclusive weekly rates are available for two- and three-bedroom suites. AE, DC, DISC, MC, V. Free parking.

One of the newest deluxe hotels to be built on the ocean, this property consists of two five-story towers within a 10-story condominium layout. Guest rooms are furnished with light woods and nautical art. One-bedroom suites can sleep two to six people, two-bedroom suites sleep six to eight, and three-bedroom suites sleep eight to ten people; all are ideal for families or extended stays. Each unit has a full kitchen including dishwasher, garbage disposal, microwave, refrigerator, and ice maker.

Dining choices include an oceanfront restaurant, indoor atrium-style cafe, and outdoor deck eatery overlooking the ocean. Facilities include an indoor pool, health club, whirlpools, saunas, tennis, gift and jewelry shops, convenience store, guest laundry, game room, and shuffleboard.

Sheraton Fontainebleau. 10100 Coastal Hwy. (at 101st St.), Ocean City, MD 21842. ☎ **800/638-2100** or 410/524-3535. Fax 410/524-3834. 250 rooms, 16 studios, 7 cabana suites. A/C TV TEL. June–Aug $130–$249 double, $295 studio, $330 cabana suite; Sept–May $95–$155 double, $210 studio, $175–$230 cabana suite. AE, CB, DC, DISC, MC, V. Free parking.

Among the chain hotels in this beachfront community, this 16-story tower is in a class by itself. It is located right on the ocean, far from the boardwalk and in the midst of the residential high-rise condo section of Ocean City. It offers oversized rooms and suites, all with views of the ocean and bay. Each room also has its own private balcony, contemporary furnishings, coffeemaker, and refrigerator. Amenities include a restaurant and two lounges overlooking the ocean, a beachside terrace, valet services, an arcade of shops, a video-game room, an indoor heated pool, and a complete spa with Jacuzzi, workout room, steam room, sauna, whirlpool, and sunrooms.

MODERATE

Brighton Suites. 12500 Coastal Hwy., Ocean City, MD 21842. ☎ **800/227-5788** or 410/250-7600. Fax 410/250-7603. 57 suites. A/C TV TEL. June–Aug $99–$189, Sept–May $69–$129 suite. AE, DC, DISC, MC, V. Free parking.

Situated on the main highway, but within easy walking distance of the beach or bay, this five-story all-suite property is ideal for families or two couples traveling together. Each suite has a bedroom with two queen-size beds or a king-size bed, a large modern bathroom with a hair dryer, and a separate living room with a pullout couch, wet bar, refrigerator-freezer, and personal safe. Most units also have a private balcony. Facilities include an indoor heated swimming pool and secure underground parking.

Castle in the Sand. 3701 Atlantic Ave., Ocean City, MD 21842. ☎ **800/552-SAND** or 410/289-6846. Fax 410/289-9446. 36 rms, 137 suites. A/C TV TEL. June–Aug $95–$172 double, $109–$209 suite; Sept–May $59–$85 double, $69–$129 suite. AE, DC, DISC, MC, V. Free parking. Closed Nov–Mar.

Nestled on the beach north of the boardwalk at 37th Street, this modern property has a mock-castle exterior complete with turrets. Standard hotel rooms are offered, as well as oceanfront rooms with kitchenettes and balconies. Outdoor amenities include an Olympic-size swimming pool, private beach, and oceanfront patio.

Comfort Inn Boardwalk. 507 Atlantic Ave. (5th St. at the oceanfront), P.O. Box 1030, Ocean City, MD 21842. ☎ **800/228-5155** or 410/289-5155. 84 rms. A/C TV TEL. June–Aug $99–$189, Sept–May $39–$139 double. AE, CB, DC, DISC, MC, V. Free parking. Closed Nov to mid-Feb.

One of the newest chain properties to be built along the boardwalk, this is a modern five-story complex of two buildings: one directly on the boardwalk and the other next to it. All of the guest rooms are decorated with light wood furnishings and sea-toned fabrics, and each has a sleeping area, kitchenette, sitting area with sofa bed, and private balcony. Facilities include a restaurant, heated outdoor and indoor pools, and a boardwalk deck.

Hampton Inn. 4201 Coastal Hwy., Ocean City, MD 21842. ☎ **800/HAMPTON** or 410/289-6488. Fax 410/289-1617. 168 rms. A/C TV TEL. June–Aug $99–$179, Sept–May $30–$120 double. AE, DC, DISC, MC, V. Free parking.

For value and convenience, this seven-story property is a good choice for families, particularly in the off-season. It is situated on the bayside of the highway 1 block from the beach and the Convention Center. The guest rooms, accessible by computer-card keys, each have a sleep-sofa as well as one or two beds. Some rooms have a microwave oven and refrigerator; all have balconies. Facilities include a game room, convenience shop, guest laundry, and fully equipped health center with glass-enclosed indoor heated swimming pool. Some units with Jacuzzis or ocean views cost extra.

Holiday Inn Oceanfront. 6600 Coastal Hwy. (oceanfront at 67th St.), Ocean City, MD 21842. ☎ **800/638-2106** or 410/524-1600. Fax 410/524-1135. 216 efficiencies. A/C TV TEL. June–Aug $69–$239, Sept–May $39–$179 double. AE, CB, DC, DISC, MC, V. Free parking.

Located in the center of Ocean City, directly on the beach, this eight-story hotel is convenient to everything. Each room has a private balcony plus a fully equipped kitchen with microwave and dishwasher. Facilities include a gourmet restaurant called Reflections (see "Dining," below), plus a poolside bar, indoor and outdoor swimming pools, Jacuzzi, saunas, exercise room, tennis court, shuffleboard, and game room.

Howard Johnson Oceanfront. 1109 Atlantic Ave., Ocean City, MD 21842. ☎ **800/926-1122** or 410/289-7251. Fax 410/289-3435. 90 rms. A/C TV TEL. June–Aug $109–$199, Sept–May $39–$89 double. AE, DC, DISC, MC, V. Free parking.

Situated on the boardwalk at 12th Street, this modern seven-story hotel has a welcoming lobby with a fireplace. The guest rooms are decorated with light woods, pastel-toned furnishings, and modern art prints. Each room has a private balcony with full or partial ocean views. Facilities include a restaurant, indoor heated pool, and gift shop.

Phillips Beach Plaza Hotel. 1301 Atlantic Ave. (between 13th and 14th sts.), Ocean City, MD 21842. ☎ **800/492-5834** or 410/289-9121. Fax 410/289-3041. 60 rms, 36 apts. A/C TV TEL. June–Aug $119–$145 double, $139–$174 apt; Sept–May $40–$60 double, $50–$75 apt. AE, DC, DISC, MC, V. Free parking.

This boardwalk hotel boasts an elegant Victorian lobby with crystal chandeliers, wrought-iron fixtures, open fireplace, and graceful statuary, all contributing to its old world ambience. The accommodations, located in an attached modern four-story bedroom block, consist of both rooms and apartments. The apartments have dining and/or living areas with full kitchens. The hotel also has a long, open porch overlooking the ocean, a top-notch on-premises seafood restaurant named Phillips by the Sea (operated by the Phillips family of Phillips Crab House renown—see "Dining," below), and a piano bar.

MODERATE/INEXPENSIVE

Comfort Inn Gold Coast. 11201 Coastal Hwy. (at 112th St.), Ocean City, MD 21842. ☎ **800/228-5150** or 410/524-3000. Fax 410/524-8255. 202 rms. A/C TV TEL. May–Aug $84.95–$164.95, Sept–Apr $29.95–$124.95 double. AE, DC, DISC, MC, V. Free parking.

For good value and great location, this hotel set back from the main road is one of the best choices among the chains. Each room has a microwave oven, refrigerator, wet bar, and an ocean or bay view. Facilities include a glass-enclosed indoor pool, Jacuzzi, sundeck, convenience store, guest laundry, and fast-food restaurant, plus an adjacent lounge and movie theater.

Talbot Inn. Talbot St. (and the bay), P.O. Box 548, Ocean City, MD 21842. ☎ **800/ 659-7703** or 410/289-9125. 36 units. A/C TV TEL. $30–$97 double. MC, V. Free parking.

A good value, this inn offers two adjacent three-story buildings: one directly on the bay (bayfront) and the other next to it (bayside). Each unit accommodates four to six people and is decorated with light woods, floral fabrics, and nautical art. Rooms have compact kitchenettes including microwaves, and most have balconies. Facilities include a marina, bar, and sportswear shop. There is a 3-day minimum on weekends in summer.

NEARBY ACCOMMODATIONS

For travelers looking for a quieter vacation, or who don't mind staying inland, Berlin, about 15 minutes away from both Ocean City and Assateague Island (depending on traffic), offers two great places to stay. To get to Berlin from Ocean City, take the Route 50 bridge out of Ocean City and follow Route 50 until you take a left on Route 113; from there you'll hit Berlin in less than a mile.

○ **Atlantic Hotel.** 2 N. Main St., Berlin, MD 21811. ☎ **410/641-3589.** Fax 410/641-4928. 16 rms. A/C TV TEL. July–Aug $85–$150, Sept–June $65–$135 double. Rates include breakfast. AE, MC, V. Free parking. From Ocean City, take Rte. 50 west to Rte. 113 (Main St.), a total of 7 miles.

This hotel in the historic town of Berlin offers a quiet old-world country inn setting within easy driving range of the beach and boardwalk attractions. Dating from 1895 and listed on the National Register of Historic Places, the Victorian three-story structure has been updated with modern amenities but still retains its original charm. The guest rooms are individually furnished with local antiques, mahogany furniture, and accessories of lace, crochet, tassels, and braids. Facilities include a reading parlor, outdoor balcony, and highly acclaimed restaurant (see "Where to Dine," below).

○ **Merry Sherwood Plantation.** 8909 Worcester Hwy. (just south of Berlin on Rte. 113), Berlin, MD 21811. ☎ **800/660-1358** or 410/641-2112. 7 rms (5 with private bath), 1 suite. A/C. May–Oct $150 double, $175 suite; winter $95 double, $125 suite. Rates include breakfast. MC, V.

This 1859 plantation home underwent 2 years of extensive restoration to turn it into the remarkably unique and elegant country inn it is today. The host, Todd Durand, can tell you all about every one of the many antiques—from the hand-carved rosewood dining room table and chairs to the inn's pride and joy, the chair made for Queen Victoria. Sound a little too prim and formal for you? Guests are encouraged to use all the antiques, so go ahead—sit in Queen Victoria's throne or play the grand piano.

Breakfast is a formal affair, complete with china, crystal, and silver. Afterward, you can take a guided tour of the inn and get a peek at the other guest rooms. All are large and uniquely decorated. The two that share a bath have the most elaborate furnishings. The honeymoon suite is decorated entirely with antique wedding memorabilia and has a whirlpool bath. Even if you can't stay here, it's worth a visit; the house is open for tours when it will not disturb the guests. Just call ahead.

WHERE TO DINE

Understandably, seafood is a favorite here. For the most part, a casual atmosphere prevails, although it is always wise to make a reservation in the better restaurants and to check on the dress code.

During summer, restaurants are rarely closed. Some open as early as 5am, dishing up hearty breakfasts for fishermen, and continue serving meals right through until 10 or 11pm.

Most restaurants have full bar facilities. Just to be safe, get a copy of the Ocean City Visitor Bureau's guide to accommodations and restaurants; it gives descriptions, hours of operation, and price guidelines for at least 50 of the best eateries.

EXPENSIVE

✪ **Atlantic Hotel Restaurant.** 2 N. Main St., Berlin. ☎ **410/641-3589.** Reservations required. Main courses $20–$29. AE, MC, V. Main dining room daily 6–10pm; Drummer's Cafe daily 11:30am–9pm. From Ocean City, take Rte. 50 west to Rte. 818 (Main St.), a total of 7 miles. INTERNATIONAL.

One of Ocean City's best restaurants is not along the beach, boardwalk, or bay, but a short 15-minute drive inland to the historic town of Berlin. The Victorian-style dining room exudes a welcoming ambience, with eager and able waiters in black tie, classical music in the background, a decor of rich colored glass, plush velvet drapes, and chandeliers with bell-shaped glass.

The creative dinner menu often includes such specialties as filet mignon with béarnaise sauce, grilled duck with walnut-garlic sauce, grilled salmon with a choice of sauces, and rack of lamb with Montrachet goat cheese. In addition, guests are encouraged to personalize menu selections. If you wish to linger, you might want to check into one of the rooms upstairs at this charming inn (see "Nearby Accommodations," above).

Bonfire. 71st St. and Coastal Hwy. ☎ **410/524-7171.** Reservations recommended on weekends. Main courses $11.95–$25.95. AE, MC, V. May–Oct daily 4–11pm, Nov–Apr 5–10pm. INTERNATIONAL.

For more than 25 years, this bayside restaurant has been drawing people for its charcoal-broiled steaks and aged prime rib, as well as surf-and-turf, lobster tails, jumbo shrimp, veal dishes, and 25 Chinese dishes ranging from Szechuan shrimp and pepper steak to orange-flavored chicken. The latest addition to the menu is an all-you-can-eat seafood and prime rib buffet. This large, elaborately decorated restaurant offers a choice of four dining rooms, filled with such eclectic furnishings as captain's chairs, plush leather banquettes, leaded- and etched-glass windows, gas lanterns, and original oil paintings. A huge oval bar sits in the center of the complex, and a live band is featured on many nights during the summer.

✪ **Fager's Island.** 60th St. (on the bay). ☎ **410/524-5500.** Reservations recommended for dinner. Main courses $15.50–$24.50; lunch $4.95–$9.95. AE, CB, DC, DISC, MC, V. Daily 11am–2am. AMERICAN.

Perched on the edge of the bay, this restaurant is surrounded by three outside decks, a pier, a pavilion, and a gazebo. With wide wraparound windows, Fager's Island is ideal for watching sunsets and is very popular at cocktail hour (when the "1812 Overture" is played). The dinner menu ranges from barbecued, blackened, or broiled seafood, to steaks and prime rib. The grilled sea bass served with a spicy corn, crabmeat, and red pepper hash is excellent. Other house specialties are roast duck in orange sauce and a "mixed grille" of filet mignon, smoked pork chop, and chef's sausage. An award-winning wine cellar offers more than 600 labels. Overstuffed sandwiches and heaping salads are available all day.

✪ **Hobbit.** 101 81st St. ☎ **410/524-8100.** Reservations recommended for dinner. Main courses $14.95–$22.95; lunch $4.95–$10.95. AE, DISC, MC, V. Daily 11am–midnight. Closed Dec 25. SEAFOOD.

One of the loveliest places to dine while watching the sunset is this restaurant right on the bay. The emphasis is on continental cuisine. Dinner entrees include flounder stuffed with lobster, rainbow trout stuffed with shrimp and crab, crab imperial, duck à l'orange, rack of lamb, and steaks. Lunch features raw-bar items, burgers, salads, stews, and sandwiches. Seating is available outside on the decks.

☉ Reflections. 6600 Coastal Hwy. (67th and Coastal Hwy.). ☎ **410/524-5252.** Reservations required. Main courses $18.95–$27.95. AE, CB, DC, DISC, MC, V. Daily 5–10pm. CONTINENTAL/AMERICAN.

Located at the Holiday Inn Oceanfront, this classy restaurant draws a devoted clientele thanks to its Chaîne des Roîtisseurs affiliation, impeccable service, and incomparable food. The decor is reminiscent of a grand European palace, with arches, alcoves, and colonnades, enhanced by brick and mirrored walls, leafy plants, globe lights, and statues.

The menu, which changes daily, blends French table-side cooking with Eastern Shore ingredients. Specialties include "symphonia de la mer" (sautéed shrimp, scallops, lobster, mushrooms, shallots, white wine, brandy, and cream), steak Diane (sautéed with shallots, Dijon mustard, mushrooms, red wine, cream, and brandy), Tijuana tuna (charbroiled with jumbo shrimp flamed in tequila and tossed with freshly made salsa), and salmon Susan (charbroiled and served with sea scallops and a saffron hollandaise sauce).

MODERATE

Bayside Skillet. 77th St. (and Coastal Hwy.). ☎ **410/524-7950.** Reservations not accepted. Main courses $6.95–$18.95. MC, V. May–Oct daily 24 hrs.; Nov–Apr daily 7am–9pm. INTERNATIONAL.

If you tire of seafood or steaks, head to this chalet-style eatery on the bayside of the main highway at 77th Street. As its name implies, it specializes in crepes, omelets, and frittatas. House specialties range from a ratatouille omelet to a "steak-n-eggs" omelet (filled with prime rib and cheese), as well as crepes filled with seafood, bacon, and spinach or strawberries and cream. Burgers, sandwiches, nachos, and salads are also offered. This wide-windowed restaurant, offering some of the best sunset views along the bay, has a cheery decor of tall beamed ceilings, knotty-pine walls, pink linens, and hanging plants.

Captain Bill Bunting's Angler. Talbot St. (and the bay). ☎ **410/289-7424.** Reservations recommended for dinner. Main courses $6.95–$27.95; lunch $3.95–$7.95. AE, MC, V. May–Oct daily 6am–11pm restaurant and 11am–2am bar. AMERICAN.

Since 1938 this spacious restaurant has been a favorite on the marina of Ocean City. It features an air-conditioned main dining room with a rustic and nautical decor, plus an outdoor patio deck overlooking the bay, an ideal spot to see the boats sailing by or the fishermen bringing back their bounty. The extensive dinner menu revolves around a variety of daily fresh fish specials, each prepared seven different ways, plus steaks and seafood platters. A free evening cruise of the bay at 7 or 9pm is included as part of the dinner price. Lunch focuses on tempting raw bar selections, fishwiches, salads, and burgers. *Note:* For early risers, doors open at 6am for breakfast.

Charlie Chiang's. 5401 Coastal Hwy. (at 54th St.). ☎ **410/723-4600.** Reservations recommended for dinner. Main courses $6.95–$17.95; lunch $4.50–$15.95. Summer daily 11:30am–11pm; winter Tues–Sun 11:30am–11pm. AE, CB, DC, DISC, MC, V. HUNAN/SZECHUAN.

Located on the bayside, at 54th Street, this restaurant is on the upper level of a two-story building, with a bright plant-filled conservatory-style decor, enhanced by Oriental screens and hangings. The menu features all the usual Chinese favorites, as well as some house specialties, such as "Charlie Chiang's chicken," deep-fried chunks of white meat sautéed with broccoli, water chestnuts, and mushrooms, in a sweet-and-sour hot sauce; "Ma La pheasant," sautéed in tangy sauce and garnished with watercress; "Treasures of the Sea," scallops and baby shrimp with onions, red and green peppers, and water chestnuts in ginger garlic sauce; and "Angel-Hair Noodles" with Taiwanese brown sauce or Singapore curry sauce.

Hanna's Marina Deck. 306 Dorchester St. ☎ **410/289-4411.** Reservations accepted for parties of 8 or more May–Sept and 6 or more Apr and Oct. Main courses $9.95–$19.95; lunch $3.95–$9.95. AE, DISC, MC, V. Apr–Oct daily 11am–11pm. SEAFOOD/AMERICAN.

Overlooking Sinepuxent Bay, the bilevel main dining room of this restaurant offers wide-windowed views of the water and passing boats, particularly memorable at sunset. There is also a smaller room facing the side street, so arrive early for a table with a view. The menu offers different "fresh catch" blackboard specials every day, prepared broiled, grilled, Cajun style, or blackened, as well as dishes such as crab-stuffed flounder, deep-fried crab cakes or soft-shell crabs, broiled lobster tails, and steamed, fried, or stuffed shrimp. Steaks, ribs, chicken, and pasta dishes are also offered. Other specialties of the house include coconut muffins and tropical salads, much in demand at lunchtime.

Harrison's Harbor Watch. Boardwalk South (overlooking the inlet). ☎ **410/289-5121.** Reservations recommended. Main courses $8.95–$19.95; lunch $4.95–$7.95. AE, DISC, MC, V. May–Oct daily 5–11pm; Jan–April and Nov Thurs–Sat 5–10pm; open for lunch Mar–Apr. SEAFOOD.

You'll get a spectacular full view of the ocean and nearby Assateague Island at this restaurant, situated at the boardwalk's southernmost point. It's a large complex (seating 400), with various levels of seating, tile floors, lots of leafy plants, and a colonial-nautical decor. A bountiful raw bar is the focus of attention at dinner, followed by entrees such as hickory-barbecued shrimp, whole local lobster, lobster linguine, crab legs, swordfish with crab imperial, steaks, and fried chicken. Lunch emphasizes lighter fare (sandwiches and salads).

Higgins' Crab House. 31st St. (and Coastal Hwy.). ☎ **410/289-2581.** Reservations accepted for parties of 8 or more. Main courses $10.95–$19.95. AE, DC, DISC, MC, V. May–Sept Mon–Fri 2:30–10pm, Sat–Sun noon–10pm; Apr and Oct Fri–Sun noon–10pm. SEAFOOD.

Owned and operated by the Higgins family, this busy spot is a sister operation to the restaurant of the same name in St. Michaels. This location serves only dinner. For a full description of the menu, see "Where to Dine," in the Talbot County section of chapter 7.

۞ Macky's Bayside Bar & Grill. 54th St. (on the bay). ☎ **410/723-5565.** Reservations not accepted in summer. Main courses $11.95–$19.95; salads and sandwiches $4.50–$9.95. AE, DISC, MC, V. Daily 11am–2am. Closed Jan. AMERICAN.

Macky's claims to have the best sunsets in town, and they certainly have the location for it. This comfortable shanty-like restaurant sits on its own patch of bay beach with a view of the mainland, the Lighthouse Club, and the Route 90 bridge. You can dine right on the sand in white plastic lawn furniture or in the partially enclosed dining area overlooking the beach. Decor is vintage beach house: Napkins and condiments are served in sand buckets, and the beach is strewn with live palm trees and lighted wire palms and dolphins. The menu touches on everything from New Orleans to southern Florida to the Eastern Shore, with a surprisingly large number of vegetarian options thrown in (try the black bean burger or the grilled garden sandwich). They even serve a few of the favorites from Tio Gringo's, a Mexican restaurant under the same ownership.

Phillips Crab House. 2004 Philadelphia Ave. ☎ **410/289-6821.** Reservations not accepted. Main courses $9.95–$24.95; lunch $4.95–$9.95. AE, DISC, MC, V. Apr–Oct daily noon–10pm. SEAFOOD.

The Phillips seafood restaurants that are so famous in Baltimore, Norfolk, and Washington, D.C., all owe their origin to a small crab carry-out started here by Shirley and Brice Phillips in 1956. That family enterprise became an Ocean City tradition and is today the town's largest restaurant, seating 1,300 people in 11 different dining rooms. Just as 40 years ago, seafood is the focus and crab is king. The extensive crab repertoire includes crab au gratin and imperial, crab cakes, soft-shell crabs, crab with Smithfield ham, and all-you-can-eat crabs. Lovers of salmon, shrimp, flounder, scallops, oysters, and lobster will also find their favorites here, prepared in a variety of ways, as well as steaks, filet mignon, and fried chicken. Lunchtime choices include sandwiches and salads.

INEXPENSIVE

Dumser's. 12305 Coastal Hwy. ☎ **410/250-5543.** Main courses $6.95–$15.95; lunch $1.95–$6.95. MC, V. Mid-June to Labor Day daily 7am–1am; Sept to mid-June daily 7am–10pm. AMERICAN.

An Ocean City favorite since 1939, this eatery originally began as an ice-cream parlor but is now equally popular as a restaurant. Dinner entrees range from steaks and prime rib to crab cakes, stuffed flounder, fried chicken, and Virginia ham. And make sure to save room for dessert, especially the ice cream, made on the premises. Lunch choices include sandwiches, salads, subs, and soups. No liquor is served. A second location, **Dumser's Drive-In,** 49th and Coastal Highway (☎ **410/524-1588**), is also open year-round, with a more limited menu. Both are good options for families with kids.

Paul Revere Smorgasbord. 2nd St. (and Boardwalk). ☎ **410/524-1776.** Buffet $7.99. MC, V. Mid-May to mid-Sept daily 3:30–9pm. AMERICAN/INTERNATIONAL.

With eight colonial-style dining rooms, this huge restaurant can accommodate up to 700 diners. One price prevails here for an all-you-can-eat buffet of more than 100 items, ranging from soups, salads, roast beef, turkey, fried chicken, ribs, seafood, and pasta to a tempting dessert bar. Beer and wine are served.

3 Assateague Island National Seashore

More than 2.5 million people come to Assateague Island each year to see the famed wild horses. To be honest, we were skeptical on our first visit, expecting crowded platforms with big telescope machines and herds of tiny ponies half a mile away. Instead, when we drove across the bridge to the island, we were greeted by half a dozen ponies grazing in the marshland a hundred yards from the road. As we drove into the park, another six or eight ponies (one or two foals among them) strolled along and across the road, and in the evening we sat on the beach as groups of ponies and a few loners migrated down the beach, passing a few feet in front of us. And as an added bonus, as we were leaving we spotted a mama sica deer and two fawns.

Ready to jump in your car right now? Well, Assateague is not without its problems. First of all, there's the 2.5 million people. The easily accessible areas of the island are always crowded during the summer, so if you come here with romantic notions of a deserted beach, inhabited only by the untamed and free ponies, you'll have to be willing to go a little out of the way, either on foot, by small boat, or by off-road vehicle. And then there's Assateague's second most famous inhabitants—the mosquitoes. They really are as bad as all the brochures, guidebooks, and park rangers tell you, so always come prepared with bug spray, citronella candles, and long sleeves. Compared to nearby Ocean City, Assateague is still a wild and primitive place—no hotels, restaurants, convenience stores, or gas stations. Just people. And ponies. And mosquitoes.

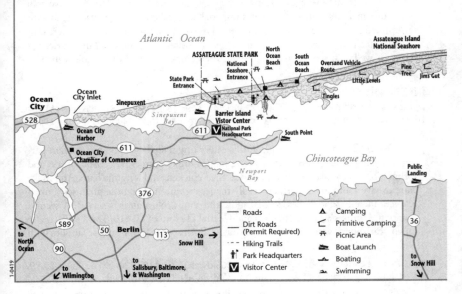

JUST THE FACTS

GETTING THERE   The only access to the Maryland side of Assateague by car is via MD Route 611 south, which meets up with Route 50 just west of Ocean City. To get to the Virginia side of the island take VA Route 175 west across Chincoteague. You cannot drive from one end of the island to the other.

VISITOR CENTERS   The national park service operates two visitor centers—the **Barrier Island Visitor Center** located on 611 before you cross the bridge onto Assateague and the **National Seashore Entrance Station** and camper registration office, which is located inside the park, so you must pay the entrance fee to get to it. The Barrier Island Visitor Center is the bigger of the two facilities and offers brochures, exhibits, two aquariums, three videos about the island and its wildlife, and a gift shop. It's open from 9am to 5pm daily. The National Seashore Entrance Station is primarily for camper registration and ORV permits, but it does have some brochures on the hiking trails and ranger programs.

FEES & REGULATIONS   Assateague State Park charges admission Memorial Day through Labor Day, Thurs–Tues $2 per person, Wed $1 per person. Admission to the National Seashore is $5 per car or $2 per person year-round and is good for a week. Most National Park regulations apply. Permits are required for backcountry camping and for use of the off-road vehicle areas. Pets are allowed only in the national park and must be on a leash. And, of course, don't feed the ponies.

SEASONS   Maryland's state park is open for day use April 1 through December 1. The National Seashore and Chincoteague National Wildlife Refuge are open year-round. There is no daily closing time on the Maryland side of the island, but

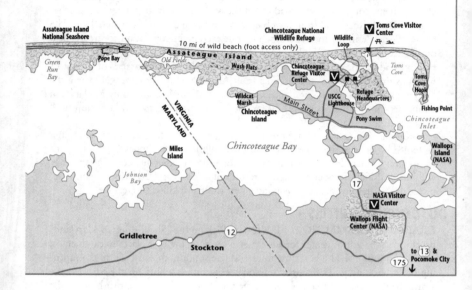

only surf fishermen and campers who are staying in designated spots are allowed to stay overnight.

AVOIDING THE CROWDS & THE BUGS   Weekends during the summer are crowded. If you plan to camp then, make reservations in the national park or come early to the state park, where reservations for less than a weeklong stay are not accepted. But the human population is not the biggest nuisance: Mosquitoes, biting flies, and ticks are abundant from April through September, and mosquitoes especially are a problem beginning at the end of July and following a heavy or steady rain. They are also much worse on the bayside of the island, so try to get an oceanside site if you're camping in the national park. Your best bet for avoiding the bugs is waiting until it gets cold enough to kill them all off.

RANGER PROGRAMS   The National Park Service offers a wide variety of ranger-led programs on a weekly basis throughout the summer, including nature hikes, surf rescue demonstrations, canoe trips, campfire programs, and surf fishing and shellfishing demonstrations. For a complete rundown of these activities pick up a copy of "Assateague Island," a visitors' guide to activities and events, at one of the visitor centers, or contact Assateague Island National Seashore, 7206 National Seashore Lane, Berlin, MD 21811 (☎ **410/641-3030** or 410/641-1441).

SEEING THE PONIES

It may come as quite a surprise to new visitors to the island that finding and viewing the famed wild horses of Assateague takes almost no effort, especially on the Maryland side of the island, where the ponies have virtually free reign. In fact, you'll probably have to stop for a few begging ponies along the side of the road as you enter the park. (For your own safety and the ponies,' roll up your car windows and *do not feed them.*) If you're camping, you may hear a pack of horses stroll right by your tent in the middle of the night or see the telltale signs in the morning. For a more picturesque setting, stop by the beach in the evening after the crowds have left; packs of four to six, and an occasional lone pony, roam the beach regularly.

On the Virginia side of the island, the ponies are less accessible; you can generally see them along the paved road called the Wildlife Tour, in the fenced marshes south of Beach Road, and from the observation platform on the Woodland Trail. The annual **Pony Penning and Auction,** a unique exercise in population control, is held on Chincoteague the last Wednesday and Thursday of July. The Chincoteague "cowboys" round up the entire Virginia herd on Wednesday, and thousands of spectators watch as the horses swim the channel from Assateague to Chincoteague where the foals are auctioned off the next day. Campsites and hotel rooms (only available on Chincoteague and the mainland) fill up fast for this event, so make reservations well ahead of time.

I would be remiss if I did not mention that these are, in fact, *wild* horses. Do not be fooled by their gentle appearance and their willingness to approach you and your car looking for handouts. The ponies are prone to unpredictable behavior and they will bite and kick, so obey the signs and do not attempt to feed or pet them. Also, please drive carefully; at least one pony a year is hit and killed by a car.

OUTDOOR ACTIVITIES

CRABBING, CLAMMING & FISHING Pick up the "Shellfishing in Maryland" brochure at the visitor center for a great map showing the best places to catch crabs, clams, and mussels. The best time to crab is late summer to early fall, in the morning or early evening. The most common method of crabbing on the island is the string, bait, and net method. Attach a piece of bony chicken or a fish head to the string (chicken necks are the preferred bait), and cast out in relatively shallow water. When you feel a tug, gently tow the line back in. If there's a crab on the end, net it before you take it out of the water, then transfer it to a basket or other container and continue crabbing.

A single collapsible crab pot or trap may also be used, if it is attended at all times. You can purchase a crab pot at bait-and-tackle shops; they look like large chicken-wire boxes. Place bait in the center of the trap, drop it in clear, shallow water, and pull it up as soon as a crab walks in. (On Assateague the crab pot has to be attended; if it weren't for the rule, you could leave it out for several hours and maybe get several crabs when you finally pulled it up.) All crabs must measure 5 inches point to point and all egg-bearing females must be returned. Limits are 1 bushel per person per day, or 2 bushels per boat per day. Crabbing is prohibited January through March.

Signing and raking are both accepted methods for clamming. The mud flats at Virginia's Toms Cove are more suitable for signing. To sign for clams, walk along the mudflats at low tide and look for small key-hole openings or "signs," indicating the presence of a clam. Then dig out the clam with a hand trowel or small digging tool. Raking can be done at any tide level, but you need a special clamming rake, which has a basket to catch the clams. Drag the rake through the mud until the tines scrape a shell; then dig up the mud, shake it loose, and catch the clam in the rake's basket. Clams must be 1 inch wide, and the limit is 1 bushel per person per day.

Mussels and oysters are relatively rare in the waters surrounding the island. Oysters are rarely found off the private leased beds (and trespassing is strictly prohibited). The park service asks that you take only what you will consume in mussels and oysters.

No saltwater license is required for surf fishing on the coast, though an after-hours permit is required on the Virginia end of the island. Fishing is prohibited on the guarded beaches and in the designated surf zones.

CANOEING, KAYAKING & BOATING The only launch facility on the island is for canoes only. It's located at the end of Ferry Landing Road on the Maryland side of the island. Larger boats can be launched either from West Ocean City Harbor; the state park facility off Route 611, across from the Barrier Island Visitor Center; South Point Boat Ramp; or the public landing at the end of Route 385 east of Snow Hill.

Waters at the Maryland end of Chincoteague Bay are usually ideal for canoeing, though the tidal currents around Chincoteague Island are strong. The bay is generally shallow, so operators of larger boats should watch for sandbars. During the summer, you can rent canoes from the concessionaire at the end of Bayside Drive. Four backcountry, canoe-in campsites are located on the Maryland end of the island. Permits are required and can be obtained in person at the ranger station on the Maryland side or at the Toms Cove Visitor Center in Virginia.

Assateague is also a great place for sea kayaking on the bay and the ocean. **Delmarva Dennis' Sea Kayaking Adventures** (☎ **302/537-5311**), located on Fenwick Island, offers daylong trips that include transportation in an off-road vehicle, lunch, and instruction on how to surf in a kayak. See "Outdoor Activities" in the "Bethany Beach & Fenwick Island" section of chapter 13.

HIKING & CYCLING Conditions and trails for hiking and biking are generally better at the Virginia end of the island, but there are three self-guided hiking trails on the Maryland end—Life of the Marsh, Life of the Forest, and Life of the Dunes. All are quite short, and all require bug repellent. Cyclists can use the 3-mile paved bike path along Bayberry Drive and the Oceanside campground.

In Virginia, about half of the 15 miles of trails are paved for cycling. The Wildlife Tour is closed to automobile traffic until 3pm each day, so hikers and bikers can have it all to themselves. The Woodland Trail, which leads to a pony observation platform, is also paved.

☺ OFF-ROAD VEHICLES The vast majority of Assateague is not accessible by car; however, off-road (or over-sand) vehicle routes run most of the length of the island. Permits are required and are issued on a yearly basis for a fee of $60. The list of regulations and conditions is long and complex, so contact the National Seashore Entrance Station and request a copy of their off-road vehicles brochure.

CAMPING

Accommodations on the island are limited to the **Assateague State Park** campground (☎ **410/641-2120** or 410/641-2918) and the two campgrounds and several backcountry campsites run by the National Park Service. The state-run facility, open April 1 through October 31, has 311 sites and offers bathhouses with flush toilets and hot and cold running water, a small camp store, and a snack bar. Reservations are accepted only for stays of a week or longer. All sites are on the oceanside of the island and cost $20 per night.

The **National Park Service** operates an oceanside campground and a bay-side campground, which are slightly more primitive than the state park facility (for information call the National Seashore Campground Office at ☎ **410/641-3030**). But they do accept reservations from May 15 through October 31, so you won't end up at the island with no place to camp if you call ahead. And do make reservations; there will not be an empty campsite to be found on the island on a summer weekend (and many weekdays). Both campgrounds have chemical toilets, drinking water, and cold showers. There are also flush toilets and cold showers at the beach bathhouse. If possible, reserve a site at the oceanside campground; the mosquitoes and biting flies are much worse on the bayside. The cost is $12 per night from May 15 through October 31, and $10 per night the rest of the year.

In addition, the park has several backcountry or canoe-in campsites strewn along the Maryland end of the island. Each site has a chemical toilet and picnic table but no drinking water. You must pick up a backcountry permit from the ranger station to use these sites, but there is no fee.

If you don't mind staying off the island, Maryland's **Pocomoke River State Park** (☎ 410/632-2566) is a less crowded and somewhat more comfortable option. It's about a 45-minute drive from either the Virginia or Maryland end of the island and offers 250 improved campsites in a wooded environment along the Pocomoke River. In addition to camping, the park offers quite a few extras: canoeing, boat rentals, a swimming pool, and hiking and biking trails. Best of all, the bugs are not as bad. Sites are $15 to $20 in summer and $10 to $15 in winter. To get there from Assateague, take Route 611 off the island, then turn left and follow Route 376 until you reach the town of Berlin; from there, take Route 113 south, and you'll hit the park a few miles south of the town of Snow Hill.

NEARBY ACCOMMODATIONS

For less primitive accommodations, you'll have to stay on the mainland or in Ocean City. The town of Berlin offers two good options: the ✪ **Atlantic Hotel** and the ✪ **Merry Sherwood Plantation.** Both are about a 15-minute drive from the island. See "Nearby Accommodations" in the Ocean City section of this chapter for details. Snow Hill, about 40 minutes from the island, has several bed-and-breakfasts, including the **River House Inn.** See "Where to Stay," below.

4 An Excursion to Snow Hill

23 miles SW of Ocean City, 19 miles SE of Salisbury

While the Disney Corporation is busy re-creating small-town America in Florida, the real thing has been quietly going about the business of life for over 300 years on the banks of the Pocomoke River. Snow Hill, the county seat of Worcester County, might well have been the model for Disney's Celebration, with its clapboard siding and white picket fences and rows of tidy cottages, gabled Victorian homes, and Federal-style manors. Close to a hundred of Snow Hill's houses and several of its churches are over a century old.

Snow Hill doesn't just look like small-town America; this is a town where everyone knows everyone, where community dances are held once a month under the full moon on the riverside and everyone shows up, and where only the world-weary tourists lock their doors at night, or during the day, for that matter. There is one fast-food joint, a McDonald's on the edge of town, and the locals were none too happy at its arrival in December 1995 (though they were quite overjoyed when Sam Walden chose to expand his empire of Wal-Marts in Pocomoke City, 15 miles south, rather than in Snow Hill). Truth be told, there's not a whole lot to do on an average day in Snow Hill, short of river excursions, antiquing, and just wandering the streets admiring the historic homes; but Furnace Town, Shad Landing and Milburn Landing State Parks, and even Assateague Island are just a short drive away, and if you can manage to be in town to see the whole community come out for one of their moonlit dances or the Annual Canoe Joust, you'll get a memorable taste of real small-town America.

ESSENTIALS

GETTING THERE   From Ocean City, take Route 50 west to Route 113 south through Berlin. From Salisbury, take MD Route 12 south. From points south, take Route 13 toward Pocomoke City and pick up Route 113 north a mile or so east of Pocomoke City.

VISITOR INFORMATION   Begin your excursion to Snow Hill by stopping by the **Worcester County Economic Development** office at 105 Pearl St. (☎ **410/ 632-3110**) or the **Julia A. Purnell Museum** at 208 W. Market St. (☎ **410/ 632-0515**), for brochures and information. Be sure to pick up a walking tour map. The **Snow Hill Area Chamber of Commerce** (☎ **410/632-0089**) is also a good source of information.

SPECIAL EVENT   The ✪ **Annual Canoe Joust** on the Pocomoke at Sturgis Park is held the first weekend in August and makes our list of most unusual sporting events.

SHOPPING

If you enter Snow Hill from the west, along Route 12, you'll be greeted by a billboard proclaiming Snow Hill the "Antiques Capital of the Shore." Not a terribly impressive title, considering that most of Maryland's Atlantic coast consists of Ocean City and Assateague, not exactly antique havens. But Snow Hill does have a fair number of antique shops, and they are all conveniently located within walking distance of each other. Generally, all the antique stores keep the same hours: Monday and Wednesday through Saturday from 10am to 5pm, Sunday from noon to 5pm.

The Cannery. 5303 Snow Hill Rd. (on the Pocomoke River). ☎ **410/632-1722.**

The Cannery is that popular crossbreed of country craft store and antique shop, featuring in the craft department candles, ironwork, furniture, woodwork, and holiday ornaments; and in the antique department, vintage clothing, furniture, and glassware. Also of note is the good-sized collection of working antique clocks.

Emporium Antiques & Collectibles. 109 Pearl St. ☎ **410/632-3012.**

Emporium's two floors are filled with an eclectic collection of smaller items: glassware, books, Oriental rugs, quilts, handkerchiefs, and linens. There is also an entire room devoted to vintage clothing, with quite a few wedding gowns, and a room full of dolls.

Goodman's Antiques. 110 W. Green St. ☎ **410/632-2686.**

This is the place to go for furniture, particularly if you're looking for oak. But Goodman's also has smaller collections of glassware, toys, decoys, and quilts.

Opera House Act II. 204 N. Washington St. ☎ **410/632-1860.**

This ever-expanding antique mall offers a little bit of everything—glassware, china, kitchen items, jewelry, and furniture. This is a good place to find unusual items.

Pusey's Country Store. 5313 Snow Hill Rd. ☎ **410/632-1992.**

Pusey's may be the closest thing Snow Hill has to a convenience store, so if you're looking for a place to stock up on provisions for a day on the river, this is your best bet. In addition to cold soda, ice, and snacks, Pusey's has a pretty good selection of microbrews, McCutcheon's jams and jellies, a small plant nursery, and a small hodgepodge collection of crafts.

THE POCOMOKE RIVER

The scenic Pocomoke River and the surrounding cypress swamp is the center of most of the county's outdoor adventures. The river, which runs the length of Worcester

County, is home to 172 species of birds and 72 families of plant life, not to mention the numerous species of mammals, reptiles, and amphibians. It's a veritable paradise for bird and nature lovers. You can access the river from several places, including the town of Snow Hill, Pocomoke River State Park (just south of Snow Hill), and Pocomoke City (13 miles south of Snow Hill and a few miles north of the river's confluence with the Chesapeake at Pocomoke Sound).

If you've been following Maryland news, you may have heard that the Pocomoke and other rivers on the Eastern Shore were in some environmental distress in the summer of 1997. Fish kills caused by the *Pfiesteria* microorganism (which has also been linked to human illness) caused the closing of several rivers including southern portions of the Pocomoke. At press time, the problem seems to have subsided, possibly due to the change of seasons, and in any case the section of the river north of Snow Hill was not affected. However, it's a good idea to pay attention to the environmental news before you plan your trip to the area. See "Health & Insurance" in chapter 3 for more information on *Pfiesteria*.

Probably the best way to see the river, and the surrounding flora and fauna, is by hopping in a canoe. **Pocomoke River Canoe Company** (☎ **410/632-3971**), located on the river in Snow Hill, rents canoes and kayaks and provides portage, guide service, and box lunches with advance notice. If you're visiting during prime bug season, that is, April through October, bring bug spray and lots of it. Better yet, unless you're looking for a deep-woods, back-to-the-elements, swamp adventure, skip the trip through the swamp north of Snow Hill. Though the scenery is breathtaking, the greenheads and mosquitoes are vicious.

If you have your own boat, there is a ramp available at **Byrd Park,** and dockage at both Byrd and **Sturgis Parks,** south of the Route 12 bridge in Snow Hill. Both parks also offer free fishing areas. Fishing from a boat requires a license, which you can pick up at the Pocomoke River Canoe Company or at **Bowen's Grocers** on West Market Street (☎ **410/632-3426**).

There are several nature trails at the Shad and Milburn Landing areas of Pocomoke River State Park, just south of Snow Hill. Nearby **Furnace Town** offers a well-marked boardwalk trail through the cypress swamp. Again, bring your bug spray. The staff at Furnace Town can give you a daily report on the insect situation along the trail.

MUSEUMS & HISTORIC SITES

The **Julia A. Purnell Museum,** 208 W. Market St. (☎ **410/632-0515**), is a good place to begin your exploration of Snow Hill. Founded in 1942 as a tribute to local legend and needlework artist Julia Purnell, this small museum expanded after Mrs. Purnell's death to include displays and exhibits depicting the town's history and culture. Along with several of Mrs. Purnell's needlework pictures, the museum features a general store exhibit, a "touching" table, items from Mrs. Purnell's sewing room, and a time line depicting the history of Worcester County in the context of U.S. history. Open April through October, Monday through Friday from 9am –5pm, Saturday and Sunday from 1 to 5pm.

Before you leave the Purnell Museum, pick up the historic walking tour brochure. There are more than 100 historic buildings still in use in Snow Hill, many of which were built prior to 1877. The walking tour includes over 50 of these buildings and provides brief descriptions of each. Unfortunately, the tour is rather long and not well thought out, so the brochure is better used as a source of information about the homes you happen to stroll or drive by on your jaunts through town.

In the heart of the Pocomoke Forest, 4 miles north of Snow Hill on Route 12, **Furnace Town Historic Site** (☎ 410/632-2032) offers a look at life in a 19th-century industrial village. A miniature Williamsburg, and somewhat more authentic, the restored village of Furnace Town surrounds the Nassawango Iron Furnace, Maryland's only bog-ore furnace. Along with a museum depicting the history of the original Furnace Town, the site features weaving, broom-making, and printing demonstrations, as well as a working blacksmith shop, woodworking shop, and kitchen garden. The site is open daily April through October from 11am to 5pm. Demonstrations are offered 2 to 4 days a week on a rotating basis, so call ahead for a schedule.

WHERE TO STAY

River House Inn. 201 E. Market St. ☎ **410/632-2722.** Fax 410/632-2866. 4 rms, 1 suite, 3 cottage suites. A/C. $100 double; $120 suite; $160–$175 cottage suite. Rates include breakfast. MC, V.

This 1860s Victorian home, highlighted on the town walking tour, sits on 2 acres of rolling riverfront land, though if you stay in the main house and are not too adventurous you may not realize the river is there. Guest lodgings are located in three buildings: the main house and two cottages. Though lacking river views, rooms in the main house are quite spacious and offer faux marble fireplaces and convenient access to the common areas: the two screened-in porches overlooking the garden, and the twin parlors with TV and VCR, games, and reading material. All three cottage suites have private screened-in porches and all the modern amenities, including whirlpool tubs, microwaves, and minifridges. But if you want a breathtaking view of the Pocomoke, stay in one of the River Hideaway suites. Discounted rates are offered in the off-season and for longer stays.

WHERE TO DINE

Bailey's Cafe. 104 Green St. ☎ **410/632-3704.** Lunch $3.85–$5.65. MC, V. Mon–Fri 7:30am–4pm, Sat–Sun 8:30am–4pm. AMERICAN.

Bailey's is conveniently located for a lunch stop after a morning of antiquing. Pastries and light lunch fare—soups, salads, and sandwiches—are the specialty, and the portions are quite generous. The tarragon and Southwestern chicken salads are our favorites. While you're waiting for your lunch, you can browse the cafe's small local-interest bookstore (it's actually two shelves in the front corner) for cookbooks, travel guides, bird and nature guidebooks, and books on area and bay history.

Snow Hill Inn and Restaurant. 104 E. Market St. ☎ **410/632-2101.** Main courses $9.95–$21.95; lunch $4.50–$8.95. AE, MC, V. Mon–Fri 11am–2pm and 5–9pm, Sat 5–9pm, Sun 4–8pm. AMERICAN/SEAFOOD.

This is Snow Hill's finest restaurant and the locals won't hesitate to tell you so. It's located in a circa-1850 home, converted to a B&B/restaurant, so there are several smallish dining areas. A newer room in the back has the feel of an enclosed porch and looks out onto the patio and garden. Surf-and-turf is the house specialty; a dish called Snow on the Hills (crab imperial served in mounds on prime rib medallions) is superb. The crab imperial, in general, is unusually good, because it is not overly rich. In addition to the regular menu, the restaurant offers an extensive selection of daily specials, often including a seafood platter with crab cakes, shrimp, and the catch of the day.

9

Western Maryland

From the green hills of Frederick to the rolling mountains of Garrett County, Western Maryland has long captured the attention of both outdoor excursionists and history buffs. The gentle farmland surrounding the historic town of Frederick is often called the Civil War Crossroads, having seen some of the bloodiest fighting of the war. Now, thousands each year flock to parks at Gettysburg, Antietam, and Harpers Ferry to hear the stories of the battles and remember those who fell. In 1996, the National Museum of Civil War Medicine opened in Frederick's historic district, giving visitors a glimpse of the medical advances made in response to the tragedies of the war.

Farther west, Garrett and Allegany counties are a boon for adventure-sports fans. Although the mountains here are not as spectacular as the Blue Ridge or Smoky Mountains, they are home to hundreds of miles of unfrequented hiking trails, trails for both downhill and cross-country skiing, numerous large protected forests, excellent camping, and two of the premier white-water rivers on the east coast: the Youghiogheny and the Savage.

SEEING WESTERN MARYLAND

A network of modern interstate highways will bring you to this relatively undiscovered part of the state. I-270 connects Washington, D.C., to Frederick. I-70 connects Baltimore to Frederick and then crosses the Pennsylvania border. The new I-68 traverses the western end of Maryland from I-70 to the West Virginia border. Route 219 intersects I-68 and heads south to Deep Creek Lake. In addition to these, Alternate Route 40, the country's first National Pike, still meanders over the entire length of the countryside, connecting Frederick to Cumberland and other points east and west.

1 The Great Outdoors in Western Maryland

Western Maryland, like its neighbor West Virginia, is mountain country, and in its forested hillsides and meandering river valleys await a myriad of outdoor activities and beautiful scenery. If you are coming to the area for the first time, don't expect huge mountains; there aren't any. Instead Maryland's mountain ranges, the Catoctin and Allegheny, rise gently from the rolling hills of Frederick County to their highest point 3,360 feet above sea level at Backbone Mountain south of Oakland. Spread out across these rumbling mountains

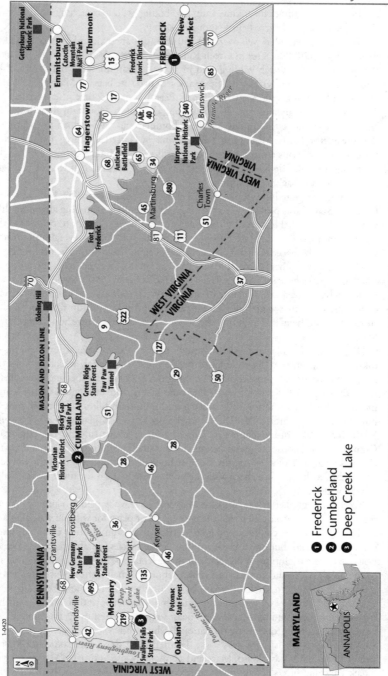

are ample opportunities for hiking, camping, biking, wildlife watching, fishing, wild river adventures, and even, believe it or not, skiing.

Western Maryland has well over 100,000 acres of state park and protected wilderness land, with 40,000 acres in Green Ridge State Forest alone. What this means is that places to hike, watch wildlife, and in general commune with nature are to be found virtually everywhere. In the Frederick area two sure bets are Maryland Heights (a steep hike with a great view of Harpers Ferry) and, of course, the Appalachian Trail, which in Maryland runs 40 miles along the South Mountain ridge from the Mason-Dixon line to the confluence of the Potomac and Shenandoah rivers just below Weaverton Cliffs. More great hiking awaits in Garrett County where favorites include the easy trails around picturesque Swallow and Muddy Creek Falls and the strenuous 17-mile Big Savage trail along the Savage Mountain ridge, an excellent place to do some backpack camping.

For those interested in camping a little closer to the road, Swallow Falls and New Germany State Parks provide a great setting and comfortable camping amenities (like warm bathhouses). However, if you like your campsite a bit more primitive, the remote Potomac–Garrett State Forest, south of Oakland, offers several unimproved sites, generously spaced so that you might not even notice if you have neighbors.

Mountain biking has been a little slow to catch on in Maryland. Even though some small local parks have set aside trails for bikers, there aren't really any of major note. Fortunately, the backwoods nature of much of Western Maryland ensures that some of the dirt roads that were intended for cars are still plenty of fun for riders with a sturdy bike and helmet. You'll find these roads in both Greenridge and Savage River State Forests.

Despite the area's lack of great mountain biking, it does have at least one major biking attraction, the 184-mile Chesapeake and Ohio Canal, which follows the Potomac River from Georgetown (in Washington, D.C.) to Cumberland. The canal's towpath is a great flat trail for both hikers and bikers, and although it can be a little messy at times, it's fine for both touring and mountain bikes. The canal goes by numerous sites, including Paw Paw Tunnel, Fort Frederick, Harpers Ferry National Historical Park, and Great Falls. The scenery is beautiful and the trip from Cumberland is almost all gently downhill. Any small portion of the canal towpath can make a great 1-day biking trip. Because flooding can make some of the towpath impassable, make sure you check with the park service to see if the route you intended to bike is clear.

Recent ecological efforts in Western Maryland have really paid off, and now, more than any time in the last 20 years, the area is a great place for wildlife watching and fishing. Whether the credit should go to better controls on hunting or on pollution can't really be said, but one thing is for sure: Some species, notably hawks and black bears, that were beginning to disappear from the landscape are now returning in force to the area's parks and forests. In Garrett County a major effort was launched to reduce the damage to the Casselman, North Branch Potomac, and Youghiogheny rivers caused by years of acid mining in the mountains above them. The effort has been a real success, and now these rivers boast some of the best fly-fishing around and have been featured prominently on national fishing shows.

While Maryland is in no way a ski destination, it does offer some fun for the winter-sports enthusiast. Wisp, Maryland's only ski resort, is situated very near Deep Creek Lake and offers several respectable downhill trails. And its cross-country skiing trails, where you can glide quietly through the snow-padded wonderland of the Allegheny forests, are some of the area's true hidden jewels. Numerous trails ranging in difficulty from easy to somewhat treacherous are open to the public at both

Herrington Manor State Park and New Germany State Park in Garrett County. Snow mobile trails are available at Savage River State Forest.

After the snow melts, Western Maryland's biggest attractions kick into high gear: white-water rafting, kayaking, and canoeing. The Youghiogheny, the North Branch Potomac, the Savage, and the Shenandoah–Potomac are the area's best-known runs. Although they can be challenging all year long, in spring after snowmelt they are at their fiercest. Both the Youghiogheny and the Shenandoah–Potomac are home to commercial raft and guide services. The dam-release-controlled Youghiogheny (pronounced "yah-ka-*gay*-nee" or "yah-ka-*hay*-nee" but often simply called the "Yock") offers a thrilling ride year-round (class IV–V on the international white-water scale of difficulty). The Shenandoah–Potomac run (class II–III) on the West Virginia border near Frederick is a more family-friendly trip in summer when the water is low. However, don't let the low rating fool you; in spring after snowmelt these two large rivers can swell and become quite a harrowing ride.

Kayakers looking to avoid the raft traffic would do well to try and visit the North Branch Potomac and Savage rivers (both class III–IV); both, however, are only runnable after heavy rains or snowmelt. For those looking to do a little open canoeing (our favorite) the Shenandoah–Potomac is great in summer and fall, and in winter and spring the scenic Casselman River (class II) to the west is quite good. Antietam Creek (class II) is a great little run year-round.

2 Civil War Sites & Excursions

Dangling on the Mason-Dixon line dividing the northern and southern halves of the United States, in the 1860s Maryland was placed at the center of the country's most bloody conflict: the American Civil War. Gen. Robert E. Lee leading the Confederate army was convinced that the key to securing the South's independence was to take the war to the north. The Rebel army's two great attempts at this led to some of the most terrible fighting of the war, at Antietam and then less than a year later at Gettysburg. But these were not the only battles, nor was fighting the only story on Maryland's Civil War front. The sites below have an air of tragic beauty about them and are ideal places to learn about and reflect on this dark time in our nation's history.

ANTIETAM NATIONAL BATTLEFIELD

Civil War buffs flock to ✪ **Antietam National Battlefield,** Route 65, north of Sharpsburg (☎ 301/432-5124), the site of the bloodiest single-day battle of the Civil War, located about 20 miles southwest of Frederick. (For a scenic trip from Frederick take alternate Route 40, which takes you through Middletown and then over South Mountain ridge where the Battle of South Mountain occurred; then turn right on Route 34 in the town of Boonsboro; this will take you into Sharpsburg.) The battlefield's quiet rolling hills and limited number of monuments make it a stark and silent contrast to the memorials of Gettysburg to the north.

Antietam is one of those places that immediately calls to mind the great schism that civil war brought to this country. Even the name is contentious: To Southerners it is still called the Battle of Sharpsburg; to the Northerners and the federal government it is Antietam. More than 23,000 men were killed or wounded here when Union forces met and stopped the first attempted Southern invasion of the North on September 17, 1862. Abraham Lincoln issued the Emancipation Proclamation as a result of this victory and made a very rare appearance at the battlefield shortly after the battle to confront the Union's reluctant General George McClellan. Clara Barton, who was to found the American Red Cross 19 years later, attended the wounded at a field hospital here. A visitor center at the battlefield offers historical exhibits, a film shown on the hour, and a slide show on the half hour. The staff provides free information and literature and can suggest tours of the battlefield and cemetery.

Be sure to stop by **Burnside Bridge,** which crosses Antietam Creek near the southern end of the battlefield. Georgia snipers stalled 12,000 Union soldiers for over 3 hours as they were trying to secure this bridge. Another oft-visited battle site, a sunken country lane near the center of the battlefield, was the scene of a 4-hour encounter that ended with no decisive winner and 4,000 casualties. This road is now known as **Bloody Lane.** The graceful stone arches of this Burnside Bridge and the harrowing sight of Bloody Lane are the among the most memorable images of the battlefield.

Admission to the battlefield is $2 for individuals, $4 per family, and free for those under 17. The visitor center is open daily June through August from 8:30am to 6pm and September through May from 8:30am to 5pm. The battlefield officially closes 20 minutes after sunset.

For a different view of the site, **Antietam Creek,** which flows the length of the park and then down to the Potomac, is an excellent novice-to-intermediate–level canoe and kayak run offering views of a small waterfall, Burnside Bridge, the ruins of Antietam Furnace, and the old C&O Canal aqueduct. River and Trail Outfitters (see "Spectator Sports & Outdoor Activities" in the Frederick section below) offers a variety of float trips down this scenic creek, and canoe and kayak rental if you'd like to try it on your own.

HARPERS FERRY NATIONAL HISTORICAL SITE

Harpers Ferry is a town rich with history, from its early years as a colonial frontier town, to its heyday as a center of industry, to its many disastrous floods. However, the town is remembered most for its unique role in the Civil War, a part that began over a year before the war itself. On October 16, 1859, abolitionist John Brown and 21 of his men raided the federal arsenal at Harpers Ferry intent on arming the nation's slaves and starting a rebellion. The raid failed, and afterward Brown was convicted of "conspiring with slaves to commit treason and murder" and was hanged. Many Northerners considered Brown a martyr. His action polarized the nation and was one of the sparks that ignited the war.

Today, **Harpers Ferry National Historical Site,** P.O. Box 65, Harpers Ferry, WV 25425 (☎ **304/535-6298**), is truly a great place to spend a day. Many of the old buildings have been restored, its cobblestone streets are still maintained, and vast portions of the town are administered by the National Park Service. Historical exhibits abound: the park service offers small museums on John Brown's raid, the town's industry, Storer College (an early African-American college established in town), and, of course, the town's direct role in the Civil War, when it changed hands between the Union and the Confederacy eight times.

Your visit to town will probably begin with a short park-provided shuttle ride from the main parking lot to the town itself. Once you're in town you'll be surrounded

---

Impressions

In the time I am writing, every stalk of corn in the northern part of the field was cut as closely as could have been done with a knife, and the slain lay in rows precisely as they had stood in their ranks a few moments before.

—Union Gen. Joseph Hooker, September 17, 1862

by sites, but a few are exceptional. The **John Brown Museum** on Shenandoah Street offers exhibits and audiovisual displays on the wild-eyed abolitionist and tracks the course of his raid, capture, and conviction. The **Harper House** is a restored dwelling that sits at the top of the stone stairs, above High Street. The oldest remaining structure in Harpers Ferry, it was built between 1775 and 1782 by town founder Robert Harper and served as a tavern for such notable guests as Thomas Jefferson and George Washington. If you can make the climb farther up the stone stairs past St. Peter's Church, ✪ **Jefferson Rock** offers a view of the confluence of the Shenandoah and Potomac rivers that the former president himself said was worth crossing the Atlantic for.

To get to Harpers Ferry, take Route 340 west from Frederick. You will cross the Potomac River Bridge (you'll see the town off the bridge to your right) into Virginia and then about three quarters of a mile later cross the Shenandoah River into West Virginia. The historical park's parking lot is about a mile past the bridge over the Shenandoah on the left. Park admission is $5 per vehicle and $3 per pedestrian or cyclist and includes the shuttle ride into town. The park is open daily from 8am to 5pm and is closed on December 25.

To experience Harpers Ferry from two entirely different vantage points, local outfitters offer white-water rafting trips down the Shenandoah right by the town and guided hikes up Maryland Heights, where you can see the town from the high cliffs on the Maryland side of the Potomac (see "Spectator Sports & Outdoor Activities" in the Frederick section below). You can also hike to Maryland Heights on your own; the trail begins directly across the walking bridge over the Potomac at Harpers Ferry. Maps are available from the park service.

FORT FREDERICK STATE PARK

Although not a major Civil War site, if you're in the area (I-70 west of Hagerstown) this unusual fortification, which served in three wars and has stood for over 240 years, is worth a look. Built in 1756 during the French and Indian War to protect Maryland's colonial frontier, this large stone fort (built at a time when every other fort on the frontier was wooden) was so well built and strategically placed that no one ever dared attack it, even during Ottawa chief Pontiac's massive Native American uprising. The fort served as a haven for British and Hessian soldiers during the American Revolution. Finally, on December 25, 1861, Confederate raiders fought a brief skirmish with Union troops who had taken over the fort from a local farmer. This was the only fighting Fort Frederick ever saw.

Now the interior barracks have been restored to look as they did during the French and Indian War, and a platform has been installed along the inside of the fort walls so that visitors can look out over the massive stone walls. During the summer, colonial reenactors tell visitors about life on the early frontier and about the fort's varied history.

For information contact **Fort Frederick State Park,** 11100 Fort Frederick Rd., Big Pool, MD 21711, or call ☎ **310/842-2155.** Admission for people 13 years of age and older is $2, children 6 to 12 years $1, and children under 6 are free. The fort is open daily April through October from 8:30am to sunset and November through March from 10am to 4pm. The park closes Thanksgiving, December 24, and December 25.

GETTYSBURG NATIONAL MILITARY PARK

Just north of the Maryland–Pennsylvania line, about 34 miles north of Frederick, Gettysburg was the "high-water mark" of the Confederate rebellion. It was here that the 70,000-strong army of Confederate soldiers under General Robert E. Lee faced 93,000 Union men under General George Meade in a 3-day conflict that would change the course of the war. After the battle Lee's army returned to Virginia defeated and exhausted and would never again be able to mount an effective attack into Union territory. Later President Lincoln would use the dedication of the National Cemetery here to deliver his poignant "Gettysburg Address," a speech that crystallized the Union's intent in fighting the war and became a classic document in American history.

The park itself is quite large and almost fully surrounds the tourist-trap town of Gettysburg. Unlike the town, however, the park is characterized by pleasant rolling hills, fences, an occasional cannon, and numerous monuments of marble, stone, and bronze. The visitor center offers maps with an 18-mile self-guided auto tour that hits all the major sites. Favorite sites include the mammoth **Pennsylvania Memorial** and **Devil's Den,** an outcropping of rocks that hid snipers during the battle. Not as frequently visited but well worth seeing are the impressive and dramatic bronze sculptures of the state memorials of North Carolina, Louisiana, and Mississippi along West Confederate Avenue.

The **Visitor Center,** Gettysburg National Military Park, P.O. Box 1080, Gettysburg, PA 17325 (☎ **717/334-1124**), is a great place to start any trip to Gettysburg. It houses a large bookstore stocked with hundreds of books on the battle and the Civil War in general, and a museum featuring audiovisual displays and a great collection of guns, cannons, ammunition, equipment, and uniforms from both sides of the war. The museum is free; however, there is a fee for the 30-minute electric map program detailing the battle ($2.50 for adults, $2 for seniors, $1 for ages 6 to 15). Park tours are offered out of the visitor center, for a fee, by the Association of **Licensed Battlefield Guides** (for information contact the visitor center above), a group set up in 1913 by Civil War veterans to ensure that visitors receive accurate information about the battle. These guides can tell you about everything from troop movements to who built the Pennsylvania Memorial and how much it cost.

One of the highlights of a trip to Gettysburg is the truly unique **Gettysburg Cyclorama.** Housed in a contemporary building next door to the visitor center, the cyclorama is an oil painting, 356 feet in circumference, giving a panoramic wraparound view of Picket's Charge, the climax of the battle. Completed in 1884 by French artist Paul Dominique Philippoteaux, this stirring work is one of only a few cycloramas left in the world today. Admission to the cyclorama, like the electric map, is $2.50 for adults, $2 for seniors, and $1 for ages 6 to 15. It includes a viewing of the painting enhanced by a sound-and-light program and narrated by actor Richard Dreyfuss.

Admission to Gettysburg National Military Park is free. The battlefield is open daily from 6am to 10pm; the visitor center and cyclorama are open daily from 8am to 5pm. Both are closed January 1, Thanksgiving, and December 25.

OTHER CIVIL WAR SITES

Civil War sites, battlefields, and museums abound throughout Maryland and Delaware. In Frederick (see "Frederick," below) the **National Museum of Civil War Medicine,** the **Barbara Fritchie House,** and **Monocacy National Battlefield** offer glimpses into that town's role in the War Between the States. Farther south, in **Fort Lincoln** in St. Mary's County (see "St. Mary's County" in chapter 6), you can see the remains of a small prison camp where 3,000 confederate soldiers died within sight of their home shores of Virginia. And **Fort Delaware** (see "Easy Excursions from

Wilmington" in chapter 10), is a large Union prison fortress on an island in the Delaware Bay.

3 Frederick

34 miles S of Gettysburg, 47 miles W of Baltimore, 45 miles NW of Washington, D.C.

In recent years, Frederick has grown from a largely agricultural community to one of the largest cities in the state, a bustling Washington suburb with a population of over 45,000, and it's still growing by leaps and bounds. Despite this growth, the city has managed to maintain its small-town charm. The 33-block historic district with its 18th- and 19th-century homes and buildings and the clustered church spires that make up Frederick's distinctive skyline are still the main attraction. The shops and restaurants here are particularly good. North and west of the city, the agricultural community still thrives: Fresh produce from the local orchards and farms is available all summer long, and in early spring newborn foals can be seen romping, playing, and sleeping in the green pastures of the county's horse farms.

ESSENTIALS

GETTING THERE   If you're driving from Washington, D.C., and points south, take I-270 to Frederick, where the interstate becomes U.S. 15 and continues north to Gettysburg and Harrisburg. From Baltimore, take I-70 west. From Cumberland and points west, take I-68 east to I-70. **Greyhound** (☎ 800/231-2222) operates regular bus service to Frederick into its depot on East All Saints Street (☎ 301/663-3311), between South Market and Carroll streets.

Plans to extend the state's **MARC** train line into Frederick from Washington, D.C., have been set in motion. Projected completion date is 1999, but that's quite tentative, so call ☎ 800/325-RAIL for information before your trip.

VISITOR INFORMATION   The **Tourism Council of Frederick County** operates an efficient, helpful visitor center at 19 E. Church St., Frederick, MD 21701 (☎ 800/999-3613 or 301/663-8687). This office not only supplies maps, brochures, and listings of accommodations and restaurants but also conducts walking tours of the historic district. Tours are operated April through December on Saturday and Sunday beginning at 1:30pm. Cost is $4.50 for adults and $3.50 for seniors. Tourist information booths are also located in the rest areas on I-70 east and west at South Mountain and on U.S. 15 south at Emmitsburg. All of these facilities are open daily from 9am to 5pm.

GETTING AROUND   Without a doubt the best way to get around in Frederick is by car—that is, if you're not walking through the historic district. Parking is cheap, when it isn't free. Downtown metered parking is 50¢ per hour and $5 per day in both of the city's two parking decks, Monday through Friday; $1 on weekends and holidays.

SPECIAL EVENTS   The most popular and beautiful time of the year here is mid- to late October, when fall colors are at their peak. That's also the peak time for special events. The **Catoctin Colorfest** in nearby Thurmont is a craft show of enormous proportions, filling all the town's parks and public areas and lining the streets. It's held annually in mid-October. Contact the Tourism Council of Frederick County (☎ 800/999-3613 or 301/663-8687) for information and exact dates.

WHAT TO SEE & DO

The focus of Frederick is its 33-block **historic district.** Not only have many of the buildings been carefully restored but the street layout today is much as it was in the

Impressions

Up from the meadows rich with corn,
Clear in the cool September morn,
The clustered spires of Frederick stand
Green-walled by the hills of Maryland.

—John Greenleaf Whittier, "Barbara Frietchie"

early days. With Courthouse Square and Old Frederick City Hall at its heart, this city is a showcase of stately mansions and elegant brick town houses. The vista also includes 18th- and 19th-century church spires, graceful Victorian parks and gardens, and the oldest and largest ginkgo tree in the United States. The Frederick Visitor Center, 19 E. Church St. (☎ 301/663-8687), distributes a map of the district and also coordinates a program of **walking tours.** Tours depart from the visitor center each Saturday and Sunday, April through December, at 1:30pm. The price is $4.50 for adults, $3.50 for seniors, and free for children under 12.

DOWNTOWN MUSEUMS & HISTORIC SITES

Barbara Fritchie House and Museum. 154 W. Patrick St. ☎ 301/698-0630. Admission $2 adults, $1.50 seniors and under age 12. Apr–Sept Mon and Thurs–Sat 10am–4pm, Sun 1–4pm; Oct–Nov Sat 10am–4pm, Sun 1–4pm. Closed Dec–Mar.

This house is a replica of the home of Frederick's premier Civil War heroine. At age 95 Barbara Fritchie bravely waved the Stars and Stripes in the path of Confederate soldiers and was immortalized in a poem by John Greenleaf Whittier as the "bravest of all in Fredericktown." A visit to the house includes a video presentation of her life and times; a collection of mementos including quilts and linens made by Barbara; her caps, shawls, and dresses; and her desk, tables, chairs, and china.

○ **Historical Society of Frederick County.** 24 E. Church St. ☎ 301/663-1188. Admission $2 adults, free under age 17. Mon–Sat 10am–4pm, Sun 1–4pm. Guided tours available year-round.

This Federal-style landmark (ca. 1820) is a good place to broaden your knowledge of area history. Main exhibits focus on local notables, such as Roger B. Taney, chief justice of the U.S. Supreme Court and author of the Dred Scott Decision; Francis Scott Key, author of the "Star-Spangled Banner"; Thomas Johnson, first governor of Maryland; and Barbara Fritchie, heroine of John Greenleaf Whittier's poem. There are also a genealogical library and formal garden.

National Museum of Civil War Medicine. 48 E. Patrick St. ☎ 800/564-1864 or 301/695-1864. Fax 301/695-6823. Free admission. Tues–Fri 10am–5pm, Sat–Sun noon–5pm.

For a brief educational respite from a day of antiquing, stop by this relatively new museum, which opened in 1996. It occupies the first floor of a three-story building that holds a macabre place in Civil War history: Several thousand dead from the Battle of Antietam were housed and embalmed here. The museum features an exhibit on black surgeons and nurses, a film, a dentistry display (including a dentist's chair from the era), a coffin that predates the war, and the "Wall of Wounded," a not-for-the-squeamish display of photos and stories of the wounded and sick. Special attention is given to the role of women in hospitals and, of course, to the Battle of Antietam, fought in nearby Sharpsburg. Because the museum is so young, it currently has few holdings, but it is continually expanding and there are plans to fill the remaining two floors as funding becomes available.

✪ **Schifferstadt.** 1110 Rosemont Ave. ☎ **301/663-3885.** Donation $2 adults. Apr to mid-Dec Tues–Sat 10am–4pm, Sun noon–4pm. Closed mid-Dec through Mar, Easter, and Thanksgiving.

On the western edge of town near U.S. 15, you'll find Frederick's oldest standing house, one of America's finest examples of German colonial architecture. Built in 1756 by the Brunner family, who named it for their homeland in Germany, this house has stone walls more than 2 feet thick and hand-hewn beams of native oak pinned together with wooden pegs. Unusual original features include an enclosed winder stairway, a vaulted cellar and chimney, wrought-iron hardware, and a perfectly preserved five-plate jamb stove. Guided tours are given throughout the day. A gift shop, featuring arts and crafts, is adjacent in a 19th-century addition to the house.

NEARBY ATTRACTIONS

Lilypons Water Gardens. 6800 Lilypons Rd., Buckeystown. ☎ **800/999-5459** or 301/874-5133. Free admission. Mar–Oct daily 9:30am–5:30pm, Nov–Feb Mon–Sat 9:30am–4:30pm. Closed Easter, Thanksgiving, and Dec 24–Jan 2. From I-270, take Rte. 85 south and turn left on Lilypons Rd.

If you want to stop and smell the lilies, be sure to check out this water garden, named for the famous opera singer Lily Pons, who visited in 1936. One of the largest suppliers of ornamental fish and aquatic plants in the world, Lilypons offers several man-made ponds filled with a myriad of colorful lilies (in season) and the gardens' other specialty, coy (large Japanese goldfish). The ponds are spread across a few acres of open fields, which you can stroll through at your leisure. You can also purchase both lilies and coy. Midsummer is the best time to see the lilies in full bloom.

Monocacy National Battlefield. 4801 Urbana Pike. ☎ **301/662-3515.** Free admission. Memorial Day–Labor Day daily 8am–4:30pm; Sept–June Wed–Sun 8am–4:30pm. Take Rte. 85 (north from I-270, south from I-70) to Rte. 355 south; entrance is on the left just before the Monocacy River.

This stretch of farmland was the site of a little-known but important Civil War encounter, the Battle of the Monocacy. Gen. Jubal Early led 18,000 Confederates against a Union force of only 5,800 under Gen. Lew Wallace. Though the Confederates won the battle, their forces were weakened considerably, and Union troops at Ft. Stevens were able to push them back away from the capital. Today the battlefield remains virtually unchanged since the battle on July 9, 1864, except for five monuments strewn throughout the site. The visitor center has an electronic map depicting the details of the battle.

✪ **National Shrine of St. Elizabeth Ann Seton.** 333 S. Seton Ave., Emmitsburg. ☎ **301/447-6606.** Free admission, but donations welcome. Apr 2–Oct 31 daily 10am–4:30pm; Nov 1–Apr 1 Tues–Sun 10am–4:30pm. Closed Jan 1, last 2 weeks of Jan, Easter, Thanksgiving, and Dec 25. Take Rte. 15 north out of Frederick; turn left at the first exit onto Business 15 and follow signs to the shrine.

For peace and tranquillity in the Catoctin Mountain Valley, visitors flock to this secluded sylvan setting, once the home of this country's first native-born canonized saint, Elizabeth Ann Seton (1774–1821). Located less than a half hour's drive north of Frederick (22 miles), the site includes a splendid basilica-style shrine that contains the relics of the saint, the building in which she established her religious community in 1809, and the White House, where she began America's Catholic parochial school system in 1810. The complex also offers a small museum on the life of Mother Seton, a 15-minute slide show, and two small shops: one selling religious items and books and the other handiwork and crafts, much of which is made by the nuns in residence, carrying on a tradition started by Mother Seton. Visitors are welcome to take a self-guided tour of the grounds.

SPECTATOR SPORTS & OUTDOOR ACTIVITIES

BASEBALL   Frederick has its own Orioles farm team, the **Frederick Keys.** They play in Harry Grove Stadium, off I-70 and Route 355 (Market Street), from May to August or early September. General admission tickets cost about $10. For tickets or information call ☎ **301/662-0088.**

BIKING   The ✪ **Chesapeake and Ohio Canal (C&O)** runs along the Potomac River for 184½ miles from Georgetown to Cumberland. Though boats no longer travel the canal, the dirt towpath, lined with floodplain forests, is a popular place for cycling. The terrain is generally flat, and since no motor vehicles are allowed on the path, it's a safe place for cyclists of all ages. In Frederick County, you can access the canal in several places: Point of Rocks, off Route 15 south; Brunswick, Route 79 off MD Route 340; and Sandy Hook, left off Route 340, just before you cross the Potomac River.

HIKING   The ✪ **Appalachian Trail** runs along the border of Frederick and Washington counties, through **Washington Monument State Park, South Mountain State Park,** and **Greenbrier State Park,** where hikers can easily access the trail. You can hike the entire Maryland portion in 3 or 4 days, but any section of it makes a great 1-day excursion. Most of the 40 miles take you along the ridge of South Mountain, offering good views and a moderately strenuous hike. At the West Virginia/Virginia border, the trail will take you to the top of **Maryland Heights,** for an excellent view of Harpers Ferry and the confluence of the Shenandoah and Potomac rivers. River and Trail Outfitters (☎ **301/695-5177**) offers guided group trips along this portion of the trail, or you can hike it yourself; the trailhead is just upriver from C&O Canal lock 33, directly across from Harpers Ferry at the walking bridge. A trail map is available from Harpers Ferry National Historical Park at the office in Harpers Ferry or at their website—**www.nps.gov/hafe/af_visit.htm.**

North of Frederick City, **Catoctin Mountain National Park,** Route 77, Thurmont (☎ **301/663-9388**), adjacent to Camp David and **Cunningham Falls State Park,** offers several miles of easy to moderately strenuous hiking trails. Several of the trails lead to overlooks, such as Wolf Rock and Chimney Rock, with fine views of the Thurmont Valley. The park also offers camping, fishing, picnic sites, and playgrounds. Admission from May through September is $3 on weekends and holidays, $2 on weekdays, except Wednesday, when it's $1. There's no admission fee the rest of the year. Take Route 15 north, about 15 miles outside of Frederick, and follow the signs to the park.

WHITE-WATER ADVENTURES   Opportunities for white-water paddling abound throughout Western Maryland, but the creeks and rivers near Frederick are great places for novices and families to get their feet wet, so to speak. ✪ **River and Trail Outfitters,** 604 Valley Rd., Knoxville, Maryland (☎ **301/695-5177**), offers half-day guided rafting trips down the Shenandoah–Potomac, a class II/III run. Experienced and informed guides lead you down Bull Falls and Washing Machine and through the Upper and Lower Staircases, all the while sharing local history, legends, and quite a few corny jokes. Prices depend on the season and the number of people in your group, but generally run about $40 to $50 per person and include a picnic lunch on the river.

Great Falls of the Potomac

Although Maryland is long on gorgeous scenery, from the dunes of Assateague Island to the mountains of Garrett County, it is surprisingly short on what you might call natural wonders, with one notable exception—Great Falls of the Potomac. Great Falls is the place where the mighty Potomac River cracks through the hard rock spine of the fall line and comes crashing down into the Mather Gorge and the coastal plain below. Interestingly enough, this cataclysm of nature can be seen every day just outside the capital beltway, in the heart of the Washington suburbs.

When you go to Great Falls for the first time, don't expect the tall, shear, white faces of Niagara Falls and other waterfalls. Great Falls is much uglier and meaner looking, and this is what gives the falls its captivating power. Water here falls not over a single drop but over many, a mass of complex rapids made up of what on smaller rivers would be considered individual waterfalls. The streams crash again and again into jagged gray rocks; they tumble downward as spotty white foam, only to regather as seething green-brown waves and swirling eddies and explode again into mist and spray.

The falls itself is split by rocky Olmsted Island. The main part of the falls, lo-cally known as the Streamers, is on the Virginia side, and the much smaller Olmsted Falls is on the Maryland side. The island can be accessed by a footbridge and trail across the narrow gorges of Olmsted Falls and two small but pretty falls within the island itself. At the end of the trail is an observation platform overlooking the Streamers, from which you can survey most of the action, except for a small hidden channel known as the Spout on the Virginia side. You'll also usually see at least a few dare-devil kayakers playing in the massive waves that form 200 yards downstream from the falls.

Expert kayakers occasionally test their skills against the many drops of Great Falls, but these attempts are rare. When they do happen, it is usually on the Virginia side before 10am, as the Spout is the "safest" of all the amazingly dangerous routes through the falls, and the park service encourages experts to run only early in the morning out of view of most tourists. The falls were first successfully run by kayakers in 1976 and later by open-canoeist Nolan Whitesell in 1986. That's right, an open canoe; I've seen pictures and still find it hard to believe.

The temptation to climb on the rocky slopes of the falls to get a better look can be overwhelming, but be warned, the waters in and around the falls are deceptive and very dangerous. Signs all over the park will remind you of the numerous drownings in the area each year. So if you do wander on the rocks, be careful.

In addition to viewing the falls, there are a few other fun things to do. This area is part of the C&O Canal Historical Park, which has several miles of pleasant but at times difficult walking trails. If you are looking for something less strenuous, a stroll along the canal towpath is always good. The park visitor center, located in an old tavern, has a display of the workings of a canal lock as well as neat pictures of recent and past flood damage to the area. To experience the canal firsthand, in summer there are canal boat tours from Wednesday through Sunday, which cost $6 for adults, $5 for seniors, and $4 for children.

To get to the park from Frederick, take I-270 south to I-495, the capital beltway. Proceed down I-495 south toward Northern Virginia and then take exit 40, the Cabin John Parkway, to Great Falls. Admission to the park is $4 per car or $2 per person. For information call the park at ☎ 301/299-3613.

If you prefer to be the captain of your own ship, River and Trail also offers canoeing and kayaking tours down the Shenandoah–Potomac and on Antietam Creek, and canoe and kayak rentals and shuttle service. They even conduct kayaking classes and run tubing trips down Antietam Creek, which takes you through Antietam National Battlefield. Call ahead for reservations and for a full list of their trip offerings. *Note:* Guides generally work for tips, as well as for their love of the river. You need only tip the guide who steers your boat; $3 to $5 per person is appropriate.

SHOPPING

The two primary reasons to visit the Frederick historic district are to eat at one of its fine restaurants and to shop. The continuing restoration of downtown has led to an ever-increasing population of antique stores, gift shops, and boutiques, and with the planned development of Carroll Creek, the shopping scene will continue to grow. The two main shopping areas are within easy walking distance.

Everedy Square and Shab Row comprise the first of these shopping areas, beginning at the corner of Patrick and East streets and continuing north about 2 1/2 blocks. The ratio of antique stores to specialty shops is much lower here; there are several gift shops specializing in country crafts and Christmas decor, a Talbots for women's clothing, and just a few antique stores.

But for the full Frederick shopping experience, you'll have to go a block or so southwest, to the main shopping district. Start at Carroll Street, just over Carroll Creek, and shop your way down Carroll to Patrick Street. Be sure to stop and take a look at the **Community Bridge** on Carroll Street; there's a rather impressive mural, created by a local artist. Turn left on Patrick. From Patrick to Market Street there's virtually nothing but antique stores and restaurants. Below we've listed only the largest and most unusual shops in both districts; this is by no means a comprehensive list. Most downtown stores are open weekdays from 10 or 11am to 5pm and weekends from noon to 6pm.

Because Frederick County is such a fertile area, it's an ideal place to shop for local produce, fruits, jams, jellies, ciders, baked goods, and more. But in most cases, you'll have to leave the historic district and head into the countryside to reach the produce markets.

ANTIQUES

Antique Cellar. 15 E. Patrick St. ☎ **301/620-0591.**

This crowded shop has some of the best prices in town on Victorian, Empire, and primitive furnishings, frames, and trunks, though a lot of the merchandise may need repair and refinishing.

Antique Imports. 125 East St. ☎ **301/662-6200.**

Located across from Shab Row, this shop houses the largest collection of British antique furniture, framed art, and lamps in the region.

Antique Station. 194 Thomas Johnson Dr. ☎ **301/695-0888.**

Housed in an old roller-skating rink, this large market contains the wares of over 140 dealers, with an emphasis on glassware and dishes, jewelry, sports memorabilia, and other smaller items.

Cannon Hill Place. 111 S. Carroll St. ☎ **301/695-9304.**

The highlight here is the two rooms crammed with vintage clothing. The rest of this large shop is filled with glassware, sports memorabilia, and in general, small, inexpensive items.

Edward & Edward Consignments. 35 S. Carroll St. ☎ **301/695-9674.**

This is a good place to get bits and pieces to finish off renovation projects. They carry lots of reasonably priced furniture, lamps, and trunks, as well as ironwork, shutters, ceramic tiles, and wooden trim work.

Emporium at Creekside. 112 E. Patrick St. ☎ **301/662-7099.**

This spacious market, housed in the old Buick dealership, displays the wares of more than 130 dealers, with a large collection of light oak furnishings, glassware and china, some vintage clothing, records, books, and magazines, and lots more.

ART & GIFTS

✪ **Flights of Fancy.** 20 East St. ☎ **301/663-9295.**

Situated in the heart of Everedy Square, this fun, colorful shop carries a little of everything: toys, jewelry, pottery, cards, candles, holiday decor, garden sculptures, and much more.

League of Maryland Craftsmen. 35 N. Market St. ☎ **301/695-1314.**

This small gallery, the league's second location, displays and sells the work of more than 100 Maryland artists, with a concentration on pottery, hand-blown glasswork, stained glass, and some paintings, etchings, and drawings. The Annapolis location has a greater selection of paintings. The shop is closed on Tuesday and Wednesday.

OUTDOOR ACCESSORIES

Trail House. 17 S. Market St., Frederick. ☎ **301/694-8448.**

For those who love the outdoors, this shop offers clothing and equipment for backpacking, camping, hiking, rock climbing, and other sporting pursuits. It also stocks local and regional maps and books, handy for walkers. Open Monday through Thursday from 9:30am to 7pm, Friday from 9:30am to 8pm.

PRODUCE MARKETS

Catoctin Mountain Orchard. 15307 Kelbaugh Rd., Thurmont. ☎ **301/271-2737.**

Situated on Route 15 north of Frederick, this farm sells a wide variety of locally grown fruits and vegetables, as well as canned fruits, preserves, maple syrups, apple and jelly packs, honey, salad dressings, relishes, and sugar-free products. Berries and cherries are also sold on a pick-your-own basis. Tours of the farm and orchards are given by appointment. Open June through October daily from 9am to 6pm; November and December daily from 9am to 5pm; and January through March Friday through Sunday from 9am to 5pm. Closed May and June.

✪ **McCutcheon's Factory Store.** 13 S. Wisner St., Frederick. ☎ **800/888-7537** or 301/662-3261.

Located downtown, off South Street, this is one of the longest established local enterprises, founded in 1938. It sells a full range of apples, nuts, and dried fruits but is best known for its apple butter, preserves, jellies, and jams, as well as honey, mustards, salad dressings, relishes, hot sauces, ciders, and juices. There is also a mail-order service, if you'd like to ship your purchases. Open Monday through Friday from 8am to 5pm and some weekends.

Pryor's Orchard. 13841 Pryor Rd., Thurmont. ☎ **301/271-2693.**

Located a half mile west of Thurmont off Route 77, this place sells a complete selection of local fruits, vegetables, cider, nuts, pear and peach butters, honey, and jellies, as well as pick-your-own berries and cherries. Open June through November daily from 9am to 6pm or later.

VINTAGE CLOTHING

Venus on the Half Shell. 151 N. Market St. ☎ **301/662-6213.**

For casual clothing from the '60s and '70s, stop by this shop. You'll find a good selection of jeans, men's shirts, ladies suits and dresses, and some nifty coats and jackets.

WHERE TO STAY

For a city of its size, Frederick has relatively few options for accommodations, with only one option in the historic district. Others are spread throughout the county. Most of the moderately priced chain hotels are conveniently located just outside the city limits. All the hotels in the area have free parking.

EXPENSIVE

Inn at Buckeystown. 3521 Buckeystown Pike (Rte. 85, 4 miles south of Frederick), Buckeystown, MD 21717. ☎ **800/272-1190** or 301/874-5755. Fax 301/874-5470. 3 rms, 2 suites, 2 cottages. A/C. $200 double; $225 suite; $250–$300 cottage. Rates include breakfast and dinner for 2; bed-and-breakfast rates available. AE, MC, V.

Situated in a quiet country village setting on the Monocacy River, this restored three-story mansion dates from 1897. The building is rich in Italianate Victorian details, with a wraparound porch, widow's walk, gables, bay windows, and ornate trim. Here you'll get both bed and board (breakfast and dinner), in the true country inn tradition. Dinner is served on Victorian china with period silver and glassware.

The interior decor is rich with antiques, Oriental rugs, chandeliers, and hand-embroidered fabrics. There are five working fireplaces. The five rooms and suites located in the main house have varying amenities and unique touches, including TV, VCR, fireplace, and balcony and/or bay window. St. John's Church, one of the cottages, is, in fact, a former church, dating from 1884, and has an outdoor hot tub, fireplace, and grand piano. The other cottage, Parson's Cottage, also has a fireplace and a kitchenette. All arrangements for lodging or dining must be made by advance phone reservation.

✪ **Stone Manor.** 5820 Carroll Boyer Rd., Middletown, MD 21769. ☎ **301/473-5454.** Fax 301/371-5622. 6 suites. A/C. $125–$250 suite. Rates include continental breakfast and chef's welcoming plate. AE, DISC, MC, V.

If you're planning a quiet, romantic getaway in the country, this is the inn for you. This historic manor, parts of which date from the 1760s, is surrounded by a 114-acre working farm—that's 114 acres of open fields, walking trails, wooded nooks, and various gardens for you to roam about undisturbed. The house, which opened as an inn and restaurant in 1991, offers a unique blend of old and new. Each suite is individually decorated with antiques and reproductions, including canopy or carved poster beds, and several feature one or two of the house's 10 original fireplaces. Yet each suite has been equipped with modern and quite luxurious amenities, including whirlpools and double multihead showers. The Trillium Room, with its antique quilts, toys, and vintage clothing, is a favorite. One suite, the Hibiscus, is wheelchair accessible and features a private entrance, fireplace, and two porches. The restaurant serves lunch, dinner, and tea by reservation only.

Tyler Spite House. 112 W. Church St., Frederick, MD 21701. ☎ **301/831-4455.** 6 rms (2 with shared bath). A/C. $100–$200 double. AE, DISC, MC, V.

Located in the heart of Frederick's historic district opposite City Hall, this three-story Federal mansion dates from 1814. It was built by Dr. John Tyler for the sole purpose of preventing the city from building a thoroughfare through the property, and hence the word *spite* was added to the name. The house's interior has 13-foot-high ceilings with intricate moldings and eight working fireplaces, many of which have carved marble mantels. The guest rooms, four of which have private baths, are individually furnished with antiques, down comforters, and Oriental carpets. Facilities include a parlor, library, music room, walled garden, and outdoor swimming pool with adjacent patio. Rates include afternoon high tea. Horse-drawn carriage rides can be arranged for an additional fee.

MODERATE

Cozy Country Inn. 103 Frederick Rd. (off Rte. 806), Thurmont, MD 21788. ☎ **301/271-4301.** 21 rms. A/C TV TEL. $40–$59 traditional rm; $52–$79 premium rm; $75–$130 executive rm. Rates include continental breakfast on weekdays. AE, DISC, MC, V.

Located about 15 miles north of Frederick at the base of the Catoctin Mountains, near the presidential retreat of Camp David, this motel has long been a popular place with families. Founded in 1929, it has recently been refurbished and upgraded, with rooms individually decorated to commemorate the style and influence unique to the presidents, political dignitaries, and news agencies that have visited Camp David and the inn. Rooms classified as "premium" have extras such as coffee/teamakers, refrigerators, hair dryers, towel warmers, and some have a VCR and wet bar. Rooms designated as "executive" all have wet bars and VCRs and all the components of the premium rooms, plus a gas fireplace and Jacuzzi. Facilities include the Cozy Restaurant (see "Where to Dine," below), pub, bakery, and a village of shops.

Hampton Inn. 5311 Buckeystown Pike, Frederick, MD 21704. ☎ **800/HAMPTON** or 301/698-2500. 160 rms. A/C TV TEL. $89–$150 double. Rates include continental breakfast. AE, DC, DISC, MC, V.

Located 2 miles south of downtown Frederick at exit 31B off I-270 at Route 85, this modern six-story hotel is a former Quality Inn with a brick facade—not the customary Hampton architecture. It is nestled beside an artificial lake and is connected by footbridge to a replica of a lighthouse that serves as an informal crab restaurant in the summer months. Many of the guest rooms also overlook the lake, and all of the rooms were renovated and the decor updated in 1997. Facilities include a lounge, outdoor pool, exercise room, and Jacuzzi. Deluxe suites with kitchenettes are also available.

Holiday Inn. 5400 Holiday Dr. (I-270 at Rte. 85), Frederick, MD 21701. ☎ **800/HOLIDAY** or 301/694-7500. Fax 301/694-0589. 155 rms. A/C TV TEL. $69–$95 double. AE, DC, MC, V.

This modern two-story brick hotel is first and foremost a conference facility and thus public areas are often bustling with activity. However, except for the handful of rooms that overlook the courtyard/restaurant, most guest rooms are separated from the public areas and are therefore relatively quiet. Rooms are slightly above standard Holiday Inn size and decor. The hotel is conveniently located for shopping—adjacent to the Francis Scott Key Mall and a short drive from the historic district. In addition, the hotel has a wide variety of recreational facilities, including an indoor pool, whirlpool, sauna, fitness center, game room, and miniature golf course, as well as a restaurant and lounge.

Spring Bank. 7945 Worman's Mill Rd., Frederick, MD 21701. ☎ **301/694-0440.** 5 rms (1 with private bath, 4 with shared bath). $80–$90 double. Rates include continental breakfast. AE, DISC, MC, V. Free parking.

Dating from 1880 and listed on the National Register of Historic Places, this sprawling red-brick Italianate and Gothic Revival bed-and-breakfast inn exudes a homey feeling. Its three stories are bedecked with gables, cupolas, double porches, bay windows, and a fish scale–patterned slate roof. Inside are high ceilings with frescoes, intricate stenciling, faux-marble mantles, antique furnishings, and William Morris wallpaper. One of the five rooms has private bath. The inn is situated north of downtown Frederick, just off Route 15, in a country setting on 10 acres. Innkeepers are Beverly and Ray Compton.

INEXPENSIVE

Comfort Inn. 420 Prospect Blvd., Frederick, MD 21701. ☎ **800/228-5150** or 301/695-6200. Fax 301/695-7895. 118 rms. A/C TV TEL. $49–$79 double. Rates include continental breakfast. AE, CB, DC, DISC, MC, V. Free parking.

What Frederick sorely needs is a moderately priced hotel within walking distance of the historic district. Unfortunately, for now, the Comfort Inn is as close as you can get, and it's about a 10-minute drive away. But this modern, two-story, brick-fronted hotel does offer good value for standard accommodations and a relatively convenient location. Facilities include a cafe, outdoor pool, and guest Laundromat.

WHERE TO DINE

What Frederick lacks in accommodations, it makes up for in its selection of good restaurants. The historic district alone is home to more than 20 fine-dining restaurants, cozy taverns, raw bars, and delis, serving everything from sushi to Wiener schnitzel to burgers and fries.

EXPENSIVE

✪ **Brown Pelican.** 5 E. Church St. ☎ **301/695-5833.** Reservations recommended for dinner. Main courses $13.95–$25.95; lunch $5.75–$9.95. AE, DISC, MC, V. Mon–Thurs 11:30am–3pm and 5–9:30pm, Fri 11:30am–3pm and 5–10pm, Sat 5–10pm, Sun 5–9:30pm. INTERNATIONAL.

Situated on the corner of Market Street in the heart of the historic district, this basement restaurant is decorated in a nautical style, with vibrant sea tones, driftwood, and yachting collectibles. The dinner menu is extensive and emphasizes seafood and veal. Some of the specialties include "Veal Brown Pelican" (with ham, mushrooms, and cream), salmon with lemon Dijon sauce, stuffed shrimp with crab imperial, and roast duckling. For lunch there are sandwiches, soups, and salads.

Red Horse Restaurant. 996 W. Patrick St. ☎ **301/663-3030.** Reservations recommended for dinner. Main courses $13.95–$19.95; with lobster, $18.95–$29.95; lunch $2.95–$12.95. AE, CB, DC, DISC, MC, V. Mon–Fri 11:30am–3pm and 4:30–10:30pm, Sat 4:30–10:30pm, Sun 4–9pm. AMERICAN.

If you crave a good cooked-to-order steak or sliced-to-order prime rib, this place is undisputedly the best in Frederick. Set along the busy Route 40 corridor west of downtown, this restaurant draws a mixed clientele of business executives, local families, and travelers. The two dining rooms are rustic and comfortable; both have stone fireplaces, and one has a glass-enclosed open kitchen where you can watch the chefs at work. In addition to beef, you'll find lamb, pork, local seafood, and hefty cold-water lobster tails. Lunch focuses on sandwiches, burgers, and salads, although steaks are much in demand here at midday too.

MODERATE

Brewer's Alley. 124 N. Market St. ☎ **301/631-0089.** Reservations recommended on weekends. Main courses $7.25–$16.95; lunch $3.95–$10.95. AE, DC, MC, V. Mon–Thurs 11:30am–2pm and 5–9pm, Fri 11:30am–2pm and 5–10:30pm, Sat 11:30am–4pm and 5–10:30pm, Sun 11:30am—4pm and 5–9pm. AMERICAN.

Frederick, like the rest of the country, has caught microbrew fever; there are two breweries in town, Blue Ridge and Brewer's Alley, the namesake of the latest addition to Restaurant Row. This place serves good, standard brew-pub fare—hearty sandwiches, burgers, and soups. The house specialty is wood-fired oven pizza—try Charlie's barbecued chicken pizza; the spicy Cajun pizza, with andouille and alligator sausages; or California Dreamin', with sun-dried tomatoes, goat cheese, and olives. Heavier entrees include grilled center-cut pork chops, dry-aged sirloin steak, and Thai chicken linguine.

Cafe Kyoko. 10 E. Patrick St. ☎ **301/696-9263.** Reservations recommended on weekends. Main courses $5.95–$13.95; lunch $5.95–$8.25. AE, MC, V. Mon–Thurs 11:30am–2pm and 5:30–9pm, Fri 11:30am–2pm and 5:30–10pm, Sat 5:30–10pm. JAPANESE/THAI.

It's easy to miss this little gem, located above the Province Too on Patrick Street, but it's the only place to get Thai food in town, and one of very few restaurants that serve sushi. The dining area is smallish but comfortable, with light wood floors, exposed wooden beams and brick walls, and the standard umbrellas and paper lanterns. Several booths line the front wall, where windows overlook Patrick Street below; you can also sit at the sushi bar in back. For a taste of everything, they have a good sushi sampler for $12.50. The Thai menu is standard, but the spicy chicken with Thai herbs is quite good.

Circa. 137 N. Market St. ☎ **301/662-2866.** Reservations recommended for dinner. Main courses $8.50–$18.50; lunch $4.95–$6.95. AE, CB, DC, DISC, MC, V. Tues–Sat 11:30am–3pm and 5–10pm, Sun noon–8pm. AMERICAN/SWISS/GERMAN.

Judging by the cuisine listed above, it would seem this is one confused establishment. Actually, Circa recently went through a major overhaul, in an effort to be more competitive with Brewer's Alley across the street, and it hasn't quite completed the transition—it used to be Alpenhof, a distinctly Swiss/German restaurant. Now the menu is lighter, with soups, sandwiches, and even some burritos and tostadas, but the specials are all still very German: Wiener schnitzel, sauerbraten, and a wurst platter with sauerkraut. Though the new menu items are good, German fare is what they do best. But most importantly, they still serve Dortmunder Union and Dark on tap in liter mugs.

Cozy Restaurant. 103 Frederick Rd. (Rte. 806), Thurmont. ☎ **301/271-7373.** Reservations recommended on weekends. Main courses $8.19–$14.99; lunch smorgasbord $5.19–$7.39; dinner buffet $7.79–$15.29. MC, V. Mon–Thurs 11am–8:45pm, Fri–Sat 8am–8:45pm, Sun 11:45am–8:45pm. AMERICAN.

Since 1929, this family-run enterprise has been a tradition in the Frederick area. Over the years, it has grown from a 12-stool lunch counter to a 675-seat full-service restaurant with a Victorian atmosphere. Known for its plentiful luncheon smorgasbords and evening buffets, it also offers à la carte dining. Entrees include country-fried chicken, roast turkey, baked ham, fried shrimp, crab cakes, surf-and-turf, lobster tails, and seafood platters. All entrees entitle you to unlimited trips to the "groaning board," a hefty table of soups, salads, breads, relishes, desserts, and cheeses.

Di Francesco's. 26 N. Market St. ☎ **301/695-5499.** Reservations recommended for dinner. Main courses $11.95–$16.95; lunch $4.95–$9.95. AE, DC, DISC, MC, V. Tues–Thurs 11:30am–3pm and 5–9:30pm, Fri–Sat 11:30am–3pm and 5–10pm, Sun noon–10pm. ITALIAN.

Decorated like a country villa, with whitewashed walls and lots of leafy plants, this restaurant exudes the flavors and ambience of Italy. The dinner menu offers more than a dozen pastas available in full or half-size orders, such as fettuccine with smoked salmon, spaghetti with anchovies and garlic, cannelloni, and lasagna. Entrees include veal saltimbocca, shrimp marinara or scampi, seafood with linguine, veal alla Marsala, chicken cacciatore, seafood and meat mixed grill, and filet mignon. Lunch features salads, omelets, pizzas, and pastas.

Jennifer's. 207 W. Patrick St., Frederick, MD 21701. ☎ **301/662-1373.** Main courses $9–$16; lunch $5–$9. AE, DC, DISC, MC, V. Mon 11:30am–9:30pm, Tues–Sat 11:30am–11pm, Sun 4–9:30pm. AMERICAN.

This neighborhood favorite is definitely worth a venture off Frederick's Restaurant Row, Market Street. Slightly off the beaten path and 1 block from the county courthouse, Jennifer's is seldom crowded and attracts the truly local locals: lawyers and businesspeople for lunch and downtown Fredericktonians for dinner. A slate fireplace facing the restaurant's two dining rooms, exposed brick walls, and a large oak bar create a warm, comfortable atmosphere, and the myriad of flags (city, state, and country) hanging from the ceiling reflect the restaurant's varied menu. Although the lunch fare is mediocre, dinner is exceptional, especially the fish and seafood offerings. The blackened catfish with Creole seasoning is excellent with warm crab dip served with fresh rye bread as an appetizer. A spa menu with lighter dishes such as shrimp fandango is also available.

La Paz. 118 Market Space. ☎ **301/694-8980.** Reservations recommended. Main courses $6–$12.50; lunch $4–$5.25. AE, MC, V. Mon–Thurs 11am–10pm, Fri 11am–11pm, Sat noon–11pm, Sun 4–11pm. MEXICAN.

Tucked away behind the parking deck on Market Street, this local favorite offers good value for an extensive menu of Mexican fare. The two smallish dining rooms fill up quickly and can be a bit loud, especially on weekends. From the main menu, you can get fajitas, flautas, the "Mexican Flag" (a crisp corn tortilla topped with chicken, cheese, guacamole, black olives, lettuce, tomatoes, and sour cream), or, our favorite, the vegetable burrito. You can also build your own combination dinner with tacos, burritos, enchiladas, or tostadas, and there's a limited children's menu. As one might expect, the margaritas are quite good.

✪ **Province.** 131 N. Market St. ☎ **301/663-1441.** Reservations required. Main courses $12.95–$18.95; lunch $4.95–$7.95. AE, DC, DISC, MC, V. Mon 11:30am–3pm, Tues–Thurs 11:30am–3pm and 5:30–9pm, Fri–Sat 11:30am–3pm and 5:30–10pm, Sun 11am–2pm and 4–8pm. INTERNATIONAL.

One of Frederick's oldest houses (ca. 1767) is the setting for this restaurant, consisting of a small bistro-style front room and a bright brick-walled room in the rear. The latter overlooks the herb garden, which produces ingredients for the kitchen. The furnishings range from snowshoe chairs to handmade quilt hangings and paintings by local artists.

Dinner entrees change daily, but a few favorite dishes are lamb chops Dijon, Parisian poulet (chicken with mushrooms and dry sherry), scallops with Irish Mist, and herb-scented filet mignon. Lunchtime selections focus on salads, quiches, omelets, crab cakes, and creative-combination sandwiches.

Tauraso's. 6 East St. (at Everedy Sq.). ☎ **301/663-6600.** Reservations not accepted on weekends; recommended for weekday dinner. Main courses $7.95–$23.95; lunch $4.95–$9.95. AE, CB, DC, DISC, MC, V. Sun–Thurs 11am–10pm, Fri–Sat 11am–11pm. ITALIAN/AMERICAN.

Bright and busy, this restaurant is the main dining choice at the Everedy Square shopping complex. There are three settings—an indoor dining room, an outdoor patio, and a pub—but the menu is the same throughout. Entrees range from Italian choices such as pastas, Tauraso's original seafood sausage, and Italian bouillabaisse, to international favorites such as crab cakes, charcoal-grilled chicken, steaks, and duck à l'orange. For lunch you'll find sandwiches, frittatas, pastas, and salads. Pizzas made in a wood-burning oven are also featured throughout the day.

INEXPENSIVE

Beans & Bagels. 49 E. Patrick St. ☎ **301/620-2165.** All items $1–$6.95. No credit cards. Mon–Fri 7am–3pm, Sat 8am–3pm, Sun 8:30am–3pm.

This unpretentious little coffee shop is one of the few places in Frederick where visitors can sit, read the paper, and enjoy gourmet coffee and a freshly baked bagel. The menu of coffees and coffee-related specialty drinks is impressive. You can also get soups and sandwiches served on croissants, bread, or, of course, bagels. Breakfast is served all day.

Province Too. 12 E. Patrick St. ☎ **301/663-3315.** All items $1.50–$6. AE, CB, DC, DISC, MC, V. Mon–Fri 7am–5pm, Sat 9am–4pm. AMERICAN.

Good for breakfast or lunch or to stock up for a picnic, this spot offers a wide variety of freshly made baked goods, stews, soups, sandwiches, and creative combination salads, plus gourmet teas and coffees.

Wags. 24 S. Market St. ☎ **301/694-8451.** Main courses $3.25–$6.25. Mon–Sat 11am–2am. No credit cards. AMERICAN.

This tiny basement bar is by far the smallest of Frederick's favorite nightspots, being only about 15 feet across at its widest point. It couldn't seat more than 35 people comfortably, but that's part of the appeal. The other part can be summed up in four words: Wags burgers and fries. The fries are served boardwalk style: greasy and in a heaping basket. The burgers are the stuff of cardiologists' nightmares: big, fattening, with dripping cheese, sour cream, or Wags special sauce. There are other equally distressing sandwiches on the menu, including the classic Reuben and ham and cheese.

FREDERICK AFTER DARK

In June, July, and August there are free open-air concerts at the **Baker Park Bandshell,** Second and Bentz streets (☎ **301/662-5161,** ext. 247). Concerts are scheduled for 8pm on Sunday evening and feature a variety of local and military bands.

Housed in an old garage just down the street from Baker Park is the **Bentz Street Raw Bar,** 6 S. Bentz St. (☎ **301/694-9134**). Admittedly, it's kind of a dive, with cement floors and a mix-and-match assortment of tables, chairs, and booths, but it's the only place in town where you can hear live music any night of the week. You'll generally hear blues, jazz, or rock, but there's also an occasional reggae band or folk singer. This is also the only place in town where the kitchen is open late, serving primarily seafood: steamed crabs and shrimp, oysters, and crawdads.

AN EXCURSION TO NEW MARKET

Six miles east of Frederick is historic **New Market,** founded in 1793 as a stop for travelers on the National Pike. Today this beautifully preserved Federal-style town is listed on the National Register of Historic Places and is known as "the antiques capital of Maryland." More than 40 different antique shops line both sides of the half-mile-long Main Street. All shops are open on the weekends, usually Saturday and Sunday from 1 to 5pm, and at other times by appointment; a few of the shops have weekday hours as noted below. The New Market Antique Dealers Association publishes a free, handy guide/map that's available throughout the town.

The Browsery. 55 W. Main St. ☎ **301/831-9644.**

Handcrafted furniture and accessories are the focus of this shop.

Fromer's Antiques. 52 W. Main St. ☎ **301/831-6712.**

Antique woodworking tools, Victorian furniture, Maxwell Parrish prints, china, and glassware are the attractions here.

Grange Hall Antiques. 1 S. Eighth Alley (off E. Main St.). ☎ **301/865-5651.**

Housed in a former Grange Hall, this shop offers an eclectic variety of graniteware, jewelry, tools, and country primitives, as well as fishing and sporting antiques and a newly acquired collection of miniatures. Open Tuesday through Sunday from 11am to 5pm.

Maria's Chalet Antiques. 2 E. Main St. ☎ **301/865-5225.**

This homey shop features German steins, teddy bears, old rugs, and clocks.

Mymanor. 25 W. Main St. ☎ **301/865-3702.**

Browse in this shop for 19th- and 20th-century sporting art and antiques.

New Market General Store. 26 W. Main St. ☎ **301/865-6313.**

This is the quintessential country store, with jars of rock candy, condiments, local honey and preserves, as well as potpourri, herbs, and baking meals and mixes. There is also a take-out food counter as well as a fine selection of antique toys. Open Monday, Tuesday, Thursday, and Friday from 9am to 5pm and Saturday and Sunday from 10am to 6pm.

Shaws of New Market. 22 W. Main St. ☎ **301/831-6010.**

Try here for period reproductions, vases, chandeliers, grandfather clocks, china dolls, and brass lamps.

Thomas' Antiques. 60 W. Main St. ☎ **301/831-6622.**

This is the place for oak furniture, brass and copper items, and equine and canine collectibles. Open Wednesday through Friday from 11am to 3:30pm, Saturday from 11am to 5pm, and Sunday from noon to 5pm.

Victorian Manor Jewelry. 33 W. Main St. ☎ **301/865-3083.**

This shop specializes in antique and estate jewelry and silver.

WHERE TO STAY

✪ **National Pike Inn.** 9–11 Main St., P.O. Box 299, New Market, MD 21774. ☎ **301/865-5055.** 5 rms (3 with bath), 1 suite. A/C. $85–$125 double; $125–$175 suite. Rates include breakfast. MC, V.

There's always a particularly warm welcome at this bed-and-breakfast, named after the famous road that passes through the town. Meticulously restored and opened as a B&B in 1986 by Tom and Terry Rimel, this sturdy Federal house was built in the early 1800s; a unique widow's watch was added in 1900. The rooms are charmingly decorated with reproductions and local antiques. Guests also enjoy the use of a country sitting room and a landscaped courtyard, as well as Terry's enthusiastic guidance on touring the area.

Strawberry Inn. 17 Main St., P.O. Box 237, New Market, MD 21774. ☎ **301/865-3318.** 5 rms. A/C. $90–$125 double. Rates include breakfast. No credit cards.

Celebrating its 25th anniversary in 1998, this lovingly restored 120-year-old bed-and-breakfast home, run by innkeepers Jane and Ed Rossig, offers cheerful antique-furnished rooms. Each room is individually decorated according to a special theme, such as the Strawberry Room or the 1776 Room. Ground-floor accommodations are available.

WHERE TO DINE

Mealey's. 8 W. Main St. ☎ **301/865-5488.** Reservations recommended for dinner. Main courses $11.95–$22.95; lunch $6.95–$11.95. AE, DISC, MC, V. Mon–Thurs 5–9pm, Fri–Sat 11:30am–2:30pm and 5–9pm, Sun noon–8pm. AMERICAN.

Even if you don't stay in New Market, it's worth a trip to dine at this restaurant tucked in a handsome three-story Federal-style brick building dating from 1793. Like a colonial house, the restaurant offers several small parlor-size rooms as well as the Pump Room, a large main dining room built around a wooden water pump that dates from 1800. The decor includes exposed brick walls, stone fireplaces, brass fixtures, and lanterns. Dinner entrees feature a blend of Maryland favorites including crab imperial, crab cakes, and fried chicken, as well as universal favorites such as prime rib and New York strip steak.

Village Tea Room. 81 W. Main St. ☎ **301/865-3450.** All items $3.75–$6.35. AE, CB, DC, MC, V. Tues–Fri 11:30am–3pm, Sat–Sun 11:30am–5pm. AMERICAN.

This delightful eatery in a two-story Victorian house on the west end of town offers homemade soups, salads, sandwiches, beaten biscuits, and more. It's ideal for lunch or for afternoon tea. Save room for dessert—22 kinds of pie, sold whole or by the slice. There is also a shop on the premises that offers period lighting, furniture, and estate jewelry.

4 Cumberland & Allegany County

137 miles W of Baltimore, 135 miles NW of Washington, D.C., 109 miles SE of Pittsburgh

Set on a tight bend of the Potomac River in the heart of the Allegheny Mountains, the small city of Cumberland looks far more like West Virginia than Maryland. As Maryland's contribution to the Rust Belt, many of its large buildings look worn and there are few major retailers or department stores in the area. However, what Cumberland does offer visitors is a strange kind of charm, a beauty born from the combination of the town's rustic frontier and industrial past and its enticingly attractive mountain setting. It is a city that, as one resident put it, "escaped urban renewal."

At the turn of the century, Cumberland was Maryland's "Queen City," second in size only to Baltimore. Many remnants of its former glory can still be seen, such as its long street of Victorian mansions, the ornate storefronts of its slowly rejuvenating shopping district, and the rising black smoke of the coal-powered train called *Mountain Thunder*.

Since the construction of I-68, making Cumberland easily accessible to the rest of the state, there has been a boom of interest in the area, much of which has centered on nearby Rocky Gap State Park. Already the home of an immensely popular country music festival, Rocky Gap will soon house both a major resort hotel and a Jack Nicklaus signature golf course. The Allegheny Mountains are of course beautiful, particularly in autumn, and the area is becoming quite popular with bikers and hikers who find Cumberland and nearby Frostburg cheaper and closer to home than the resort areas of Deep Creek Lake to the west.

ESSENTIALS

GETTING THERE The completion of I-68 in the early 1990s opened up Western Maryland and made driving there infinitely safer and hours faster. I-68 runs right through the center of Cumberland and is the fastest route by car from either the east or west. From the east and north, I-70 will take you to I-68. For a more scenic drive, you can get off I-70 or I-68 onto the Old National Pike (U.S. 40).

Cumberland is served by the **Cumberland Regional Airport,** Route 28, just over the border in West Virginia (☎ 304/738-0002). Flights are operated by **US Airways Commuter** (☎ 800/428-4322) from Pittsburgh International Airport.

Greyhound (☎ 800/231-2222) operates regular bus service into Cumberland, stopping at 201 Glenn St. (☎ 301/722-6226), and **Amtrak** operates limited passenger service through Cumberland from points east and west, stopping at a station on East Harrison Street. For full information call ☎ **800/872-7245** or 301/724-8890.

VISITOR INFORMATION   Walking-tour brochures, maps, and general information about Cumberland and the surrounding area are available from the **Allegany County Visitors Bureau's** two walk-in locations. The larger one is at the **Western Maryland Station Center,** Mechanic and Harrison streets, Cumberland, MD 21502 (☎ **800/508-4748** or 301/777-5905). It's open Monday through Friday from 9am to 5pm and Saturday and Sunday from 10am to 4pm. A smaller center is operated out of **Rocky Gap State Park** (☎ **301/478-3124**), off I-68, which is open Monday to Friday 8am to 4pm.

If you're coming from the east, the ✪ **Sidling Hill Exhibition Center,** off I-68 about 20 miles east of Cumberland, is a great place to stop for brochures, information, and an incredible view.

SPECIAL EVENTS   By far the biggest event in Allegany County and maybe all of Western Maryland is the ✪ **Rocky Gap Country/Bluegrass Music Festival** (☎ **888/762-5942**), held the first weekend in August each year at Rocky Gap State Park. An average of 10,000 to 20,000 people attend to hear such nationally known artists as Willie Nelson, Travis Tritt, Kathy Mattea, and Hank Williams Jr.

WHAT TO SEE & DO
ATTRACTIONS

C&O Canal Boat Replica. At North Branch of C&O Canal Park, PPG Rd. ☎ **301/729-3136** or 301/777-5905. Free admission, but donations welcome. June–Aug Sun 1–4pm, and other times by appointment.

This 93-foot boat is a full-scale replica of a C&O Canal boat like the ones that used to move along the 184¹/₂-mile canal between Georgetown and Cumberland. The boat features a captain's cabin with furnishings from the canal era, a hay house where feed was stored for the mules, and an onboard mule stable. Canal lock no. 75 and a restored log-cabin lock house are located nearby. Guided tours are conducted by volunteers. The replica is located 5 miles south of Cumberland off Route 51.

Chesapeake & Ohio Canal National Historical Park. 13 Canal St. ☎ **301/722-8226.** Free admission. Visitor center, June–Aug Tues–Sun 9am–5pm, Sept–May Tues–Sat 9am–5pm.

The C&O Canal came to this area in 1850, after 184¹/₂ miles of ditch and towpath had been constructed, originating near Washington at Georgetown. For more than 75 years it was an important transport line and had a major impact on the early development of Cumberland. Start a visit at the Canal Visitor Center, in the Western Maryland Station Center at track level, to see the background exhibits on the history of the canal and pick up a brochure on the canal. Then explore the towpath, a nearly level trail for walkers, hikers, and bikers. There are remnants of locks, dams, lock houses, and other historical features along the way.

Emmanuel Episcopal Church. 16 Washington St. ☎ **301/777-3364.** Services Thurs 10:30am, Sun 8am and 10am; open by appointment or prior arrangement at other times.

This church is built on the foundations of Fort Cumberland, where George Washington began his military career; earthworks from the fort (ca. 1755) still lie beneath the church. Although the Emmanuel parish dates from 1803, the cornerstone of the present native sandstone building was laid in 1849 and was completed in 1851. The church, which contains original Tiffany stained-glass windows from three different periods and a scale model of Fort Cumberland, is not normally open to the public except for services, by tour, or by appointment; but the grounds are part of the Fort Cumberland Walking Trail, signposted with plaques and detailed in a leaflet available from the visitor center.

George Washington's Headquarters. In Riverside Park, Greene St. (at the junction of Wills Creek and the Potomac River). ☎ **301/777-5905.** Free admission. Open by appointment and on certain holidays. Exterior viewing at all times.

This log cabin, believed to be the only remaining structure from the original Fort Cumberland, was used by then Col. George Washington as his official quarters during the French and Indian War. The cabin is not open to the public but does have a viewing window and a tape-recorded description that plays when activated by a push button.

History House. 218 Washington St. ☎ **301/777-8678.** Admission $3 adults, $1 students over 12. May–Oct Tues–Sat 11am–4pm, Sun 1:30–4pm; Nov–Apr Tues–Sat 11am–4pm.

Originally built as a private residence in 1867 for the president of the C&O Canal, this house is now in the hands of the Allegany County Historical Society. The restored 18-room dwelling contains antique furnishings such as a Victorian courting couch and an 1840 square grand piano. Other features include a research room, an early-19th-century brick-walled garden, and a basement kitchen with authentic cooking utensils, fireplace, coal stove, dishes, and pottery.

✪ Paw Paw Tunnel. Rte. 51 and the Potomac River. ☎ **301/739-4200.** Free admission. Open year-round dawn to dusk.

Anyone who starts to explore some of Allegany County's lesser-known attractions will realize very quickly that many of them are well . . . *spooky.* Paw Paw Tunnel, part of the C&O Canal National Historical Park, is the best of the spooky Allegany County sites and, better yet, it's fun for the whole family. It all started in 1836 when engineers decided to build the C&O Canal right through, rather than around, an intervening mountain. The result was a tunnel lined with over 6 million bricks and passing three quarters of a mile through the darkness of the hill.

All there is to do at Paw Paw is walk through the tunnel, which takes about 20 minutes (one way). The park service suggests bringing a flashlight. That might be a good idea—though to tell the truth, we've never met anyone in the tunnel with a flashlight. Walking the tunnel is not for people who are afraid of the dark (because it gets quite dark) or the claustrophobic (because you must walk down a narrow towpath bounded by a guard railing and the canal on one side and a sloping brick wall on the other). But, if you are up for an easy adventure, pass through the enormous brick arch into the damp darkness, then head for the light at the end of the tunnel.

Thrasher Carriage Museum. 19 Depot St., Depot Center, Frostburg. ☎ **301/689-3380.** Admission $2 adults, $1.75 seniors, $1 under age 12. May–Sept Tues–Sun 11am–3pm, Oct daily 11am–6pm, Nov–Dec and Apr weekends 11am–3pm.

Housed in a renovated warehouse opposite the steam-train depot in Frostburg, this museum displays an extensive collection of late 19th- and early 20th-century horse-drawn carriages, featuring over 50 vehicles from the private collection of the late James R. Thrasher. Highlights include the inaugural coach used by Teddy Roosevelt, several Vanderbilt sleighs, elaborately decorated funeral wagons, formal closed vehicles, milk wagons, surreys, and open sleighs. If you take the trip on the Western Maryland Scenic Railroad (see below) admission to this museum is free.

Toll Gate House. Rte. 40A (Old National Rd., at LaVale). ☎ **301/729-3047.** Free admission. May–Oct Sat–Sun 1:30–4:30pm, and by appointment.

Built in 1836, this historic toll gate house is the last of its kind to remain in Maryland. When this country's first national road was built, federal funds were used. Afterward, ownership was turned over to the states and tolls were collected at this site.

✪ **Western Maryland Scenic Railroad.** Western Maryland Station Center, 13 Canal St. ☎ **800/TRAIN-50** or 301/759-4400. Tickets May–Sept $16 adults, $14.50 seniors, $9.75 ages 2–12; Oct–Dec $18 adults, $17.50 seniors, $10.75 children. Reservations are required. May–Sept Tues–Sun 11:30am; Oct Mon–Thurs 11am, Fri–Sun 1 and 4pm; Nov to mid-Dec Sat–Sun 11:30am. From I-68, take the Downtown Cumberland exit 43C (westbound) or the Johnson St. exit 43A (eastbound) and follow signs to Western Maryland Station Center.

It's worth a trip to Western Maryland just to board this vintage steam train and ride the 32-mile round-trip between Cumberland and Frostburg. A genuine delight for young and old alike, this excursion—enhanced by an informative live commentary—follows a scenic mountain valley route through the Cumberland Narrows, Helmstetter's Horseshoe Curve, Brush Tunnel, many panoramic vistas, and a 1,300-foot elevation change between the two destinations. All trains depart and terminate at Cumberland. The trip takes 3 hours, including a 1 1/2-hour layover in Frostburg, where you can visit the Thrasher Carriage Museum, a complex of shops, a restaurant, and an active turntable where the train engine is turned in full view of the public for the Cumberland-bound segment of the journey.

Organized Tours & Excursions

One of the highlights of a visit to Cumberland is a stroll or a drive through the **Victorian Historic District,** primarily along Washington Street on the western side of town. This area includes the site of the original Fort Cumberland (now the Emmanuel Episcopal Church) and more than 50 residential and public buildings, built primarily in the 1800s when Cumberland was at its economic peak. Placed on the National Register of Historic Places in 1973, this street is a showcase of homes with elaborate stained-glass windows, graceful cupolas, and sloping mansard roofs. You'll see architectural styles ranging from Federal, Queen Anne, Empire, Colonial Revival, Italianate, and English Country Gothic to Georgian Revival, Gothic Revival, and Greek Revival. Most of the houses are not open to the public, but a self-guided walking tour of the neighborhood is described in a brochure available free from the tourist information office.

Shircliffe Express Tours, P.O. Box 624, Cumberland, MD 21501 (☎ **301/ 759-0510**), designs individual guided sightseeing tours to suit visitors' interests. Tours are conducted in a van or horse-drawn carriage by Ansel Shircliffe, a knowledgeable local tourism official who often dons a Revolutionary War uniform to enhance the experience. Specialties include local history, colonial and Victorian landmarks, craft shopping, fall foliage, and more. Tours operate year-round, with prices averaging $15 per hour, depending on exact requirements. Advance reservations are required.

Outdoor Activities

BIKING   The Cumberland area, nestled beside the scenic C&O Canal, is ideal for bicycling. **Allegany Adventures,** 14419 National Hwy., LaVale, MD 21501 (☎ **301/729-4719**), operates 1-day, weekend, or 5-day guided cycling tours along the canal towpath and wildlife areas from April through October. One-day trips, which last from 4 to 6 hours and include bike rental and a catered lunch, cost $25 to $40 per person; weekend trips, which include bike rental, overnight camping accommodations, meals, and a support vehicle, average $100 per person per day. Hiking/biking trips can also be booked. Advance reservations are required. If you prefer just to rent a bike and explore the area on your own, bike rentals can also be arranged for $5 per hour or $25 per day.

GOLF   Allegany County will soon be home to the much-awaited **Rocky Gap Lodge and Golf Resort** (see "Where to Stay," below), scheduled to open in spring

1998. Its pride will be an 18-hole Jack Nicklaus signature course, which promises to be truly world class. However, heavy rains in the summer of 1997 have delayed the course's completion. The front nine should be open for play in early August 1998 and the course is scheduled to have its full debut October 1, 1998.

HIKING & CAMPING   To commune with nature or enjoy a walk in the forest, ✪ **Rocky Gap State Park,** exit 50 off I-68 (☎ **301/777-2139**), and its sister to the east, the expansive **Green Ridge State Forest,** exit 64 off I-68 (☎ **301/478-3124**), are ideal. Rocky Gap offers views of beautiful Lake Habeeb, mountain overlooks, and a stout trail up Evitts Mountain to the remains of a 1784 homestead. The park has over 270 campsites but is terribly popular, so call ahead for reservations in summer (☎ **301/777-2138**).

Green Ridge is almost 40,000 acres of state-owned wilderness housing abundant wildlife, from deer to wild turkeys. Primitive camping is available. There are several scenic vistas over the Potomac River. At the forest's southern end you'll find the intriguing Paw Paw Tunnel (see "Attractions," above) on the C&O Canal.

SHOPPING

Allegany Arts Council Artists Co-Op Gallery. Western Maryland Station Center, 13 Canal St., Cumberland. ☎ **301/777-ARTS.**

Housed in the Western Maryland Station Center, this gallery features the works of more than 30 Western Maryland artists and craftspeople. The wares range from a wide selection of original oils, acrylics, and watercolors, to historic and limited-edition prints, wood carvings, stained glass, quilted items, and collectible Santas. Open Monday through Friday from 10am to 4pm and Saturday and Sunday from 10am to 2pm.

Book Center. 15–17 N. Centre St., Cumberland. ☎ **301/722-2284.**

Located just off Cumberland's pedestrian mall, this shop has a large selection of books on Maryland and local history as well as volumes on railroading and canals. In addition, there are postcards, gifts, and out-of-state newspapers. Open Monday and Thursday from 8am to 9pm, Tuesday, Wednesday, Friday, and Saturday from 8am to 6pm, and Sunday from 9am to 4pm.

Gallery on Greene. 8 Greene St., Cumberland. ☎ **301/724-7936.**

Situated beside Wills Creek, this restored Victorian house features a gallery and working artist's studio with a selection of works by Maryland artists—landscapes, still lifes, florals, portraits, and local and historic scenes, plus stained glass and prints. Open Tuesday through Friday from noon to 4pm, Saturday from 11am to 3pm, or by appointment.

Historic Cumberland Antique Mall. 55 Baltimore St., Cumberland. ☎ **301/777-2979.**

Ensconced in a former department store in the center of the city's pedestrian mall, this antique emporium offers Victorian furniture, china, toys, decorated stoneware, glassware, primitives, clocks, jewelry, railroad and military memorabilia, quilts, brass, copper, tools, and more. Open Monday through Saturday from 10am to 5pm and Sunday from noon to 5pm.

Manhattan Centre. 69 Baltimore St., Cumberland. ☎ **301/722-2130.**

This center is a recent and happy addition to Cumberland's shopping district. It houses an art gallery, design studio, and coffee shop, offering shoppers original artwork, posters, prints, decorative vases and plates, and even cappuccino. Open Monday through Saturday from 9am to 5pm.

WHERE TO STAY

The Cumberland–Frostburg area offers an inviting blend of historic inns, modern hotels and motels, and homey bed-and-breakfast lodgings. Take your pick—most are moderately priced and offer very good value. All have free parking.

Best Western Braddock Motor Inn. 1268 National Hwy., LaVale, MD 21502. ☎ **800/ 296-6006** or 301/729-3300. Fax 301/729-3300. 108 rms. A/C TV TEL. $66–$108 double. AE, CB, DC, DISC, MC, V.

A tree-shaded country setting adds to the rural atmosphere of this two-story motel, just off I-68 and east of the historic LaVale Toll Gate. Rooms are furnished in contemporary style. Facilities include a restaurant, lounge, indoor heated swimming pool, Jacuzzi, sauna, exercise room, and game room. Complimentary shuttle service is provided from the airport, bus station, and train station.

Comfort Inn. 1100 New Georges Creek Rd., Frostburg Industrial Park, Frostburg, MD 21532. ☎ **800/228-5150** or 301/689-2050. 100 rms. A/C TV TEL. $51–$73 double. Rates include continental breakfast. AE, DC, DISC, MC, V. Free parking.

Sitting on a hillside outside of town, with lovely views of the valley in all directions, this modern two-story inn is built in a hacienda style with a white brick exterior. Guest rooms have dark woods, pastel-tone fabrics, separate sitting areas, and a choice of king- or queen-size beds. Facilities include a fitness center and sauna.

✪ Failinger's Hotel Gunter. 11 W. Main St., Frostburg, MD 21532. ☎ **301/689-6511.** 17 rms. A/C TV TEL. $55–$80 double. Rates include continental breakfast. AE, DC, MC, V.

Originally opened in 1897 as the Gladstone Hotel, this four-story landmark was revived and restored several years ago by the present owners, the Kermit Failinger family. The guest rooms are masterfully done, as are the public areas and the main staircase, the centerpiece of the hotel. The restoration has added modern conveniences, but it has not altered the hotel's Victorian style or its original oak doors and brass fixtures, claw-foot bathtubs, intricate wall trim, vintage pictures and prints, smoked-glass lantern-style lamps, and delicate wall sconces.

The guest rooms are individually furnished, with canopy or four-poster beds, armoires, laces and frills, and pastel fabrics. The one exception is no. 307, decorated starkly in black and white, and named the Roy Clark Room, after the country-western entertainer who stayed in it during a 1990 visit. Throughout the corridors, there are collectibles, dried-flower assortments, and hanging plants. Facilities include a restaurant, lounge, unique basement area that houses a sports bar (which still has a gamecock fighting arena, though it's no longer used as such), and the remnants of an old jail.

Holiday Inn. S. George St., Cumberland, MD 21502. ☎ **800/HOLIDAY** or 301/724-8800. Fax 301/724-4001. 130 rms. A/C TV TEL. $79–$84 double. AE, DC, DISC, MC, V.

This modern six-story hotel sits at the east end of Cumberland's shopping promenade, giving its guests easy walking access to the downtown area. Although in the past this hotel didn't have the best reputation, it went through a major interior design makeover in 1997, and its new clean look, good facilities, and good location have quickly overshadowed its past. Rooms are clean and comfortable, as you would expect from a Holiday Inn. Railroad enthusiasts might like one of the rooms overlooking the nearby railroad tracks; everyone else will prefer the town side of the hotel, where there's less noise. Facilities include fax and copying services, meeting rooms, a restaurant, a bar, and an outdoor pool.

☉ Inn at Walnut Bottom. 120 Greene St., Cumberland, MD 21502. ☎ **800/286-9718** or 301/777-0003. Fax 301/777-8288. 12 rms (4 with shared bath), 2 suites. A/C TV TEL. $79–$105 double; $110–$180 suite. Rates include breakfast. AE, DISC, MC, V.

Nestled in a quiet downtown residential area just a block from historic Washington Street, this bed-and-breakfast inn is composed of two restored 19th-century homes: the Cowden House (1820) and the Dent House (1890). The inn is furnished with antiques and period reproductions including four-poster and brass beds, tapestry rugs, and down comforters. The guest rooms are spacious, with high ceilings and large windows, and include some ground-floor accommodations. Ten rooms have private baths. Facilities include an independently operated restaurant called Oxford House (see "Where to Dine," below), two parlors, a gift shop, and free use of the inn's bikes. The innkeepers are Grant Irvin and Kirsten Hansen.

Rocky Gap Lodge and Golf Resort. P.O. Box 1199, Cumberland, MD 21501-1199. ☎ **800/724-0828** or 301/724-4437. 194 rms, 26 suites. A/C MINIBAR TV TEL. $89–$129 double; $130–$305 suite. AE, DC, MC, V. Free parking.

As this book goes to press, workers are putting the finishing touches on the Rocky Gap Lodge, an attractive modern brick structure overlooking a beautiful lake, surrounded by the mountains of Rocky Gap State Park. It is to be the area's first 4-star hotel, and although not yet complete, clearly it will be one of the biggest things to hit Allegany County since the B&O Railroad. The grand opening of the lodge is set for April 17, 1998; however, the golf course will be opening a little later (see "Outdoor Activities," above). We toured the unfinished lodge and found it quite worthy of all the hoopla. As you walk into the hotel's expansive lobby you are greeted by high ceilings, towering stonework, and a panoramic view of the lake. A variety of rooms are available, from standard doubles to the two large multiroom Presidential suites. Facilities will include conference centers, ballrooms, a lakefront restaurant, indoor/outdoor pool, fitness center, tennis courts, pro shop, and an 18-hole Jack Nicklaus signature golf course.

WHERE TO DINE
EXPENSIVE

☉ Au Petit Paris. 86 E. Main St., Frostburg. ☎ **301/689-8946.** Reservations required. Main courses $10.50–$31.50. AE, CB, DC, DISC, MC, V. Tues–Sat 6–9:30pm. FRENCH.

The interior of this restaurant is delightfully Parisian thanks to French murals and posters and bistro-style furnishings. Established more than 35 years ago, this restaurant is a local favorite for such dishes as trout with almonds, frog's legs, duck à l'orange, coq au vin, steak Diane or au poivre, chateaubriand, veal cordon bleu, and a signature dish of lamb noisettes with Madeira sauce.

MODERATE

Giuseppe's Italian Restaurant. 11 Bowery St., Frostburg. ☎ **301/689-2220.** Reservations recommended on weekends. Main courses $8.95–$15.95. AE, DISC, MC, V. Mon–Thurs 4:30–10pm, Fri–Sun 3–11pm. ITALIAN.

In the heart of town and a block from the Frostburg State University campus, this two-floor dining spot is popular with the college community and is staffed by many of the students and locals. The decor is eclectic, with colorful posters of herbs and plants, and the food is first-rate. Entrees include all the usual Italian favorites, such as pizza, pastas, chicken cacciatore, shrimp scampi, and sausage and peppers. There's also a surprising array of nightly specials, including fresh seafood, such as trout stuffed with crab imperial or orange roughy.

L'Osteria. Ali Ghan Rd., off I-68 (exit 46E/W). ☎ **301/777-3553.** Reservations required. Main courses $8.95–$18.95. AE, DC, DISC, MC, V. Mon–Thurs 5–9pm, Fri–Sat 5–10pm. ITALIAN/ INTERNATIONAL.

An "Old Cumberland" ambience prevails at this mid-19th-century structure, located in a country setting east of downtown. The interior includes original woodwork and antiques, but the menu is thoroughly contemporary. The restaurant is open only for dinner. Entrees include veal saltimbocca or pizzaiola, filet of beef au poivre, shrimp Parmesan, blackened red fish prepared following a Paul Prudhomme recipe, and chicken cacciatore with peppers and onions in tomato and wine sauce. More than a half-dozen pastas are also offered. There is also a nightclub, the Wine Cellar, located beneath the restaurant.

✪ **Oxford House.** 118 Greene St. ☎ **301/777-7101.** Reservations recommended for dinner. Main courses $10.95–$18.95; lunch $3.95–$7.95. AE, MC, V. Mon–Fri 11am–2:30pm and 5–9pm, Sat 5–9:30pm, brunch the last Sunday of each month 10am–3pm. INTERNATIONAL.

Housed in the Inn at Walnut Bottom, this restaurant has three small dining rooms decorated with original oil paintings and reproductions, floral linens, and plants. Classical music plays in the background. The menu is varied and offers the diner everything from European flair to local Maryland flavor. A particularly unique treat in the mountains, the chicken Annapolis is tender chicken breast stuffed with tasty ham and Swiss cheese and a crab cake. Another dish worth trying is the shrimp and scallops Victoria, served over pasta in a rich white sauce. One small but significant detail: The house salad is exceptional, just as the menu claims. And be sure to check out the wine list.

MODERATE/INEXPENSIVE

✪ **Mason's Barn and J.B.'s Steak Cellar.** I-68 (exit 46E/W). ☎ **301/722-6155** for Mason's, **301/722-6060** for J.B.'s. Main courses $7.95–$22.95; lunch $3.95–$7.95; breakfast $2.59–$6.49. AE, CB, DC, DISC, MC, V. Mason's, 7am–10pm daily; J.B.'s, 11am–11pm daily. AMERICAN.

Two great local favorites at one easy-to-find location, 1 mile east of Cumberland. Mason's Barn was established in 1954 as a small roadside diner, and this dependable restaurant has been growing ever since, thanks to the friendly and attentive supervision of owners Ed Mason and his son, Mike. As its name implies, it offers an authentic barnlike setting, with a decor of farming tools, local antiques, and an eclectic collection of Maryland memorabilia. Entrees include steaks and seafood dishes as well as barbecued ribs, chicken, veal, and pasta items. All of them have a distinctively home-cooked flavor. Lunch choices range from salads and homemade soups to sandwiches (the crab-cake sandwich is a standout). Breakfast is also available.

In order to showcase their skills at charbroiled beef and seafood dishes, the Masons opened the saloon-style J.B.'s Steak Cellar downstairs from the barn. Here in a slightly more formal atmosphere you can chomp on more expensive fare, including lobster by the pound, grilled jumbo shrimp, and a 20-ounce Angus, center-cut T-bone steak.

Pennywhistle's. 25 N. Centre St. ☎ **301/724-6626.** All items $3–$5.95. MC, V. Mon–Fri 8am–5pm, Sat 8:30am–3pm. AMERICAN.

Situated just off the city's pedestrian mall, this is an ideal spot for a snack or lunch while browsing downtown. The menu offers a creative blend of soups, salads, and sandwiches. Sandwich specialties include roast beef with cream cheese and pepper jelly on a croissant; smoked turkey with cranberry relish; sprouts on whole-grain bread; and a classic peanut butter with raisins, apple, nuts, and honey on a croissant.

CUMBERLAND AFTER DARK

The **Allegany Arts Council,** 74 Baltimore St. (☎ **301/777-ARTS**), publishes a monthly newsletter detailing upcoming concerts and cultural events in the Cumberland area. You can also stop by their office for an update on events; the council is open weekdays from 10am to 4pm.

The **Cumberland Theatre,** 103 Johnson St. (☎ **301/759-4990**), housed in a renovated church, presents a truly enjoyable professional program of Broadway musicals and comedies as well as mysteries and dramas, from June through November. Performances are staged Wednesday through Sunday, and tickets average $11 to $15.

5 Deep Creek Lake & Garrett County

50 miles SW of Cumberland, 190 miles W of Baltimore, 100 miles SE of Pittsburgh

During the heyday of the B&O Railroad, Garrett, with its mild summer temperatures and beautiful mountains and countryside, became a summer resort for Maryland and Washington, D.C. Huge hotels, like the Loch Lynn and the Deer Park Inn, sprung up in Deer Park, Oakland, and other communities along the rail line, attracting such notable guests as President Cleveland and his wife, who spent a week of their honeymoon here. Unfortunately, the demise of the railroad isolated Garrett County, and in the ensuing decades all the great hotels were demolished or burned to the ground.

With the formation of Deep Creek Lake in the 1920s, Garrett County has slowly reemerged, eventually becoming the four-season resort it is today. It offers the state's only downhill skiing as well as water sports, golf, and, in the nearby state parks and forests, white-water paddling, cross-country skiing, mountain biking, and other outdoor adventures.

ESSENTIALS

GETTING THERE   From the east or west, take I-68 to Keyser's Ridge and then head south on Route 219.

VISITOR INFORMATION   The **Deep Creek Lake–Garrett County Promotion Council,** in the Garrett County Courthouse, 200 S. Third St., Oakland, MD 21550 (☎ **301/334-1948** or 301/387-6171), is an invaluable source of information and brochures. From mid-May through mid-October, an Information Booth is located on Route 219, at Deep Creek Lake, south of Deep Creek Lake Bridge (☎ **301/ 387-6171**). In the winter, ski condition information is available from Wisp Resort (☎ **301/387-4000**). Be sure to pick up or write ahead for a copy of the county's vacation guide; it's a hefty magazine with hotel, restaurant, and service listings and general helpful information. The council also produces a free, very detailed map of the county and of the Deep Creek Lake region. If you're going to do any exploring outside the resort area, be sure to pick up one of these.

SPECIAL EVENTS   Thousands of visitors flock to Oakland for the annual ✪ **Autumn Glory Festival.** It's a 4-day celebration held in early October and features the Maryland State Band and Fiddle Championships, a tournament of bands, arts and antique vendors, and the Fireman's Parade. The **McHenry Highland Festival,** held annually in early June, celebrates McHenry's Scottish history, with bagpipe, harp, and fiddle performances throughout the day, as well as dance competitions, workshops, sheepdog exhibitions, and athletic contests. For information and a complete calendar of events, contact the Deep Creek Lake–Garrett County Promotion Council at ☎ **301/334-1948.**

DEEP CREEK LAKE

Nestled in the heart of the Allegheny Mountains, Deep Creek Lake has long been a popular year-round recreational area. It's the state's largest freshwater lake, nearly 12 miles in length, with 65 miles of shoreline lined with private vacation homes and chalets. Summer temperatures average a comfortable 65.9°F. But in winter months, Deep Creek Lake really comes into its own, as Maryland's premier ski resort, with an average temperature of 28°F and a yearly snowfall of more than 80 inches.

OUTDOOR ACTIVITIES

BOATING　Summer activities focus on water sports, with every type of boat from sailboats to speedsters on the lake. Nearly all marinas around the lake have craft for rent, 7 days a week. Paddleboats or canoes average $6 an hour; fishing boats, $15 an hour; pontoon boats, from $20 to $30 an hour; and ski boats and runabouts, from $16 to $32 an hour, depending on horsepower. Some of the leading firms at Deep Creek Lake along Route 219 are **Echo Marina** (☎ 301/387-BOAT), **Bill's Marine Service** (☎ 301/387-5536), **Crystal Waters** (☎ 301/387-5515), **Blue Anchor** (☎ 301/387-5677), **Deep Creek Outfitters** (☎ 301/387-6977), and **S&H Marina** (☎ 301/387-5616). Rowboats and canoes can also be rented from the camper/information office at **Deep Creek Lake State Park.**

FISHING　Deep Creek Lake is home to approximately 22 different species of fish, including yellow perch, bass, bluegill, catfish, crappie, chain pickerel, northern pike, walleye, and trout. Fishing is best April through June, but ice-fishing in January and February is also becoming popular in the area. Maryland requires a fishing license, which costs $10 for residents and $20 for nonresidents and can be bought at most tackle shops. Try **Johnny's Bait House** on Route 219 in McHenry (☎ **301/387-FISH**) or **Deep Creek Outfitters** at 1899 Deep Creek Dr. in McHenry (☎ **301/387-6977**).

GOLF　The **Golf Club at Wisp,** Wisp Resort Golf Course, 290 Marsh Hill Rd., McHenry (☎ **301/387-4911**), is an 18-hole championship facility nestled between the Allegheny Mountains and Deep Creek Lake. Open from April through mid-October, the course welcomes guests 7 days a week. Greens fees are about $32 per person, $55 with cart. There is a fully stocked pro shop on the grounds. In addition, the **Oakland Golf Club,** Sang Run Road, Oakland (☎ **301/334-3883**), invites visitors to play on its 18-hole championship course on weekdays. Call ahead for greens and cart fees.

HIKING　Five hiking trails ranging from easy to challenging are available at **Deep Creek Lake State Park** (☎ **301/387-5563**), south of McHenry on State Park Road. The Indian Turnip Trail, approximately 2$^1/_2$ miles long, is the most scenic of the trails, winding along Meadow Mountain and across the ridge top. Admission is free; the park is open daily 8am until sunset.

MOUNTAIN BIKING　The ever-expanding **Wisp Resort** now has mountain bike trails and all the trimmings. Chairlifts can take you to the top of Marsh Mountain, the location of all their trails. **Rudy's** (☎ **301/387-4640**), Wisp's outfitter, offers bike rentals and guided 2-hour or 4-hour expeditions. Access to the trails, including a map, costs $2.50 per day. If you rent a bike from Rudy's, access to the trails is included. Bike rentals start at $13.50 for 2 hours and go up to $24 per day. Guided tours range from $10 to $25 per person. Bike rentals are also available from **High Mountain Sports** (☎ **301/387-4199**), located on Route 219 at Trader's Landing.

SKIING　Deep Creek Lake is the home of Maryland's only ski area. With an elevation of 3,080 feet and a vertical rise of 610 feet, the **Wisp Resort** offers 23 ski runs and trails on 85 acres of skiable terrain. The longest single run is 2 miles. Slope fees range from $30 on weekdays to $37 on weekends, with reduced rates for night skiing, 2-day tickets, early- or late-season skiing, and children. The ski season opens at the end of November and closes in mid-March. The Wisp also operates an on-premises ski school, a rental service, and a ski shop. For full information, contact the Wisp Resort, 290 Marsh Hill Rd., Deep Creek Lake, MD 21541 (☎ **301/387-4911**).

Cross-country ski trails are available at several of Garrett County's nearby state parks. See "Outdoor Adventures in Greater Garrett County," below.

SWIMMING   Deep Creek Lake State Park (☎ **301/387-5563**) features a 700-foot guarded sandy beach with bathhouses and lockers nearby. Admission is $2 per person, with seniors and children in restraint seats allowed in free. The park is open 8am until sunset.

ATTRACTIONS IN NEARBY GRANTSVILLE

Whether you're on your way in or out of Deep Creek Lake/McHenry or just need a break from all the outdoor recreation, the historic sites of Grantsville are worth a visit. From I-68, take exit 19 to U.S. 40 east, and you'll soon come to the **Casselman River Bridge.** This impressive structure was the largest single-span stone arch in the United States when it was built in 1813. It's no longer in use to vehicular traffic, but you can walk across the bridge to visit Grantsville's other attraction, **Spruce Forest Artisan Village** (☎ **301/895-3332**). This reconstructed village consists of several cabins, a school house, a church, and other buildings from Western Maryland and Pennsylvania, some of which date from the Revolutionary War era. From mid-May through October these structures are the workshops of local artisans: a blacksmith, potter, weaver, basket-maker, stained-glass artist, and several others. Their works and the works of other Allegheny artists can be purchased from the Penn Alps Restaurant and Craft Shop adjacent to the village (see "Where to Dine," below). The village is open Memorial Day through the last Saturday in October, Monday through Saturday from 10am to 5pm.

Grantsville is also home to the most unique shopping experience in Garrett County, **Yoder's Country Market,** Route 669, Grantsville (☎ **800/321-5148** or 301/895-5148). Started as a Mennonite family farm enterprise in 1932, the market has grown from a one-room butcher shop to an extensive specialty market. It's known for a variety of fresh and natural food items such as jams, jellies, relishes, honey, maple syrup, molasses, fruits, nuts, baked goods, cereals and grains, meats, cheeses, herbs, and spices. In addition, there are cookbooks featuring Amish and Mennonite recipes and Pennsylvania Dutch crafts. It's open Monday through Saturday from 8am to 6pm.

WHERE TO STAY

Aside from the hotels and inns listed below, the Deep Creek Lake area offers lots of vacation rental properties—cabins, town homes, and mountain chalets—for rent by the week or in 2- or 3-day intervals. Most of the homes are individually owned and rented through real estate/rental agencies. Two reputable rental agencies are **Railey Rentals** (☎ **800/447-3034**) and **Mountain Lake Rentals** (☎ **800/846-RENT**).

Moderate

Alpine Village. 19638 Garrett Hwy. (at Glendale Rd.), Oakland, MD 21550. ☎ **800/343-5253** or 301/387-5534. 29 rms, 14 chalets. TV TEL. $60–$80 double; $90–$160 chalet. AE, DC, DISC, MC, V. Free parking.

Views of the lake and mountains are part of the charm at this inn nestled on 30 wooded acres. The facility offers a choice of lodge-style rooms and chalets. Rooms have queen-size beds and sundecks; many also have cathedral ceilings, fireplaces, and kitchenettes. The chalets have living rooms, patios, and complete kitchens, in addition to at least two bedrooms, and can accommodate up to six people. All rooms have air-conditioning; the chalets, however, do not. Guests also enjoy docking facilities, beach swimming, and a heated outdoor pool (in summer).

○ **Wisp Resort.** 290 Marsh Hill Rd. (off U.S. 219, on the north side of the lake), Deep Creek Lake, MD 21541. ☎ **800/462-9477** or 301/387-5581. Fax 301/387-4127. 67 rms, 100 suites. A/C TV TEL. $65–$169 unit. AE, DC, DISC, MC, V. Free parking.

A mecca for skiers in winter and golfers in summer, this resort is Deep Creek Lake's center of activity. In addition to an 18-hole championship golf course and a 23-trail ski area, the amenities include an indoor swimming pool and whirlpool, tennis court, and fitness center. The guest rooms have a queen-size bed, a sofa bed, and a small refrigerator. Some units also have small kitchenettes or fireplaces. Dining and entertainment facilities include a restaurant (see "Where to Dine," below), coffee shop/pizzeria, and two lounges. Another favorite feature is Willy Wisp, the hotel's childcare and education facility for kids ages 2 to 11. Wisp specializes in providing complete vacation packages, so if there's some activity you want to try—mountain biking, white-water paddling, orienteering—let the staff know, and they'll usually be able to make all the necessary arrangements.

Moderate/Inexpensive

Carmel Cove Inn. P.O. Box 644, Oakland, MD 21550. ☎ **301/387-0067.** 10 rms. A/C. $70–$100 double. Rates include breakfast. MC, V. Free parking.

For off-the-beaten-path seclusion, head to this little bed-and-breakfast inn, tucked in a wooded area off Glendale Road and Route 219. It sits on the edge of a 53-acre residential community within walking distance of a private cove along Deep Creek Lake. The inn is the former monastery of the Discalced Carmelite Fathers and has steeples, a clock tower, and a chapel-like facade. The guest rooms are simply furnished. There are no telephones or TVs in the rooms, but a common parlor has a stacked stone fireplace and a TV for guest use. Innkeepers Peter and Mary Bender prepare hearty buffet breakfasts, often including Belgian waffles, cheesy sausage mushroom quiche, and griddle cakes with Maryland maple syrup. Guests can use the fishing poles, canoe, bikes, tennis court, and sundeck.

○ **Harley Farm.** 16766 Garrett Hwy., Oakland, MD 21550. ☎ and fax **301/387-9050.** 5 rms. $60–$80 double. Rates include breakfast. MC, V. Free parking.

Located about 5 miles south of Deep Creek Lake and signposted off Route 219, this two-story bed-and-breakfast inn sits in a scenic valley surrounded by a 65-acre horse farm. The guest rooms, furnished in contemporary country style, are all in a newly built addition to the original brick farmhouse. Public areas include a downstairs gathering room with fireplace and a wraparound porch overlooking a wildflower meadow.

Innlet Motor Lodge. 2001 Deep Creek Dr., P.O. Box 178, McHenry, MD 21541. ☎ **800/540-0763** or 301/387-5596. 20 rms. A/C TV TEL. $65–$78 double. AE, DISC, MC, V. Free parking.

For a room with a view, try this dependable two-story motel facing Deep Creek Lake and the Wisp ski area. Each room has contemporary furniture with dark woods and rustic colors, and a balcony or patio. About half of the units have fireplaces. Facilities include a private beach, boat dock, and picnic tables.

Point View Inn. Rte. 219, P.O. Box 100, McHenry, MD 21541. ☎ **301/387-5555.** 22 rms. TV TEL. $50–$75 double; $80–$95 double with kitchenette. AE, DISC, MC, V. Free parking.

Right on the shores of Deep Creek Lake, this lodging offers motel-style rooms with porches or private terraces overlooking the lake. Most units have Victorian or antique furnishings, some with fireplaces. Facilities include a boat dock, a private beach, an informal cafe/lounge, and a full-service dining room that overlooks the lake.

WHERE TO DINE

Note: Garrett County liquor regulations prohibit restaurants from serving any alcoholic beverages, including wine, on Sunday.

Expensive/Moderate

Deer Park Inn. 65 Hotel Rd., Deer Park, MD 21550. ☎ **301/334-2308.** Reservations required. Main courses $14.50–$21.50. AE, DISC, MC, V. Memorial Day–Labor Day Mon–Sat 5:30–9:30pm, September–May daily 5:30–9:30pm. FRENCH/COUNTRY.

For fine dining in an authentic turn-of-the-century atmosphere, it's hard to beat this lovely inn, originally built in 1889 as a 17-room summer home for a prominent Baltimore architect, Josiah Pennington. Although the cottage was left dormant for many years, it was restored several years ago and is now listed on the National Register of Historic Places. Furnished with Victorian antiques, many of which are original to the building and other nearby estates, it is now the setting for candlelight dining, prepared by chef-owner John Gonzales, formerly executive chef at the Watergate and Ritz-Carlton Hotels in Washington, D.C.

House specialties include a mixed grill of jumbo shrimp wrapped in prosciutto, swordfish, and beef tenderloin; sautéed veal tenderloin with apples and calvados; warm salad of sea scallops, snow peas, and bell peppers on mixed greens with walnut vinaigrette; and roast rabbit on a bed of fresh fennel. The main drawback is that the inn is in the middle of nowhere, deep in the country (though well signposted), about 9 miles southeast of the Deep Creek Lake Bridge, off Sand Flat Road and Route 135. If you want to stay overnight, the inn does offer three rooms with private bath upstairs (from $65 to $85).

Moderate

Bavarian Room. 290 Marsh Hill Rd., Deep Creek Lake. ☎ **301/387-4911.** Main courses $11.95–$18.95. AE, DC, DISC, MC, V. Sun–Thurs 5–10pm, Fri–Sat 5–10:30pm. INTERNATIONAL.

Part of the Wisp Resort, this restaurant offers an Alpine decor and old-world atmosphere, with a fireplace. The menu includes such varied dishes as barbecued ribs, charcoal-grilled steaks, and Wiener schnitzel, as well as design-yourself pasta dishes. Unlimited trips to the soup-and-salad bar come with your choice of entree.

Dr. Willy's Great American Seafood Co. 178 Quarry Rd. (off Rte. 219), Deep Creek Lake. ☎ **301/387-7380.** Reservations not accepted. Main courses $9.95–$15.95. MC, V. June–Sept daily 5–9pm, Oct and Jan–May Sat–Sun 5–9pm. SEAFOOD.

When a restaurant has a seafood market on the premises, you can expect the freshest of seafood. Named after a legendary seafaring parrot, this rustic establishment is a real find for fish lovers on this side of Maryland. The menu changes with the seasons, but crab cakes and crab soup are usually available, as are other Maryland seafood specialties, various kinds of shrimp, and fish shipped daily from afar. If you prefer a picnic, take-out is also available from the market. Although the original Dr. Willy is no longer around, owner Willy Hughes is ever-present and happy to answer any questions on the day's catch.

McClive's. Deep Creek Dr., McHenry. ☎ **301/387-6172.** Reservations not accepted. Main courses $8.95–$33. AE, CB, DC, DISC, MC, V. Sun–Tues 5–10pm, Fri–Sat 5–11pm; also open for lunch late June to Labor Day. Closed Thanksgiving and Dec 25. AMERICAN.

Perched on the lakefront, this modern restaurant offers panoramic views of the lake and of ski trails at Wisp from its indoor dining room or the outside deck. The menu presents a wide choice of seafood dishes such as blackened roughy, soft-shell crabs Dijon, garlic scallops, mussels Provençal, applewood smoked trout, shrimp and scallops Florentine, and mesquite-grilled swordfish or salmon. In addition, there is blackened prime rib, lemon chicken, lamb and pork chops, and a variety of pastas. Nightly specials offer particularly good value.

✪ Silver Tree. Glendale Rd., Oakland. ☎ **301/387-4040.** Reservations not accepted. Main courses $5.99–$24.99. AE, CB, DC, DISC, MC, V. Mon–Thurs 5–10pm, Fri–Sat 5–11pm, Sun 4–10pm. ITALIAN.

This lakefront restaurant has an 1890s decor of knotty-pine walls, beamed ceilings, colored-glass lamps, and open fireplaces. Wide picture windows add a contemporary touch, framing views of the lake and surrounding woodlands. The specialty here is Italian food—veal parmigiana, spaghetti with a choice of sauces, lasagna, and manicotti. In addition, there is a wide selection of seafood entrees, ranging from crab imperial and crab soufflé to seafood Newburg and fish combination platters. Prime rib and charbroiled steaks are also on the menu. In summer, light fun-food meals are also served at Silver Tree Harbor, a lakeside seafood bar on the restaurant grounds.

Moderate/Inexpensive

Uno Restaurant. 19814 Garrett Hwy., Deep Creek Lake. ☎ **301/387-4866.** Reservations not accepted. Main courses $5.95–$18.95. AE, DC, MC, V. Mon–Thurs 11am–midnight, Fri–Sat 11am–1am, Sun 11am–11pm. AMERICAN.

Situated in a beautiful lakefront setting on Route 219, this is one of the few chain operations in the Deep Creek area. The layout includes a central fireplace, booth seating on two levels, and framed posters of theater and movie personalities. In warm weather there is additional seating on an outdoor deck. The menu specializes in multi-ingredient pizzas and pastas. Burgers, soups, sandwiches, salads, wings, and ribs are also available.

NEARBY DINING

✪ Penn Alps Restaurant and Craft Shop. 125 Casselman Rd., Grantsville. ☎ **301/895-5985.** Reservations not accepted. Main courses $7.95–$11.95; lunch $3.25–$6.95. DISC, MC, V. Nov to day before Memorial Day Mon–Thurs 7am–7pm, Fri–Sat 7am–8pm, Sun 7am–3pm; Memorial Day–Oct 31 Mon–Sat 7am–8pm, Sun 7am–3pm. Closed several days at Christmas. PENNSYLVANIA DUTCH.

Don't leave the mountainous countryside of Western Maryland without a stop at this welcoming oasis. Situated between an 18th-century gristmill and an old stone arch bridge along Alt. Route 40, this unique restaurant and shop is housed in a remodeled log stagecoach inn dating back to 1818. There are five dining rooms, all with an old-world atmosphere, serving Pennsylvania Dutch–style cooking, such as roast pork and sauerkraut and hickory smoked ham, as well as roast beef, fried chicken, steaks, and seafood. Lighter items are also available, including sandwiches, soups, salads, and burgers.

OUTDOOR ADVENTURES IN GREATER GARRETT COUNTY

Because of its long, cold winters and difficult mountainous terrain, Garrett County, and Western Maryland in general, has historically been an isolated, backwater community. But as roads and transportation have improved and especially since the opening of I-68, this beautiful, unspoiled region has become a haven for adventure-sports enthusiasts. In fact, Garrett County is home to the only college-degree adventure-sports program in the country. There's almost nothing the intrepid explorer can't do here, from hiking and mountain biking to navigating some of the wildest white water on the east coast.

Garrett County has a large complex of state parks and forests, and their names will pop up quite often in the activities listings below. On the eastern side of the county, **Savage River State Forest** (☎ **301/895-5759**) comprises 53,000 acres along the Savage River and the reservoir. Within the state forest there are two state parks: **New Germany** (☎ **301/895-5453**) and **Big Run** (☎ **301/895-5453**). Route 495 off I-68 runs through the state forest and provides access to both parks. For information about all three, write to 349 Headquarters Lane, Grantsville, MD 21536.

Potomac–Garrett State Forest (☎ **301/334-2038**) is actually two forests run by the same office. Its land, totaling some 18,000 acres, is spread out in patches in the southern and western parts of the county. Call ☎ **301/334-2038** or write to 1431 Potomac Camp Rd., Oakland, MD 21550, for information and brochures. On the western edge of the state are some of the most popular spots in the county, **Swallow Falls State Park** (☎ **301/387-6938**) and **Herrington Manor State Park** (☎ **301/334-9180**), providing access to the Youghiogheny and lots of cross-country skiing. For information on both these parks, write to 222 Herrington Lane, Oakland, MD 21550.

Perhaps the most unique offering in Garrett County is its **Adventuresports Institute.** This division of Garrett Community College offers an associate's degree in adventure sports, but its classes are open to nonmatriculant students. So if you want to learn how to paddle white water rather than just riding along in a raft, enroll in one of the institute's 2- or 3-day kayaking classes. The institute also teaches classes in sports that you won't readily find outfitters equipped for, like mountaineering and rock climbing or orienteering. For a list of course offerings and prices, call ☎ **301/387-3032** or write to Adventuresports Institute, Garrett Community College, P.O. Box 151, 687 Mosser Rd., McHenry, MD 21541.

CROSS-COUNTRY SKIING   Trails and facilities for cross-country skiing are available at **Herrington Manor State Park** (☎ **301/334-9180**) and **New Germany State Park** (☎ **301/895-5453**). Both offer equipment rental, cabins (see "Where to Stay," below), and large stone "warming rooms" where skiers can grab a snack and some hot cocoa to revive themselves. There are 10 miles of groomed, marked trails at Herrington Manor and 12 miles at New Germany. Trails and rental facilities are open from 8am to 4pm during good, safe skiing conditions.

FISHING   A massive cleanup effort launched by the small towns of Garrett County and the Maryland Bureau of Mines has brought fly-fishing back to the "three sisters"—the Youghiogheny, Casselman, and North Branch of the Potomac. The region has become such a popular area for fly-fishing that it's been featured on national fly-fishing shows and public TV segments. The ✪ **Casselman River** is a particularly fertile catch-and-release river; anglers here have been known to catch 40 fish a day. The Youghiogheny supports a strong population of brown and rainbow trout, but be aware that damn releases cause substantial increases in the water level below the Deep Creek Lake power plant. Call ☎ **824/533-8911** for a damn-release schedule.

For tackle and bait, stop by **Johnny's Bait House** on Route 219 in McHenry (☎ **301/387-FISH**) or **Deep Creek Outfitters** at 1899 Deep Creek Dr. in McHenry (☎ **301/387-6977**).

HIKING   Nearly all the designated skiing and mountain biking trails in the state parks can be used by foot travelers, but there are also worthwhile designated hiking trails in **Savage River State Forest** (☎ **301/895-5759**) and ✪ **Swallow Falls State Park** (☎ **301/387-6938**). Savage River is the largest of Maryland's state forests, with about 53,000 acres, and features many miles of rugged and challenging hiking trails. The longest one, Big Savage, follows a 17-mile linear path along the ridge of Big

Savage Mountain at an average elevation of 2,500 feet. Another popular trail is Monroe Run, which traverses the forest between New Germany and Big Run State Parks.

The trails at Swallow Falls State Park are considerably less strenuous but are worthwhile for the excellent views of Swallow Falls, Tolliver Falls, and Muddy Creek Falls, which drops a precipitous 63 feet. The main hike follows the Youghiogheny River through one of Maryland's last virgin forests of giant pines and hemlocks. Ten miles of other trails wind through the park, and there's also a $5^{1}/_{2}$-mile footpath that ends at Herrington Manor State Park.

I would be remiss if I did not mention that the highest point in Maryland, **Hoye Crest** on **Backbone Mountain,** is in Garrett County. You can hike to the top, but you have to start in Monongahela National Forest in West Virginia, off Route 219. The trail is rough, and surprisingly the view from the top is not spectacular, but there are several impressive vistas along the way.

MOUNTAIN BIKING   Again, several trails in each state park are multiuse and can be used by bikers. However, **Potomac–Garrett State Forest** (☎ 301/334-2038) has 8 miles of designated mountain biking trails, and all the trails at **Savage River State Forest** (☎ 301/895-5759) except Big Savage and Monroe Run may be used by mountain bikers. You can rent bikes from **Rudy's** (☎ 301/387-4640) at the Wisp Resort in McHenry or from **High Mountain Sports** (☎ 301/387-4199).

SNOWMOBILING   There are designated snowmobile trails at **Potomac–Garrett State Forest** (☎ **301/334-2038**) and **Savage River State Forest** (☎ **301/ 895-5759**). Off-road vehicle permits are required and can be obtained at each park's headquarters.

WHITE-WATER RAFTING & KAYAKING   In 1976 the Youghiogheny River between Millers Run and Friendsville became Maryland's first officially designated Wild River. This portion, known as the Upper Yough, contains approximately 20 class IV and V rapids. Fortunately for the inexperienced traveler, outfitters have sprung up all over the area, willing to take people down this potentially dangerous and certainly exciting river. If you'd prefer a little less excitement, the Middle Yough offers class I and II rapids, and the Lower Yough is a class III run. And there are also several rivers just across the border in West Virginia—the Cheat, the Gauley, Big Sandy, and Russell Fork—that are also rated at class IV+. Most outfitters run raft trips on several or all of these rivers.

Precision Rafting (☎ **800/477-3723**), conveniently located in Friendsville, Maryland, offers raft trips down all the above-mentioned rivers as well as paddling lessons, for those interested in learning to kayak. Rafting trips include a riverside barbecue lunch and cost from $90 to $115 per person for an Upper Yough trip. Friendsville is at the intersection of I-68, Route 42, and the Youghiogheny River; from Deep Creek Lake, take Route 219 north to Route 42 and follow it into town.

There are several outfitters based in nearby Ohiopyle, Pennsylvania, that offer similar trips, including **Mountain Streams** (☎ **800/RAFT-NOW**) and **Laurel Highlands River Tours** (☎ **800/4RAFTIN**). To get to Ohiopyle from Deep Creek Lake, take U.S. 219 north to U.S. 40 west (just past the intersection with I-68). Go into Pennsylvania, and turn right onto Route 381 (north), which will take you to Ohiopyle. It's about an hour from Deep Creek Lake. *Note:* Whichever outfitter you choose, remember to tip your guide: $3 to $5 per person is appropriate.

WHERE TO STAY: CAMPING & CABINS

Garrett County's state parks offer accommodation options to suit just about everyone's needs, from heated, furnished log cabins to primitive camping.

CAMPING Campsites with varying levels of facilities are available at all the state parks and forests except Herrington Manor. On the eastern side of the state, ✪ **New Germany State Park** (☎ **301/895-5453**) has 39 improved campsites with exceptionally clean bathhouses and hot showers. All sites sit in a wooded glen and are large and private. Unfortunately, the camping area is only open April through October; cost is $12 per night. Just down the road, **Big Run State Park** (☎ **301/895-5453**) offers 30 unimproved sites with chemical toilets and running water. Some of the sites are in wooded areas along Monroe Run and Big Run; the remainder sit on the shore of the Savage River Reservoir. Sites at Big Run are open year-round and cost $8 per night.

In **Savage River State Forest** (☎ **301/895-5759**), which surrounds New Germany and Big Run, there are 42 primitive sites spread throughout the forest, each with a lantern pole, fire pit, and table. Backwoods camping is also permitted. Campsites are generally placed along the roads throughout the forest but are spread out. You'll likely not encounter many other campers. Camping is permitted year-round at a rate of $5 per night; you must pick up a permit at B.J.'s Store or the forest headquarters.

In the southern and western parts of the county, ✪ **Potomac–Garrett State Forest** (☎ **301/334-2038**) offers five primitive camping areas, open year-round if you can get to them. These sites are particularly beautiful and generously spaced. However, the roads to the sites are not well maintained. Cost is $5 per night. **Swallow Falls State Park** (☎ **301/387-6938**) features the area's largest camping facility with 65 improved sites and modern bathhouses with showers and laundry tubs. Camping fee is $11 to $15 per night; reservations can be made up to a year in advance.

CABINS **Herrington Manor State Park** (☎ **301/334-9180**) and **New Germany State Park** (☎ **301/895-5453**) both have furnished, heated log cabins available for rent by the week or by the night, though a 2-night minimum stay applies during the fall, winter, and spring. All cabins have a woodstove and some firewood is provided. Herrington Manor has 20 cabins, able to sleep two, four, or six people. Rates range from $325 to $425 per week or $65 to $85 per night. New Germany's 11 cabins are a little newer and more generously spaced, though the park itself is smaller. The newest of the cabins, completed in 1997, sleeps eight people. Weekly rates range from $350 to $550, and nightly rates from $70 to $110. The cabins in both parks are quite popular and must be reserved ahead of time, up to a year in advance.

10 Wilmington

Wilmington lives in the shadows of its neighbor, Philadelphia, to the north and of its own majestic suburb, the Brandywine Valley. But those who have visited Wilmington know that what makes this little city neat is how well it supplies all the amenities of a big city—great museums, good theater, a lovely opera house, fine restaurants, and, of course, the famous Hotel du Pont. To top it off, in 1997 the revitalization of Wilmington's waterfront began with the launching of the *Kalmar Nyckel,* a replica of the ship that brought the first Swedish settlers to the area. All this comes without all the big city hubbub. That's why many people stay here as a launching point for visits to the Brandywine Valley—so that they can visit Winterthur or Nemours, hit the opera, and then sleep in style. You might even begin to feel a little like a du Pont yourself.

1 Orientation

ARRIVING

BY PLANE Most people flying into the Northern Delaware area use the **Philadelphia International Airport** (☎ 215/492-3000), within a half hour's ride of downtown Wilmington. Many Wilmington hotels operate courtesy transfer services to and from the airport. Car-rental agencies at the airport include **Avis** (☎ 215/492-0900), **Budget** (☎ 215/492-9400), and **Hertz** (☎ 615/492-7232).

In addition, **SuperShuttle** (☎ 800/562-4094) operates a 24-hour transfer system between Philadelphia International Airport and any address in Delaware. The company has counters in all airport terminals and telephones located on courtesy phone boards at the airport. Rates per person range from $12 to $28, depending on pickup or drop-off point (based on ZIP code). Departures are scheduled from the Philadelphia airport every 5 to 20 minutes 24 hours a day.

BY TRAIN Wilmington is a major stop on **Amtrak's** Northeast Corridor line (☎ 800/USA-RAIL), with Metroliner and unreserved trains stopping here several times daily. The Wilmington Amtrak station is located at Martin Luther King Boulevard and French Street, on the city's southern edge, adjacent to the Christina River. There's a taxi stand outside the station.

Downtown Wilmington

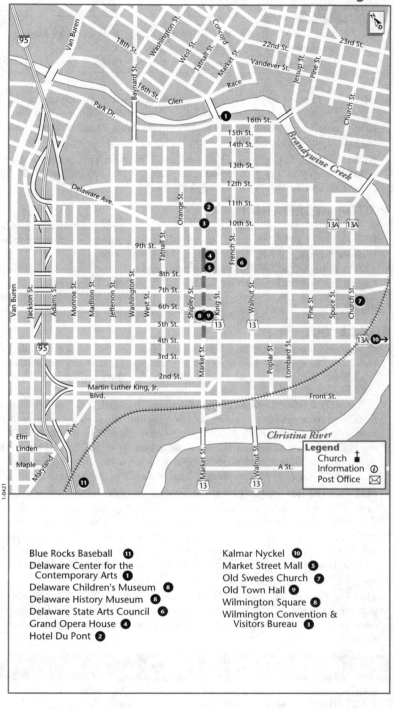

Legend
- Church †
- Information ⓘ
- Post Office ✉

Blue Rocks Baseball ⑪
Delaware Center for the Contemporary Arts ①
Delaware Children's Museum ⑧
Delaware History Museum ⑧
Delaware State Arts Council ⑥
Grand Opera House ④
Hotel Du Pont ②

Kalmar Nyckel ⑩
Market Street Mall ⑤
Old Swedes Church ⑦
Old Town Hall ⑨
Wilmington Square ⑧
Wilmington Convention & Visitors Bureau ③

*The Delaware ideal . . . is that life is best lived on a scale where everyone's hand leaves
a print, and that a future without the best of the past isn't worth a darn.*
                                                    —Jane Vessels, *National Geographic*, August 1983

BY CAR   The best way to drive to Wilmington is via I-95, which cuts across the
city's center. The Delaware Memorial Bridge also connects Wilmington to the New
Jersey Turnpike and points north. From the south, Route 13 will bring you into the
city via Virginia and Southern Delaware.

BY BUS   Daily service is provided into the **Wilmington Transportation Center**
at 101 N. French St. (☎ **302/655-6111** or 302/652-7391) by **Greyhound** (☎ **800/
231-2222**) and **Trailways** (☎ **800/343-9999**).

VISITOR INFORMATION

A complete selection of literature about Wilmington, the Brandywine Valley, and
Historic New Castle is available from the **Greater Wilmington Convention and
Visitors Bureau,** 100 W. 10th St., Suite 20, Wilmington, DE 19801 (☎ **800/
422-1181** or 302/652-4088). For motorists passing through the area, the bureau
maintains a **Visitors Information Center** on I-95 (☎ **302/737-4059**). It is located
just south of the city, in the service area between Routes 273 and 896, and operates
from 8am to 8pm; an automatic hotel-reservation system is provided.

CITY LAYOUT

Wilmington is surrounded by three rivers: the Brandywine, the Christina, and the
Delaware. The compact downtown business area, wedged between the Brandywine
and Christina rivers, is laid out in an almost square grid system, less than 20 blocks
wide or long.

   A word of caution: Even though the downtown area is relatively small, the attractions, restaurants, and hotels are spread out, even into the northern suburbs. Aside
from a few museums and shops along the Market Street Mall, you really can't or
wouldn't want to walk between the major attractions. There isn't really a tourist area
downtown (the Brandywine Valley is the city's greatest attraction), and the waterfront, despite the revitalization process, is still mainly a working waterfront.

MAIN ARTERIES & STREETS   Market Street runs from north to south in downtown Wilmington. The east–west cross streets are numbered from 1st to 16th, with
the lowest number on the southern end; the north–south streets bear the names of
presidents, local heroes, and trees, in no definable order or system. Most streets are
one-way, except for Market and 4th streets. I-95 enters Wilmington via two main
avenues: Delaware Avenue (Route 52) on the north end of the city and Martin Luther
King Boulevard on the south.

MAPS   "Greater Wilmington's Guide to the Brandywine Valley," a booklet produced and distributed by the Greater Wilmington Convention and Visitors Bureau,
has a fairly detailed map of downtown Wilmington, with all the major attractions
marked.

2 Getting Around

BY BUS   Wilmington has no subway, but it does have a bus system known as
DART (Delaware Administration for Regional Transit). Blue-and-white signs indicating DART stops are located throughout the city, and regular routes can take you

to hotels, museums, theaters, and parks, as well as popular sights such as Winterthur and New Castle. Fares are based on a zone system; the minimum fare for one zone is $1.15. Exact change is required. You can obtain complete information on schedules and applicable fares at most banks or by calling DART First State (☎ **302/ 577-3278** or 302/652-3278).

BY SHUTTLE   DART also operates the **Downtowner,** a free minibus shuttle service in Wilmington. Shuttles run from the Wilmington Amtrak station to Hercules Plaza, weekdays from 7:30am to 6pm. The route goes up Walnut Street north via Rodney Square and West Street to 13th Street and then down Market Street and King Street to the starting point. Service is provided every 20 minutes during off-peak hours (7:30 to 11am and 2 to 6pm) and every 10 minutes between the peak hours of 11am and 2pm.

BY CAR   Because downtown Wilmington lacks a real tourist center—its attractions and restaurants are spread across the city—and most people who visit here travel out to the Brandywine Valley, a car is really something of a necessity. If you aren't driving into the area, you can rent one from either **Avis,** 903 Washington St. (at 9th Street) (☎ **302/654-0379**), or **Budget,** 100 N. Walnut St. (☎ **302/764-3300**).

BY TAXI   There are taxi stands at the Amtrak station, which is across the street from the bus station. If you wish to order a cab, call **Yellow Cab Delaware** (☎ **302/ 656-8151**).

FAST FACTS: Wilmington

Airports   See "Arriving," earlier in this chapter.

American Express   Contact **Delaware Travel Agency,** 4001 Concord Pike, at ☎ **302/479-0200.**

Area Code   Wilmington's area code is 302.

Buses   See "Getting Around," earlier in this chapter.

Camera Repair   For camera repair, supplies, or photo processing, try **Lincoln Camera Shop,** Delaware Avenue and Union Street (☎ **302/654-6241**), or **Ritz Camera,** 108 W. 9th St. (☎ **302/655-4459**).

Car Rentals   See "Getting Around," earlier in this chapter.

Climate   See "When to Go," in chapter 3.

Dentists   Call the **Wilmington Dental Referral Service** (☎ **800/91-SMILE**).

Doctors   Call the **New Castle County Medical Society Physician Referral Service** (☎ **302/658-3168**).

Emergencies   Dial ☎ **911** for fire, police, or ambulance.

Eyeglass Repair   The most convenient downtown location is **Wilmington Optical,** 616 Market St. Mall (☎ **302/654-0530**).

Hospitals   **Wilmington Hospital,** 14th and Washington streets (☎ **302/ 733-1000**), or **St. Francis Hospital,** 7th and Clayton streets (☎ **302/421-4100**).

Information   See "Visitor Information," earlier in this chapter.

Libraries   **Wilmington Central Library** is at 10th and Market streets (☎ **302/ 571-7415**).

Newspapers/Magazines   The city's daily newspaper is the *News-Journal.* The best monthly magazine is *Delaware Today.*

Pharmacies   A local chain with more than a dozen locations in the area is **Happy Harry Discount Drugs;** there are two downtown stores—900 Orange St. (☎ **302/654-1834**) and Trolley Square Shopping Center, Delaware Avenue (☎ **302/655-6397**).

Police   For nonemergencies, call ☎ **302/571-4404.** For emergencies, dial ☎ **911.**

Post Office   The main downtown post office branch is at Rodney Square Station, 1101 N. King St. (☎ **302/656-0196**).

Taxes   There is no sales tax in Delaware, but an 8% lodging tax applies to stays at city hotels.

Taxis   See "Getting Around," earlier in this chapter.

Transit Information   Call **DART First State** (☎ 302/577-3278).

3 Accommodations

No matter where you go in Delaware, when you hear people refer to the "hotel," you can be sure they mean the Hotel du Pont in Wilmington. For more than 80 years, this hotel has dominated the Delaware lodging scene. Consequently, there are relatively few other full-service hotels in downtown Wilmington. In recent years, however, as the Wilmington suburbs have grown, several new hotels and motels have sprung up in the surrounding areas.

Wilmington hotels, like other city hotels, charge top prices during the Sunday-through-Thursday period. The best way to save money is to reserve a 1- or 2-night weekend package (Friday and Saturday), which, in many cases, can represent a 50% reduction off normal midweek room rates.

DOWNTOWN
VERY EXPENSIVE

✪ **Hotel du Pont.** 11th and Market sts., Wilmington, DE 19801. ☎ **800/441-9019** or 302/594-3100. Fax 302/294-3108. 217 rms, 10 suites. A/C MINIBAR TV TEL. $219–$279 double; $295–$495 suite. Weekend packages available. AE, CB, DC, DISC, MC, V. Parking $13.

Opened in 1913 and owned by E. I. du Pont de Nemours and Company, this is the benchmark for all other Delaware hotels. The palatial 12-story Italian Renaissance structure, located in the heart of the city, is a showcase of polished marble, elegant coffered ceilings, richly carved walnut, oak paneling, original artwork, and genteel service.

The guest rooms, recently refurbished and enlarged to the tune of $40 million, are in a class by themselves and have merited an International Gold Key Design Award. Each unit has mahogany reproduction furniture and built-in cabinetry, original artwork, and double-glazed windows. Most of the fabrics, fibers, and fittings are made of the latest Du Pont products. Special amenities include a computer port in the phone system, voice mail in three languages, and a wall safe.

Dining/Entertainment: The hotel has two fine restaurants: the highly regarded Green Room (see "Dining," below) and the smaller Brandywine Room (see "Dining," below). In addition, the imposing old-world Lobby Lounge is a popular spot for cocktails, afternoon tea, or people watching. The Grill offers casual cafeteria-style dining.

Services: Concierge, 24-hour room service, valet and laundry service, complimentary morning newspapers, nightly turndown service, express checkout, valet parking, shoe shine.

Facilities: VCRs, fitness center, business center, conference facilities, bank, brokerage, barbershop, beauty salon, gift shops and boutiques, jewelry shop, theater.

EXPENSIVE

✪ **Sheraton Suites.** 422 Delaware Ave., Wilmington, DE 19801. ☎ **800/325-3535** or 302/654-8300. Fax 302/654-6036. 230 suites. A/C TV TEL. $180–$210 double. Weekend packages available. AE, DC, DISC, MC, V. Parking $9.

In the heart of Wilmington's corporate and financial section, this contemporary 16-story hotel is decorated in subdued art deco tones. The lobby is rich in columns, mirrors, and marble flooring. Each unit has a full bedroom, separate living room, large well-lit bathroom with hair dryer and TV, and dressing area. Amenities include two telephones with call-waiting services and computer access lines, a dining and work table, desk, wet bar, coffeemaker, and refrigerator with complimentary soft drinks.

Dining/Entertainment: The conservatory-style restaurant and lounge offer moderately priced food and drinks on the lobby level.

Services: Room service, dry-cleaning and valet service, baby-sitting.

Facilities: Exercise room, indoor swimming pool, sauna, conference rooms, self-service Laundromat, gift shop.

MODERATE

Brandywine Suites. 707 King St., Wilmington, DE 19801. ☎ **302/656-9300.** Fax 302/656-2459. 49 suites. A/C MINIBAR TV TEL. $99–$159 suite. Rates include buffet breakfast. Weekend packages available. AE, CB, DC, MC, V. Valet parking $7.50.

If your taste in lodging runs to homey rather than opulent, your best choice is this hotel next to historic Market Street Mall. Opened in 1987, it was created from a cluster of vintage three- and four-story brick buildings that were thoroughly renovated and then linked together with a central atrium and two elevators.

The result is a small all-suite hotel with a nouveau European decor. Each guest unit has a parlor, bedroom, and well-equipped bathroom, as well as a refrigerator, two TVs, and three telephones. On the ground floor, there's a small lobby with an open fireplace and a skylit sitting area. Facilities include a bistro-style restaurant and an exercise room.

Courtyard by Marriott/Wilmington Downtown. 1102 West St., Wilmington, DE 19801. ☎ **800/228-9390** or 302/429-7600. Fax 302/429-9167. 126 rms. A/C TV TEL. $114 double. Weekend packages available. AE, DC, DISC, MC, V. Parking $7.50.

Converted from a 10-story former office building, this hotel does not fit the usual mold of the Marriott chain. It does, however, offer good value for downtown. Guest rooms vary in size and configuration, but all have contemporary furniture, dark woods, a wet bar, coffeemaker, refrigerator, and large desk; 18 rooms also have a whirlpool bath and a microwave. The facilities include a restaurant/pub.

SUBURBS
EXPENSIVE

✪ **Christiana Hilton.** 100 Continental Dr., Newark, DE 19713. ☎ **800/HILTONS** or 302/454-1500. Fax 302/454-0233. 266 rms. A/C TV TEL. $99–$200 double. Weekend packages available. AE, CB, DC, DISC, MC, V. Free parking.

This hotel, nestled amid grassy grounds off exit 4B of I-95, is a good choice for a suburban location. Located in a burgeoning area near Delaware's university at Newark and a variety of shopping malls, it boasts a modernized four-story brick exterior, surrounded by topiary gardens with a brick-lined courtyard, gazebo, and pond that a family of swans calls home. The bedrooms are decorated in the Old Williamsburg tradition, with dark wood reproduction furniture and colonial prints and colors.

The hotel provides concierge service, room service, same-day valet service, nightly turndown, free shuttle service to downtown Wilmington, and express checkout. Its facilities include two restaurants, a lounge, an outdoor swimming pool, and a health and fitness room.

✪ **Inn at Montchanin Village.** Rte. 100 and Kirk Rd., Montchanin, DE 19710. ☎ **800/ COWBIRD** or 302/888-2133. Fax 302/888-0389. 37 units. $150–$170 double; $180–$325 suite. Rates include continental breakfast. AE, DC, MC, V. Free parking.

Proximity and atmosphere make this a great place from which to explore the Brandywine Valley as well as Wilmington. Yet another piece of du Pont history, Montchanin Village was once home to many of the workers from the nearby black powder mills and factories along the Brandywine. What remains of the village, 11 buildings completed between 1870 and 1910, became the Inn at Montchanin Village in June 1996, after several years of painstaking restoration. Nine of the buildings, once the workers' residences, have been converted into the 37 guest rooms and suites. The old blacksmith shop and barn are now the inn's restaurant called Krazy Kat's (see "Dining," below) and the reception area; the railroad station is a gourmet take-out shop.

Each guest room is uniquely designed and decorated. One- and two-level suites range from one to four bedrooms. All units have access to an outdoor sitting area, and first-level rooms and suites have private gardens. The whole place is warm and inviting. The owners provide such luxuries as towel warmers, lighted magnifying mirrors, umbrellas, coffeemakers, microwaves, and dual-line telephones.

Wilmington Hilton. 630 Naamans Rd. at I-95, Wilmington, DE 19703. ☎ **800/HILTONS** or 302/792-2700. Fax 302/798-6182. 193 rms. A/C TV TEL. $119–$159 double; $300 suite. Weekend packages available. AE, CB, DC, DISC, MC, V. Free parking.

Built in 1974, this modern eight-story hotel is continually being improved (the latest refurbishment was done in 1995). It's popular for business travelers because of its handy location, 5 miles north of Wilmington and 12 miles south of Philadelphia Airport at exit 11 off I-95, across from the Tri-State industrial complex and next to the Brandywine Corporate Center. The contemporary rooms are configured in various ways. Among the amenities are a restaurant, lounge, outdoor swimming pool, exercise room, basketball court, and volleyball court. The hotel also provides room service, same-day valet and laundry service, daily shoe shine, and complimentary shuttle service to and from the airport or train station.

MODERATE

Best Western Brandywine Valley Inn. 1807 Concord Pike (Rte. 202), Wilmington, DE 19803. ☎ **800/537-7772** or 302/656-9436. Fax 302/656-8564. 95 rms. A/C TV TEL. $79–$100 double. Weekend packages available. AE, CB, DC, DISC, MC, V. Free parking.

Situated north of downtown at the gateway to the Brandywine Valley, this modern motor inn is next to a shopping center but set back from the main road. The lobby features a Winterthur reproduction gallery, a collection of 15 furnishings commissioned by the nearby museum. This creative theme is carried through to the guest rooms, which have Georgian-style furnishings and Andrew Wyeth prints. Many rooms face an outdoor swimming pool and gardens in a central courtyard.

Courtyard by Marriott. 48 Geoffrey Dr., Newark, DE 19713. ☎ **800/321-2211** or 302/ 456-3800. Fax 302/456-3824. 152 rms, 12 suites. A/C TV TEL. $124 double; $144–154 suite. Weekend packages available. AE, CB, DC, DISC, MC, V. Free parking.

Opened in 1991, this four-story property was the first of the Marriott chain to open in the state. The layout follows the usual Courtyard plan, with sliding glass windows and balconies or patios facing a central landscaped terrace. Guest units are spacious, with a separate sitting area, a desk, and coffeemaking facilities. Hotel facilities include a restaurant, lounge, elevator, indoor swimming pool, and whirlpool.

Radisson Hotel Wilmington. 4727 Concord Pike (U.S. Rte. 202), Wilmington, DE 19803. ☎ **800/333-3333** or 302/478-6000. Fax 302/478-6000. 149 rms. A/C TV TEL. $109 double. Weekend packages available. AE, CB, DC, DISC, MC, V. Free parking.

Popular with business travelers during the week and families on weekends, this modern seven-story structure is on the busy Route 202 corridor, just north of downtown Wilmington and a few miles from the major historic museums and gardens. The bedrooms have a Brandywine Valley flavor, with dark reproduction furniture and local art. The facilities include two restaurants, an outdoor swimming pool, a fitness room, and a lounge with evening entertainment. There's a courtesy limousine service to downtown.

INEXPENSIVE

Fairfield Inn. 65 Geoffrey Dr., Newark, DE 19713. ☎ **800/228-2800** or 302/292-1500. Fax 302/292-1500. 105 rms. A/C TV TEL. $49–$69 double. Rates include continental breakfast. AE, CB, DC, MC, V. Free parking.

This three-story property offers comfortable and attractively furnished accommodations at low prices, in a very accessible location. There are three types of bedrooms: a compact single-bed room ideal for a lone traveler, a standard double, and a larger double with a king-size bed. All units have a full-length mirror, lounge chair, and reading light with a work desk. Complimentary coffee and newspapers are offered in the lobby. Facilities include an outdoor swimming pool, computer-card keys, and a meeting room.

Tally Ho Motor Lodge. 5209 Concord Pike, Wilmington, DE 19803. ☎ **302/478-0300.** 135 rms. A/C TV TEL. $42–$48 double. AE, CB, DC, DISC, MC, V. Free parking.

Located on the busy Route 202 strip just south of Naamans Road, this modern two-story motel is a popular choice for families. The rooms have standard furnishings and are equipped with one or two double beds or a king-size bed. Some rooms have a kitchenette. Among the facilities are an outdoor swimming pool and a guest Laundromat.

4 Dining

DOWNTOWN
EXPENSIVE

✪ **Brandywine Room.** In the Hotel du Pont, 11th and Market sts. ☎ **302/594-3156.** Reservations required. Main courses $22–$30. AE, CB, DC, DISC, MC, V. Sun–Thurs 5–10pm. AMERICAN/REGIONAL.

This is the Hotel du Pont's smaller and more clubby restaurant, with rich wood paneling, original artworks by three generations of the Wyeth family, and classical music playing in the background. Although the atmosphere here is slightly less formal than at the Green Room, the service is just as solicitous and the food equally outstanding. The emphasis is on local specialties, such as crab imperial with orange hazelnut Hollandaise sauce and veal Chesapeake, a thin scaloppini topped with jumbo lump crab and béarnaise sauce. For meat lovers, the Brandywine Mixed Grill offers a combination not often seen on menus—venison chop, sausage, and steak in juniper and rosemary juice. Our favorite is a succulent roast baby rack of lamb with a pecan crust.

✪ **Columbus Inn.** 2216 Pennsylvania Ave. ☎ **302/571-1492.** Reservations recommended for dinner. Main courses $12.95–$26.95; lunch $6.95–$13.95. AE, CB, DC, DISC, MC, V. Mon–Fri 11:30am–1am, Sat 5pm–1am, Sun 11am–1pm. AMERICAN/REGIONAL.

One of the city's oldest buildings dating from 1798, this stone house is set on a hill overlooking the main route (Route 52) to the Brandywine Valley at Woodlawn Avenue. The decor is a blend of dark woods, brick walls, book-filled shelves, brass fixtures, and photos of jazz stars—a perfect setting for live jazz sessions on Thursday through Saturday nights and on Sunday during brunch. This is a popular midday spot for Wilmington businesspeople, who enjoy the lunch choices of hot beef and seafood entrees, salads, sandwiches, or burgers.

The new chef, Dave Peterson, has added more fresh seafood to the menu, including fresh Florida yellowtail snapper. The rest of the dinner menu includes several house specialties—among them lobster scampi, lobster chunks sautéed in scampi sauce and served over linguine and spinach—as well as such regular favorites as Dover sole, steaks, and rack of lamb. There are also a few dishes promoting the jazz atmosphere, such as linguine Ellington, veal chop Fitzgerald, and chicken Satchmo. This restaurant is particularly known for its snapper soup, doused with sherry, and its Caesar salad, prepared tableside.

Constantinou's House of Beef. 1616 Delaware Ave. ☎ **302/652-0653.** Reservations recommended for dinner. Main courses $16.95–$30.95; lunch $6.95–$15.95. AE, CB, DC, DISC, MC, V. Mon–Thurs 11am–10pm, Fri 11am–11pm, Sat 4–11pm, Sun 4–9pm. INTERNATIONAL.

For the best steak in town, head here. You'll also enjoy the Victorian decor, filled with original tankards, prints, and bric-a-brac from around the world. Flags of all nations, American eagles, gold-framed mirrors, and tuxedoed waiters add to the charm. Lunch offerings include prime rib and steak teriyaki, as well as seafood platters, salads, and hearty sandwiches. Aged tender beef takes center stage at night with a variety of cuts of prime Kansas steaks as well as cut-to-order prime rib. Other favorites include rack of lamb, surf-and-turf, lobster tails, shrimp scampi, and jumbo crab imperial. A raw bar is featured on Wednesday, Thursday, and Friday evenings.

✪ **Green Room.** In the Hotel du Pont, 11th and Market sts. ☎ **302/594-3154.** Reservations required. Jackets required for men on Fri and Sat. Main courses $21–$29; lunch $9.95–$16.95; fixed-price brunch $29.50. AE, CB, DC, MC, V. Mon–Thurs 6:30–11am and 11:30am–2pm; Fri 6:30–11am, 11:30am–2pm, and 5:45–10pm; Sat 7–11am, 11:30am–2pm, and 5:45–10pm; Sun brunch 10am–2:15pm. FRENCH/CONTINENTAL.

The prices here are steep, but it's not your average restaurant—Delawareans consider this to be the state's top spot for a memorable meal. The Green Room is known for its impressive decor of tall arching windows, walls of quartered oak paneling, and handcrafted golden chandeliers from Spain. To complete the tableau, tuxedoed waiters provide impeccable service and a classical harpist plays in the background. Best of all, the chefs and the food are top rate. Entrees range from poached Maine lobster and sautéed Arctic char to rack of venison with portobello mushrooms or roast veal loin with sweetbreads. Even if you can't spend a night at the Hotel du Pont, treat yourself to a meal here. If you come for brunch, don't miss the "Good Morning America" omelet, filled with lobster, wild mushrooms, and smoked tomato sauce.

Shipley Grill. 913 Shipley St. ☎ **302/652-7797.** Reservations recommended for dinner. Main courses $17.95–$23.95; lunch $4.95–$11.95. AE, CB, DC, DISC, MC, V. Mon–Fri 11am–3pm and 5–11pm, Sat 5–11pm, Sun 5–9pm. INTERNATIONAL.

Situated just half a block from the Hotel du Pont, this brick-fronted restaurant has an old-world atmosphere with banquette seats, dark woods, brass lighting fixtures, ceiling fans, and a round marble bar. Lunch items include soups, salads, sandwiches, burgers, and pastas. At dinnertime, the locals flock here for thick and juicy steaks or the signature dish, Shipley's mixed grill. Grilled salmon, served with a red onion confit and watercress mousse, is also a favorite. Diners can choose from their extensive all-American wine list, which offers over 30 wines by the glass as well as by the bottle.

✪ **The Silk Purse & the Sow's Ear.** 1307 N. Scott St. ☎ **302/654-7666.** Reservations recommended. Main courses $17–$27. MC, V. Tues–Sat 6–9:30pm. INTERNATIONAL.

For many years, the Silk Purse has been heralded as one of Wilmington's best restaurants, drawing people north of downtown to an unlikely location, tucked in the middle of a quiet residential block in a private house. The restaurant presents an adventurous cuisine with good service amid a contemporary decor of fresh flowers, graceful glass lamps, framed gallery prints, and rattan furniture. About 5 years ago, the owners went one step further, adding the Sow's Ear upstairs, as a more informal and lower-priced extension. In early 1995, however, both restaurants came together to offer the same menu and the same prices. The menu changes daily and is never boring. Choices might include fried squid with spicy Vietnamese dipping sauce; seared sea scallops with leeks, tomatoes, and cream; and corn-coated oysters on salsa fresca with a chipotle cream—not to mention roasted garlic and goat cheese soufflé.

MODERATE

Kid Shelleen's. 1801 W. 14th St. (at Scott St.). ☎ **302/658-4600.** Main courses $8.95–$16.95. AE, CB, DC, DISC, MC, V. Mon–Sat 11am–midnight, Sun 10am–midnight. AMERICAN.

Tucked in a residential area on the city's north side, this lively indoor-outdoor restaurant is known for its casual atmosphere and open charcoal grill. The decor is highlighted by oil paintings of Old Wilmington and New Castle on brick and wood walls. Entrees include grilled salmon, barbecued chicken, baby-back ribs, Black Angus strip steaks, and pastas. The bar here is known for its large-screen TV showing the latest sports action.

Tavola Toscana. 1412 N. Du Pont St. ☎ **302/654-8001.** Reservations recommended. Main courses $13–$24; lunch $11–$14. AE, DISC, MC, V. Mon–Fri 11:30am–2pm and 5:30–10pm, Sat 5:30–10pm, Sun 5:30–9pm. TUSCAN/ITALIAN.

As soon as you step into this restaurant, you know it has to be good by the excited din of the customers, the bustle of the waiting staff, the piquant aromas flowing from the open kitchen and the wood-burning oven, and the constant attention displayed by the ever-present owner and chef, Daniel Butler. Specialties include charcoal-grilled veal chop with oregano and lime; Tuscan mixed grill of veal, sausage, chicken liver, and sage-seasoned chicken; and T-bone steaks grilled with a splash of lemon and Tuscan olive oil. Freshly made pastas and individual pizzas with exotic toppings are also on the menu. The restaurant is a little out of the way, at the Rockford Shops, 14th Street off Delaware Avenue, but there's rarely an empty table.

Tiffin. 1210 N. Market St. ☎ **302/571-1133.** Reservations recommended for dinner. Main courses $15.95–$23.95; lunch $6.95–$10.95. MC, V. Mon–Thurs 11:30am–2:30pm and 5:30–10pm, Fri 11:30am–2pm and 5:30–11pm, Sat 5:30–11pm. AMERICAN.

Conveniently situated just 2 blocks north of the Hotel du Pont, this trendy eatery has a bright and airy atmosphere, with pastel linens, light woods, wicker seats, mirrored walls, and lots of plants. The menu changes each spring and fall, but you'll generally find such tempting choices as spicy Louisiana catfish; breast of duck with thyme and pear cranberry chutney; jumbo lump crab cakes; and breast of chicken with rosemary and garlic; as well as steaks, grilled salmon, and tuna. Lunch items include sandwiches, burgers, and a good selection of salads.

Waterworks Cafe. 16th and French sts. ☎ **302/652-6022.** Reservations recommended for dinner. Main courses $13.95–$24.95; lunch $5.95–$14.95. AE, DISC, MC, V. Tues–Fri 11:30am–2:30pm and 5:30–10pm, Sat 5:30–10pm. AMERICAN/INTERNATIONAL.

Overlooking the Brandywine, the trendy Waterworks Cafe, housed in the former water-station buildings on the banks of the river, is touted as Wilmington's only waterfront restaurant. The decor is colorful and contemporary. Outdoors there's a roofed deck and patio seating in good weather. For lunch there's a variety of fish and meat entrees, omelets, and cold platters—try the Great Oceans salad. At dinnertime the selections include roast duckling Brandywine, veal Oscar, chicken Marsala, prime rib, surf-and-turf, lobster tails, and Alaskan salmon steak.

INEXPENSIVE

✪ **Govatos.** 800 Market St. Mall. ☎ **302/652-4082.** Breakfast $2.95–$4.95; lunch $4.95–$7.95. MC, V. Mon–Fri 8am–3:30pm, Sat 8am–3pm. AMERICAN.

Established in 1894, this old-world-style eatery is a Wilmington tradition and an ideal choice in midcity for breakfast or lunch. The menu offers sandwiches, burgers, salads, and hot platters of Delaware favorites, such as honey-dipped chicken and shrimp in a basket. The main attractions, however, are the desserts and other confections, since this place produces Delaware's largest selection of homemade chocolates and candies. Govatos has a second restaurant located in the Talleyville Shopping Center, 4105 Concord Pike (☎ **302/478-5324**).

Temptations. 11A Trolley Sq., Delaware Ave. ☎ **302/429-9162.** All items $2.95–$6.95. AE, CB, DC, DISC, MC, V. Mon–Thurs 10am–9pm, Fri–Sat 10am–10pm. AMERICAN/ICE CREAM.

If you have a sweet tooth, you'll want to try this ice-cream parlor and restaurant. It serves sandwiches, salads, and burgers in addition to an extensive selection of ice creams. The menu includes more than a dozen sundaes, among them the appropriately named "Original Sin"—a huge banana split, with fig leaves in season.

SUBURBS
EXPENSIVE

Krazy Kat's. Rte. 100 and Kirk Rd. ☎ **302/888-2133.** Reservations recommended. Jackets requested for men. Main courses $23–$25; lunch $9–$14. AE, DC, MC, V. Mon–Fri 7–9am, 11am–2pm, and 5:30–11pm; Sat 8–11am and 5:30–10pm; Sun 8am–noon and 5:30–10pm. CONTINENTAL.

If you want a fine-dining experience without the formal, stuffy atmosphere, give Krazy Kat's a try. Located in the old blacksmith shop at the Inn at Montchanin Village, Krazy Kat's was once the home of an eccentric cat lover, hence the name and the cartoonlike cat art that adorns the walls. Leopard-print chairs and china with a jungle motif finish off the comfortably elegant decor. Menu items focus on fresh local ingredients. Mushrooms of all shapes and sizes pop up everywhere, from the petite filet mignon with grilled portobello mushroom cap to the sautéed French escargots with shiitake mushrooms and roasted garlic and red peppers. The crab cakes and shrimp mousseline are good, and the mixed grill of duck, lamb, and ostrich is superb. The wine list here, which features about 100 carefully chosen vintages, was recently awarded a Wine Spectator Award of Excellence. If you're not a wine connoisseur, the staff will gladly help you choose one you'll enjoy.

✪ **Picciotti's.** 3001 Lancaster Ave. ☎ **302/652-3563.** Reservations recommended. Main courses $16.95–$25.95. AE, CB, DISC, DC, MC, V. Sun–Thurs 5–9pm, Fri–Sat 5–10pm. INTERNATIONAL.

This 60-year-old restaurant is known for outstanding beef. It was first established at 4th Street and Du Pont Street but moved to its present location, at the intersection of Cleveland Avenue, about 20 years ago. The exterior is unpretentious, but inside great culinary things happen. Most people come here for the filet mignon, touted as the best in Delaware and beyond; we heartily concur—Picciotti's filets are as tender and flavorful as any you'll find elsewhere. If beef, however, is not your dish, you may choose from a selection of other entrees, such as chicken cordon bleu, roast fillet of lamb, calves' liver, baked salmon, grilled tuna, pastas, and a house specialty of crab cakes.

✪ **Sal's Petite Marmite.** 603 N. Lincoln St. ☎ **302/652-1200.** Reservations suggested. Main courses $15–$29; lunch $8.95–$16.95. AE, CB, DC, DISC, MC, V. Mon–Fri 11:30am–2pm and 5–10pm, Sat 5–10pm. NORTHERN ITALIAN/CLASSICAL FRENCH.

Although tucked away in the heart of Little Italy, this restaurant is not a typical pasta and pizza spot. Founded more than 20 years ago by master chef Sal Buono, it is an elegant and award-winning culinary enclave with a country-club ambience, blending French and Italian cuisine amid a decor of rich leather furnishings. Great care is taken to obtain the freshest and best ingredients daily; all the tomatoes and herbs, for example, are grown in the owner's private garden.

Lunch focuses on salads and light entrees such as grilled chicken with fresh spinach and sun-dried tomatoes and spicy pasta primavera. Dinner, more of an event, depends on what is in season but can often include smoked duck and foie gras, garlic-seared shrimp and sea scallops, and pepper-seared chicken tenderloin, sautéed with spinach, tomatoes, olives, and white wine. The Cigar Room, an adjacent cigar and martini bar, has an impressive martini menu, with over 20 types of martinis.

EXPENSIVE/MODERATE

Feby's Fishery. 3701 Lancaster Pike. ☎ **302/998-9501.** Reservations recommended for dinner. Main courses $10.95–$21.95; lobster dishes $22.95–$29.95; lunch $5.95–$14.95. AE, MC, V. Mon–Thurs 11am–9pm, Fri 11am–10pm, Sat–Sun 4–9pm. SEAFOOD.

Situated on the city's southwest side, just west of the junction of Route 100 south, this nautically themed restaurant also has a seafood market, a sure sign of fresh fish on the premises. The menu features a variety of crab, shrimp, lobster, and scallop dishes, as well as daily fish specials and creative combinations, such as salmon with tarragon sauce and crab imperial Florentine. The menu also offers Italian seafood dishes, such as cioppino—a stew of mussels, clams, oysters, shrimp, and fish in seasoned red sauce with fettuccine Alfredo. For landlubbers, there's filet mignon and Delmonico steak.

Ristorante Carucci. 504 Greenhill Ave. ☎ **302/654-2333.** Reservations required. Main courses $12.95–$18.95; lunch $12.95–$18.95. AE, DC, MC, V. Tues–Fri 11:30am–2:30pm and 5pm–midnight, Sat 5pm–midnight. ITALIAN.

The theme of this contemporary art deco–style restaurant is music—piano tunes as background for lunch and opera arias performed by the waiting staff in the evening. The menu changes with the season, but it's always offered with a flourish: Waiters present meats and fish on platters for you before you select what you want and how you want it cooked. Wines are likewise introduced and described in detail before being chosen and uncorked. The cuisine is innovative, with the choices often including black shrimp ravioli and lobster sauce, baked red snapper with tomato and oyster mushrooms, braid of coho salmon and rainbow trout with tomato-basil cream sauce, rack of lamb, and homemade pastas.

MODERATE

DiNardo's. 405 N. Lincoln St. ☎ **302/656-3685.** Reservations not accepted. Main courses $8.95–$21.95; lunch $3.95–$15.95. AE, CB, DC, DISC, MC, V. Mon–Sat 11am–11:30pm, Sun 3–10pm. SEAFOOD.

Crabs are the pièce de résistance at this small, casual, family-run restaurant, a tradition in Delaware since 1938—and the place to go if you enjoy cracking your own crustaceans. DiNardo's even flies the crabs in from New Orleans when they're out of season locally. Lunchtime choices include crab and shellfish platters, salads, and pastas. Dinner entrees, in addition to crabs in the shell, include a variety of other crab dishes—crab cakes, crab claws, crab legs, and crab imperial—as well as shrimp, lobster, flounder, scallops, oysters, and, for landlubbers, steaks. There are also combination platters.

Terrace at Greenhill. 800 N. Du Pont Rd. ☎ **302/575-1990.** Reservations recommended for dinner. Main courses $9.95–$17.95; lunch $4.95–$7.95. AE, DC, MC, V. Mon–Thurs 11:30am–2:30pm and 5–9pm, Fri–Sat 11:30am–2:30pm and 5–10pm, Sun 10am–2:30pm and 4–8:30pm. INTERNATIONAL.

Situated west of downtown in a residential area off Pennsylvania Avenue (Route 52), this restaurant overlooks the Ed "Porky" Oliver Golf Course and is a favorite with local golfers. The decor is bright and airy, with light wood and rattan furnishings, lots of plants and greenery, and walls full of watercolors by local artists. Like the setting, the food is fun and varied. Lunch items include Southwest chicken sauté, turkey burger, and salmon cake, as well as salads, soups, omelets, quiches, pizzas, crepes, and sandwiches. For dinner there's a selection of steaks and seafood, such as rainbow trout amandine or blackened red snapper, as well as several specialty items, among them jambalaya and chicken scampi.

5 Attractions

Though many visitors to Wilmington travel out to the Brandywine Valley attractions, the downtown area has several museums and sites of interest. Most of these sites, as well as the city's shops and restaurants, revolve around the Market Street Mall, a 5-block pedestrian area that stretches from 6th Street to 11th Street. On the waterfront, the *Kalmar Nyckel* and the Delaware Grand Exhibition Hall are at present the only tourist attractions, but efforts are under way to revitalize that area by adding a historic village, carriage rides, and a shopping complex, so look for some significant changes in the next few years.

✪ **Delaware Art Museum.** 2301 Kentmere Pkwy. ☎ **302/571-9590.** Admission $5 adults, $3 seniors and over age 6, $2.50 college students, free on Wed night. Tues and Thurs–Sat 9am–4pm, Wed 9am–9pm, Sun 10am–5pm. From I-95, take Rte. 52 north. Turn right onto Bancroft Pkwy., then left onto Kentmere, and follow signs to the museum.

Renowned for its holdings of American art (from 1840 to the present), this prestigious museum is located just north of downtown in Rockford Park, a residential area of the city. It houses the largest collection of works by Howard Pyle, the father of American illustration and founder of the Brandywine school of painting, as well as many works by his followers, including the Wyeths, Frank Schoonover, Elizabeth Shippen Green, and Maxfield Parrish. It also contains outstanding examples of American sculpture, photography, and traditional and contemporary craft, as well as the largest display of pre-Raphaelite English art in the United States.

Delaware Center for the Contemporary Arts. 103 E. 16th St. ☎ **302/656-6466.** Free admission. Tues–Fri 11am–5pm, Sat 1–5pm. Closed Aug.

Nestled beside the Brandywine, this impressive gallery focuses on contemporary visual arts that reflect everyday life, including controversial and provocative issues. The exhibits include paintings, drawings, sculptures, photographs, and crafts of various sorts by both national and local artists. The center has more than two dozen

---

Especially for Kids

The **Delaware Children's Theater,** 1014 Delaware Ave. (☎ **302/655-1014**), presents plays based on fairy tales and other stories familiar to children of all ages. Admission is $9, with performances on Saturday and Sunday at 2pm. *Note:* Even for adult visitors without children, this ornate three-story building is worth a look for its historic and architectural value. Listed on the National Register of Historic Places, it was designed in 1892 by a woman exclusively as a women's club. The building today continues to be owned and operated by women.

---

exhibits a year, among them an art auction in early April, a kitchen tour in October, and a studio tour in November.

Delaware Grand Exhibition Hall. On the Christina River next to the minor league baseball stadium. ☎ **888/395-0005.** Admission $12.50 adults, $11 seniors, $4 ages 5–16, $7.50 college students, free under age 5. Exhibition daily 9am–8pm (last entry at 6pm); box office daily June–July 9am–5pm, Aug–Dec 8:30am–6pm.

Even though as of this printing the building is not yet finished, the Grand Exhibition Hall and its first upcoming exhibit, *Nicholas and Alexandra: The Last Imperial Family of Tsarist Russia,* are all the buzz in the city of Wilmington. The Exhibition Hall is to be a focal point on Wilmington's Christina River waterfront and a spark for the revitalization effort under way there. The *Nicholas and Alexandra* exhibit is slated to run from August 1 to December 31, 1998; advanced tickets go on sale in June (for ticket information call ☎ 888/395-0005). The exhibit will take up 14 galleries and comprise over 400 objects, all on loan from the Hermitage Museum in St. Petersburg, Russia, including elegant court gowns, military uniforms, icons and chalices of the Russian Orthodox Church, and a number of decorative pieces designed by Karl Fabergè. Ticket prices include timed entry to the exhibit, an 8-minute orientation presentation, and an individual recorded tour. After December 1998 the *Nicholas and Alexandra* exhibit will be replaced with other exhibits for which the hours, admission, and tour program should be similar. Be sure to call ahead to find out what (and if) something is showing.

Delaware History Museum. 504 Market St. (at the south end of the Market St. Mall). ☎ **302/656-0637** or 302/655-7161. Free admission. Tues–Fri noon–4pm, Sat 10am–4pm.

Housed in a restored 1941 F. W. Woolworth Co. building, once the third largest Woolworth store in America, this museum tells the story of Delaware. It features changing interactive exhibits on different phases of history and social development and permanent displays of regional decorative arts, paintings, children's toys, and items of local interest. The Discovery Room, featuring *Grandma's Attic,* gives children a place to dress up, touch and handle artifacts, and hear storytellers. The gift shop specializes in Delaware-handcrafted items and souvenirs.

Kalmar Nyckel Foundation. 1124 E. 7th St. ☎ **302/429-7447.** Admission $5 adults and age 13 and over, $4 seniors, $2 ages 6–12. Mon–Sat 10am–4pm, Sun noon–4pm. *Note:* Parties of more than five persons need an appointment at any time. Take Martin Luther King Blvd. to King St. and then turn right on 4th St. Continue until turning left on Swedes Landing Rd. before the Wincester Bridge, and then right on 7th St.

Set on the shores of the Christina River near Old Swedes Church and Fort Christina Park, the *Kalmar Nyckel* Foundation, named after one of the ships that brought the first Swedish settlers to the New World in the 1630s, aims to re-create the story of the Swedes' arrival in the Delaware Valley. After several years of construction and many hours of work from volunteer and professional blacksmiths, shipbuilders, and carvers, the new ship *Kalmar Nyckel* was finally launched in late September 1997, though it is far from complete. Visitors can watch as workers continue construction, and when weather and working conditions permit, can tour the ship, as well as the working shipyard, which has a blacksmith shop and carving workshop.

✪ Old Swedes Church. 606 Church St. ☎ **302/652-5629.** Free admission, but donations welcome. Mon, Wed, and Fri–Sat 1–4pm. Take Martin Luther King Blvd. to 4th St. Turn right on 4th St., left on Church St.; church is 2 blocks on right.

Located near the Christina River, this is one of the oldest churches in the United States. The church remains in its original 1698 form (and still maintains its extensive genealogical records) and is still regularly used for religious services. Highlights of the interior include stained-glass windows installed from 1885 to 1897 and a church chest dating from 1713, as well as herringbone bricks in the main aisle and a black-walnut canopied pulpit, one of the oldest of its kind in the United States. The church yard, which predates the church by 60 years, was used as a burying ground for early settlers of Fort Christina and its community. A nearby reconstructed farmhouse depicts the everyday life of the early Swedish settlers.

Old Town Hall. 512 Market St. ☎ **302/655-7161.** Free admission, but donations welcome. Tues–Fri noon–4pm, Sat 10am–4pm. From I-96, take Rte. 52 south; turn left on 11th St.; turn right onto King St.; building is 5 blocks on right.

This landmark Georgian-style building in the heart of the city, built from 1798 to 1800, functioned as the center of political and social activities during the height of Wilmington's mercantile-milling economy. It is now operated by the Historical Society of Delaware and features permanent and rotating exhibits depicting life in Delaware over the centuries. Don't miss the restored jail cells in the basement.

FORT DELAWARE STATE PARK

One of the state's most unusual parks, **✪ Fort Delaware State Park,** Pea Patch Island, Delaware City (☎ **302/834-7941**), lies about 16 miles south of Wilmington, in the Delaware River. To get there, take Route 13 or I-95 south from Wilmington to Route 9 (turn left), which will take you to Delaware City. The park surrounds a massive five-sided granite fortress that served as a detention center during the Civil War. Inside there's a museum, 19th-century cells and armaments, and an audiovisual presentation about the history of the island. Other facilities include an observation tower for bird watchers (the island is a popular nesting spot for egrets, herons, and other marsh fowl) and an assortment of nature trails and picnic sites. You can visit the island by taking a 10-minute boat ride from Delaware City. The ferry departs every hour on the hour from Battery Park at the end of Clinton Road. Boat fare, which includes admission to the park, is $6 for adults and $4 for children 13 and under.

When you arrive on the island, a tractor-pulled tram will take you from the dock to the fort, where, if you're visiting during a living history weekend, you'll be greeted by a Confederate prisoner/reenactor. The site is open June through September, Wednesday through Sun from 10am to 6pm and on weekends April through June and during October from 10am to 6pm. Reenactments and living history demonstrations are held throughout the summer, so try to plan your visit to coincide with these events. Guided tours by Confederate and Union reenactors and musket, artillery, and cannon demonstrations are great (though a bit loud) for children and adults.

To get a schedule of events, contact the **Fort Delaware Society,** P.O. Box 553, Delaware City, DE 19706 (☎ **302/834-1630**).

6 Spectator Sports & Outdoor Activities

BASEBALL   When it comes to the national pastime, Wilmington cheers for the **Blue Rocks,** 801 S. Madison St. (☎ **302/888-2015**), a minor league baseball team first organized in the 1940s and revived with much fanfare in 1993. The team plays at the 5,900-seat Daniel S. Frawley Stadium, situated beside I-95, just south of downtown. Box seats cost $7 and reserved seats cost $6; general admission is $4 and admission for children, seniors, and military personnel is $2. Parking is free.

GOLF   The rolling hills around Wilmington make for challenging golf. The following are a few of the best clubs that welcome visitors:

Delcastle Golf Club, 802 McKennan's Church Rd. (☎ **302/995-1990**), located southwest of the city near Delaware Park racetrack, offers an 18-hole championship course, pro shop, driving range, and miniature golf course. Greens fees are $16 weekdays and $20 weekends; carts are $22. The club is open daily, dawn to dusk, except January 1 and December 25.

Ed "Porky" Oliver Golf Course, 800 N. Du Pont Rd. (☎ **302/571-9041**), is situated in a residential area west of downtown and off Route 52 (Pennsylvania Avenue). The club has an 18-hole championship course, driving range, pro shop, and restaurant (see Terrace at Greenhill in "Dining," above); it also provides lessons and group clinics. Tee times are accepted by phone 1 week in advance. Greens fees are $16 on weekdays and $20 on weekends; a cart is $11 per person. The course is open daily, year-round, dawn to dusk.

The **Three Little Bakers Golf Course,** 3542 Foxcroft Dr. (☎ **302/737-1877**), nestled in the Pike Creek Valley southwest of Wilmington, is a semiprivate, 18-hole, par-71 course open daily to the public except after 3pm on Thursday and Friday. Facilities include a pro shop, club rental, golf lessons, and bag storage. Greens fees, including cart, are $40 Monday through Thursday and $45 Friday, Saturday, and Sunday; carts rent for $11 per person.

HORSE RACING   For almost 60 years, racing fans have placed their bets at **Delaware Park,** Route 7, off I-95 exit 4B, Stanton (☎ **302/994-2521**), a picturesque tree-lined setting about 5 miles south of Wilmington. From April through November, there is daytime thoroughbred racing on various days of the week. Post time is 12:45pm; admission is free. During the rest of the year, Delaware Park offers simulcast races from other east coast tracks and a wide variety of coin-operated and video slot machines, from 25¢ to $5.

PARKS   Wilmington's playground is **Bellevue State Park,** 800 Carr Rd. (☎ **302/ 577-3390**). Located on the northeast perimeter of the city, this 270-acre park was once the home of the William du Pont family. Facilities include picnic areas, garden paths for walking, and fitness trails for jogging. Admission is free except from Memorial Day through Labor Day and weekends and holidays in May, September, and October, when the entrance fee is $5 for each out-of-state vehicle and $2.50 for each Delaware-registered car. Tours of Bellevue Mansion, located on the premises, are scheduled throughout the summer. Cost is $3.50 per person.

Southwest of Wilmington is **Lums Pond State Park,** 1068 Howell School Rd., off Route 71, Bear, Delaware (☎ **302/368-6989**). Stretching along the Chesapeake and Delaware Canal, this 1,757-acre park encompasses the state's largest freshwater pond, a home to several beaver colonies and waterfowl. For humans, the pond offers swimming, fishing, and boating. You can either bring your own boat or rent a rowboat, canoe, paddleboat, or sailboat from the park during the summer and on weekends in May and September. Rates range from $3.50 to $9 per hour, depending on the type of boat. The surrounding parklands include hiking and walking trails, a nature center, picnic areas, football, soccer, and baseball fields, basketball and tennis courts, and camping sites. Admission charges are the same as for Bellevue State Park, described above, but are in effect from the beginning of May through the end of October.

7 Shopping

THE SHOPPING SCENE

Wilmington and the surrounding area has dozens of extensive malls and shopping centers, such as **Concord Mall,** 4737 Concord Pike (☎ **302/478-9271**), and **Christiana Mall,** 715 Christiana Mall, Route 7 at I-95 exit 4S (☎ **302/731-9815**). The downtown area also offers good shopping, particularly on **9th Street** and along **Market Street Mall.**

SHOPPING A TO Z

ART

Hardcastle Gallery. Frederick Country Center, Rte. 52, Centreville, DE. ☎ **302/655-5230.**

For original oil paintings and watercolors, as well as prints and sculptures, visit this gallery, located in the Frederick Country shopping center. Open Monday through Thursday from 10am to 6pm, Friday from 10am to 8pm, and Saturday from 10am to 4pm.

BOOKS

Encore Books. 827–829 N. Market St. Mall. ☎ **302/656-3112.**

In the heart of Wilmington's historic pedestrian mall, this shop carries a variety of discounted books on local history and sights. It also has a good selection of maps. Open weekdays from 9am to 6pm, Saturday from 10am to 6pm.

Ninth Street Book Shop. 104 W. 9th St. ☎ **302/652-3315.**

This shop offers a large selection of books on Delaware and local history, as well as travel books and maps. Other well-stocked categories include mysteries, children's books, and cookbooks, as well as a selection of books on African-American history and culture. Open Monday through Friday from 8:30am to 5:30pm and Saturday from 10am to 3pm.

CHOCOLATES & CANDIES

Govatos. 800 N. Market St. Mall. ☎ **302/652-4082.**

Since 1894, this shop has been selling Delaware's largest selection of homemade chocolates and candies. All sweets are available by the piece or the pound. Open weekdays from 8am to 5pm, Saturday from 8am to 3pm.

FASHIONS

Handbags 'n Things. 205 9th St. ☎ **302/654-5910.**

This little shop stocks ladies' hats, jewelry, and shoes. It's located on a street lined with art and antique shops and also a bank called, appropriately enough, the Artisans Savings Bank. Open Monday through Saturday from 10am to 6pm.

Wright & Simon. 911 Market St. Mall. ☎ **302/658-7345.**

A traditional haberdashery, this store carries fine suits and coats for men, including tailored and made-to-measure clothing. Open weekdays from 9am to 5:30pm, Saturday from 9am to 4:30pm.

JEWELRY & TIMEPIECES
The Watchmaker. 107 W. 9th St. ☎ **302/429-8463.**

This inviting shop is known for its unusual timepieces and jewelry created on the premises. Restoration and repair services for antique jewelry are also provided. Open weekdays from 8:30am to 5pm.

8   Wilmington After Dark

For the latest information about evening entertainment in the Wilmington area, consult the Friday edition of the Wilmington *News-Journal,* which features a weekend entertainment guide, "55 Hours." The city's monthly *Out & About* magazine also lists entertainment events. Both publications are available at newsstands. In addition, the **Delaware State Arts Council,** Carvel State Office Building, 820 N. French St. (☎ **302/577-8278**), publishes *ARTLINE,* a free bimonthly newsletter covering major arts events. It lists concerts, theater events, art exhibits, and cultural programs.

For many Wilmington area performing arts events, tickets are available at **B&B Tickettown,** 322 W. 9th St. (☎ **302/656-9797**), at the corner of West Street, behind the Sheraton Suites Hotel.

THE PERFORMING ARTS

For such a small city, Wilmington has a surprisingly lively performing arts scene, and the ✪ **Grand Opera House,** 818 N. Market St., is the center of it. Built in 1871 as part of a Masonic temple, this impressive restored Victorian showplace is nestled in the heart of the downtown pedestrian mall. On the exterior you'll see some of the finest examples of cast-iron architecture in America. The facility seats 1,100 and is home to OperaDelaware and the Delaware Symphony Orchestra. It also offers an ever-changing program of guest artists in ballet, jazz, chamber music, pop concerts, and theatrical productions. Tickets range from $10 to $51; call ☎ **302/658-7897** for information or **800/37-GRAND** or 302/652-5577 for tickets.

The city's other large venue, **The Playhouse,** 10th and Market streets, has brought the finest of touring Broadway shows to downtown Wilmington for more than 80 years. Located next to the Hotel du Pont, it has a 1,239-seat capacity amid a vintage Victorian decor. Over the years, audiences have applauded stars from Sarah Bernhardt to Kathleen Turner; recent shows have included *Cats* and *Les Misérables.* In addition, local companies, such as the Brandywine Ballet, often perform in the Playhouse. Ticket prices range from $22 to $55. For information or tickets call ☎ **302/656-4401.**

Two smaller venues enhance the city's offerings. The **Delaware Center for the Contemporary Arts,** 103 E. 16th St. (☎ **302/656-6466**), beside the Brandywine Creek, features chamber music and classical music concerts, as well as a performing arts series, throughout the year. Tickets cost $10 to $12 for most events. Founded more than 50 years ago, the **Christina Cultural Arts Center,** 705 N. Market St. Mall (☎ **302/652-0101**), offers innovative programs that involve the community and celebrate the diversity of the city. Currently, they host "Ebony Rain," an open poetry night on the second and fourth Fridays of each month, usually at 8pm. It costs $5.

CLASSICAL MUSIC

In recent years, under the direction of maestro Stephen Gunzenhauser, the **Delaware Symphony Orchestra** has gained national recognition as a model regional orchestra. The DSO presents over 90 performances a year, ranging from classical and chamber to pops. Performances are held in the Grand Opera House in Wilmington, but the orchestra also recently began a traveling series, performing in Kent and Sussex County. For ticket information, contact the Grand Opera House at ☎ **800/ 37GRAND** or 302/652-5577.

The **Wilmington Music School,** 4101 Washington St. (☎ **302/762-1132**), offers frequent concerts and recitals by the Wilmington Community Orchestra and the Wilmington Festival Players. It also sponsors performances by faculty members, guest artists, and students. Admission is free to some events; others range from $3 to $5.

THEATER

Candlelight Music Dinner-Theatre. 2208 Millers Rd., Ardentown, DE. ☎ **302/475-2313.** Tickets $25–$29.

A big red barn is the setting for the Candlelight, Delaware's first dinner theater, which started more than 25 years ago. Among its productions have been the musicals *Camelot, Gigi, My Fair Lady, Man of La Mancha,* and *Fiddler on the Roof.* The price of admission includes a buffet dinner, with members of the cast doubling as waiters and waitresses. The theater is located in the suburb of Arden, near the Hilton Hotel, and is signposted off Harvey Road. Open Thursday through Saturday, with the buffet at 6pm and the show at 8:15pm; Sunday, buffet at 5pm and show at 7:15pm.

Delaware Theatre Company. 200 Water St. ☎ **302/594-1104;** box office 302/594-1100. Tickets $19.50–$33.

Situated at the foot of Orange Street, this is a modern, 389-seat, state-of-the-art facility; no seat is more than 12 rows from the stage. The theater is home to Delaware's only resident professional company, which presents an ever-changing program of classic and contemporary plays throughout the year. Evening shows are Tuesday through Saturday at 8pm; matinees are Wednesday at 1pm and Saturday at 2pm.

Three Little Bakers Dinner-Theatre. 3540 Foxcroft Dr. ☎ **800/368-3303.** Dinner/show $23.95–$31.95.

Located southeast of Wilmington off Route 7, this suburban theater presents Broadway shows as well as celebrity specials featuring well-known stars and bands. Some of the productions put on here have been *The Sound of Music, Music Man, Evita,* and *West Side Story.* The price of admission includes a buffet dinner with French and Swiss pastries, dancing, and preshow entertainment. The theater is named after its three founders: Al, Nick, and Hugo Immediato, all originally bakers by profession. Open Wednesday, Friday, and Saturday, with dinner at 5:30pm and show at 8pm; Thursday and Sunday matinee, with buffet at 11:30am and show at 2pm.

THE CLUB & MUSIC SCENE

The Wilmington music and dancing scene got a big boost with the recent opening of the Big Kahuna. You can't miss it; it's the club with the big volcano out front. Several nationally known rock artists have played here recently. In the rest of the city, the nightlife is still pretty mellow, dominated by jazz, folk music, and the hotel piano bars.

Big Kahuna. 550 S. Madison St. ☎ **302/571-8402.** Cover $5. Take exit 6 (Maryland Ave.) off I-95 and look for the volcano.

This audacious club, Wilmington's biggest and newest night club, features live rock on Friday, deejay dance nights on Saturday, and Monday night football in season. For a schedule and information on their restaurant, Kahunaville, check out the website at **www.kahunaville.com.**

Bourbon Street Cafe. 105 Kirkwood Sq., Kirkwood Hwy. ☎ **302/633-1944.** No cover or $3–$5 for some acts.

For a bit of New Orleans decor, atmosphere, and music in Wilmington, try this place, located next to the entrance of Delaware Park racetrack. It offers live jazz and blues every night except Monday.

Cavanaugh's. 703 N. Market St. ☎ **302/656-4067.** Cover $2–$5.

Located in a historic building in the heart of the city, on the main pedestrian mall, this place offers a variety of music on most nights, from live jazz, bluegrass, and rock to a sing-along piano bar.

Comedy Cabaret. 1001 Jefferson St. ☎ **302/652-6873.** Cover about $12.

This club presents professional comedy shows on Friday and Saturday at 9:30pm.

Kelly's Logan House. 1701 Delaware Ave. ☎ **302/65-LOGAN.** Cover $3–$5.

Built in 1864, this place claims to be the oldest tavern in the city. It has all the trappings of an old Irish pub, including original pressed-tin ceilings and exposed brick walls. Its name comes from a famous Union army general, John A. Logan, who instituted Memorial Day; the "Kelly" part derives from the family that has owned the house since 1889. This is one of the best places in the city for live entertainment in an intimate setting. There's usually rhythm-and-blues music Thursday through Saturday nights.

O'Friel's. 600 Delaware Ave. ☎ **302/654-9952.** No cover for most sessions.

This is the city's classic Irish pub, with beers from the "ould sod" on tap and traditional and contemporary Irish music on many nights. There's usually a session of Irish traditional music at 9pm every Thursday, Friday, and Saturday night.

Porky's Dance Club. 1206 N. Union St. ☎ **302/429-6633.** Cover $2–$5.

Dubbed Wilmington's "hottest over-30 dance club," this lively spot offers a variety of entertainment to appeal to different tastes: karaoke on Sunday, country dance lessons on Thursday, oldies on Wednesday, and contemporary live bands and deejay music on Thursday, Friday, and Saturday.

11

The Brandywine Valley & Historic New Castle

The Brandywine Valley is a great expanse of Delaware countryside at its best—sparkling river waters, rolling hills, lush landscapes, enchanting gardens, and wonderful estates and museums. Historic New Castle, nestled beside the Delaware River, is a masterfully preserved 18th-century town with cobblestone streets, brick walkways, and Federal town houses. It manages to thrive today while still retaining the charm of its days as Delaware's original capital and a major colonial seaport. Both these destinations are a vital part of the overall Wilmington experience, as well as outstanding travel destinations in their own right.

1 The Brandywine Valley

10 miles N of Wilmington, 35 miles W of Philadelphia, 90 miles N of Baltimore

Meandering north from Wilmington, the scenic and historic Brandywine Valley has a long and storied history. The river and its valley provided for early settlers, powered the first great du Pont industry, and inspired some of the country's great artists. To the Native Americans who inhabited the area first, the river was known as the Wawset or Suspecoughwit and was cherished as a bountiful shad fishing source. The Swedes and Danes who settled here also used the river for fishing, calling it the Fishkill. The Quakers and other English settlers, who renamed it Brandywine, used the river for power, making the Brandywine an important milling center in the 18th and 19th centuries. At its peak, more than 100 water-powered mills along the Brandywine corridor produced everything from flour, paper, and textiles to snuff and, of course, black powder, where the American du Ponts first made their fortune. In more recent times, the valley has been home to a whole school of artists and illustrators, beginning with Howard Pyle and Frank Schoonover, and including the Wyeth family—N.C.; Andrew, who still lives and paints here; and Jamie.

Today, the Brandywine Valley is a tourist mecca—a blend of historical museums, art galleries, idyllic gardens, welcoming inns, and gourmet restaurants. It stretches across the Delaware border into Pennsylvania—for the full Brandywine experience, you really must see the sites of both states. As such, we've included Pennsylvania attractions, inns, and restaurants in this chapter as well.

The Brandywine Valley & Historic New Castle

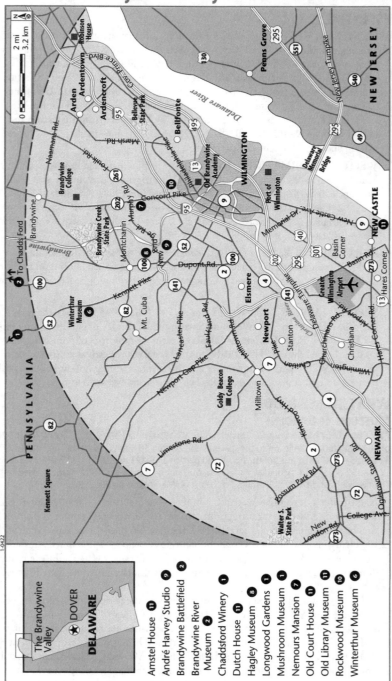

Amstel House ⑪
André Harvey Studio ⑨
Brandywine Battlefield ②
Brandywine River Museum ②
Chaddsford Winery ①
Dutch House ⑪
Hagley Museum ⑧
Longwood Gardens ①
Mushroom Museum ①
Nemours Mansion ⑦
Old Court House ⑪
Old Library Museum ⑪
Rockwood Museum ⑩
Winterthur Museum ⑥

ESSENTIALS

GETTING THERE   The valley's attractions in Delaware are spread out north of Wilmington, but most of them are along or near Delaware Route 100. If you're traveling by car, take I-95 into Wilmington to Delaware Route 52 north, which will take you to Route 100. The main attractions in Pennsylvania are all along U.S. Route 1. From Wilmington, follow the above directions and take Route 100 to U.S. Route 1, or take I-95 to U.S. Route 202, which will take you all the way to U.S. Route 1.

From Wilmington, **bus** service is provided by **Delaware Administration for Regional Transit/DART** (☎ 302/577-3278). See "Arriving" in chapter 10 for information about rail and air transportation.

VISITOR INFORMATION   For all types of helpful maps and brochures about the Brandywine Valley, contact the **Greater Wilmington Convention and Visitors Bureau,** 100 W. 10th St., Suite 20, Wilmington, DE 19801 (☎ **800/422-1181** or 302/652-4088), or the **Brandywine Valley Tourist Information Center,** Route 1 at the entrance to Longwood Gardens, P.O. Box 910, Kennett Square, PA 19348 (☎ **800/228-9933** or 610/388-2900).

AREA CODE   Like the rest of Delaware, the Brandywine Valley attractions located in the Wilmington suburbs have the 302 area code. Many neighboring sights, inns, and restaurants on the Pennsylvania side of the border, however, have the 610 area code.

SPECIAL EVENTS   Longwood Gardens (☎ **800/737-5500**) has changing displays for each season. The **Welcome Spring** indoor display of colorful spring bulbs is a favorite, as is the **Christmas Display,** featuring hundreds of poinsettias and an outdoor lighted display. The **Old-Fashioned Ice Cream Festival** at Rockwood Museum (☎ **302/761-4340**) is another favorite event, featuring hot-air balloons, baby parades, and, of course, ice cream. It's held the second weekend in July.

WHAT TO SEE & DO
MUSEUMS & GARDENS

✪ **Winterthur Museum and Gardens.** Rte. 52, Winterthur, DE 19735. ☎ **800/448-3883** or 302/888-4600. Admission to the galleries and garden $8 adults, $6 seniors and ages 12–18, $4 ages 5–11. Guided tours of the house and garden $13–$21 adults, $11–$19 seniors and ages 12–18, $9 ages 5–11. Mon–Sat 9am–5pm, Sun noon–5pm (last tour at 4pm). Closed Jan 1, Thanksgiving, and Dec 25. Six miles northwest of Wilmington on Rte. 52.

Named after a town in Switzerland, this nine-story mansion and country estate is the Brandywine Valley's star attraction, ranked as the world's premier collection of American antiques and decorative arts. The estate was once the country home of the late Henry Francis du Pont, a collector of furniture, who made the initial acquisitions. The objects, including Chippendale furniture, silver tankards by Paul Revere, and a dinner service made for George Washington, are displayed in more than 175 period rooms.

A visit to Winterthur can start either directly in the period rooms or in The Galleries, the new $20 million two-story pavilion designed to prepare visitors for the experience. The first of the galleries features a 10-minute audiovisual presentation and a series of interactive exhibits that provide background information about Winterthur's treasures. The second, the Henry S. McNeil Gallery, offers an exhibition of tools and workshops used in furniture making. The third, the Thomas A. Graves Jr. Gallery, houses rotating exhibitions. Adding to the splendid aura of the house, the 980-acre grounds are meticulously landscaped with native and exotic plants, and can be toured on foot or by tram.

The museum staff conducts several guided tours, including an introductory tour, 1-hour and 2-hour in-depth decorative arts tours, and a garden walk. There is also an annual Yuletide tour, offered from mid-November through January. Facilities include two restaurants (traditional afternoon tea is a special treat), an extensive museum store, and a bookshop. Be advised that children under 5 are not permitted in this museum.

✪ **Nemours Mansion and Gardens.** Rockland Rd., P.O. Box 109, Wilmington, DE 19899. ☎ **302/651-6912.** Admission $10 adults (under age 16 not permitted). May–Nov Tues–Sat, tours at 9am, 11am, 1pm, and 3pm; Sun tours at 11am, 1pm, and 3pm. Take Rte. 202 north; turn left on Rockland Rd.

This 300-acre estate was the home of Alfred I. du Pont. Built in 1909 and 1910 and named after the du Pont ancestral home in north-central France, the 102-room, Louis XVI–style château contains antique furnishings, Oriental rugs, tapestries, paintings dating from the 15th century, and a spectacular musical clock built for Marie Antoinette. The gardens, which extend almost a third of a mile from the mansion, represent one of the finest examples of formal French-style gardens in America. Guided tours of the mansion take a minimum of 2 hours. Following the mansion tour visitors can stroll through the gardens on their own or take a guided bus tour, which includes a walk through the family garage containing, among other vintage vehicles, two Rolls Royces. Reservations are recommended, especially for weekend tours. Visitors must be over 16 years of age.

André Harvey Studio. 101 Stone Block Row, Greenville, DE. Mailing address: Box 8, Rockland Rd., Rockland, DE 19732. ☎ **302/656-7955.** Free admission. Mon–Sat 10am–5pm, or by appointment.

Housed in an 1814 stone mill building just downstream from the Hagley Museum gates, this studio features realistic bronze sculptures of people and animals by André Harvey. The museum also displays jewelry made in collaboration with goldsmith Donald Pywell. A separate gallery shows the different stages of casting.

Brandywine Battlefield. Rte. 1, P.O. Box 202, Chadds Ford, PA 19317. ☎ **610/459-3342.** Free admission to battlefield; house tour $3.50 adults, $2.50 seniors, $1.50 ages 6–12. Tues–Sat 9am–5pm, Sun noon–5pm.

Set amid 50 acres of rolling countryside, this is the site of a 1777 Revolutionary War battle, where Washington's troops fought with the British for control of strategic territory near Philadelphia. Though the revolutionaries lost, their courageous stand helped convince the French to form an alliance with them, a union that turned the tide of the war. The site includes a visitor center with exhibits and dioramas as well as two historic Quaker farmhouses that housed the officers during the battle.

✪ **Brandywine River Museum.** Rte. 1, P.O. Box 141, Chadds Ford, PA 19317. ☎ **610/459-1900.** Admission $5 adults, $2.50 seniors and ages 6–12. Daily 9:30am–4:30pm. Closed Dec 25. Just south of Rte. 100 on the Brandywine River.

Housed in a Civil War–era restored gristmill on the Brandywine River, this museum is surrounded by a nature trail and wildflower gardens dotted with sculptures. The museum's four galleries display the best of Brandywine area artists, with paintings by Howard Pyle, Frank Schoonover, and three generations of Wyeths (N.C., Andrew, and his sisters Henriette and Carolyn, and his son Jamie), as well as works by other American artists and illustrators. One gallery is devoted entirely to the works of Andrew Wyeth, who still lives and paints in the Brandywine Valley and occasionally stops in to touch up, move, remove, or otherwise make adjustments to his paintings or the gallery. The well-stocked museum store offers a large selection of books, reproductions, and posters, primarily Wyeth-related, but other regional artists are also represented.

Chaddsford Winery. Rte. 1, Chadds Ford, PA 19317. ☎ **610/388-6221.** Free admission. *Note:* There is a $5 per person fee to participate in a full tasting session. Apr–Dec daily noon–6pm, Jan–Mar Tues–Sun noon–6pm. Five miles south of Rte. 202, just past the Brandywine River Museum.

Housed in a restored barn, this small winery produces some lovely oak-aged chardonnays, pinot noirs, and cabernet sauvignons, as well as table wines. Visitors are encouraged to tour on their own, free of charge. Guided tours are conducted on the hour on weekends between noon and 5pm, and at 1pm and 3pm on weekdays.

Delaware Museum of Natural History. 4840 Kennett Pike (Rte. 52), Wilmington, DE 19807. ☎ **302/652-7600** or 302/658-9111. Admission $5 adults, $4 seniors, $3 ages 3–17. Mon–Sat 9:30am–4:30pm, Sun noon–5pm. Five miles northwest of Wilmington on Rte. 52.

Located on the main route between Wilmington and Winterthur, the Museum of Natural History houses more than 100 exhibits of birds, shells, and mammals from far and near, including displays of the Great Barrier Reef, an African water hole, and various Delaware fauna. For young visitors, there's a hands-on Discovery Room, as well as a continuous showing of nature films. The museum has acquired and assembled for display the skeletal remains of two rare Chinese dinosaurs, making it one of only a few museums in the United States to have Chinese dinosaurs in its permanent collection.

✪ **Hagley Museum.** Rte. 141, Wilmington, DE 19807. ☎ **302/658-2400.** Admission $9.75 adults, $7.50 students and seniors, $3.50 ages 6–14. Mar 15–Dec daily 9:30am–4:30pm; Jan–Mar 14 Mon–Fri, 1 guided tour at 1:30pm, Sat–Sun 9:30am–4:30pm. Closed Thanksgiving, Dec 25, and Dec 31. From Wilmington, take Rte. 52 north to Rte. 100 north. Follow Rte. 100 to Rte. 141 north. The museum is on the right, $1/8$ mile from the intersection.

If you plan to visit several du Pont homes or museums, stop by this one first; it'll give you a firm grasp on the family history, and you'll get to see the progression in the size and opulence of the family homes. This serene, wooded grove along the Brandywine River is where French émigré Eleuthère Irénée du Pont de Nemours started the gunpowder mill that got the du Pont family established in the United States in 1802. Today, this 240-acre outdoor museum site re-creates the original 19th-century mill village through a series of restored buildings and gardens and displays and demonstrations of the inner workings of the mill and the making of black gunpowder. Videos, narrated bus tours, and educated guides and staff explain the history of the du Pont family in Delaware and the workings of the mill itself. The highlight of the museum is Eleutherian Mills, the first (1803) du Pont home in America, a Georgian-style residence furnished to reflect five generations of du Ponts.

✪ **Longwood Gardens.** Rte. 1, Kennett Sq., PA 19348. ☎ **610/388-1000.** Admission $12 adults ($8 on Tues), $6 ages 16–20, $2 ages 6–15, free under age 6. Apr–Oct daily 9am–6pm, Nov–Mar daily 9am–5pm, extended evening hrs. during the Christmas Display and the Summer Festival of Fountains. On Rte. 1, just south of the intersection with Rte. 52.

One of the world's most celebrated horticultural displays, Longwood showcases more than 11,000 different types of plants and flowers amid 1,050 acres of outdoor gardens and woodlands. On the grounds you'll find an indoor conservatory, illuminated fountains, an open-air theater, and a chiming tower. Unique displays include an indoor children's garden with a maze, an idea garden for home gardeners, a completely restored Italian Water Garden, a new indoor Cascade Garden by the Brazilian landscape designer Robert Burle Marx, and an indoor Mediterranean Garden. The land originally belonged to Pierre S. du Pont, who designed most of the gardens; the

What to Do in Wilmington & the Brandywine Valley with Kids

Wilmington and its beautiful suburbs, the Brandywine Valley and New Castle, are home to palatial residences, elegant hotels, and immense gardens. But for those of us who can't afford to send our kids away with a nanny, getting the most out of this trip can be difficult. Two of the area's top attractions, Winterthur and Nemours, have minimum age requirements. At Winterthur it's 5; at Nemours it's 16. Fortunately, there are several sites in the Greater Wilmington area that welcome kids (all listed fully in "What to See & Do" in this chapter, except the Delaware History Museum and Fort Delaware State Park, both listed in chapter 10).

Delaware History Museum   This museum of First State history is housed in an old F. W. Woolworth store in Wilmington. It features a great hands-on Discovery Room, where kids can handle artifacts and listen to storytellers.

Delaware Museum of Natural History   This neat museum has exhibits of birds, shells, mammals, and even skeletal dinosaurs. There's also a Discovery Room and lots of nature films. What kid wouldn't love it?

Fort Delaware State Park   It's a long way from old-world elegance, but kids will love this Civil War prison fort on an island in the Delaware Bay. Not only is there a boat ride to the island and then a tractor-pulled tram ride to the fort but also reenactors, donning deep Southern accents, lead guided tours and even give artillery and cannon demonstrations in the summer months.

Hagley Museum   The family-friendly Hagley Museum, set on a beautiful park on the Brandywine River, tells the story of the du Pont family's early gun-powder mill. Kids love the gun-powder testing demonstration—*bang*—and both kids and parents can explore the lovely grounds, the first du Pont home, and an early workers' village.

Longwood Gardens   The greatest of the du Pont gardens, this is a sprawling landscape with fountains, animal-shaped hedges, and greenhouses for you and the children to explore. Inside the greenhouses are usually at least a few wandering performers to entertain you, and there's also a children's garden that small children can explore without holding your hand. It's expensive, but you can save a little money by visiting on a Tuesday, when adult admission is discounted to $8.

Peirce–du Pont House, on the grounds, is also open to the public. Longwood's attractions include not only ever-changing seasonal plant displays (the Christmas Display is one of the most popular) but also more than 300 performing arts events each year. There is a large museum shop and a restaurant that offers good cafeteria-style fare with garden views.

Mushroom Museum at Phillips Place. 909 E. Baltimore Pike (Rte. 1), Kennett Sq., PA 19348. ☎ 610/388-6082. Admission $1.25 adults, 75¢ seniors, 50¢ ages 7–12. Daily 10am–6pm. Closed major holidays. On Rte. 1, 1/2 mile south of Longwood Gardens.

A good place to learn about mushroom farming, this museum explains the history, lore, and development of mushrooms, from the ordinary to the exotic. There is also a shop selling fresh mushrooms and specializing in exotics and gift items with mushroom motifs.

۞ Rockwood Museum. 610 Shipley Rd., Wilmington, DE. ☎ **302/761-4340.** Free admission for self-guided garden tour. Guided home and grounds tours $6 adults, $5 seniors, $2 ages 5–16. Mar–Dec Tues–Sun 11am–4pm, Jan–Feb Tues–Sat 11am–4pm (last tour at 3pm). From

I-95 north, take exit 9 (Marsh Rd.); turn right onto Carr Rd., right again onto Washington St. Ext., and then right onto Shipley Rd. Museum is on the left. From I-95 south, take exit 9; turn left on Marsh Rd., right onto Washington St. Ext., and follow directions above.

A Victorian theme prevails at this rural gothic mansion, situated on 72 tree-filled acres between Route 202 and Marsh Road northeast of downtown Wilmington. Inspired by an English country house, it was built in 1851 by Joseph Shipley, one of the city's early merchant bankers. The mansion was acquired in 1892 by the Bringhursts, a wealthy family, who furnished it with a lavish mélange of 17th-, 18th-, and 19th-century decorative arts from the United States, Britain, and Continental Europe. The elaborate conservatory features a brilliant array of Victorian flora that reflects the 6 acres of exotic foliage and landscape surrounding the manor. Among the outside buildings are a porter's lodge, gardener's cottage, and carriage house and barn. Seasonal programs include a summer concert series in May and June, a Victorian Ice Cream Festival in July, and a changing Christmas exhibit each December.

WHERE TO STAY

Most Wilmington-area hotels are convenient bases from which to tour the Brandywine Valley, so check the "Accommodations" section in chapter 10 for more places to stay. Below are some of the inns and hotels on the Pennsylvania side of the border.

Abbey Green Motor Lodge. 1036 Wilmington Pike (Rte. 202), West Chester, PA 19382. ☎ **610/692-3310.** 18 rms. A/C TV TEL. $49–$59 double. AE, DC, DISC, MC, V. Free parking.

This family-run motel, situated just north of the Brandywine Battlefield Park and close to scenic Routes 52 and 100, is an excellent budget choice in the Brandywine region. Designed in a courtyard style, it's set back from the road on its own grounds, with picnic tables, a gazebo, and an outdoor fireplace. All rooms have a refrigerator; six units have their own fireplace. The owners also operate a gift shop on the premises.

✪ **Brandywine River Hotel.** Rtes. 1 and 100, P.O. Box 1058, Chadds Ford, PA 19317. ☎ **610/388-1200.** Fax 610/388-1200, ext. 301. 40 rms, 10 suites. A/C TV TEL. $125 double; $149–$169 suite. Rates include continental breakfast and afternoon tea. AE, CB, DC, DISC, MC, V. Free parking.

This hotel, perched on a hillside in the heart of the valley, was built to meld perfectly with this scenic and historic region. Two stories high, with a facade of brick and cedar shingle, it is set beside a cluster of rustic shops, art galleries, and an artisans' cooperative. The historic Chadds Ford Inn restaurant is just a few steps away via a brick-lined path. The lobby and reception area offers a huge stone, open fireplace and a homey ambience. The guest rooms are decorated with colonial-style cherry wood furnishings, brass fixtures, chintz fabrics, and paintings in the Brandywine tradition. Some of the suites have an individual fireplace and a Jacuzzi. Breakfast is served in an attractive "hospitality room" with a fireplace and old-world furnishings.

Longwood Inn. 815 E. Baltimore Pike (Rte. 1), Kennett Sq., PA 19348. ☎ **610/444-3515.** Fax 610/444-4285. 28 rms. A/C TV TEL. $75–$85 double. Rates include continental breakfast. AE, CB, DC, DISC, MC, V. Free parking.

Situated half a mile southwest of Longwood Gardens, this inn is surrounded by beautifully landscaped flower beds and gardens. The accommodations are modern, almost motel style, with a colonial reproduction motif and garden views. At press time, the restaurant in the hotel was closed for renovations; no projected date for a reopening was available.

Mendenhall Hotel. Rte. 52, P.O. Box 208, Mendenhall, PA 19357. ☎ **610/388-2100.** Fax 610/388-1184. 70 rms, 4 suites. A/C TV TEL. $109 double; $145–$195 suite. Rates include continental breakfast. AE, DC, DISC, MC, V. Free parking.

Deep in the heart of the Brandywine Valley, this property is part of an original Penn land grant purchased by Benjamin Mendenhall in 1703. The current complex is a blend of old and new—the Mendenhalls' 1796 lumber mill, which is now part of the restaurant structure, and an adjacent three-story complex of modern bedrooms with conference center. The guest rooms have country-style furnishings, with pine headboards or four-posters, desks, armoires, and cabinets, and also more modern touches, such as hair dryers, bathroom telephones, and computer-card keys. The freestanding restaurant, traditionally known as the Mendenhall Inn, offers country French and American cuisine in five different dining rooms and a tavern setting for a more informal atmosphere. The hotel has an exercise room and lovely gardens for strolling.

WHERE TO DINE
EXPENSIVE/MODERATE

✪ **Chadds Ford Inn.** Rtes. 1 and 100, Chadds Ford, PA. ☎ **610/388-7361.** Reservations recommended for dinner. Main courses $13.95–$22.95; lunch $5.95–$12.95. AE, DC, DISC, MC, V. Mon–Thurs 11:30am–2pm and 5:30–10pm, Fri–Sat 11:30am–2pm and 5–10:30pm, Sun 11am–2pm and 4–9pm. INTERNATIONAL.

Dating from the early 1700s, this sturdy stone building was first the home of the Chadsey family and then a tavern and a hotel. Although it's been renovated, the inn still retains much of its colonial charm, with antique furnishings and century-old memorabilia. The walls display reproductions of paintings by local artists, including works by Andrew and Jamie Wyeth. Salads, sandwiches, pizzas, burgers, and pastas make up the lunch menu. Dinner entrees include a variety of fish and meat dishes, such as baked salmon with potato-and-celery crust, Pennsylvania brook trout, shrimp and lobster sauté over pasta, roast free-range chicken, pork tenderloin with spaetzle, and herb-roasted prime rib.

Cuisines Restaurant. 200 Wilmington–West Chester Pike (Rte. 202), Chadds Ford, PA. ☎ **610/459-3390.** Reservations recommended for dinner. Main courses $11.95–$23.95; lunch $4.95–$10.95. AE, MC, V. Mon–Fri 11:30am–2pm and 5:30–10pm, Sat 5:30–10pm. INTERNATIONAL.

Furnished with a relaxing blend of earth-toned fabrics, plush chairs, light wood trim, and plenty of glass and brass, Cuisines offers foods from many lands, including paella, sole buerre blanc, curry chicken, sirloin steak Creole, shepherd's pie, hot-pepper linguine and mussels with lemon-butter sauce, Black Angus steaks, and veal saltimbocca. Cuisines is located at the junction of Routes 202 and 491.

✪ **Dilworthtown Inn.** 1390 Old Wilmington Pike and Brinton Bridge Rd. (off Rte. 202), West Chester, PA. ☎ **610/399-1390.** Reservations recommended for dinner. Main courses $13.95–$26.95. AE, CB, DC, DISC, MC, V. Mon–Sat 5:30–10:30pm, Sun 3–9pm. INTERNATIONAL.

Located on the road that was once the principal connection between Wilmington and West Chester, this establishment was built as a house by James Dilworth in 1758; because of its strategic position, it soon became a tavern. Restored in 1972, the restaurant now has 12 dining rooms, including the house's original kitchen and an outside stable area for warm-weather dining. The decor consists of Early American furniture, hand-stenciled walls, 11 fireplaces, gas and candlelight lamps, and Andrew Wyeth paintings. The menu features a gourmet medley of entrees, such as filet mignon Beaujolais and smoked chicken and lobster, as well as several delectable house specialties, such as Dilworthtown seafood sauté (shrimp and scallops sautéed in roasted garlic, oregano, spinach, and sun-dried tomatoes) and grilled breast of Lancaster County chicken with an apricot and ginger glaze. The extensive wine cellar offers 900 different labels.

Lenape Inn. Rtes. 52 and 100, West Chester, PA. ☎ **610/793-2005.** Reservations recommended for dinner. Main courses $14.50–$29.95; lunch $6.95–$12.95. AE, DC, DISC, MC, V. Tues–Sat 11:30am–3pm and 4:30–10:30pm, Sun 2–9pm. AMERICAN/CONTINENTAL.

Diners love the expansive views of the Brandywine River from within this multilevel brick-facade restaurant with a modern decor, including newly renovated copper fireplaces. But views are not everything here—service is very attentive and the cuisine is artfully prepared. New chef Jon Blum has added an extensive selection of pasta dishes to the regular menu. Evening selections also include a house special of veal picante with prosciutto ham and shiitake mushrooms, salmon with golden caviar poached in court bouillon, duckling flamed in peach-brandy sauce, breast of capon with creamed leek and garlic sauce, rack of lamb, surf-and-turf, and prime western sirloin steaks.

MODERATE

✪ Buckley's Tavern. 5812 Kennett Pike, Centreville, DE. ☎ **302/656-9776.** Reservations recommended for dinner. Main courses $5.95–$19.95; lunch $3.95–$9.95. AE, CB, DC, MC, V. Mon–Wed 11:30am–2:30pm and 5:30–9:30pm, Thurs–Fri 11:30am–2:30pm and 5:30–10pm, Sat 11:30am–3pm and 5:30–10pm, Sun 11am–3pm and 5–9pm. AMERICAN.

Situated on the main road (Route 52) from Wilmington, this old house has a long history dating from 1817. It was first a private residence, then a stagecoach stop with a tollgate in front, later a taproom and bar, and finally an ice-cream store. In 1951 Dennis Buckley turned it into a restaurant. Much of the decor retains an old-world country inn charm, with a fireplace, a plant-filled greenhouse room, and an outdoor porch.

The menu is an innovative blend of fresh ingredients: crab cakes with a rémoulade sauce, black olive tapenade ravioli with artichoke hearts and roasted bell peppers, chicken with asparagus in a lemon-herb vinaigrette, and filet mignon with a five-mushroom ragoût. Lunch items range from sandwiches, salads, burgers, pastas, and pizzas to hearty soups and stews.

INEXPENSIVE

Crossroads Cafe at Winterthur. Rte. 52, Winterthur, DE. ☎ **302/888-4826.** Reservations not accepted. Main courses $4.95–$5.75. Daily 8am–4pm (hot food available 10:30am–2:30pm). AMERICAN.

This latest addition to the Winterthur facilities offers visitors more relaxed, modified cafeteria-style dining. The restaurant features a variety of food stations where diners can choose from made-to-order salads, sandwiches, fresh pasta, or even fajitas. You can enter the restaurant without visiting the museum and gardens, so no entrance fee is required.

✪ Garden Restaurant & Tea Room at Winterthur. Rte. 52, Winterthur, DE. ☎ **302/888-4600.** Reservations not required except for afternoon tea (required for parties of 6 or more). Most items $2–$7; Sun brunch $18.95 adults, $12.95 ages 5–9; afternoon tea $9.25. AE, MC, V. Mon–Sat 11:30am–1:30pm, Sun 10am–1:30pm; daily 3–4:30pm for afternoon tea. AMERICAN.

This pavilion-style restaurant with lovely garden views offers lunch and snacks. Afternoon tea is a special treat, with six types of tea, Victorian-style scones, traditional sandwiches (cucumber, smoked salmon, egg, and watercress), pastries, and fresh fruits. Sunday brunch includes omelets cooked to order, Belgian waffles, leg of lamb, seafood Creole, chicken Mornay, desserts, and chilled mimosas or champagne. You don't have to pay the museum admission fee to dine here.

2 Historic New Castle

7 miles S of Wilmington, 40 miles SW of Philadelphia, 70 miles NE of Baltimore

New Castle was Delaware's original capital and a major colonial seaport. The area was first purchased from the Indians in 1651 by Peter Stuyvesant, who established here a Dutch settlement named Fort Casimir. (It's said that Stuyvesant designed the town's central Green by "pegging it off" with his wooden leg.) Later captured by the Swedes and then the English, who renamed it New Castle, this stretch of land along the west bank of the Delaware River remains much the way it was in the 17th and 18th centuries. Original houses and public buildings have been restored and preserved, and the sidewalks are still made of brick and the streets of cobblestones.

New Castle is ideal for walking. In less than an hour, you can stroll past old homes and churches and such historic sights as Packet Alley, a well-worn pathway named after the many packet boats that used to come here in the 18th and 19th centuries. If you get tired, take a break on one of the benches by the river and watch the boats go by.

ESSENTIALS

GETTING THERE   From Wilmington, either take Route 13 south to Route 273 east to New Castle, or take Route 9 south directly to New Castle.

VISITOR INFORMATION   You can obtain brochures and information by writing or calling the **New Castle Visitors Bureau,** P.O. Box 465, New Castle, DE 19720 (☎ **800/758-1550** or 302/322-8411).

SPECIAL EVENTS   **A Day in Old New Castle,** held annually the third Saturday in May, gives visitors a chance to tour the town's private homes and gardens, as well as the public buildings, gardens, and museums. The town also hosts several Christmas events, featuring house tours, carolers, carriage rides, and reenactors. Contact the **New Castle Visitors Bureau** (☎ **302/322-8411**) or the **New Castle Historical Society** (☎ **302/322-2794**) for more information.

WHAT TO SEE & DO
ATTRACTIONS

Amstel House. 4th and Delaware sts. ☎ **302/322-2794.** Admission $2 per person (*note:* can be combined with a visit to the Dutch House for a reduced charge of $3.50 for both). Mar–Dec Tues–Sat 11am–4pm, Sun 1–4pm; Jan–Feb Sat 11am–4pm, Sun 1–4pm.

Dating from the 1730s, this house, once the home of Nicholas Van Dyke, a state governor, is a fine example of 18th-century Georgian architecture. It was likely the most elegant house in town at the time of its construction. Today it's furnished with antiques and decorative arts of the period.

Dutch House Museum. Third St., on the Green. ☎ **302/322-9168.** Admission $2 per person (*note:* can be combined with a visit to the Amstel House for a reduced rate of $3.50 for both). Mar–Dec Tues–Sat 11am–4pm, Sun 1–4pm; Jan–Feb Sat 11am–4pm, Sun 1–4pm.

One of the oldest brick houses in Delaware, this building has remained almost unchanged since its construction around 1700. The early Dutch furnishings include a hutch table and a courting bench. On display is a 16th-century Dutch Bible. During various seasonal celebrations, the dining table is set with authentic foods and decorations.

Immanuel Episcopal Church. 100 Harmony St., on the Green. ☎ **302/328-2413.** Free admission. Daily 9am–4pm.

Built in 1703, this was the first parish of the Church of England in Delaware. The church was burned in 1980, but it has been carefully restored. The adjoining graveyard has tombstones dating from 1707.

○ Old Court House. 211 Delaware St., on the Green. ☎ **302/323-4453.** Free admission, but donations welcome. Tues–Sat 10am–3:30pm, Sun 1:30–4:30pm.

This building was Delaware's colonial capital and the meeting place of the state assembly until 1777. Built in 1732, on the fire-charred remains of an earlier courthouse, it's been restored and modified over the years, though always maintaining its place as the focal point of the town. The building's cupola is at the center of a 12-mile circle that marks the northern boundary between Delaware and Pennsylvania. Inside the Court House you'll find portraits of men important to Delaware's early history, the original speaker's chair, and excavated artifacts. Tours are conducted free of charge.

Old Library Museum. 40 E. Third St. ☎ **302/328-2923.** Free admission. Mar–Dec Thurs–Sun 1–4pm; Jan–Feb Sat 11am–4pm, Sun 1–4pm.

This unique hexagonal building, erected in 1892 by the New Castle Library Society, is now used for exhibits by the New Castle Historical Society. The design of this house, a fine example of fanciful Victorian architecture, is attributed to William Eyre.

○ Read House and Garden. 42 The Strand. ☎ **302/322-8411.** Admission $4 adults, $3.50 seniors and students, $2 children. Mar–Dec Tues–Sat 10am–4pm, Sun noon–4pm; Jan–Feb Sat 10am–4pm, Sun noon–4pm.

This 22-room house, built between 1791 and 1804 near the banks of the Delaware, is a fine example of Federal architecture in a garden setting. It features elaborately carved woodwork, relief plasterwork, gilded fanlights, and silver door hardware, all reflecting the height of Federal fashion. The surrounding 2 1/2-acre formal garden dates from 1847 and is the oldest surviving garden in Delaware. The Read House is named after a prominent lawyer and son of a signer of the Declaration of Independence.

WHERE TO STAY

New Castle provides a charming and convenient base for touring the Brandywine Valley and visiting Wilmington, only 7 miles away.

Ramada Inn–New Castle. I-295 and Rte. 13, P.O. Box 647, Manor Branch, New Castle, DE 19720. ☎ **800/2-RAMADA** or 302/658-8511. Fax 302/658-3071. 130 rms. A/C TV TEL. $78–$84 double. AE, CB, DC, DISC, MC, V. Free parking.

Close to the Delaware Memorial Bridge, wedged between I-295 and Route 13, this busy two-story property sits on its own grounds, set back from the main roads but still within sight of the constant traffic. Although not in the historic district, it is convenient for those in transit and is popular with a business clientele. The building is designed in a modernized colonial motif. The rooms are decorated with watercolors of local attractions and reproduction furniture, including desks in work areas. Among the guest facilities are an outdoor swimming pool, a lounge, and a full-service restaurant.

Rodeway Inn. 111 S. Du Pont Hwy., New Castle, DE 19720. ☎ **800/321-6246** or 302/328-6246. Fax 302/328-9493. 40 rms. A/C TV TEL. $50–$65 double. Rates include continental breakfast. AE, DC, DISC, MC, V. Free parking.

Positioned along the main highway outside of the historic district, this distinctive motel is laid out like a little village of individual cottage units, with Amsterdam-style tile roofs and facades and front gardens. It's popular with seniors and families because of its homey atmosphere and because all rooms are at ground-floor level, with car parking right outside each door. The facilities include a steak-house restaurant.

Terry House. 130 Delaware St., New Castle, DE 19720. ☎ **302/322-2505.** 4 rms. A/C TV TEL. $60–$98 double. Rates include continental breakfast. AE, MC, V. Free parking on street.

Located in the heart of the historic district across from the courthouse, this three-story brick Federal town house dates from 1860. It was occupied by the Terry family for more than 60 years. The spacious guest rooms, which look out over either the Delaware River or the town square and courthouse, are furnished with antiques and reproductions. Each room has a queen-size bed. There are two porches in the back of the house that overlook Battery Park and the Delaware River.

WHERE TO DINE

The New Castle area is the site of a county airport and several commercial industries. Consequently, restaurants conveniently line Route 13, otherwise known as the Du Pont Highway.

Air Transport Command. 143 N. Du Pont Hwy. ☎ **302/328-3527.** Reservations recommended for dinner. Main courses $12.95–$24.95; lunch $4.95–$12.95. AE, CB, DC, MC, V. Mon–Thurs 11am–10pm, Fri–Sat 11am–11pm, Sun 9:30am–10pm. INTERNATIONAL.

Authentic air force memorabilia set the tone at Air Transport Command, appropriately located close to the runways of New Castle County Airport. The flying heroes and heroines of World War II are commemorated with old uniforms, newspaper clippings, pictures, and flying equipment. You can even pick up a set of headphones and listen to the ground-to-air instructions at the nearby control tower. Music from the 1940s adds to the vintage atmosphere. Dinner entrees include veal saltimbocca, rack of lamb, prime rib, shrimp and lobster stir-fry, farmhouse chicken, and roast duckling.

Lynnhaven Inn. 154 N. Du Pont Hwy. ☎ **302/328-2041.** Reservations recommended for dinner. Main courses $6.95–$26.95; lunch $4.25–$12.95. AE, DC, DISC, MC, V. Mon–Thurs 11:30am–9:30pm, Fri 10:30am–10pm, Sat 4–10pm, Sun 1–9pm. AMERICAN/SEAFOOD.

For more than 40 years, this restaurant has been winning raves from locals and travelers alike. The decor includes a changing collection of decoy and wildlife wood carvings and displays of ship models and nautical antiques. Lunchtime selections range from sandwiches and salads to burgers and hot seafood dishes. The dinner menu offers more than a dozen seafood selections, from local crab cakes, crab imperial, and crab-stuffed flounder to blackened redfish, shrimp Aegean (sautéed in butter sauce with oregano, garlic, tomato, green onions, and feta cheese), and imported warm-water lobster tails. Meat choices include steaks, prime rib, and veal dishes.

12 Dover & Central Delaware

Delaware visitors and natives alike often think of Kent County and central Delaware as the no-man's-land between metropolitan Wilmington and the beaches, but in reality this region has a lot to offer. Dover, the capital of Delaware, has a wealth of historic sites—you can visit the tavern where Delaware delegates ratified the U.S. Constitution, tour the Old State House, or visit a number of museums and galleries. For a little excitement, there's Dover Downs, where you can play the slots year-round and in season see NASCAR racing and harness racing.

Outside Dover, the countryside is quietly picturesque. As you travel through central Delaware on Route 13, the main thoroughfare, you'll be surrounded on both sides by vast, green farmland. Look for the roadside produce stands where local farmers sell their wares and the tax-free markets where the sizable Amish community sells its fresh produce, baked goods, and handmade quilts and baskets. There are no beaches along the coasts, only coastal marshes and wetlands, home to thousands of geese, ducks, egrets, and other migratory birds. A highlight for nature lovers is the Bombay Hook National Wildlife Refuge, which gives visitors access to the marshes for bird watching, hiking, and photography.

1 Dover

45 miles S of Wilmington

Plotted in 1717 according to a charter rendered by William Penn, Dover was originally designed as the courthouse seat for Kent County, a rich grain-farming area. By 1777, however, this agrarian community's importance had increased greatly, and the state's legislature, seeking a safe inland location as an alternative to the old capital of New Castle on Delaware Bay, relocated itself to Dover. Dover's major claim to fame is that on December 7, 1787, the state's delegates assembled at the Golden Fleece Tavern on the Dover Green to ratify the new Constitution of the United States, making Delaware the first state to do so.

Today, Dover continues to be a hub of state government and business. Its boundaries have expanded far beyond the original historic district to a busy north–south corridor along Routes 13 and 113. The small agrarian community of the 18th century has grown

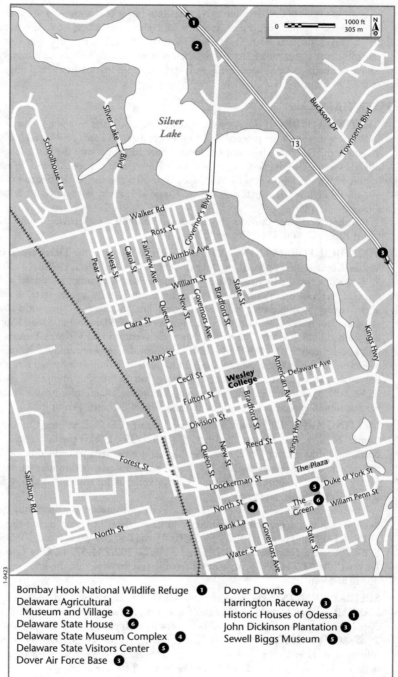

Dover

0 1000 ft
   305 m

N

Silver Lake Blvd

Schoolhouse La

Silver Lake

Silver Lake

Buckson Dr

Townsend Blvd

13

Kings Hwy

Walker Rd

Ross St

Pear St

West St

Carol St

Fairview Ave

Columbia Ave

Governor's Blvd

William St

New St

Governors Ave

Bradford St

State St

Clara St

Queen St

Mary St

Cecil St

Wesley College

American Ave

Delaware Ave

Fulton St

Bradford St

Division St

Reed St

Forest St

Salisbury Rd

Queen St

New St

Kings Hwy

The Plaza

Loockerman St

❺ Duke of York St

The Green ❻

Willam Penn St

North St ❹

Bank La

North St

Governors Ave

Water St

State St

1-0423

Bombay Hook National Wildlife Refuge ❶
Delaware Agricultural
  Museum and Village ❷
Delaware State House ❻
Delaware State Museum Complex ❹
Delaware State Visitors Center ❺
Dover Air Force Base ❸

Dover Downs ❶
Harrington Raceway ❸
Historic Houses of Odessa ❶
John Dickinson Plantation ❸
Sewell Biggs Museum ❺

to become a center of modern industry; at least 20 major companies—among them International Playtex, Scott Paper, and General Foods—are located here. Also in the area is Dover Air Force Base, the largest airport facility on the east coast. Yet visitors can still catch a glimpse of Dover's agrarian past in the area's Amish community, which maintains the traditions, dress, and mode of transportation (horse and buggy) of the 19th century.

ESSENTIALS

GETTING THERE   If you're driving from points north and northwest, take I-95 to Wilmington and then proceed south on Route 1 (a toll road) or Route 13 (also known as the Du Pont Highway) to Dover. Route 13, which runs the entire length of Delaware, is also the best way to approach Dover from the south. From Washington, D.C., and points directly west, take Route 50 across the Bay Bridge to Route 301 north. Follow 301 to 302 east, then to Route 454. From 454 take Route 8 into Dover.

Carolina Trailways provides regular bus service into Dover, arriving at 650 Bay Court Plaza (☎ **800/334-1590** or 302/734-1417).

VISITOR INFORMATION   Begin your visit to Dover at the **Delaware State Visitor Center,** 406 Federal St. at Duke of York Street, Dover, DE 19901 (☎ **302/ 739-4266**). Centrally located on the Green, this well-stocked office provides a wide range of literature on the attractions of the city, Kent County, and the state, as well as two changing exhibits on Delaware history, fashion, and arts and crafts, and a large gift shop. Its hours are Monday through Saturday from 8:30am to 4:30pm and Sunday from 1:30 to 4:30pm. The **Kent County Convention and Visitor's Bureau** at 9 E. Loockerman St. (☎ **800/233-KENT**) also provides brochures and information.

Eleven miles north of Dover on the road to or from Wilmington, you'll find the **Smyrna Visitors Center,** 5500 Du Pont Hwy., off Route 13, Smyrna (☎ **302/ 653-8910**). This is an excellent place to stop for brochures and information. It also has rest rooms, gardens, and picnic tables, and is open 24 hours a day.

GETTING AROUND   **Central Delaware Transit (CDT),** Blue Hen Corporate Center, 655 Bay Rd., Dover, DE 19901 (☎ **302/739-3278**), a public bus system operating in the greater Dover area, provides service between posted stops within downtown and major residential, shopping, and college areas, Monday through Friday from 7am to 6pm. The fare is 75¢ for adults, 50¢ for students, and 30¢ for seniors. Exact change is required.

The most convenient way to get around the city and surrounding areas is by car. Some of the major **car-rental agencies** that have offices in Dover include **Avis,** 1615 N. Du Pont Hwy. (☎ **302/734-5550**); **Hertz,** 650 Bay Court Plaza (☎ **302/ 678-0700**); and **National,** Routes 13 and 113 (☎ **302/734-5774**). **City Cab of Dover** (☎ **302/734-5968**) operates a reliable taxi service, with 24-hour radio-dispatched vehicles.

SPECIAL EVENTS   The biggest events in Dover are the two "Monster Mile" **NASCAR weekends,** held in May and September, at Dover Downs International Speedway. The names and lengths of the races vary each year; contact Dover Downs at ☎ **800/441-RACE** or 302/734-RACE for tickets, or ☎ 302/674-4600 for information. Hotels start booking up for these weekends 8 months in advance, so make reservations well ahead of time and be prepared for rate hikes.

Visitors interested in the historical sites of Dover should try to visit during **Old Dover Days,** held the first weekend in May, when several of the city's privately owned historical homes and gardens are open to the public. Guides dress in period costumes to greet visitors, and maypole dancing, craft demonstrations, refreshments, and general merriment take place on the Green. Contact the Friends of Old Dover, P.O. Box 44, Dover, DE 19903 (☎ 302/322-5744), for tickets and tour information.

EXPLORING DOVER

Most of Dover's historic sites, government buildings, and museums are located around or within walking distance of **the Green.** From Route 13, follow signs for the historic district and take State Street, which goes right through the center of the Green. I've listed below only those sites open to the public, but many of the buildings surrounding the Green are of historic significance and are designated with plaques and signs. You can pick up a map of the Green and the surrounding area at the **Delaware State Visitor Center,** located on the northeast corner of the Green, near the State House.

The remaining attractions, along with Dover's hotels and motels, are concentrated east of the historic district, along Route 13, otherwise known as Du Pont Highway. This strip, which is home to Dover Downs, the Delaware Agricultural Museum and Village, and the Dover Air Force Base, extends for several miles, so you'll need a car to get from place to place.

MUSEUMS & HISTORIC SITES

✪ **Delaware Agricultural Museum and Village.** 866 N. Du Pont Hwy., Dover, DE 19901. ☎ **302/734-1618.** Admission $3 adults, $2 seniors and ages 6–17, free under age 6. Jan–Mar Mon–Fri 10am–4pm; Apr–Dec Tues–Sat 10am–4pm, Sun 1–4pm. Across from Dover Downs on Rte. 13.

For insight into Delaware's rich agricultural heritage, this museum is well worth a visit. The large main building, which was expanded in 1997, houses permanent and temporary displays on the last 200 years in the local poultry, dairy, and produce industries. There are more than 6,000 artifacts, including a 1941 crop-duster, an 18th-century log house, and a 1912 incubator capable of holding 6,000 eggs, as well as the "Whittlin' Room," featuring the whittled folk art of Jehu Camper, and "A Touch of History," a room full of objects you (and your kids) are allowed and encouraged to touch. On the grounds behind the main building, there's a re-creation of an 1890s village, with a one-room schoolhouse, church, mill, blacksmith shop, and farmhouse. There's also a gift shop where you can buy books and general souvenirs.

✪ **Johnson Victrola Museum.** 316 S. Governors Ave. ☎ **302/739-4266.** Free admission. Tues–Sat 10am–3:30pm. One block west of the Green, off Bank Lane and behind the Meeting House Galleries.

This unusual museum, part of the Delaware State Museum Complex, which also includes the Meeting House Galleries, is a tribute to Delaware-born and Dover-raised Eldridge R. Johnson, inventor and founder of the Victor Talking Machine Company, now known as RCA. The museum houses not only a large number of Victrolas of all makes and models but also a display on Nipper, the dog that made RCA a household name in the early 20th century, including Johnson's copy of *His Master's Voice,* the oil painting that made Nipper famous. One room of the museum is designed as a 1920s Victrola dealer's store and contains an extensive collection of talking machines and early recordings, which a volunteer will gladly play for you.

Meeting House Galleries. 316 S. Governors Ave. ☎ **302/739-4266.** Free admission. Tues–Sat 10am–3:30pm. One block west of the Green, between North St. and Bank Lane.

The Meeting House Galleries, part of the Delaware State Museum Complex, which also includes the Johnson Victrola Museum, are housed in two historic buildings:

a 1790 Presbyterian Church and its 1880 Sunday school building. Meeting House Gallery I contains exhibits on Delaware archaeology, including artifacts from the Island Field Site, a Native American burial ground near Bowers Beach. Meeting House Gallery II focuses on Delaware communities and culture of the early 1900s and is set up to depict "Main Street Delaware." This exhibit includes a general store and post office, printing shop, pharmacy, and woodworking shop.

☉ Old State House. The Green. ☎ **302/739-4266.** Fax 302/739-3943. Free admission. Tues–Sat 10am–4:30pm, Sun 1:30–4:30pm.

Built in 1792, Delaware's State House is one of the oldest state houses in the United States and makes a sharp contrast to the more ornate Maryland State House in Annapolis. As part of Delaware's bicentennial celebration in 1976, the State House, a Federal-style building, was restored to its original appearance. It now contains the 18th-century courtroom and legislative chambers, a ceremonial governor's office, displays on Delaware history and the history of the building, and county offices. Although the state's legislature, the General Assembly, moved to the nearby Legislative Hall in 1934, the State House still remains Delaware's symbolic capitol.

Sewell C. Biggs Museum of American Art. 406 Federal St. ☎ **302/739-6711** or 302/674-5133. Free admission. Wed–Sat 10am–4pm, Sun 1:30–4:30pm.

Housed on the second and third floors of the Delaware State Visitor Center, this museum has a large collection of American paintings, sculptures, and decorative arts. The majority of works are by artists from the Delaware Valley region, such as Frank Schoonover, Thomas Cole, and the Janvier family. Other pieces include tall clocks by area craftsmen and antiques that once belonged to noted 18th-century Delaware families, such as the Reads, the Loockermans, and the Finneys. The museum also offers a scavenger hunt activity sheet for children, an evening lecture series for which a small fee is charged, and a series of changing exhibits.

NEARBY ATTRACTIONS

Dover Air Force Base Museum. 1301 Heritage Rd. (off Rte. 113). ☎ **302/677-5939.** Fax 302/677-5940. Free admission. Mon–Sat 9am–4pm. Take Rte. 13 south to Rte. 113, which runs along the west side of the base. Enter at the south gate to reach the museum.

This museum, which recently relocated to a restored World War II hangar listed in the National Register of Historic Places, houses a fine collection of vintage aircraft and artifacts. Exhibits reflect the evolution and history of Dover Air Force Base, which has been the hub of strategic airlift in the eastern United States. The museum's first plane, a C-47A used in the 1944 D-Day paratroop drop over Normandy, France, was rejected in 1986 by other museums as "hopeless to repair." Nonetheless, it is now on display, immaculately restored. The latest addition to the museum is an F-16 *Fighting Falcon,* acquired in May 1996. And there's a little of everything in between— one of the few remaining B-17Gs from the 1948 Flying Bomb project, an O-2 Forward Air Control plane used in Vietnam, and, when mission requirements allow, the enormous C-5 *Galaxy.* Picture taking is encouraged, even with flash equipment. The adjacent gift shop offers unique aviation-related books, posters, patches, and souvenirs.

John Dickinson Plantation. Kitts Hummock Rd. ☎ **302/739-3277.** Free admission. Jan–Feb Tues–Sat 10am–3:30pm; Mar–Dec Tues–Sat 10am–3:30pm, Sun 1:30–4:30pm. Take Rte. 113 south from Dover to Kitts Hummock Rd., just past the Dover Air Force Base.

This is the reconstructed boyhood home of John Dickinson, one of Delaware's foremost statesmen of the Revolutionary and Federal periods and a framer and signer of the U.S. Constitution. The original brick house, dating from 1740, was destroyed by fire in 1804, but the home was rebuilt in 1896. Several reconstructed outbuildings and a slave/tenement house stand along with it on the property today. Guides dressed in period clothing give visitors a glimpse of daily life of the Dickinson family, tenants, and slaves.

SPECTATOR SPORTS & OUTDOOR ACTIVITIES

HARNESS HORSE RACING In addition to stock-car racing, Dover Downs offers harness horse racing from November through March. Post time in November through January is 1pm Friday, Saturday, and Sunday, 3pm Monday and Tuesday; in February through May it's 3pm Tuesday and Thursday. **Harrington Raceway,** Route 13, Harrington (☎ **302/398-3269**), one of the oldest pari-mutuel racing tracks in the United States, schedules races September through November, Thursday through Sunday from 7 to 11pm. The track is situated on the state fair grounds, about 15 miles south of Dover. Admission is free.

STOCK CAR RACING Without a doubt, Dover's biggest sporting activity is stock-car racing. Fans from far and near flock to the "Monster Mile" at **Dover Downs International Speedway,** Route 13, P.O. Box 843, Dover, DE 19903 (☎ **800/441-RACE** or 302/734-RACE for tickets, or ☎ 302/674-4600 for information), the home of two top auto races, drawing some of the world's top stock-car drivers. Ticket prices for adults range from $20 for general admission (with limited view) to $72 for renewable tickets. Mail orders are accepted.

If you want to get even closer to the action, **Reds Kagle's Monster Racing Excitement** (☎ **800/468-6946**) will let you get behind the wheel to "tame the Monster" yourself at Dover Downs. You must call ahead to schedule a drive time. Packages range from $75 for a four-lap passenger seat ride with an instructor, to $550 for the chance to drive a race car yourself for 20 laps.

SILVER LAKE & KILLENS POND STATE PARK

Dover's beautiful **Silver Lake** is the core of a park-side recreation area in the heart of the city. Biking, swimming, and picnicking are among the favorite activities here. In addition, the park has a boat ramp, exercise circuit, volleyball court, and walking/ jogging trail. The park is open year-round from sunrise to sundown, with entrances on State Street and Kings Highway. The swimming area is open Memorial Day through Labor Day from 11am to 7pm. Complete information is available from the **City of Dover Parks and Recreation Division,** P.O. Box 475, Dover, DE 19903 (☎ **302/736-7050**).

Some 13 miles south of Dover, about a half mile east of Route 13, is Kent County's only state park, **Killens Pond State Park,** County Road 426, R.D. 1, Box 858, Felton (☎ **302/284-4526**). Covering approximately 1,040 acres, with a 66-acre mill pond at its core, Killens Pond is a natural inland haven and Kent County's summer playground. Its facilities include picnic areas, shuffleboard courts and horseshoe pits, biking and hiking trails, volleyball courts, boat rentals, pond fishing, camping, and the Killens Pond Water Park, which features a guarded main pool, two water slides, a wading pool, and the "Tot Lot," a kiddie water park. Admission to the state park is $2.50 for Delaware-registered cars and $5 for out-of-state vehicles. Entrance to the water park is an additional $1.50 for adults and $1 for children under age 16.

Camping facilities at Killens Pond are quite modern, though at times a bit too close for comfort. In addition to campsites, the park offers six cabins and one water-view cottage. Campsites are on a first-come first-served basis and fill up quite quickly on summer weekends with mostly families in campers and trailers. Sites cost $11 to $17.

Seventeen primitive sites are available for tents only, though quite a few are in an open field rather than in the nearby wooded glen. The park and campground are open year-round; the water park is open Memorial Day through Labor Day.

WHERE TO STAY

Dover doesn't boast grand or historic hotels. It has a few modern motels and motor inns, open year-round, with ample parking facilities. The major properties are on Route 13 (Du Pont Highway).

The rates for accommodations, in general, are moderate. Prices can be hiked on some weekends, however, and surcharges often run as high as $30 a night during the May and September races at Dover Downs. For some inexplicable reason (perhaps runover from the beaches), Dover's hotels tend to book up on summer weekends, so it's best to check in advance.

Best Western Galaxy Inn. 1700 E. Lebanon Rd., Dover, DE 19901. ☎ **800/528-1234** or 302/735-4700. Fax 302/735-1604. 64 rms. A/C TV TEL. $60–$75 double. AE, DC, DISC, MC, V.

Though situated across from Dover Air Force Base's north gate, at the junction of busy Route 113 and Route 10, this two-story motel is set back from the road on a small hillside. Rooms are decorated in contemporary style with standard furnishings. The facilities include a lounge and an outdoor (seasonal) swimming pool. A choice of fast-food restaurants is nearby. It's a popular motel for businesspeople and tourists interested in easy access to the air force base.

Comfort Inn of Dover. 222 S. Du Pont Hwy. (Rte. 13), Dover, DE 19901. ☎ **800/228-5150** or 302/674-3300. Fax 302/674-3300. 94 rms. A/C TV TEL. $55–$70 double. Rates include continental breakfast. AE, DC, DISC, MC, V.

Businesspeople and families are attracted to this motel, just off the Route 13 corridor at Loockerman Street. The closest motel to the city's historic district, the brick-fronted Comfort Inn is laid out in two adjoining bilevel wings. The decor and furnishings are typical of the Comfort chain. The facilities include an outdoor swimming pool and an exercise room. A branch of the TGIF restaurant chain is adjacent.

✪ **Sheraton Dover Hotel.** 1570 N. Du Pont Hwy. (Rte. 13), Dover, DE 19901. ☎ **302/678-8500.** Fax 302/678-9073. 156 rms. A/C TV TEL. $75–$96 double. AE, CB, DC, DISC, MC, V.

A favorite lodging spot for traveling business executives and conference attendees, this seven-story motor hotel is the most complete facility along the main north–south corridor. Guest rooms, revamped in 1994 and 1995, are furnished in a traditional motif with mahogany reproduction furniture, historically themed art, and such extras as a coffeemaker and an iron with ironing board. The hotel offers varied dining and entertainment choices: Tango's Bistro, a full-service, upscale restaurant with a casual atmosphere; the Starlight Lounge, a rooftop lounge with a view of Dover and live bands Tuesday through Saturday; and the Hub Rock Cafe, featuring karaoke on weekdays and a deejay on weekends. Facilities include an indoor swimming pool, a hot tub, and an exercise room.

WHERE TO DINE
MODERATE

✪ **Blue Coat Inn.** 800 N. State St. ☎ **302/674-1776.** Reservations recommended on weekends. Main courses $8.95–$24.95; lunch $4.95–$8.95. AE, CB, DC, DISC, MC, V. Tues–Thurs 11:30am–4pm and 4:30–9pm, Fri–Sat 11:30am–3pm and 4:30–10pm, Sun noon–9pm. AMERICAN/REGIONAL.

Nestled on Silver Lake just north of downtown in a garden setting, this colonial-style restaurant, originally a private home, offers lovely waterside views. It takes its name from the uniform worn by the Delaware Regiment that marched from Dover Green in July 1776 to join General Washington's army. Four original stone fireplaces, weathered timbers, and antiques from the area enhance the interior. At lunchtime there's an extensive menu of hot and cold entrees, including crab imperial, crab cakes, stuffed flounder, and filet mignon. Dinner entrees range from seafood combination platters to Southern crab couplet (Maryland blue crab with Virginia Smithfield ham), shrimp Rockefeller, and prime rib. For after-meal browsing, there's a Gift Shoppe and Countrie Store, both housed in what used to be a stable for thoroughbred horses.

Paradiso Ristorante. 1151 E. Lebanon Rd., Rte. 10 Plaza. ☎ **302/697-3055.** Reservations recommended. Main courses $13.95–$22.95; lunch $6.95–$9.95. AE, DC, DISC, MC, V. Mon–Fri 11am–2pm and 5–10pm, Sat 5–10pm. NORTHERN ITALIAN.

Tucked in a shopping center just west of the Dover Air Force Base, the Paradiso could easily be overlooked by visitors, but it's a favorite of locals. The interior features murals, paintings, and statuary reminiscent of a Roman palazzo. Featured dishes include filetto Veneziano, filet mignon with wild mushrooms in Chianti wine; osso bucco alla Milanese, veal shank with Arborio rice; aragosta alla Genovese, egg-dipped lobster in lemon sauce; and saltimbocca alla Romano, medaillons of veal with prosciutto and cheese. There are also more than a dozen pastas made fresh daily, including a signature dish of tortellini Marco Polo con tonno, little hats with fresh tuna, capers, and olives in red sauce. Be ready to spend a few hours here.

Village Inn. Rte. 9, Little Creek. ☎ **302/734-3245.** Reservations recommended for dinner. Main courses $12.95–$23.95; lunch $4.95–$7.95. DISC, MC, V. Tues–Fri 11am–2pm and 4:30–10pm, Sat 11am–10pm, Sun noon–9pm. SEAFOOD.

It's worth the slight detour, about 4 miles east of Dover past several cornfields, to try this restaurant, situated in the town of Little Creek, on the Mahon and Little rivers off Delaware Bay. Founded more than 20 years ago and still run by a local family, this restaurant has built its reputation on its ever-fresh seafood. The specialty is fresh flounder, served in a variety of ways: stuffed with crab, breaded, poached, or however else you might want it. Other seafood entrees are oyster pot pie, crab cakes, crab imperial, stuffed butterflied gulf shrimp, and a steamed seafood pot containing king crab legs, clams, scallops, and shrimp. Steaks, chicken, veal, duck, and prime rib are also available. Lunch consists mainly of sandwiches, salads, chowders, and seafood platters. The interior is a cheery blend of nautical and floral decor, with local handcrafts and grapevine wreaths.

✪ W.T. Smithers. 140 S. State St. ☎ **302/674-8875.** Reservations recommended for dinner. Main courses $10.95–$23.95; lunch $4.95–$6.95. CB, MC, V. Mon–Sat 11am–1am. INTERNATIONAL.

Housed in a Victorian-style building in the heart of Dover's historic district, W.T. Smithers is named in honor of a local hero who was, at various times, a baseball player, a lawyer, a member of the state's 1897 constitutional convention, and one of Teddy Roosevelt's Rough Riders. The interior offers a homey turn-of-the-century atmosphere, with a choice of eight different dining rooms, including a library, parlor, tavern, trophy room, outdoor deck, and "anniversary" room, ideal for special dinners for two to four persons. The menu at lunch features double-decker sandwiches, burgers, pasta, and vegetarian platters. Dinner entrees include steaks, surf-and-turf, crab imperial, shrimp scampi, blackened chicken, and pastas.

INEXPENSIVE

Blue Coat Inn Pancake House. 950 N. State St. ☎ **302/674-8310.** Breakfast $2.45–$6.95; lunch $2.95–$6.95; dinner $5.95–$9.95. MC, V. Mon–Sat 6am–8pm, Sun 6am–3pm. AMERICAN.

Set overlooking Silver Lake on the edge of town, the Blue Coat Inn Pancake House, a sister operation of the more formal Blue Coat Inn next door, is a good choice for an inexpensive hearty meal in a simple cottage setting. Not surprisingly, the specialty is pancakes—served in traditional style or with fruit and nut toppings—as well as waffles and omelets. The restaurant also serves soup and sandwiches, as well as dinner entrees such as fried chicken, steaks, ribs, and traditional crab cakes. Take-out is available.

McDowell–Collins Storehouse. 408 S. State St. ☎ **302/734-5154.** All items $1.50–$4. No credit cards. Mon–Fri 7am–3:30pm. AMERICAN.

If you're looking for a quick snack or a light lunch in an Old Dover atmosphere, step into this 2¹/₂-story, early 19th-century frame house opposite the County Courthouse. Restored in 1975 as a museum by the Dover Heritage Trail, it has had a varied history including a stint as a general store from 1883 to 1907, operated by Robert Collins. The menu isn't fancy, just old-fashioned—BLT or tuna sandwiches, hot dogs, burgers, hearty soups, salads, and daily specials.

2 Bombay Hook National Wildlife Refuge

Because of its abundance of wildlife refuges, the Delmarva Peninsula has become a haven not only for migrating birds but for bird watchers as well. Bombay Hook, established in 1937 as part of a chain of waterfowl refuges extending from Canada to the Gulf of Mexico, is the largest of Delaware's refuges (though not the largest on the peninsula), with nearly 16,000 acres of wetlands. Though the primary (and loudest) inhabitants/visitors of the refuge are migratory ducks and geese, Bombay Hook also hosts several species of herons, egrets, sandpipers, willets, and the occasional bald eagle, as well as the more permanent mammal, amphibian, and reptile population.

If you've visited Maryland's Blackwater National Wildlife Refuge, the largest and most popular in terms of tourism of the Delmarva refuges, Bombay Hook will be quite a contrast. The facilities here are considerably more primitive—the roads are not paved, the trails are well marked but not well worn, and there are fewer trails, ranger programs, and visitor services. But all this means there are also fewer human visitors, so, especially in the off-season, you may have the place all to yourself.

JUST THE FACTS

GETTING THERE Take Route 13 north of Dover to Route 42 (Fast Landing Road); travel east on Route 42 to Route 9 and then north on Route 9 for 2 miles to Whitehall Neck Road. (Route 82), which leads to the refuge entrance.

VISITOR INFORMATION The visitor center/ranger station is located at the entrance, off Whitehall Neck Road. Here you will find displays on the wildlife, maps and information on the trails, and rest rooms. Open weekdays 8am to 4pm and on fall and spring weekends from 9am to 5pm. Be aware that the visitor center is closed on weekends in summer and winter, though a map of the refuge is posted outside.

FEES & REGULATIONS The park is open year-round during daylight hours. Entrance fees are $4 per car or $2 per person walking or cycling. There is no charge for children under 16. Hunting is permitted under special regulations on designated portions of the refuge during the regular Delaware hunting season.

SEEING THE HIGHLIGHTS

Like most wildlife refuges, much of Bombay Hook is not accessible to the public. However, the 12-mile round-trip auto tour route, several nature trails, and three observation towers offer ample opportunity for observing the waterfowl and other wildlife.

The driving tour route, which can also be used by cyclists, begins and ends at the visitor center and takes you by the three major wetland pools in the refuge: Raymond Pool, Shearness Pool, and Bear Swamp Pool. The roads are well marked and offer plenty of spots to pull off and park. Cyclists especially should note that the roads throughout the refuge are not paved—they're dirt and gravel—though they are flat. Interpretive audiocassettes for use with the auto tour may be rented at the visitor center.

BIRD WATCHING   As one might imagine, the best time to see migratory birds is fall and spring, specifically, October through November and mid-February through March. Canada and snow geese begin to arrive in early October, and duck populations—pintail, mallard, American widgeon, blue-winged and green-winged teal, and others—increase until they peak in November. Shorebird migration begins in April, and their populations in the refuge peak in May and June.

The refuge is also home to bald eagles. Though not easily spotted, they are present in the refuge throughout the year. Eggs begin hatching in April, and in June the baby eagles begin to leave their nests. Shearness Pool serves as their roosting and nesting area. Parson Point Trail will take you to the back of the pool for a closer look. However, during mating and nesting season, and at the refuge manager's discretion, this trail may be closed to protect the eagles.

Of course, birds can be seen all along the auto tour, but for the best vantage point hike out to one of the three 30-foot observation towers, one overlooking each of the pools. The trail to Bear Swamp Observation Tower is wheelchair accessible, and though the tower itself is not accessible, an observation platform at ground level below the tower provides a good view of the feeding wood ducks, snow geese, egrets, and the occasional muskrat. In addition to the observation towers, a photography blind is available by advance request.

HIKING   Hiking in the refuge is primarily a means of observing and photographing wildlife, so the three nature trails aren't terribly strenuous or long. All the trails are flat, and the longest is only about a mile round-trip. The Bear Swamp Trail, which leads to the Bear Swamp observation tower, is paved and partially wheelchair accessible. The other two trails are fairly primitive. Mosquitoes, ticks, and biting flies are a problem July through September, so bring insect repellent and wear long sleeves and pants. Parson Point Trail, the longest of the three trails, may be the best place in the refuge to spy bald eagles because it ends at the back side of Shearness Pool, a roosting and nesting area for the eagles. However, it is closed to the public during nesting season (November through June). The Boardwalk Trail offers visitors a look at four different refuge habitats—woodland, freshwater pond, brackish pond, and saltmarsh—and the widest variety of wildlife.

3 Odessa

23 miles N of Dover; 22 miles S of Wilmington

Soon after the town of Cantwell's Bridge was founded in 1731, it became a bustling and important center of trade, a vital link between Philadelphia and the farmers of central Delaware. The streets were lined with shops and hotels, and the town even had its own tannery and furniture maker. Today, the streets of Odessa, as the town was renamed in 1855, are quiet. There are few businesses, and certainly no trading is done at the little boat landing off Main Street on the Appoquinimink Creek (or "the crick" as the natives call it). But you can still see something of Odessa's heyday in the brick-lined walkways and more than 30 historic and elegant homes and buildings that make up the town's historic district.

There are officially 32 historic homes and buildings, spanning 3 centuries and at least four architectural styles, in the village of Odessa. The houses range from the modest Collins–Sharp House, a colonial-style cabin dating from the early 1700s, to immense and stately Federal and Georgian homes and elaborate Victorians. All the homes and buildings stand within the town's small historic district, which begins at Front Street along the banks of the Appoquinimink and extends 4 blocks to Fourth Street—an ideal walking tour. Most of the homes are private residences and are only open to the public for special events, but four of the buildings are open for guided tours from March through December. These four are collectively known as the Historic Houses of Odessa and are owned and operated by Winterthur Museum. (So when you see a brochure for the Historic Houses of Odessa, it is actually referring only to the homes run by Winterthur.)

ESSENTIALS

GETTING THERE   Take Route 13 north from Dover or south from Wilmington or New Castle to Odessa and follow signs to the historic district.

VISITOR INFORMATION   Unfortunately, there is no official visitor center in Odessa. Maps and limited brochures are posted outside the Brick Hotel on Main Street, and the office inside for Historic Houses of Odessa (where you buy tickets for the house tours) can also answer questions and provide some brochures. For information before your visit, contact Historic Houses of Odessa, P.O. Box 507, Odessa, DE 19730 (☎ 302/378-4069).

SPECIAL EVENTS   The Women's Club of Odessa sponsors **Yuletide in Odessa,** held annually the first Saturday in December. Several of the private residences are open to the public for this event. The Winterthur houses also celebrate the season, in a somewhat unusual way. To honor the Quaker history of the houses and the region, staff here deck these houses out not in the traditional fashion but rather to portray a selected Victorian children's classic (this year it was *Oliver Twist*).

TOURING THE HISTORIC DISTRICT

If you'd like to see the entire historic district (from the outside), you really have just one option: Pick up a copy of "Stroll Through Odessa," a brochure produced by the Odessa Arts Council, and walk, bike, or drive the self-guided tour. Since the tour only covers 3 or 4 blocks, we recommend parking your car along Main Street or Front Street and walking or biking. The brochure maps out the district, labels all 32 structures, and gives a very brief description of each one. Stop by the covered bulletin board outside the Brick Hotel at the corner of Main and Second streets to pick up the brochure.

To tour the inside of some of these great old homes, you also have only one option. Winterthur's four **Historic Houses of Odessa** (☎ 302/378-4069) are open to the public from March through December, Tuesday through Saturday from 10am to 4pm and Sunday from 1 to 4pm. The **Brick Hotel** at the corner of Main and Second streets is the first of these houses and also hosts the museum offices and reception area, as well as the country's largest collection of Belter-style Victorian furniture. Stop in here to buy tickets and begin the tours. You can tour all the properties, or just one or two, and the price varies accordingly. For three houses, the price for adults is $8, and for students and seniors it's $7. Admission for children ages 5 to 11 is $3, and children 4 and under are free. For more information, contact Historic Houses of Odessa, P.O. Box 502, Odessa, DE 19730.

The **Collins–Sharp House,** a log-and-frame cabin, is the oldest of the four buildings, dating from the 1700s. The museum uses this building for its educational programs, hosting living history demonstrations on hearth cooking, gardening, and other aspects of early colonial life. It is open to the public only when the museum is sponsoring some special program or demonstration, so call ahead for the schedule.

The **Wilson–Warner House,** built in 1769 by David Wilson, a prosperous merchant, is a fine example of Delaware–Georgian architecture. When the Wilson family went bankrupt in 1829, a complete inventory of the family's possessions was made and all the contents of the house were sold at auction. Luckily the inventory survived, and Winterthur was able to furnish the house much as it would have been in the early 1800s.

The **Corbit–Sharp House,** built 5 years after the Wilson–Warner House, is an early example of one neighbor trying to outdo another—surpassing the Joneses, so to speak. William Corbit built his considerably larger Georgian home next door to the Wilsons. It features an impressive frontispiece, a widow's walk, and a view of the Appoquinimink that can't be beat.

13 The Delaware Beaches

Strewn along 25 miles of ocean and bay shoreline, Delaware's five beach towns—Lewes, Rehoboth Beach, Dewey Beach, Bethany Beach, and Fenwick Island—are each distinct communities, with their own personalities, ambiences, and repeat visitors. Whether you prefer the rich history and quaint boutiques and antique shops in Lewes to the fine restaurants and huge outlet complex in Rehoboth to the clean, well-kept, and relatively uncommercialized beaches of Bethany, you're likely to find just the right beach scene for you and your family. And if you don't, the next resort, with its own unique character, is just a short drive up or down the coast.

1 The Great Outdoors in Southern Delaware

For such a small state, Delaware has great expanses of open land, long stretches of beach, and lots of accessible waterways. All this allows a wide variety of outdoor activities. If you can't find exactly what you're looking for in Southern Delaware, across the border Ocean City and Assateague (see chapter 8) offer similar activities, with a few variations.

In at least one aspect, Southern Delaware bests Ocean City: **bicycling.** In Ocean City, biking is useful for avoiding traffic and parking, but it's really a good means of transportation rather than an enjoyable, relaxing activity. Delaware's level terrain, smaller towns, and many back roads make biking a fun and relatively safe day's excursion. The wide and quiet back roads of inland Southern Delaware are especially biker-friendly. The Delaware Department of Transportation distributes free maps designating safe, scenic roads (it also tells you which roads to avoid). For family excursions, Cape Henlopen State Park has lots of well-marked, paved bicycle trails usually away from park traffic.

Several parks and refuges along the Delaware coast provide ample opportunities for **wildlife and bird watching.** The town of Lewes, with Prime Hook National Wildlife Refuge to its north and Cape Henlopen just next door, is the best base of operation for birders. The entire point of Cape Henlopen is prime breeding ground for the endangered piping plover. (Of course, access to the cape is restricted certain times of the year to protect the nesting grounds.) Whales and dolphins appear regularly off the coast of Cape Henlopen, though usually a little farther south, closer to the Great Dune. The Prime

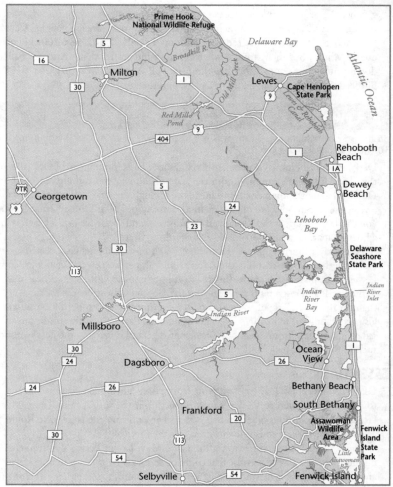

Hook refuge has a greater variety of wildlife and shorebirds and a 7-mile canoe trail to get you to those lesser-visited parts of the refuge—though you'll have to provide your own canoe.

Another great way to view wildlife is on a **sea kayak** on the water surrounding Burton's Island in Rehoboth Bay. If you're an experienced kayaker, you can rent a boat and paddle around on your own. Or, if you need a little more guidance, contact Delmarva Dennis in Rehoboth. He offers a variety of sea-kayaking adventures in Rehoboth Bay and the waters surrounding Assateague Island, and even whale- and dolphin-watching trips on the ocean.

Fishing is one of the most popular outdoor activities on the Atlantic coast. Everyone has a favorite spot where the fish are always biting. Lately, the conventional wisdom among anglers has favored the waters off Cape Henlopen. But ask around when you arrive; the good spots tend to change from year to year. As for facilities, Cape Henlopen has an enormous fishing pier right next to a bait-and-tackle shop. For charter fishing in Delaware, Lewes is the base for nearly all operations, though there's a much larger fleet in Ocean City to the south.

Since the people of inland Sussex County couldn't really compete with the shore's fishing, they've come up with their own little adventures, showing people Delaware from above. The **First State Hot Air Balloon Team** (☎ **302/684-2002**) operates out of Milton, but their trips go wherever the wind carries them. And if a balloon doesn't move fast enough for you, the **Free Fall Academy** (☎ **301/261-0188** or 302/875-3804) will take you up in a plane and then toss you out.

2 Lewes

86 miles SE of Wilmington, 34 miles N of Ocean City, 121 miles E of Washington, D.C., 107 miles SE of Baltimore

Delaware's northernmost and oldest beach resort, Lewes (pronounced LOO-is) is also the oldest European community in the state. The town was founded in 1681 as a Dutch whaling station named Zwaanendael. Though this first settlement lasted only a year, the community even today maintains strong ties to its Dutch heritage, which you can learn about at the Zwaanendael Museum, and to the sea—as a beach resort, a boating marina, and a port for dozens of fishing fleets.

For today's tourists, Lewes is a unique beach resort experience. Located on the Delaware Bay where it meets the Atlantic and along the Lewes–Rehoboth Canal, Lewes's shopping and historic district are as important to visitors as its beach. Most of the hotels and restaurants are located in the shopping district across the canal rather than on the beach side of town—in fact, for swimming and other beach activities, visitors often head to nearby Cape Henlopen State Park. Nightlife within this more sedate atmosphere is minimal, but fortunately it gets a lot better at the nearby resorts, such as Rehoboth, just 7 miles south.

ESSENTIALS

GETTING THERE   If you're driving from points north, take Routes 113 and 13 to Route 1 and then to Route 9 into town. From the south, take Route 113 to Georgetown, and then take Route 9 east to Lewes. From the west, take Route 50 across the Bay Bridge to Route 404 east, and then to Route 9.

Many visitors come to Lewes via the **Cape May–Lewes Ferry,** a convenient 70-minute Delaware Bay minicruise that connects southern New Jersey to mid-Delaware and saves considerable driving mileage for north- or southbound passengers along the Atlantic coast. In operation since 1964, this ferry service maintains a fleet of five vessels, each holding up to 800 passengers and 100 cars. Departures are operated daily year-round, from early morning until evening, with almost hourly service in the summer months from 6:20am to midnight.

Passenger rates are $4.50 for adults and $2.25 for ages 6 to 12 per trip; vehicle fares, calculated by car length, range from $18 for most cars to $64 for large trucks, with reduced prices for motorcycle and bicycle passengers and off-peak reduced rates from December to March. Reservations are recommended. The Lewes Terminal (☎ **302/644-6030**) is next to the Cape Henlopen State Park entrance, about a mile from the center of town. The New Jersey terminal is in Cape May, at the end of the Garden State Parkway. Call ☎ **800/64-FERRY** for reservations or ☎ 302/426-1155 for rates and information.

Carolina Trailways provides regular bus service into the Rehoboth Bus Center, 251 Rehoboth Ave., Rehoboth Beach (☎ **302/227-7223**), about 5 miles south of Lewes.

Visitors arriving by **plane** should fly into the **Salisbury/Ocean City Regional Airport.** See "Getting There" in chapter 8.

and even some real bargains. Don't expect great merchandising. Several (though not all) of these shops are cluttered, dusty warehouse-size buildings, and you may have to do considerable searching. Then again, that's what bargain-hunting is all about. In general, the farther away from the shore you go, the greater the dust and clutter—and the better your chances of finding a bargain.

We've arranged the tour in a circle, so you can begin and end in Lewes. If you have limited time, consider just covering the Route 9 portion of the trip; that's where the majority of the shops are located. For an even more comprehensive list of shops, pick up a copy of "Adventures in Antiquing," if you can find it. Ask your hotel or innkeeper. Unfortunately, there aren't any great places to stop for lunch along the way, so you may want to stop by **A Taste of Heaven** (see "Where to Dine," below) on the way out of town for carry-out.

Start: Downtown Lewes
Finish: Downtown Lewes
Time: Depends on your shopping style and prowess, but for thorough coverage of all the shops, you'll probably need a full morning or afternoon.

When you leave Lewes, head north on Route 1, and in 2 or 3 miles you'll come to a giant among the area antique malls.

1. Antique Village at Red Mill (☎ **302/645-1940** or 302/644-0842), on your right. This three-building complex houses the wares of 110 dealers. The front building has a Federal Room, a Victorian Room, an Art Deco Room, and a Country Room, with pieces from the respective periods. The remaining buildings hold a variety of smaller items—china, cut-glass items, kitchenware, and a large collection of Barbies.

Just north of the Antique Village, on the opposite side, is its smaller neighbor.

2. Heritage Antique Market (☎ **302/645-2309**) houses just 50 dealers. But this makes it much easier to shop here. Each booth has a distinct flavor and most concentrate on a single period or item. There are two booths full of books and lots of fine 18th-century and Victorian furnishings. Another portion of the store is devoted to modern collectibles, such as Department 56 items.

When you leave Heritage, head north on Route 1 and take the next left. This winding country road will take you into Milton. Turn right onto Union Street (Route 5), which will take you into the center of town.

3. Jail House Antiques at 106 Union St. (☎ **302/684-8660**) falls into the cluttered category but still offers some fine smaller items, such as dishes and glassware, tea sets, and kitchenware.

Continue your drive through Milton and at the intersection of Route 16 you'll see

4. A Walk Thru Time (☎ **302/684-3306**). This is a store with the sort of high-quality pieces and merchandising you'd expect to find in downtown Lewes. Items on display include fine period furnishings, jewelry, decorative items, lamps, and glassware. There's even a "Gentlemen's Room" with sports memorabilia and trains.

Turn left onto Route 16, and then left again, less than a mile down the road, at Route 30. Route 30 will take you back to Route 9. Turn right onto Route 9 and in less than a mile you'll come to

5. Signs of the Past (☎ **302/856-9189**), on the right. The outside of this ramshackle building is covered in old tin signs and advertisements for everything from Penzoil to RC Cola. This place is the king of clutter and dust, but if you're looking for signs, old cola bottles, spice jars, lithographs, or even furniture and musical instruments (which will undoubtedly need repair), this is the place to shop.

Lewes Antique Driving Tour

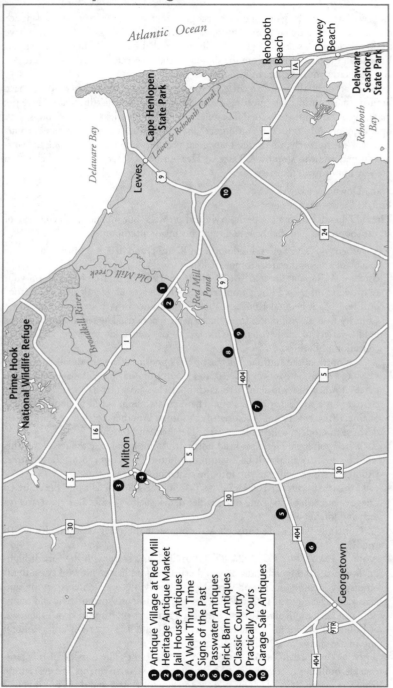

1. Antique Village at Red Mill
2. Heritage Antique Market
3. Jail House Antiques
4. A Walk Thru Time
5. Signs of the Past
6. Passwater Antiques
7. Brick Barn Antiques
8. Classic Country
9. Practically Yours
10. Garage Sale Antiques

Continue west on Route 9, just a bit farther, and you'll see
6. ✪ **Passwater Antiques** (☎ **302/856-6667**). Look for the big white missile mounted on the front of the building. The highlight of this large multidealer complex is its collection of lunch boxes and thermoses. And it's not just the same old Peanuts and Superfriends boxes you see everywhere; when we were there, they had the Hardy Boys, the Bionic Woman, and our favorite, H.R. Puffinstuff. But that's only one booth. You'll also find old video equipment, toys, dishes, crocks, crates, magazines, and more.

Turn right onto Route 9, heading east, and 4 or 5 miles down the road you'll come to the aptly named
7. **Brick Barn Antiques** (☎ **302/684-4442**). This two-story barn is filled with fine Empire, Victorian, and Edwardian furniture, with a few pieces of china and glassware thrown in. You'll find several large china cabinets, as well as dining tables and chairs, chandeliers, and quite a few complete bedroom sets upstairs.

Continue east on Route 9 and in about a mile you'll run into
8. **Classic Country** (☎ **302/684-3285**). It looks small from the outside, but inside there are two floors displaying the wares of about 30 dealers. The focus here is on country primitive items, including furniture, kitchenware, shipping crates, and quilts.

Just up the road, on the right, is
9. ✪ **Practically Yours** (☎ **302/684-8936**), where you'll be greeted by Kelly, an English sheepdog, and Reuben, a basset hound, both sporting baseball caps. This is a well-merchandised multidealer establishment, neither cluttered nor dusty. In addition to the usual furnishings and dishes, you might find some unusual items, such as a wicker casket and several sets of golf clubs.

That's the last official stop on the tour; Route 9 will take you back into Lewes. On the way, if you haven't stopped in earlier, you may want to visit **Garage Sale Antiques** (see "Shopping," below), on Route 1 just south of the Route 9 intersection.

SHOPPING

Lewes is the best shopping destination on the shore for unusual arts and crafts, collectibles, and antiques. We've categorized the shops based on the bulk of their merchandise, but many of them carry a little of everything. All the places listed below are in Lewes or very close by, but if you're interested in antiques, check out the driving tour above; it covers the inland antique shops and malls, and the prices are generally lower outside of town.

ANTIQUES

Auntie M's Emporium. 203-B Second St. and 116 Third St. ☎ **302/644-2242** or 302/644-1804.

The Second Street store, which fronts on Market Street behind King's Ice Cream, has a large collection of used books, antique kitchenware, and seasonal gifts. The Third Street location has more kitchenware, rare books, including children's books, larger furniture, and garden sculptures. Open daily 11am to 5pm, with reduced hours in winter.

Copper Penny Antiques. 109 Market St. ☎ **302/645-2983.**

This small, somewhat cluttered shop carries a wide selection of beautifully polished copper and brass pieces, and they're all antiques—no reproductions here. In addition, the shop carries small pieces of furniture, kitchenware, and some handmade wooden bowls and decor. Open Thursday through Monday 10am to 5pm.

Garage Sale Antiques. Rte. 1 (just south of Rte. 9 into Lewes). ☎ **302/645-1205.**

This is the place that furnished the Blue Water House Inn (see "Where to Stay," below). It specializes in unusual furniture, lamps, garden sculptures, and collectibles. Look for the bright yellow house on the southbound side of Route 1. Open daily year-round 11am to 6pm.

✪ **Swan's Nest.** 107 Kings Hwy. ☎ **302/645-8403.**

I've listed it under antiques, but this place is really a hodgepodge, with several rooms of antiques (with an emphasis on fine 18th- and 19th-century cabinet work), one room devoted to Christmas ornaments and decorations, a room of art supplies, and a front lawn full of cast-aluminum garden sculptures and ironwork. And that doesn't cover all the rooms. Open Monday through Saturday 10am to 5pm and Sunday 1 to 4:30pm.

Thistles. 203 Second St. ☎ **302/644-2323.**

One of the pricier places in town, this shop carries fine, unusual furniture, including Tiffany-style lamps, pottery, glassware, and silver pieces. The shop does carry some reproductions and some modern giftware. Open daily year-round from 10am to 5pm, with extended hours in the summer on Thursday through Saturday until 8pm.

ART & HANDCRAFTS

✪ **Peninsula Collection.** 520 Savannah Rd. ☎ **302/645-0551.**

Located across the canal below the Beacon Hotel, this art gallery and framing shop displays mainly works by regional artists, supplemented by national and international artists. Though the shop carries a lot of watercolor, there are also some oils, photography, and even sculpture. Open Tuesday through Saturday from 10am to 5pm and Sunday from 11am to 3pm.

Preservation Forge. 114 W. Third St. ☎ **302/645-7987.**

This fully operational blacksmith shop sells the handcrafted ironwork of John Austin Ellsworth—weathervanes, pokers, gates, hinges, hooks, door latches, and more. It's a great place to stop by just to see the blacksmith at work. Open Monday, Tuesday, and Thursday through Saturday 8am to 4pm.

✪ **Stepping Stone.** 107 W. Market St. ☎ **302/645-1254.**

Traditional and contemporary American handcrafts are the focal point of this shop, including the work of many local artisans. The wares range from wooden ship models and unusual musical instruments to hand-painted scarves, pottery, jewelry, candles, etched glassware, and blown-glass items. Open daily from 10am to 5pm.

GIFTS

✪ **Saxon Swan.** 101 Second St. ☎ **302/645-7488.**

The Saxon Swan offers a potpourri of figurines, pottery, sculptures, ornaments, etchings, and watercolors. It also has an array of international Nativity scenes and Santas, as well as menorahs and Judaica collectibles. Open Monday through Saturday from 10am to 5pm, Sunday from 11am to 5pm.

Sugar & Spice Collection. 107 Second St. ☎ **302/645-0189.**

This large shop defies definition. It has an extensive collection of kitchenware—everything from cutting boards and utensils to hand-blown glasses—as well as seasonal gifts and decorations, Department 56 items, frames, garden supplies and ornaments, and even birdhouses. Open Monday through Friday 10am to 6pm, Saturday 10am to 8pm, and Sunday 11am to 6pm.

Union Jack. 107 W. Market St. ☎ **302/645-1254.**

This gift shop specializes in items from the British Isles, from tea and all its accessories to Irish tin whistles. Foodstuffs from Great Britain fill most of the shelves, but you can also find books, maps, and videos of British shows and movies. Open daily from 10am to 5pm.

TOYS

Puzzles. 111 Second St. ☎ **302/645-8013.**

Intriguing games and puzzles of all kinds are on sale at this shop, including jigsaws, crosswords, brain-teasers, mazes, and metal and wooden puzzles. Open daily from 10am to 9:30pm in the summer, 10am to 6pm in the shoulder season, and 11am to 4pm in January, February, and March. Call in the winter to verify hours.

WHERE TO STAY IN LEWES

Lewes's choices for accommodation include handsome downtown inns as well as traditional motels. Prices, in general, are in the moderate-to-expensive range in the summer months and in the moderate-to-inexpensive range at other times of the year. Check what rate is in effect at the time you plan to visit and whether any minimum-night stays are required. Reservations are required in the summer months and recommended at other times, since the total room capacity in town barely exceeds 300.

EXPENSIVE/MODERATE

✪ **Blue Water House Inn.** 407 E. Market St. (across the canal on the bayside of town). ☎ **800/493-2080** for reservations or 302/645-7832 for information. 6 rms. $80–$120 double. Rates include breakfast. MC, V. Free parking.

Fun, early '70s beach garage sale is how I'd describe the room decor of this unique lighthouse-shaped bed-and-breakfast. (Our room had an incredible 3-foot daisy-shaped aluminum mirror. Where do they find this stuff?) In fact, innkeepers Chuck and Karen Ulrich and Charlie and Kayla, their two children, regularly stop by Garage Sale Antiques (see "Shopping," above) looking for new additions for the inn. The comfortable guest rooms, all on the second level, are quite large, have private baths, and open onto a covered porch. The "Lookout" on the upper level provides panoramic views and a good place to relax, play games, and watch TV. The ground-level patio is home to "Captain Chuck's World Famous Conga Bar" where you can lie back in a hammock and sip a margarita.

The Ulrich family has created a casual, kick-your-shoes-off atmosphere that makes their guests feel right at home. Families with children are welcome and well accommodated; two or three rooms can be converted to suites and baby-sitting is available. In addition, the inn has a large selection of bikes, beach balls, and boogie boards for guest use. For more information (and pictures), check out their web page at **www.lewes-beach.com**.

✪ **Inn at Canal Square.** 122 Market St., Lewes, DE 19958. ☎ **800/222-7902** or 302/645-8499. Fax 302/645-7083. 21 rms, 1 houseboat. A/C TV TEL. $75–$135 double courtyard rm, $90–$165 double in main building; $175–$250 houseboat. Rates include continental breakfast. AE, DC, DISC, MC, V. Free parking.

This four-story inn overlooking its own marina has a casual, country-inn atmosphere with the amenities of a large full-service hotel and marina. The generously sized guest rooms are furnished in 18th-century English style, with reproduction headboards, nightstands, armoires, brass lamps, and comfortable armchairs, as well as designer fabrics, waterfowl art prints, and live plants. Best of all, most rooms have a balcony or porch overlooking the water. The modern bathrooms, each with separate vanity area and hair dryers, have sleek black-and-white marble and tile appointments. Facilities include a sitting room and parlor, a conference center, and an adjacent marina with boat slips available for guests. For those looking for a different experience, the inn also rents a custom-designed, two-bedroom houseboat, permanently moored on the marina. The houseboat has a full galley, sundeck, and fireplace and sleeps four adults.

✪ **New Devon Inn.** 142 Second St. (at Market St.), Lewes, DE 19958. ☎ **800/824-8754** or 302/645-6466. 24 rms, 2 suites. A/C TEL. $45–$120 double; $90–$170 suite. Rates include continental breakfast. AE, DC, DISC, MC, V. Free parking.

Dating from the 1920s, this restored, three-story brick hotel sits right in the heart of Lewes. Guests relax in a modern sitting room with art deco tones and a baby grand piano, in the adjacent Music Room, or in the wicker and plant-filled Garden Room. The guest rooms, located on the second and third floors, are individually furnished with local antiques, crystal or brass lamps, and fine comforters and linens. The hotel facilities include The Buttery, a full-service restaurant (see "Where to Dine," below), and a half-dozen shops on the main and lower levels. In addition, the inn has a concierge desk, twice-daily maid service, and turndown service. Ask about the package deals available here, including the Biking Inn-to-Inn tour (see "Offbeat & Outdoor Adventures" in the Inland Southern Delaware section, below). *Note:* Because of the many expensive antique furnishings, this hotel may not be suitable for children under 16.

Wild Swan Inn. 525 Kings Hwy., Lewes, DE 19958. ☎ **302/645-8550.** Fax 302/645-8550. 3 rms (all with private bath). A/C. $85–$120 double. Rates include breakfast. No credit cards. Free parking.

This bed-and-breakfast, located a half mile from town and a mile from the beach, opposite the Lewes Library on Adams Avenue, is a standout for turn-of-the-century ambience and 1990s comfort. Built in 1910 as a lightship captain's house in classic Queen Anne Victorian style, it's rich in ornate gingerbread and fancy finials. The common rooms and guest rooms are also Victorian, with high ceilings and vivid colors, lavish wallpaper, antique brass lighting fixtures, and antique furnishings. In honor of the house's name, the innkeepers have filled the rooms with swan-motif accessories, from china swans to swan toilet paper. All the rooms have queen-size beds. The facilities include a wraparound veranda and an outdoor swimming pool; bicycles are available for guest use. There's also a well-tended garden and gazebo.

MODERATE/INEXPENSIVE

Angler's Motel. 110 Anglers Rd. (at Market St.), Lewes, DE 19958. ☎ **302/645-2831.** 25 rms. A/C TV TEL. $65–$95 double. AE, MC, V. Free parking.

One of the oldest lodgings in the area, this well-kept motel is a favorite with fishing guests and families. Most of the rooms have views of the wharf and marina. Outside there's a pleasant sundeck, a pool, grills, and a picnic area. All rooms have a kitchenette or unstocked refrigerator. A 2-day minimum stay applies on summer weekends; reduced rates are in effect from mid-September to mid-May.

Beacon Motel. 514 Savannah Rd., P.O. Box 609, Lewes, DE 19958. ☎ **800/735-4888** or 302/645-4888. 66 rms. A/C TV TEL. $45–$105 double. AE, MC, V. Free parking. Closed late Dec to Mar.

This motel, opened in 1989, occupies the top two floors of a three-story property, with the ground level devoted to shops and a reception area. The bright and cheery rooms feature standard furnishings and seashell art, plus a refrigerator and a small balcony with sliding glass doors. The facilities include an outdoor swimming pool and a sundeck.

Cape Henlopen Motel. Savannah and Anglers rds., P.O. Box 243, Lewes, DE 19958. ☎ **800/447-3158** or 302/645-2828. 28 rms. A/C TV TEL. $40–$95 double. AE, DC, MC, V. Free parking.

Located directly across from Fisherman's Wharf, this modern, two-story, L-shaped motel has fully carpeted and wood-paneled rooms, some with beach-style furniture. All second-floor rooms have balconies. There's a 2-night minimum stay on weekends and a 3-night minimum during holiday weekends in the summer. Open all year.

INEXPENSIVE

Savannah Inn. 330 Savannah Rd. (Rte. 9), Lewes, DE 19958. ☎ **302/645-5592.** 7 rms (with shared baths). $40–$70 double. Rates include breakfast. No credit cards. Free parking. Closed Oct to late May.

Innkeepers Richard and Susan Stafursky give you the ambience of a bygone era. A gracious, semi-Victorian brick house with a wraparound enclosed porch, this bed-and-breakfast is conveniently situated in the heart of midtown Lewes at the corner of Orr Street. Bedrooms are of varying size and decor, all with shared baths but private basins. The rates include a bountiful breakfast of local fruits, homemade breads or muffins and jams, and a choice of hot beverage. There's a 2-night minimum on weekends and a 3-night minimum on holidays. Some rooms can accommodate three or four persons, at a rate of $55 to $65. (*Note:* Rooms are available at reduced rates without breakfast during the off-season.)

NEARBY ACCOMMODATIONS

For travelers more interested in a subdued setting than in immediate access to the beach, nearby Milton offers two charming bed-and-breakfasts.

۞ Captain William Russell House. 320 Union St., Milton, DE 19968. ☎ **302/684-2504.** 3 rms. May–Sept $80–$90 double; Oct–Mar $65–$80 double. Rates include breakfast. No credit cards. Free parking.

Situated on the main street in Milton, about a block from the Broadkill River, this mid-19th-century painted lady offers a relaxed bed-and-breakfast atmosphere with a distinctly British flair. Afternoon tea and pastries are served daily by your English butler, innkeeper Tony Boyd-Heron, who dons an accent and, for special occasions, tails and bow tie. Breakfast, also served by Tony, is so good and filling that most of their guests do not need lunch. Specialties include breakfast burritos, baked grapefruit, and quiche. Guest rooms, each with private bath, are decorated with turn-of-the-century antiques and have a somewhat nautical flair. The two rooms in the back of the house have private patios with lovely views of an old black walnut tree. All guests can relax in the sunroom, where breakfast and tea are served in the warmer months.

The Hollies. 313 Reed St., Milton, DE 19968. ☎ **302/684-8905.** 2 rms (with shared bath). $65 double. Rates include breakfast. No credit cards. Free parking.

Almost directly behind the Captain Russell House stands this warm and homey bed-and-breakfast. There is nothing pretentious about this place. Owner and innkeeper Joan Nagy really strives to make her guests feel as though they are staying with a close friend. She has succeeded so completely that some of her repeat customers call her

"Grammy Joan." The house itself is over 100 years old and offers guests a large sunroom, a cozy sitting room with a woodstove, and a smallish yard with a lovely herb and flower garden out back. Breakfast, served in the eat-in kitchen, is a real treat, with freshly baked breads and pastries, including Joan's specialty, raspberry cream cheese coffee cake. Two-night stays are the minimum for holiday weekends.

CAMPING

For summertime family outings, camping at ✪ **Cape Henlopen State Park** (☎ 302/ 645-2103) is a good, inexpensive option. The 159 campsites sit on pine-covered dunes and all have water hookup and access to clean bathhouses with showers. The sites are all fairly spacious, but the ones in the center loops are not terribly private. The largest and most private sites are located in the back loop, but they aren't well suited for trailers or motor homes. (To get to these sites, continue straight along the main road into the camping area until you have to veer left onto the gravel and dirt road.) The campground is open April 1 through October 31 on a first-come first-served basis. Rates are $18 per night. As with all camping on the Atlantic coast, mosquitoes can be a problem (though not nearly as bad as at Assateague), so bring bug repellent.

WHERE TO DINE
EXPENSIVE

✪ **The Buttery.** 142 Second St. ☎ **302/645-7755.** Reservations recommended. Main courses $16–$26; lunch $5.95–$9.50. DISC, MC, V. Tues–Sat 11am –2:30pm and 5–10pm, Sun 10:30am–2:30pm and 5–9pm. NOUVEAU FRENCH.

The Buttery at the New Devon Inn is one of the newest additions to the fine-dining scene in Lewes, having opened its doors in 1993. This is as close as you'll get to a Paris bistro on the Delaware and Maryland shore. There are two candlelit dining rooms set in white linens. The outer dining room has a bar and coffee bar for lunch, while the back room is slightly more formal, with contemporary decor and Matisse-like prints on the walls. The menu, like most in the area, has a wide selection of seafood—crab cakes, pan-seared yellowfin tuna, and bouillabaisse—with a few beef and poultry options, including an exceptional grilled breast of chicken with Thai pepper-peanut sauce. This is also a great place for a champagne Sunday brunch. But perhaps the best deal is the early-bird three-course fixed-price special, every night until 6:30pm, for $14.95.

Gilligan's. 134 Market St. (at Front St.). ☎ **302/645-7866.** Reservations recommended for dinner. Main courses $14–$23; lunch $5–$9.50. AE, MC, V. Apr–Oct daily 11am–11pm. SEAFOOD.

One of the unique dining spots in Lewes is Gilligan's, next to the Inn at Canal Square and right on the water. The restaurant consists of a refurbished diving boat anchored on the marina and attached to a renovated chicken coop on the dock. Although it sounds outlandish, the result is a charming harborfront structure with a trendy deck bar and a glass-walled dining room, all decorated in a tropical island motif. Unfortunately, the indoor dining area is rather small and can get a bit crowded and loud at times. Seafood dominates the dinner menu, with such choices as crab cakes, soft-shell crabs, hoisin-glazed salmon, and grilled sea scallops with Japanese eggplant. For landlubbers, there's also a variety of chicken, veal, pork, steak, and pasta dishes.

✪ **Kupchick's.** 3 E. Bay Ave. ☎ **302/645-0420.** Reservations recommended for dinner. Main courses $13.95–$25. AE, CB, DC, MC, V. Daily 5–10pm with reduced hrs. in winter. SEAFOOD/STEAK.

This beachfront restaurant, opened in 1985, carries on a tradition of fine food started in 1913 when the present owners' grandparents, immigrants from Romania, began the first Kupchick's in Toronto and later added a second restaurant in Montreal. There are two dining rooms on the ground floor, each with a European ambience and decor, and a more casual upper-level open deck for sea-view meals on warm summer days. Dinner entrees include crab imperial, shrimp scampi, chicken piccata, lobster, fresh swordfish, and certified Angus steaks. Kupchick's is also known for its chowder and desserts—Key lime cheesecake, chocolate walnut pie, and raspberry soufflé. The restaurant usually has a half-price entree night weekly, especially in the fringe seasons, so call ahead or check with your innkeeper or hotel.

MODERATE

La Rosa Negra. 128 Second St. ☎ **302/645-1980.** Reservations recommended for dinner. Main courses $6.50–$18.95; lunch $2.50–$6. AE, DISC, MC, V. Mon–Thurs 11am–2pm and 4–9:30pm, Fri–Sat 11am–2pm and 4–10pm, Sun 4–9:30pm. ITALIAN.

In a town known for seafood, this small shopfront restaurant is a pleasant change of pace. The decor is highlighted by a black rose *(rosa negra)* etched on stained glass in the front window; the table settings carry on the same theme with black-and-white linens and pottery. Local art enlivens the white walls. Specialties include chicken Florentine Gorgonzola, scampi alle ceci (with chickpeas, black olives, and white wine over linguine), and fettuccine puttanesca (with chopped olives, garlic, and tomatoes, over linguine pesto), as well as vegetarian pastas such as manicotti and ravioli served with marinara sauce.

Lighthouse Restaurant. Savannah and Anglers rds. ☎ **302/645-6271.** Reservations accepted only for parties of 8 or more. Main courses $11.95–$24.95; lunch $3.95–$13.95. MC, V. Mar–Oct Sun–Thurs 7am–4pm and 5–9pm, Fri–Sat 7am–4pm and 5–10pm. SEAFOOD.

Pleasant views of the marina and a casual nautical decor are the features at this restaurant. There's seating both indoors and outside, under a covered deck. An all-day menu features soups, salads, sandwiches, and platters; especially worth trying are the seaside salads (greens topped with sautéed shrimp, scallops, and crab). The dinner menu emphasizes a selection of fish dishes, such as crab cakes, combination platters, and lobster, as well as steaks, ribs, and fried chicken.

Rose and Crown Restaurant and Pub. 108 Second St. ☎ **302/645-2373.** Reservations recommended for dinner. Main courses $8.95–$20.95; lunch $3.95–$7.95. AE, MC, V. Daily 11am–1am. INTERNATIONAL.

Housed in the historic 1930s Walsh Building, this restaurant offers a pub atmosphere in three separate eating areas: a bright, plant-filled front room with large windows overlooking busy Second Street; a clubby bar area with brass fixtures, skylit ceiling, and wall hangings from England and Ireland; and a cozy back room with dark wood trim, exposed-brick walls, and a tin ceiling. Lunch fare includes pub salads, home-made soups, quiches, shepherd's pie, Welsh rabbit, and fish-and-chips. Dinner features such entrees as London broil, English cottage beef pie, pork stew in cider, and crab imperial.

INEXPENSIVE

⭐ **A Taste of Heaven.** 107 Savannah Rd. ☎ **302/644-1992.** All items $4.95–$6.95. AE, MC, V. Wed–Mon 9am–5pm. GOURMET DELI.

For quick and casual but exceptionally good lunch fare, try this gourmet deli. It has a good selection of sandwiches and salads, including three or four daily specials and lots of options for vegetarians. I recommend their roasted eggplant sandwich, with roasted red peppers and fresh mozzarella on french bread, and their peppered turkey breast on seven-grain. You can dine inside or outside on the small sidewalk cafe area, or carry out.

3 Rehoboth & Dewey Beaches

88 miles SE of Wilmington, 27 miles N of Ocean City, 124 miles SE of Washington, D.C., 110 miles SE of Baltimore

Of all the Delaware Beach resorts, Rehoboth is by far the most popular and it is not hard to see why. Rehoboth has struck an amazing balance between small-town beach resort fun and sophisticated style. Away from its fine beachfront hotels, condominiums, and boardwalk, Rehoboth is a town of pleasant turn-of-the-century cottages and tree-lined streets perfect for a relaxing bike ride or stroll. It offers a plethora of shopping as well as numerous restaurants specializing in everything from local seafood to French cuisine. And, if all this hasn't sparked your interest, just outside of Rehoboth is one of the largest retail outlet centers in the nation, offering about as much tax-free shopping as anyone could desire.

Dewey Beach, Rehoboth's younger cousin, is situated to the south, between Rehoboth's lovely Silver Lake and the Delaware Seashore State Park. Dewey in many ways functions as Rehoboth South and is connected to the larger town by a trolley service that runs all summer long. Not without charms of its own, Dewey, which is only 2 blocks wide from the Atlantic to the Rehoboth Bay, affords plenty of public beach space as well as several options for bayfront dining.

ESSENTIALS

GETTING THERE   If you're driving from points north, take Routes 113 and 13 to Route 1, and then Route 1A into Rehoboth. From the south, take Route 113 north to Route 26 east to Bethany Beach. From there take Route 1 north to Rehoboth. From the west, take Route 50 across the Bay Bridge to Route 404 east; then take Route 9 east to Route 1 south.

Carolina Trailways provides regular bus service into the Rehoboth Bus Center, 251 Rehoboth Ave., Rehoboth Beach (☎ **800/441-1329** or 302/227-7223).

For visitors arriving by plane, the nearest airport is **Salisbury/Ocean City Regional Airport.** See "Getting There" in chapter 8.

VISITOR INFORMATION   Sightseeing brochures, maps, descriptions of accommodations, and restaurant listings are available from the **Rehoboth Beach–Dewey Beach Chamber of Commerce,** P.O. Box 216, Rehoboth Beach, DE 19971 (☎ **800/441-1329** or 302/227-2233). The office, located in the old Rehoboth Railroad Station at 502 Rehoboth Ave., is open year-round Monday through Friday from 9am to 5pm and Saturday from 9am to noon; in addition, from Memorial Day through Labor Day there are Sunday hours from 9am to noon.

GETTING AROUND   By Public Transportation   From Memorial Day through Labor Day, Delaware Resort Transit/DRT (☎ **302/739-3278** or 302/226-2001) operates daily **bus shuttle service** between Route 1 and the Rehoboth Beach boardwalk and other nearby beach points. The daily cost is $1 per person or $4 per car, which includes parking, with unlimited reboarding privileges.

The **Jolly Trolley** (☎ **302/227-1197**), an independent firm, also operates a shuttle service between Rehoboth Beach, starting at the Boardwalk and Rehoboth Avenue, and Dewey Beach. The service runs daily Memorial Day through Labor Day from 7am to 2am, on the hour and half hour; in May and September it operates on weekends only. The cost is $1 per ride for adults ($2 after midnight) and free for children under 6. You can board at any signposted stop along the route.

By Car   Parking in Rehoboth Beach can be difficult. Metered parking is in effect (either 30 minutes, hourly, or up to 12 hours, with the majority of machines programmed for the first two time limits). This system operates from 10am to midnight from mid-May through mid-September. Parking at nonmetered spots is by permit only from 10am to 5pm. The number of spaces can rarely accommodate the demand; to ease the situation, most lodging places offer free parking to their guests and many people choose to park their car and leave it at the hotel or motel until going home. Rehoboth is small enough that walking usually proves to be the best way to get around.

SPECIAL EVENTS   The big event in the Rehoboth/Dewey area is the annual **Sea Witch Halloween Festival and Fiddler's Convention,** held at the end of October. This 2-day event features a costume parade, trick-or-treating, a broom-tossing contest, a 5K foot race, and, of course, a fiddling contest. For information contact the Rehoboth Beach–Dewey Beach Chamber of Commerce (☎ **800/441-1329** or 302/227-2233).

WHAT TO SEE & DO

Rehoboth and Dewey offer a somewhat quieter, more relaxed alternative to Ocean City, but with a little nightlife and stores that stay open past 5pm, which you won't find at Bethany, Lewes, or Fenwick Island. There are two main attractions here: the beach and the outlets.

OUTDOOR ACTIVITIES

BEACHES   Swimming at Rehoboth's and Dewey's wide sandy beaches is one of the area's top activities. All the beaches have public access and are guarded, but there are no bathhouses.

The 10-mile-long beach at **Delaware Seashore State Park Inlet 850,** Route 1 (☎ 302/227-2800), located 2 miles south of Rehoboth Beach, offers both the crashing surf of the Atlantic and the gentle waters of Rehoboth Bay. Its facilities include lifeguard-supervised swimming, surfing, and fishing. In addition, it has a full-service boating marina and a bay-shore campground with more than 300 sites for RVs and trailers. Admission to the park is $2.50 for Delaware cars and $5 for out-of-state vehicles.

BICYCLING   With its flat terrain and shady streets, Rehoboth is ideal for bicycling. Bikes are allowed on the Boardwalk between 5 and 10am from May 15 to September 15. Three companies offer rentals to visitors. **Bob's Bicycle Rentals,** 30 Maryland Ave. at First Street (☎ **302/227-7966**), rents one-speed touring bikes, mountain bikes, and tandems. Bob's is open Memorial Day through Labor Day, daily

Especially for Kids

Rehoboth Summer Children's Theatre, at 18 Baltimore Ave. (☎ 215/886-9341), performs favorites such as *Snow White, Robin Hood,* and *Peter Pan.* Curtain time is at 7:30pm on Tuesday, Wednesday, and Thursday. Prices range from $4.50 to $7, depending on the event.

Rehoboth Beach has three summertime family amusement areas: **Funland,** situated at the Boardwalk and Delaware Avenue, which has rides and games (opens at 1pm daily); and **Playland,** at the Boardwalk and Wilmington Avenue, which features video games for all ages (open from 10am to midnight). About 1½ miles north of town there's also **Sports Complex,** Route 1 and Country Club Road (☎ 302/227-8121). This is a family-fun park with go-kart tracks, miniature golf, a water slide, bumper boats, kiddie canoes, and other outdoor rides. Open weekends May and September and daily from Memorial Day to Labor Day, 10am to 11pm.

9am to 6pm or later; hours vary the rest of the year. **Wheels Bicycle Shop,** 318 Rehoboth Ave. (☎ 302/227-6807), is conveniently situated on the main thoroughfare. This well-stocked shop rents a variety of cruising bikes. In the peak season, it also operates a rental station on the Boardwalk at Virginia Avenue (☎ 302/227-8520), open daily 9am to 6pm or later Memorial Day through Labor Day (hours vary the rest of the year). **Rehoboth Sport & Kite Company** (☎ 302/227-6996), located on the Boardwalk at Virginia Avenue, also rents bikes. Generally, rates for bike rentals at all shops range from $2 to $7 per hour and $7 to $20 per day, depending on the type of bike.

WATER SPORTS   Bay Sports, 11 Dickinson St., Dewey Beach (☎ 302/226-2677 or 302/227-7590), rents Windsurfers, Sunfish sailboats, and jet skis by the half hour or hour or by the day. Rates for a Windsurfer or Sunfish are $22 for 1 hour, $32 for 2 hours, and $42 for 3 hours; and jet skis are $30 to $60 for a half hour. Sailing and windsurfing lessons can also be arranged.

SHOPPING THE OUTLETS & THE BOARDWALK

Thanks to the **Rehoboth Outlets** (☎ 800/832-3590), Rehoboth Beach is no longer just a summer destination. The 140 tax-free outlets in the three shopping centers along Route 1, about a mile north of Rehoboth, draw a huge holiday shopping crowd, keeping many area hotels full through December. Whenever you decide to visit, pick up a map and listing of stores at one of the outlet centers so that you can make the best use of your time.

Center 1 (it's farthest north on Route 1) is the oldest of the shopping centers and has most of the fashion designers—Jones New York, Liz Claiborne, Ann Taylor, and Tommy Hilfiger—as well as a lot of the housewares stores, such as Lenox and Pfaltzgraff. The next outlet center you'll come to as you move south is center 3, the largest of the three, hosting Levi's, Guess, J. Crew, OshKosh B'Gosh, Mikasa, Oneida, Waterford, Wedgwood, and more. Center 2, the farthest south along Route 1 and the smallest of the centers, has a Leather Loft, Carter's Childrenswear, Corning Revere, Bass, and others. All three centers are open May through December, Monday through Saturday from 10am to 9pm and Sunday from 10am to 6pm; during the off-season (January through April) they're open Sunday through Thursday from 10am to 6pm and Friday and Saturday from 10am to 9pm.

In downtown Rehoboth the shopping is concentrated on the mile-long Boardwalk and on Rehoboth Avenue, which intersects the Boardwalk at its midpoint. Most of the stores are open from 10am to 6pm, with extended evening hours in the summer.

Christmas Spirit. 129 Rehoboth Ave. ☎ **302/227-6872.**

It's Christmas year-round in this delightful shop, stocked full of trees, lights, handcrafted ornaments from around the world, angel tree tops, tree skirts, vintage Victorian decorations, candles, nutcrackers, character Santas, lighted villages and figurines, gift wrap, and more.

Mizzen Mast. 149 Rehoboth Ave. ☎ **302/227-3646.**

Dedicated to the good nature in all of us, this shop features environmentally friendly and recycled products, such as Birkenstock footprint sandals, nature music, T-shirts, pottery, notepads, stickers, mugs, cards, posters, games, stuffed animals, and hand-painted birds.

Olde Salt Gift Shop. 42 Rehoboth Ave. ☎ **302/227-1210.**

Tucked in the Penny Lane Mall, this shop stocks nautically themed gifts, such as books on Chesapeake Bay, illustrated maps, watercolors, and miniature lighthouses, as well as Christmas items, Dickens Village collectibles, and baking tools. Open January through March, Saturday and Sunday from 11am to 5pm; April through December, daily from 10am to 5pm.

Sea Shell Shop. 119 Rehoboth Ave. ☎ **302/227-6666.**

This shop is a treasure trove of seashell art, lamps, jewelry, and gifts, as well as loose shells, sponges, coral, and hermit crab souvenirs. Other locations are at Bellevue Street and Highway 1, Dewey Beach (☎ **302/227-6695**), and 4405 Coastal Hwy. (☎ **302/227-4323**).

Wild Birds Unlimited. 49 Baltimore Ave. ☎ **302/227-5850.**

For nature lovers, this shop offers bird-themed stained glass, chimes, art, and books, as well as birdhouses and bird-feeding equipment. Open June through August, Wednesday through Monday from 10am to 10pm; September through May, Wednesday through Monday from 10am to 5pm.

ATTRACTIONS

If the weather turns cloudy or your skin turns too red, move off the beach and see what else Rehoboth has to offer. The **Rehoboth Art League** (☎ **302/227-8408**), at 12 Dodds Lane, is a great place to visit even on sunny days. Nestled in the Henlopen Acres section of town amid 3 acres of gardens and walking paths and an outdoor sculpture area, this facility includes three galleries, a teaching studio, and a restored cottage. It offers exhibits by local and nationally known talent, art classes, workshops, and cultural performances. Admission is usually free, though for special events there may be a charge, ranging from $1 to $10. Open May through September, Monday through Saturday from 10am to 4pm and Sunday from 1 to 4pm; in October and February through April, weekdays from 10am to 4pm.

The **Anna Hazzard Museum** (☎ **302/226-1119**), located at 17 Christian St. (on Martin's Lawn, off Rehoboth Ave.), is one of the original "tent" buildings erected in the days when Rehoboth was a summer resort/retreat for Methodists. It's a good place from which to gain a perspective on Rehoboth and its history. Admission is free but by appointment only.

WHERE TO STAY

Most of the accommodations in Rehoboth and Dewey are moderately priced. In July and August, however, you may encounter difficulty finding any room (single or double occupancy) near the beach for under $100 a night; if you must be by the water, be ready to pay for it. Even though Rehoboth and Dewey are seasonal destinations, don't expect dramatic off-season discounts like you'll find in Ocean City. The outlets are a huge attraction for holiday shoppers, so the shoulder season in this area extends through December (but ask your hotel about weekday packages). In any case, reservations are always necessary in the summer and strongly recommended through the holiday shopping season.

REHOBOTH BEACH

Very Expensive/Expensive

✪ Atlantic Sands Hotel & Suites. 101 N. Boardwalk, Rehoboth Beach, DE 19971. ☎ **800/ 422-0600** or 302/227-2511. Fax 302/227-9476. 114 rms. A/C TV TEL. $60–$259 double. AE, DISC, MC, V. Free parking.

Ideally situated on the Boardwalk between Baltimore and Maryland avenues, the five-story Atlantic Sands is Rehoboth's largest hotel and the only oceanfront property in town with an outdoor ground-level swimming pool. Its guest rooms are all newly refurbished and have a balcony and view of the water. Each unit is furnished with light woods or rattan furniture, brass fixtures, seashell art and accessories, silk and dried floral arrangements, and fabrics of sea, sky, and sand tones. Some rooms also have a Jacuzzi bath, a wet bar, and a refrigerator. In the summer months, the hotel operates a buffet-style restaurant, featuring all-you-can-eat breakfasts and dinners. Among the facilities are a hot tub and a rooftop sundeck.

Boardwalk Plaza. Olive Ave. and the Boardwalk, Rehoboth Beach, DE 19971. ☎ **800/ 33-BEACH** or 302/227-7169. Fax 302/227-0561. 33 rms., 45 suites. A/C TV TEL. $55–$325 standard double; $65–$360 ocean-view double; $110–$445 oceanfront deluxe double; $77–$375 ocean-view suite; $88–$425 oceanfront suite. AE, CB, DC, DISC, MC, V. Free parking.

With a fanciful pink-and-white gingerbread facade, this four-story Victorian-style hotel stands out on the Boardwalk. The Victorian theme continues inside, with an antique-filled lobby complete with live talking parrots in gilded cages and guest rooms decorated with rich, dark-wood antique and reproduction furniture and frilly fabrics. The hotel offers a variety of rooms with different amenities and services. Rooms on the concierge level come with newspaper delivery, turndown service, hair dryers, and bath robes. Many of the rooms have a balcony, with a full or partial view of the ocean, some have Jacuzzis, and all have stocked minibars and coffeemakers. The hotel's facilities include Victoria's, an oceanfront restaurant, an indoor-outdoor heated spa pool, a rooftop and a poolside sundeck, and an exercise room.

Expensive/Moderate

✪ Brighton Suites Hotel. 34 Wilmington Ave., Rehoboth Beach, DE 19971. ☎ **800/ 227-5788** or 302/227-5780. Fax 302/227-6815. 66 suites. A/C TV TEL. $59–$219 suite. AE, DC, DISC, MC, V. Free parking.

For families or two couples traveling together, this all-suite hotel is a good choice, a short walk from the beach, at the corner of First Street. Each unit in this sandy pink four-story property has a bedroom with a king-size bed, a large bathroom, and a separate living room with sleep-sofa. In-room features include a wet bar, refrigerator, safe, and hair dryer. A 3-night minimum stay applies for holidays and summer weekends. In the summer months, child-care service is provided on some evenings. There is a heated indoor pool on the premises.

⚫ Comfort Inn. 4439 Hwy. 1, Rehoboth Beach, DE 19971. ☎ **800/228-5150** or 302/226-1515. 97 rms, 3 suites. A/C TV TEL. $59–$150 double; $99–$250 suite. Rates include continental breakfast. AE, CB, DC, DISC, MC, V. Free parking.

Located on Route 1 within sight of the Rehoboth outlets, this new addition to the hotel scene is perfectly located for serious outlet shoppers. It opened in 1996 and immediately added on a new wing, which opened in 1997, so guest rooms are newly furnished, clean, and comfortable. Standard guest rooms are large and suites are very roomy; many have a refrigerator and/or microwave, and some have whirlpool tubs. Rooms with king-size beds generally have a sitting area with a sofa bed. It's a short drive away from the beach, but the hotel makes up for it by requiring only a 2-night minimum stay on summer weekends (many area hotels have a 3-night minimum).

⚫ Henlopen Hotel. 511 N. Boardwalk, Rehoboth Beach, DE 19971. ☎ **800/441-8450** or 302/227-2551. Fax 302/227-8147. 92 rms. A/C TV TEL. $55–$140 standard; $75–$170 studio; $95–$195 oceanfront. AE, CB, DC, MC, V. Free parking. Closed Nov–Mar.

Situated between Lake Avenue and Grenoble Place, on the north end of the Boardwalk, this beachfront lodging has a tradition dating from 1879, when the first Henlopen Hotel was built on this site. The present modern structure has 12 oceanfront rooms and 80 rooms with ocean view, each with its own balcony. All rooms have a coffeemaker, and some come with a microwave and refrigerator. Dining facilities include Rehoboth's only rooftop restaurant and lounge, overlooking the beach and the boardwalk. There's a 2-night minimum for all weekend bookings and a 3-night minimum for holiday weekend reservations.

Moderate

Admiral Motel. 2 Baltimore Ave., Rehoboth Beach, DE 19971. ☎ **800/428-2424** or 302/227-2103. 73 rms. A/C TV TEL. $45–$139 double. AE, DISC, MC, V. Free parking.

In the heart of the beach district, this modern five-story motel is a favorite with families—children under 11 stay free in their parents' room. It has an indoor-outdoor rooftop swimming pool and a sundeck with a Jacuzzi. All rooms have a partial ocean view, refrigerator, and coffeemaker; most units have a private balcony. There are 2- and 3-night minimum stays in the summer and supplementary charges for some peak or holiday weekends.

Oceanus Motel. 6 Second St., P.O. Box 324, Rehoboth Beach, DE 19971. ☎ **800/852-5011** or 302/227-8200. 38 rms. A/C TV TEL. $49–$159 double. Rates include continental breakfast. DISC, MC, V. Free parking. Closed Nov to late Mar.

This L-shaped three-story motel lies 2 blocks from the beach and just off Rehoboth Avenue in a quiet neighborhood. Each room is outfitted with extra-long beds and a refrigerator; most rooms have a balcony overlooking the pool. Guest facilities include an outdoor swimming pool and patio area and a self-service Laundromat. At certain times, weekend supplements of $10 to $20 a night prevail.

Sandcastle Motel. 123 Second St., off Rehoboth Ave., Rehoboth Beach, DE 19971. ☎ **800/372-2112** or 302/227-0400. 60 rms. A/C TV TEL. $42–$125 double. AE, DISC, MC, V. Free parking. Closed Jan–Feb.

Built in the shape of a sugary white sand castle, this unique five-story motel is situated 2 blocks from the beach and right off the main shop-lined thoroughfare. Each of the large and well-laid-out rooms has a private balcony and a refrigerator. The motel's facilities include an enclosed parking garage, an elevated sundeck, and an indoor swimming pool with lifeguard. Minimum stays apply during peak season.

Dewey Beach

Expensive/Moderate

Atlantic Oceanside Motel. 1700 Hwy. 1, Dewey Beach, DE 19971. ☎ **800/422-0481** or 302/227-8811. Fax 302/227-4039. 60 rms. A/C TV TEL. $49–$159 double peak season; $35–$109 double off-season. AE, CB, DC, DISC, MC, V. Free parking. Closed Nov–Apr.

Situated between Dagsworth and McKinley streets, this modern three-story structure is set on the main north–south beach highway and enjoys equal distance from the bay and the ocean (both about a block away). The rooms are of the standard motel variety, but each has a coffeemaker, microwave oven, and refrigerator. The facilities include an outdoor heated pool and a sundeck. A weekend surcharge is in effect at certain periods, and a 3-night minimum stay is required for summer weekends. Atlantic Oceanside recently opened a second location, 2¹/₂ blocks from the beach, offering exclusively suites and rooms with kitchenettes. For information and reservations, contact the motel at the number above.

✪ **Bay Resort.** Bellevue St., P.O. Box 461, Dewey Beach, DE 19971. ☎ **800/922-9240** or 302/227-6400. 68 rms. A/C TV TEL. $45–$139 double. Rates include continental breakfast. DISC, MC, V. Free parking. Closed Nov to late Mar.

The ideal place from which to watch the sun go down on Rehoboth Bay is at this three-story motel complex, located on a strip of land between the bay and the ocean. Guest units, each with a small kitchenette and a balcony, face either the pool or the bay. The facilities include an outdoor pool, water-sports center, private beach, and 250-foot pier on the bay. Depending on the time of year, there can also be a weekend surcharge of $15 to $25 per night and a 3-night minimum on holidays.

Best Western Gold Leaf. 1400 Hwy. 1, Dewey Beach, DE 19971. ☎ **800/422-8566,** 800/528-1234, or 302/226-1100. Fax 302/226-9785. 76 rms. A/C TV TEL. $48–$178 double. AE, DC, DISC, MC, V. Free parking.

Located 1 block from both the beach and the bay, this modern four-story motel is situated across the street from the Ruddertowne complex. It offers bright, contemporary rooms with a balcony and a view of the bay, ocean, or both. All rooms are also equipped with a refrigerator and a safe, and the newly remodeled king rooms now have two-person whirlpool tubs. Facilities include enclosed parking, a rooftop swimming pool, and a sundeck. There's a weekend surcharge and 2- and 3-night minimums in the summer. Complimentary coffee is provided for guests in the lobby. Look for reduced-rate packages November through March.

WHERE TO DINE

Some motels do not have restaurants, so here are the two best bets for a morning meal: **Royal Treat** (8 to 11:30am) and the **Lamp Post** (7 to 11am). For addresses and telephone numbers, see below.

Rehoboth Beach

Expensive

Back Porch Cafe. 59 Rehoboth Ave. ☎ **302/227-3674.** Reservations recommended on weekends. Main courses $20–$26; lunch $8–$10. MC, V. June–Sept daily 11am–3pm and 6–10pm; Apr–May and Oct Sat–Sun 11am–3pm and 6–10pm. INTERNATIONAL.

For more than 20 years, a Key West atmosphere has prevailed at this restaurant, where the emphasis is on fresh foods creatively prepared and presented. The dining area includes indoor alcoves and three outdoor decks, all decorated with an eclectic collection of plants and handmade tables. Lunch items include various omelets, lemon-basil chicken salad, pan-fried fish cakes, and Jamaican pork pie. Dinner entrees include rosemary-marinated lamb loin, spice-crusted tenderloin of beef, pan-seared salmon, grilled loin of yellowfin tuna, and portobello mushroom terrine with baby spinach.

Blue Moon. 35 Baltimore Ave. ☎ **302/227-6515.** Reservations required. Main courses $16–$26. AE, CB, DC, DISC, MC, V. Feb–Dec Mon–Sat 6–11pm, Sun noon–3pm and 6–11pm. AMERICAN/INTERNATIONAL.

Located off the main thoroughfare, between First and Second streets, this restaurant is housed in an eye-catching blue-and-mango-colored beach cottage. The interior features curved banquettes, indirect lighting, exotic flower arrangements, and rotating art exhibits by local and international artists. California and Pacific Rim styles of cooking are the specialties here. The chef buys from a local grower who specializes in gourmet herbs. Entrees range from braided salmon and sole with saffron risotto in champagne sauce to Thai-seasoned duck breast with coconut-curry sauce. Seared beef tenderloin with a dry vermouth and Dijon mustard sauce and a variety of pastas are also available.

✪ **Chez La Mer.** 210 Second St. ☎ **302/227-6494.** Reservations recommended. Main courses $15–$28. AE, DC, DISC, MC, V. June–Sept Mon–Thurs 5:30–10pm, Fri–Sat 5:30–10:30pm; Apr–May and Oct Thurs–Sun 5–10pm. CONTINENTAL.

Although this area is full of good restaurants, Chez La Mer is the only one with French country inn decor, cuisine, and service—it's no wonder that the three intimate little dining rooms fill up quickly. The menu changes several times during the year, but specialties often include veal sweetbreads, soft-shell crabs, and a spicy bouillabaisse. All dishes are cooked to order, and special diets, such as low sodium, can be accommodated. Neat attire is a must.

Club Potpourri. 316 Rehoboth Ave. ☎ **302/227-4227.** Reservations recommended on weekends. Main courses $18–$24. AE, DISC, MC, V. June–Sept Mon–Thurs 5–11pm, Fri–Sat 5pm–midnight; Oct–April Wed–Sat 5–10pm. INTERNATIONAL.

A classy cafe ambience prevails at this restaurant, a mecca for fans of live jazz as well as good food. The decor blends brass, globe lanterns, skylights, mirrored walls, and lots of garden plants. The dinner menu ranges from jambalaya and Southwest grilled chicken to pan-roasted rib of veal, filet mignon, and rack of lamb. Early-bird specials are featured from 5 to 7pm.

La La Land. 22 Wilmington Ave. ☎ **302/227-3887.** Reservations required. Main courses $18–$24. CB, DISC, MC, V. May–Oct Sun–Thurs 6–10pm, Fri–Sat 6–11pm. INTERNATIONAL.

Located on a side street off the Boardwalk, this highly acclaimed restaurant specializes in blending California influence with Asian and Southwestern overtones. There's seating indoors in an art-filled pink, purple, and periwinkle-toned dining room and outdoors on a patio with a bamboo garden setting. The menu offers a variety of creative choices: cured salmon tartare with cucumbers, basil cream, and black olives; sautéed Norwegian salmon wrapped in rice paper; seared noisettes of lamb with wild-rice custard; striped bass sautéed in pine nuts; crisp-skin Canadian salmon; and mixed grill of rack of lamb with duck breast.

Expensive/Moderate

✪ **Sea Horse.** 330 Rehoboth Ave. ☎ **302/227-7451.** Reservations recommended for dinner. Main courses $12.95–$26.95; lunch $4.95–$12.95. AE, DC, DISC, MC, V. Mon–Thurs 11:30am–10pm, Fri–Sat 11:30am–11pm. INTERNATIONAL.

A mainstay for more than 25 years in Rehoboth Beach, the Sea Horse is hard to beat for quality food and hefty portions. The plush and welcoming dining rooms are filled with sturdy captain's chairs, copper lanterns, a huge stone fireplace, mirrored panels, carpeted walls, and floral prints. Lunch ranges from burgers to crab imperial. For dinner there's a wide selection of beef (from prime rib to chateaubriand) and seafood (gulf shrimp, crab cakes, snow crab legs, scallops Dijon, rock lobster tails, and many local fresh fish). The restaurant provides a large guest parking lot.

Summer House. 228 Rehoboth Ave. ☎ **302/227-3895.** Main courses $9.95–$23.95; light fare $5.95–$8.95. AE, CB, DC, DISC, MC, V. Apr–Oct daily 5–10pm. SEAFOOD.

Situated on the main thoroughfare next to the Rehoboth Public Library and across from the Convention Hall, this restaurant exudes a festive resort atmosphere in its Gazebo and Aspen dining rooms. The menu of over 100 items emphasizes seafood, with such choices as crab Rolande (lump crab with green and red peppers, mozzarella, hollandaise, and onion) and a house "treasure" consisting of broiled crab cake, shrimp, scallops, swordfish, and brandied clams casino. In addition, there are more than a half-dozen steak, filet mignon, and chicken dishes. Burgers, sandwiches, and other light items are also offered for more informal dining at lower prices, and the "Kids Korner" section of the menu features child-size pizzas, pastas, and even filet mignon, as well as the old standby sandwiches.

✪ **Sydney's Blues & Jazz Restaurant.** 25 Christian St. ☎ **800/808-1924** or 302/227-1339. Reservations recommended on weekends. Main courses $14–$19; grazing portions $10–$13. AE, DC, DISC, MC, V. May–Oct daily 4pm–1am; Nov–April Thurs–Sun 4pm–1am. LOUISIANAN.

Located in an old schoolhouse and run by Sydney Arzt, a former schoolteacher, this restaurant is known for its nightly jazz and blues sessions as well as its unique grazing menu, allowing customers to sample more than one main course. Entrees include St. Charles soft-shell crab, stuffed with shrimp and topped with a crawfish, tasso, and cream sauce; crawfish and shrimp Monica served with roasted red pepper, garlic, and shallot cream sauce over penne pasta; and filet of beef with pearl onions and port wine. The candlelit decor is also an attraction, with black-and-white photos of Hollywood stars on the walls and a skylit ceiling from which gold and silver mobile ornaments are suspended.

Moderate

Ann Marie's Italian and Seafood Restaurant. 208 Second St. (on the corner of Wilmington Ave.). ☎ **302/227-9902.** Reservations not accepted. Main courses $7.95–$19.95. DISC, MC, V. June–Aug Mon–Thurs 5–10pm, Fri–Sun 5–11pm; May and Sept–Oct Thurs–Sat 5–10pm, Sun 4–10pm. ITALIAN.

Established in 1977, this beach-house restaurant brings the atmosphere and flavors of Italy to the beach. It offers a wide variety of freshly made pastas, especially homemade lasagna, a family recipe and a Rehoboth culinary icon for some 20 years. Other mainstays include veal (Parmesan, alla Marsala, and piccata), prime rib, lobster, surf-and-turf, shrimp and seafood cacciatore, shrimp and scallops in marinara sauce, and crab cakes.

Lamp Post. Rtes. 1 and 24. ☎ **302/645-9132.** Reservations not accepted. Main courses $8.95–$25; lunch $3.95–$11.95; breakfast $2.50–$8.95. AE, DISC, MC, V. Daily 7am–10pm. SEAFOOD/STEAK.

Far from the Boardwalk and the action of downtown Rehoboth, this restaurant sits along the main highway, 3 miles north of town. It's convenient for a change of pace from beachfront life or if you're in transit along the coast. Opened in 1953 as the Drexel Diner by award-winning restaurateur Ruth Steele, this friendly spot has been expanded by three generations of the Steele family. Tables are handcrafted from authentic hatch-cover tops from the *Liberty* ships of World War II. The menu focuses on fresh local flounder served in a variety of ways, including "Henlopen" style (stuffed with shrimp, sea scallops, provolone cheese, and seasonings), as well as a half-dozen types of hand-cut steaks and prime rib (weekends only). House specials also include chicken Delaware (sautéed breast of chicken topped with a grilled slice of ham, mushrooms, and melted cheddar cheese) and Delaware seafood chowder.

Obie's by the Sea. On the Boardwalk (at Olive Ave.). ☎ **302/227-6261.** Main courses $4.95–$14.95. AE, MC, V. Daily 11:30am–1am. Closed Nov–Apr. AMERICAN.

You can't dine any closer to the ocean than at this restaurant, situated beside the Boardwalk between Virginia and Olive avenues. A casual seaside atmosphere prevails here, with an all-day menu of sandwiches, burgers, ribs, salads, and "clam bakes" (steamed clams, spiced shrimp, barbecued chicken, corn on the cob, and muffins). There's deejay music and dancing on weekends.

Inexpensive

Dream Cafe. 26 Baltimore Ave. ☎ **302/226-CAFE.** All items 75¢–$6.25. CB, DC, DISC, MC, V. May–Oct daily 7am–10pm; Nov–Apr daily 7am–4pm. AMERICAN.

Conveniently situated between the Boardwalk and First Street, this bright and airy cafe offers a fine selection of fresh-baked breads, baguettes, bagels, croissants, and pastries, as well as gourmet salads, homemade soups, sandwiches, pâtés, quiches, pastas, vegetarian selections, and tempting desserts. Exotic coffees, herbal teas, and a fresh juice bar are also available. Eat-in and take-out service is provided.

Royal Treat. 4 Wilmington Ave. ☎ **302/227-6277.** All items $2–$7. No credit cards. May–Oct breakfast daily 8–11:30am; ice cream daily 1–11:30pm. AMERICAN.

For breakfast and refreshing snacks, try this restored Rehoboth landmark, an airy restaurant/ice-cream parlor next to the Boardwalk. Breakfast favorites include pancakes, French toast, and old-fashioned omelets.

DEWEY BEACH

Moderate

✪ **Rusty Rudder.** 113 Dickinson St. (on the bay). ☎ **302/227-3888.** Main courses $11.95–$25.95; lunch $4.95–$7.95. MC, V. Daily 11:30am–11pm; Sun brunch 10am–2pm. SEAFOOD/ AMERICAN.

Opened in 1979, this large California-style restaurant is a favorite gathering place for young beachgoers. Situated right on the bay, it offers great water views from indoor and outdoor dining rooms, open decks, and terraces. Dinner entrees, which allow for unlimited trips to the bountiful salad bar, include chicken cordon bleu, Parmesan pan-fried backfin crab cakes, and prime rib, as well as enormous seafood and shellfish platters. Lunches range from salads and sandwiches to Cajun catfish and other fish specials. There's also nightly entertainment, with frequent big-name concerts on weekends.

Starboard. 2009 Hwy. 1. ☎ **302/227-4600.** Breakfast and lunch items $2.95–$10.95; main courses $7.95–$13.95. AE, DISC, MC, V. Mid-Mar to late Oct daily 7am–1am. AMERICAN.

A popular Dewey Beach gathering spot for more than 30 years, this informal restaurant is situated on the bayside of the main highway at the corner of Saulsbury Street. It's famous for its large collection of hot sauces (more than 2,000) and for its Bloody Mary breakfasts with make-your-own omelets and pancakes with fruit toppings. Menu choices range from daily fresh-fish specials, cooked to order and served with a variety of sauces, to popular favorites such as shrimp salad, seafood lasagna, chicken cordon bleu, veal Parmesan, spaghetti and meatballs, and prime rib.

Waterfront. McKinley St. (on the bay). ☎ **302/227-9292.** Main courses $7.95–$16.95; lunch $2.95–$6.95. AE, MC, V. Daily noon–1am. Closed Oct–Apr. AMERICAN.

Bay-side sunsets and charcoal-grilled meats and seafood are the main draws at this restaurant, which boasts an open deck, a gazebo, and wide-windowed dining rooms overlooking the water. For lunch, it offers both shrimp and burgers barbecued in its outdoor, open-pit grill, as well as soups, salads, and sandwiches. Dinner entrees include barbecued ribs, chicken, steaks, and shish kebabs, as well as 1-pound lobsters and a variety of other steamed, baked, and broiled seafood.

Moderate/Inexpensive

Crabbers' Cove. Dickenson St. (on the bay in the Ruddertowne complex). ☎ **302/227-3888.** Main courses $9.95–$19.95. AE, DC, DISC, MC, V. May–Sept daily 4–9pm. SEAFOOD.

This casual open-air family seafood restaurant features a variety of all-you-can-eat specials. Entrees include steak, fried chicken, barbecued ribs, fresh fish, shrimp-in-a-basket, and steamed hard crabs, as well as fillet of flounder, grilled tuna steak, baked sea trout, gulf shrimp, steamed mussels, and crab cakes. The "Little Crabbers" menu offers several kids' favorites, some for just $1.

REHOBOTH & DEWEY BEACHES AFTER DARK

Sandwiched between the quiet family resorts of Bethany Beach and Fenwick Island to the south and Lewes to the north, Rehoboth and Dewey Beaches offer the only consistent nightlife on the Delaware coast.

CLUBS & BARS

Nationally known jazz and blues artists entertain year-round at **Sydney's,** 25 Christian St. (☎ **302/227-1339**). Shows are nightly except Wednesday from mid-May through mid-September and on Friday and Saturday nights at other times. Cover charge is $8 on weekends, but there is no cover for dinner guests.

The lilting sing-along sounds of Ireland are heard Thursday through Saturday in the summer at **Irish Eyes,** 15 Wilmington Ave. (☎ **302/227-2888**). Classic rock-and-roll or deejay music is played on other nights. Cover charge varies.

CONCERT HALLS/THEATERS

There's always music in the air at Rehoboth and Dewey, whether indoors or outdoors. The ۞ **Rehoboth Beach Memorial Bandstand,** an open-air pavilion at Rehoboth Avenue and the Boardwalk (☎ **302/227-2233**), hosts more than 40 free concerts and other musical events during the summer. Concerts are generally held Friday through Sunday at 8pm. Check with the Chamber of Commerce office for an up-to-date schedule.

4 Bethany Beach & Fenwick Island

100 miles SE of Wilmington, 130 miles SE of Washington, D.C., 120 miles SE of Baltimore

Nicknamed "the quiet resorts," Bethany Beach and Fenwick Island boast by far the most laid-back and relaxed atmosphere of any of the Maryland and Delaware beach areas. This pleasant stretch of condominium communities, state parks, public and private beaches, and almost no high-rise resort towers offers families and other travelers an impressively calm alternative to the bustle of Ocean City to the south and the sophistication and shopping of Rehoboth to the north. It's a great place to just sit back and enjoy the beach.

You won't find much nightlife here, but outdoor activities abound, from swimming to bicycling to bird watching to a romantic walk on the relatively uncommercialized Bethany Beach Boardwalk. And if after a few days of unwinding you find yourself longing for a little more excitement, try hopping over to nearby Rehoboth (see above) where nighttime fun is almost always brewing.

ESSENTIALS

GETTING THERE   Whether you're approaching Bethany Beach and Fenwick Island from points north or south, it is best to take Route 113 and to avoid the frequently crowded (particularly in July and August) Route 1. To reach Bethany Beach, at Dagsboro take Route 26 east; to reach Fenwick Island from the north, take Route 20 south (just outside of Dagsboro); and to get to Fenwick from the south, turn west on Route 54 at Selbyville. From the west, take Route 50 across the Bay Bridge to Route 404 east, and then turn south on Route 113 and follow the directions above.

Carolina Trailways provides regular bus service during the summer season, stopping at Bethany Rental Services, 201 Central Blvd., Bethany Beach (☎ **302/ 539-6244**).

Visitors arriving by plane can fly into the **Salisbury/Ocean City Regional Airport.** See "Getting There" in chapter 8.

VISITOR INFORMATION   The **Bethany–Fenwick Area Chamber of Commerce,** P.O. Box 1450, Bethany Beach, DE 19930 (☎ **800/962-7873** or 302/ 539-2100), is situated on Route 1 (known also as Coastal Highway), adjacent to the Fenwick Island State Park at the Fenwick line at Lewes Street. The office is designed like a beach house, with wide windows overlooking the ocean and snow-white sands. The chamber publishes a helpful booklet called "The Quiet Resorts" and also stocks brochures from motels, restaurants, and other visitor services. Open year-round Monday through Friday from 9am to 5pm and Saturday and Sunday from 10am to 4pm.

GETTING AROUND   Since Bethany Beach and Fenwick Island are within 5 miles of each other, the predominant mode of transport is car (although bicycles and in-line skates are not uncommon). Most visitors bring their own vehicles or rent cars from nearby Ocean City. Like Rehoboth, many Bethany and Fenwick streets are subject to meter or permit parking, and the rules are strictly enforced. Fortunately, all the motels provide free parking for guests and most of the restaurants also have access to plentiful parking for customers.

ORIENTATION   These quiet resorts comprise three resort communities: Bethany Beach and South Bethany to the north, and Fenwick Island to the south, separated from Bethany by Fenwick Island State Park. The resorts share a barrier island/ peninsula with Ocean City, Maryland, and are surrounded by water, with the Atlantic Ocean to the east and the Indian River Bay, the Assawoman Canal, and the Little Assawoman Bay to the west.

Bethany Beach and South Bethany are very much connected communities (the two are commonly referred to simply as Bethany or Bethany Beach), and bicycling or walking between the two is not terribly difficult. Bethany Beach proper, however, does possess the lion's share of shopping, as well as the boardwalk and the public beach. South Bethany, primarily condominiums and rental home communities, borders the public beaches of Fenwick Island State Park to the south.

The town of Fenwick Island is a small strip of land sandwiched between Ocean City and Fenwick Island State Park and offers easy access to both the excitements of Ocean City (see chapter 8) and the more restful fun of the nearby State Park.

WHAT TO SEE & DO

The 1-mile-long **Bethany Beach Boardwalk,** relatively free of commercial enterprises, is perfect for those looking for a quiet beach-side walk and unobstructed views of the wide-open strand. Most of the shops and fast-food eateries are located on Garfield Parkway, perpendicular to the Boardwalk, which it intersects in the middle.

Especially for Kids

The **Viking Golf Theme Park**, Routes 1 and 54, Fenwick Island (☎ **302/539-1644**), is an inland amusement park across the street from the Fenwick Island Lighthouse. This summertime attraction features a water slide, miniature golf, and bumper-boat and go-kart rides. Hours are 9am to midnight, Memorial Day through Labor Day. Viking miniature golf is open year-round, but hours vary (for more on miniature golf see "Minigolf Mania" in chapter 8).

Fenwick, while lacking a boardwalk, has a wide-open beach with gentle dunes. There are no concessions or fast-food outlets along the shoreline, only private homes and rental properties. Most of the shops and business enterprises are concentrated 1 block inland along Route 1.

OUTDOOR ACTIVITIES

BICYCLING   The windswept flat land along Route 1 in Bethany Beach and Fenwick Island is ideal for bicycling; however, during peak traffic season (July, August, and summer holidays) caution is advised. For a change of scenery, nearby **Assawoman Wildlife Area** offers several sandy but bikeable roads that wind through attractive tidal marshland and forests. To reach the wildlife area take Route 26 west and turn left on Road 361; then turn right on Road 362, go about 1¹/₂ miles, and turn right on Road 363; then turn left on Road 364 and follow the signs for Camp Barnes.

   Birdies and Pars golf shop, Market Place at Sea Colony, Route 1, Bethany Beach (☎ **302/539-4922**), rents single-speed cruiser bikes for $5 per hour, $10 per day, and $30 per week. The shop is open Memorial Day through Labor Day, daily 8am to 7pm and 9:30am to 5pm during the rest of the year.

   Bethany Cycle and Fitness Shop, Route 26 Mall, Route 26, Bethany Beach (☎ **302/537-9982**), rents beach-cruiser bikes with one to five speeds for $5 per hour, $10 per day, or $30 per week. They are open Memorial Day through Labor Day, daily 8am to 8pm; Thursday through Monday 10am to 6pm the rest of the year.

HIKING & BIRD WATCHING   During the off-season both **Fenwick Island** and **Delaware Seashore State Parks** (both on Route 1) are great places to hike on nearly deserted windswept beaches. However, in-season when these beaches are covered with sunbathers, it's best for walking enthusiasts to head at least a little inland (and remember: Bring bug spray). Delaware Seashore State Park's **Burton's Island** boasts a 1¹/₂-mile nature trail and many opportunities to spot wildfowl, from the ever-present great blue herons to the rare piping plover.

   Assawoman Wildlife Area (for directions see "Bicycling," above) welcomes hikers on its few miles of dirt roads through beautiful tidal marsh and forests. In addition, an observation tower and duck blinds make it easy to view a wide variety of shorebirds.

HITTING THE BEACHES   Ideal for swimming and sunning, **Bethany Beach** is free and open to the public. **Bethany Rental Service,** 201 Central Ave. (☎ **302/539-6244**), operates a rental concession on the beach, offering 8-foot umbrellas, surf mats, boogie boards, highback or lounge chairs, and more.

   Fenwick Island State Park, Route 1 (☎ **302/539-9060**), just south of Bethany Beach, offers public space for swimming, sunbathing, surfing, and general beach frolic. The facilities include shower and changing rooms, a first-aid room, lifeguards, and a boardwalk with a gift shop, picnic tables, and refreshments. Admission is $5 for out-of-state cars and $2.50 for Delaware cars. Admission is free weekdays during spring and fall and all week in winter.

To the north, **Delaware Seashore State Park,** Route 1 (☎ 302/227-2800), offers 10 miles of public beach featuring two ocean beach swimming areas with bathhouse facilities and lifeguards in summer, a surfing area, and a bay beach swimming area at Tower Road near the north end of the park. Like Fenwick Island State Park, admission is $5 for out-of-state cars, $2.50 for Delaware cars, and free weekdays during spring and fall and all week in the winter.

SEA KAYAKING   Whether you're surfing waves on the Atlantic or paddling through the beautiful maze of Delaware's inland tidal waters, sea kayaking is a great way to enjoy this section of the Atlantic coast. ✪ **Delmarva Dennis Sea Kayaking Adventures** offers a myriad of tours and summer float trips, from circumnavigating Burton's Island in the Indian River Bay to paddling with dolphins in the ocean or surfing the waves off Assateague Island. Your guide, naturalist Dennis Little, who is well versed in everything from ecology to shipwrecks and treasure beaches, makes sure that these no-experience-necessary adventures are informative as well as exciting. If you're up for something really different, Dennis will take you saltwater fishing from your kayak. (*Be warned:* When the fish pulls, you follow.) For information call ☎ **302/537-5311** or write P.O. Box 234, Ocean View, DE, 19970, or e-mail **deldenmb@dmv.com.**

For those looking to hit the water on their own, kayaks can be rented from **Bay Sports Watersports Rental and Lessons** (see "Water Sports," below).

SURF FISHING   A major draw in this area, fishing in Delaware's tidal waters requires no license. The Bethany–Fenwick Chamber of Commerce sponsors two surf fishing tournaments a year, in early May and in early October; for information call ☎ **800/962-7873** or 302/539-2100.

Fenwick Island State Park has 3 miles of seacoast beach, much of which is open to surf fishing, and considerable tracks of open bayfront, ideal for both fishing and crabbing. There are also several dune crossings set up for off-road vehicles; a surf-fishing vehicle permit is required. For vehicle permits and maps of surf-fishing areas call ☎ **302/539-9060.** Similar facilities are also available at **Delaware Seashore State Park** (☎ **302/227-2800**).

For more about fishing see "Outdoor Activities" in chapter 8.

TENNIS   Although there's not much tennis for the general public in Bethany–Fenwick, **Sea Colony Resort** (see "Where to Stay," below) is the largest tennis resort on the east coast, sporting 26 courts, including four outdoor lighted courts, four clay courts, and four indoor courts.

WATER SPORTS   Adjacent to Fenwick Island State Park on the bayside is **Bay Sports Watersports Rental and Lessons,** Route 1, Fenwick Island (☎ **302/226-2677**), which rents sailboats from $35 an hour and catamarans in three sizes, from $35 to $40 an hour. Jet skis, kayaks, paddleboats, and WaveRunners are also available. Sailing lessons can be arranged from $20 and up an hour. Open late May to early September, daily from 9am to sunset.

ATTRACTIONS

Chief among the sights here is the **Fenwick Island Lighthouse on the Transpeninsular Line,** Route 54, about a quarter mile west of Route 1. Built in 1859, this is one of the Delaware shore's oldest landmarks. The lighthouse is still in operation today; its beams can be seen for 15 miles.

On the south side of the lighthouse you'll see the **First Stone of the Transpeninsular Line,** between Route 1 and Route 54, on the Delaware–Maryland border. This stone monument, erected on April 26, 1751, marks the eastern end of the Transpeninsular Line surveyed in 1750 and 1751 by John Watson and William

Parsons of Pennsylvania and John Emory and Thomas Jones of Maryland. This line established the east–west boundary between Pennsylvania's "Three Lower Counties" (now Delaware) and the Colony of Maryland. The Transpeninsular Line served as the basis for the later Mason-Dixon line.

If you've ever wondered what sunken treasure really looks like, you won't want to miss **Discoveries from the Sea Museum** (☎ 302/539-9366), a very small but worthwhile private museum, located oddly enough above the Sea Shell City shop at Route 1 and Bayard Street, Fenwick Island. The collection includes jewelry, coins, and china recovered from local shipwrecks and treasure beaches, as well as silver and gold bars, and a jeweled dagger and other weapons. We liked the nifty display of both common and rare seashells, useful in identifying the shells you find on the beach. Admission is free. Hours are daily 9am to 9pm, Memorial Day through Labor Day; 11am to 4pm, September through October and April through May; and Saturday and Sunday, 11am to 4pm, November through March.

SHOPPING

Most of the shopping in this area is in Bethany Beach along or near Garfield Parkway and the Boardwalk. Shops are generally open daily from 10am to 5pm with extended hours in summer.

Bethany Beach Books. Garfield Pkwy., Bethany Beach. ☎ **302/539-2522.**

Just off the Bethany Beach Boardwalk, this is the perfect place to pick up some reading for the beach. Well stocked with best-sellers, summer-scorchers, literature, and local interest, the store also features staff reviews and suggestions placed below many of the titles.

Japanesque. 16 Pennsylvania Ave., Bethany Beach. ☎ **302/539-2311.**

Bringing the aura of the Far East to the Delaware beach, this shop carries a wide selection of Japanese jewelry, banners, kimonos, obi, hand-painted scarves, fans, gyotaku items (the art of the Japanese fish rub), folk toys, miniature Zen rock gardens, gift wrap, note cards, hangings, tea kettles, chopsticks, and books.

Sea Crest Gift and Gallery. Atlantic Ave. and Garfield Pkwy., Bethany Beach. ☎ **302/ 539-7621.**

Gifts and crafts that pertain to the sea are featured here, from dolphin, seagull, and dove art mobiles to framed sea art, as well as seashell-motif jewelry, wind chimes, pottery, music boxes, and colored glass.

Seaport Antique Village. Rte. 54 (at the bridge), Fenwick Island. ☎ **302/436-8962.**

This store claims to have one of the largest privately owned antique collections in the United States. All the art and furnishings are for sale. Items include paintings, china, chandeliers, jewelry, wicker, furniture, and objects made of crystal, sterling, brass, and bronze.

WHERE TO STAY

Like other Delaware coastal resorts, Bethany Beach and Fenwick Island are packed in the summer peak season. In July and August, rooms are booked months in advance, cost more, and often come with weekend surcharges and 2- or 3-night minimum stays. Motels that otherwise would be considered in the moderate or budget category might charge between $70 and $100 for a double. So if you'd like to keep the costs reasonable, come during midweek or consider a visit in May, June, September, or October, when the weather can be almost as warm.

BETHANY BEACH

Moderate

Bethany Arms Motel and Apts. Atlantic Ave. and Hollywood St., P.O. Box 1600, Bethany Beach, DE 19930. ☎ **302/539-9603.** 52 units. A/C TV TEL. $40–$100 double; $50–$140 apartment. MC, V. Free parking. Closed late Oct to early Mar.

Ideal for families who want to be close to the ocean, this modern complex offers basic motel units with a refrigerator and apartments with a fully equipped kitchen and an oceanfront view. The complex consists of two buildings right on the boardwalk and three situated just behind the first two, between the boardwalk and Atlantic Avenue; all are two or three stories high. A 2-night minimum is in effect on summer weekends. During holiday periods (such as Memorial Day and Labor Day weekends), 3-night minimums and some surcharges apply.

Harbor View Motel. Rte. 1, R.D. 1, Box 102, Bethany Beach, DE 19930. ☎ **302/539-0500.** Fax 302/539-5170. 60 rms, 8 efficiencies. A/C TV TEL. $35–$100 double; $50–$115 efficiency. Rates include continental breakfast. AE, DISC, MC, V. Free parking. Closed Nov to mid-Mar.

Located 3 miles north of Bethany Beach at the southern edge of the Delaware Seashore State Park, this modern two-story motel on the bayside offers views of the bay as well as the ocean. It has both rooms and efficiencies; some are equipped with an individual Jacuzzi, and all have a balcony. The guest facilities include an outdoor swimming pool, a sundeck on the bay, barbecue grills, a launderette, and a restaurant. There are weekend surcharges and 3-day minimums in season.

Westward Pines. 10 Kent Ave. (1 block west of Rte. 1), Bethany Beach, DE 19930. ☎ **302/ 539-7426.** 14 rms. A/C TV. $55–$70 double; $60–$85 for units with Jacuzzi and fireplace. No credit cards. Free parking.

If you want comfort in a secluded setting, consider this ranch-style motel situated in a residential area 4 blocks from the beach. It's surrounded by tall trees and leafy shrubs. The guest units, all on ground-floor level, have standard furnishings plus a small refrigerator and a coffeemaker; some have a fireplace and a Jacuzzi. A minimum stay may be required on weekends.

FENWICK ISLAND

Moderate

Fenwick Islander. Rte. 1 and South Carolina Ave. (between South Carolina and West Virginia aves.), Fenwick Island, DE 19944. ☎ **800/346-4520** or 302/539-2333. 63 units. A/C TV TEL. $30–$105 double. AE, DISC, MC, V. Free parking. Closed Nov–Mar.

Situated on the bayside of the highway, just north of the Maryland–Delaware state line, this bright, modern three-story motel is ideal for families. All of the units are equipped with refrigerator and kitchenette facilities; second- and third-floor rooms have balconies. Children under 5 stay free; ages 6 to 16 are charged just $5 each per night. Guest amenities include an outdoor swimming pool and a Laundromat. Weekend and holiday rates are subject to surcharges and minimum-stay requirements.

Fenwick Sea Charm Motel and Ric-Mar Apartments. Oceanfront and Lighthouse Rd. (just north of the Delaware–Maryland border), Fenwick Island, DE 19944. ☎ **302/539-9613.** 37 units. A/C TV. $50–$80 double; $55–$150 apartment. DISC, MC, V. Free parking. Closed Nov to mid-May.

The homey Sea Charm, a three-story inn with wraparound porches, is the epitome of a vintage beach cottage. It may be a little timeworn and frayed around the edges, but it's the only place on Fenwick Island that has accommodations right on the beach. A favorite with families, which come back year after year, it offers a choice of motel rooms, oceanfront efficiencies, and one- to three-bedroom ocean-view apartments, some of which have a balcony. Facilities include an outdoor swimming pool and a ground-level patio and sundeck with picnic furniture and outdoor grills. Sea Charm has also recently acquired the 18-unit Ric-Mar Apartments (one- and two-bedroom) located adjacent to the old building on the beach. A 3-night minimum reservation is required throughout the season, and some surcharges apply on weekends.

Sands Motel. Rte. 1 (between Indian and James sts.), Fenwick Island, DE 19944. ☎ **302/ 539-7745;** Dec–Mar ☎ 410/213-2152. 21 rms, 16 apts and efficiencies. A/C TV. $39–$73 double; $40–$110 apt and efficiency. AE, DC, DISC, MC, V. Free parking. Closed Nov–Mar.

Situated on the ocean side of the Coastal Highway but not directly on the oceanfront, the Sands offers a choice of standard rooms, efficiencies, and apartments. It has a kidney-shaped outdoor pool and easy access to the beach, and welcomes well-behaved pets. Rates are subject to a 3-day minimum stay in season, holidays, and weekends; surcharges also apply for certain weekend bookings.

CONDOMINIUMS & RENTALS

Perhaps the most popular sort of accommodations in Bethany–Fenwick is condominiums and rentals. From oceanfront flats to single-family homes, a wide variety is available. During summer, most must be reserved well in advance and for at least a week; however, weekend rates and discounts are common during the off-season. If you decide to go the rental route, be sure to ask the Realtor if you'll need to bring your own towels, sheets, toiletries, and other necessities. Also, remember that the decor and upkeep of rental properties is dependent upon the tastes of the individual owners and not the Realtors.

Some reputable local Realtors include **Long & Foster,** Route 1, Bethany Beach (☎ **302/539-9040); Tansey–Warner, Inc.,** Pennsylvania Avenue, across from Sea Colony (P.O. Box 337), Bethany Beach (☎ **302/539-3001);** and **Tidewater Realty, Ltd.,** 5 Starboard Center, Bethany Beach (☎ **302/539-7500).**

One particularly interesting rental option is Bethany Beach's ✪ **Sea Colony Resort.** This large and attractive resort community is one of the premier tennis resorts on the east coast, with 26 courts, including four lighted outdoor courts, four clay courts, and four indoor courts. It also offers a wide range of rental accommodations, including oceanside condominium towers and single-family homes overlooking one of Sea Colony's many man-made lakes. Other facilities include numerous swimming pools (two of them indoors), a first-rate fitness center and sauna, supervised activities for the kids (during the summer), and concierge service. Rates in peak season (July 10 to August 20) range from $835 per week for an inland one-bedroom tennis villa to $2,015 per week for a three-bedroom oceanfront unit. Rates decrease during off-peak summer periods and are considerably less during the off-season. For information, contact the Sea Colony Rental Office located in the Market Place at Sea Colony, Route 1, Bethany Beach, by calling ☎ **800/SEA-COLONY** or 302/539-6965.

WHERE TO DINE

The restaurants of the Bethany Beach and Fenwick Island area provide a pleasant blend of waterside and inland dining, all at fairly moderate prices. Because these two resorts are popular with families, there are also some fine lower-priced restaurants that offer quality, ambience, and creative cooking. Most restaurants serve alcohol, unless otherwise noted. *Note:* In Bethany, alcoholic beverages are available only in restaurants—there are no bars.

Since most motels in Bethany and Fenwick do not serve breakfast, check some of the places below for breakfast, particularly **Holiday House, Libby's,** and **Warren Station.**

BETHANY BEACH

Moderate

Harbor Lights. Rte. 1 (north of central Bethany). ☎ **302/539-3061.** Reservations recommended on weekends. Main courses $12.95–$20.95. AE, DISC, MC, V. Apr–Oct daily 5–10pm. SEAFOOD.

This restaurant is nestled on the bayside of the main highway, with views of the water. The menu emphasizes fresh crab (crab cakes, soft-shell crabs, crabmeat au gratin or imperial) and local fish platters, steaks, and surf-and-turf combinations. Two of the house signature dishes are veal Oscar and Harbor Lights Seafood Stew, made with shrimp, scallops, flounder, and garden vegetables.

Holiday House Seafood Restaurant. Garfield Pkwy. and the Boardwalk. ☎ **302/539-7298.** Reservations recommended for dinner. Main courses $8.95–$21.95; lunch $5–$10. AE, DISC, MC, V. Apr–Oct daily 8am–2pm and 5–9pm. SEAFOOD.

For oceanfront dining, try this restaurant on the Bethany Beach Boardwalk. Light fare, sandwiches, and salads are available for lunch, but at dinner the emphasis is on seafood—sautéed shrimp scampi, broiled scallops, local soft-shell crabs, and broiled crab-stuffed flounder. On many nights, a seafood buffet is featured. For meat eaters, the menu also includes prime rib, Delaware fried chicken, baked ham, and pork dishes.

Magnolia's Restaurant. Cedar Neck Rd. (2 miles west of Bethany Beach off Rte. 26 and Central Ave.), Ocean View. ☎ **302/539-5671.** Reservations recommended for dinner. Main courses $11.95–$21.95; lunch $2.95–$11.95. AE, DISC, MC, V. Daily 5–10pm. SOUTHERN.

This restaurant features Carolina-style cuisine and ambience. There are no great sea views or wide windows here, but there is an elegant decor of lace curtains and tablecloths, light woods, colored glass, and lots of leafy plants and flowers. The dinner menu is a medley of dishes influenced by the Old South—from baked Dixie chicken and scallops Savannah to Cajun-style stuffed flounder and seafood Norfolk. A light menu is also available, in an adjoining pub room, from 11am to 12:45am.

○ Old Mill Crab House. Cedar Neck Rd., Ocean View, Bethany Beach. ☎ **302/537-2240.** Reservations not accepted. Main courses $7.50–$24. AE, MC, V. Mon–Fri 5–9pm, Sat 4–10pm, Sun 3–8pm. Take Rte. 26 west from Bethany Beach; turn right on Cedar Neck Rd., and then turn left down the long driveway just past Rd. 360. SEAFOOD.

In Delaware, this is the place for crabs. The Old Mill Crab House is a large and popular family restaurant overlooking the Indian River Bay. From the comfort of your paper-lined table you can really dig into Old Mill's Crab Special, which includes all-you-can-eat steamed crabs, hush puppies, clam crisps, shrimp crisps, corn on the cob (roasted in the husk), and fried chicken (cooked Eastern Shore style, i.e., greasy) for $19.95. Large trash cans are provided at the ends of all the tables for getting rid of spent crab shells. They also have wonderful, no-nonsense crab cakes and a children's menu for those 10 years and under. (*Note:* The original Old Mill Crab House, the reputation of which launched the Old Mill Crab House in Ocean View, is located inland at the town of Delmar on the Delaware–Maryland border, Route 54 West and Waller Road; call ☎ **302/846-2808.**

Inexpensive

Cottage Café. Rte. 1, Bethany Beach. ☎ **302/539-8710.** All items $2.95–$13.95. AE, MC, V. Sun–Thurs 11am–9pm, Fri–Sat 11am–10pm. AMERICAN.

This homey restaurant and pub has a country cottage–style facade and interior. It displays the works of Maryland artist Joseph Craig English (his paintings and prints portray everyday scenes of the region). The varied menu offers everything from old-fashioned pot roast and country fried chicken to black beans and rice, meat loaf, steaks, burgers, sandwiches, and pastas.

McCabe's Gourmet Market. Rte. 1 (in the York Beach Mall, just north of Fenwick Island State Park), South Bethany. ☎ **302/539-8550.** Sandwiches $3.95–$5.95. AE, DISC, MC, V. Daily 7:30am–5pm, with extended hrs. in summer. DELI.

This coffee bar and deli is a local favorite for delicious gourmet deli sandwiches and salads. There's a small seating area for those who need a break from the sun.

FENWICK ISLAND
Expensive/Moderate

✪ **Harpoon Hanna's.** Rte. 54 (on the bay). ☎ **302/539-3095.** Reservations not accepted. Main courses $9.95–$21.95; lunch $4.95–$9.95. AE, DISC, MC, V. Daily 11am–11pm. SEAFOOD.

Dining in Delaware while looking at Maryland is all part of the experience at this restaurant, located on Assawoman Bay near the state line. The half-dozen large and lively dining rooms have a nautical decor. Lunch ranges from salads to sandwiches and omelets (try the Harpoon Seafood Omelet, overflowing with shrimp, crab, mild cheddar, tomatoes, and sautéed mushrooms). In the evening fresh fish heads the menu: swordfish, sea trout, tuna, tilefish, shrimp, crab, and lobster.

✪ **Nantuckets.** Rte. 1 and Atlantic Ave. (1 block from the beach). ☎ **800/362-3463** or 302/539-2607. Reservations recommended. Main courses $15.95–$23.95. AE, DISC, MC, V. Daily 4–10pm tap room, 5–10pm dining room. SEAFOOD.

A New England cottage atmosphere prevails at this restaurant, with its four cozy dining rooms. Chef-owner David Twinning is known for innovative dishes, such as Madaket Beach Fish Stew (a potpourri of shrimp, scallops, crab, clams, mussels, and fresh fish in a tomato-saffron broth) and Veal Homard à la David (veal and lobster medaillons with brandy, hearts of palm, Dijon mustard, and cream). Other house favorites are quahog (clam) chowder (a rich scallop-and-clam chowder with traditional red potatoes and corn), lobster and scallops coquille, and jumbo shrimp sautéed with garlic, ginger, and chutney. If seafood is not your thing, there are center-cut loin lamb chops with a fine horseradish-mint sauce and breast of chicken with crab and artichokes. The service is top-notch. Early-bird specials are available daily to those seated by 5:45.

✪ **Tom & Terry's.** Rte. 54 (1¹/₂ miles west of Rte. 1, on Assawoman Bay). ☎ **302/436-4161.** Main courses $15.95–$26.95; lunch $6.95–$10.95. DISC, MC, V. Daily 11:30am–4pm and 5–10pm. SEAFOOD/AMERICAN.

This tropical-style restaurant with great views of the Ocean City skyline offers seating in a wide-windowed dining room or on an outside deck. The menu focuses largely on seafood (there's a seafood market on the premises, too), including crab-stuffed lobster tails, backfin crab cakes, soft-shell crabs, grilled tuna and swordfish steaks, and stuffed flounder. Steaks, prime rib, and chicken Marsala are also offered. There are early-bird specials from 5 to 6pm each night.

Moderate

Uncle Raymond's Ocean Grill. Rte. 1 and Atlantic Ave. ☎ **302/539-1388.** Reservations not accepted. Main courses $9–$16; lunch $2.50–$7.50. DISC, MC, V. Apr–Sept daily 11am–1am. SEAFOOD/AMERICAN.

This casual restaurant is popular for its large 200-seat outside deck, with picnic table seating, overlooking the main highway. The uncomplicated menu offers steamed hard crabs, backfin crab cakes, fried shrimp, charbroiled tuna or swordfish, and a house specialty of Seafood Raymond (shrimp, lobster, crab sautéed in spicy seafood gravy of wine, onion, peppers, and mushrooms). Surf-and-turf and lobster tails are also available at higher prices. You can even get pizza here.

Inexpensive

Libby's. Ocean Hwy. (between Dagsboro and Cannon sts.). ☎ **302/539-7379.** Reservations not accepted. Main courses $6.95–$18.95; lunch $2.95–$7.95; breakfast $2.65–$5.95. AE, DISC, MC, V. Daily 8am–8pm. Closed Dec–Feb. AMERICAN.

Known far and wide for its polka-dot facade, this restaurant is a particular favorite for breakfast. Choices include "pancakes with personality" (royal cherry, Georgia pecan, chocolate chip), old-fashioned buckwheat cakes, waffles, French toast, and omelets, as well as low-calorie fare. Lunch features a variety of overstuffed sandwiches, burgers, and salads. Dinner entrees, which come with a huge salad bar, range from soft-shell crabs and shrimp to steaks and chicken-in-the-basket.

Warren Station. Ocean Hwy. (Rte. 1, between Indian and Houston sts.). ☎ **302/539-7156.** Reservations not accepted. Main courses $6.50–$15; lunch $2–$6.50; breakfast $2–$6.25. DISC, MC, V. Mid-May to early Sept daily 8am–9pm. AMERICAN.

For more than 30 years, wholesome cooking at reasonable prices has been the trademark of this homey and casual restaurant. Designed to duplicate the look of the old Indian River Coast Guard Station, the decor features light woods, lots of windows, and bright blue canvas dividers. Turkey is the specialty of the house, roasted fresh daily and hand-carved to order, priced from $7.50 and up for a complete dinner. Other entrees include fried chicken, sugar-cured ham with raisin sauce, charbroiled T-bone steaks, crab cutlets, and flounder stuffed with crab imperial. Complete dinners—with appetizer or soup, salad, two vegetables, and beverage—range from $8 to $15. Sandwiches, burgers, soups, and salads are available for lunch. No alcohol is served.

5 Inland Southern Delaware

Not many people venture inland from the Delaware beaches. Western Sussex County is a land of small towns, back-to-back soybean and cornfields, cypress swamps, and the inevitable chicken farms. Nothing much of interest to the average beachgoing tourist. But for the adventurous traveler, hidden in this rural farming region are some unique and interesting opportunities, from biking the back roads to paddling through a cypress swamp to a relaxing free fall from a moving plane.

ESSENTIALS

GETTING THERE   Route 13 is the main north–south route through western Sussex County and is near most of the attractions and towns. More detailed instructions are given with specific activities below; however, don't set out without a decent map. The Southern Delaware Tourism Office puts out a free, very detailed road map (the best we've found). If you can't find one at the visitor center, contact the commission at ☎ **800/357-1818** or 302/856-1818. The map for bicycle users is also quite good. See "Bicycling," below.

VISITOR INFORMATION   The only walk-in **visitor center** in western Sussex County is the new facility in Bridgeville (☎ **302/337-8877**), located at the intersection of Routes 404 and 13. Here you can pick up brochures, maps, and discount coupons, and there's even a reservation service. Unfortunately, the center isn't conveniently located if you're staying on the beach and are venturing inland for the day. You can also contact the **Southern Delaware Tourism Office** (☎ **800/357-1818** or 302/856-1818), P.O. Box 240, Georgetown, DE 19947.

SPECIAL EVENTS   The **Delmarva Hot Air Balloon Festival and Craft Festival,** held annually in Milton on the second Saturday of May, attracts over 20 balloons and 125 craft, antique, and food vendors. There's also live entertainment, games and rides for kids, and tethered balloon rides. Admission is free. Proceeds benefit the American Diabetes Foundation. For more information call ☎ 302/684-8404.

OFFBEAT & OUTDOOR ADVENTURES

BICYCLING   Southern Delaware is a great place to bike. The terrain is flat; the views of the surrounding farmland, rural villages, and wetlands are refreshing and pleasant; and most roads are wide, with good shoulders for bikers. (The only drawback is the occasional odor from the chicken farms.) The **Delaware Bicycle Council**, P.O. Box 778, Dover, DE 19903, produces a map of Sussex and Kent counties called "Delaware Maps for Bicycle Users." All the roads are marked and color-coded according to their suitability for cyclists, so there's no guesswork involved in planning your route.

For an organized biking tour, **Biking Inn to Inn Delaware** is a 4-day/3-night package that provides cyclists with accommodations in three different inns or bed-and-breakfasts (one each in Laurel, Lewes, and Greenwood), plus breakfast, dinner, and snacks each day, luggage transfer, and detailed maps of the route. Cyclists travel about 35 miles each day, with alternate routes provided for those who need a greater challenge. The inns on the route are Spring Garden Bed and Breakfast and Eli's Country Inn, both listed below, and the New Devon Inn, listed in the Lewes section above. The tour costs $300 to $330, depending on the season. For more information contact Ambassador Travel, 1008 W. Stein Hwy., Seaford, DE 19973 (☎ 800/845-9939 or 302/629-9604).

CANOEING   The creeks and ponds of Sussex County make for lovely canoe excursions. A well-maintained 5-mile canoe trail along the Hitch Pond and James Branches of the Nanticoke River will take you past the two largest trees in Delaware, one of which is estimated to be around 750 years old. The trail begins at **Trap Pond State Park,** R.D. 2, Box 331, Laurel, DE 19956 (☎ 302/875-5153), where you can rent canoes for $4.50 an hour if you don't have your own. Put in at the dam, and follow the wooden signs that designate the trail. The trail ends at the state boat launch on Records Pond.

A visit to this area would not be complete without a stop at **Trussum Pond,** which looks and feels more like the Florida everglades or the bayou than Southern Delaware. From Route 24, take Route 449, which goes by the entrance to Trap Pond State Park, to Road 72, or Trussom Pond Road. There's a small park and parking area next to the pond, and if you're feeling adventurous you can paddle amongst the abundant lily pads and graceful bald cypress (Sussex County is home to the northernmost stand of bald cypress in the country). But you'll have to do the navigating yourself; there aren't any trail markers.

HOT-AIR BALLOONING   Open fields, flat terrain, and predictable wind patterns off the Atlantic make Sussex County well suited for hot-air ballooning. The **First State Hot Air Balloon Team** (☎ 302/684-2002), Delaware's state balloon team, will take you up for a 45-minute to 1-hour ride for $100 per person. Because weather conditions have to be just so for the balloon to launch, scheduling a trip is a bit difficult. For visitors from out of town, call ahead to let the team know when you'll be in the area and they'll schedule a ride with you when the weather permits (it helps if you have several days available). If you live in the area and have a flexible schedule, call and have your name put on their waiting list; when the weather is suitable for a launch, the team will start calling people on the list.

Visitors can also take a ride in a balloon at the **Delmarva Hot Air Balloon and Craft Festival,** held annually in Milton. Several balloons are available for untethered rides

Taking to the Sky in Southern Delaware: Hot-Air Ballooning

Perhaps this piece could have been called "The Joys of Floating" because to most people that's what ballooning is all about. But there's a lot more to this sport. Ballooning is at once bizarre and marvelous. There is nothing natural about levitating 3,000 feet over a cornfield, but there are few things as glorious as the 360° panoramic view of the fields, towns, rivers, and even the sea below. If this is starting to intrigue you, then you will be happy to hear that Southern Delaware is a great place to try ballooning for the first time. Call the **First State Hot Air Balloon Team** (☎ **302/684-2002**), listed above. Here is a little of what you might experience on your first flight with them.

At the launch site, things will happen quickly. You will be asked to sign a waiver and don what looks very much like a bicycle helmet. Meanwhile, the ground team will lay out the balloon, attach it to the basket, and begin inflating it with a giant fan. At this point you might be tempted to ask, "Where are we going to land?" The ever-calm balloonist will undoubtedly answer, as he did before our first ride, "Well, that's the thing. We don't really know."

Once in the air, the first thing you'll notice is that it's all very calm, not at all like flying in an airplane. You are floating. When the balloonist fires the torch, it lets out a roar, and the balloon sails higher. With his passengers in awe, maybe even still shaking a little because there's nothing beneath them for hundreds of feet except the inch-thick board at the bottom of the basket, the balloonist begins to explain things. He'll tell you ballooning is like three-dimensional sailing because balloons rely on the wind to move them. If the balloonist doesn't like the direction the wind is blowing, he moves the balloon higher or lower to a level where the wind is blowing the "right" direction. Everything happens slowly; any action the balloonist takes will have its consequences about 5 minutes later.

Gradually you loft up to 1,000 feet, where the cornfields are reduced to rows of black-and-tan lines, cars and trucks look like toys, and in the distance you can see Rehoboth, Lewes, and the Atlantic. Enjoy the view. The rest of the adventure is landing: trying to avoid trees, highways, power lines, chicken farms, valuable crops, and wandering livestock. But the balloonist has done this before. Good luck.

(reservations required) and tethered rides (first come, first served). For information on the festival and for reservations, call ☎ **302/684-8408**. For more on ballooning, see "Taking to the Sky in Southern Delaware," below.

SKYDIVING For the truly adventurous, Southern Delaware offers a most unusual and spectacular vista, a 360° view encompassing the Chesapeake Bay and the Atlantic Ocean—all you have to do is jump out of a plane at about 13,500 feet. The Free Fall Academy, P.O. Box 3312, Crofton, MD 21114 (☎ **301/261-0188** or 302/875-3804), offers skydiving instruction and several options for first-time and experienced jumpers. They use an FAA-designated drop zone (DZ) at the Laurel Airport, 2 miles west of Laurel, Delaware on Route 24. Oddly enough, it's considerably easier to make arrangements to go sky-diving than it is to plan a hot-air balloon ride. The academy offers jumps 7 days a week, weather permitting. You can call ahead to make reservations or just show up, but in any case expect a wait on beautiful spring and summer days. All jumps require some ground training, from 1 to 8 hours depending on the type of jump, so be sure to plan for that time.

First-time jumpers can choose between a tandem jump, a static-line jump, and an accelerated free-fall jump. For the tandem jump, the most popular for first-timers, you are harnessed to an instructor, and the two of you jump from about 13,500 feet, free-fall for 40 to 60 seconds, and enjoy a 3- to 4-minute canopy ride on a parachute built for two people. This jump requires about an hour of ground training and preparation and costs around $175. A static-line jump is a solo jump that takes you up to about 3,000 feet. The parachute opens automatically, so there's no free fall. A first-time static-line jump costs about $160 and requires 4 to 6 hours of ground training. An accelerated free-fall first jump is something of a combination of the two other options. You jump from about 13,500 feet, with the same free fall and canopy ride as the tandem jump, but you have your own parachute, though two instructors do jump with you using a harness-hold technique. This jump costs about $290. For all jumps, be sure to ask about discounts for groups, military personnel, and students.

WHERE TO STAY

There aren't many options for accommodations in inland Sussex County, but the few country inns and bed-and-breakfasts boast hospitable hosts, big breakfasts, and good value. In addition to the places listed below, the **Captain William Russell House** and **The Hollies** in Milton are excellent inland options, especially if you're visiting during the hot-air balloon festival or want to be close to the beach. For reviews of these inns, see "Where to Stay" in the Lewes section above.

✪ **Eli's Country Inn.** Rte. 36, Greenwood–Milford Rd., P.O. Box 779, Greenwood, DE 19950. ☎ **800/594-0048** or 302/349-4265. Fax 302/349-9340. 8 rms. A/C. $70.20–$81 double. Rates include breakfast. DISC, MC, V.

Old-fashioned country hospitality is what this inn is all about. When you arrive you'll be greeted by one or maybe several of the seven sisters who own and operate the inn, which is housed in the big white farmhouse that their father, Eli, built. Guests can relax in the spacious great room, the downstairs sitting room, the TV lounge or reading room upstairs, or on one of the three porches. Guest rooms are spacious and homey, and all have private baths.

The mailing address here is Greenwood, Delaware, but there's nothing resembling a town in sight. The fields and yard surrounding the house are favorite launching and landing sites of the First State Hot Air Balloon Team, so on clear days guests are occasionally surprised by a hot-air balloon passing just outside their windows. This is a place to get away from the hustle and bustle of city and suburban life, to enjoy peace and tranquillity, the occasional passing balloon, and the company of this gracious family.

Spring Garden Bed and Breakfast. R.D. 5, Box 283A, Delaware Ave. Ext., Laurel, DE 19956. ☎ **302/875-7015.** 4 rms (2 with bath), 1 suite. A/C. $65–$75 double; $85 suite. Rates include breakfast. No credit cards.

This inn is ideally located for fishermen and canoeists, just minutes from Trap Pond State Park and Trussum Pond. Since the innkeeper, Gwen North, envisioned and founded the Biking Inn to Inn program (see "Biking," above), Spring Garden is usually the first stop on the tour. The 18th-century country manor sits on 3 acres with a secluded wooded stream and a lovely garden, in bloom spring through fall. Gwen has decorated each of the guest rooms in period furnishings. Two favorites are the Song Bird Suite, a Victorian room where guests awake to the songs of the birds in the plum tree outside the window; and Naomi's Room, a colonial room with a large canopy bed, fireplace, sitting area, and private bath. A full country breakfast awaits each morning, with fresh fruit, whole-grain cereals, and some of Gwen's specialties such as Scotch eggs, crepes, and Belgian waffles. For antique enthusiasts, there's a shop right on the premises, in the old post-and-beam barn in the back.

Index

FROMMER'S® COMPLETE TRAVEL GUIDES

(Comprehensive guides to destinations around the world, with
selections in all price ranges—from deluxe to budget)

Acapulco, Ixtapa &
   Zihuatenejo
Alaska
Amsterdam
Arizona
Atlanta
Australia
Austria
Bahamas
Barcelona, Madrid &
   Seville
Belgium, Holland &
   Luxembourg
Bermuda
Boston
Budapest & the Best of
   Hungary
California
Canada
Cancún, Cozumel & the
   Yucatán
Cape Cod, Nantucket &
   Martha's Vineyard
Caribbean
Caribbean Cruises & Ports
   of Call
Caribbean Ports of Call
Carolinas & Georgia
Chicago
China
Colorado
Costa Rica
Denver, Boulder &
   Colorado Springs
England

Europe
Florida
France
Germany
Greece
Hawaii
Hong Kong
Honolulu, Waikiki & Oahu
Ireland
Israel
Italy
Jamaica & Barbados
Japan
Las Vegas
London
Los Angeles
Maryland & Delaware
Maui
Mexico
Miami & the Keys
Montana & Wyoming
Montréal & Québec City
Munich & the Bavarian Alps
Nashville & Memphis
Nepal
New England
New Mexico
New Orleans
New York City
Northern New England
Nova Scotia, New
   Brunswick
   & Prince Edward Island
Oregon
Paris

Philadelphia & the Amish
   Country
Portugal
Prague & the Best of the
   Czech Republic
Provence & the Riviera
Puerto Rico
Rome
San Antonio & Austin
San Diego
San Francisco
Santa Fe, Taos &
   Albuquerque
Scandinavia
Scotland
Seattle & Portland
Singapore & Malaysia
South Pacific
Spain
Switzerland
Thailand
Tokyo
Toronto
Tuscany & Umbria
USA
Utah
Vancouver & Victoria
Vienna & the Danube
   Valley
Virgin Islands
Virginia
Walt Disney World &
   Orlando
Washington, D.C.
Washington State

FROMMER'S® DOLLAR-A-DAY GUIDES

(The ultimate guides to comfortable low-cost travel)

Australia from $50 a Day
California from $60 a Day
Caribbean from $60 a Day
Costa Rica & Belize
   from $35 a Day
England from $60 a Day
Europe from $50 a Day
Florida from $50 a Day
Greece from $50 a Day
Hawaii from $60 a Day
India from $40 a Day

Ireland from $50 a Day
Israel from $45 a Day
Italy from $50 a Day
London from $60 a Day
Mexico from $35 a Day
New York from $75 a Day
New Zealand from $50 a Day
Paris from $70 a Day
San Francisco from $60 a Day
Washington, D.C., from
   $60 a Day

FROMMER'S® PORTABLE GUIDES

(Pocket-size guides for travelers who want everything in a nutshell)

Bahamas
California Wine Country
Charleston & Savannah
Chicago

Dublin
Las Vegas
London
Maine Coast
New Orleans

Puerto Vallarta, Manzanillo
& Guadalajara
San Francisco
Venice
Washington, D.C.

FROMMER'S® NATIONAL PARK GUIDES

(Everything you need for the perfect park vacation)

Grand Canyon
National Parks of the American West
Yellowstone & Grand Teton

Yosemite & Sequoia/
Kings Canyon
Zion & Bryce Canyon

FROMMER'S® IRREVERENT GUIDES

(Wickedly honest guides for sophisticated travelers)

Amsterdam
Chicago
London

Manhattan
New Orleans
Paris

San Francisco
Santa Fe

Walt Disney World
Washington, D.C.

FROMMER'S® BY NIGHT GUIDES

(The series for those who know that life begins after dark)

Amsterdam
Chicago
Las Vegas
London

Los Angeles
Madrid
& Barcelona
Manhattan

Miami
New Orleans
Paris

Prague
San Francisco
Washington, D.C.

THE COMPLETE IDIOT'S TRAVEL GUIDES

(The ultimate user-friendly trip planners)

Cruise Vacations
Las Vegas
New Orleans

New York City
Planning Your Trip
to Europe

San Francisco
Walt Disney World

SPECIAL-INTEREST TITLES

Arthur Fommer's New World of Travel
The Civil War Trust's Official Guide to
the Civil War Discovery Trail
Frommer's Caribbean Hideaways
Frommer's Complete Hostel Vacation
Guide to England, Scotland & Wales
Frommer's Europe's Greatest
Driving Tours
Frommer's Food Lover's Companion
to France
Frommer's Food Lover's Companion to
Italy
Israel Past & Present
New York City with Kids
New York Times Weekends

Outside Magazine's Adventure Guide
to New England
Outside Magazine's Adventure Guide
to Northern California
Outside Magazine's Adventure Guide
to the Pacific Northwest
Outside Magazine's Adventure Guide
to Southern California & Baja
Outside Magazine's Guide to Family Vacations
Places Rated Almanac
Retirement Places Rated
Washington, D.C., with Kids
Wonderful Weekends from New York City
Wonderful Weekends from San Francisco
Wonderful Weekends from Los Angeles

WHEREVER
YOU TRAVEL,
*H*ELP IS NEVER
FAR AWAY.

From planning your trip to

providing travel assistance along

the way, American Express®

Travel Service Offices are always

there to help you do more.

For the office nearest you, call
1-800-AXP-3429.